PHILOSOPHY

IN THE AGE

OF CRISIS

Harper's Philosophy Series
UNDER THE EDITORSHIP OF FRANK A. TILLMAN

PHILOSOPHY

IN THE AGE

OF CRISIS

Edited by

Eleanor Kuykendall

STATE UNIVERSITY OF NEW YORK
COLLEGE AT NEW PALTZ

Harper & Row, Publishers
NEW YORK, EVANSTON, AND LONDON

PHILOSOPHY IN THE AGE OF CRISIS

LIBRARY OF CONGRESS CATALOG CARD NUMBER: 71-113489

Contents

Preface

Recent social and political upheavals have offered a new challenge to the ancient discipline of philosophy. Philosophers have always clarified concepts; now they may apply their analysis to the events of contemporary life. The philosophers and philosophically inclined thinkers who contribute to this book undertake to do just that. This book introduces philosophy by showing how philosophical reflection can give sense and significance to those events which constitute a crisis in our age.

It is no secret that there is a crisis in our age. What passes for a discussion of it, however, often fails. Warnings of impending disaster tell us neither why particular events are so critical nor what we ought to do to change patterns of racial discrimination, urban violence, or declining religion. We are overwhelmed by descriptions of the latest advances in computer design and by statistics listing the latest casualties in Vietnam, but mere descriptions tell us neither whether nor why we ought to think these events important. We want to know what difference these events make in our lives and how we can live to meet their challenge.

What we want to know most about the events of the current crisis is that which philosophers are most concerned to discover. First, philosophers want to identify crisis events. Not every social, political, or technological change generates a crisis. Those that threaten human dignity, human rights, or personal identity—those that impair the quality and authenticity of human existence—are crisis events. These events immediately engage philosophers' concern.

Second, philosophers begin their analysis with a concern for what is human, and perhaps uniquely human. It is true that for some time the "analytic philosophy" practiced in English-speaking countries seemed aloof from human concerns, but this is no longer the case. Philosophers of every methodological persuasion—analytic, existentialist, and even Marxist—now take the nature and quality of human existence as a point of departure for even their most abstract speculations. Whether they begin with the nature of human communication, the contents of human consciousness, or the organization of human society, philosophers begin their analysis, in every case, with the human.

Finally, the outcome of philosophical analysis again reveals philosophers' concern with what is human. The concepts which philosophers finally clarify—concepts like human dignity or personal identity—are concepts essential to a discussion and evaluation of human existence. In this sense philosophical activity is itself uniquely human, for only man attempts to give significance to his existence by clarifying the concepts he uses to characterize it.

Accordingly, the authors represented in these pages identify the contemporary events which challenge human life, clarify concepts needed to characterize human life, and show what gives life significance in the present age. Their writings are divided into four major sections, each of which is occupied with a different facet of contemporary life.

Section I, "The Primacy of the Person," establishes the nature of human dignity as a standard for assessing contemporary events. Its authors identify several elements of social and technological change which contribute to the current crisis. In the final subsection, "Freedom," they discuss the nature and extent of our ability to direct our lives to meet the challenge of present events.

Section II, "Political Action," analyzes the nature and basis of human rights. Its authors assess the sources of governmental authority, the right of citizens to oppose their governments, and the means they may justly take to bring changes about. Revolution is both opposed and advocated; restructuring the government and altering its policies from within are both considered; and both violent and nonviolent protest are compared at length.

Section III, "Man and World," explores the concept of personal identity. Its authors present contrasting definitions of the self and contrasting answers to the question Can I know another person's experiences? They offer several alternative solutions to the problem of establishing our place as expressive, perceiving human beings in an inanimate world.

Finally, in Section IV, "Religious Commitment," the authors consider a more permanent basis for belief in human dignity, human rights, and personal identity despite our own death. They analyze religious experiences induced by drugs, reported by mystics, and described by a famous scientist. They discuss doubt as it affects both Christians and Jews, and they present and evaluate proofs for the existence of God.

Thus the four sections of this book are concerned with the clarification of such concepts as human dignity, human rights, personal identity, and immortality. We constantly appeal to such concepts to assess events and justify actions in our own lives. What is significant about contemporary events the philosopher helps us to discover.

I am glad to thank Professor Larry Holmes, Chairman of the Philosophy Department, State University College at New Paltz, for encouraging me in this project. For patiently commenting on several early versions of the reading list I should like to thank not only Professor Holmes but also Professor Barry Blose, now of American University, and Professors Amiya Chakravarty, Price Charlson, John Kirk, and Stanley Newburger, all of New Paltz. Also I am glad to thank Hilda A. Kuykendall for her careful reading of the introductions. Of course I alone bear responsibility for problems that remain.

ELEANOR KUYKENDALL

January, 1970
New Paltz, New York

Section I

THE PRIMACY

OF THE PERSON

What gives worth and authenticity to human existence? Amidst their outcry against the "dehumanization" wrought by social change and technological upheaval, people ask—with some justice—to be treated as names instead of numbers. They also ask —again with some justice—to conduct their lives unrestricted by society so long as they don't hurt anybody else. Their surprisingly individual appeal evokes the long-lost ideal of the primacy of the person. Present events now challenge us to revitalize this standard, which once gave life significance.

The opening essay is Plato's dramatic recital of the trial and death of Socrates. We might suppose that the trial of a philosopher convicted for his eccentricities in the fourth century before Christ would have no bearing on our present crisis, but the case of Socrates is unique. Socrates was sentenced to death for leading the youth of Athens to question the official gods. Today, the youth lead philosophers to question the official gods. Socrates testified that he was seeking a well-hidden truth; today, the truth remains as well hidden as it was in Athens. Socrates chose to die in his quest rather than to try to escape. In his life and death he displayed the dignity of his quest and his existence. It is this dignity which men still seek.

What, then, is human dignity? Two complementary answers are presented in the subsection that bears that title. In "Treating Others as Persons, not Things"

Immanuel Kant presents human dignity as a respect for persons, and as the ultimate test of morality. According to Kant, any of my actions is moral if it would be moral for all persons; any of my actions is moral if it results in my treating other persons as ends, or ultimate values, rather than as means, or things. In "The Limits to the Authority of Society over the Individual" John Stuart Mill presents human dignity as individual integrity. My actions must promote the happiness of others, but the actions which affect no one else ought to remain private and unregulated by society: in my own person, I deserve respect. Thus human dignity may be characterized as that which evokes respect and that which expresses integrity and individuality. Human dignity is the primacy of the person.

These characterizations of human dignity help us to identify the more pressing issues of the curent crisis. Some, like racial discrimination, raise immediate political questions and receive extended discussion in Section II, "Political Action." Others, like war, may be considered as questions for both political and individual decision. The individual aspects of war, like the questions raised by the "new morality" and by the effect of technological change on individual action, are discussed in the subsection "The Crisis in Human Values."

Local wars such as those in Vietnam and Biafra, because they have taken the lives of many defenseless noncombatants, have aroused widespread moral indignation. All wars involve cruelty and killing, but who is responsible? The faceless governments? The citizens who elect these officials? The citizens who fail to oppose them? The military officers who issue orders? Or the draftees who obey orders? In "War Guilt" J. Glenn Gray soberly considers all these questions and concludes that it is no easier to condemn than to condone those who give the orders or those who carry them out.

That uniquely personal aspect of human relationships, the sexual, has been increasingly affected by the "new morality," which asserts that society ought not to regulate sexual behavior as it once did. This leaves us with no standard for sexual relationships, beyond the immediacy of desire. Is there an aspect in the sexual relationship itself that expresses one's awareness of the other person as well as one's own sensations? Does it make a genuine interpersonal relationship possible?

In "Love and Sexual Desire" Jean-Paul Sartre argues that in the sexual relationship one does manifest his consciousness of the other person. Yet, Sartre concludes all personal relationships are of unequal balance. One person (not always the same one) dominates the other, if only by a look. No reciprocal exchange is possible, so all true interpersonal relationships, including the sexual, are doomed.

On the other hand, in "Sexual Perversion" Thomas Nagel tries to show that an equal interpersonal recognition is possible between lovers. Each lover perceives the other as a person, and each lover can recognize that the other perceives him in the same way. Thus sexual morality is exemplified by sexual relationships (whether condoned by traditional standards or not) in which such interpersonal communication is complete. Sexual perversion is impaired, or incomplete, communication.

Technological change also threatens the quality and authenticity of human life. For example, in "The Ethical Dimension of Scientific Research" Nicholas Rescher points out that a scientist may discover tension between his acts as a professional and as a private citizen. As a private citizen he may question the allocation of government funds to space research rather than to domestic programs, while as a scientist he seeks government funds to further his work. As an individual he may oppose war, but as a scientist he makes discoveries which may be applied to the development of new weapons.

Moreover, technological developments infringe increasingly upon what we might call individual integrity, that is, our privacy. In "Philosophical Reflections on Experimenting with Human Subjects" Hans Jonas questions research on incurable disease and expresses concern about organ transplants made without the knowledge of the patient. In dealing with people as if they were mere collections of symptoms, Jonas points out, medical researchers may forget that they are dealing with more than bodily organs.

In "Privacy and Freedom" Alan F. Westin describes in great detail the intrusions on privacy occasioned by advances in electronic and computer technology. When information about one's income, travel, and associates can be readily obtained from a computer data bank, then one risks being treated merely as data. The actions of electronic technicians or computer operators may affect us from a distance. So, Westin concludes, we must now seek ways of regulating their actions and the actions of others who never confront us directly as persons.

But it is idle to offer standards, evaluate actions, or try to change the course of events unless it is indeed possible to act freely. If a person can act freely, he can be held morally responsible for his actions. If he cannot act freely, he cannot be responsible. Can man, then, act freely? This question is discussed in the third subsection, "Freedom."

The difficulty of this question has always been that we do not know where to begin our analysis. We know neither what actions are nor what freedom is, and yet these issues are intertwined. Two centuries ago David Hume proposed some initial distinctions which still evoke debate and offer a useful starting point. In "Liberty and Necessity" he suggests that all events are caused; that is, so far as we know, each type of event is regularly preceded by another identifiable type of event (for Hume's questions about causation see his essay, "The Passive Mind: Custom and Convention," in Section III, "Man and World"). The events which are said to be caused by a man acting freely must, accordingly, follow other events which the agent initiates. In fact, only some events do. Some so-called actions are compelled by external events over which the so-called agent has no control, as is the case when the prisoner is compelled to remain in his cell because he has been placed in chains. On the other hand, most events said to be the actions of someone are caused by the internal event of his willing to act. These, according to Hume, are free actions for which the agent is responsible.

Talk of internal causes of action takes on a new twist when Sigmund Freud talks of the origin of conscience, or "the moral sense," in "The Unconscious." One's personality can be thought of as divided into three parts: the superego, which issues moral edicts; the ego, which we usually take to be the true self; and the id, the repository of forbidden desires. Yet the superego is formed primarily by early parental training; both it and the ego have areas that are unconscious and thus beyond our knowledge or control. Moreover, we cannot control the id at all. Under these circumstances, Freud concludes, responsible action at best must be the product of constant conflict among the parts of the personality and the external world.

If Freud is right, as John Hospers contends in "What Means This Freedom?," then the individual's motives, which are unconscious, cause his actions. But if one's motives are unconscious one can neither know what they are nor control them: One is responsible neither for one's motives nor for the actions which they cause. Thus the traditional notion of moral responsibility has to be replaced by another notion that might be called accountability to society. We will jail, but not blame, those who become hopeless criminals and endanger society because of illnesses initiated in their babyhood. We cannot so much offer to change what we or others do as to tolerate so far as possible their inability to do otherwise.

In contrast, Jean-Paul Sartre argues in "Freedom as Choosing Oneself" that Freud is quite wrong in postulating an unconscious. According to Sartre, everyone is completely conscious or can choose to be conscious; thus one can consciously choose his actions. Since he defines a person as the sum of the actions he has consciously chosen and is now choosing, Sartre regards a person as free to choose both his acts and the kind of person he wishes to be. Anyone who claims that he lacks this freedom, according to Sartre, is deceiving himself and acting out of self-deception, or "bad faith" (*mauvaise foi*); it is our misfortune, but also our responsibility, that most of the time we choose to flee responsibility in bad faith. In any case we remain totally free and totally responsible for our actions, Sartre asserts.

These quite different conceptions of freedom vary in both their appeal and their defensibility. Sartre's position is exhilarating but exceedingly difficult to defend, for he does not show that his conception of bad faith accounts for all of the phenomena which Freud invoked his theory of the unconscious to explain. Hospers' and Freud's positions, on the other hand, restrict our quest to change the course of events. Hume's position falls between these extremes. The issues are still very entangled, and philosophical analysis of the concepts of freedom and of human action continues. At present whether human beings are free remains an open question.

What is at stake in each of these intensive discussions of human dignity, the present crisis in human values, and human freedom is the primacy of the person. We invoke what is uniquely human as a standard to evaluate human actions, and we seek what is uniquely human to describe these actions as free.

PLATO

The Trial and Death of Socrates

Plato (c. 427–327 B.C.) was the most famous
student of Socrates and the author of the
philosophical dialogues in which Socrates'
conversations are recorded.

THE TRIAL

I do not know what effect my accusers have had upon you, gentlemen, but for my
own part I was almost carried away by them—their arguments were so convincing.
On the other hand, scarcely a word of what they said was true. I was especially
astonished at one of their many misrepresentations; I mean when they told you
that you must be careful not to let me deceive you—the implication being that I am
a skillful speaker. I thought that it was peculiarly brazen of them to tell you this
without a blush, since they must know that they will soon be effectively confuted, when
it becomes obvious that I have not the slightest skill as a speaker—unless, of course,
by a skillful speaker they mean one who speaks the truth. If that is what they mean,
I would agree that I am an orator, though not after their pattern.

My accusers, then, as I maintain, have said little or nothing that is true, but
from me you shall hear the whole truth—not, I can assure you, gentlemen, in flowery
language like theirs, decked out with fine words and phrases. No, what you will
hear will be a straightforward speech in the first words that occur to me, confident
as I am in the justice of my cause, and I do not want any of you to expect anything
different. It would hardly be suitable, gentlemen, for a man of my age to address you
in the artificial language of a schoolboy orator. One thing, however, I do most ear-
nestly beg and entreat of you. If you hear me defending myself in the same language
which it has been my habit to use, both in the open spaces of this city—where many
of you have heard me—and elsewhere, do not be surprised, and do not interrupt. Let
me remind you of my position. This is my first appearance in a court of law, at the
age of seventy, and so I am a complete stranger to the language of this place. Now
if I were really from another country, you would naturally excuse me if I spoke in
the manner and dialect in which I had been brought up, and so in the present case
I make this request of you, which I think is only reasonable, to disregard the manner
of my speech—it may be better or it may be worse—and to consider and concentrate
your attention upon this one question, whether my claims are fair or not. That is
the first duty of the juryman, just as it is the pleader's duty to speak the truth.

The proper course for me, gentlemen of the jury, is to deal first with the earliest

From *Apology* and *Phaedo*, by Plato, translated by Hugh Tredennick from *The Last Days of
Socrates*, Penguin Books, Ltd., 1954. Reprinted by permission of the publishers.

charges that have been falsely brought against me, and with my earliest accusers, and then with the later ones. I make this distinction because I have already been accused in your hearing by a great many people for a great many years, though without a word of truth, and I am more afraid of those people than I am of Anytus and his colleagues, although they are formidable enough. But the others are still more formidable. I mean the people who took hold of so many of you when you were children and tried to fill your minds with untrue accusations against me, saying, There is a wise man called Socrates who has theories about the heavens and has investigated everything below the earth, and can make the weaker argument defeat the stronger.

It is these people, gentlemen, the disseminators of these rumors, who are my dangerous accusers, because those who hear them suppose that anyone who inquires into such matters must be an atheist. Besides, there are a great many of these accusers, and they have been accusing me now for a great many years. And what is more, they approached you at the most impressionable age, when some of you were children or adolescents, and they literally won their case by default, because there was no one to defend me. And the most fantastic thing of all is that it is impossible for me even to know and tell you their names, unless one of them happens to be a playwright. All these people, who have tried to set you against me out of envy and love of slander—and some too merely passing on what they have been told by others—all these are very difficult to deal with. It is impossible to bring them here for cross-examination; one simply has to conduct one's defense and argue one's case against an invisible opponent, because there is no one to answer. So I ask you to accept my statement that my critics fall into two classes, on the one hand my immediate accusers, and on the other those earlier ones whom I have mentioned, and you must suppose that I have first to defend myself against the latter. After all, you heard them abusing me longer ago and much more violently than these more recent accusers.

Very well, then, I must begin my defense, gentlemen, and I must try, in the short time that I have, to rid your minds of a false impression which is the work of many years. I should like this to be the result, gentlemen, assuming it to be for your advantage and my own; and I should like to be successful in my defense, but I think that it will be difficult, and I am quite aware of the nature of my task. However, let that turn out as God wills. I must obey the law and make my defense.

Let us go back to the beginning and consider what the charge is that has made me so unpopular, and has encouraged Meletus to draw up this indictment. Very well, what did my critics say in attacking my character? I must read out their affidavit, so to speak, as though they were my legal accusers: Socrates is guilty of criminal meddling, in that he inquires into things below the earth and in the sky, and makes the weaker argument defeat the stronger, and teaches others to follow his example. It runs something like that. You have seen it for yourselves in the play by Aristophanes, where Socrates goes whirling round, proclaiming that he is walking on air, and uttering a great deal of other nonsense about things of which I know nothing whatsoever. I mean no disrespect for such knowledge, if anyone really is versed in it—I do not want any more lawsuits brought against me by Meletus—but the fact is, gentlemen, that I take no interest in it. What is more, I call upon the greater part of you as witnesses to my statement, and I appeal to all of you who have ever listened to me talking—and there are a great many to whom this applies—to clear your neighbors' minds on this point. Tell one another whether any one of you has ever heard me discuss such questions briefly or at length, and then you will realize that the other popular reports about me are equally unreliable.

The fact is that there is nothing in any of these charges, and if you have heard anyone say that I try to educate people and charge a fee, there is no truth in that either. I wish that there were, because I think that it is a fine thing if a man is qualified to teach, as in the case of Gorgias of Leontini and Prodicus of Ceos and Hippias of Elis. Each one of these is perfectly capable of going into any city and actually persuading the young men to leave the company of their fellow citizens, with any of whom they can associate for nothing, and attach themselves to him, and pay money for the privilege, and be grateful into the bargain.

There is another expert too from Paros who I discovered was here on a visit; I happened to meet a man who has paid more in Sophists' fees than all the rest put together—I mean Callias, the son of Hipponicus. So I asked him—he has two sons, you see—Callias, I said, if your sons had been colts or calves, we should have had no difficulty in finding and engaging a trainer to perfect their natural qualities, and this trainer would have been some sort of horse dealer or agriculturalist. But seeing that they are human beings, whom do you intend to get as their instructor? Who is the expert in perfecting the human and social qualities? I assume from the fact of your having sons that you must have considered the question. Is there such a person or not?

Certainly, said he.

Who is he, and where does he come from? said I. And what does he charge?

Evenus of Paros, Socrates, said he, and his fee is five minas.

I felt that Evenus was to be congratulated if he really was a master of this art and taught it at such a moderate fee. I should certainly plume myself and give myself airs if I undersood these things, but in fact, gentlemen, I do not.

Here perhaps one of you might interrupt me and say, But what is it that you do, Socrates? How is it that you have been misrepresented like this? Surely all this talk and gossip about you would never have arisen if you had confined yourself to ordinary activities, but only if your behavior was abnormal. Tell us the explanation, if you do not want us to invent it for ourselves.

This seems to me to be a reasonable request, and I will try to explain to you what it is that has given me this false notoriety. So please give me your attention. Perhaps some of you will think that I am not being serious, but I assure you that I am going to tell you the whole truth.

I have gained this reputation, gentlemen, from nothing more or less than a kind of wisdom. What kind of wisdom do I mean? Human wisdom, I suppose. It seems that I really am wise in this limited sense. Presumably the geniuses whom I mentioned just now are wise in a wisdom that is more than human. I do not know how else to account for it. I certainly have no knowledge of such wisdom, and anyone who says that I have is a liar and willful slanderer. Now, gentlemen, please do not interrupt me if I seem to make an extravagant claim, for what I am going to tell you is not my own opinion. I am going to refer you to an unimpeachable authority. I shall call as witness to my wisdom, such as it is, the god at Delphi.

You know Chaerephon, of course. He was a friend of mine from boyhood, and a good democrat who played his part with the rest of you in the recent expulsion and restoration. And you know what he was like, how enthusiastic he was over anything that he had once undertaken. Well, one day he actually went to Delphi and asked this question of the god—as I said before, gentlemen, please do not interrupt—he asked whether there was anyone wiser than myself. The priestess replied that there was no one. As Chaerephon is dead, the evidence for my statement will be supplied by his brother, who is here in court.

Please consider my object in telling you this. I want to explain to you how the attack upon my reputation first started. When I heard about the oracle's answer, I said to myself, What does the god mean? Why does he not use plain language? I am only too conscious that I have no claim to wisdom, great or small. So what can he mean by asserting that I am the wisest man in the world? He cannot be telling a lie; that would not be right for him.

After puzzling about it for some time, I set myself at last with considerable reluctance to check the truth of it in the following way. I went to interview a man with a high reputation for wisdom, because I felt that here if anywhere I should succeed in disproving the oracle and pointing out to my divine authority, You said that I was the wisest of men, but here is a man who is wiser than I am.

Well, I gave a thorough examination to this person—I need not mention his name, but it was one of our politicians that I was studying when I had this experience—and in conversation with him I formed the impression that although in many people's opinion, and especially in his own, he appeared to be wise, in fact he was not. Then when I began to try to show him that he only thought he was wise and was not really so, my efforts were resented both by him and by many of the other people present. However, I reflected as I walked away, Well, I am certainly wiser than this man. It is only too likely that neither of us has any knowledge to boast of, but he thinks that he knows something which he does not know, whereas I am quite conscious of my ignorance. At any rate it seems that I am wiser than he is to this small extent, that I do not think that I know what I do not know.

After this I went on to interview a man with an even greater reputation for wisdom, and I formed the same impression again, and here too I incurred the resentment of the man himself and a number of others.

From that time on I interviewed one person after another. I realized with distress and alarm that I was making myself unpopular, but I felt compelled to put my religious duty first. Since I was trying to find out the meaning of the oracle, I was bound to interview everyone who had a reputation for knowledge. And by dog, gentlemen, for I must be frank with you, my honest impression was this. It seemed to me, as I pursued my investigation at the god's command, that the people with the greatest reputations were almost entirely deficient, while others who were supposed to be their inferiors were much better qualified in practical intelligence.

I want you to think of my adventures as a sort of pilgrimage undertaken to establish the truth of the oracle once for all. After I had finished with the politicians I turned to the poets, dramatic, lyric, and all the rest, in the belief that here I should expose myself as a comparative ignoramus. I used to pick up what I thought were some of their most perfect works and question them closely about the meaning of what they had written, in the hope of incidentally enlarging my own knowledge. Well, gentlemen, I hesitate to tell you the truth, but it must be told. It is hardly an exaggeration to say that any of the bystanders could have explained those poems better than their actual authors. So I soon made up my mind about the poets too. I decided that it was not wisdom that enabled them to write their poetry, but a kind of instinct or inspiration, such as you find in seers and prophets who deliver all their sublime messages without knowing in the least what they mean. It seemed clear to me that the poets were in much the same case, and I also observed that the very fact that they were poets made them think that they had a perfect understanding of all other subjects, of which they were totally ignorant. So I left that line of inquiry too with the same sense of advantage that I had felt in the case of the politicians.

Last of all I turned to the skilled craftsmen. I knew quite well that I had practically no technical qualifications myself, and I was sure that I should find them full of impressive knowledge. In this I was not dissappointed. They understood things which I did not, and to that extent they were wiser than I was. But, gentlemen, these professional experts seemed to share the same failing which I had noticed in the poets. I mean that on the strength of their technical proficiency they claimed a perfect understanding of every other subject, however important, and I felt that this error more than outweighed their positive wisdom. So I made myself spokesman for the oracle, and asked myself whether I would rather be as I was—neither wise with their wisdom nor stupid with their stupidity—or possess both qualities as they did. I replied through myself to the oracle that it was best for me to be as I was.

The effect of these investigations of mine, gentlemen, has been to arouse against me a great deal of hostility, and hostility of a particularly bitter and persistent kind, which has resulted in various malicious suggestions, including the description of me as a professor of wisdom. This is due to the fact that whenever I succeed in disproving another person's claim to wisdom in a given subject, the bystanders assume that I know everything about that subject myself. But the truth of the matter, gentlemen, is pretty certainly this, that real wisdom is the property of God, and this oracle is his way of telling us that human wisdom has little or no value. It seems to me that he is not referring literally to Socrates, but has merely taken my name as an example, as if he would say to us, The wisest of you men is he who has realized, like Socrates, that in respect of wisdom he is really worthless.

That is why I still go about seeking and searching in obedience to the divine command, if I think that anyone is wise, whether citizen or stranger, and when I think that any person is not wise, I try to help the cause of God by proving that he is not. This occupation has kept me too busy to do much either in politics or in my own affairs. In fact, my service to God has reduced me to extreme poverty.

There is another reason for my being unpopular. A number of young men with wealthy fathers and plenty of leisure have deliberately attached themselves to me because they enjoy hearing other people cross-questioned. These often take me as their model, and go on to try to question other persons. Whereupon, I suppose, they find an unlimited number of people who think that they know something, but really know little or nothing. Consequently their victims become annoyed, not with themselves but with me, and they complain that there is a pestilential busybody called Socrates who fills young people's heads with wrong ideas. If you ask them what he does, and what he teaches that has this effect, they have no answer, not knowing what to say. But as they do not want to admit their confusion, they fall back on the stock charges against any philosopher, that he teaches his pupils about things in the heavens and below the earth, and to disbelieve in gods, and to make the weaker argument defeat the stronger. They would be very loath, I fancy, to admit the truth—which is that they are being convicted of pretending to knowledge when they are entirely ignorant. So, jealous, I suppose, for their own reputation, and also energetic and numerically strong, and provided with a plausible and carefully worked-out case against me, these people have been dinning into your ears for a long time past their violent denunciations of myself.

There you have the causes which led to the attack upon me by Meletus and Anytus and Lycon, Meletus being aggrieved on behalf of the poets, Anytus on behalf of the professional men and politicians, and Lycon on behalf of the orators. So, as I said at the beginning, I should be surprised if I were able, in the short time that I have, to rid your minds of a misconception so deeply implanted.

There, gentlemen, you have the true facts, which I present to you without any concealment or suppression, great or small. I am fairly certain that this plain speaking of mine is the cause of my unpopularity, and this really goes to prove that my statements are true, and that I have described correctly the nature and the grounds of the calumny which has been brought against me. Whether you inquire into them now or later, you will find the facts as I have just described them.

So much for my defense against the charges brought by the first group of my accusers. I shall now try to defend myself against Meletus—high-principled and patriotic as he claims to be—and after that against the rest.

Let us first consider their deposition again, as though it represented a fresh prosecution. It runs something like this: Socrates is guilty of corrupting the minds of the young, and of believing in deities of his own invention instead of the gods recognized by the state. Such is the charge. Let us examine its points one by one.

First it says that I am guilty of corrupting the young. But I say, gentlemen, that Meletus is guilty of treating a serious matter with levity, since he summons people to stand their trial on frivolous grounds, and professes concern and keen anxiety in matters about which he has never had the slightest interest. I will try to prove this to your satisfaction.

Come now, Meletus, tell me this. You regard it as supremely important, do you not, that our young people should be exposed to the best possible influence?

I do.

Very well, then, tell these gentlemen who it is that influences the young for the better. Obviously you must know, if you are so much interested. You have discovered the vicious influence, as you say, in myself, and you are now prosecuting me before these gentlemen. Speak up and inform them who it is that has a good influence upon the young. . . . You see, Meletus, that you are tongue-tied and cannot answer. Do you not feel that this is discreditable, and a sufficient proof in itself of what I said, that you have no interest in the subject? Tell me, my friend, who is it that makes the young good?

The laws.

That is not what I mean, my dear sir. I am asking you to name the *person* whose first business it is to know the laws.

These gentlemen here, Socrates, the members of the jury.

Do you mean, Meletus, that they have the ability to educate the young, and to make them better?

Certainly.

Does this apply to all jurymen, or only to some?

To all of them.

Excellent! A generous supply of benefactors. Well, then, do these spectators who are present in court have an improving influence, or not?

Yes, they do.

And what about the members of the Council?

Yes, the councilors too.

But surely, Meletus, the members of the Assembly do not corrupt the young? Or do all of them too exert an improving influence?

Yes, they do.

Then it would seem that the whole population of Athens has a refining effect upon the young, except myself, and I alone demoralize them. Is that your meaning?

Most emphatically, yes.

This is certainly a most unfortunate quality that you have detected in me. Well, let me put another question to you. Take the case of horses. Do you believe that those who improve them make up the whole of mankind, and that there is only one person who has a bad effect on them? Or is the truth just the opposite, that the ability to improve them belongs to one person or to very few persons, who are horse trainers, whereas most people, if they have to do with horses and make use of them, do them harm? Is not this the case, Meletus, both with horses and with all other animals? Of course it is, whether you and Anytus deny it or not. It would be a singular dispensation of fortune for our young people if there is only one person who corrupts them, while all the rest have a beneficial effect. But I need say no more. There is ample proof, Meletus, that you have never bothered your head about the young, and you make it perfectly clear that you have never taken the slightest interest in the cause for the sake of which you are now indicting me.

Here is another point. Tell me seriously, Meletus, is it better to live in a good or in a bad community? Answer my question, like a good fellow; there is nothing difficult about it. Is it not true that wicked people have a bad effect upon those with whom they are in the closest contact, and that good people have a good effect?

Quite true.

Is there anyone who prefers to be harmed rather than benefited by his associates? Answer me, my good man; the law commands you to answer. Is there anyone who prefers to be harmed?

Of course not.

Well, then, when you summon me before this court for corrupting the young and making their characters worse, do you mean that I do so intentionally or un-intentionally?

I mean intentionally.

Why, Meletus, are you at your age so much wiser than I at mine? You have discovered that bad people always have a bad effect, and good people a good effect, upon their nearest neighbors. Am I so hopelessly ignorant as not even to realize that by spoiling the character of one of my companions I shall run the risk of getting some harm from him? Because nothing else would make me commit this grave offense in-tentionally. No, I do not believe it, Meletus, and I do not suppose that anyone else does. Either I have not a bad influence, or it is unintentional, so that in either case your accusation is false. And if I unintentionally have a bad influence, the correct procedure in cases of such involuntary misdemeanors is not to summon the culprit before this court, but to take him aside privately for instruction and reproof, because obviously if my eyes are opened, I shall stop doing what I do not intend to do. But you deliberately avoided my company in the past and refused to enlighten me, and now you bring me before this court, which is the place appointed for those who need punishment, not for those who need enlightenment.

It is quite clear by now, gentlemen, that Meletus, as I said before, has never shown any degree of interest in this subject. However, I invite you to tell us, Meletus, in what sense you make out that I corrupt the minds of the young. Surely the terms of your indictment make it clear that you accuse me of teaching them to believe in new deities instead of the gods recognized by the state. Is not that the teaching of mine which you say has this demoralizing effect?

That is precisely what I maintain.

Then I appeal to you, Meletus, in the name of these same gods about whom we are speaking, to explain yourself a little more clearly to myself and to the jury, because I cannot make out what your point is. Is it that I teach people to believe in some gods—which implies that I myself believe in gods, and am not a complete atheist, so that I am not guilty on that score—but in different gods from those recognized by the state, so that your accusation rests upon the fact that they are different? Or do you assert that I believe in no gods at all, and teach others to do the same?

Yes, I say that you disbelieve in gods altogether.

You surprise me, Meletus. What is your object in saying that? Do you suggest that I do not believe that the sun and moon are gods, as is the general belief of all mankind?

He certainly does not, gentlemen of the jury, since he says that the sun is a stone and the moon a mass of earth.

Do you imagine that you are prosecuting Anaxagoras, my dear Meletus? Have you so poor an opinion of these gentlemen, and do you assume them to be so illiterate as not to know that the writings of Anaxagoras of Clazomenae are full of theories like these? And do you seriously suggest that it is from me that the young get these ideas, when they can buy them on occasion in the market place for a drachma at most, and so have the laugh on Socrates if he claims them for his own, to say nothing of their being so silly? Tell me honestly, Meletus, is that your opinion of me? Do I believe in no god?

No, none at all, not in the slightest degree.

You are not at all convincing, Meletus—not even to yourself, I suspect. In my opinion, gentlemen, this man is a thoroughly selfish bully, and has brought this action against me out of sheer wanton aggressiveness and self-assertion. He seems to be devising a sort of intelligence test for me, saying to himself, Will the infallible Socrates realize that I am contradicting myself for my own amusement, or shall I succeed in deceiving him and the rest of my audience?

It certainly seems to me that he is contradicting himself in this indictment, which might just as well run: Socrates is guilty of not believing in the gods, but believing in the gods. And this is pure flippancy.

I ask you to examine with me, gentlemen, the line of reasoning which leads me to this conclusion. You, Meletus, will oblige us by answering my questions. Will you all kindly remember, as I requested at the beginning, not to interrupt if I conduct the discussion in my customary way?

Is there anyone in the world, Meletus, who believes in human activities, and not in human beings? Make him answer, gentlemen, and don't let him keep on making these continual objections. Is there anyone who does not believe in horses, but believes in horses' activities? Or who does not believe in musicians, but believes in musical activities? No, there is not, my worthy friend. If you do not want to answer, I will supply it for you and for these gentlemen too. But the next question you must answer. Is there anyone who believes in supernatural activities and not in supernatural beings?

No.

How good of you to give a bare answer under compulsion by the court! Well, do you assert that I believe and teach others to believe in supernatural activities? It does not matter whether they are new or old. The fact remains that I believe in them according to your statement; indeed you solemnly swore as much in your affidavit. But if I believe in supernatural activities, it follows inevitably that I also believe in supernatural beings. Is not that so? It is. I assume your assent, since you do not answer. Do we not hold that supernatural beings are either gods or the children of gods? Do you agree or not?

Certainly.

Then if I believe in supernatural beings, as you assert, if these supernatural beings are gods in any sense, we shall reach the conclusion which I mentioned just now when I said that you were testing my intelligence for your own amusement, by stating first that I do not believe in gods, and then again that I do, since I believe in supernatural beings. If on the other hand these supernatural beings are bastard children of the gods by nymphs or other mothers, as they are reputed to be, who in the world would believe in the children of gods and not in the gods themselves? It would be as ridiculous as to believe in the young of horses or donkeys and not in horses and donkeys themselves. No, Meletus, there is no avoiding the conclusion that you brought this charge against me as a test of my wisdom, or else in despair of finding a genuine offense of which to accuse me. As for your prospect of convincing any living person with even a smattering of intelligence that belief in supernatural and divine activities does not imply belief in supernatural and divine beings, and vice versa, it is outside all the bounds of possibility.

As a matter of fact, gentlemen, I do not feel that it requires much defense to clear myself of Meletus' accusation. What I have said already is enough. But you know very well the truth of what I said in an earlier part of my speech, that I have incurred a great deal of bitter hostility, and this is what will bring about my destruction, if anything does—not Meletus nor Anytus, but the slander and jealousy of a very large section of the people. They have been fatal to a great many other innocent men, and I suppose will continue to be so; there is no likelihood that they will stop at me. But perhaps someone will say, Do you feel no compunction, Socrates, at having followed a line of action which puts you in danger of the death penalty?

I might fairly reply to him, You are mistaken, my friend, if you think that a man who is worth anything ought to spend his time weighing up the prospects of life and death. He has only one thing to consider in performing any action—that is, whether he is acting rightly or wrongly, like a good man or a bad one. On your view the heroes who died at Troy would be poor creatures, especially the son of Thetis. He, if you remember, made light of danger in comparison with incurring dishonor when his goddess mother warned him, eager as he was to kill Hector, in some such words as these, I fancy: My son, if you avenge your comrade Patroclus' death and kill Hector, you will die yourself—'Next after Hector is thy fate prepared.' When he heard this warning, he made light of his death and danger, being much more afraid of an ignoble life and of failing to avenge his friends. 'Let me die forthwith,' said he, 'when I have requited the villain, rather than remain here by the beaked ships to be mocked, a burden on the ground.'[1] Do you suppose that he gave a thought to death and danger?

The truth of the matter is this, gentlemen. Where a man has once taken up his stand, either because it seems best to him or in obedience to his orders, there I believe he is bound to remain and face the danger, taking no account of death or anything else before dishonor.

This being so, it would be shocking inconsistency on my part, gentlemen, if, when the officers whom you chose to command me assigned me my position at Potidaea and Amphipolis and Delium, I remained at my post like anyone else and faced death, and yet afterward, when God appointed me, as I supposed and believed, to the duty of leading the philosophical life, examining myself and others, I were then through fear of death or of any other danger to desert my post. That would indeed be shocking, and then I might really with justice be summoned into court for not believing in the gods, and disobeying the oracle, and being afraid of death, and thinking that I am wise when I am not. For let me tell you, gentlemen, that to be afraid of death is only another form of thinking that one is wise when one is not; it is to think that one knows what one does not know. No one knows with regard to death whether it is not really the greatest blessing that can happen to a man, but people dread it as though they were certain that it is the greatest evil, and this ignorance, which thinks that it knows what it does not, must surely be ignorance most culpable. This, I take it, gentlemen, is the degree, and this the nature of my advantage over the rest of mankind, and if I were to claim to be wiser than my neighbor in any respect, it would be in this—that not possessing any real knowledge of what comes after death, I am also conscious that I do not possess it. But I do know that to do wrong and to disobey my superior, whether God or man, is wicked and dishonorable, and so I shall never feel more fear or aversion for something which, for all I know, may really be a blessing, than for those evils which I know to be evils.

Suppose, then, that you acquit me, and pay no attention to Anytus, who has said that either I should not have appeared before this court at all, or, since I have appeared here, I must be put to death, because if I once escaped your sons would all immediately become utterly demoralized by putting the teaching of Socrates into practice. Suppose that, in view of this, you said to me, Socrates, on this occasion we shall disregard Anytus and acquit you, but only on one condition, that you give up spending your time on this quest and stop philosophizing. If we catch you going on in the same way, you shall be put to death.

Well, supposing, as I said, that you should offer to acquit me on these terms, I should reply, Gentlemen, I am your very grateful and devoted servant, but I owe

[1] *Iliad* 18.96 sq.

a greater obedience to God than to you, and so long as I draw breath and have my faculties, I shall never stop practicing philosophy and exhorting you and elucidating the truth for everyone that I meet. I shall go on saying, in my usual way, My very good friend, you are an Athenian and belong to a city which is the greatest and most famous in the world for its wisdom and strength. Are you not ashamed that you give your attention to acquiring as much money as possible, and similarly with reputation and honor, and give no attention or thought to truth and understanding and the perfection of your soul?

And if any of you disputes this and professes to care about these things, I shall not at once let him go or leave him. No, I shall question him and examine him and test him; and if it appears that in spite of his profession he has made no real progress toward goodness, I shall reprove him for neglecting what is of supreme importance, and giving his attention to trivialities. I shall do this to everyone that I meet, young or old, foreigner or fellow citizen, but especially to you, my fellow citizens, inasmuch as you are closer to me in kinship. This, I do assure you, is what my God commands, and it is my belief that no greater good has ever befallen you in this city than my service to my God. For I spend all my time going about trying to persuade you, young and old, to make your first and chief concern not for your bodies nor for your possessions, but for the highest welfare of your souls, proclaiming as I go, Wealth does not bring goodness, but goodness brings wealth and every other blessing, both to the individual and to the state.

Now if I corrupt the young by this message, the message would seem to be harmful, but if anyone says that my message is different from this, he is talking nonsense. And so, gentlemen, I would say, You can please yourselves whether you listen to Anytus or not, and whether you acquit me or not. You know that I am not going to alter my conduct, not even if I have to die a hundred deaths.

Order, please, gentlemen! Remember my request to give me a hearing without interruption. Besides, I believe that it will be to your advantage to listen. I am going to tell you something else, which may provoke a storm of protest, but please restrain yourselves. I assure you that if I am what I claim to be, and you put me to death, you will harm yourselves more than me. Neither Meletus nor Anytus can do me any harm at all; they would not have the power, because I do not believe that the law of God permits a better man to be harmed by a worse. No doubt my accuser might put me to death or have me banished or deprived of civic rights, but even if he thinks— as he probably does, and others too, I dare say—that these are great calamities, I do not think so. I believe that it is far worse to do what he is doing now, trying to put an innocent man to death. For this reason, gentlemen, so far from pleading on my own behalf, as might be supposed, I am really pleading on yours, to save you from misusing the gift of God by condemning me. If you put me to death, you will not easily find anyone to take my place. It is literally true, even if it sounds rather comical, that God has specially appointed me to this city, as though it were a large thorough-bred horse which because of its great size is inclined to be lazy and needs the stimula-tion of some stinging fly. It seems to me that God has attached me to this city to perform the office of such a fly, and all day long I never cease to settle here, there, and everywhere, rousing, persuading, reproving every one of you. You will not easily find another like me, gentlemen, and if you take my advice you will spare my life. I suspect, however, that before long you will awake from your drowsing, and in your annoyance you will take Anytus' advice and finish me off with a single slap, and then you will go on sleeping till the end of your days, unless God in his care for you sends someone to take my place.

If you doubt whether I am really the sort of person who would have been sent to this city as a gift from God, you can convince yourselves by looking at it in this way. Does it seem natural that I should have neglected my own affairs and endured the humiliation of allowing my family to be neglected for all these years, while I busied myself all the time on your behalf, going like a father or an elder brother to see each one of you privately, and urging you to set your thoughts on goodness? If I had got any enjoyment from it, or if I had been paid for my good advice, there would have been some explanation for my conduct, but as it is you can see for yourselves that although my accusers unblushingly charge me with all sorts of other crimes, there is one thing that they have not had the impudence to pretend on any testimony, and that is that I have ever exacted or asked a fee from anyone. The witness that I can offer to prove the truth of my statement is, I think, a convincing one —my poverty.

It may seem curious that I should go round giving advice like this and busying myself in people's private affairs, and yet never venture publicly to address you as a whole and advise on matters of state. The reason for this is what you have often heard me say before on many other occasions—that I am subject to a divine or supernatural experience, which Meletus saw fit to travesty in his indictment. It began in my early childhood—a sort of voice which comes to me, and when it comes it always dissuades me from what I am proposing to do, and never urges me on. It is this that debars me from entering public life, and a very good thing too, in my opinion, because you may be quite sure, gentlemen, that if I had tried long ago to engage in politics, I should long ago have lost my life, without doing any good either to you or to myself. Please do not be offended if I tell you the truth. No man on earth who conscientiously opposes either you or any other organized democracy, and flatly prevents a great many wrongs and illegalities from taking place in the state to which he belongs, can possibly escape with his life. The true champion of justice, if he intends to survive even for a short time, must necessarily confine himself to private life and leave politics alone.

I will offer you substantial proofs of what I have said—not theories, but what you can appreciate better, facts. Listen while I describe my actual experiences, so that you may know that I would never submit wrongly to any authority through fear of death, but would refuse even at the cost of my life. It will be a commonplace story, such as you often hear in the courts, but it is true.

The only office which I have ever held in our city, gentlemen, was when I was elected to the Council. It so happened that our group was acting as the executive when you decided that the ten commanders who had failed to rescue the men who were lost in the naval engagement should be tried en bloc, which was illegal, as you all recognized later. On this occasion I was the only member of the executive who insisted that you should not act unconstitutionally, and voted against the proposal; and although your leaders were all ready to denounce and arrest me, and you were all urging them on at the top of your voices, I thought that it was my duty to face it out on the side of law and justice rather than support you, through fear of prison or death, in your wrong decision.

This happened while we were still under a democracy. When the oligarchy came into power, the Thirty Commissioners in their turn summoned me and four others to the Round Chamber and instructed us to go and fetch Leon of Salamis from his home for execution. This was of course only one of many instances in which they issued such instructions, their object being to implicate as many people as possible in their wickedness. On this occasion, however, I again made it clear not by my words but by my actions that death did not matter to me at all—if that is not too strong an expression—but that it mattered all the world to me that I should do nothing wrong or wicked. Powerful as it was, that government did not terrify me into doing a wrong action. When we came out of the Round Chamber, the other four went off to Salamis and arrested Leon, and I went home. I should probably have been put to death for this, if the government had not fallen soon afterward. There are plenty of people who will testify to these statements.

Do you suppose that I should have lived as long as I have if I had moved in the sphere of public life, and conducting myself in that sphere like an honorable man, had always upheld the cause of right, and conscientiously set this end above all other things? Not by a very long way, gentlemen; neither would any other man. You will find that throughout my life I have been consistent in any public duties that I have performed, and the same also in my personal dealings. I have never countenanced any action that was incompatible with justice on the part of any person, including those whom some people maliciously call my pupils. I have never set up as any man's teacher, but if anyone, young or old, is eager to hear me conversing and carrying out my private mission, I never grudge him the opportunity; nor do I charge a fee for talking to him, and refuse to talk without one. I am ready to answer questions for rich and poor alike, and I am equally ready if anyone prefers to listen to me and answer my questions. If any given one of these people becomes a good citizen or a bad one, I cannot fairly be held responsible, since I have never promised or imparted any teaching to anybody, and if anyone asserts that he has ever learned or heard from me privately anything which was not open to everyone else, you may be quite sure that he is not telling the truth.

But how is it that some people enjoy spending a great deal of time in my company? You have heard the reason, gentlemen; I told you quite frankly. It is because they enjoy hearing me examine those who think that they are wise when they are not—an experience which has its amusing side. This duty I have accepted, as I said, in obedience to God's commands given in oracles and dreams and in every other way that any other divine dispensation has ever impressed a duty upon man. This is a true statement, gentlemen, and easy to verify. If it is a fact that I am in process of corrupting some of the young, and have succeeded already in corrupting others, and if it were a fact that some of the latter, being now grown up, had discovered that I had ever given them bad advice when they were young, surely they ought now to be coming forward to denounce and punish me. And if they did not like to do it themselves, you would expect some of their families—their fathers and brothers and other near relations—to remember it now, if their own flesh and blood had suffered any harm from me. Certainly a great many of them have found their way into this court, as I can see for myself—first Crito over there, my contemporary and near neighbor, the father of this young man Critobulus, and then Lysanias of Sphettus, the father of Aeschines here, and next Antiphon of Cephisus, over there, the father of Epigenes. Then besides there are all those whose brothers have been members of our circle—Nicostratus, the son of Theozotides, the brother of Theodotus, but Theodotus is dead, so he cannot appeal to his brother, and Paralus here, the son of Demodocus, whose brother was Theages. And here is Adimantus, the son of Ariston, whose brother Plato is over there, and Aeantodorus, whose brother Apollodorus is here on this side. I can name many more besides, some of whom Meletus most certainly ought to have produced as witnesses in the course of his speech. If he forgot to do so then, let him do it now—I am willing to make way for him. Let him state whether he has any such evidence to offer. On the contrary, gentlemen, you will find that they are all prepared to help me—the corrupter and evil genius of their nearest and dearest relatives, as Meletus and Anytus say. The actual victims of my corrupting influence might perhaps be excused for helping me; but as for the uncorrupted, their relations of mature age, what other reason can they have for helping me except the right and proper one, that they know Meletus is lying and I am telling the truth?

There, gentlemen, that, and perhaps a little more to the same effect, is the substance of what I can say in my defense. It may be that some one of you, remembering his own case, will be annoyed that whereas he, in standing his trial upon a less serious charge than this, made pitiful appeals to the jury with floods of tears, and had his infant children produced in court to excite the maximum of sympathy, and many of his relatives and friends as well, I on the contrary intend to do nothing of the sort, and that, although I am facing, as it might appear, the utmost danger. It may be that one of you, reflecting on these facts, will be prejudiced against me, and being irritated by his reflections, will give his vote in anger. If one of you is so disposed—I do not expect it, but there is the possibility—I think that I should be quite justified in saying to him, My dear sir, of course I have some relatives. To quote the very words of Homer, even I am not sprung 'from an oak or from a rock,'[2] but from human parents, and consequently I have relatives—yes, and sons too, gentlemen, three of them, one almost grown up and the other two only children—but all the same I am not going to produce them here and beseech you to acquit me.

Why do I not intend to do anything of this kind? Not out of perversity, gentlemen, nor out of contempt for you; whether I am brave or not in the face of death has nothing to do with it. The point is that for my own credit and yours and for the credit of the state as a whole, I do not think that it is right for me to use any of these methods at my age and with my reputation—which may be true or it may be false, but at any rate the view is held that Socrates is different from the common run of mankind. Now if those of you who are supposed to be distinguished for wisdom or courage or any other virtue are to behave in this way, it would be a disgrace. I have often noticed that some people of this type, for all their high standing, go to extraordinary lengths when they come up for trial, which shows that they think it will be a dreadful thing to lose their lives—as though they would be immortal if you did not put them to death! In my opinion these people bring disgrace upon our city. Any of our visitors might be excused for thinking that the finest specimens of Athenian manhood, whom their fellow citizens select on their merits to rule over them and hold other high positions, are no better than women. If you have even the smallest

[2] *Odyssey* 19.163.

reputation, gentlemen, you ought not to descend to these methods; and if we do so, you must not give us license. On the contrary, you must make it clear that anyone who stages these pathetic scenes and so brings ridicule upon our city is far more likely to be condemned than if he kept perfectly quiet.

But apart from all question of appearances, gentlemen, I do not think that it is right for a man to appeal to the jury or to get himself acquitted by doing so; he ought to inform them of the facts and convince them by argument. The jury does not sit to dispense justice as a favor, but to decide where justice lies, and the oath which they have sworn is not to show favor at their own discretion, but to return a just and lawful verdict. It follows that we must not develop in you, nor you allow to grow in yourselves, the habit of perjury; that would be sinful for us both. Therefore you must not expect me, gentlemen, to behave toward you in a way which I consider neither reputable nor moral nor consistent with my religious duty, and above all you must not expect it when I stand charged with impiety by Meletus here. Surely it is obvious that if I tried to persuade you and prevail upon you by my entreaties to go against your solemn oath, I should be teaching you contempt for religion, and by my very defense I should be accusing myself of having no religious belief. But that is very far from the truth. I have a more sincere belief, gentlemen, than any of my accusers, and I leave it to you and to God to judge me as it shall be best for me and for yourselves.

There are a great many reasons, gentlemen, why I am not distressed by this result—I mean your condemnation of me—but the chief reason is that the result was not unexpected. What does surprise me is the number of votes cast on the two sides. I should never have believed that it would be such a close thing, but now it seems that if a mere thirty votes had gone the other way, I should have been acquitted. Even as it is, I feel that so far as Meletus' part is concerned I have been acquitted, and not only that, but anyone can see that if Anytus and Lycon had not come forward to accuse me, Meletus would actually have forfeited his one thousand drachmas for not having obtained one fifth of the votes.

However, we must face the fact that he demands the death penalty. Very good. What alternative penalty shall I propose to you, gentlemen? Obviously it must be adequate. Well, what penalty do I deserve to pay or suffer, in view of what I have done?

I have never lived an ordinary quiet life. I did not care for the things that most people care about—making money, having a comfortable home, high military or civil rank, and all the other activities, political appointments, secret societies, party organizations, which go on in our city. I thought that I was really too strict in my principles to survive if I went in for this sort of thing. So instead of taking a course which would have done no good either to you or to me, I set myself to do you individually in private what I hold to be the greatest possible service. I tried to persuade each one of you not to think more of practical advantages than of his mental and moral well-being, or in general to think more of advantage than of well-being in the case of the state or of anything else. What do I deserve for behaving in this way? Some reward, gentlemen, if I am bound to suggest what I really deserve, and what is more, a reward which would be appropriate for myself. Well, what is appropriate for a poor man who is a public benefactor and who requires leisure for giving you moral encouragement? Nothing could be more appropriate for such a person than free maintenance at the state's expense. He deserves it much more than any victor in the races at Olympia, whether he wins with a single horse or a pair or a team of four. These people give you the semblance of success, but I give you the reality; they do not need maintenance, but I do. So if I am to suggest an appropriate penalty which is strictly in accordance with justice, I suggest free maintenance by the state.

Perhaps when I say this I may give you the impression, as I did in my remarks about exciting sympathy and making passionate appeals, that I am showing a deliberate perversity. That is not so, gentlemen. The real position is this. I am convinced that I never wrong anyone intentionally, but I cannot convince you of this, because we have had so little time for discussion. If it was your practice, as it is with other nations, to give not one day but several to the hearing of capital trials, I believe that you might have been convinced, but under present conditions it is not easy to dispose of grave allegations in a short space of time. So, being convinced that I do no wrong to anybody, I can hardly be expected to wrong myself by asserting that I deserve something bad, or by proposing a corresponding penalty. Why should I? For fear of suffering this penalty proposed by Meletus, when, as I said, I do not know whether it is a good thing or a bad? Do you expect me to choose something which I know very well is bad by making my counterproposal? Imprisonment? Why should I spend my days in prison, in subjection to the periodically appointed officers of the law? A fine, with imprisonment until it is paid? In my case the effect would be just the same, because I have no money to pay a fine. Or shall I suggest banishment? You would very likely accept the suggestion.

I should have to be desperately in love with life to do that, gentlemen. I am not so blind that I cannot see that you, my fellow citizens, have come to the end of your patience with my discussions and conversations. You have found them too irksome and irritating, and now you are trying to get rid of them. Will any other people find them easy to put up with? That is most unlikely, gentlemen. A fine life I should have if I left this country at my age and spent the rest of my days trying one city after another and being turned out every time! I know very well that wherever I go the young people will listen to my conversation just as they do here, and if I try to keep them off, they will make their elders drive me out, while if I do not, the fathers and other relatives will drive me out of their own accord for the sake of the young.

Perhaps someone may say, But surely, Socrates, after you have left us you can spend the rest of your life in quietly minding your own business.

This is the hardest thing of all to make some of you understand. If I say that this would be disobedience to God, and that is why I cannot 'mind my own business,' you will not believe that I am serious. If on the other hand I tell you that to let no day pass without discussing goodness and all the other subjects about which you hear me talking and examining both myself and others is really the very best thing that a man can do, and that life without this sort of examination is not worth living, you will be even less inclined to believe me. Nevertheless that is how it is, gentlemen, as I maintain, though it is not easy to convince you of it. Besides, I am not accustomed to think of myself as deserving punishment. If I had money, I would have suggested a fine that I could afford, because that would not have done me any harm. As it is, I cannot, because I have none, unless of course you like to fix the penalty at what I could pay. I suppose I could probably afford a mina. I suggest a fine of that amount.

One moment, gentlemen. Plato here, and Crito and Critobulus and Apollodorus, want me to propose thirty minas, on their security. Very well, I agree to this sum, and you can rely upon these gentlemen for its payment.

Well, gentlemen, for the sake of a very small gain in time you are going to earn the reputation—and the blame from those who wish to disparage our city—of having put Socrates to death, 'that wise man'—because they will say I am wise even if I am not, these people who want to find fault with you. If you had waited just a little while, you would have had your way in the course of nature. You can see that I am well on in life and near to death. I am saying this not to all of you but to those who voted for my execution, and I have something else to say to them as well.

No doubt you think, gentlemen, that I have been condemned for lack of the arguments which I could have used if I had thought it right to leave nothing unsaid or undone to secure my acquittal. But that is very far from the truth. It is not a lack of arguments that has caused my condemnation, but a lack of effrontery and impudence, and the fact that I have refused to address you in the way which would give you most pleasure. You would have liked to hear me weep and wail, doing and saying all sorts of things which I regard as unworthy of myself, but which you are used to hearing from other people. But I did not think then that I ought to stoop to servility because I was in danger, and I do not regret now the way in which I pleaded my case. I would much rather die as the result of this defense than live as the result of the other sort. In a court of law, just as in warfare, neither I nor any other ought to use his wits to escape death by any means. In battle it is often obvious that you could escape being killed by giving up your arms and throwing yourself upon the mercy of your pursuers, and in every kind of danger there are plenty of devices for avoiding death if you are unscrupulous enough to stick at nothing. But I suggest, gentlemen, that the difficulty is not so much to escape death; the real difficulty is to escape from doing wrong, which is far more fleet of foot. In this present instance I, the slow old man, have been overtaken by the slower of the two, but my accusers, who are clever and quick, have been overtaken by the faster— by iniquity. When I leave this court I shall go away condemned by you to death, but they will go away convicted by truth herself of depravity and wickedness. And they accept their sentence even as I accept mine. No doubt it was bound to be so, and I think that the result is fair enough.

Having said so much, I feel moved to prophesy to you who have given your vote against me, for I am now at the point where the gift of prophecy comes most readily to men—at the point of death. I tell you, my executioners, that as soon as I am dead, vengeance shall fall upon you with a punishment far more painful than your killing of me. You have brought about my death in the belief that through it you will be delivered from submitting your conduct to criticism, but I say that the result will be just the opposite. You will have more critics, whom up till now I have restrained without your knowing it, and being younger they will be harsher to you and will cause you more annoyance. If you expect to stop denunciation of your wrong way of life by putting people to death, there is something amiss with your reasoning. This way of escape is neither possible nor creditable. The best and easiest way is not to stop the mouths of others, but to make yourselves as good men as you can. This is my last message to you who voted for my condemnation.

As for you who voted for my acquittal, I should very much like to say a few words to reconcile you to the result, while the officials are busy and I am not yet on my way to the place where I must die. I ask you, gentlemen, to spare me these few moments. There is no reason why we should not exchange fancies while the law permits. I look upon you as my friends, and I want you to understand the right way of regarding my present position.

Gentlemen of the jury—for *you* deserve to be so called—I have had a remarkable experience. In the past the prophetic voice to which I have become accustomed has always been my constant companion, opposing me even in quite trivial things if I was going to take the wrong course. Now something has happened to me, as you can see, which might be thought and is commonly considered to be a supreme calamity; yet neither when I left home this morning, nor when I was taking my place here in the court, nor at any point in any part of my speech did the divine sign oppose me. In other discussions it has often checked me in the middle of a sentence, but this time it has never opposed me in any part of this business in anything that I have said or done. What do I suppose to be the explanation? I will tell you. I suspect that this thing that has happened to me is a blessing, and we are quite mistaken in supposing death to be an evil. I have good grounds for thinking this, because my accustomed sign could not have failed to oppose me if what I was doing had not been sure to bring some good result.

We should reflect that there is much reason to hope for a good result on other grounds as well. Death is one of two things. Either it is annihilation, and the dead have no consciousness of anything, or, as we are told, it is really a change—a migration of the soul from this place to another. Now if there is no consciousness but only a dreamless sleep, death must be a marvelous gain. I suppose that if anyone were told to pick out the night on which he slept so soundly as not even to dream, and then to compare it with all the other nights and days of his life, and then were told to say, after due consideration, how many better and happier days and nights than this he had spent in the course of his life—well, I think that the Great King himself, to say nothing of any private person, would find these days and nights easy to count in comparison with the rest. If death is like this, then, I call it gain, because the whole of time, if you look at it in this way, can be regarded as no more than one single night. If on the other hand death is a removal from here to some other place, and if what we are told is true, that all the dead are there, what greater blessing could there be than this, gentlemen? If on arrival in the other world, beyond the reach of our so-called justice, one will find there the true judges who are said to preside in those courts, Minos and Rhadamanthus and Aeacus and Triptolemus and all those other half-divinities who were upright in their earthly life, would that be an unrewarding journey? Put it in this way. How much would one of you give to meet Orpheus and Musaeus, Hesiod and Homer? I am willing to die ten times over if this account is true. It would be a specially interesting experience for me to join them there, to meet Palamedes and Ajax, the son of Telamon, and any other heroes of the old days who met their death through an unfair trial, and to compare my fortunes with theirs—it would be rather amusing, I think.

And above all I should like to spend my time there, as here, in examining and searching people's minds, to find out who is really wise among them, and who only thinks that he is. What would one not give, gentlemen, to be able to question the leader of that great host against Troy, or Odysseus, or Sisyphus, or the thousands of other men and women whom one could mention, to talk and mix and argue with whom would be unimaginable happiness? At any rate I presume that they do not put one to death there for such conduct, because apart from the other happiness in which their world surpasses ours, they are now immortal for the rest of time, if what we are told is true.

You too, gentlemen of the jury, must look forward to death with confidence, and fix your minds on this one belief, which is certain—that nothing can harm a good man either in life or after death, and his fortunes are not a matter of indifference to the gods. This present experience of mine has not come about mechanically. I am quite clear that the time had come when it was better for me to die and be released from my distractions. That is why my sign never turned me back. For my own part I bear no grudge at all against those who condemned me and accused me, although it was not with this kind intention that they did so, but because they thought that they were hurting me; and that is culpable of them. However, I ask them to grant me one favor. When my sons grow up, gentlemen, if you think that they are putting money or anything else before goodness, take your revenge by plaguing them as I plagued you; and if they fancy themselves for no reason, you must scold them just as I scolded you, for neglecting the important things and thinking that they are good for something when they are good for nothing. If you do this, I shall have had justice at your hands, both I myself and my children.

Now it is time that we were going, I to die and you to live, but which of us has the happier prospect is unknown to anyone but God.

SOCRATES' DEATH

There is one way, then, in which a man can be free from all anxiety about the fate of his soul—if in life he has abandoned bodily pleasures and adornments, as foreign to his purpose and likely to do more harm than good, and has devoted himself to the pleasures of acquiring knowledge, and so by decking his soul not with a borrorowed beauty but with its own—with self-control, and goodness, and courage, and liberality, and truth—has fitted himself to await his journey to the next world. You, Simmias and Cebes and the rest, will each make this journey someday in the future, but for me the fated hour, as a tragic character might say, calls even now. In other words, it is about time that I took my bath. I prefer to have a bath before drinking the poison, rather than give the women the trouble of washing me when I am dead.

When he had finished speaking, Crito said, Very well, Socrates. But have you no directions for the others or myself about your children or anything else? What can we do to please you best?

Nothing new, Crito, said Socrates, just what I am always telling you. If you look after yourselves, whatever you do will please me and mine and you too, even if you don't agree with me now. On the other hand, if you neglect yourselves and fail to follow the line of life as I have laid it down both now and in the past, however fervently you agree with me now, it will do no good at all.

We shall try our best to do as you say, said Crito. But how shall we bury you?

Any way you like, replied Socrates, that is, if you can catch me and I don't slip through your fingers.

He laughed gently as he spoke, and turning to us went on, I can't persuade Crito that I am this Socrates here who is talking to you now and marshaling all the arguments. He thinks that I am the one whom he will see presently lying dead, and he asks how he is to bury me! As for my long and elaborate explanation that when I have drunk the poison I shall remain with you no longer, but depart to a state of heavenly happiness, this attempt to console both you and myself seems to be wasted on him. You must give an assurance to Crito for me—the opposite of the one which he gave to the court which tried me. He undertook that I should stay, but you must assure him that when I am dead I shall not stay, but depart and be gone. That will help Crito to bear it more easily, and keep him from being distressed on my account when he sees my body being burned or buried, as if something dreadful were happening to me, or from saying at the funeral that it is Socrates whom he is laying out or carrying to the grave or burying. Believe me, my dear friend Crito, misstatements are not merely jarring in their immediate context; they also have a bad effect upon the soul. No, you must keep up your spirits and say that it is only my body that you are burying, and you can bury it as you please, in whatever way you think is most proper.

With these words he got up and went into another room to bathe, and Crito went after him, but told us to wait. So we waited, discussing and reviewing what had been said, or else dwelling upon the greatness of the calamity which had befallen us, for we felt just as though we were losing a father and should be orphans for the rest of our lives. Meanwhile, when Socrates had taken his bath, his children were brought to see him—he had two little sons and one big boy—and the women of his household, you know, arrived. He talked to them in Crito's presence and gave them directions about carrying out his wishes. Then he told the women and children to go away, and came back himself to join us.

It was now nearly sunset, because he had spent a long time inside. He came and sat down; fresh from the bath, and he had only been talking for a few minutes when the prison officer came in, and walked up to him.

Socrates, he said, at any rate I shall not have to find fault with you, as I do with others, for getting angry with me and cursing when I tell them to drink the poison—carrying out government orders. I have come to know during this time that you are the noblest and the gentlest and the bravest of all the men that have ever come here, and now especially I am sure that you are not angry with me, but with them, because you know who are responsible. So now—you know what I have come to say—good-by, and try to bear what must be as easily as you can.

As he spoke he burst into tears, and turning round, went away.

Socrates looked up at him and said, Good-by to you, too. We will do as you say.

Then addressing us he went on, What a charming person! All the time I have been here he has visited me, and sometimes had discussions with me, and shown me the greatest kindness—and how generous of him now to shed tears for me at parting! But come, Crito, let us do as he says. Someone had better bring in the poison, if it is ready-prepared; if not, tell the man to prepare it.

But surely, Socrates, said Crito, the sun is still upon the mountains; it has not gone down yet. Besides, I know that in other cases people have dinner and enjoy their wine, and sometimes the company of those whom they love, long after they receive the warning, and only drink the poison quite late at night. No need to hurry. There is still plenty of time.

It is natural that these people whom you speak of should act in that way, Crito, said Socrates, because they think that they gain by it. And it is also natural that I should not, because I believe that I should gain nothing by drinking the poison a little later—I should only make myself ridiculous in my own eyes if I clung to life and hugged it when it has no more to offer. Come, do as I say and don't make difficulties.

At this Crito made a sign to his servant, who was standing near by. The servant went out and after spending a considerable time returned with the man who was to administer the poison. He was carrying it ready-prepared in a cup.

When Socrates saw him he said, Well, my good fellow, you understand these things. What ought I to do?

Just drink it, he said, and then walk about until you feel a weight in your legs, and then lie down. Then it will act of its own accord.

As he spoke he handed the cup to Socrates, who received it quite cheerfully, Echecrates, without a tremor, without any change of color or expression, and said, looking up under his brows with his usual steady gaze, What do you say about pouring a libation from this drink? Is it permitted, or not?

We only prepare what we regard as the normal dose, Socrates, he replied.

I see, said Socrates. But I suppose I am allowed, or rather bound, to pray the gods that my removal from this world to the other may be prosperous. This is my prayer, then, and I hope that it may be granted.

With these words, quite calmly and with no sign of distaste, he drained the cup in one breath.

Up till this time most of us had been fairly successful in keeping back our tears, but when we saw that he was drinking, that he had actually drunk it, we could do so no longer. In spite of myself the tears came pouring out, so that I covered my face and wept brokenheartedly—not for him, but for my own calamity in losing such a friend. Crito had given up even before me, and had gone out when he could not restrain his tears. But Apollodorus, who had never stopped crying even before, now broke out into such a storm of passionate weeping that he made everyone in the room break down, except Socrates himself, who said, Really, my friends, what a way to behave! Why, that was my main reason for sending away the women, to prevent this sort of disturbance, because I am told that one should make one's end in a tranquil frame of mind. Calm yourselves and try to be brave.

This made us feel ashamed, and we controlled our tears. Socrates walked about, and presently, saying that his legs were heavy, lay down on his back—that was what the man recommended. The man—he was the same one who had administered the poison—kept his hand upon Socrates, and after a little while examined his feet and legs, then pinched his foot hard and asked if he felt it. Socrates said no. Then he did the same to his legs, and moving gradually upward in this way let us see that he was getting cold and numb. Presently he felt him again and said that when it reached his heart, Socrates would be gone.

The coldness was spreading about as far as his waist when Socrates uncovered his face, for he had covered it up, and said—they were his last words—Crito, we ought to offer a cock to Asclepius. See to it, and don't forget.

No, it shall be done, said Crito. Are you sure that there is nothing else?

Socrates made no reply to this question, but after a little while he stirred, and when the man uncovered him, his eyes were fixed. When Crito saw this, he closed the mouth and eyes.

Such, Echecrates, was the end of our comrade, who was, we may fairly say, of all those whom we knew in our time, the bravest and also the wisest and most upright man.

Human

Dignity

———

IMMANUEL KANT

Treating Others as Persons, not Things

Immanuel Kant (1724–1804) was the German
philosopher whose theories of ethics and knowledge
changed the course of Western thought and remain
influential today. Among his other works is the
Critique of Pure Reason, from which an additional
selection is printed in Section III, "Man and World."

There is therefore only a single categorical imperative and it is this: *'Act only on that maxim through which you can at the same time will that it should become a universal law'.*

Now if all imperatives of duty can be derived from this one imperative as their principle, then even although we leave it unsettled whether what we call duty may not be an empty concept, we shall still be able to show at least what we understand by it and what the concept means.

Since the universality of the law governing the production of effects constitutes what is properly called *nature* in its most general sense (nature as regards its form)—that is, the existence of things so far as determined by universal laws—the universal imperative of duty may also run as follows: *'Act as if the maxim of your action were to become through your will a universal law of nature.'*

We will now enumerate a few duties, following their customary division into duties towards self and duties towards others and into perfect and imperfect duties.

1. A man feels sick of life as the result of a series of misfortunes that has mounted to the point of despair, but he is still so far in possession of his reason as to ask himself whether taking his own life may not be contrary to his duty to himself. He now applies the test 'Can the maxim of my action really become a universal law of nature?' His maxim is 'From self-love I make it my principle to shorten my life if its continuance threatens more evil than it promises pleasure.' The only further question to ask is whether this principle of self-love can become a universal law of nature. It is then seen at once that a system of nature by whose law the very same feeling whose function (*Bestimmung*) is to stimulate the furtherance of life should actually destroy life would contradict itself and consequently could not subsist as a system of nature. Hence this maxim cannot possibly hold as a universal law of nature and is therefore entirely opposed to the supreme principle of all duty.

2. Another finds himself driven to borrowing money because of need. He well knows that he will not be able to pay it back; but he sees too that he will get no loan unless he gives a firm promise to pay it back within a fixed time. He is inclined to

From *Groundwork of the Metaphysics of Morals,* by Immanuel Kant, in *The Moral Law,* translated by H. J. Paton, Hutchinson University Library, 1948. Reprinted by permission of the publishers.

make such a promise; but he has still enough conscience to ask 'Is it not unlawful and contrary to duty to get out of difficulties in this way?' Supposing, however, he did resolve to do so, the maxim of his action would run thus: 'Whenever I believe myself short of money, I will borrow money and promise to pay it back, though I know that this will never be done'. Now this principle of self-love or personal advantage is perhaps quite compatible with my own entire future welfare; only there remains the question 'Is it right?' I therefore transform the demand of self-love into a universal law and frame my question thus: 'How would things stand if my maxim became a universal law?' I then see straight away that this maxim can never rank as a universal law of nature and be self-consistent, but must necessarily contradict itself. For the universality of a law that every one believing himself to be in need can make any promise he pleases with the intention not to keep it would make promising, and the very purpose of promising, itself impossible, since no one would believe he was being promised anything, but would laugh at utterances of this kind as empty shams.

3. A third finds in himself a talent whose cultivation would make him a useful man for all sorts of purposes. But he sees himself in comfortable circumstances, and he prefers to give himself up to pleasure rather than to bother about increasing and improving his fortunate natural aptitudes. Yet he asks himself further 'Does my maxim of neglecting my natural gifts, besides agreeing in itself with my tendency to indulgence, agree also with what is called duty?' He then sees that a system of nature could indeed always subsist under such a universal law, although (like the South Sea Islanders) every man should let his talents rust and should be bent on devoting his life solely to idleness, indulgence, procreation, and, in a word, to enjoyment. Only he cannot possibly *will* that this should become a universal law of nature or should be implanted in us as such a law by a natural instinct. For as a rational being he necessarily wills that all his powers should be developed, since they serve him, and are given him, for all sorts of possible ends.

4. Yet a *fourth* is himself flourishing, but he sees others who have to struggle with great hardships (and whom he could easily help); and he thinks 'What does it matter to me? Let every one be as happy as Heaven wills or as he can make himself; I won't deprive him of anything; I won't even envy him; only I have no wish to contribute anything to his well-being or to his support in distress!' Now admittedly if such an attitude were a universal law of nature, mankind could get on perfectly well—better no doubt than if everybody prates about sympathy and goodwill, and even takes pains, on occasion, to practise them, but on the other hand cheats where he can, traffics in human rights, or violates them in other ways. But although it is possible that a universal law of nature could subsist in harmony with this maxim, yet it is impossible to *will* that such a principle should hold everywhere as a law of nature. For a will which decided in this way would be in conflict with itself, since many a situation might arise in which the man needed love and sympathy from others, and in which, by such a law of nature sprung from his own will, he would rob himself of all hope of the help he wants for himself.

· · ·

Suppose, however, there were something *whose existence* has *in itself* an absolute value, something which as *an end in itself* could be ground of determinate laws; then in it, and in it alone, would there be the ground of a possible categorical imperative—that is, of a practical law.

Now I say that man, and in general every rational being, *exists* as an end in himself, *not merely as a means* for arbitrary use by this or that will: he must in all his actions, whether they are directed to himself or to other rational beings, always be viewed *at the same time as an end*. All the objects of inclination have only a conditioned value; for if there were not these inclinations and the needs grounded on them, their object would be valueless. Inclinations themselves, as sources of needs, are so far from having an absolute value to make them desirable for their own sake that it must rather be the universal wish of every rational being to be wholly free from them. Thus the value of all objects that can *be produced* by our action is always conditioned. Beings whose existence depends, not on our will, but on nature, have none the less, if they are non-rational beings, only a relative value as means and are consequently called *things*. Rational beings, on the other hand, are called *persons* because their nature already marks them out as ends in themselves— that is, as something which ought not to be used merely as a means—and consequently imposes to that extent a limit on all arbitrary treatment of them (and is an object of reverence). Persons, therefore, are not merely subjective ends whose existence as an object of our actions has a value *for us:* they are *objective ends*—that is, things whose existence is in itself an end, and indeed an end such that in its place we can put no other end to which they should serve *simply* as means; for unless this is so, nothing at all of *absolute* value would be found anywhere. But if all value were conditioned—that is, contingent—then no supreme principle could be found for reason at all.

If then there is to be a supreme practical principle and—so far as the human will is concerned—a categorical imperative, it must be such that from the idea of something which is necessarily an end for every one because it is an *end in itself* it forms an *objective* principle of the will and consequently can serve as a practical law. The ground of this principle is this: *Rational nature exists as an end in itself.* This is the way in which a man necessarily conceives his own existence: it is therefore so far a *subjective* principle of human actions. But it is also the way in which every other rational being conceives his existence on the same rational ground which is valid also for me; hence it is at the same time an *objective* principle, from which, as a supreme practical ground, it must be possible to derive all laws for the will. The practical imperative will therefore be as follows: *Act in such a way that you always treat humanity, whether in your own person or in the person of any other, never simply as a means, but always at the same time as an end*. We will now consider whether this can be carried out in practice.

Let us keep to our previous examples.

First, as regards the concept of necessary duty to oneself, the man who contemplates suicide will ask 'Can my action be compatible with the Idea of humanity *as an end in itself?*' If he does away with himself in order to escape from a painful situation, he is making use of a person merely as *a means* to maintain a tolerable state of affairs till the end of his life. But man is not a thing—not something to be used *merely* as a means: he must always in all his actions be regarded as an end in himself. Hence I cannot dispose of man in my person by maiming, spoiling, or killing. (A more precise determination of this principle in order to avoid all misunderstanding—for example, about having limbs amputated to save myself or about exposing my life to danger in order to preserve it, and so on—I must here forego: this question belongs to morals proper.)

Secondly, so far as necessary or strict duty to others is concerned, the man who has a mind to make a false promise to others will see at once that he is intending to make use of another man *merely as a means* to an end he does not share. For the man whom I seek to use for my own purposes by such a promise cannot possibly agree with my way of behaving to him, and so cannot himself share the end of the action. This incompatibility with the principle of duty to others leaps to the eye more obviously when we bring in examples of attempts on the freedom and property of others. For then it is manifest that a violator of the rights of man intends to use the person of others merely as a means without taking into consideration that, as rational beings, they ought always at the same time to be rated as ends—that is, only as beings who must themselves be able to share in the end of the very same action.

Thirdly, in regard to contingent (meritorious) duty to oneself, it is not enough that an action should refrain from conflicting with humanity in our own person as an end in itself: it must also *harmonize with this end.* Now there are in humanity capacities for greater perfection which form part of nature's purpose for humanity in our person. To neglect these can admittedly be compatible with the *maintenance* of humanity as an end in itself, but not with the *promotion* of this end.

Fourthly, as regards meritorious duties to others, the natural end which all men seek is their own happiness. Now humanity could no doubt subsist if everybody contributed nothing to the happiness of others but at the same time refrained from deliberately impairing their happiness. This is, however, merely to agree negatively and not positively with *humanity as an end in itself* unless every one endeavours also, so far as in him lies, to further the ends of others. For the ends of a subject who is an end in himself must, if this conception is to have its *full* effect in me, be also, as far as possible, *my* ends.

This principle of humanity, and in general of every rational agent, *as an end in itself* (a principle which is the supreme limiting condition of every man's freedom of action) is not borrowed from experience; firstly, because it is universal, applying as it does to all rational beings as such, and no experience is adequate to determine universality; secondly, because in it humanity is conceived, not as an end of man (subjectively)—that is, as an object which, as a matter of fact, happens to be made an end—but as an objective end—one which, be our ends what they may, must, as a law, constitute the supreme limiting condition of all subjective ends and so must spring from pure reason. That is to say, the ground for every enactment of practical law lies *objectively in the rule* and in the form of universality which (according to our first principle) makes the rule capable of being a law (and indeed a law of nature); *subjectively,* however, it lies in the *end;* but (according to our second principle) the subject of all ends is to be found in every rational being as an end in himself. From this there now follows our third practical principle for the will—as the supreme condition of the will's conformity with universal practical reason—namely, the Idea *of the will of every rational being as a will which makes universal law.*

By this principle all maxims are repudiated which cannot accord with the will's own enactment of universal law. The will is therefore not merely subject to the law, but is so subject that it must be considered as also *making the law* for itself and precisely on this account as first of all subject to the law (of which it can regard itself as the author).

JOHN STUART MILL

The Limits to the Authority of Society over the Individual

John Stuart Mill (1806–1873) was a British ethical theorist and philosopher of science. He also wrote *Utilitarianism* and *A System of Logic.*

What, then, is the rightful limit to the sovereignty of the individual over himself? Where does the authority of society begin? How much of human life should be assigned to individuality, and how much to society?

Each will receive its proper share, if each has that which more particularly concerns it. To individuality should belong the part of life in which it is chiefly the individual that is interested; to society, the part which chiefly interests society.

Though society is not founded on a contract, and though no good purpose is answered by inventing a contract in order to deduce social obligations from it, every one who receives the protection of society owes a return for the benefit, and the fact of living in society renders it indispensable that each should be bound to observe a certain line of conduct towards the rest. This conduct consists, first, in not injuring the interests of one another; or rather certain interests, which, either by express legal provision or by tacit understanding, ought to be considered as rights; and secondly, in each person's bearing his share (to be fixed on some equitable principle) of the labors and sacrifices incurred for defending the society or its members from injury and molestation. These conditions society is justified in enforcing at all costs to those who endeavor to withhold fulfillment. Nor is this all that society may do. The acts of an individual may be hurtful to others, or wanting in due consideration for their welfare, without going the length of violating any of their constituted rights. The offender may then be justly punished by opinion, though not by law. As soon as any part of a person's conduct affects prejudicially the interests of others, society has jurisdiction over it, and the question whether the general welfare will or will not be promoted by interfering with it, becomes open to discussion. But there is no room for entertaining any such question when a person's conduct affects the interests of no persons besides himself, or needs not affect them unless they like (all the persons concerned being of full age, and the ordinary amount of understanding). In all such cases there should be perfect freedom, legal and social, to do the action and stand the consequences.

It would be a great misunderstanding of this doctrine to suppose that it is one of selfish indifference, which pretends that human beings have no business with each other's conduct in life, and that they should not concern themselves about the well-doing or well-being of one another, unless their own interest is involved. Instead of any diminution, there is need of a great increase of disinterested exertion to promote the good of others. But disinterested benevolence can find other instruments to persuade people to their good, than whips and scourges, either of the literal or the metaphorical sort. I am the last person to undervalue the self-regarding virtues; they are only second in importance, if even second, to the social. It is equally the business of education to cultivate both. But even education works by conviction and persuasion as well as by compulsion, and it is by the former only that, when the period of education is past, the self-regarding virtues should be inculcated. Human beings owe to each other help to distinguish the better from the worse, and encouragement to choose the former and avoid the latter. They should be for ever stimulating each other to increased exercise of their higher faculties, and increased direction of their feelings and aims towards wise instead of foolish, elevating instead of degrading, objects and contemplations. But neither one person, nor any number of persons, is warranted in saying to another human creature of ripe years, that he shall not do with his life for his own benefit what he chooses to do with it. He is the person most interested in his own well-being: the interest which any other person, except in cases of strong personal attachment, can have in it, is trifling, compared with that which he himself has; the interest which society has in him individually (except as to his conduct of others) is fractional, and altogether indirect: while, with respect to his own feelings and circumstances, the most ordinary man or woman has means of knowledge immeasurably surpassing those that can be possessed by any one else. The interference of society to overrule his judgment and purposes in what only regards himself, must be grounded on general presumptions; which may be altogether wrong, and even if right, are as likely as not to be misapplied to individual cases, by persons no better acquainted with the circumstances of such cases than those are who look at them merely from without. In this department, therefore, of human affairs, Individuality has its proper field of action. In the conduct of human beings towards one another, it is necessary that general rules should for the most part be observed, in order that people may know what they have to expect; but in each person's own concerns, his individual spontaneity is entitled to free exercise. Considerations to aid his judgment, exhortations to strengthen his will, may be offered to him, even obtruded on him, by others; but he himself is the final judge. All errors which he is likely to commit against advice and warning, are far outweighed by the evil of allowing others to constrain him to what they deem his good.

I do not mean that the feelings with which a person is regarded by others, ought not to be in any way affected by his self-regarding qualities or deficiencies. This is neither possible nor desirable. If he is eminent in any of the qualities which conduce to his own good, his is, so far, a proper object of admiration. He is so much the nearer to the ideal perfection of human nature. If he is grossly deficient in those qualities, a sentiment the opposite of admiration will follow. There is a degree of folly, and a degree of what may be called (though the phrase is not unobjectionable) lowness or depravation of taste, which, though it cannot justify doing harm to the person who manifests it, renders him necessarily and properly a subject of distaste, or, in extreme cases, even of contempt: a person could not have the opposite qualities in due strength without entertaining these feelings. Though doing no wrong to any one, a person may so act as to compel us to judge him, and feel to him, as a fool, or as a being of an inferior order: and since this judgment and feeling are a fact which he would prefer to avoid, it is doing him a service to warn him of it beforehand, as of any other disagreeable consequence to which he exposes himself. It would be well, indeed, if this good office were much more freely rendered than the common notions of politeness at present permit, and if one person could honestly point out to another that he thinks him in fault, without being considered unmannerly or presuming. We have a right, also, in various ways, to act upon our unfavorable opinion of any one, not to the oppression of his individuality, but in the exercise of ours. We are not bound, for example, to seek his society; we have a right to avoid it (though not to parade the avoidance), for we have a right to choose the society most acceptable to us. We have a right, and it may be our duty, to caution others against him, if we think his example or conversation likely to have a pernicious effect on those with whom he associates. We may give others a preference over him in optional good offices, except those which tend to his improvement. In these various modes a person may suffer very severe penalties at the hands of others, for faults which directly concern only himself; but he suffers these penalties only in so far as they are the natural, and, as it were, the spontaneous consequences of the faults themselves, not because they are purposely inflicted on him for the sake of punishment. A person who shows rashness, obstinacy, self-conceit—who cannot live within moderate means who cannot restrain himself from hurtful indulgences—who pursues animal pleasures at the expense of those of feeling and intellect—must expect to be lowered in the opinion of others, and to have a less share of their favorable sentiments; but of this he has no right to complain, unless he has merited their favor by special excellence in his social relations, and has thus established a title to their good offices, which is not affected by his demerits towards himself.

What I contend for is, that the inconveniences which are strictly inseparable from the unfavorable judgment of others, are the only ones to which a person should ever be subjected for that portion of his conduct and character which concerns his own good, but which does not affect the interests of others in their relations with him. Acts injurious to others require a totally different treatment. Encroachment on their rights; infliction on them of any loss or damage not justified by his own rights; falsehood or duplicity in dealing with them; unfair or ungenerous use of advantages over them; even selfish abstinence from defending them against injury—these are fit objects of moral reprobation, and, in grave cases, of moral retribution and punishment. And not only these acts, but the dispositions which lead to them, are properly immoral, and fit subjects of disapprobation which may rise to abhorrence. Cruelty of disposition; malice and ill nature; that most antisocial and odious of all passions, envy; dissimulation and insincerity; irascibility on insufficient cause, and resentment disproportioned to the provocation; the love of domineering over others; the desire to engross more than one's share of advantages (the πλεονεξία of the Greeks); the pride which derives gratification from the abasement of others; the egotism which thinks self and its concerns more important than everything else, and decides all doubtful questions in its own favor;—these are moral vices, and constitute a bad and odious moral character: unlike the self-regarding faults previously mentioned, which are not properly immoralities, and to whatever pitch they may be carried, do not constitute wickedness. They may be proofs of any amount of folly, or want of personal dignity and self-respect; but they are only a subject of moral reprobation when they involve a breach of duty to others, for whose sake the individual is bound to have care for himself. What are called duties to ourselves are not socially obligatory, unless circumstances render them at the same time duties to others. The term duty to oneself, when it means anything more than prudence, means self-respect or self-development; and for none of these is any one accountable to his fellow creatures, because for none of them is it for the good of mankind that he be held accountable to them.

The distinction between the loss of consideration which a person may rightly incur by defect of prudence or of personal dignity, and the reprobation which is due to him for an offense against the rights of others, is not a merely nominal distinction. It makes a vast difference both in our feelings and in our conduct towards him, whether he displeases us in things in which we think we have a right to control him, or in things in which we know that we have not. If he displeases us, we may express our distaste, and we may stand aloof from a person as well as from a thing that displeases us; but we shall not therefore feel called on to make his life uncomfortable. We shall reflect that he already bears, or will bear, the whole penalty of his error; if he spoils his life by mismanagement, we shall not, for that reason, desire to spoil it still further: instead of wishing to punish him, we shall rather endeavor to alleviate his punishment, by showing him how he may avoid or cure the evils his conduct tends to bring upon him. He may be to us an object of pity, perhaps of dislike, but not of anger or resentment; we shall not treat him like an enemy of society: the worst we shall think ourselves justified in doing is leaving him to himself, if we do not interfere benevolently by showing interest or concern for him. It is far otherwise if he has infringed the rules necessary for the protection of his fellow creatures, individually or collectively. The evil consequences of his acts do not then fall on himself, but on others; and society, as the protector of all its members, must retaliate on him; must inflict pain on him for the express purpose of punishment, and must take care that it be sufficiently severe. In the one case, he is an offender at our bar, and we are called on not only to sit in judgment on him, but, in one shape or another, to execute our own sentence; in the other case, it is not our part to inflict any suffering on him, except what may incidentally follow from our using the same liberty in the regulation of our own affairs, which we allow to him in his.

The distinction here pointed out between the part of a person's life which concerns only himself, and that which concerns others, many persons will refuse to admit. How (it may be asked) can any part of the conduct of a member of society be a matter of indifference to the other members? No person is an entirely isolated being; it is impossible for a person to do anything seriously or permanently hurtful to himself, without mischief reaching at least to his near connections, and often far beyond them. If he injures his property, he does harm to those who directly or indirectly derived support from it, and usually diminishes, by a greater or less amount, the general resources of the community. If he deteriorates his bodily or mental faculties, he not only brings evil upon all who depended on him for any portion of their happiness, but disqualifies himself for rendering the services which he owes to his fellow creatures generally; perhaps becomes a burthen on their affection or benevolence; and if such conduct were very frequent, hardly any offense that is committed would detract more from the general sum of good. Finally, if by his vices or follies a person does no direct harm to others, he is nevertheless (it may be said) injurious by his example; and ought to be compelled to control himself, for the sake of those whom the sight or knowledge of his conduct might corrupt or mislead.

And even (it will be added) if the consequences of misconduct could be confined to the vicious or thoughtless individual, ought society to abandon to their own guidance those who are manifestly unfit for it? If protection against themselves is confessedly due to children and persons under age, is not society equally bound to afford it to persons of mature years who are equally incapable of self-government? If gambling, or drunkenness, or incontinence, or idleness, or uncleanliness, are as injurious to happiness, and as great a hindrance to improvement, as many or most of the acts prohibited by law, why (it may be asked) should not law, so far as is consistent with practicability and social convenience, endeavor to repress these also? And as a supplement to the unavoidable imperfections of law, ought not opinion at least to organize a powerful police against these vices, and visit rigidly with social penalties those who are known to practice them? There is no question here (it may be said) about restricting individuality, or impeding the trial of new and original experiments in living. The only things it is sought to prevent are things which have been tried and condemned from the beginning of the world until now; things which experience has shown not to be useful or suitable to any person's individuality. There must be some length of time and amount of experience, after which a moral or prudential truth may be regarded as established: and it is merely desired to prevent generation after generation from falling over the same precipice which has been fatal to their predecessors.

I fully admit that the mischief which a person does to himself may seriously affect, both through their sympathies and their interests, those nearly connected with him, and in a minor degree, society at large. When, by conduct of this sort, a person is led to violate a distinct and assignable obligation to any other person or persons, the case is taken out of the self-regarding class, and becomes amenable to moral disapprobation in the proper sense of the term. If, for example, a man, through intemperance or extravagance, becomes unable to pay his debts, or, having undertaken the moral responsibility of a family, becomes from the same cause incapable of supporting or educating them, he is deservedly reprobated, and might be justly punished; but it is for the breach of duty to his family or creditors, not for the extravagance. If the resources which ought to have been devoted to them, had been diverted from them for the most prudent investment, the moral culpability would have been the same. George Barnwell murdered his uncle to get money for his mistress, but if he had done it to set himself up in business, he would equally have been hanged. Again, in the frequent case of a man who causes grief to his family by addiction to bad habits, he deserves reproach for his unkindness or ingratitude; but so he may for cultivating habits not in themselves vicious, if they are painful to those with whom he passes his life, or who from personal ties are dependent on him for their comfort. Whoever fails in the consideration generally due to the interests and feelings of others, not being compelled by some more imperative duty, or justified by allowable self-preference, is a subject of moral disapprobation for that failure, but not for the cause of it, nor for the errors, merely personal to himself, which may have remotely led to it. In like manner, when a person disables himself, by conduct purely self-regarding, from the performance of some definite duty incumbent on him to the public, he is guilty of a social offense. No person ought to be punished simply for being drunk; but a soldier or a policeman should be punished for being drunk on duty. Whenever, in short, there is a definite damage, or a definite risk of damage, either to an individual or to the public, the case is taken out of the province of liberty, and placed in that of morality or law.

The Crisis

in Human Values

J. GLENN GRAY

War Guilt

J. Glenn Gray, who
teaches philosophy at
Colorado State College,
was a U.S. intelligence
officer during World
War II. This selection
combines passages from
his war diary with his
philosophical reflections
on them ten years later.

It is a crucial moment in a soldier's life when he is ordered to perform a deed that
he finds completely at variance with his own notions of right and good. Probably
for the first time, he discovers that an act someone else thinks to be necessary is for
him criminal. His whole being rouses itself in protest, and he may well be forced
to choose in this moment of awareness of his freedom an act involving his own life
or death. He feels himself caught in a situation that he is powerless to change yet
cannot himself be part of. The past cannot be undone and the present is inescapable.
His only choice is to alter himself, since all external features are unchangeable.

What this means in the midst of battle can only inadequately be imagined by
those who have not experienced it themselves. It means to set oneself against others
and with one stroke lose their comforting presence. It means to cut oneself free of
doing what one's superiors approve, free of being an integral part of the military
organism with the expansion of the ego that such belonging brings. Suddenly the
soldier feels himself abandoned and cast off from all security. Conscience has isolated
him, and its voice is a warning. If you do this, you will not be at peace with me in
the future. You can do it, but you ought not. You must act, as a man and not as an
instrument of another's will.

I shall always remember the face of a German soldier when he described such
a drastic awakening as this. At the time we picked him up for investigation in the
Vosges in 1944, he was fighting with the French Maquis against his own people.
To my question concerning his motives for deserting to the French Resistance, he
responded by describing his earlier involvement in German reprisal raids against
the French. On one such raid, his unit was ordered to burn a village and to allow
none of the villagers to escape. (Possibly the village was Oradour and the soldier

From *The Warriors*, by J. Glenn Gray, Harper Torchbooks, 1967; first published in 1959. Reprinted
by permission of the author.

was one of the participants in that grisly atrocity; at that time we knew little of what was happening elsewhere and I did not ask him for names.) As he told how women and children were shot as they fled screaming from the flames of their burning homes, the soldier's face was contorted in painful fashion and he was nearly unable to breathe. It was quite clear that this extreme experience had shocked him into full awareness of his own guilt, a guilt he feared he would never atone. At the moment of that awakening he did not have the courage or resolution to hinder the massacre, but his desertion to the Resistance soon after was evidence of a radically new course. Terrible as was his self-reproach at what now could not be undone, he had won himself through this experience and would never again be available as a functionary.

In the Netherlands, the Dutch tell of a German soldier who was a member of an execution squad ordered to shoot innocent hostages. Suddenly he stepped out of rank and refused to participate in the execution. On the spot he was charged with treason by the officer in charge and was placed with the hostages, where he was promptly executed by his comrades. In such an act the soldier has abandoned once and for all the security of the group and exposed himself to the ultimate demands of freedom. He responded in the crucial moment to the voice of conscience and was no longer driven by external commands. In this case we can only guess what must have been the influence of his deed on slayers and slain. At all events, it was surely not slight, and his example on those who hear of the episode cannot fail to be inspiriting. Were it not for the revelation of nobility in mankind, which again and again appears in time of war, we could scarcely endure reading the literature of combat.

These are, of course, extreme examples and not to be taken as typical. Normally, the awakening of guilt is much more gradual, and the achievement of clarity about duty to one's country and duty to oneself a matter of anguished doubt, sometimes lasting for months or years. But the primary realization is the same in all cases: there is a line that a man dare not cross, deeds he dare not commit, regardless of orders and the hopelessness of the situation, for such deeds would destroy something in him that he values more than life itself. He may decide that his commander, his army, or his people may justly demand his life but may not command him to do what is in violation of his deepest self. However clear he may be about this momentous conclusion in moments of quiet and repose, the soldier is not thereby steeled against anxiety and fear of death. In the melee of conflict he may at times feel as do his unawakened comrades, that life is all he has, after all. Personal resolution is constantly attacked by the strain and disorder of combat life. His body, he discovers, is not always subject to his will. Impulses and emotions sweep him away, causing him to act again and again contrary to his sense of right. Against his innermost desire, he involves himself in guilt. Conscience within him is a voice long before it is a power; he desires to respond long before he has the required resolution. Though the voice is insistent, more clamorous impulses are able to dominate him in moments of violent action.

Nevertheless, his conscience has established an image of the ideal, a man who will acquit himself in whatever situation with independence and dignity. His inner history henceforth in combat will be the struggle to live up to this ideal. It may be that the soldier is contending against fear that he will involuntarily desert his comrades in a critical moment and be responsible for their death. It may be that he has qualms against killing enemy soldiers. Or he may be utterly persuaded of the justice of his country's cause and of the necessity of destroying lives to realize that cause, yet strongly opposed to this or that means his side is employing. He may be struggling to acquit himself well in a tangle of personal relationships common to military organizations in times of tension and peril. The occasions and situations are manifold in which the soldier who can no longer pass responsibility for his acts to others must struggle to gain full possession of himself. The voice of conscience is forever convicting him of inadequacy and insufficiency, urging him to better efforts. The ideal of acquitting himself like a man comes to appear utopian when he is confronted with certain situations.

Guilt is likely to come upon him in many other ways than as a consequence of natural fear of pain or death. Modern wars are full of border situations where a soldier is forced to choose between evils and where every choice is likely leaping into the dark because its consequences are unforeseeable. Rarely will he find a situation as clearly wrong as the shooting of hostages or the strafing of fleeing civilians. On the contrary, he will often have to choose between helping a wounded comrade to safety or remaining at his post to protect others whom he does not know. Sometimes he will have to choose the welfare of his unit at the expense of other units or the civilian populace. Hunger and cold and animal needs are everywhere in war in the midst of superfluity of food and warmth and delicacies. When he gives up his food or warm room in favor of some pitiful urchin or haggard mother, such charity can hardly comfort him because it is so transient. In the face of the need, his efforts will seem inconsequential to the point of futility. Even though the soldier may become a relatively selfless man in the service of the civil populace and his weaker comrades, he will seldom be at ease with himself. In some degree he will feel guilty of omitting to do what he ought, or doing what he ought not. This is inevitable, of course, for he is an individual who thinks of himself and others as ends in themselves in a situation where human beings are means for superpersonal goals. Men are materials to be expended for national interests, real or imagined. All the awakened soldier can hope to do in such a society is to meliorate the lot of the less fortunate, to act in an inhumane environment as humanely as possible. Opportunities to be humane are ordinarily plentiful enough in combat zones, but his freedom is constricted on all sides. It is like moving on a rack.

Such a soldier is likely to suffer most of all from the commands of military superiors when they are close to the border zone of the forbidden, that is, when they transgress the line that he cannot cross if he is to live with his conscience. The satisfaction that the unawakened conscience takes in making itself an instrument of higher wills is for the awakened conscience a leading source of its misery. To be required to carry out orders in which he does not believe, given by men who are frequently far removed from the realities with which the orders deal and often motivated by abstract hatred—this is the familiar lot of the combat soldier. The man of conscience can survive morally only by following the letter of such orders and disobeying their intention.

It is a great boon of front-line positions that this disobedience is frequently possible, since supervision is not very exact where danger of death is present. Many a conscientious soldier has discovered he could reinterpret military orders in his own spirit before obeying them. The fortunate ones have escaped difficulties with their commanders; the unfortunate have often ended in disciplinary barracks or even a death cell. At all events, the tension in such a soldier between the voice of conscience and the demands made upon him as a means and instrument of higher authority will rarely relax. The alternatives to this tension are for him either the surrender of his conscience to superiors or open defiance of their orders with fateful consequences to his life and freedom. Both alternatives he will seek to avoid as long as possible.

Here is a personal example. For several months in World War II, I was attached to an infantry division whose divisional intelligence officer, a colonel, was an insensitive military tyrant. He was pleased to have our detachment of six men under his control and at the same time was deeply resentful of our superior educational backgrounds and independence of mind. He liked to meddle with our somewhat specialized job of interrogating the civilian populace in the search for spies and saboteurs the retreating Germans might have left behind or sent over the front. Increasingly, I found myself resenting and resisting his often harsh orders for civilian restrictions and prohibitions. As linguists, we were his only means of communication with the civilian populace, who were regarded by him as an infernal nuisance to be tolerated only because they could not be conveniently expelled from combat areas.

When our division entered the first towns of Alsace, we encountered numerous young Alsatians in civilian clothes who had deserted from the German armies when on furlough and hidden out at the risk of their lives while awaiting our advance. The Alsatians had helped to hide these youths from the ruthless clutches of the Gestapo. Some of them had previously served with the French against the Germans, but when Alsace and Lorraine were incorporated in Germany with the defeat of France in 1940, they had been conscripted into Hitler's armies, only to desert at the first opportunity. There was, of course, much rejoicing now that they could at last leave their hiding places and greet old friends and neighbors publicly once more. Many of them came to us and offered their help in intelligence work. Hard pressed as we were for help (only two in our detachment knew German well enough to be effective), we found much for them to do.

But the colonel had noticed the appearance of young men on the streets here in contrast to France, where male youth had been conspicuously absent. He called our detachment commander by telephone and demanded an explanation. With our briefing, the captain gave him the facts of the situation. The colonel's response was immediate: "Do they have discharge papers from the German Army?" It was explained to him that deserters were never supplied with discharge papers, that being contrary to the usage of the German Army. His conclusion was breath-taking. In that case, these men were prisoners of war, and we were to round them up and ship them in prisoner trucks through regular channels to the huge camps in France. The colonel insisted on quick action. Our captain, who was sympathetic with us but afraid of the colonel, begged us to arrest the deserters the next day as ordered.

I was fortunate in having as a German-speaking colleague a strong-minded and intelligent young man of Boston Irish descent. He was profane, not overly scrupulous on moral issues, but fair-minded. He and I determined not to obey the order. To obey it would be the one way to alienate completely this friendly and much-mistreated Alsatian people. For parents to see their sons, who had risked their lives escaping from the German Army, loaded on the same trucks with hated

German soldiers and transported to prison camps would be to embitter relations with their "liberators" from the beginning. Moreover, the orders were manifestly unjust to these young men, who felt themselves to be allies and wanted in every way to aid our cause. The two of us hoped to avoid the issue by simply ignoring the order and continuing our other work, of which we had more than enough. But the colonel called again and was this time insulting and insistent. Still we ignored him, though our captain begged us to act. The third day, the colonel was threatening us with court-martial and worse for disobeying a direct order.

What were we to do? The two of us talked it over and decided to continue to refuse. It was not so much courage on my part as physical weariness and moral disgust at the injustices of warfare. In the most obscene language, my associate declared that the Army could court-marital him a hundred times and he would not obey such a stupid, senseless command. His mood was one of weary, sullen resistance to the vast stupidity of higher headquarters. He had been much longer in the war than I, having served with distinction in Africa and Sicily as well as in Italy and France. If his concern with the injustice of the order was not as great as mine, his resoluteness was greater, and fortified me. I had visions of the forbidding disciplinary barracks we had glimpsed in North Africa, of a dishonorable discharge and the disgrace it would bring on my aged father, who would not be able to understand why I had to disobey. Still, I knew that if I did not draw the line here I would be unable to draw it anywhere. If I did not refuse to become a party to the arrest of innocent, wronged men, I could not refuse to do anything that this or any other colonel ordered. I felt myself to be at the end of a tether. This was to be a showdown, and I had little doubt as to the winner. The loneliness and isolation of spirit that swept over me served to teach me how much I had hitherto been sustained by the silent approval of "the others." Even my partner in disobedience could not lift from me the heavy spiritual burden, for he was bitter and cynical about the whole affair.

Fortunately, things turned out in very different fashion from the expected. The colonel decided to call up army headquarters and report our insubordination before taking further action. He chanced to reach an intelligent officer who knew us both slightly, and this officer wanted to know why we persisted in disobeying orders. This the colonel had never stopped to determine, but when he did communicate the cause, Army Intelligence found our reasons good and within a day or two sent through an order that all Alsatian deserters were to be left with their families and in no case to be transported anywhere with German prisoners of war.

We had unexpectedly won the day and drew comfort afterward from the report that where our division had gone through Alsace the population was distinctly more pro-American than in other parts of Alsace-Lorraine. In areas where the deserters had been arrested, they had been forced to undergo manifold hardships and humiliations in prisoner-of-war camps, ironically enough because they were not in uniform, and were treated by our troops as cowardly and unworthy the respect accorded regular prisoners.

This was only an incident of war, not objectively important except as it influenced sectors of a population for or against the Allied cause. But subjectively it was for me a kind of turning point. As a result of it, I gained no great confidence in my ability to withstand extreme pressures from official authority, yet I had determined that a line could be drawn between personal rights and military demands. Though I knew that sheer good fortune had prevented the normal consequences of disobedience from falling upon me, I felt, nevertheless, immensely strengthened for a possible second refusal. More important, the incident cleared my mind on the vexed question of the relation of the individual to his state. Hard as they were to assert, I now felt convinced that the individual had his absolute rights even in the desperate struggle for survival that is modern war. And survival without integrity of conscience is worse than perishing outright, or so it seemed to me. Nothing had furthered my self-knowledge so much since my encounter with the old man of the mountain in Italy the year before.

I have no doubt that many others have found themselves in much more crucial difficulties in warfare than this example illustrates. Yet, curiously enough, most contemporary war novels deal with nearly every agony of combat except this one. Where matters of conscience are taken up, as in the immensely popular *Caine Mutiny,* there is frequently an ambivalence in the attitude of the author toward the rights of conscience against military organization. In Wouk's novel, for instance, the reader is left in doubt about the moral justification for "the mutiny," despite the fact that the captain of the *Caine* is portrayed in the worst possible light. He is cowardly, completely neurotic, a pathological liar, and incapable of giving orders that will save his ship from destruction. Yet, the author reminds us, he is a commander in the United States Navy, of long service, and as such an early fighter against the evil enemies of his country. Perhaps he should be obeyed despite his incapacity, since the principles of obedience and discipline count for more in a war of survival than individual conscience and private morality. This is typical of the modern confusion about the spheres of individual right and state authority in the era of total war.

However, the man of awakened conscience actually caught in this dilemma, as contrasted with the author writing a book about it, will usually be clear that duty to himself prohibits him from acting contrary to his voice, regardless of his fears and the personal consequences. He may obey such orders, but at the cost of his moral integrity. The safe observer has no right to blame him, for the sternest self-discipline is demanded. Few men in any age have had the moral stamina of a Socrates, who many centuries ago decided for himself that it was a right and duty to disobey his state and people when he felt they were wrong, but not his right to flee from their punishment for that disobedience. If few young men can be expected to attain the resolution of a mature Socrates, the reflective soldier is nearly certain to share the Socratic trust in the reliability of his conscience when it is in conflict with the group will.

This is particularly true of the conscience that is supported by faith in its divine origin. A secure religious faith has enabled many a soldier to act in defiance of unjust commands or to overcome the temptation to save himself at the cost of others. As I have pointed out elsewhere, the testimony of those condemned officers and soldiers who struck against Hitler in 1944 is eloquent and instructive evidence of this fact. Judging from their last letters to friends and family members, not all of them had religious support for their consciences. Those who had no religious faith or hope for life after death acted as courageously as the others and faced the end with confidence in the justice of their cause. Nevertheless, their sadness stands in sharp contrast with the tranquillity and even exaltation of those who were believers. Both groups seemed immensely relieved to be freed from the pressure of conformity to a system and a party they had learned to despise. The difference between them was that those of religious faith took leave of their lives as though the physical end was the beginning of something mysterious yet marvelous.

There is a kind of guilt that transcends the personal responsibility of the sensitive conscience and burdens that soldier particularly who retains faith in the cause and the country for which he is fighting. It is the guilt the individual shares as a member of a military unit, a national fighting force, a people at war. We may call it social or political or collective guilt; it is not essentially different for the civilian than for the soldier, and it is inescapable. No matter how self-contained and isolated in spirit the man of conscience may feel, he cannot avoid the realization that he is a participant in a system and an enterpirse whose very essence is violence and whose spirit is to win at whatever cost. For the soldier, it is his squad or company or division that performs deeds abhorrent to him. No matter how strongly he abjures personal responsibility for this or that deed, he cannot escape social responsibility. So long as he wears the same uniform as his fellows, he will be regarded by outsiders as one of them. His fellows, too, treat him as a member of the fraternity of men at arms. The conscience within him may be more and more appalled by the heedlessness of group behavior and the mechanical ruthlessness of an organization whose dedication to violence gives it an unholy character. I was appalled and yet I could not escape it. I wrote in my journal one day at the height of the war:

> Yesterday we caught two spies, making our recent total five. We are getting a reputation as a crack detachment. One had to be severely beaten before he confessed. It was pretty horrible, and I kept away from the room where it was done . . . though I could not escape his cries of pain. . . . I lay awake until three o'clock this morning. . . . I thought of the Hamlet line as most appropriate, "Tis bitter cold and I am sick at heart."

A soldier with an awakened conscience who is a member of such a community, coarse, vulgar, heedless, violent, realizes with overpowering clarity the possibility of being alienated from his own kind. This uniformed, machine-like monster, the combat unit, drives him back into himself and repels him utterly. Toward individuals who make it up, he can gain many relationships, but the collectivity itself chokes him without mercy.

Toward his nation as a nation he may well come to experience in his innermost self the same lack of relationship. A state of war reveals itself to the penetrating eye in its clearest light and the spectacle is not beautiful. Nietzsche's likeness of it to a cold snake is, from one perspective, not greatly exaggerated. The awakened conscience will recognize a part of this spirit of the nation in the hate-filled speeches of politician-patriots, in the antipathy toward dissenting opinions about the utter virtue of its cause, in the ruthlessness with which the individual is sacrificed for real or alleged national advantages. It will despise the fanaticism with which this state makes morally dubious and historically relative ends into absolutes, its perversity in maintaining pride at whatever price in human misery.

At the same time, justice will force this soldier to admit that these are his people, driven by fear and hatred, who are directing this vast mechanism. If he is honest with himself he will admit that he, too, is a violent man on occasion and capable of enjoying the fruits of violence. Legally, and more than legally, he belongs to the community of soldiers and to the state. At some level of his being he can understand why they perform as they do and can find it in his heart to feel sorry for some of the politicians and higher officers. In their place he wonders if he would do any better than they. He is bound to reflect that his nation has given him refuge and sustenance, provided him whatever education and property he calls his own. He belongs and will always belong to it in some sense, no matter where he goes or how hard he seeks to alter his inheritance. The crimes, therefore, that his nation or one of its units commits cannot be indifferent to him. He shares the guilt as he shares the satisfaction in the generous deeds and worthy products of nation or army. Even if he did not consciously will them and was unable to prevent them, he cannot wholly escape responsibility for collective deeds.

He belongs and yet he does not belong. "I did not ask to be born," he is likely to tell himself while struggling with his responsibility for collective deeds, "and I did not choose my nation. Had I been given a choice of places to grow up at various stages in my education I might have chosen other than the nation in which I was accidentally born. I am, of course, a citizen of this nation and am willing to expose my life in its defense. But in my inner being I belong only to the community that I have freely chosen, my friends, my club, my church, my profession. All other associations of mine are external and accidental, however little I may have realized it earlier. This does not free me from the guilt that this nation is heaping upon itself, so long as I participate in its defense. I shall always be guilty as long as I belong to a nation at all. Yet there is no good life apart from some nation or other."

It is clear to him that his political guilt is of a different sort from the personal, since the latter stems from his freedom in a direct way, the former only in part. The nation was in being long before him and will presumably continue in being after his death. Hence his capacity to change its course is immeasurably limited by its history as well as by his own powers. For the politically conscious soldier, this does not mean, however, that it is negligible. Insofar as his political guilt is in direct relation to his freedom, he will become conscious of what he has done or failed to do to promote or hinder the humanizing of military or political means and objectives. He will be certain at all events that he has not done enough. On this or that occasion he has been silent when he should have spoken out. In his own smaller or larger circle of influence he has not made his whole weight felt. Had he brought forth the civil courage to protest in time, some particular act of injustice might have been avoided. Whatever the level of influence the soldier commands, from the squad or platoon to the command of armies, in some manner he is able to affect the course of group action.

When the nation for which he is fighting has enjoyed a free government and been previously responsive to its citizens' wishes, he will be conscious of greater responsibility than will the soldier whose government is authoritarian or totalitarian. The greater the possibility of free action in the communal sphere, the greater the degree of guilt for evil deeds done in the name of everyone. Still, the degrees of guilt are impossible to assess for anyone else, and hardly any two people share an equal burden of communal guilt. The soldier may have been too young as a civilian to have exerted much influence on events or he may have been too poorly informed or confused to know where his political duty lay. As a soldier, he may be in too isolated or insignificant a location to make effective use of his freedom. No citizen of a free land can justly accuse his neighbor, I believe, of political guilt, of not having done as much as he should to prevent the state of war or the commission of this or that state crime. But each can—and the man of conscience will—accuse himself in proportion to the freedom he had to alter the course of events.

The peculiar agony of the combat soldier's situation is that, even more than in his struggle with his own ideal self, he is aware of the puniness of his individual powers to effect a change. War not only narrows the limits of personal freedom, but it likewise constricts the individual's communal liberty, his capacity to make his power felt in significant ways. The sense of impotence will weigh upon him day after day. Though the man of awakened conscience will hardly believe that the war is a natural catastrophe, he will not know how any individual can alter its seemingly inexorable course. Personal guilt can be in some measure atoned and the struggle to improve can be taken up every morning anew. But communal guilt comes upon him in ever increasing measure in any war, and he is likely to feel utterly inadequate either to atone for it or prevent its accumulation.

For instance, when the news of the atomic bombing of Hiroshima and Nagasaki came, many an American soldier felt shocked and ashamed. The combat soldier knew better than did Americans at home what those bombs meant in suffering and injustice. The man of conscience wherever he was realized intuitively that the vast majority of the Japanese in both cities were no more, if no less, guilty of the war than were his own parents, sisters, or brothers. In his shame, he may have said to himself, as some of us did: "The next atomic bomb, dropped in anger, will probably fall on my own country and we will have deserved it." Such a conviction will hardly relieve him of the heavy sense of wrong that his nation committed and the responsibility for which he must now in some measure share. All the arguments used in justification—the shortening of the war by many months and the thousands of American lives presumably saved—cannot alter the fact that his government was the first to use on undefended cities, without any warning, a monstrous new weapon of annihilation.

Worst of all about such deeds is that millions accepted and felt relief. Hearing this near-exultation in the enemy's annihilation, one can only conclude that political guilt has another source than the freedom of the individual to affect group action. It lies in the degree of his identification with the goals and the means of realizing them that his nation adopts. The person who inwardly approves an immoral action of his government or military unit testifies to his own probable decision that he possessed the freedom and opportunity of the actors. Freedom is possible, therefore, not only in the power to do or prevent, but also in inner assent and consent to action by others. With a relative criterion like this it is, of course, impossible to be exact in estimating even one's own guilt. Yet the jubilation in evil deeds allows little room for doubt that inner consent is often forthcoming. So do thousands of people increase their political guilt in wartime beyond the range of their direct action.

To some extent after World War I and explicitly after World War II, doctrines of collective guilt have become common. The German nation, for example, and particularly the German Army is often said to be guilty for having fought for Hitler in his aggressive wars of conquest and rapine. However innocent the individual soldier may have been of any personal misconduct, the fact that he was a member of a criminal conspiracy to deprive other peoples of their independence by violent means made him guilty. What justice is there in such a claim? To what extent is a German soldier in the last war guilty who kept himself free of personal crimes but was forced to experience, more or less directly, atrocities committed by his fellow soldiers and who was not blind to Hitler's mad ambitions? Is he not in an utterly different position from the soldier of a nation like ours who fought the war defensively to repel aggression?

In terms of what I have previously said, the answer can only be that no outsider has a moral right to make such an accusation about either the soldiery or the people as a whole. For an anti-Nazi soldier to have interfered with some act of injustice carried out by his fellow countrymen would have resulted in his prompt execution, as enough recorded instances prove. Apart from the demands of courage and determination that such an act requires, the question that tormented some soldiers in this situation was: What political purpose will my sacrifice serve? Many a conscientious German soldier might have screwed up his courage to open interference had he seen clearly in what way his death would have helped prevent further crimes. Fortunate soldiers found the right moment and the right deed with which to strike against the system they despised, and their chance to witness made them content to die. Others fought to the end of the war without such opportunities or without the necessary courage. Only those who sacrificed themselves in similar situations have the right to accuse them, and probably few of them would care to do so, if they were alive and able. For my own deeds I am responsible and can be held accountable, even if I act under the orders of another. For the deeds of my fellow men, specifically my fellow countrymen, my responsibility cannot be a public or legal one, for it is too dependent on my estimate of my ability to hinder criminal acts and of my inner consent to their commission.

Yet if accusations of collective guilt are unjustified, the sensitive German soldier could hardly escape the consciousness of his own political guilt. A burning sense of shame at the deeds of his government and the acts of horror committed by German soldiers and police was the mark of a conscientious German at the close of the war. "I am ashamed to be a German" was a not infrequent remark when friend was speaking to friend as the revelations of what the Third Reich had done became generally known. To be sure, those without conscience considered that they had atoned sufficiently for their political "mistakes" by their suffering during and after the war, and rejected with indignation any imputation of collective guilt. They wanted to hear nothing of their vicarious part in the crimes of their fellow citizens.

The reflective man knows in his heart what rarely crosses his lips, that the sins of his fellows are not so remote from him as he would like. If he is a soldier, he, too, has yielded at times to the temptations of power and the license that violence evokes in all of us. However free he may have kept himself from external participation in evil deeds and however foreign cruelty may be to his better nature, he will be aware that there is in nearly all men the capacity for criminal deeds and the obscure yearning for license to act without consequences, hence his recognition of the chains of communal responsibility and his knowledge that atonement in this sphere is largely chimerical. No human power could atone for the injustice, suffering, and degradation of spirit of a single day of warfare.

JEAN-PAUL SARTRE

Love and Sexual Desire

Jean-Paul Sartre, French
existentialist philosopher,
novelist, and playwright, has
also written *No Exit* and
Nausea. His latest writings are
Search for a Method and *La
Critique de la Raison
Dialectique,* in which he
attempts to reconcile
existentialism with Marxism.

Everything which may be said of me in my relations with the Other applies to
him as well. While I attempt to free myself from the hold of the Other, the Other
is trying to free himself from mine; while I seek to enslave the Other, the Other
seeks to enslave me. We are by no means dealing with unilateral relations with an
object-in-itself, but with reciprocal and moving relations. The following descriptions
of concrete behavior must therefore be envisaged within the perspective of *conflict.*
Conflict is the original meaning of being-for-others.

If we start with the first revelation of the Other as a *look,* we must recognize
that we experience our inapprehensible being-for-others in the form of a *possession.*
I am possessed by the Other; the Other's look fashions my body in its nakedness,
causes it to be born, sculptures it, produces it as it *is,* sees it as I shall never see it.
The Other holds a secret—the secret of what I am. He makes me be and thereby he
possesses me, and this possession is nothing other than the consciousness of possessing
me. . . .

. . . Why does the lover want to be *loved*? If Love were in fact a pure desire for
physical possession, it could in many cases be easily satisfied. Proust's hero, for
example, who installs his mistress in his home, who can see her and possess her at
any hour of the day, who has been able to make her completely dependent on him
economically, ought to be free from worry. Yet we know that he is, on the contrary,
continually gnawed by anxiety. Through her consciousness Albertine escapes Marcel
even when he is at her side, and that is why he knows relief only when he gazes
on her while she sleeps. It is certain then that the lover wishes to capture a "consciousness." But why does he wish it? And how?

The notion of "ownership," by which love is so often explained, is not actually
primary. Why should I want to appropriate the Other if it were not precisely that

From *Being and Nothingness,* by Jean-Paul Sartre, translated by Hazel E. Barnes, Philosophical
Library, 1956. Reprinted by permission of the publishers.

the Other makes me be? But this implies precisely a certain mode of appropriation; it is the Other's freedom as such that we want to get hold of. Not because of a desire for power. The tyrant scorns love, he is content with fear. If he seeks to win the love of his subjects, it is for political reasons; and if he finds a more economical way to enslave them, he adopts it immediately. On the other hand, the man who wants to be loved does not desire the enslavement of the beloved. He is not bent on becoming the object of passion which flows forth mechanically. He does not want to possess an automaton, and if we want to humiliate him, we need only try to persuade him that the beloved's passion is the result of a psychological determinism. The lover will then feel that both his love and his being are cheapened. If Tristan and Isolde fall madly in love because of a love potion, they are less interesting. The total enslavement of the beloved kills the love of the lover. The end is surpassed; if the beloved is transformed into an automaton, the lover finds himself alone. Thus the lover does not desire to possess the beloved as one possesses a thing; he demands a special type of appropriation. He wants to possess a freedom as freedom.

On the other hand, the lover can not be satisfied with that superior form of freedom which is a free and voluntary engagement. Who would be content with a love given as pure loyalty to a sworn oath? Who would be satisfied with the words, "I love you because I have freely engaged myself to love you and because I do not wish to go back on my word." Thus the lover demands a pledge, yet is irritated by a pledge. He wants to be loved by a freedom but demands that this freedom as freedom should no longer be free. He wishes that the Other's freedom should determine itself to become love—and this not only at the beginning of the affair but at each instant—and at the same time he wants this freedom to be captured *by itself*, to turn back upon itself, as in madness, as in a dream, so as to will its own captivity. This captivity must be a resignation that is both free and yet chained in our hands. In love it is not a determinism of the passions which we desire in the Other nor a freedom beyond reach; it is a freedom which *plays the role of* a determinism of the passions and which is caught in its own role. For himself the lover does not demand that he be the cause of this radical modification of freedom but that he be the unique and privileged occasion of it. In fact he could not want to be the cause of it without immediately submerging the beloved in the midst of the world as a tool which can be transcended. That is not the essence of love. On the contrary, in Love the Lover wants to be "the whole World" for the beloved. This means that he puts himself on the side of the world: he is the one who assumes and symbolizes the world; he is a *this* which includes all other *thises*. He is and consents to be an *object*. But on the other hand, he wants to be the object in which the Other's freedom consents to lose itself.

. . .

. . . Each one of the lovers wants to be the object for which the Other's freedom is alienated in an original intuition; but this intuition which would be love in the true sense is only a contradictory ideal of the for-itself. Each one is alienated only to the exact extent to which he demands the alienation of the other. Each one wants the other to love him but does not take into account the fact that to love is to want to be loved and that thus by wanting the other to love him, he only wants the other to want to be loved in turn. Thus love relations are a system of indefinite reference —analogous to the pure "reflection-reflected" of consciousness—under the ideal standard of the *value* "live"; that is, in a fusion of consciousnesses in which each of them would preserve his otherness in order to found the other. This state of affairs is due to the fact that consciousnesses are separated by an insurmountable nothingness, a nothingness which is both the internal negation of the one by the other and a factual nothingness between the two internal negations. Love is a contradictory effort to surmount the factual negation while preserving the internal negation. I demand that the Other love me and I do everything possible to realize my project; but if the Other loves me, he radically deceives me by his very love. I demanded of him that he should found my being as a privileged object by maintaining himself as pure subjectivity confronting me; and as soon as he loves me he experiences me as subject and is swallowed up in his objectivity confronting my subjectivity.

· · ·

. . . Man, it is said, is a sexual being because he possesses a sex. And if the reverse were true? If sex were only the instrument and, so to speak, the *image* of a fundamental sexuality? If man possessed a sex only because he is originally and fundamentally a sexual being as a being who exists in the world in relation with other men? Infantile sexuality precedes the physiological maturation of the sex organs. Men who have become eunuchs do not thereby cease to feel desire. Nor do many old men. The fact of being able to *make use of* a sex organ fit to fertilize and to procure enjoyment represents only one phase and one aspect of our sexual life. There is one mode of sexuality "with the possibility of satisfaction," and the developed sex represents and makes concrete this possibility. But there are other modes of sexuality of the type which can not get satisfaction, and if we take these modes into account we are forced to recognize that sexuality appears with birth and disappears only with death. Moreover neither the tumescence of the penis nor any other physiological phenomenon can ever explain or provoke sexual desire— no more than the vaso-constriction or the dilation of the pupils (or the simple consciousness of these physiological modifications) will be able to explain or to provoke fear. In one case as in the other although the body plays an important role, we must —in order to understand it—refer to being-in-the-world and to being-for-others. I desire a human being, not an insect or a mollusk, and I desire him (or her) as he is and as I am in situation in the world and as he is an Other for me and as I am an Other for him.

The fundamental problem of sexuality can therefore be formulated thus: is sexuality a contingent accident bound to our physiological nature, or is it a necessary structure of being-for-itself-for-others? From the sole fact that the question can be posited in these terms, we see that we must go back to ontology to decide it. Moreover ontology can decide this question only by determining and fixing the meaning of sexual existence for-the-Other. To have sex means—in accordance with the description of the body which we attempted in the preceding chapter—to exist sexually for an Other who exists sexually for me. And it must be well understood that at first this Other is not necessarily *for me*—nor I for him—a *heterosexual* existent but only a being who has sex. Considered from the point of view of the For-itself, this apprehension of the Other's sexuality could not be the pure disinterested contemplation of his primary or secondary sexual characteristics. *My first* apprehension of the Other as having sex does not come when I conclude from the distribution of his hair, from the coarseness of his hands, the sound of his voice, his strength that he is of the masculine sex. We are dealing there with derived conclusions which refer to an original state. The first apprehension of the Other's sexuality in so far as it is lived and suffered can be only *desire;* it is by desiring the Other (or by discovering myself as incapable of desiring him) or by apprehending his desire for me that I discover his being-sexed. Desire reveals to me simultaneously *my* being-sexed and *his* being-sexed, *my* body as sex and *his* body. Here therefore in order to decide the nature and ontological position of sex we are referred to the study of desire. What therefore is desire?

And first, desire of *what?*

We must abandon straight off the idea that desire is the desire of pleasure or the desire for the cessation of a pain. For we can not see how the subject could get out of this state of immanence so as to "attach" his desire to an object. Every subjectivist and immanentist theory will fail to explain how we desire a particular woman and not simply our sexual satisfaction. It is best therefore to define desire by its transcendent object. Nevertheless it would be wholly inaccurate to say that desire is a desire for "physical possession" of the desired object—if by "possess" we mean here "to make love to." Of course the sexual act for a moment frees us from desire, and in certain cases it can be posited explicitly as the hoped-for issue of the desire—when desire, for example, is painful and fatiguing. But in this case it is necessary that the desire itself be the object which is posited as "to be overcome," and this can be accomplished only by means of a reflective consciousness. But desire by itself is nonreflective; therefore it could never posit itself as an object to be overcome. Only a roué represents his desire to himself, treats it as an object, excites it, "turns it off," varies the means of assuaging it, *etc.* But in this case, we must observe, it is the desire itself which becomes the desirable. The error here stems from the fact that we have learned that the sexual act suppresses the desire. We have therefore added on a bit of knowledge to the desire and from outside we have added pleasure as desire's normal satisfaction—for reasons external to the essence of desire (*e.g.,* procreation, the sacred character of maternity, the exceptional strength of the pleasure provoked by ejaculation, the symbolic value attached to the sexual act). Thus the average man through mental sluggishness and desire to conform can conceive of no other goal for his desire than ejaculation. This is what has allowed people to conceive of desire as an instinct whose origin and end are strictly physiological since in man, for example, it would have as its cause the erection and as its final limit the ejaculation. But desire by itself by no means implies the sexual act; desire does not thematically posit it, does not even suggest it in outline, as one sees when it is a question of the desire of very young children or of adults who are ignorant of the "technique" of love. Similarly desire is not a desire of any special amorous practice; this is sufficiently proved by the diversity of sexual practices, which vary with social groups. In a general way desire is not a desire of *doing.* The "doing" is after the event, is added on to the desire from outside and necessitates a period of apprenticeship; there is an amorous technique which has its own ends and means. Therefore since desire can not posit its suppression as its supreme end nor single out for its ultimate goal any particular act, it is purely and simply the desire of a transcendent object. Here again we find that affective intentionality of which we spoke in preceding chapters and which Scheler and Husserl have described.

But what is the object of desire? Shall we say that desire is the desire of a *body?* In one sense this can not be denied. But we must take care to understand this correctly. To be sure it is the body which disturbs us: an arm or a half-exposed breast or perhaps a leg. But we must realize at the start that we desire the arm or the uncovered breast only on the ground of the presence of the whole body as an organic totality. The body itself as totality may be hidden. I may see only a bare arm. But the body is there. It is from the standpoint of the body that I apprehend the arm as an arm. The body is as much present, as adherent to the arm which I see as the designs of the rug, which are hidden by the feet of the table, are present and adherent to those designs which I see. And my desire is not mistaken; it is addressed not to a sum of physiological elements but to a total form—better yet, to a form *in situation*. A particular attitude, as we shall see later, does much to provoke desire. Now along with the attitude the surroundings are given and finally the world. But here suddenly we are at the opposite pole from a simple physiological pruritus; desire posits the world and desires the body in terms of the world and the beautiful hand in terms of the body. There follows exactly the procedure which we described in the preceding chapter, that by which we apprehended the Other's body from the standpoint of his situation in the world. Moreover there is nothing in this which should surprise us since desire is nothing but one of the great forms which can be assumed by the revelation of the Other's body. Yet precisely for this reason we do not desire the body as a purely material object; a purely material object is not *in situation*. Thus this organic totality which is immediately present to desire is desirable only in so far as it reveals not only life but also an appropriate consciousness. Nevertheless, as we shall see, the Other's being-in-situation which desire reveals is of an entirely original type. Furthermore the consciousness here considered is still only one *property* of the desired object; that is, it is nothing but the sense of flow of the objects in the world, precisely in so far as this flow is cut off, localized, and made a part of my world. To be sure, one can desire a woman who is asleep, but one desires her in so far as this sleep appears on the ground of consciousness. Consciousness therefore remains always at the horizon of the desired body; it makes the meaning and the unity of the body. A living body as an organic totality in situation with consciousness at the horizon: such is the object to which desire *is addressed*. What does desire wish from this object? We can not determine this until we have answered a preliminary question: *Who* is the one who desires?

The answer is clear. *I am* the one who desires, and desire is a particular mode of my subjectivity. Desire is consciousness since it can be only as a non-positional consciousness of itself. Nevertheless we need not hold that the desiring consciousness differs from the cognitive consciousness, for example, only in the nature of its object. For the For-itself, to choose itself as desire is not to produce a desire while remaining indifferent and unchanged—as the Stoic cause produces its effect. The For-itself puts itself on a certain plane of existence which is not the same, for example, as that of a For-itself which chooses itself as a metaphysical being. Every consciousness, as we have seen, supports a certain relation with its own facticity. But this relation can vary from one mode of consciousness to another. The facticity of a pain-consciousness, for example, is a facticity discovered in a perpetual flight. The case is not the same for the facticity of desire. The man who desires *exists* his body in a particular mode and thereby places himself on a particular level of existence. In fact everyone will agree that desire is not only *longing,* a clear and translucent *longing* which directs itself through our body toward a certain object. Desire is defined as *trouble.* The notion of "trouble" can help us better to determine the nature of desire. We contrast troubled water with transparent water, a troubled look with a clear look. Troubled water remains water; it preserves the fluidity and the essential characteristics of water; but its translucency is "troubled" by an inapprehensible presence which makes one with it, which is everywhere and nowhere, and which is given as a clogging of the water by itself. To be sure, we can explain the troubled quality by the presence of fine solid particles suspended in the liquid, but this explanation is that of the *scientist.* Our original apprehension of the troubled water is given us as changed by the presence of an invisible *something* which is not itself distinguished and which is manifested as a pure factual resistance. If the desiring consciousness is *troubled,* it is because it is analogous to the troubled water.

To make this analogy precise, we should compare sexual desire with another form of desire—for example, with hunger. Hunger, like sexual desire, supposes a certain state of the body, defined here as the impoverishment of the blood, abundant salivary secretion, contractions of the tunica, *etc.* These various phenomena are described and classified from the point of view of the Other. For the For-itself they are manifested as pure facticity. But this facticity *does not compromise* the nature of the For-itself, for the For-itself immediately flees it toward its possibles; that is, toward a certain state of satisfied-hunger which, as we have pointed out in Part Two, is the In-itself-for-itself of hunger. Thus hunger is a pure surpassing of corporal facticity; and to the extent that the For-itself becomes conscious of this facticity in a non-thetic form, the For-itself becomes conscious of it as a surpassed facticity. The body here is indeed the *past, the passed-beyond.* In sexual desire, to be sure, we can find that structure common to all appetites—a state of the body. The Other can note various physiological modifications (the erection of the penis, the turgescence of the nipples of the breasts, changes in the circulatory system, rise in temperature, *etc.*) The desiring consciousness exists this facticity; it is *in terms of this facticity*—we could even say *through* it—that the desired body appears as desirable. Nevertheless if we limited ourselves to this description, sexual desire would appear as a *distinct and clear desire,* comparable to the desire of eating and drinking. It would be a pure flight from facticity toward other possibles. Now everyone is aware that there is a great abyss between sexual desire and other appetites. We all know the famous saying, "Make love to a pretty woman when you want her just as you would drink a glass of cold water when you are thirsty." We know also how unsatisfactory and even shocking this statement is to the mind. This is because when we do desire a woman, we do not keep ourselves wholly outside the desire; the desire *compromises* me; I am the accomplice of my desire. Or rather the desire has fallen wholly into complicity with the body. Let any man consult his own experience; he knows how consciousness is clogged, so to speak, by sexual desire; it seems that one is invaded by facticity, that one ceases to flee it and that one slides toward a *passive* consent to the desire. At other moments it seems that facticity invades consciousness in its very flight and renders consciousness opaque to itself. It is like a yeasty tumescence of fact.

The expressions which we use to designate desire sufficiently show its specificity. We say that it *takes hold of* you, that it *overwhelms* you, that it *paralyzes* you. Can one imagine employing the same words to designate hunger? Can one think of a hunger which "would overwhelm" one? Strictly speaking, this would be meaningful only when applied to impressions of emptiness. But, on the contrary, even the feeblest desire is already overwhelming. One can not hold it at a distance as one can with hunger and "think of something else" while keeping desire as an undifferentiated tonality of non-thetic consciousness which would be desire and which would serve as a sign of the body-as-ground. But *desire is consent to desire.* The heavy, fainting consciousness slides toward a languor comparable to sleep. Every one has been able to observe the appearance of desire in another. Suddenly the man who desires becomes a heavy tranquillity which is frightening; his eyes are fixed and appear half-closed, his movements are stamped with a heavy and sticky sweetness; many seem to be falling asleep. And when one "struggles against desire," it is precisely this languor which one resists. If one succeeds in resisting it, the desire before disappearing will become wholly distinct and clear, like hunger. And then there will be "an awakening." One will feel that one is lucid but with heavy head and beating heart. Naturally all these descriptions are inexact; they show rather the way in which we interpret desire. However they indicate the primary fact of desire: in desire consciousness chooses to exist its facticity on another plane. It no longer flees it; it attempts to subordinate itself to its own contingency—as it apprehends another body—*i.e.,* another contingency—as desirable. In this sense desire is not only the revelation of the Other's body but the revelation of my own body. And this, not in so far as this body *is an instrument* or *a point of view,* but in so far as it is pure facticity; that is, a simple contingent form of the necessity of my contingency. I *feel* my skin and my muscles and my breath, and I feel them not in order to transcend them toward something as in emotion or appetite but as a living and inert datum, not simply as the pliable and discrete instrument of my action upon the world but as a *passion* by which I am engaged in the world and in danger in the world. The For-itself is *not* this contingency; it continues to exist but it experiences the vertigo of its own body. Or, if you prefer, this vertigo is precisely its way of existing its body. The non-thetic consciousness allows itself to go over to the body, *wishes* to be the body and to be only body. In desire the body instead of being only the contingency which the For-itself flees toward possibles which are peculiar to it, becomes at the same time the most immediate possible of the For-itself. Desire is not only the desire of the Other's body; it is—within the unity of a single act—the non-thetically lived project of being swallowed up in the body. Thus the final state of sexual desire can be swooning as the final stage of consent to the body. It is in this sense that desire can be called the desire of one body for another body. It is in fact an appetite directed *toward* the Other's body, and it is lived as the vertigo of the For-itself before its own body. The being which desires is consciousness *making itself body.*

But granted that desire is a consciousness which makes itself body in order to appropriate the Other's body apprehended as an organic totality in situation with consciousness on the horizon—what then is the meaning of desire? That is, why does consciousness make itself body—or vainly attempt to do so—and what does it expect from the object of its desire? The answer is easy if we realize that in desire I make myself flesh *in the presence of the Other in order to appropriate* the Other's flesh. This means that it is not merely a question of my grasping the Other's shoulders or thighs or of my drawing a body over against me: it is necessary as well for me to apprehend them with this particular instrument which is the body as it produces a clogging of consciousness. In this sense when I grasp these shoulders, it can be said not only that my body is a means for touching the shoulders but that the Other's shoulders are a means for my discovering my body as the fascinating revelation of facticity—that is, as flesh. Thus desire is the desire to appropriate a body as this appropriation reveals to me my body as flesh. But this body which I wish to appropriate, I wish to appropriate as *flesh*. Now at first the Other's body is not flesh for me; it appears as a synthetic form in action. As we have seen, we can not perceive the Other's body as pure flesh; that is, in the form of an isolated object maintaining external relations with other *thises*. The Other's body is originally a body in situation; flesh on the contrary, appears as the *pure contingency of presence*. Ordinarily it is hidden by cosmetics, clothing, etc.; in particular it is hidden by *movements*. Nothing is less "in the flesh" than a dancer even though she is nude. Desire is an attempt to strip the body of its movements as of its clothing and to make it exist as pure flesh; it is an attempt to *incarnate* the Other's body.

It is in this sense that the caress is an appropriation of the Other's body. It is evident that if caresses were only a stroking or brushing of the surface, there could be no relation between them and the powerful desire which they claim to fulfill; they would remain on the surface like looks and could not *appropriate* the Other for me. We know well the deceptiveness of that famous expression, "The contact of two epidermises." The caress does not want simple *contact;* it seems that man alone can reduce the caress to a contact, and then he loses its unique meaning. This is because the caress is not a simple stroking; it is a *shaping*. In caressing the Other I cause her[1] flesh to be born beneath my caress, under my fingers. The caress is the ensemble of those rituals which *incarnate* the Other. But, someone will object, was the Other not already incarnated? To be precise, no. The Other's flesh did not exist explicitly for me since I grasped the Other's body in situation; neither did it exist for her since she transcended it toward her possibilities and toward the object. The caress causes the Other to be born as flesh for me and for herself. And by flesh we do not mean that a *part* of the body such as the dermis, the connective tissues or, specifically, epidermis; neither need we assume that the body will be "at rest" or dozing although often it is thus that its flesh is best revealed. But the caress reveals the flesh by stripping the body of its action, by cutting it off from the possibilities which surround it; the caress is designed to uncover the web of inertia beneath the action—*i.e.,* the pure "being-there"—which sustains it. For example, by *clasping* the Other's hand and *caressing* it, I discover underneath the act of *clasping,* which this hand is *at first,* an extension of flesh and bone which can be

---

[1] The pronouns in French are masculine because they refer to *autrui* (the Other) which may stand for either man or woman but which, grammatically, is masculine. The feminine sounds more natural in English. Tr.

grasped; and similarly my look caresses when it discovers underneath this leaping which is at first the dancer's legs, the curved extension of the thighs. Thus the caress is in no way distinct from the desire: to caress with the eyes and to desire are one and the same. *Desire is expressed by the caress as thought is by language.* The caress reveals the Other's flesh as flesh to myself and to the Other. But it reveals this flesh in a very special way. To take hold of the Other reveals to her inertia and her passivity as a transcendence-transcended; but this is not to caress her. In the caress it is not my body as a synthetic form in action which caresses the Other; it *is* my body as flesh which causes the Other's flesh to be born. The caress is designed to cause the Other's body to be born, through pleasure, for the Other—and for myself —as a *touched* passivity in such a way that my body is made flesh in order to touch the Other's body with its own passivity; that is, by caressing itself with the Other's body rather than by caressing her. This is why amorous gestures have a language which could almost be said to be studied; it is not a question so much of taking hold of a part of the Other's body as of placing one's own body against the Other's body. Not so much to push or to touch in the active sense but to place against. It seems that I lift my own arm as an inanimate object and that I *place* it against the flank of the desired woman, that my fingers which I run over her arm are inert at the end of my hand. Thus the revelation of the Other's flesh is made through my own flesh; in desire and in the caress which expresses desire, I incarnate myself in order to realize the incarnation of the Other. The caress by *realizing* the Other's incarnation reveals to me my own incarnation; that is, I make myself flesh in order to impel the Other to realize *for-herself* and *for me* her own flesh, and my caresses cause my flesh to be born for me in so far as it is for the Other *flesh causing her to be born as flesh.* I make her enjoy my flesh through her flesh in order to compel her to feel herself flesh. And so possession truly appears as a *double reciprocal incarnation.* Thus in desire there is an attempt at the incarnation of consciousness (this is what we called earlier the clogging of consciousness, a troubled consciousness, etc.) in order to realize the incarnation of the Other.

.   .   .

We are now in a position to make explicit the profound meaning of desire. In the primordial reaction to the Other's look I constitute myself as a look. But if I look at his look in order to defend my self against the Other's freedom and to transcend it as freedom, then both the freedom and the look of the Other collapse. I see eyes; I see a being-in-the-midst-of-the-world. Henceforth the Other escapes me. I should like to act upon his freedom, to appropriate it, or at least, to make the Other's freedom recognize my freedom. But this freedom is death; it is no longer absolutely *in the world* in which I encounter the Other-as-object, for his characteristic is to be transcendent to the world. To be sure, I can *grasp* the Other, grab hold of him, knock him down. I can, providing I have the power, compel him to perform this or that act, to say certain words. But everything happens as if I wished to get hold of a man who runs away and leaves only his coat in my hands. It is the coat, it is the outer shell which I possess. I shall never get hold of more than a body, a psychic object in the midst of the world. And although all the acts of this body can be interpreted in terms of freedom, I have completely lost the key to this interpretation; I can act only upon a facticity. If I have preserved my awareness of a transcendent freedom in the Other, this awareness provokes me to no purpose by indicating a reality which is on principle beyond my reach and by revealing to me every instant the fact that I *am missing* it, that everything which I do is done "blindly" and takes on a meaning elsewhere in a sphere of existence from which I am on principle excluded. I can make the Other beg for mercy or ask my pardon, but I shall always be ignorant of what this submission means for and in the Other's freedom.

THOMAS NAGEL

Sexual Perversion

Thomas Nagel teaches
philosophy at Princeton
University. He has
written several articles
on topics in the
philosophy of mind.

There is something to be learned about sex from the fact that we possess a concept of sexual perversion. I wish to examine the concept, defending it against the charge of unintelligibility and trying to say exactly what about human sexuality qualifies it to admit of perversions. Let me make some preliminary comments about the problem before embarking on its solution.

Some people do not believe that the notion of sexual perversion makes sense, and even those who do disagree over its application. Nevertheless I think it will be widely conceded that, if the concept is viable at all, it must meet certain general conditions. First, if there are any sexual perversions, they will have to be sexual desires or practices that can be plausibly described as in some sense unnatural, though the explanation of this natural/unnatural distinction is of course the main problem. Second, certain practices will be perversions if anything is, such as shoe fetishism, bestiality, and sadism; other practices, such as unadorned sexual intercourse, will not be; about still others there is controversy. Third, if there are perversions, they will be unnatural sexual *inclinations* rather than merely unnatural practices adopted not from inclination but for other reasons. I realize that this is at variance with the view, maintained by some Roman Catholics, that contraception

"Sexual Perversion," by Thomas Nagel, from *The Journal of Philosophy*, Vol. 76, No. 1, Jan. 16, 1969. Reprinted by permission of the publishers and the author.

is a sexual perversion. But although contraception may qualify as a deliberate perversion of the sexual and reproductive functions, it cannot be significantly described as a *sexual* perversion. A sexual perversion must reveal itself in conduct that expresses an unnatural *sexual* preference. And although there might be a form of fetishism focused on the employment of contraceptive devices, that is not the usual explanation for their use.

I wish to declare at the outset my belief that the connection between sex and reproduction has no bearing on sexual perversion. The latter is a concept of psychological, not physiological interest, and it is a concept that we do not apply to the lower animals, let alone to plants, all of which have reproductive functions that can go astray in various ways. (Think of seedless oranges.) Insofar as we are prepared to regard higher animals as perverted, it is because of their psychological, not their anatomical similarity to humans. Furthermore, we do not regard as a perversion every deviation from the reproductive function of sex in humans: sterility, miscarriage, contraception, abortion.

Another matter that I believe has no bearing on the concept of sexual perversion is social disapprobation or custom. Anyone inclined to think that in each society the perversions are those sexual practices of which the community disapproves, should consider all the societies that have frowned upon adultery and fornication. These have not been regarded as unnatural practices, but have been thought objectionable in other ways. What is regarded as unnatural admittedly varies from culture to culture, but the classification is not a pure expression of disapproval or distaste. In fact it is often regarded as a *ground* for disapproval, and that suggests that the classification has an independent content.

I am going to attempt a psychological account of sexual perversion, which will depend on a specific psychological theory of sexual desire and human sexual interactions. To approach this solution I wish first to consider a contrary position, one which provides a basis for skepticism about the existence of any sexual perversions at all, and perhaps about the very significance of the term. The skeptical argument runs as follows:

"Sexual desire is simply one of the appetites, like hunger and thirst. As such it may have various objects, some more common than others perhaps, but none in any sense 'natural'. An appetite is identified as sexual by means of the organs and erogenous zones in which its satisfaction can be to some extent localized, and the special sensory pleasures which form the core of that satisfaction. This enables us to recognize widely divergent goals, activities, and desires as sexual, since it is conceivable in principle that anything should produce sexual pleasure and that a nondeliberate, sexually charged desire for it should arise (as a result of conditioning, if nothing else). We may fail to empathize with some of these desires, and some of them, like sadism, may be objectionable on extraneous grounds, but once we have observed that they meet the criteria for being sexual, there is nothing more to be said on *that* score. Either they are sexual or they are not: sexuality does not admit of imperfection, or perversion, or any other such qualification—it is not that sort of affection."

This is probably the received radical position. It suggests that the cost of defending a psychological account may be to deny that sexual desire is an appetite.

But insofar as that line of defense is plausible, it should make us suspicious of the simple picture of appetites on which the skepticism depends. Perhaps the standard appetites, like hunger, cannot be classed as pure appetites in that sense either, at least in their human versions.

Let us approach the matter by asking whether we can imagine anything that would qualify as a gastronomical perversion. Hunger and eating are importantly like sex in that they serve a biological function and also play a significant role in our inner lives. It is noteworthy that there is little temptation to describe as perverted an appetite for substances that are not nourishing. We should probably not consider someone's appetites as *perverted* if he liked to eat paper, sand, wood, or cotton. Those are merely rather odd and very unhealthy tastes: they lack the psychological complexity that we expect of perversions. (Coprophilia, being already a sexual perversion, may be disregarded.) If on the other hand someone liked to eat cookbooks, or magazines with pictures of food in them, and preferred these to ordinary food— of if when hungry he sought satisfaction by fondling a napkin or ashtray from his favorite restaurant—then the concept of perversion might seem appropriate (in fact it would be natural to describe this as a case of gastronomical fetishism). It would be natural to describe as gastronomically perverted someone who could eat only by having food forced down his throat through a funnel, or only if the meal were a living animal. What helps in such cases is the peculiarity of the desire itself, rather than the inappropriateness of its object to the biological function that the desire serves. Even an appetite, it would seem, can have perversions if in addition to its biological function it has a significant psychological structure.

In the case of hunger, psychological complexity is provided by the activities that give it expression. Hunger is not merely a disturbing sensation that can be quelled by eating; it is an attitude toward edible portions of the external world, a desire to relate to them in rather special ways. The method of ingestion: chewing, savoring, swallowing, appreciating the texture and smell, all are important components of the relation, as is the passivity and controllability of the food (the only animals we eat live are helpless mollusks). Our relation to food depends also on our size: we do not live upon it or burrow into it like aphids or worms. Some of these features are more central than others, but any adequate phenomenology of eating would have to treat it as a relation to the external world and a way of appropriating bits of that world, with characteristic affection. Displacements or serious restrictions of the desire to eat could then be described as perversions, if they undermined that direct relation between man and food which is the natural expression of hunger. This explain why it is easy to imagine gastronomical fetishism, voyeurism, exhibitionism, or even gastronomical sadism and masochism. Indeed some of these perversions are fairly common.

If we can imagine perversions of an appetite like hunger, it should be possible to make sense of the concept of sexual perversion. I do not wish to imply that sexual desire is an appetite—only that being an appetite is no bar to admitting of perversions. Like hunger, sexual desire has as its characteristic object a certain relation with something in the external world; only in this case it is usually a person rather than an omelet, and the relation is considerably more complicated. This added complication allows scope for correspondingly complicated perversions.

The fact that sexual desire is a feeling about other persons may tempt us to take a pious view of its psychological content. There are those who believe that sexual desire is properly the expression of some other attitude, like love, and that when it occurs by itself it is incomplete and unhealthy—or at any rate subhuman. (The extreme Platonic version of such a view is that sexual practices are all vain attempts to express something they cannot in principle achieve: this makes them all perversions, in a sense.) I do not believe that any such view is correct. Sexual desire is complicated enough without having to be linked to anything else as a condition for phenomenological analysis. It cannot be denied that sex may serve various functions—economic, social, altruistic—but it also has its own content as a relation between persons, and it is only by analyzing that relation that we can understand the conditions of sexual perversion.

I believe it is very important that the object of sexual attraction is a particular individual, who transcends the properties that make him attractive. When different persons are attracted to a single person for different reasons: eyes, hair, figure, laugh, intelligence—we feel that the object of their desire is nevertheless the same, namely that person. There is even an inclination to feel that this is so if the lovers have different sexual aims, if they include both men and women, for example. Different specific attractive characteristics seem to provide enabling conditions for the operation of a single basic feeling, and the different aims all provide expressions of it. We approach the sexual attitude toward the person through the features that we find attractive, but these features are not the objects of that attitude.

This is very different from the case of an omelet. Various people may desire it for different reasons, one for its fluffiness, another for its mushrooms, another for its unique combination of aroma and visual aspect; yet we do not enshrine the transcendental omelet as the true common object of their affections. Instead we might say that several desires have accidentally converged on the same object: any omelet with the crucial characteristics would do as well. It is not similarly true that any person with the same flesh distribution and way of smoking can be substituted as object for a particular sexual desire that has been elicited by those characteristics. It may be that they will arouse attraction whenever they recur, but it will be a new sexual attraction with a new particular object, not merely a transfer of the old desire to someone else. (I believe this is true even in cases where the new object is unconsciously identified with a former one.)

The importance of this point will emerge when we see how complex a psychological interchange constitutes the natural develoment of sexual attraction. This would be incomprehensible if its object were not a particular person, but rather a person of a certain *kind*. Attraction is only the beginning, and fulfillment does not consist merely of behavior and contact expressing this attraction, but involves much more.

The best discussion of these matters that I have seen appears in part III of Sartre's *Being and Nothingness*.[1] Since it has influenced my own views, I shall say a few

---

[1] Translated by Hazel E. Barnes (New York: Philosophical Library: 1956). [Article reprinted here on pp. 49–58—*Ed.*]

things about it now. Sartre's treatment of sexual desire and of love, hate, sadism, masochism, and further attitudes toward others, depends on a general theory of consciousness and the body which we can neither expound nor assume here. He does not discuss perversion, and this is partly because he regards sexual desire as one form of the perpetual attempt of an embodied consciousness to come to terms with the existence of others, an attempt that is as doomed to fail in this form as it is in any of the others, which include sadism and masochism (if not certain of the more impersonal deviations) as well as several nonsexual attitudes. According to Sartre, all attempts to incorporate the other into my world as another subject, i.e., to appre-hend him at once as an object for me and as a subject for whom I am an object, are unstable and doomed to collapse into one or other of the two aspects. Either I reduce him entirely to an object, in which case his subjectivity escapes the possession or appropriation I can extend to that object; or I become merely an object for him, in which case I am no longer in a position to appropriate his subjectivity. Moreover, neither of these aspects is stable; each is continually in danger of giving way to the other. This has the consequence that there can be no such thing as a *successful* sexual relation, since the deep aim of sexual desire cannot in principle be accom-plished. It seems likely, therefore, that the view will not permit a basic distinction between successful or complete and unsuccessful or incomplete sex, and therefore cannot admit the concept of perversion.

I do not adopt this aspect of the theory, nor many of its metaphysical under-pinnings. What interests me is Sartre's picture of the attempt. He says that the type of possession that is the object of sexual desire is carried out by "a double reciprocal incarnation" and that this is accomplished, typically in the form of a caress, in the following way: "I make myself flesh in order to impel the Other to realize *for-herself* and *for me* her own flesh, and my caresses cause my flesh to be born for me in so far as it is for the Other *flesh causing her to be born as flesh*" ([p. 57 of this text] italics Sartre's). The incarnation in question is described variously as a clogging or troubling of consciousness, which is inundated by the flesh in which it is embodied.

The view I am going to suggest, I hope in less obscure language, is related to this one, but it differs from Sartre's in allowing sexuality to achieve its goal on occasion and thus in providing the concept of perversion with a foothold.

Sexual desire involves a kind of perception, but not merely a single perception of its object, for in the paradigm case of mutual desire there is a complex system of superimposed mutual perceptions—not only perceptions of the sexual object, but perceptions of oneself. Moreover, sexual awareness of another involves consider-able self-awareness to begin with—more than is involved in ordinary sensory per-ception. The experience is felt as an assault on oneself by the view (or touch, or what-ever) of the sexual object.

Let us consider a case in which the elements can be separated. For clarity we will restrict ourselves initially to the somewhat artificial case of desire at a distance. Suppose a man and a woman, whom we may call Romeo and Juliet, are at opposite ends of a cocktail lounge, with many mirrors on the walls which permit unobserved observation, and even mutual unobserved observation. Each of them is sipping a martini and studying other people in the mirrors. At some point Romeo notices

Juliet. He is moved, somehow, by the softness of her hair and the diffidence with which she sips her martini, and this arouses him sexually. Let us say that *X senses Y* whenever *X* regards *Y* with sexual desire. (*Y* need not be a person, and *X*'s apprehension of *Y* can be visual, tactile, olfactory, etc., or purely imaginary; in the present example we shall concentrate on vision.) So Romeo senses Juliet, rather than merely noticing her. At this stage he is aroused by an unaroused object, so he is more in the sexual grip of his body than she of hers.

Let us suppose, however, that Juliet now senses Romeo in another mirror on the opposite wall, though neither of them yet knows that he is seen by the other (the mirror angles provide three-quarter views). Romeo then begins to notice in Juliet the subtle signs of sexual arousal: heavy-lidded stare, dilating pupils, faint flush, et cetera. This of course renders her much more bodily, and he not only notices but senses this as well. His arousal is nevertheless still solitary. But now, cleverly calculating the line of her stare without actually looking her in the eyes, he realizes that it is directed at him through the mirror on the opposite wall. That is, he notices, and moreover senses, Juliet sensing him. This is definitely a new development, for it gives him a sense of embodiment not only through his own reactions but through the eyes and reactions of another. Moreover, it is separable from the initial sensing of Juliet; for sexual arousal might begin with a person's sensing that he is sensed and being assailed by the perception of the other person's desire rather than merely by the perception of the person.

But there is a further step. Let us suppose that Juliet, who is a little slower than Romeo, now senses that he senses her. This puts Romeo in a position to notice, and be aroused by, her arousal at being sensed by him. He senses that she senses that he senses her. This is still another level of arousal, for he becomes conscious of his sexuality through his awareness of its effect on her and of her awareness that this effect is due to him. Once she takes the same step and senses that he senses her sensing him, it becomes difficult to state, let alone imagine, further iterations, though they may be logically distinct. If both are alone, they will presumably turn to look at each other directly, and the proceedings will continue on another plane. Physical contact and intercourse are perfectly natural extensions of this complicated visual exchange, and mutual touch can involve all the complexities of awareness present in the visual case, but with a far greater range of subtlety and acuteness.

Ordinarily, of course, things happen in a less orderly fashion—sometimes in a great rush—but I believe that some version of this overlapping system of distinct sexual perceptions and interactions is the basic framework of any full-fledged sexual relation and that relations involving only part of the complex are significantly incomplete. The account is only schematic, as it must be to achieve generality. Every real sexual act will be psychologically far more specific and detailed, in ways that depend not only on the physical techniques employed and on anatomical details, but also on countless features of the participants' conceptions of themselves and of each other, which become embodied in the act. (It is a familiar enough fact, for example, that people often take their social roles and the social roles of their partners to bed with them.)

The general schema is important, however, and the proliferation of levels of mutual awareness it involves is an example of a type of complexity that typifies human interactions. Consider aggression, for example. If I am angry with some-one, I want to make him feel it, either to produce self-reproach by getting him to see himself through the eyes of my anger, and to dislike what he sees—or else to produce reciprocal anger or fear, by getting him to perceive my anger as a threat or attack. What I want will depend on the details of my anger, but in either case it will involve a desire that the object of that anger be aroused. This accomplishment constitutes the fulfillment of my emotion, through domination of the object's feelings.

Another example of such reflexive mutual recognition is to be found in the phenomenon of meaning, which appears to involve an intention to produce a belief or other effect in another by bringing about his recognition of one's intention to produce that effect. (That result is due to H. P. Grice,[2] whose position I shall not attempt to reproduce in detail.) Sex has a related structure: it involves a desire that one's partner be aroused by the recognition of one's desire that he or she be aroused.

It is not easy to define the basic types of awareness and arousal of which these complexes are composed, and that remains a lacuna in this discussion. I believe that the object of awareness is the same in one's own case as it is in one's sexual awareness of another, although the two awarenesses will not be the same, the difference being as great as that between feeling angry and experiencing the anger of another. All stages of sexual perception are varieties of identification of a person with his body. What is perceived is one's own or another's *subjection* to or *immersion* in his body, a phenomenon which has been recognized with loathing by St. Paul and St. Augustine, both of whom regarded "the law of sin which is in my members" as a grave threat to the dominion of the holy will.[3] In sexual desire and its expression the blending of involuntary response with deliberate control is extremely important. For Augustine, the revolution launched against him by his body is symbolized by erection and the other involuntary physical components of arousal. Sartre too stresses the fact that the penis is not a prehensile organ. But mere involuntariness characterizes other bodily processes as well. In sexual desire the involuntary responses are com-bined with submission to spontaneous impulses: not only one's pulse and secretions but one's actions are taken over by the body; ideally, deliberate control is needed only to guide the expression of those impulses. This is to some extent also true of an appetite like hunger, but the takeover there is more localized, less pervasive, less extreme. One's whole body does not become saturated with hunger as it can with desire. But the most characteristic feature of a specifically sexual immersion in the body is its ability to fit into the complex of mutual perceptions that we have described. Hunger leads to spontaneous interactions with food; sexual desire leads to spontaneous interactions with other persons, whose bodies are asserting their sovereignty in the same way, producing involuntary reactions and spontaneous impulses in *them*. These reactions are perceived, and the perception of them is per-ceived, and that perception is in turn perceived; at each step the domination of the person by his body is reinforced, and the sexual partner becomes more possessible by physical contact, penetration, and envelopment.

Desire is therefore not merely the perception of a preexisting embodiment of

[2] "Meaning," *Philosophical Review*, LXVI, 3 (July 1957): 377–388.
[3] See Romans, VII, 23; and the *Confessions*, Book 8, v.

the other, but ideally a contribution to his further embodiment which in turn enhances the original subject's sense of himself. This explains why it is important that the partner be aroused, and not merely aroused, but aroused by the awareness of one's desire. It also explains the sense in which desire has unity and possession as its object: physical possession must eventuate in creation of the sexual object in the image of one's desire, and not merely in the object's recognition of that desire, or in his or her own private arousal. (This may reveal a male bias: I shall say something about that later.)

To return, finally, to the topic of perversion: I believe that various deviations constitute truncated or incomplete versions of the complete configuration, and may therefore be regarded as perversions of the central impulse.

In particular, narcissistic practices and intercourse with animals, infants, and inanimate objects seem to be stuck at some primitive version of the first stage. If the object is not alive, the experience is reduced entirely to an awareness of one's own sexual embodiment. Small children and animals permit awareness of the embodiment of the other, but present obstacles to reciprocity, to the recognition by the sexual object of the subject's desire as the source of his (the object's) sexual self-awareness.

Sadism concentrates on the evocation of passive self-awareness in others, but the sadist's engagement is itself active and requires a retention of deliberate control which impedes awareness of himself as a bodily subject of passion in the required sense. The victim must recognize him as the source of his own sexual passivity, but only as the active source. De Sade claimed that the object of sexual desire was to evoke involuntary responses from one's partner, especially audible ones. The infliction of pain is no doubt the most efficient way to accomplish this, but it requires a certain abrogation of one's own exposed spontaneity. All this, incidentally, helps to explain why it is tempting to regard as sadistic an excessive preoccupation with sexual technique, which does not permit one to abandon the role of agent at any stage of the sexual act. Ideally one should be able to surmount one's technique at some point.

A masochist on the other hand imposes the same disability on his partner as the sadist imposes on himself. The masochist cannot find a satisfactory embodiment as the object of another's sexual desire, but only as the object of his control. He is passive not in relation to his partner's passion but in relation to his nonpassive agency. In addition, the subjection to one's body characteristic of pain and physical restraint is of a very different kind from that of sexual excitement: pain causes people to contract rather than dissolve.

Both of these disorders have to do with the second stage, which involves the awareness of oneself as an object of desire. In straightforward sadism and masochism other attentions are substituted for desire as a source of the object's self-awareness. But it is also possible for nothing of that sort to be substituted, as in the case of a masochist who is satisfied with self-inflicted pain or of a sadist who does not insist on playing a role in the suffering that arouses him. Greater difficulties of classification are presented by three other categories of sexual activity: elaborations of the sexual act; intercourse of more than two persons; and homosexuality.

If we apply our model to the various forms that may be taken by two-party heterosexual intercourse, none of them seem clearly to qualify as perversions. Hardly anyone can be found these days to inveigh against oral-genital contact, and the merits of buggery are urged by such respectable figures as D. H. Lawrence and Norman Mailer. There may be something vaguely sadistic about the latter technique (in Mailer's writings it seems to be a method of introducing an element of rape), but it is not obvious that this has to be so. In general, it would appear that any bodily contact between a man and a woman that gives them sexual pleasure, is a possible vehicle for the system of multi-level interpersonal awareness that I have claimed is the basic psychological content of sexual interaction. Thus a liberal platitude about sex is upheld.

About multiple combinations, the least that can be said is that they are bound to be complicated. If one considers how difficult it is to carry on two conversations simultaneously, one may appreciate the problems of multiple simultaneous interpersonal perception that can arise in even a small-scale orgy. It may be inevitable that some of the component relations should degenerate into mutual epidermal stimulation by participants otherwise isolated from each other. There may also be a tendency toward voyeurism and exhibitionism, both of which are incomplete relations. The exhibitionist wishes to display his desire without needing to be desired in return; he may even fear the sexual attentions of others. A voyeur, on the other hand, need not require any recognition by his object at all: certainly not a recognition of the voyeur's arousal.

It is not clear whether homosexuality is a perversion if that is measured by the standard of the described configuration, but it seems unlikely. For such a classification would have to depend on the possibility of extracting from the system a distinction between male and female sexuality; and much that has been said so far applies equally to men and women. Moreover, it would have to be maintained that there was a natural tie between the type of sexuality and the sex of the body, and also that two sexualities of the same type could not interact properly.

Certainly there is much support for an aggressive-passive distinction between male and female sexuality. In our culture the male's arousal tends to initiate the perceptual exchange, he usually makes the sexual approach, largely controls the course of the act, and of course penetrates whereas the woman receives. When two men or two women engage in intercourse they cannot both adhere to these sexual roles. The question is how essential the roles are to an adequate sexual relation. One relevant observation is that a good deal of deviation from these roles occurs in heterosexual intercourse. Women can be sexually aggressive and men passive, and temporary reversals of role are not uncommon in heterosexual exchanges of reasonable length. If such conditions are set aside, it may be urged that there is something irreducibly perverted in attraction to a body anatomically like one's own. But alarming as some people in our culture may find such attraction, it remains psychologically unilluminating to class it as perverted. Certainly if homosexuality is a perversion, it is so in a very different sense from that in which shoe-fetishism is a perversion, for some version of the full range of interpersonal perceptions seems perfectly possible between two persons of the same sex.

In any case, even if the proposed model is correct, it remains implausible to describe as perverted every deviation from it. For example, if the partners in heterosexual intercourse indulge in private heterosexual fantasies, that obscures the recognition of the real partner and so, on the theory, constitutes a defective sexual relation. It is not, however, generally regarded as a perversion. Such examples suggest that a simple dichotomy between perverted and unperverted sex is too crude to organize the phenomena adequately.

I should like to close with some remarks about the relation of perversion to good, bad, and morality. The concept of perversion can hardly fail to be evaluative in some sense, for it appears to involve the notion of an ideal or at least adequate sexuality which the perversions in some way fail to achieve. So, if the concept is viable, the judgment that a person or practice or desire is perverted will constitute a sexual evaluation, implying that better sex, or a better specimen of sex, is possible. This in itself is a very weak claim, since the evaluation might be in a dimension that is of little interest to us. (Though, if my account is correct, that will not be true.)

Whether it is a moral evaluation, however, is another question entirely—one whose answer would require more understanding of both morality and perversion than can be deployed here. Moral evaluation of acts and of persons is a rather special and very complicated matter, and by no means all our evaluations of persons and their activities are moral evaluations. We make judgments about people's beauty or health or intelligence which are evaluative without being moral. Assessments of their sexuality may be similar in that respect.

Furthermore, moral issues aside, it is not clear that unperverted sex is necessarily *preferable* to the perversions. It may be that sex which receives the highest marks for perfection *as sex* is less enjoyable than certain perversions; and if enjoyment is considered very important, that might outweigh considerations of sexual perfection in determining rational preference.

That raises the question of the relation between the evaluative content of judgments of perversion and the rather common *general* distinction between good and bad sex. The latter distinction is usually confined to sexual acts, and it would seem, within limits, to cut across the other: even someone who believed, for example, that homosexuality was a perversion could admit a distinction between better and worse homosexual sex, and might even allow that good homosexual sex could be better *sex* than not very good unperverted sex. If this is correct, it supports the position that, if judgments of perversion are viable at all, they represent only one aspect of the possible evaluation of sex, even *qua sex*. Moreover it is not the only important aspect: certainly sexual deficiencies that evidently do not constitute perversions can be the object of great concern.

Finally, even if perverted sex is to that extent not so good as it might be, bad sex is generally better than none at all. This should not be controversial: it seems to hold for other important matters, like food, music, literature, and society. In the end, one must choose from among the available alternatives, whether their availability depends on the environment or on one's own constitution. And the alternatives have to be fairly grim before it becomes rational to opt for nothing.

NICHOLAS RESCHER

The Ethical Dimension of Scientific Research

Nicholas Rescher, Professor of Philosophy at the University of
Pittsburgh, is the editor of the *American Philosophical
Quarterly* and the author of *Distributive Justice.*

It has been frequently asserted that the creative scientist is distinguished by his
objectivity. The scientist—so it is said—goes about his work in a rigidly impersonal
and unfeeling way, unmoved by any emotion other than the love of knowledge and
the delights of discovering the secrets of nature.

This widely accepted image of scientific inquiry as a cold, detached, and un-
humane affair is by no means confined to the scientifically uninformed and to
scientific outsiders, but finds many of its most eloquent spokesmen within the scientific
community itself. Social scientists in particular tend to be outspoken supporters of
the view that the scientist does not engage in making value judgments, and that
science, real science, deals only with what is, and has no concern with what ought
to be. Any recitation of concrete instances in which the attitudes, values, and temperaments of scientists have influenced their work or affected their findings is dismissed with the scornful dichotomy that such matters may bear upon the psychology
or sociology of scientific inquiry, but have no relevance whatever to the *logic* of
science.

This point of view that science is "value free" has such wide acceptance as to
have gained for itself the distinctive, if somewhat awesome, label as the thesis of the
value neutrality of science.

Now the main thesis that I propose is simply that this supposed division between
the evaluative disciplines on the one hand and the nonevaluative sciences on the other
is based upon mistaken views regarding the nature of scientific research. In paying
too much attention to the abstract logic of scientific inquiry, many students of scientific method have lost sight of the fact that science is a human enterprise, carried out
by flesh and blood men, and that scientific research must therefore inevitably exhibit some normative complexion. It is my aim to examine the proposition that
evaluative, and more specifically *ethical,* problems crop up at numerous points within
the framework of scientific research. I shall attempt to argue that the scientist does
not, and cannot put aside his common humanity and his evaluative capabilities when
he puts on his laboratory coat.

ETHICAL ISSUES AND THE COLLECTIVIZATION OF SCIENTIFIC RESEARCH

Before embarking on a consideration of the ethical dimension of scientific research, a number of preliminary points are in order.

In considering ethical issues within the sciences, I do not propose to take any notice at all of the various moral problems that arise in relation to what is *done with* scientific discoveries once they have been achieved. I want to concern myself with scientific work as such, and insofar as possible to ignore the various technological and economic applications of science. We shall not be concerned with the very obviously ethical issues that have to do with the use of scientific findings for the production of the instrumentalities of good or evil. The various questions about the morality of the *uses* to which scientific discoveries are put by men other than the scientists themselves—questions of the sort that greatly exercise such organizations as, for example, the Society for Social Responsibility in Science—are substantially beside the point. We all know that the findings of science can be used to manufacture wonder drugs to promote man's welfare, or bacteriological weapons to promote his extermination. Such questions of what is done with the fruits of the tree of science, both bitter and sweet, are not problems that arise *within* science, and are not ethical choices that confront the scientist himself. This fact puts them outside of my limited area of concern. They relate to the exploitation of scientific research, not to its pursuit, and thus they do not arise *within* science in the way that concerns us here.

Before turning to a description of some of the ethical issues that affect the conduct of research in the sciences, I should like to say a word about their reason for being. Ethical questions—that is, issues regarding the rightness and wrongness of conduct—arise out of people's dealings with each other, and pertain necessarily to the duties, rights, and obligations that exist in every kind of interpersonal relationship. For a Robinson Crusoe, few, if any, ethical problems present themselves. One of the most remarkable features of the science of our time is its joint tendency toward collectivization of effort and dispersion of social involvement.

The solitary scientist laboring in isolation in his study or laboratory has given way to the institutionalized laboratory, just as the scientific paper has become a thing of almost inevitably multiple authorship, and the scientific calculation has shifted from the back of an envelope to the electronic computer. Francis Bacon's vision of scientific research as a group effort has come to realization. The scientist nowadays usually functions not as a detached individual unit, but as part of a group, as a "member of the team."

This phenomenon of the collectivization of scientific research leads increasingly to more prominent emphasis upon ethical considerations within science itself. As the room gets more crowded, if I may use a simile, the more acute becomes the need for etiquette and manners; the more people involved in a given corner of scientific research, the more likely ethical issues are apt to arise. It seems that these phenomena of the collectivization and increasing social diffusion of modern science are the main forces that have resulted in making a good deal of room for ethical considerations within the operational framework of modern science.

ETHICAL PROBLEMS REGARDING RESEARCH GOALS

Perhaps the most basic and pervasive way in which ethical problems arise in connection with the prosecution of scientific research is in regard to the choice of research problems, the setting of research goals, and the allocation of resources (both human and material) to the prosecution of research efforts. This ethical problem of choices relating to research goals arises at all levels of aggregation—the national, the institutional, and the individual. I should like to touch upon each of these in turn.

The National Level. As regards the national level, it is a commonplace that the United States government is heavily involved in the sponsorship of research. The current level of federal expenditure on research and development is 8.4 billion dollars, which is around 10 per cent of the federal budget, and 1.6 per cent of the gross national product. If this seems like a modest figure, one must consider the historical perspective. The rate of increase of this budget item over the past ten years has been 10 per cent per annum, which represents a doubling time of seven years. Since the doubling time of our GNP is around twenty years, at these present rates our government will be spending all of our money on science and technology in about sixty-five years. But even today, long before this awkward juncture of affairs is reached, our government, that is to say our collective selves, is heavily involved in the sponsorship of scientific work. And since the man who pays the piper inevitably gets to call at least some of the tune, our society is confronted with difficult choices of a squarely ethical nature regarding the direction of these research efforts. Let me cite a few instances.

In the Soviet Union, 35 per cent of all research and academic trained personnel is engaged in the engineering disciplines, compared with 10 per cent in medicine and pharmaceutical science. Does this 3.5 to 1 ratio of technology to medicine set a pattern to be adopted by the United States? Just how are we to "divide the pie" in allocating federal support funds among the various areas of scientific work?

In our country, the responsibility for such choices is, of course, localized. The President's Science Advisory Committee and the Federal Council for Science and Technology give a mechanism for establishing an overall science budget and thereby for making the difficult decisions regarding resource allocation. These decisions, which require weighing space probes against biological experimentation and atomic energy against oceanography are among the most difficult choices that have to be made by, or on behalf of, the scientific community. The entrance of political considerations may complicate, but cannot remove, the ethical issues that are involved in such choices.

What is unquestionably the largest ethical problem of scientific public policy today is a question of exactly this type. I refer to the difficult choices posed by the fantastic costs of the gadgetry of space exploration. The costs entailed by a systematic program of manned space travel are such as to necessitate major sacrifices in the resources our society can commit both to the advancement of knowledge as such in areas other than space and to medicine, agriculture, and other fields of technology bearing directly upon human welfare. Given the fact, now a matter of common knowledge, that modern science affords the means for effecting an almost infinite improvement in the material conditions of life for at least half the population of our planet, are we morally justified in sacrificing this opportunity to the supposed necessity of producing cold war spectaculars? No other question could more clearly illustrate the ethical character of the problem of research goals at the national level.

The Institutional Level. Let me now turn to the institutional level—that of the laboratory or department or research institute. Here again the ethical issue regarding research goals arises in various ways connected with the investment of effort, or, to put this same matter the other way around, with the selection of research projects.

One very pervasive problem at this institutional level is the classical issue of pure, or basic, versus applied, or practical, research. This problem is always with us and is always difficult, for the more "applied" the research contribution, the more it can yield immediate benefits to man; the more "fundamental," the deeper is its scientific significance and the more can it contribute to the development of science itself. No doubt it is often the case unfortunately that the issue is not dealt with on this somewhat elevated plane, but is resolved in favor of the applied end of the spectrum by the mundane, but inescapable, fact that this is the easier to finance.

I need scarcely add that this ethical issue can also arise at the institutional level in far more subtle forms. For instance, the directorship of a virology laboratory may have to choose whether to commit its limited resources to developing a vaccine which protects against a type of virus that is harmless as a rule but deadly to a few people, as contrasted with a variant type of virus that, while deadly to none, is very bothersome to many.

The Individual Level. The most painful and keenly felt problems are often not the greatest in themselves, but those that touch closest to home. At the level of the individual, too, the ethical question of research goals and the allocation of effort— namely that of the individual himself—can arise and present difficulties of the most painful kind. To cite one example, a young scientist may well ponder the question of whether to devote himself to pure or to applied work. Either option may present its difficulties for him, and these can, although they need not necessarily, be of an ethical nature.

Speaking now just of applied science, it is perfectly clear that characteristically ethical problems can arise for the applied scientist in regard to the nature of the application in question. This is at its most obvious in the choice of a military over against a nonmilitary problem context—A-bombs versus X-rays, poison gas versus pain killers. On this matter of the pressure of ethical considerations upon the conscience of an individual, I cannot forbear giving a brief, but eloquent, autobiographical quotation from C. P. Snow:

> I was an official for twenty years. I went into official life at the beginning of the war, for the reason that prompted my scientific friends to begin to make weapons. I stayed in that life until a year ago, for the same reason that made my scientific friends turn into civilian soldiers. The official's life in England is not quite so disciplined as a soldier's, but it is very nearly so. I think I know the virtues, which are very great, of the men who live that disciplined life. I also know what for me was the moral trap. I, too, had got onto an escalator. I can put the result in a sentence: I was coming to hide behind the institution; I was losing the power to say no.[1]

How many scientists in our day are passengers riding along on Snow's escalator and have dulled their moral sensitivities to this question of personal goals? I have

[1] *Science,* Vol. CXXXIII (1961), 258–259.

myself known more than one scientist who has forgone the chance of being a public benefactor in favor of the more immediate opportunity to be a public servant.

ETHICAL PROBLEMS REGARDING THE STAFFING OF RESEARCH ACTIVITIES

The recruitment and assignment of research personnel to particular projects and activities poses a whole gamut of problems of an ethical nature. I will confine myself to two illustrations.

It is no doubt a truism that scientists become scientists because of their interest in science. Devotion to a scientific career means involvement with scientific work: *doing* science rather than *watching* science done. The collectivization of science creates a new species—the science administrator whose very existence poses both practical and ethical problems. Alvin Weinberg, director of the Oak Ridge National Laboratory, has put it this way:

> Where large sums of public money are being spent there must be many administrators who see to it that the money is spent wisely. Just as it is easier to spend money than to spend thought, so it is easier to tell other scientists how and what to do than to do it oneself. The big scientific community tends to acquire more and more bosses. The Indians with bellies to the bench are hard to discern for all the chiefs with bellies to the mahogany desks. Unfortunately, science dominated by administrators is science understood by administrators, and such science quickly becomes attenuated, if not meaningless.[2]

The facts adduced by Weinberg have several ethical aspects. For one thing there is Weinberg's concern with what administrationitis may be doing to science. And this is surely a problem with ethical implications derived from the fact that scientists have a certain obligation to the promotion of science itself as an ongoing human enterprise. On the other hand, there is the ethical problem of the scientist himself, for a scientist turned administrator is frequently a scientist lost to his first love.

My second example relates to the use of graduate students in university research. There seems to me to be a very real problem in the use of students in the staffing of research projects. We hear a great many pious platitudes about the value of such work for the training of students. The plain fact is that the kind of work needed to get the project done is simply not always the kind of work that is of optimum value for the basic training of a research scientist in a given field. Sometimes instead of doing the student a favor by awarding him a remunerative research fellowship, we may be doing him more harm than good. In some instances known to me, the project work that was supposedly the training ground of a graduate student in actuality derailed or stunted the development of a research scientist.

ETHICAL PROBLEMS REGARDING RESEARCH METHODS

Let me now take up a third set of ethical problems arising in scientific research—those having to do with the *methods* of the research itself. Problems of this kind

[2] *Ibid.*, Vol. CXXXIV (1961), 162.

arise perhaps most acutely in biological or medical or psychological experiments involving the use of experimental animals. They have to do with the measures of omission and commission for keeping experimental animals from needless pain and discomfort. In this connection, let me quote Margaret Mead:

> The growth of importance of the study of human behavior raises a host of new ethical problems, at the head of which I would place the need for consent to the research by both observer and subject. Studies of the behavior of animals other than man introduced a double set of problems: how to control the tendency of the human observer to anthropomorphize, and so distort his observations, and how to protect both the animal and the experimenter from the effects of cruelty. In debates on the issue of cruelty it is usually recognized that callousness toward a living thing may produce suffering in the experimental subject, but it is less often recognized that it may produce moral deterioration in the experimenter.[3]

It goes without saying that problems of this sort arise in their most acute form in experiments that risk human life, limb, well-being, or comfort.

Problems of a somewhat similar character come up in psychological or social science experiments in which the possibility of a compromise of human dignity or integrity is present, so that due measures are needed to assure treatment based on justice and fair play.

ETHICAL PROBLEMS REGARDING STANDARDS OF PROOF

I turn now to a further set of ethical problems relating to scientific research—those that are bound up with what we may call the standards of proof. These have to do with the amount of evidence that a scientist accumulates before he deems it appropriate to announce his findings and put forward the claim that such-and-so may be regarded as an established fact. At what juncture should scientific evidence be reasonably regarded as strong enough to give warrant for a conclusion, and how should the uncertainties of this conclusion be presented?

This problem of standards of proof is ethical, and not merely theoretical or methodological in nature, because it bridges the gap between scientific understanding and action, between thinking and doing. The scientist cannot conveniently side-step the whole of the ethical impact of such questions by saying to the layman, "I'll tell you the scientific facts and then *you* decide on the proper mode of action." These issues are usually so closely interconnected that it is the scientific expert alone who can properly adjudge the bearing of the general scientific considerations upon the particular case in hand.

Every trained scientist knows, of course, that "scientific knowledge" is a body of statements of varying degrees of certainty—including a great deal that is quite unsure as well as much that is reasonably certain. But in presenting particular scientific results, and especially in presenting his own results, a researcher may be under a strong temptation to fail to do justice to the precise degree of certainty and uncertainty involved.

On the one hand, there may be some room for play given to a natural human tendency to exaggerate the assurance of one's own findings. Moreover, when much

---

[3] *Ibid.*, Vol. CXXXIII (1961), 164.

money and effort have been expended, it can be embarrassing—especially when talking with the nonscientific sponsors who have footed the bill—to derogate from the significance or suggestiveness of one's results by dwelling on the insecurities in their basis. The multiple studies and restudies made over the past ten years in order to assess the pathological and genetic effects of radioactive fallout afford an illustration of a struggle to pinpoint the extent of our knowledge and our ignorance in this area.

On the other hand, it may in some instances be tempting for a researcher to underplay the certainty of his findings by adopting an unreasonably high standard of proof. This is especially possible in medical research, where life-risking actions may be based upon a research result. In this domain, a researcher may be tempted to "cover" himself by hedging his findings more elaborately than the realities of the situation may warrant.

Especially when communicating with the laity, this matter of indicating in a convincing way the exact degree of assurance that attaches to a scientific opinion may be a task of great complexity and difficulty. Let me illustrate this by a quotation from W. O. Baker, Vice President for Research at Bell Laboratories:

> I happened to be one of a task force that was gathered officially, with State Department sanction, at the very beginning of 1946, to prepare a detailed scientific estimate . . . about the probable duration of the United States nuclear monopoly. We found, of course, the engineering truth that another country, explicitly the Soviet Union, would have nuclear weapons in a certain number of years after 1946—a number which we carefully estimated. Our estimate, which is a matter of record, was off by little more than a year, and it was, indeed, too conservative an estimate. But it was by no means trusted, and—an equally sorry circumstance—we lacked the skill to make people believe and heed it.[4]

ETHICAL PROBLEMS REGARDING THE DISSEMINATION OF RESEARCH FINDINGS

A surprising variety of ethical problems revolve around the general topic of the dissemination of research findings. It is so basic a truth as to be almost axiomatic that, with the possible exception of a handful of unusual cases in the area of national security classification, a scientist has not only the right, but even the duty, to communicate his findings to the community of fellow scientists, so that his results may stand or fall in the play of the open market place of ideas. Modern science differs sharply in this respect from science in Renaissance times, when a scientist shared his discoveries only with trusted disciples, and announced his findings to the general public only in cryptogram form, if at all.

This ethical problem of favoritism in the sharing of scientific information has come to prominence again in our day. Although scientists do generally publish their findings, the processes of publication consume time, so that anything between six months and three years may elapse between a scientific discovery and its publication in the professional literature. It has become a widespread practice to make pre-publication announcements of findings, or even pre-prepublication announcements. The ethical problem is posed by the extent and direction of such exchanges, for there

[4] *Ibid.*, Vol. CXXXIII (1961), 261.

is no doubt that in many cases favoritism comes into the picture, and that some workers and laboratories exchange findings in a preferential way that amounts to a conspiracy to maintain themselves ahead of the state of the art in the world at large. There is, of course, nothing reprehensible in the natural wish to overcome publication lags or in the normal desire for exchanges of ideas with fellow workers. But when such practices tend to become systematized in a prejudicial way, a plainly ethical problem comes into being.

Let us consider yet another ethical problem regarding the dissemination of research findings. The extensive dependence of science upon educated public opinion, in connection with its support both by the government and the foundations, has already been touched upon. This factor has a tendency to turn the reporting of scientific findings and the discussion of issues relating to scientific research into a kind of journalism. There is a strong incentive to create a favorable climate of public opinion for certain pet projects or concepts. Questions regarding scientific or technical merits thus tend to get treated not only in the proper forum of the science journals, but also in the public press and in Congressional or foundation committee rooms. Not only does this create the danger of scientific pressure groups devoted to preconceived ideas and endowed with the power of retarding other lines of thought, but it also makes for an unhealthy emphasis on the spectacular and the novel, unhealthy, that is, from the standpoint of the development of science itself. For such factors create a type of control over the direction of scientific research that is disastrously unrelated to the proper issue of strictly scientific merits.

The fact is that science has itself become vulnerable in this regard through its increasing sensitivity to public relations matters. Let me cite just one illustration— that of the issue of the fluoridation of municipal water supplies. Some scientists appear to have chosen this issue as a barricade at which to fight for what (to use a political analogue) might be called the "grandeur" of science.

Not long ago, local referenda in the state of Massachusetts gave serious defeats to the proponents of fluoridation. Not only were proposals to introduce this practice defeated in Wellesley and Brookline, but Andover, where fluoridation had been in effect for five years, voted discontinuance of the program. These defeats in towns of the highest educational and socioeconomic levels caused considerable malaise in the scientific community, and wails of anguish found their way even into *Science,* official journal of the American Association for the Advancement of Science. This annoyance over what is clearly not a *scientific* setback, but merely a failure in public relations or political effectiveness, sharply illustrates the sensitivity that scientists have developed in this area.

ETHICAL PROBLEMS REGARDING THE CONTROL OF SCIENTIFIC "MISINFORMATION"

Closely bound up with the ethical problems regarding the dissemination of scientific information are what might be thought of as the other side of the coin—the control, censorship, and suppression of scientific misinformation. Scientists clearly have a duty to protect both their own colleagues in other specialties and the lay public against the dangers of supposed research findings that are strictly erroneous, particularly in regard to areas such as medicine and nutrition, where the public health and welfare are concerned. And quite generally, of course, a scientist has an obligation to maintain the professional literature of his field at a high level of content and quality. The editors and editorial reviewers in whose hands rests access to the media of scientific publication clearly have a duty to preserve their readership from errors of fact and trivia of thought. But these protective functions must always be balanced by respect for the free play of ideas and by a real sensitivity to the possible value of the unfamiliar.

To give just one illustration of the importance of such considerations, I will cite the example of the nineteenth-century English chemist J. J. Waterson. His groundbreaking papers on physical chemistry, anticipating the development of thermodynamics by more than a generation, were rejected by the referees of the Royal Society for publication in its *Proceedings,* with the comment (among others) that "the paper is nothing but of nonsense." As a result, Waterson's work lay forgotten in the archives of the Royal Society until rescued from oblivion by Rayleigh some forty-five years later. Let me quote J. S. Haldane, whose edition of Waterson's works in 1928 decisively rehabilitated this important researcher:

> It is probable that, in the long and honorable history of the Royal Society, no mistake more disastrous in its actual consequences for the progress of science and the reputation of British science than the rejection of Waterson's papers was ever made. The papers were foundation stones of a new branch of scientific knowledge, molecular physics, as Waterson called it, or physical chemistry and thermodynamics as it is now called. There is every reason for believing that, had the papers been published, physical chemistry and thermodynamics would have developed mainly in this country [i.e., England], and along much simpler, more correct, and more intelligible lines than those of their actual development.[5]

Many other examples could be cited to show that it is vitally important that the gatekeepers of our scientific publications be keenly alive to the possible but unobvious value of unfamiliar and strange seeming conceptions.

It is worth emphasizing that this matter of "controlling" the dissemination of scientific ideas poses special difficulties due to an important, but much underrated, phenomenon: *the resistivity to novelty and innovation by the scientific community itself.* No feature of the historical course of development of the sciences is more damaging to the theoreticians' idealized conception of science as perfectly objective—the work of almost disembodied intellects governed by purely rational considerations and actuated solely by an abstract love of truth. The mere assertion that scientists can resist, and indeed frequently have resisted, acceptance of scientific discoveries clashes sharply with the stereotyped concept of the scientist as the purely objective, wholly rational, and entirely open-minded man. Although opposition to scientific findings by social groups other than scientists has been examined by various investigators, the resistance to scientific discoveries by scientists themselves is just beginning to attract the attention of sociologists.[6]

The history of science is, in fact, littered with examples of this phenomenon. Lister, in a graduation address to medical students, bluntly warned against blindness to new ideas such as he had himself encountered in advancing his theory of anti-

[5] Quoted by Stephen G. Brush in *American Scientist,* Vol. XLIX (1961), 211–212.

[6] To anyone interested in this curious topic, I refer the eye-opening article by Bernard Barber, "Resistance by Scientists to Scientific Discovery," *Science,* Vol. CXXXIV (1961).

sepsis. Pasteur's discovery of the biological character of fermentation was long opposed by chemists, including the eminent Liebig, and his germ theory met with sharp resistance from the medical fraternity of his day. No doubt due in part to the very peculiar character of Mesmer himself, the phenomenon of hypnosis, or mesmerism, was rejected by the scientifically orthodox of his time as so much charlatanism. At the summit of the Age of Reason, the French Academy dismissed the numerous and well-attested reports of stones falling from the sky (meteorites, that is to say) as mere folk stories. And this list could be prolonged *ad nauseam*.

Lord Rayleigh, the rediscoverer of J. J. Waterson, who had also himself been burned by scientific opposition to his research findings, became so pessimistic about the difficulties that new conceptions encounter before becoming established in science that he wrote:

> Perhaps one may . . . say that a young author who believes himself capable of great things would usually do well to secure the favorable recognition of the scientific world by work whose scope is limited, and whose value is easily judged, before embarking on greater flights.[7]

(The value of Rayleigh's advice is, of course, very questionable, in view of the fact that it is more than likely that any young scientist of promise who fritters away the maximally creative years of youthful freshness and enthusiasm by doing work of routine drudgery will almost inevitably blunt the keen edge of his productive capacities to a point where "great things" are simply no longer within his grasp.)

Those scientists who have themselves fallen victim to the resistance to new ideas on the part of their colleagues have invariably felt this keenly, and have given eloquent testimony to the existence of this phenomenon. Oliver Heaviside, whose important contributions to mathematical physics were slighted for over twenty-five years, is reported to have exclaimed bitterly that "even men who are not Cambridge mathematicians deserve justice." And Max Planck, after encountering analogous difficulties, wrote:

> This experience gave me also an opportunity to learn a new fact—a remarkable one in my opinion: A new scientific truth does not triumph by convincing its opponents and making them see the light, but rather because its opponents eventually die, and a new generation grows up that is familiar with it.[8]

In summary, the prominence, even in scientific work, of the human psychological tendency to resist new ideas must temper the perspective of every scientist when enforcing what he conceives to be his duty to safeguard others against misinformation and error.

At no point, however, does the ethical problem of information control in science grow more difficult and vexatious than in respect to the boundary line between proper science on the one hand and pseudo-science on the other. The plain fact is that truth is to be found in odd places, and that scientifically valuable materials turn up in unexpected spots.

No one, of course, would for a moment deny the abstract thesis that there is

[7] Quoted by Brush, *op. cit.,* 210.
[8] Quoted by Barber, *op. cit.*

such a thing as pseudo-science, and that it must be contested and controlled. The headache begins with the question of just what is pseudo-science and what is not. We can all readily agree on some of the absurd cases so interestingly desribed in Martin Gardner's wonderful book *Fads and Fallacies in the Name of Science* (New York: Dover Publications, Inc., 1957). But the question of exactly where science ends and where pseudo-science begins is at once important and far from simple. There is little difficulty indeed with Wilbur Glenn Voliva, Gardner's Exhibit No. 1, who during the first third of this century thundered out of Zion (Illinois) that "the earth is flat as a pancake." But parapsychology, for example, is another study and a much more complicated one. And the handful of United States geneticists who, working primarily with yeasts, feel that they have experimental warrant for Lamarckian conclusions, much to the discomfort of the great majority of their professional colleagues, exemplify the difficulties of a hard and fast compartmentalization of pseudo-science in a much more drastic way. Nobody in the scientific community wants to let pseudo-science make headway. But the trouble is that one man's interesting possibility may be another man's pseudo-science.

On the one hand, reputable scientists have often opposed genuine scientific findings as being pseudo-scientific. Lord Bacon, the high priest of early modern science, denounced Gilbert's treatise *On the Magnet as* "a work of inconclusive writing," and he spoke disparagingly of the "electric energy concerning which Gilbert told so many fables." A more recent, if less clearcut, example is the extensive opposition encountered by psychoanalysis, particularly in its early years.

But on the other hand, we have the equally disconcerting fact that reputable scientists have advanced, and their fellow scientists accepted, findings that were strictly fraudulent. One instructive case is that of the French physicist René Blondlot, which is interestingly described in Derek Price's book *Science Since Babylon* (New Haven: Yale University Press, 1961). Blondlot allegedly discovered "N-rays," which were supposed to be something like X-rays. His curious findings attracted a great deal of attention, and earned for Blondlot himself a prize from the French government. But the American physicist Robert W. Wood was able to show by careful experimental work that Blondlot and all who concurred in his findings were deluded. It is thus to be recognized not only that pseudo-science exists, but that it sometimes even makes its way into the sacred precincts of highly orthodox science. This, of course, does not help to simplify the task of discriminating between *real* and *pseudo-*science.

But let us return to the ethical issues involved. These have to do not with the uncontroversial thesis that pseudo-science must be controlled, but with procedural questions of the *means* to be used for the achievement of this worthy purpose. It is with this problem of the means for its control that pseudo-science poses real ethical difficulties for the scientific community.

The handiest instrumentalities to this end and the most temptingly simple to use are the old standbys of thought control—censorship and suppression. But these are surely dire and desperate remedies. It is no doubt highly unpleasant for a scientist to see views that he regards as "preposterous" and "crackpot" to be disseminated and even to gain a considerable public following. But surely we should never lose sensitivity to the moral worth of the methods for achieving our ends or forget that good ends do not justify questionable means. It is undeniably true that scientists have the duty to prevent the propagation of error and misinformation. But this duty has to be acted on with thoughtful caution. It cannot be construed to fit the conveniences of the moment. And it surely cannot be stretched to give warrant to the suppression of views that might prove damaging to the public "image" of science or to justify the protection of one school of thought against its critics. Those scientists who pressured the publisher of Immanuel Velikovsky's fanciful *Worlds in Collision* by threatening to boycott the firm's textbooks unless this work were dropped from its list resorted to measures that I should not care to be called on to defend, but the case is doubtless an extreme one. However, the control exercised by editors and guardians of foundation purse-strings is more subtle, but no less effective and no less problematic.

The main point in this regard is one that needs little defense or argument in its support. Surely scientists, of all people, should have sufficient confidence in the ability of truth to win out over error in the market place of freely interchanged ideas as to be unwilling to forgo the techniques of rational persuasion in favor of the unsavory instrumentalities of pressure, censorship, and suppression.

ETHICAL PROBLEMS REGARDING THE ALLOCATION OF CREDIT FOR SCIENTIFIC RESEARCH ACHIEVEMENTS

The final set of ethical problems arising in relation to scientific research that I propose to mention relate to the allocation of credit for the achievements of research work. Moral philosophers as well as students of jurisprudence have long been aware of the difficulties in assigning to individuals the responsibility for corporate acts, and thus to allocate to individual wrongdoers the blame for group misdeeds. This problem now faces the scientific community in its inverse form—the allocation to individuals of credit for the research accomplishments resulting from conjoint, corporate, or combined effort. Particularly in this day of collectivized research, this problem is apt to arise often and in serious forms.

Let no one be put off by stories about scientific detachment and disinterestedness. The issue of credit for their findings has for many centuries been of the greatest importance to scientists. Doubts on this head are readily dispelled by the prominence of priority disputes in the history of science. Their significance is illustrated by such notorious episodes as the bitter and long-continuing dispute between Newton and Leibniz and their followers regarding priority in the invention of the calculus—a dispute that made for an estrangement between English and continental mathematics which lasted through much of the eighteenth century, considerably to the detriment of the quality of British mathematics during that era.

But to return to the present, the problem of credit allocation can come up nowadays in forms so complex and intricate as to be almost inconceivable to any mind not trained in the law. For instance, following out the implications of an idea put forward as an idle guess by X, Y, working under W's direction in Z's laboratory, comes up with an important result. How is the total credit to be divided? It requires no great imagination to think up some of the kinds of problems and difficulties that can come about in saying who is to be credited with what in this day of corporate and collective research. This venture lends itself to clever literary exploitation in the hands of a master like C. P. Snow.

RETROSPECT ON THE ETHICAL DIMENSION
OF SCIENTIFIC RESEARCH

Let us now pause for a moment to survey the road that we have traveled thus far. The discussion to this point has made a guided tour of a major part of the terrain constituting the ethical dimension of scientific research. In particular, we have seen that questions of a strictly ethical nature arise in connection with scientific research at the following crucial junctures:

1. the choice of research goals
2. the staffing of research activities
3. the selection of research methods
4. the specification of standards of proof
5. the dissemination of research findings
6. the control of scientific misinformation
7. the allocation of credit for research accomplishments

In short, it seems warranted to assert that, at virtually every junction of scientific research work, from initial inception of the work to the ultimate reporting of its completed findings, issues of a distinctively ethical character may present themselves for resolution.

It is a regrettable fact that too many persons, both scientists and students of scientific method, have had their attention focused so sharply upon the abstracted "logic" of an idealized "scientific method" that this ethical dimension of science has completely escaped their notice. This circumstance seems to me to be particularly regrettable because it has tended to foster a harmful myth that finds strong support in both the scientific and the humanistic camps—namely, the view that science is antiseptically devoid of any involvement with human values. Science, on this way of looking at the matter, is so purely objective and narrowly factual in its concerns that it can, and indeed should, be wholly insensitive to the emotional, artistic, and ethical values of human life.

I hope that my analysis of the role of ethical considerations within the framework of science has been sufficiently convincing to show that this dichotomy, with its resultant divorce between the sciences and the humanities, is based on a wholly untenable conception of the actual division of labor between these two areas of intellectual endeavor. It is my strong conviction that both parties to this unasked for divorce must recognize the spuriousness of its alleged reasons for being, if the interests of a wholesome unity of human understanding are to be served properly.

The humanist, for his part, must not be allowed to forget that in the whole course of the intellectual history of the West, from Aristotle and his predecessors to Descartes, Newton, Kant, James, and Einstein, science has been a part of the cultural tradition in its larger sense. Throughout the whole course of the development of our civilization, science has always merited the historic epithet of "natural philosophy." No matter how much our way of describing the facts may change, there is little doubt that this basic circumstance of the formative role of science in molding the *Weltanschauung* basic to all of our areas of thought will remain invariant.

On the other hand, the scientist, for his part, should realize science has worth and status enough in its own right that its devotees can dispense with claiming that, although the handiwork of imperfect humans, it is somehow mysteriously endowed with virtually superhuman powers, such as are implied by claims of actual achievement of what in fact are remote ideals, and in some instances unworkable idealizations, like pure open-mindedness, complete objectivity, and perfect rationality.

From the standpoint of a realistic appreciation of the nature of science as a human creation and activity, it seems to me that a heightened awareness of the humanistic dimension of science—which I have tried to illustrate on the ethical side —can serve the best interests of both of these two important working areas of the human intellect. Instead of being nearly separable, these domains are interpenetrating and interdependent. Rather than being strange bedfellows, the sciences and the humanities are ancient and mutually beneficial partners in that pre-eminently humane enterprise of leading man to a better understanding both of himself and of the world in which he lives.

HANS JONAS

Philosophical Reflections on Experimenting with Human Subjects

Hans Jonas, Alvin Johnson Professor of Philosophy at the New School for Social Research, has also written *The Phenomenon of Life* and *The Western Tradition and Technological Man.*

When I was first asked to comment "philosophically" on the subject of human experimentation, I had all the hesitation natural to a layman in the face of matters on which experts of the highest competence have had their say and still carry on their dialogue. As I familiarized myself with the material, any initial feeling of moral rectitude that might have facilitated my task quickly dissipated before the awesome complexity of the problem, and a state of great humility took its place. Nevertheless, because the subject is obscure by its nature and involves fundamental, transtechnical issues, any attempt at clarification can be of use, even without novelty. Even if the philosophical reflection should in the end achieve no more than the realization that in the dialectics of this area we must sin and fall into guilt, this insight may not be without its own gains.

Reprinted by permission from *Dædalus, Journal of the American Academy of Arts and Sciences,* Boston, Massachusetts, Volume 98, Number 2.

THE PECULIARITY OF HUMAN EXPERIMENTATION

Experimentation was originally sanctioned by natural science. There it is performed on inanimate objects, and this raises no moral problems. But as soon as animate, feeling beings become the subjects of experiment, as they do in the life sciences and especially in medical research, this innocence of the search for knowledge is lost and questions of conscience arise. The depth to which moral and religious sensibilities can become aroused is shown by the vivisection issue. Human experimentation must sharpen the issue as it involves ultimate questions of personal dignity and sacro-sanctity. One difference between the human experiments and the physical is this: The physical experiment employs small-scale, artificially devised substitutes for that about which knowledge is to be obtained, and the experimenter extrapolates from these models and simulated conditions to nature at large. Something deputizes for the "real thing"—balls rolling down an inclined plane for sun and planets, electric discharges from a condenser for real lightning, and so on. For the most part, no such substitution is possible in the biological sphere. We must operate on the original itself, the real thing in the fullest sense, and perhaps affect it irreversibly. No simu-lacrum can take its place. Especially in the human sphere, experimentation loses entirely the advantage of the clear division between vicarious model and true object. Up to a point, animals may fulfill the proxy role of the classical physical experiment. But in the end man himself must furnish knowledge about himself, and the com-fortable separation of noncommittal experiment and definitive action vanishes. An experiment in education affects the lives of its subjects, perhaps a whole generation of schoolchildren. Human experimentation for whatever purpose is always *also* a responsible, nonexperimental, definitive dealing with the subject himself. And not even the noblest purpose abrogates the obligations this involves.

Can both that purpose and this obligation be satisfied? If not, what would be a just compromise? Which side should give way to the other? The question is in-herently philosophical as it concerns not merely pragmatic difficulties and their arbi-tration, but a genuine conflict of values involving principles of a high order. On prin-ciple, it is felt, human beings *ought not* to be dealt with in that way (the "guinea pig" protest); on the other hand, such dealings are increasingly urged on us by con-siderations, in turn appealing to principle, that claim to override those objections. Such a claim must be carefully assessed, especially when it is swept along by a mighty tide. Putting the matter thus, we have already made one important assumption rooted in our "Western" cultural tradition: The prohibitive rule is, to that way of thinking, the primary and axiomatic one; the permissive counter-rule, as qualifying the first, is secondary and stands in need of justification. We must justify the infringement of a primary inviolability, which needs no justification itself; and the justification of its infringement must be by values and needs of a dignity commensurate with those to be sacrificed.

"INDIVIDUAL VERSUS SOCIETY" AS THE CONCEPTUAL FRAMEWORK

The setting for the conflict most consistently invoked in the literature is the polarity of individual versus society—the possible tension between the individual good and the common good, between private and public welfare. Thus, W. Wolfensberger speaks of "the tension between the long-range interests of society, science, and progress, on one hand, and the rights of the individual on the other." Walsh Mc-Dermott says: "In essence, this is a problem of the rights of the individual versus the rights of society." Somewhere I found the "social contract" invoked in support of claims that science may make on individuals in the matter of experimentation. I have grave doubts about the adequacy of this frame of reference, but I will go along with it part of the way. It does apply to some extent, and it has the advantage of being familiar. We concede, as a matter of course, to the common good some pragmatically determined measure of precedence over the individual good. In terms of rights, we let some of the basic rights of the individual be overruled by the acknowledged rights of society—as a matter of right and moral justness and not of mere force or dire necessity (much as such necessity may be adduced in defense of that right). But in making that concession, we require a careful clarification of what the needs, interests, and rights of society are, for society—as distinct from any plurality of individuals—is an abstract and as such is subject to our definition, while the individual is the primary concrete, prior to all definition, and his basic good is more or less known. Thus, the unknown in our problem is the so-called common or public good and its potentially superior claims, to which the individual good must or might sometimes be sacrificed, in circumstances that in turn must also be counted among the unknowns of our question. Note that in putting the matter in this way—that is, in asking about the right of society to individual sacrifice—the consent of the sacrificial subject is no necessary part of the *basic* question.

"Consent," however, is the other most consistently emphasized and examined concept in discussions of this issue. This attention betrays a feeling that the "social" angle is not fully satisfactory. If society has a right, its exercise is not contingent on volunteering. On the other hand, if volunteering is fully genuine, no public right to the volunteered act need be construed. There is a difference between the moral or emotional appeal of a cause that elicits volunteering and a right that demands compliance—for example, with particular reference to the social sphere, between the *moral claim* of a common good and society's *right* to that good and to the means of its realization. A moral claim cannot be met without consent; a right can do without it. Where consent is present anyway, the distinction may become immaterial. But the awareness of the many ambiguities besetting the "consent" actually available and used in medical research prompts recourse to the idea of a public right conceived independently of (and valid prior to) consent; and, vice versa, the awareness of the problematic nature of such a right makes even its advocates still insist on the idea of consent with all its ambiguities: An uneasy situation exists for both sides.

Nor does it help much to replace the language of "rights" by that of "interests" and then argue the sheer cumulative weight of the interests of the many over against those of the few or the single individual. "Interests" range all the way from the most marginal and optional to the most vital and imperative, and only those sanctioned by particular importance and merit will be admitted to count in such a calculus—which simply brings us back to the question of right or moral claim. Moreover, the appeal to numbers is dangerous. Is the number of those afflicted with a particular disease great enough to warrant violating the interests of the nonafflicted? Since the number of the latter is usually so much greater, the argument can actually turn around to the contention that the cumulative weight of interest is on *their* side. Finally, it may well be the case that the individual's interest in his own inviolability is itself a public interest such that its publicly condoned violation, irrespective of numbers, violates the interest of all. In that case, its protection in *each* instance would be a paramount interest, and the comparison of numbers will not avail.

These are some of the difficulties hidden in the conceptual framework indicated by the terms "society-individual," "interest," and "rights." But we also spoke of a moral call, and this points to another dimension—not indeed divorced from the societal sphere, but transcending it. And there is something even beyond that: true sacrifice from highest devotion, for which there are no laws or rules except that it must be absolutely free. "No one has the right to choose martyrs for science" was a statement repeatedly quoted in the November, 1967, *Dædalus* conference. But no scientist can be prevented from making himself a martyr for his science. At all times, dedicated explorers, thinkers, and artists have immolated themselves on the altar of their vocation, and creative genius most often pays the price of happiness, health, and life for its own consummation. But no one, not even society, has the shred of a right to expect and ask these things. They come to the rest of us as a *gratia gratis data*.

THE SACRIFICIAL THEME

Yet we must face the somber truth that the *ultima ratio* of communal life is and has always been the compulsory, vicarious sacrifice of individual lives. The primordial sacrificial situation is that of outright human sacrifices in early communities. These were not acts of blood-lust or gleeful savagery; they were the solemn execution of a supreme, sacral necessity. One of the fellowship of men had to die so that all could live, the earth be fertile, the cycle of nature renewed. The victim often was not a captured enemy, but a select member of the group: "The king must die." If there was cruelty here, it was not that of men, but that of the gods, or rather of the stern order of things, which was believed to exact that price for the bounty of life. To assure it for the community, and to assure it ever again, the awesome *quid pro quo* had to be paid ever again.

Far be it from me, and far should it be from us, to belittle from the height of our enlightened knowledge the majesty of the underlying conception. The particular *causal* views that prompted our ancestors have long since been relegated to the realm of superstition. But in moments of national danger we still send the flower of our young manhood to offer their lives for the continued life of the community, and if it is a just war, we see them go forth as consecrated and strangely ennobled by a sacrifical role. Nor do we make their going forth depend on their own will and consent, much as we may desire and foster these: We conscript them according to law. We conscript the best and feel morally disturbed if the draft, either by design or in effect, works so that mainly the disadvantaged, socially less useful, more expendable, make up those whose lives are to buy ours. No rational persuasion of the pragmatic necessity here at work can do away with the feeling, mixed of gratitude and guilt, that the sphere of the sacred is touched with the vicarious offering of life for life. Quite apart from these dramatic occasions, there is, it appears, a persistent and constitutive aspect of human immolation to the very being and prospering of human society—an immolation in terms of life and happiness, imposed or voluntary, of few for many. What Goethe has said of the rise of Christianity may well apply to the nature of civilization in general: *"Opfer fallen hier, / Weder Lamm noch Stier, / Aber Menschenopfer unerhoert."* We can never rest comfortably in the belief that the soil from which our satisfactions sprout is not watered with the blood of martyrs. But a troubled conscience compels us, the undeserving beneficiaries, to ask: Who is to be martyred? in the service of what cause? and by whose choice?

Not for a moment do I wish to suggest that medical experimentation on human subjects, sick or healthy, is to be likened to primeval human sacrifices. Yet something sacrificial is involved in the selective abrogation of personal inviolability and the ritualized exposure to gratuitous risk of health and life, justified by a presumed greater, social good. My examples from the sphere of stark sacrifice were intended to sharpen the issues implied in that context and to set them off clearly from the kinds of obligations and constraints imposed on the citizen in the normal course of things or generally demanded of the individual in exchange for the advantages of civil society.

THE "SOCIAL CONTRACT" THEME

The first thing to say in such a setting-off is that the sacrificial area is not covered by what is called the "social contract." This fiction of political theory, premised on the primacy of the individual, was designed to supply a rationale for the *limitation* of individual freedom and power required for the existence of the body politic, whose existence in turn is for the benefit of the individuals. The principle of these limitations is that their *general* observance profits all, and that therefore the individual observer, assuring this general observance for his part, profits by it himself. I observe property rights because their general observance assures my own; I observe traffic rules because their general observance assures my own safety; and so on. The obligations here are mutual and general; no one is singled out for special sacrifice. For the most part, *qua* limitations of my liberty, the laws thus deducible from the hypothetical "social contract" enjoin me from certain actions rather than obligate me to positive actions (as did the laws of feudal society). Even where the latter is the case, as in the duty to pay taxes, the rationale is that I am myself a beneficiary of the services financed through these payments. Even the contributions levied by the welfare state, though not originally contemplated in the liberal version of the social contract theory, can be interpreted as a personal insurance policy of one sort or another—be it against the contingency of my own indigence, the dangers of disaffection from the laws in consequence of widespread unrelieved destitution, or the disadvantages of a diminished consumer market. Thus, by some stretch, such contributions can still be subsumed under the principle of enlightened self-interest. But no complete abrogation of self-interest at any time is in the terms of the social contract, and so pure sacrifice falls outside it. Under the putative terms of the contract alone, I cannot be required to die for the public good. (Thomas Hobbes made this forcibly clear.) Even short of this extreme, we like to think that nobody is entirely and one-sidedly the victim in any of the renunciations exacted under normal circumstances by society "in the general interest"—that is, for the benefit of others. "Under normal circumstances," as we shall see, is a necessary qualification. Moreover, the "contract" can legitimize claims only on our overt public actions and not on our invisible private being. Our powers, not our persons, are beholden to the commonweal. In one important respect, it is true, public interest and control do extend to the private sphere by general consent: in the compulsory education of our children. Even there, the assumption is that the learning and what is learned, apart from all future social usefulness, are also for the benefit of the individual in his own being. We would not tolerate education to degenerate into the conditioning of useful robots for the social machine.

Both restrictions of public claim in behalf of the "common good"—that concerning one-sided sacrifice and that concerning the private sphere—are valid only, let us remember, on the premise of the primacy of the individual, upon which the whole idea of the "social contract" rests. This primacy is itself a metaphysical axiom or option peculiar to our Western tradition, and the whittling away of this axiom would threaten the tradition's whole foundation. In passing, I may remark that systems adopting the alternative primacy of the community as their axiom are naturally less bound by the restrictions we postulate. Whereas we reject the idea of "expendables" and regard those not useful or even recalcitrant to the social purpose as a burden that society must carry (since their individual claim to existence is as absolute as that of the most useful), a truly totalitarian regime, Communist or other, may deem it right for the collective to rid itself of such encumbrances or to make them forcibly serve some social end by conscripting their persons (and there are effective combinations of both). We do not normally—that is, in nonemergency conditions—give the state the right to conscript labor, while we do give it the right to "conscript" money, for money is detachable from the person as labor is not. Even less than forced labor do we countenance forced risk, injury, and indignity.

But in time of war our society itself supersedes the nice balance of the social contract with an almost absolute precedence of public necessities over individual rights. In this and similar emergencies, the sacrosanctity of the individual is abrogated, and what for all practical purposes amounts to a near-totalitarian, quasi-Communist state of affairs is *temporarily* permitted to prevail. In such situations, the community is conceded the right to make calls on its members, or certain of its members, entirely different in magnitude and kind from the calls normally allowed. It is deemed right that a part of the population bears a disproportionate burden of risk of a disproportionate gravity; and it is deemed right that the rest of the community accepts this sacrifice, whether voluntary or enforced, and reaps its benefits—difficult as we find it to justify this acceptance and this benefit by any normal ethical categories. We justify it transethically, as it were, by the supreme collective emergency, formalized, for example, by the declaration of a state of war.

Medical experimentation on human subjects falls somewhere between this overpowering case and the normal transactions of the social contract. On the one hand, no comparable extreme issue of social survival is (by and large) at stake. And no comparable extreme sacrifice or foreseeable risk is (by and large) asked. On the other hand, what is asked goes decidedly beyond, even runs counter to, what it is otherwise deemed fair to let the individual sign over of his person to the benefit of the "common good." Indeed, our sensitivity to the kind of intrusion and use involved is such that only an end of transcendent value or overriding urgency can make it arguable and possibly acceptable in our eyes.

HEALTH AS A PUBLIC GOOD

The cause invoked is health and, in its more critical aspect, life itself—clearly superlative goods that the physician serves directly by curing and the researcher indirectly by the knowledge gained through his experiments. There is no question about the good served nor about the evil fought—disease and premature death. But a good to whom and an evil to whom? Here the issue tends to become somewhat clouded. In the attempt to give experimentation the proper dignity (on the problematic view that a value becomes greater by being "social" instead of merely individual), the health in question or the disease in question is somehow predicated of the social whole, as if it were society that, in the persons of its members, enjoyed the one and suffered the other. For the purposes of our problem, public interest can then be pitted against private interest, the common good against the individual good. Indeed, I have found health called a national resource, which of course it is, but surely not in the first place.

In trying to resolve some of the complexities and ambiguities lurking in these conceptualizations, I have pondered a particular statement, made in the form of a question, which I found in the *Proceedings* of the November *Dædalus* conference: "Can society afford to discard the tissues and organs of the hopelessly unconscious patient when they could be used to restore the otherwise hopelessly ill, but still salvageable individual?" And somewhat later: "A strong case can be made that society can ill afford to discard tissues and organs of the hopelessly unconscious patient; they are greatly needed for study and experimental trial to help those who can be salvaged." I hasten to add that any suspicion of callousness that the "commodity" language of these statements may suggest is immediately dispelled by the name of the speaker, Dr. Henry K. Beecher, for whose humanity and moral sensibility there can be nothing but admiration. But the use, in all innocence, of this language gives food for thought. Let me, for a moment, take the question literally. "Discarding implies proprietary rights—nobody can discard what does not belong to him in the first place. Does society then own my body? "Salvaging" implies the same and, moreover, a use-value to the owner. Is the life-extension of certain individuals then a public interest? "Affording" implies a critically vital level of such an interest—that is, of the loss or gain involved. And "society" itself—what is it? When does a need, an aim, an obligation become social? Let us reflect on some of these terms.

WHAT SOCIETY CAN AFFORD

"Can Society afford . . . ?" Afford what? To let people die intact, thereby withholding something from other people who desperately need it, who in consequence will have to die too? These other, unfortunate people indeed cannot afford not to have a kidney, heart, or other organ of the dying patient, on which they depend for an extension of their lease on life; but does that give them a right to it? Does it oblige society to procure it for them? What is it that *society* can or cannot afford—leaving aside for the moment the question of what it has a *right* to? It surely can afford to lose members through death; more than that, it is built on the balance of death and birth decreed by the order of life. This is too general, of course, for our question, but perhaps it is well to remember. The specific question seems to be whether society can afford to let some people die whose death might be deferred by particular means if these were authorized by society. Again, if it is merely a question of what society can or cannot afford, rather than of what it ought or ought not to do, the answer must be: Of course, it can. If cancer, heart disease, and other organic, noncontagious ills, especially those tending to strike the old more than the young, continue to exact their toll at the normal rate of incidence (including the toll of private anguish and misery), society can go on flourishing in every way.

Here, by contrast, are some examples of what, in sober truth, society cannot afford. It cannot afford to let an epidemic rage unchecked: a persistent excess of deaths over births, but neither too great an excess of births over deaths; too low an average life-expectancy even if demographically balanced by fertility, but neither too great a longevity with the necessitated correlative dearth of youth in the social body; a debilitating state of general health; and things of this kind. These are plain cases where the whole condition of society is critically affected, and the public interest can make its imperative claims. The Black Death of the Middle Ages was a *public* calamity of the acute kind; the life-sapping ravages of endemic malaria or sleeping sickness in certain areas are a public calamity of the chronic kind. A society as a whole can truly not "afford" such situations, and they may call for extraordinary remedies, including, perhaps, the invasion of private sacrosanctities.

This is not entirely a matter of numbers and numerical ratios. Society, in a subtler sense, cannot "afford" a single miscarriage of justice, a single inequity in the dispensation of its laws, the violation of the rights of even the tiniest minority, because these undermine the moral basis on which society's existence rests. Nor can it, for a similar reason, afford the absence of atrophy in its midst of compassion and of the effort to alleviate suffering—be it widespread or rare—one form of which is the effort to conquer disease of any kind, whether "socially" significant (by reason of number) or not. And in short, society cannot afford the absence among its members of *virtue* with its readiness to sacrifice beyond defined duty. Since its presence—that is to say, that of personal idealism—is a matter of grace and not of decree, we have the paradox that society depends for its existence on intangibles of nothing less than a religious order, for which it can hope, but which it cannot enforce. All the more must it protect this most precious capital from abuse.

For what objectives connected with the medico-biological sphere should this reserve be drawn upon—for example, in the form of accepting, soliciting, perhaps even imposing the submission of human subjects to experimentation? We postulate that this must be not just a worthy cause, as any promotion of the health of anybody doubtlessly is, but a cause qualifying for transcendent social sanction. Here one thinks first of those cases critically affecting the whole condition, present and future, of the community. Something equivalent to what in the political sphere is called "clear and present danger" may be invoked and a state of emergency proclaimed, thereby suspending certain otherwise inviolable prohibitions and taboos. We may observe that averting a disaster always carries greater weight than promoting a good. Extraordinary danger excuses extraordinary means. This covers human experimentation, which we would like to count, as far as possible, among the extraordinary rather than the ordinary means of serving the common good under public auspices. Naturally, since foresight and responsibility for the future are of the essence of institutional society, averting disaster extends into long-term prevention, although the lesser urgency will warrant less sweeping licenses.

SOCIETY AND THE CAUSE OF PROGRESS

Much weaker is the case where it is a matter not of saving but of improving society. Much of medical research falls into this category. A permanent death rate from heart failure or cancer does not threaten society. So long as certain statistical ratios are maintained, the incidence of disease and of disease-induced mortality is not (in the strict sense) a "social" misfortune. I hasten to add that it is not therefore less of a human misfortune, and the call for relief issuing with silent eloquence from each victim and all potential victims is of no lesser dignity. But it is misleading to equate the fundamentally human response to it with what is owed to society: It is owed by man to man—and it is thereby owed by society to the individuals as soon as the adequate ministering to these concerns outgrows (as it progressively does) the scope of private spontaneity and is made a public mandate. It is thus that society assumes responsibility for medical care, research, old age, and innumerable other things not originally of the public realm (in the original "social contract"), and they become duties toward "society" (rather than directly toward one's fellow man) by the fact that they are socially operated.

Indeed, we expect from organized society no longer mere protection against harm and the securing of the conditions of our preservation, but active and constant improvement in all the domains of life: the waging of the battle against nature, the enhancement of the human estate—in short, the promotion of progress. This is an expansive goal, one far surpassing the disaster norm of our previous reflections. It lacks the urgency of the latter, but has the nobility of the free, forward thrust. It surely is worth sacrifices. It is not at all a question of what society can afford, but of what it is committed to, beyond all necessity, by our mandate. Its trusteeship has become an established, ongoing, institutionalized business of the body politic. As eager beneficiaries of its gains, we now owe to "society," as its chief agent, our individual contribution toward its *continued pursuit*. Maintaining the existing level requires no more than the orthodox means of taxation and enforcement of professional standards that raise no problems. The more optional goal of pushing forward is also more exacting. We have this syndrome: Progress is by our choosing an acknowledged interest of society, in which we have a stake in various degrees; science is a necessary instrument of progress; research is a necessary instrument of science; and in medical science experimentation on human subjects is a necessary instrument of research: Therefore, human experimentation has come to be a societal interest.

The destination of research is essentially melioristic. It does not serve the preservation of the existing good from which I profit myself and to which I am obligated. Unless the present state is intolerable, the melioristic goal is in a sense gratuitous, and not only from the vantage point of the present. Our descendants have a right to be left an unplundered planet; they do not have a right to new miracle cures. We have sinned against them if by our doing we have destroyed their inheritance—which we are doing at full blast; we have not sinned against them if by the time they come around arthritis has not yet been conquered (unless by sheer neglect). And generally, in the matter of progress, as humanity had no claim on a Newton, a Michelangelo, or a St. Francis to appear, and no right to the blessings of their unscheduled deeds, so progress, with all our methodical labor for it, cannot be budgeted in advance and its fruits received as a due. Its coming-about at all and its turning out for good (of which we can never be sure) must rather be regarded as something akin to grace.

THE MELIORISTIC GOAL, MEDICAL RESEARCH, AND INDIVIDUAL DUTY

Nowhere is the melioristic goal more inherent than in medicine. To the physician, it is not gratuitous. He is committed to curing and thus to improving the power to cure. Gratuitous we called it (outside disaster conditions) as a *social* goal, but noble at the same time. Both the nobility and the gratuitousness must influence the manner in which self-sacrifice for it is elicited and even its free offer accepted. Freedom is certainly the first condition to be observed here. The surrender of one's body to medical experimentation is entirely outside the enforceable "social contract."

Or can it be construed to fall within its terms—namely, as repayment for benefits from past experimentation that I have enjoyed myself? But I am indebted for these benefits not to society, but to the past "martyrs," to whom society is indebted itself, and society has no right to call in my personal debt by way of adding new to its own. Moreover, gratitude is not an enforceable social obligation; it anyway does not mean that I must emulate the deed. Most of all, if it was wrong to exact such sacrifice in the first place, it does not become right to exact it again with the plea of the profit it has brought me. If, however, it was not exacted, but entirely free, as it ought to have been, then it should remain so, and its precedence must not be used as a social pressure on others for doing the same under the sign of duty.

Indeed, we must look outside the sphere of the social contract, outside the whole realm of public rights and duties, for the motivations and norms by which we can expect ever again the upwelling of a will to give what nobody—neither society, nor fellow man, nor posterity—is entitled to. There are such dimensions in man with trans-social wellsprings of conduct, and I have already pointed to the paradox, or mystery, that society cannot prosper without them, that it must draw on them, but cannot command them.

What about the moral law as such a transcendent motivation of conduct? It goes considerably beyond the public law of the social contract. The latter, we saw, is founded on the rule of enlightened self-interest: *Do ut des*—I give so that I be given to. The law of individual conscience asks more. Under the Golden Rule, for example, I am required to give as I wish to be given to under like circumstances, but not in order that I be given to and not in expectation of return. Reciprocity, essential to the social law, is not a condition of the moral law. One subtle "expectation" and "self-interest," but of the moral order itself, may even then be in my mind: I prefer the environment of a moral society and can expect to contribute to the general morality by my own example. But even if I should always be the dupe, the Golden Rule holds. (If the social law breaks faith with me, I am released from its claim.)

MORAL LAW AND TRANSMORAL DEDICATION

Can I, then, be called upon to offer myself for medical experimentation in the name of the moral law? *Prima facie,* the Golden Rule seems to apply. I should wish, were I dying of a disease, that enough volunteers in the past had provided enough knowledge through the gift of their bodies that I could now be saved. I should wish, were I desperately in need of a transplant, that the dying patient next door had agreed to a definition of death by which his organs would become available to me in the freshest possible condition. I surely should also wish, were I drowning, that somebody would risk his life, even sacrifice his life, for mine.

But the last example reminds us that only the negative form of the Golden Rule ("Do not do unto others what you do not want done unto yourself") is fully prescriptive. The positive form ("Do unto others as you would wish them to do unto you"), in whose compass our issue falls, points into an infinite, open horizon where prescriptive force soon ceases. We may well say of somebody that he ought to have come to the succor of B, to have shared with him in his need, and the like. But we may not say that he ought to have given his life for him. To have done so would be praiseworthy; not to have done so is not blameworthy. It cannot be asked of him; if he fails to do so, he reneges on no duty. But *he* may say of himself, and only he, that he ought to have given his life. *This* "ought" is strictly between him and himself, or between him and God; no outside party—fellow man or society—can appropriate its voice. It can humbly receive the supererogatory gifts from the free enactment of it.

We must, in other words, distinguish between moral obligation and the much larger sphere of moral value. (This, incidentally, shows up the error in the widely held view of value theory that the higher a value, the stronger its claim and the greater the duty to realize it. The highest are in a region beyond duty and claim.) The ethical dimension far exceeds that of the moral law and reaches into the sublime solitude of dedication and ultimate commitment, away from all reckoning and rule—in short, into the sphere of the *holy.* From there alone can the offer of self-sacrifice genuinely spring, and this—its source—must be honored religiously. How? The first duty here falling on the research community, when it enlists and uses this source, is the safeguarding of true authenticity and spontaneity.

THE "CONSCRIPTION" OF CONSENT

But here we must realize that the mere issuing of the appeal, the calling for volunteers, with the moral and social pressures it inevitably generates, amounts even under the most meticulous rules of consent to a sort of *conscripting.* And some soliciting is necessarily involved. This was in part meant by the earlier remark that in this area sin and guilt can perhaps not be wholly avoided. And this is why "consent," surely a non-negotiable minimum requirement, is not the full answer to the problem. Granting then that soliciting and therefore some degree of conscripting are part of the situation, who may conscript and who may be conscripted? Or less harshly expressed: Who should issue appeals and to whom?

The naturally qualified issuer of the appeal is the research scientist himself, collectively the main carrier of the impulse and the only one with the technical competence to judge. But his being very much an interested party (with vested interests, indeed, not purely in the public good, but in the scientific enterprise as such, in "his" project, and even in his career) makes him also suspect. The ineradicable dialectic of this situation—a delicate incompatibility problem—calls for particular controls by the research community and by public authority that we need not discuss. They can mitigate, but not eliminate the problem. We have to live with the ambiguity, the treacherous impurity of everything human.

SELF-RECRUITMENT OF THE RESEARCH COMMUNITY

To whom should the appeal be addressed? The natural issuer of the call is also the first natural addressee: the physician-researcher himself and the scientific confraternity at large. With such a coincidence—indeed, the noble tradition with which the whole business of human experimentation started—almost all of the associated legal, ethical, and metaphysical problems vanish. If it is full, autonomous identification of the subject with the purpose that is required for the dignifying of his serving as a subject—here it is; if strongest motivation—here it is; if fullest understanding—here it is; if freest decision—here it is; if greatest integration with the person's total, chosen pursuit—here it is. With self-solicitation, the issue of consent in all its insoluble equivocality is bypassed *per se*. Not even the condition that the particular purpose be truly important and the project reasonably promising, which must hold in any solicitation of others, need be satisfied here. By himself, the scientist is free to obey his obsession, to play his hunch, to wager on chance, to follow the lure of ambition. It is all part of the "divine madness" that somehow animates the ceaseless pressing against frontiers. For the rest of society, which has a deep-seated disposition to look with reverence and awe upon the guardians of the mysteries of life, the profession assumes with this proof of its devotion the role of a self-chosen, consecrated fraternity, not unlike the monastic orders of the past; and this would come nearest to the actual, religious origins of the art of healing.

It would be the ideal, but not a real solution to keep the issue of human experimentation within the research community itself. Neither in numbers nor in variety of material would its potential suffice for the many-pronged, systematic, continual attack on disease into which the lonely exploits of the early investigators have grown. Statistical requirements alone make their voracious demands; were it not for what I have called the essentially "gratuitous" nature of the whole enterprise of progress, as against the mandatory respect for invasion-proof selfhood, the simplest answer would be to keep the whole population enrolled, and let the lot, or an equivalent of draft boards, decide which of each category will at any one time be called up for "service." It is not difficult to picture societies with whose philosophy this would be consonant. We are agreed that ours is not one such and should not become one. The specter of it is indeed among the threatening utopias on our own horizon from which we should recoil, and of whose advent by imperceptible steps we must beware. How then can our mandatory faith be honored when the recruitment for experimentation goes outside the scientific community as it must in honoring another commitment of no mean dignity? We simply repeat the former question: To whom should the call be addressed?

"IDENTIFICATION" AS THE PRINCIPLE OF RECRUITMENT IN GENERAL

If the properties we adduced as the particular qualifications of the members of the scientific fraternity itself are taken as general criteria of selection, then one should look for additional subjects where a maximum of identification, understanding, and spontaneity can be expected—that is, among the most highly motivated, the most highly educated, and the least "captive" members of the community. From this naturally scarce resource, a descending order of permissibility leads to greater abundance and ease of supply, whose use should become proportionately more hesitant as the exculpating criteria are relaxed. An inversion of normal "market" behavior is demanded here—namely, to accept the lowest quotation last (and excused only by the greatest pressure of need), to pay the highest price first.

As such a rule of selection is bound to be rather hard on the number-hungry research industry, it will be asked: Why all the fuss? At this point we had better spell out some of the things we have been tacitly presupposing all the time. What is wrong with making a person an experimental subject is not so much that we make him thereby a means (which happens in social contexts of all kinds), as that we make him a thing—a passive thing merely to be acted on, and passive not even for real action, but for token action whose token object he is. His being is reduced to that of a mere token or "sample." This is different from even the most exploitative situations of social life; there the business is real, not fictitious. The subject, however much abused, remains an agent and thus a "subject" in the other sense of the word. The soldier's case, referred to earlier, is instructive: Subject to most unilateral discipline, forced to risk mutilation and death, conscripted without, perhaps against, his will—he is still conscripted with his capacities to act, to hold his own or fail in situations, to meet real challenges for real stakes. Though a mere "number" to the High Command, he is not a token and not a thing. (Imagine what he would say if it turned out that the war was a game staged to sample observations on his endurance, courage, or cowardice.

These compensations of personhood are denied to the subject of experimentation, who is acted upon for an extraneous end without being engaged in a real relation where he would be the counterpoint to the other or to circumstance. Mere "consent" (mostly amounting to no more than permission) does not right this reification. The "wrong" of it can only be made "right" by such authentic identification with the cause that it is the subject's as well as the researcher's cause—whereby his role in its service is not just permitted by him, but *willed*. That sovereign will of his which embraces the end as his own restores his personhood to the otherwise depersonalizing context. To be valid it must be autonomous and informed. The latter condition can, outside the research community, only be fulfilled by degrees; but the higher the degree of the understanding regarding the purpose and the technique, the more valid becomes the endorsement of the will. A margin of mere trust inevitably remains. Ultimately, the appeal for volunteers should seek this free and generous endorsement, the appropriation of the research purpose into the person's own scheme of ends. Thus, the appeal is in truth addressed to the one, mysterious, and sacred source of any such generosity of the will—"devotion," whose forms and objects of commitment are various and may invest different motivations in different individuals. The following, for instance, may be responsive to the "call" we are discussing: compassion with human suffering, zeal for humanity, reverence for the Golden Rule, enthusiasm for progress, homage to the cause of knowledge, even longing for sacrificial justification (do not call that "masochism," please). On all these, I say, it is defensible and right to draw when the research objective is worthy enough; and it is a prime duty of the research community (especially in view of what we called the "margin of trust") to see that this sacred source is never abused for frivolous ends. For a less than adequate cause, not even the freest, unsolicited offer should be accepted.

THE RULE OF THE "DESCENDING ORDER" AND ITS COUNTER-UTILITY SENSE

We have laid down what must seem to be a forbidding rule. Having faith in the transcendent potential of man, I do not fear that the "source" will ever fail a society that does not destroy it—and only such a one is worthy of the blessings of progress. But "elitistic" the rule is (as is the enterprise of progress itself), and elites are by nature small. The combined attribute of motivation and information, plus the absence of external pressures, tends to be socially so circumscribed that strict adherence to the rule might numerically starve the research process. This is why I spoke of a descending order of permissibility, which is itself permissive, but where the realization that it is a *descending* order is not without pragmatic import. Departing from the august norm, the appeal must needs shift from idealism to docility, from high-mindedness to compliance, from judgment to trust. Consent spreads over the whole spectrum. I will not go into the casuistics of this penumbral area. I merely indicate the principle of the order of preference: The poorer in knowledge, motivation, and freedom of decision (and that, alas, means the more readily available in terms of numbers and possible manipulation), the more sparingly and indeed reluctantly should the reservoir be used, and the more compelling must therefore become the countervailing justification.

Let us note that this is the opposite of a social utility standard, the reverse of the order by "availability and expendability": The most valuable and scarcest, the least expendable elements of the social organism, are to be the first candidates for risk and sacrifice. It is the standard of *noblesse oblige;* and with all its counter-utility and seeming "wastefulness," we feel a rightness about it and perhaps even a higher "utility," for the soul of the community lives by this spirit. It is also the opposite of what the day-to-day interests of research clamor for, and for the scientific community to honor it will mean that it will have to fight a strong temptation to go by routine to the readiest sources of supply—the suggestible, the ignorant, the dependent, the "captive" in various senses. I do not believe that heightened resistance here must cripple research, which cannot be permitted; but it may slow it down by the smaller numbers fed into experimentation in consequence. This price—a possibly slower rate of progress—may have to be paid for the preservation of the most precious capital of higher communal life.

EXPERIMENTATION ON PATIENTS

So far we have been speaking on the tacit assumption that the subjects of experimentation are recruited from among the healthy. To the question "Who is conscriptable?" the spontaneous answer is: Least and last of all the sick—the most available source as they are under treatment and observation anyway. That the afflicted should not be called upon to bear additional burden and risk, that they are society's special trust and the physician's particular trust—these are elementary responses of our moral sense. Yet the very destination of medical research, the conquest of disease, requires at the crucial stage trial and verification on precisely the sufferers from the disease, and their total exemption would defeat the purpose itself. In acknowledging this inescapable necessity, we enter the most sensitive area of the whole complex, the one most keenly felt and most searchingly discussed by the practitioners themselves. This issue touches the heart of the doctor-patient relation, putting its most solemn obligations to the test. Some of the oldest verities of this area should be recalled.

THE FUNDAMENTAL PRIVILEGE OF THE SICK

In the course of treatment, the physician is obligated to the patient and to no one else. He is not the agent of society, nor of the interests of medical science, the patient's family, the patient's co-sufferers, or future sufferers from the same disease. The patient alone counts when he is under the physician's care. By the simple law of bilateral contract (analogous, for example, to the relation of lawyer to client and its "conflict of interest" rule), he is bound not to let any other interest interfere with that of the patient in being cured. But manifestly more sublime norms than contractual ones are involved. We may speak of a sacred trust; strictly by its terms, the doctor is, as it were, alone with his patient and God.

There is one normal exception to this—that is, to the doctor's not being the agent of society vis-à-vis the patient, but the trustee of his interests alone—the quarantining of the contagious sick. This is plainly not for the patient's interest, but for that of others threatened by him. (In vaccination, we have a combination of both: protection of the individual and others.) But preventing the patient from causing harm to others is not the same as exploiting him for the advantage of others. And there is, of course, the abnormal exception of collective catastrophe, the analogue to a state of war. The physician who desperately battles a raging epidemic is under a unique dispensation that suspends in a nonspecifiable way some of the strictures of normal practice, including possibly those against experimental liberties with his patients. No rules can be devised for the waiving of rules in extremities. And as with the famous shipwreck examples of ethical theory, the less said about it the better. But what is allowable there and may later be passed over in forgiving silence cannot serve as a precedent. We are concerned with non-extreme, non-emergency conditions where the voice of principle can be heard and claims can be adjudicated free from duress. We have conceded that there are such claims, and that if there is to be medical advance at all, not even the superlative privilege of the suffering and the sick can be kept wholly intact from the intrusion of its needs. About this least palatable, most disquieting part of our subject, I have to offer only groping, inconclusive remarks.

THE PRINCIPLE OF "IDENTIFICATION" APPLIED TO PATIENTS

On the whole, the same principles would seem to hold here as are found to hold with "normal subjects": motivation, identification, understanding on the part of the subject. But it is clear that these conditions are peculiarly difficult to satisfy with regard to a patient. His physical state, psychic preoccupation, dependent relation to the doctor, the submissive attitude induced by treatment—everything connected with his condition and situation makes the sick person inherently less of a sovereign person than the healthy one. Spontaneity of self-offering has almost to be ruled out; consent is marred by lower resistance or captive circumstance, and so on. In fact, all the factors that make the patient, as a category, particularly accessible and welcome for experimentation at the same time compromise the quality of the responding affirmation that must morally redeem the making use of them. This, in addition to the primacy of the physician's duty, puts a heightened onus on the physician-researcher to limit his undue power to the most important and defensible research objectives and, of course, to keep persuasion at a minimum.

Still, with all the disabilities noted, there is scope among patients for observing the rule of the "descending order of permissibility" that we have laid down for normal subjects, in vexing inversion of the utility order of quantitative abundance and qualitative "expendability." By the principle of this order, those patients who most identify with and are cognizant of the cause of research—members of the medical profession (who after all are sometimes patients themselves)—come first; the highly motivated and educated, also least dependent, among the lay patients come next; and so on down the line. An added consideration here is seriousness of condition, which again operates in inverse proportion. Here the profession must fight the tempting sophistry that the hopeless case is expendable (because in prospect already expended) and therefore especially usable; and generally the attitude that the poorer the chances of the patient the more justifiable his recruitment for experimentation (other than for his own benefit). The opposite is true.

NONDISCLOSURE AS A BORDERLINE CASE

Then there is the case where ignorance of the subject, sometimes even of the experimenter, is of the essence of the experiment (the "double blind"-control group-placebo syndrome). It is said to be a necessary element of the scientific process. Whatever may be said about its ethics in regard to normal subjects, especially volunteers, it is an outright betrayal of trust in regard to the patient who believes that he is receiving treatment. Only supreme importance of the objective can exonerate it, without making it less of a transgression. The patient is definitely wronged even when not harmed. And ethics apart, the practice of such deception holds the danger of undermining the faith in the *bona fides* of treatment, the beneficial intent of the physician—the very basis of the doctor-patient relationship. In every respect, it follows that concealed experiment on patients—that is, experiment under the guise of treatment—should be the rarest exception, at best, if it cannot be wholly avoided.

This has still the merit of a borderline problem. This is not true of the other case of necessary ignorance of the subject—that of the unconscious patient. Drafting him for nontherapeutic experiments is simply and unqualifiedly impermissible; progress or not, he must never be used, on the inflexible principle that utter help-lessness demands utter protection.

When preparing this paper, I filled pages with a casuistics of this harrowing field, but then scratched out most of it, realizing my dilettante status. The shadings are endless, and only the physician-researcher can discern them properly as the cases arise. Into his lap the decision is thrown. The philosophical rule, once it has admitted into itself the idea of a sliding scale, cannot really specify its own applica-tion. It can only impress on the practitioner a general maxim or attitude for the exercise of his judgment and conscience in the concrete occasions of his work. In our case, I am afraid, it means making life more difficult for him.

It will also be noted that, somewhat at variance with the emphasis in the litera-ture, I have not dwelt on the element of "risk" and very little on that of "consent." Discussion of the first is beyond the layman's competence; the emphasis on the second has been lessened because of its equivocal character. It is a truism to say that one should strive to minimize the risk and to maximize the consent. The more demanding concept of "identification," which I have used, includes "consent" in its maximal or authentic form, and the assumption of risk is its privilege.

NO EXPERIMENTS ON PATIENTS UNRELATED TO THEIR OWN DISEASE

Although my ponderings have, on the whole, yielded points of view rather than definite prescriptions, premises rather than conclusions, they have led me to a few unequivocal yeses and noes. The first is the emphatic rule that patients should be experimented upon, if at all, *only* with reference to *their* disease. Never should there be added to the gratuitousness of the experiment as such the gratuitousness of service to an unrelated cause. This follows simply from what we have found to be the *only* excuse for infracting the special exemption of the sick at all—namely, that the scientific war on disease cannot accomplish its goal without drawing the sufferers from disease into the investigative process. If under this excuse they become subjects of experiment, they do so *because,* and only because, of *their* disease.

This is the fundamental and self-sufficient consideration. That the patient can-not possibly benefit from the unrelated experiment therapeutically, while he might from experiment related to his condition, is also true, but lies beyond the problem area of pure experiment. Anyway, I am discussing nontherapeutic experimentation only, where *ex hypothesi* the patient does not benefit. Experiment as part of therapy —that is, directed toward helping the subject himself—is a different matter altogether and raises its own problems, but hardly philosophical ones. As long as a doctor can say, even if only in his own thought: "There is no known cure for your condition (or: You have responded to none); but there is promise in a new treatment still under investigation, not quite tested yet as to effectiveness and safety; you will be taking a chance, but all things considered, I judge it in your best interest to let me try it on you"—as long as he can speak thus, he speaks as the patient's physician and may err, but does not transform the patient into a subject of experimentation. Introduction of an untried therapy into the treatment where the tried ones have failed is not "experimentation on the patient."

Generally, there is something "experimental" (because tentative) about every individual treatment, beginning with the diagnosis itself; and he would be a poor doctor who would not learn from every case for the benefit of future cases, and a poor member of the profession who would not make any new insights gained from his treatments available to the profession at large. Thus, knowledge may be advanced in the treatment of any patient, and the interest of the medical art and all sufferers from the same affliction as well as the patient may be served if something happens to be learned from his case. But this gain to knowledge and future therapy is incidental to the *bona fide* service to the present patient. He has the right to expect that the doctor does nothing to him just in order to learn.

In that case, the doctor's imaginary speech would run, for instance, like this: "There is nothing more I can do for you. But you can do something for me. Speaking no longer as your physician but on behalf of medical science, we could learn a great deal about future cases of this kind if you would permit me to perform certain experiments on you. It is understood that you yourself would not benefit from any knowledge we might gain; but future patients would." This statement would express the purely experimental situation, assumedly here with the subject's concurrence and with all cards on the table. In Alexander Bickel's words: "It is a different situation when the doctor is no longer trying to make [the patient] well, but is trying to find out how to make others well in the future."

But even in the second case of the nontherapeutic experiment where the patient does not benefit, the patient's own disease is enlisted in the cause of fighting that disease, even if only in others. It is yet another thing to say or think: "Since you are here—in the hospital with its facilities—under our care and observation, away from your job (or, perhaps, doomed), we wish to profit from your being available for some other research of great interest we are presently engaged in." From the standpoint of merely medical ethics, which has only to consider risk, consent, and the worth of the objective, there may be no cardinal difference between this case and the last one. I hope that my medical audience will not think I am making too fine a point when I say that from the standpoint of the subject and his dignity there is a cardinal difference that crosses the line between the permissible and the impermissible, and this by the same principle of "identification" I have been invoking all along. Whatever the rights and wrongs of any experimentation on any patient—in the one case, at least that residue of identification is left him that it is his own affliction by which he can contribute to the conquest of that affliction, his own kind of suffering which he helps to alleviate in others; and so in a sense it is his own cause. It is totally indefensible to rob the unfortunate of this intimacy with the purpose and make his misfortune a convenience for the furtherance of alien concerns. The observance of this rule is essential, I think, to attenuate at least the wrong that nontherapeutic experimenting on patients commits in any case.

ON THE REDEFINITION OF DEATH

My other emphatic verdict concerns the question of the redefinition of death—acknowledging "irreversible coma as a new definition for death." I wish not to be misunderstood. As long as it is merely a question of when it is permitted to cease the artificial prolongation of certain functions (like heartbeat) traditionally regarded as signs of life, I do not see anything ominous in the notion of "brain death." Indeed, a new definition of death is not even necessary to legitimize the same result if one adopts the position of the Roman Catholic Church, which here for once is eminently reasonable—namely that "when deep unconsciousness is judged to be permanent, extraordinary means to maintain life are not obligatory. They can be terminated and the patient allowed to die." Given a clearly defined negative condition of the brain, the physician is allowed to allow the patient to die his own death by *any* definition, which of itself will lead through the gamut of all possible definitions. But a disquietingly contradictory purpose is combined with this purpose in the quest for a new definition of death, in the will to *advance* the moment of declaring him dead: Permission not to turn off the respirator, but, on the contrary, to keep it on and thereby maintain the body in a state of what would have been "life" by the older definition (but is only a "simulacrum" of life by the new)—so as to get at his organs and tissues under the ideal conditions of what would previously have been "vivisection."

Now this, whether done for research or transplant purposes, seems to me to overstep what the definition can warrant. Surely it is one thing when to cease delaying death, but another when to start doing violence to the body; one thing when to desist from protracting the process of dying, but another when to regard that process as complete and thereby the body as a cadaver free for inflicting on it what would be torture and death to any living body. For the first purpose, we need not know the exact borderline with absolute certainty between life and death —we leave it to nature to cross it wherever it is, or to traverse the whole spectrum if there is not just one line. All we need to know is that coma is irreversible. For the second purpose we must know the borderline; and to use any definition short of the maximal for perpetrating on a *possibly* penultimate state what only the ultimate state can permit is to arrogate a knowledge which, I think, we cannot possibly have. *Since we do not know the exact borderline between life and death,* nothing less than the maximum definition of death will do—brain death plus heart death plus any other indication that may be pertinent—before final violence is allowed to be done.

It would follow then, for this layman at least, that the use of the definition should itself be defined, and this in a restrictive sense. When only permanent coma can be gained with the artificial sustaining of functions, by all means turn off the respirator, the stimulator, any sustaining artifice, and let the patient die; but let him die all the way. Do not, instead, arrest the process and start using him as a mine while, with your own help and cunning, he is still kept this side of what may in truth be the final line. Who is to say that a shock, a final trauma, is not administered to a sensitivity diffusely situated elsewhere than in the brain and still vulnerable to suffering? a sensitivity that we ourselves have been keeping alive? No fiat of definition can settle this question. But I wish to emphasize that the question of possible suffering (easily brushed aside by a sufficient show of reassuring expert consensus) is merely a subsidiary and not the real point of my argument; this, to reiterate, turns on the indeterminacy of the boundaries between *life and death,* not between sensitivity and insensitivity, and bids us to lean toward a maximal rather than a minimal determination of death in an area of basic uncertainty.

There is also this to consider: The patient must be absolutely sure that his doctor does not become his executioner, and that no definition authorizes him ever to become one. His right to this certainty is absolute, and so is his right to his own body with all its organs. Absolute respect for these rights violates no one else's rights, for no one has a right to another's body. Speaking in still another, religious vein: The expiring moments should be watched over with piety and be safe from exploitation.

I strongly feel, therefore, that it should be made quite clear that the proposed new definition of death is to authorize *only* the one and *not* the other of the two opposing things: only to break off a sustaining intervention and let things take their course, not to keep up the sustaining intervention for a final intervention of the most destructive kind.

There would now have to be said something about nonmedical experiments on human subjects, notably psychological and genetic, of which I have not lost sight. But having overextended my limits of space by the most generous interpretation, I must leave this for another occasion. Let me only say in conclusion that if some of the practical implications of my reasonings are felt to work out toward a slower rate of progress, this should not cause too great dismay. Let us not forget that progress is an optional goal, not an unconditional commitment, and that its tempo in particular, compulsive as it may become, has nothing sacred about it. Let us also remember that a slower progress in the conquest of disease would not threaten society, grievous as it is to those who have to deplore that their particular disease be not yet conquered, but that society would indeed be threatened by the erosion of those moral values whose loss, possibly caused by too ruthless a pursuit of scientific progress, would make its most dazzling triumphs not worth having. Let us finally remember that it cannot be the aim of progress to abolish the lot of mortality. Of some ill or other, each of us will die. Our mortal condition is upon us with its harshness but also its wisdom—because without it there would not be the eternally renewed promise of the freshness, immediacy, and eagerness of youth; nor, without it, would there be for any of us the incentive to number our days and make them count. With all our striving to wrest from our mortality what we can, we should bear its burden with patience and dignity.

ALAN F. WESTIN

Privacy and Freedom

Alan F. Westin is Professor of
Public Law and Government
at Columbia University. He
has also written *The Anatomy
of a Constitutional Law Case,
Freedom Now!: The Civil
Rights Struggle in America,*
and many articles.

To begin, let me restate the main conclusions that have been presented, since it is on these foundations that I shall rest my analysis of the "forces" and "choices" that confront us.

1. A technological breakthrough in techniques of physical surveillance now makes it possible for government agents and private persons to penetrate the privacy of homes, offices, and vehicles; to survey individuals moving about in public places; and to monitor the basic channels of communication by telephone, telegraph, radio, television, and data line. Most of the "hardware" for this physical surveillance is cheap, readily available to the general public, relatively easy to install, and not presently illegal to own. As of the 1960's, the new surveillance technology is being used widely by government agencies of all types and at every level of government, as well as by private agents for a rapidly growing number of businesses, unions, private organizations, and individuals in every section of the United States. Increasingly, permanent surveillance devices have been installed in facilities used by employees or the public. While there are defenses against "outside" surveillance, these are so costly and complex and demand such constant vigilance that their use is feasible only where official or private matters of the highest security are to be protected. Finally, the scientific prospects for the next decade indicate a continuing increase in the range and versatility of the listening and watching devices, as well as the possibility of computer processing of recordings to identify automatically the speakers or topics under surveillance. These advances will come just at the time when personal contacts, business affairs, and government operations are being channeled more and more into electronic systems such as data-phone lines and computer communications.

2. In the field of psychological surveillance, techniques such as polygraphing and personality testing that probe the intimate thought processes of their subjects

have swept into widespread use since World War II. Because they are supposed to offer "scientific" examination of individuals, these techniques have become commonplace in the personnel-selection systems of many corporations, private organizations, and government agencies, and are used for a variety of other purposes as well. At the same time, advances in drug research indicate that we may be approaching the point at which the administration of a drug (with or without the subject's knowledge) may render him a truthful person under questioning; already, arguments in favor of such narco-analysis under new drugs have appeared in police and legal journals. Finally, research in brain-wave analysis establishes that "reading" certain signals of the brain is now possible; if in the coming decades this progresses to the ability to distinguish the more complex messages involved in thoughts and emotions, direct interrogation of the mind may become the "ultimate weapon" in penetration of privacy.

3. In the area I have called data surveillance, the rapid pace of computer development and usage throughout American society means that vast amounts of information about individuals and private groups in the nation are being placed in computer-usable form. More and more information is being gathered and used by corporations, associations, universities, public schools, and governmental agencies. And as "life-long dossiers" and interchange of information grow steadily, the possibilities increase that agencies employing computers can accomplish heretofore impossible surveillance of individuals, businesses, and groups by putting together all the now scattered pieces of data. This danger is augmented by current proposals from some private and government spokesmen who advocate the adoption of a fully-computerized and automatic credit system to replace cash transactions, a single-identifying-number system for every person in his dealings with public authorities, and similar "total" computer systems.

4. In each of these areas of surveillance, most of the scientific advances did not arise through efforts to develop instruments for invading the privacy of the citizenry. Rather, they grew out of research to solve broad problems of American society—space travel and communication, medical research, diagnosis and treatment of mental illness, mobile television broadcasts, rapid analysis and use of general data, and a host of similar purposes. Once the scientific advances were made, however, often at levels of cost that only government could supply in the stages of basic research and prototype development, many of the techniques were then adopted swiftly by both government agencies and private interests for purposes of physical, psychological, or data surveillance. The technology we have been discussing has thus been "socially useful" in origin, and potentially "neutral" in relation to privacy. Yet the ease with which the new techniques have been used for penetration of privacy, their relatively low cost in relation to the resources of those wishing to employ these techniques for surveillance, and the ready accessibility of the "parts" or "processes" indicate that existing legal and social rules for policing the borderline between "proper" and "improper" use have proved inadequate. Furthermore, the test psychologists and computer scientists involved in applying the new surveillance techniques have often been so sure of their own purposes and ethics that they have been insufficiently sensitive to the issues of privacy created by the uses of these processes. This preoccupation with scientific solutions to social problems has sometimes tended to place the professionals in various fields in opposition to what they

regard as "unscientific" and "emotional" positions asserting "new" claims of privacy.

5. The response of American society to these technological and scientific developments since 1945 has been uneven and often without the consistency that comes with self-consciousness. But the studies of civic reactions to five key problems—subliminal suggestion, electronic eavesdropping, polygraphs, personality testing, and the computer—show steadily growing sensitivity to privacy claims in the press and among national civic groups. Group positions vary, depending on who is doing the surveillance, who is being surveyed, and the purpose for intruding. But so many areas have been affected by the new techniques and so many group interests have been directly threatened that statements deploring the erosion of privacy and the tactics of "Big Brother" have been issuing steadily from every position along the ideological spectrum, from extreme right to radical left. While some might read the record differently, I conclude from the five depth-studies that a "minimum position" in support of privacy is emerging. This unites both liberal and conservative camps, and awaits only a clear enunciation of basic standards and the development of a creative evaluative process before it becomes a national consensus which can be drawn upon by legislators, judges, and private authorities to deal with the specific problems of privacy under technological pressure.

6. In probing the functions which privacy serves in democratic systems—its psychological, sociological, and political utility—we found that privacy is an irreducibly critical element in the operations of individuals, groups, and government in a democratic system with a liberal culture. For the individual, there is a need to keep some facts about himself wholly private, and to feel free to decide for himself who shall know other facts, at what time, and under what conditions. At the same time, there is an equally powerful need in each person to disclose "personal" or "private" matters to others, as well as a strong impulse to penetrate the privacy of others, not only in terms of his peers and local gossip but also by "eavesdropping" on the activities of leading elites of the society through exposés by the press, government investigations, court trials, etc. While some aspects of this urge for penetration of another's privacy can be considered "voyeuristic" in the personal sense and "populistic" in their political aspect, this is so clearly a fact of behavior, and serves such a key role in a mass society, that its presence must be noted by anyone seriously concerned with privacy norms in our society. There is also a close correlation between the availability of privacy from hostile surveillance and the achievement of creativity, mental health, and ethical self-development, though there is always a shifting standard of balance in these matters and a heavy layer of cultural relativism.

Privacy as a need in organizational life was amply demonstrated in considering the internal affairs of businesses, civic groups, and ideological protest movements. Without time for preparation and internal rationalization of views and differences, private groups cannot fulfill the independent role envisaged for them by the values of a pluralistic, democratic society. Whether to allow such nutritive privacy for a particular group, and how much, are always policy questions for law and government. Thus a scale of privacy depending on the social prestige and assumed social contributions of groups has been a standard feature of our society, with the major religious organizations placed at one end of the scale and "subversive" groups at the other. In addition to the need of individual groups for privacy, there is also a need for privacy in negotiations *between* private groups, such as labor-management bargaining sessions, intercorporate negotiations, and a variety of similar relations in the civic and political sphere.

A core area of privacy is also essential to the successful conduct of democratic government, whether the setting is the private conference of the Supreme Court, meetings of the White House staff with the President, executive sessions of legislative committees, the conference-committee stage of legislation in Congress, exploratory negotiations with foreign governments, or "frank" sessions behind the scenes at international conferences or at the UN. In situations of all types, privacy is a critical ingredient for the process of accommodation and resolution upon which peaceful settlement of conflicting interests rests. In most instances, the privacy required is a temporary one, and the interests of a democratic society in knowing what its elected and appointed officials are doing can be properly served by pulling back the curtain of privacy after the bargains have been struck and implemented. At that stage, democratic statesmen are held responsible for their acts. Just when the time for disclosure has been reached, and whether privacy is proper at all for a particular process of government, are issues that will receive different answers according to the type of problem, the degree of agreement in the nation on the policies being pursued, the presence of built-in conflicts over privacy created by our separation-of-powers system, and many other factors already discussed. But the need for privacy in democratic government, and the dangers of mislabeling this need by calling it "secrecy," have been the burden of the discussion. . . .

7. Finally . . . it was seen that concern for protecting privacy has been part of American constitutional law, common law, federal and state legislation, and administrative rules from the very beginning of our national history. A deliberate concept of balancing competing interests was at the heart of American privacy law, as in the "reasonable man" standard for common-law privacy rules and in the federal and state constitutions' ban against "unreasonable" searches. This chapter (and the case studies on civic reactions) showed that the current legal framework is now inadequate to defend the American equilibrium on privacy from new surveillance techniques. However, there has been a strong ferment in American law in the past decade, a beginning of the process necessary to develop in law and social norms what was once assured by physical and technological realities in the older republican society. Despite this recognition that American law is in the process of change, two deep concerns remain: first, that the new legal doctrines should reflect sensitively the needs for both privacy and disclosure; and, second, that major attention should be paid to the role of voluntary, privacy-supporting actions by private authorities and organizations, especially in areas where legal intervention is unlikely or would probably be ineffective.

DEVELOPING CRITERIA FOR WEIGHING CONFLICTING INTERESTS

If privacy is to receive its proper weight on the scales in any process of balancing competing values, what is needed is a structured and rational weighing process, with definite criteria that public and private authorities can apply in comparing the claims for disclosure or surveillance through new devices with the claims to privacy. The following are suggested as the basic steps of such a process: measuring the seriousness of the need to conduct surveillance; deciding whether there are alternative methods to meet the need; deciding what degree of reliability will be required of the surveillance instrument; determining whether true consent to surveillance has been given; and measuring the capacity for limitation and control of the surveillance if it is allowed. Each step is discussed here only briefly; the next section shows how the weighing process would actually be applied to the main problems of privacy and surveillance currently facing American society.

The Seriousness of the Need to Conduct Surveillance. Though surveillance devices are sometimes used for satisfying personal voyeuristic urges and as illegitimate weapons in political or private affairs, the more typical and important use is to solve problems of genuine social importance. Police forces want to solve crimes, corporations to control theft, employers to select more successful employees, educators to identify personality problems in school children, behavioral scientists to observe real-life situations. But if all that has to be done to win legal and social approval for surveillance is to point to a social problem and show that surveillance would help to cope with it, then there is no balancing at all, but only a qualifying procedure for a license to invade privacy. The need must be serious enough to overcome the very real and presently rising risk of jeopardizing the public's confidence in its daily freedom from unreasonable invasions of privacy.

Weighing the seriousness of the need to use surveillance devices might lead American society to deal more frankly than it usually has done with some of its laws against deviant moral or political conduct. For example, we make it criminal to engage in gambling, prostitution, and homosexual solicitation; yet we know that such laws are broken continually by many people who do not regard such activities as immoral. We also know that law enforcement is highly selective, often pursuing the "little lawbreaker" while leaving the more powerful violators untouched. Organized criminal syndicates thrive on providing these services, and too many public officials are corrupted into giving protection to these activities because of public ambivalence toward the acts involved. If the real function of these laws is to hold some social boundaries on such conduct, to prevent it from spreading further than society wishes, we should weigh carefully whether we want to use new surveillance technology in such areas of moral departure. Already police have started installing hidden color cameras and closed-circuit TV in public rest rooms to obtain evidence of homosexual solicitations,[1] have been planting listening devices surreptitiously in such public places as restaurants and motels to investigate prostitution,[2] and have wiretapped for months public telephones where bookmakers place calls.[3] The real question is whether the containment function of our vice laws can justify the spread of surveillance into the large areas of public life that are bound to be involved.

A similar re-examination of need ought to take place over the question of how much public or private employers need to know about the emotions, attitudes, and beliefs of their employees working in ordinary, non-sensitive positions. If our social attitudes toward work are changing as much as they seem to be, if we are coming to believe that objective performance rather than race, color, or religion is our

---

[1] Kyler, "Camera Surveillance of Sex Deviates," *Law and Order,* November, 1963, 16; *Time,* November 12, 1965, 59–61.

[2] *The New York Times,* February 5, 1964.

[3] Samuel Dash, *The Eavesdroppers,* New York, 1959, 69–70.

criterion, then judgments about religious, political and sexual adjustment made covertly by psychologists in the interests of institutional clients may also be found to be unnecessary for selection among applicants and evaluation of the performance of existing employees.

Alternative Methods To Meet the Need: The Burden of Proof. Much of life as well as law depends on deciding who has the burden of proof in any situation in which action is to be taken. In deciding whether there are alternative methods less violative of individual and organizational privacy than proposed surveillance devices and processes, the burden of proof that other techniques are not available should be on those seeking authorization. For example, the need to resort to wiretapping or bugging during the course of criminal investigation in modern American society, with our patterns of mobility, swift communication, and so on, is stated as a conclusion by the majority of law-enforcement witnesses before legislative committees.[4] Cases are usually cited in which this was said to have been the fact. But there has never been a detailed presentation by any law-enforcement agency, in terms that the educated public could judge, to prove this view on a crime-by-crime analysis. My own belief, after talking to almost a hundred law-enforcement officials, is that such a case could be made for crimes such as extortion and kidnapping, where the consent of one party (the victim) to the key conversations would be obtainable anyway, and in certain national-security investigations, including the need for positive security checks and offensive intelligence operations. But this case has never been made in public. Until it is, with the opportunity for opponents of eavesdropping to challenge the presentation in the public forum, law-enforcement spokesmen have not proved the positive need for the use of surreptitious listening and watching devices.

The same approach to alternative methods should apply in such matters as personality testing. Record analysis, interviews that stay within decent boundaries of privacy, aptitude and achievement tests (including simulation tests), and on-the-job trial testing seem to provide completely adequate available alternatives to the use of personality tests. There has never been evidence secured under scientific control procedures, in either industry or government, to show that employees selected by personality measures are more successful than those selected without such tests. Nor has there been the slightest proof that employees selected by organizations which do not use personality testing are less effective, successful, or well adjusted than those from companies which have bought the fad of personality testing. The survey that I conducted in 1965 of 208 industrial firms showed that 53.6 per cent were not using personality tests (indicating, happily, a trend away from such use, compared to the 1950's).[5] Among the companies operating without such tests are American Motors, Bristol-Myers, DuPont, Florida Power & Light, A&P, Gulf Oil, Litton Industries, Metropolitan Life Insurance, Northern Pacific Railroad, Pabst Brewing, and RCA, none of which—or the other thousands of companies like them—seem to be centers for emotionally disturbed employees or executives.

---

[4] See, for example, the statements by Frank Hogan and Daniel Sullivan on Hearings on S. 2183 and S. 1495, before the Senate Committee on the Judiciary, 87th Cong., 2nd Sess. 173, 195–98, 1962.

[5] See the descriptions of this survey in Ch. 6 of this work, pp. 136 ff.

To give just one more example, control of petty thefts in industry is a serious problem. Studies have shown that the rising levels of white-collar crime and pilfering have seriously injured industry, with employee thefts amounting to millions of dollars annually for some companies.[6] Yet such techniques as tool and inventory controls, physical inspection of parcels and purses at exit gates, electronic scanning devices that will register certain types of objects, and similar methods, all supplemented by standard investigations of high-loss locations by company investigators (which can include sending in investigators disguised as regular employees), offer adequate alternatives to the periodic polygraphing that has been adopted by some companies in their quest for theft control. The simple proof is that most companies do not use polygraphs, and those firms relying on other security measures, even in high-loss industries, have not been destroyed by their failure to adopt polygraphing.

Reliability of the Instrument. The reliability required of a surveillance device or process will depend on the purpose for which the inquiry is conducted. If acceptance of polygraph reports or narco-analysis as evidence in criminal trials is involved, the courts should take as conclusive scientific tests showing that it is possible for many persons to lie under narco-analysis, or that polygraph readings by average operators are wrong (for example, that they fail to identify lies, or identify as lies testimony that is true) in a significant percentage of trials. When new drugs make it impossible to lie, or computer readings of advanced emotional-sensing equipment increase levels of accuracy to the 95- or 99-per-cent mark, the test of reliabilty will be met. At that point, however, the issue of admissibility in court would still be subject to inquiry on other grounds.

On the other hand, if intelligence agencies are seeking to choose five men to volunteer for a dangerous mission, or if defectors from a Communist country seek asylum here and want to work for our intelligence agencies, the use of polygraphs or narco-analysis might be justified, even assuming present levels of reliability. Where crucial interests of national security are involved, the issues of judicially determined guilt or innocence are not present, a 75-per-cent accuracy ratio might be sufficient reliability on which to select among candidates or decide whether to trust a report.

As already indicated, no body of data proves that personality tests of any kind, objective or projective, can predict the future performance of individuals in an employment situation in percentages significantly greater than other existing selection methods. Given the fact that the questions used in such tests intrude into otherwise protected areas of personal life and private beliefs, and that preserving an attitude of nonconfession toward authorities is a high social goal in American society, the privacy-invading type of personality test fails to meet minimum reliability requirements.

Realistically, the issue of whether a particular surveillance device or technique "works" will be a continuous inquiry, not a one-time test. New types of emotional sensors, and monitors to read their output, are continually being developed, for instance, as are new psychological tests for predicting behavior. A technique might fail the test of scientific validity for decades, then be perfected to accuracy. Therefore a sensible approach would be to think in terms of a scientific threshold that any

[6] *Business Week,* Feb. 27, 1960, 109; *ibid,* June 18, 1960, 98, 105.

privacy-invading process must pass before American society should have to reach the next question of whether the process should be permitted even though it *is* wholly scientific. Until such a threshold is passed, both law and social sanctions should require that unproved processes be used only in situations in which individuals freely consent to their use.

The Issue of Consent: Expressed, Implied, or Coerced?   A central aspect of privacy is that individuals and organizations can determine for themselves which matters they want to keep private and which they are willing—or need—to reveal. Similarly, society can require consent to various general regulations as a condition for receiving government benefits. Furthermore, the needs of social order may require certain levels of exposure and confession even if these are involuntary. Consent is thus to be analyzed in the specific context of the purpose of surveillance and the use to be made of the information so obtained. Neither law nor public pressure should force anyone to have privacy if that person, assuming he is an adult of sound mind, wants to give up his privacy for psychological, commercial, or humanitarian reasons. There is no violation of the right to privacy when persons give general consent to be recorded or watched as part of a scientific experiment, an educational study, a test of a new food or product, or a study of physical or emotional reaction to an entertainment performance; submit to psychological tests for counseling or medical purposes, or to perfect a test; take experimental drugs; give personal data to a private or governmental survey; and the like. This is true as long as the subject is told in advance, the experiment is not one that demeans a civilized society, and there will be no serious harm done to the person. Individuals should be free to take polygraph or personality tests as volunteers for special government missions as long as they will not be penalized if they do not volunteer. Persons should be free, with full consent, to give up their privacy in ways that would be shocking and wholly unacceptable for non-consenters. For example, during 1963 a furor was created by reports that investigators under a National Institutes of Health grant were going to record the conversations of newlyweds in their apartments, to study personal interaction during the early stages of married life.[7] Several Congressmen and editors asked angrily how far the scientific Big Brother would go to penetrate our most sacred retreats. Closer inquiry revealed the following facts: In return for free rent, the couples had agreed in advance to allow recording of conversations in the living room, dining room, and kitchen of the house. No monitoring of bedrooms or bathrooms was involved, and full ground rules were set down as to the hours when the monitoring would be carried out and as to the use to be made of the recordings. This being the case, there was no unreasonable violation of privacy. Indeed, a few moments' reflection about the effect on scientific inquiry of forbidding such volunteer experiments will suggest how unwise intervention by prohibitory legislation would be in this area.

A more difficult problem is deciding when consent is implied by acceptance of a given type of employment or the carrying on of a certain activity. For instance, it is customary for schoolteachers to be visited by principals and division heads to observe classroom performance, just as it has been typical to have ordinary window-

[7] New York *Herald Tribune,* Sept. 28, 1963.

glass panels in the doors of classrooms, through which persons in the corridor can see inside. Does the teachers' consent to this customary practice, and the general relation of teachers to administrative supervision, include the right of the administration to install in each classroom loudspeaker boxes which can be switched on silently by the principal to listen to what is going on in that classroom? If the visit could be made in person or from the hall, what difference does it make that the observation will now be unannounced, will be carried out by a mechanical device, and will not disturb the class by a physical intrusion? My answer is that the findings about visibility and conformity discussed earlier indicate such a harmful effect on teacher and student morale, academic freedom, and the sense of personal dignity in schools that these outweigh the benefits of efficiency in observation. One way to convince school administrators who have been using such listening boxes of the need to balance values more sensitively would be to suggest that the school board and the city council should also have a box in the principal's office, to ensure that his standard of performance with teachers, students, and parents is up to the desired levels of excellence.

A harder case is presented when employers, whether private or governmental require scientific tests that invade privacy for hiring or advancement. When refusal to take the tests means loss of the job, and when the particular type of tests becomes a commonplace in the industry or field, a withholding of consent may jeopardize one's basic ability to practice his profession. Moreover, in certain areas of special importance, American law does not allow individuals to consent to waive their rights when there is inequality in the bargaining position, as with statutes outlawing "yellow dog" contracts by which workers promised not to join unions as a condition of employment and continued employment. This suggests that we should examine the nature of consent carefully in each instance, to see how freely or how coerced the consent is in that context.

Finally, it should be recognized that consent to reveal information to a particular person or agency, for a particular purpose, is not consent for that information to be circulated to all or used for other purposes. The individual may consent to tell things to his teacher or professor that ought not be circulated as part of student records without the student's consent. Information given to life-insurance companies, credit agencies, survey researchers, or government regulatory and welfare agencies ought not to be shared, in ways that identify the particular individual, without notice of the additional use and consent to it. Unless this principle of consent is well understood and accepted as the controlling principle for information flow in a data-stream society, we will be in for serious problems of privacy in the future.

To conclude that consent is not freely given in such circumstances does not mean that such scientific techniques may never be used in these areas. It simply distinguishes true conditions of consent from nonconsent, and carries our analysis to the next stage of inquiry: when can these devices be used without the knowledge or real consent of the subjects, and under what safeguards?

Capacity for Limitation and Control. Whether or not to authorize the use of surveillance devices or processes must, finally, depend on the specific system proposed for authorization and control of the surveillance. Though there will be variations according to the type of instrument, I would suggest that four basic criteria must be met. First, rules must be set limiting those who may carry out the surveillance. For example, the history of police-force use of eavesdropping is sufficiently stained with misconduct throughout the nation that use of physical surveillance devices at the state level should be strictly limited to district attorneys' offices and state attorney generals' offices, and at the federal level to the FBI and military agencies. Administration of acceptable psychological tests ought to be limited to accredited psychologists specially licensed by state boards of psychology to engage in this practice. Private investigators should be specifically forbidden to engage in physical surveillance with the new listening and watching devices, and owners of property to which the public is invited should be forbidden to install or use secret surveillance, even for safeguarding persons and property, unless notices are prominently displayed to that effect.

Second, detailed regulations should be set for the *scope, duration,* and *operations* of the surveillance. Rules of scope will determine the questions that may be asked and those that are forbidden (on privacy grounds) in psychological and personality examinations, and which questions may not be obtained by government for general data pools. In the case of physical surveillance, rules of scope will determine the types of crime for which surveillance is permitted and the places that may be surveyed. The rules of duration will determine, for example, how long physical surveillance may be carried on (the ideal policy being for short, renewable periods). Rules of operation should specify the way in which the surveillance should be carried out—the type of monitoring equipment to be used and methods of identifying and preserving recordings; the types of tests approved for psychological examinations; the equipment approved for polygraphing and how the results should be read; and others.

Third, some general agency ought to be created to set the standards for surveillance, supervise practices under the rules, investigate compliance, and hear complaints about misconduct. If law-enforcement officials are involved, a system of judicial order should be used, though much more careful rules would have to be set for proving need to use physical surveillance than have prevailed to date under warrant systems. In the case of personality testing, some combination of public board and private psychologists' association might be established to set standards and hear complaints.

Having set rules for the surveillance itself—who can employ the device or process, how, and under what review authority—the fourth step is to set rules to govern disclosure and use of the information obtained. Use in court—whether in criminal trials or civil cases—ought to be strictly reserved for information gathered in full conformity with the control system; refusal to permit use of evidence obtained in violation of the control system is the simplest and most practical way of building respect for the rules. Beyond this, regulations should be developed for each surveillance process, to insure that the information obtained is used only for the purpose for which it was secured and is seen only by those who must have access to it for that specific purpose. Systems of maintenance and disposal ought to be fashioned to guarantee this protection of privacy, with penalties enforced against unauthorized disclosure or use.

Freedom

DAVID HUME

Liberty and Necessity

David Hume (1711–1776) has
greatly influenced contemporary discussions in the
philosophy of science. Two
other selections from Hume
are presented in Section III,
"Man and World."

. . . The most irregular and unexpected resolutions of men may frequently be
accounted for by those who know every particular circumstance of their character
and situation. A person of an obliging disposition gives a peevish answer: But he
has the toothache, or has not dined. A stupid fellow discovers an uncommon alacrity
in his carriage: But he has met with a sudden piece of good fortune. Or even when
an action, as sometimes happens, cannot be particularly accounted for, either by the
person himself or by others; we know, in general, that the characters of men are,
to a certain degree, inconstant and irregular. This is, in a manner, the constant
character of human nature; though it be applicable, in a more particular manner,
to some persons who have no fixed rule for their conduct, but proceed in a continued
course of caprice and inconstancy. The internal principles and motives may operate
in a uniform manner, notwithstanding these seeming irregularities; in the same
manner as the winds, rain, clouds, and other variations of the weather are supposed
to be governed by steady principles; though not easily discoverable by human
sagacity and enquiry.

Thus it appears, not only that the conjunction between motives and voluntary
actions is as regular and uniform as that between the cause and effect in any part
of nature; but also that this regular conjunction has been universally acknowledged
among mankind, and has never been the subject of dispute, either in philosophy or
common life. Now, as it is from past experience that we draw all inferences concerning the future, and as we conclude that objects will always be conjoined together
which we find to have always been conjoined; it may seem superfluous to prove
that this experienced uniformity in human actions is a source whence we draw
inferences concerning them. But in order to throw the argument into a greater
variety of lights we shall also insist, though briefly, on this latter topic.

The mutual dependence of men is so great in all societies that scarce any human
action is entirely complete in itself, or is performed without some reference to the
actions of others, which are requisite to make it answer fully the intention of the

From *An Essay Concerning Human Understanding*, by David Hume, 1768.

agent. The poorest artificer, who labours alone, expects at least the protection of the magistrate, to ensure him the enjoyment of the fruits of his labour. He also expects that, when he carries his goods to market, and offers them at a reasonable price, he shall find purchasers, and shall be able, by the money he acquires, to engage others to supply him with those commodities which are requisite for his subsistence. In proportion as men extend their dealings, and render their intercourse with others more complicated, they always comprehend, in their schemes of life, a greater variety of voluntary actions, which they expect, from the proper motives, to co-operate with their own. In all these conclusions they take their measures from past experience, in the same manner as in their reasonings concerning external objects; and firmly believe that men, as well as all the elements, are to continue, in their operations, the same that they have ever found them. A manufacturer reckons upon the labour of his servants for the execution of any work as much as upon the tools which he employs, and would be equally surprised were his expectations disappointed. In short, this experimental inference and reasoning concerning the actions of others centers so much into human life, that no man, while awake, is ever a moment without employing it. Have we not reason, therefore, to affirm that all mankind have always agreed in the doctrine of necessity affording to the foregoing definition and explication of it?

Nor have philosophers ever entertained a different opinion from the people in this particular. For, not to mention that almost every action of their life supposes that opinion, there are even few of the speculative parts of learning to which it is not essential. What would become of *history,* had we not a dependence on the veracity of the historian according to the experience which we have had of mankind? How could *politics* be a science, if laws and forms of government had not a uniform influence upon society? Where would be the foundation of *morals,* if particular characters had no certain or determinate power to produce particular sentiments, and if these sentiments had no constant operation on actions? And with what pretence could we employ our *criticism* upon any poet or polite author, if we could not pronounce the conduct and sentiments of his actors either natural or unnatural to such characters, and in such circumstances? It seems almost impossible, therefore, to engage either in science or action of any kind without acknowledging the doctrine of necessity, and this *inference* from motive to voluntary actions, from characters to conduct.

And indeed, when we consider how aptly *natural* and *moral* evidence link together, and form only one chain of argument, we shall make no scruple to allow that they are of the same nature, and derived from the same principles. A prisoner who has neither money nor interest, discovers the impossibility of his escape, as well when he considers the obstinacy of the gaoler, as the walls and bars with which he is surrounded; and, in all attempts for his freedom, chooses rather to work upon the stone and iron of the one, than upon the inflexible nature of the other. The same prisoner, when conducted to the scaffold, foresees his death as certainly from the constancy and fidelity of his guards, as from the operation of the axe or wheel. His mind runs along a certain train of ideas: The refusal of the soldiers to consent to his escape; the action of the executioner; the separation of the head and body; bleeding, convulsive motions, and death. Here is a connected chain of natural causes and voluntary actions; but the mind feels no difference between them in passing from one link to another: Nor is less certain of the future event than if it were connected with the objects present to the memory or senses, by a train of causes, cemented together by what we are pleased to call a *physical* necessity. The same experienced union has the same effect on the mind, whether the united objects be motives, volition, and actions; or figure and motion. We may change the name of things; but their nature and their operation on the understanding never change.

Were a man, whom I know to be honest and opulent, and with whom I live in intimate friendship, to come into my house, where I am surrounded with my servants, I rest assured that he is not to stab me before he leaves it in order to rob me of my silver standish; and I no more suspect this event than the falling of the house itself, which is new, and solidly built and founded.—*But he may have been seized with a sudden and unknown frenzy.*—So may a sudden earthquake arise, and shake and tumble my house about my ears. I shall therefore change the suppositions. I shall say that I know with certainty that he is not to put his hand into the fire and hold it there till it be consumed: And this event, I think I can foretell with the same assurance, as that, if he throw himself out at the window, and meet with no obstruction, he will not remain a moment suspended in the air. No suspicion of an unknown frenzy can give the least possibility to the former event, which is so contrary to all the known principles of human nature. A man who at noon leaves his purse full of gold on the pavement at Charing-Cross, may as well expect that it will fly away like a feather, as that he will find it untouched an hour after. Above one half of human reasonings contain inferences of a similar nature, attended with more or less degrees of certainty proportioned to our experience of the usual conduct of mankind in such particular situations. . . .

But to proceed in this reconciling project with regard to the question of liberty and necessity; the most contentious question of metaphysics, the most contentious science; it will not require many words to prove, that all mankind have ever agreed in the doctrine of liberty as well as in that of necessity, and that the whole dispute, in this respect, also has been hitherto merely verbal. For what is meant by liberty, when applied to voluntary actions? We cannot surely mean that actions have so little connexion with motives, inclinations, and circumstances, that one does not follow with a certain degree of uniformity from the other, and that one affords no inference by which we can conclude the existence of the other. For these are plain and acknowledged matters of fact. By liberty, then, we can only mean *a power of acting or not acting, according to the determinations of the will;* that is, if we choose to remain at rest, we may; if we choose to move, we also may. Now this hypothetical liberty is universally allowed to belong to every one who is not a prisoner and in chains. Here, then, is no subject of dispute. . . .

SIGMUND FREUD

The Unconscious

Sigmund Freud
(1865–1939) founded
psychoanalysis. The
selection below is taken
from his last writings
on the ego, superego,
and id.

. . . From the very first we have said that human beings fall ill of a conflict
between the claims of instinctual life and the resistance which arises within them
against it; and not for a moment have we forgotten this resisting, repelling, repressing agency, which we thought of as equipped with its special forces, the ego-
instincts, and which coincides with the ego of popular psychology. The truth was
merely that, in view of the laborious nature of the progress made by scientific
work, even psycho-analysis was not able to study every field simultaneously and to
express its views on every problem in a single breath. But at last the point was
reached when it was possible for us to divert our attention from the repressed to
the repressing forces, and we faced this ego, which had seemed so self-evident, with
the secure expectation that here once again we should find things for which we could
not have been prepared. It was not easy, however, to find a first approach; and that
it what I intend to talk to you about to-day.

I must, however, let you know of my suspicion that this account of mine of
ego-psychology will affect you differently from the introduction into the psychical
underworld which preceded it. I cannot say with certainty why this should be so.
I thought first that you would discover that whereas what I reported to you previously
were, in the main, facts, however strange and peculiar, now you will be listening
principally to opinions—that is, to speculations. But that does not meet the position.
After further consideration I must maintain that the amount of intellectual working
over of the factual material in our ego-psychology is not much greater than it was
in the psychology of the neuroses. I have been obliged to reject other explanations
as well of the result I anticipate: I now believe that it is somehow a question of the
nature of the material itself and of our being unaccustomed to dealing with it. In
any case, I shall not be surprised if you show yourselves even more reserved and
cautious in your judgment than hitherto.

From *New Introductory Lectures on Psycho-Analysis,* by Sigmund Freud. Translated from the Ger-
man and edited by James Strachey. Copyright 1933 by Sigmund Freud, copyright renewed 1961 by
W. J. H. Sprott, copyright © 1965, 1964, by James Strachey. Reprinted by permission of W. W. Norton
& Company, Inc.

The situation in which we find ourselves at the beginning of our enquiry may be expected to point the way for us. We wish to make the ego the matter of our enquiry, our very own ego. But is that possible? After all, the ego is in its very essence a subject; how can it be made into an object? Well, there is no doubt that it can be. The ego can take itself as an object, can treat itself like other objects, can observe itself, criticize itself, and do Heaven knows what with itself. In this, one part of the ego is setting itself over against the rest. So the ego can be split; it splits itself during a number of its functions—temporarily at least. Its parts can come together again afterwards. That is not exactly a novelty, though it may perhaps be putting an unusual emphasis on what is generally known. On the other hand, we are familiar with the notion that pathology, by making things larger and coarser, can draw our attention to normal conditions which would otherwise have escaped us. Where it points to a breach or a rent, there may normally be an articulation present. If we throw a crystal to the floor, it breaks; but not into haphazard pieces. It comes apart along its lines of cleavage into fragments whose boundaries, though they were invisible, were predetermined by the crystal's structure. Mental patients are split and broken structures of this same kind. Even we cannot withhold from them something of the reverential awe which peoples of the past felt for the insane. They have turned away from external reality, but for that very reason they know more about internal, psychical reality and can reveal a number of things to us that would otherwise be inaccessible to us.

We describe one group of these patients as suffering from delusions of being observed. They complain to us that perpetually, and down to their most intimate actions, they are being molested by the observation of unknown powers—presumably persons—and that in hallucinations they hear these persons reporting the outcome of their observation: 'now he's going to say this, now he's dressing to go out' and so on. Observation of this sort is not yet the same thing as persecution, but it is not far from it; it presupposes that people distrust them, and expect to catch them carrying out forbidden actions for which they would be punished. How would it be if these insane people were right, if in each of us there is present in his ego an agency like this which observes and threatens to punish, and which in them has merely become sharply divided from their ego and mistakenly displaced into external reality?

I cannot tell whether the same thing will happen to you as to me. Ever since, under the powerful impression of this clinical picture, I formed the idea that the separation of the observing agency from the rest of the ego might be a regular feature of the ego's structure, that idea has never left me, and I was driven to investigate the further characteristics and connections of the agency which was thus separated off. The next step is quickly taken. The content of the delusions of being observed already suggests that the observing is only a preparation for judging and punishing, and we accordingly guess that another function of this agency must be what we call our conscience. There is scarely anything else in us that we so regularly separate from our ego and so easily set over against it as precisely our conscience. I feel an inclination to do something that I think will give me pleasure, but I abandon it on the ground that my conscience does not allow it. Or I have let myself to be persuaded by too great an expectation of pleasure into doing something to which the voice of conscience has objected and after the deed my conscience punishes me with distressing reproaches and causes me to feel remorse for the deed. I might simply say that the special agency which I am beginning to distinguish in the ego is conscience. But it is more prudent to keep the agency as something independent and to suppose that conscience is one of its functions and that self-observation, which is an essential preliminary to the judging activity of conscience, is another of them. And since when we recognize that something has a separate existence we give it a name of its own, from this time forward I will describe this agency in the ego as the 'super-ego'.

I am now prepared to hear you ask me scornfully whether our ego-psychology comes down to nothing more than taking commonly used abstractions literally and in a crude sense, and transforming them from concepts into things—by which not much would be gained. To this I would reply that in ego-psychology it will be difficult to escape what is universally known; it will rather be a question of new ways of looking at things and new ways of arranging them than of new discoveries. So hold to your contemptuous criticism for the time being and await further explanations. The facts of pathology give our efforts a background that you would look for in vain in popular psychology. So I will proceed.

Hardly have we familiarized ourselves with the idea of a super-ego like this which enjoys a certain degree of autonomy, follows its own intentions and is independent of the ego for its supply of energy, than a clinical pictures forces itself on our notice which throws a striking light on the severity of this agency and indeed its cruelty, and on its changing relations to the ego. I am thinking of the condition of melancholia, or more precisely, of melancholic attacks, which you too will have heard plenty about, even if you are not psychiatrists. The most striking feature of this illness, of whose causation and mechanism we know much too little, is the way in which the super-ego—'conscience', you may call it, quietly—treats the ego. While a melancholic can, like other people, show a greater or lesser degree of severity to himself in his healthy periods, during a melancholic attack his super-ego becomes over-severe, abuses the poor ego, humiliates it and ill-treats it, threatens it with the direst punishments, reproaches it for actions in the remotest past which had been taken lightly at the time—as though it had spent the whole interval in collecting accusations and had only been waiting for its present access of strength in order to bring them up and make a condemnatory judgement on their basis. The super-ego applies the strictest moral standard to the helpless ego which is at its mercy; in general it represents the claims of morality, and we realize all at once that our moral sense of guilt is the expression of the tension between the ego and the super-ego. It is a most remarkable experience to see morality, which is supposed to have been given us by God and thus deeply implanted in us, functioning [in these patients] as a periodic phenomenon. For after a certain number of months the whole moral fuss is over, the criticism of the super-ego is silent, the ego is rehabilitated and again enjoys all the rights of man till the next attack. In some forms of the disease, indeed, something of a contrary sort occurs in the intervals; the ego finds itself in a blissful state of intoxication, it celebrates a triumph, as though the super-ego had lost all its strength or had melted into the ego; and this liberated, manic ego permits itself a truly uninhibited satisfaction of all its appetites. Here are happenings rich in unsolved riddles!

No doubt you will expect me to give you more than a mere illustration when

I inform you that we have found out all kinds of things about the formation of the super-ego—that is to say, about the origin of conscience. Following a well-known pronouncement of Kant's which couples the conscience within us with the starry Heavens, a pious man might well be tempted to honour these two things as the masterpieces of creation. The stars are indeed magnificent, but as regards conscience God has done an uneven and careless piece of work, for a large majority of men have brought along with them only a modest amount of it or scarcely enough to be be worth mentioning. We are far from overlooking the portion of psychological truth that is contained in the assertion that conscience is of divine origin; but the thesis needs interpretation. Even if conscience is something 'within us,' yet it is not so from the first. In this it is a real contrast to sexual life, which is in fact there from the beginning of life and not only a later addition. But, as is well known, young children are amoral and possess no internal inhibitions against their impulses striving for pleasure. The part which is later taken on by the super-ego is played to begin with by an external power, by parental authority. Parental influence governs the child by offering proofs of love and by threatening punishments which are signs to the child of loss of love and are bound to be feared on their own account. This realistic anxiety is the precursor of the later moral anxiety. So long as it is dominant there is no need to talk of a super-ego and of a conscience. It is only subsequently that the secondary situation develops (which we are all too ready to regard as the normal one), where the external restraint is internalized and the super-ego takes the place of the parental agency and observes, directs and theatens the ego in exactly the same way as earlier the parents did with the child.

The super-ego, which thus takes over the power, function and even the methods of the parental agency, is however not merely its successor but actually the legitimate heir of its body. It proceeds directly out of it, we shall learn presently by what process. First, however, we must dwell upon a discrepancy between the two. The super-ego seems to have made a one-sided choice and to have picked out only the parents' strictness and severity, their prohibiting and punitive function, whereas their loving care seems not to have been taken over and maintained. If the parents have really enforced their authority with severity we can easily understand the child's in turn developing a severe super-ego. But, contrary to our expectation, expe-rience shows that the super-ego can acquire the same characteristic of relentless severity even if the upbringing had been mild and kindly and had so far as possible avoided threats and punishments. We shall come back later to this contradiction when we deal with the transformations of instinct during the formation of the super-ego.

I cannot tell you as much as I should like about the metamorphosis of the parental relationship into the super-ego, partly because that process is so complicated that an account of it will not fit into the framework of an introductory course of lectures such as I am trying to give you, but partly also because we ourselves do not feel sure that we understand it completely. So you must be content with the sketch that follows.

The basis of the process is what is called an 'identification'—that is to say, the assimilation of one ego to another one, as a result of which the first ego behaves like the second in certain respects, imitates it and in a sense takes it up into itself. Identification has been not unsuitably compared with the oral, cannibalistic incorporation of the other person. It is a very important form of attachment to someone else, probably the very first, and not the same thing as the choice of an object. The difference between the two can be expressed in some such way as this. If a boy identifies himself with his father, he wants to *be like* his father; if he makes him the object of his choice, he wants to *have* him, to possess him. In the first case his ego is altered on the model of his father; in the second case that is not necessary. Identification and object-choice are to a large extent independent of each other; it is however possible to identify oneself with someone whom, for instance, one has taken as a sexual object, and to alter one's ego on his model. It is said that the influencing of the ego by the sexual object occurs particularly often with women and is characteristic of femininity. I must already have spoken to you in my earlier lectures of what is by far the most instructive relation between identification and object-choice. It can be observed equally easily in children and adults, in normal as in sick people. If one has lost an object or has been obliged to give it up, one often compensates oneself by identifying onself with it and by setting it up once more in one's ego, so that here object-choice regresses, as it were, to identification.

I myself am far from satisfied with these remarks on identification; but it will be enough if you can grant me that the installation of the super-ego can be described as a successful instance of identification with the parental agency. The fact that speaks decisively for this view is that this new creation of a superior agency within the ego is most intimately linked with the destiny of the Oedipus complex, so that the super-ego appears as the heir of that emotional attachment which is of such importance for childhood. With his abandonment of the Oedipus complex a child must, as we can see, renounce the intense object-cathexes which he has deposited with his parents, and it is as a compensation for this loss of objects that there is such a strong intensification of the identifications with his parents which have probably long been present in his ego. Identifications of this kind as precipitates of object-cathexes that have been given up will be repeated often enough later in the child's life; but it is entirely in accordance with the emotional importance of this first instance of such a transformation that a special place in the ego should be found for its outcome. Close investigation has shown us, too, that the super-ego is stunted in its strength and growth if the surmounting of the Oedipus complex is only incompletely successful. In the course of development the super-ego also takes on the influences of those who have stepped into the place of parents—educators, teachers, people chosen as ideal models. Normally it departs more and more from the original parental figures; it becomes, so to say, more impersonal. Nor must it be forgotten that a child has a different estimate of its parents at different periods of its life. At the time at which the Oedipus complex gives place to the super-ego they are something quite magnificent; but later they lose much of this. Identifications then come about with these later parents as well, and indeed they regularly make important contributions to the formation of character; but in that case they only affect the ego, they no longer influence the super-ego, which has been determined by the earliest parental imagos.

. . . The super-ego is the representative for us of every moral restriction, the advocate of a striving towards perfection—it is, in short, as much as we have been able to grasp psychologically of what is described as the higher side of human life. Since it itself goes back to the influence of parents, educators and so on, we learn still more of its significance if we turn to those who are at its sources. As a rule parents and authorities analogous to them follow the precepts of their own super-egos in educating children. Whatever understanding their ego may have come to with their super-ego, they are severe and exacting in educating children. They have forgotten the difficulties of their own childhood and they are glad to be able now to identify themselves fully with their own parents who in the past laid such severe restrictions upon them. Thus a child's super-ego is in fact constructed on the model not of its parents but of its parents' super-ego; the contents which fill it are the same and it becomes the vehicle of tradition and of all the time-resisting judgements of value which have propagated themselves in this manner from generation to generation. You may easily guess what important assistance taking the super-ego into account will give us in our understanding of the social behaviour of mankind—in the problem of delinquency, for instance—and perhaps even what practical hints on education. It seems likely that what are known as materialistic views of history sin in under-estimating this factor. They brush it aside with the remark that human 'ideologies' are nothing other than the product and superstructure of their contemporary economic conditions. That is true, but very probably not the whole truth. Mankind never lives entirely in the present. The past, the tradition of the race and of the people, lives on in the ideologies of the super-ego, and yields only slowly to the influences of the present and to new changes; and so long as it operates through the super-ego it plays a powerful part in human life, independently of economic conditions.

In 1921 I endeavoured to make use of the differentiation between the ego and the super-ego in a study of group psychology. I arrived at a formula such as this: a psychological group is a collection of individuals who have introduced the same person into their super-ego and, on the basis of this common element, have identified themselves with one another in their ego. This applies, of course, only to groups that have a leader. If we possessed more applications of this kind, the hypothesis of the super-ego would lose its last touch of strangeness for us, and we should become completely free of the embarrassment that still comes over us when, accustomed as we are to the atmosphere of the underworld, we move in the more superficial, higher strata of the mental apparatus. We do not suppose, of course, that with the separation off of the super-ego we have said the last word on the psychology of the ego. It is rather a first step; but in this case it is not only the first step that is hard.

Now, however, another problem awaits us—at the opposite end of the ego, as we might put it. It is presented to us by an observation during the work of analysis, an observation which is actually a very old one. As not infrequently happens, it has taken a long time to come to the point of appreciating its importance. The whole theory of psycho-analysis is, as you know, in fact built up on the perception of the resistance offered to us by the patient when we attempt to make his unconscious conscious to him. The objective sign of this resistance is that his associations fail or depart widely from the topic that is being dealt with. He may also recognize the resistance *subjectively* by the fact that he has distressing feelings when he approaches the topic. But this last sign may also be absent. We then say to the patient that we infer from his behaviour that he is now in a state of resistance; and he replies that he knows nothing of that, and is only aware that his associations have become more difficult. It turns out that we were right; but in that case his resistance was unconscious too, just as unconscious as the repressed, at the lifting of which we were working. We should long ago have asked the question: from what part of his mind does an unconscious resistance like this arise? The beginner in psycho-analysis will be ready at once with the answer: it is, of course, the resistance of the unconscious. An ambiguous and unserviceable answer! If it means that the resistance arises from the repressed, we must rejoin: certainly not! We must rather attribute to the repressed a strong upward drive, an impulsion to break through into consciousness. The resistance can only be a manifestation of the ego, which originally put the repression into force and now wishes to maintain it. That, moreover, is the view we always took. Since we have come to assume a special agency in the ego, the super-ego, which represents demands of a restrictive and rejecting character, we may say that repression is the work of this super-ego and that it is carried out either by itself or by the ego in obedience to its orders. If then we are met by the case of the resistance in analysis not being conscious to the patient, this means either that in quite important situations the super-ego and the ego can operate unconsciously, or—and this would be still more important—that portions of both of them, the ego and the super-ego themselves, are unconscious. In both cases we have to reckon with the disagreeable discovery that on the one hand (super-) ego and conscious and on the other hand repressed and unconscious are far from coinciding.

And here, Ladies and Gentlemen, I feel that I must make a pause to take breath—which you too will welcome as a relief—and, before I go on, to apologize to you. My intention is to give you some addenda to the introductory lectures on psycho-analysis which I began fifteen years ago, and I am obliged to behave as though you as well as I had in the interval done nothing but practise psycho-analysis. I know that that assumption is out of place; but I am helpless, I cannot do otherwise. This is no doubt related to the fact that it is in general so hard to give anyone who is not himself a psycho-analyst an insight into psycho-analysis. You can believe me when I tell you that we do not enjoy giving an impression of being members of a secret society and of practising a mystical science. Yet we have been obliged to recognize and express as our conviction that no one has a right to join in a discussion of psycho-analysis who has not had particular experiences which can only be obtained by being analysed oneself. When I gave you my lectures fifteen years ago I tried to spare you certain speculative portions of our theory; but it is precisely from them that are derived the new acquisitions of which I must speak to you to-day.

I return now to our topic. In face of the doubt whether the ego and super-ego are themselves unconscious or merely produce unconscious effects, we have, for good reasons, decided in favour of the former possibility. And it is indeed the case that large portions of the ego and super-ego can remain unconscious and are normally unconscious. That is to say, the individual knows nothing of their contents and it requires an expenditure of effort to make them conscious. It is a fact that ego and conscious, repressed and unconscious do not coincide. We feel a need to make a fundamental revision of our attitude to the problem of consious-unconscious. At first we are inclined greatly to reduce the value of the criterion of being conscious since it has shown itself so untrustworthy. But we should be doing it an injustice. As may be said of our life, it is not worth much, but it is all we have. Without the illumination thrown by the quality of consciousness, we should be lost in the obscurity of depth-psychology; but we must attempt to find our bearings afresh.

There is no need to discuss what is to be called conscious: it is removed from all doubt. The oldest and best meaning of the word 'unconscious' is the descriptive one; we call a psychical process unconscious whose existence we are obliged to assume —for some such reason as that we infer it from its effects—, but of which we know nothing. In that case we have the same relation to it as we have to a physical process in another person, except that it is in fact one of our own. If we want to be still more correct, we shall modify our assertion by saying that we call a process unconscious if we are obliged to assume that it is being activated *at the moment* though *at the moment* we know nothing about it. This qualification makes us reflect that the majority of conscious processes are conscious only for a short time; very soon they become *latent,* but can easily become conscious again. We might also say that they had become unconscious, if it were at all certain that in the condition of latency they are still something psychical. So far we should have learnt nothing new; nor should we have acquired the right to introduce the concept of an unconscious into psychology. But then comes the new observation that we were already able to make in parapraxes. In order to explain a slip of the tongue, for instance, we find ourselves obliged to assume that the intention to make a particular remark was present in the subject. We infer it with certainty from the interference with his remark which has occurred; but the intention did not put itself through and was thus unconscious. If, when we subsequently put it before the speaker, he recognizes it as one familiar to him, then it was only temporarily unconscious to him; but if he repudiates it as something foreign to him, then it was permanently unconscious. From this experience we retrospectively obtain the right also to pronounce as something unconscious what had been described as latent. A consideration of these dynamic relations permits us now to distinguish two kinds of unconscious—one which is easily, under frequently occurring circumstances, transformed into something conscious, and another with which this transformation is difficult and takes place only subject to a considerable expenditure of effort or possibly never at all. In order to escape the ambiguity as to whether we mean the one or the other unconscious, whether we are using the word in the descriptive or in the dynamic sense, we make use of a permissible and simple way out. We call the unconscious which is only latent, and thus easily becomes conscious, the 'preconscious' and retain the term 'unconscious' for the other. We now have three terms, 'conscious,' 'preconscious' and 'unconscious,' with which we can get along in our description of mental phenomena. Once again: the preconscious is also unconscious in the purely descriptive sense, but we do not give it that name, except in talking loosely or when we have to make a defence of the existence in mental life of unconscious processes in general.

You will admit, I hope, that so far that is not too bad and allows of convenient handling. Yes, but unluckily the work of psycho-analysis has found itself compelled to use the word 'unconscious' in yet another, third, sense, and this may, to be sure, have led to confusion. Under the new and powerful impression of there being an extensive and important field of mental life which is normally withdrawn from the ego's knowledge so that the processes occurring in it have to be regarded as unconscious in the truly dynamic sense, we have come to understand the term 'unconscious' in a topographical or systematic sense as well; we have come to speak of a 'system' of the preconscious and a 'system' of the unconscious, of a conflict between the ego and the system *Ucs.*, and have used the word more and more to denote a mental province rather than a quality of what is mental. The discovery, actually an inconvenient one, that portions of the ego and super-ego as well are unconscious in the dynamic sense, operates at this point as a relief—it makes possible the removal of a complication. We perceive that we have no right to name the mental region that is foreign to the ego 'the system *Ucs.*', since the characteristic of being unconscious is not restricted to it. Very well; we will no longer use the term 'unconscious' in the systematic sense and we will give what we have hitherto so described a better name and one no longer open to misunderstanding. Following a verbal usage of Nietzsche's and taking up a suggestion by Georg Groddeck [1923],[1] we will in future call it the 'id'.[2] This impersonal pronoun seems particularly well suited for expressing the main characteristic of this province of the mind—the fact of its being alien to the ego. The super-ego, the ego and the id—these, then, are the three realms, regions, provinces, into which we divide an individual's mental apparatus, and with the mutual relations of which we shall be concerned in what follows.

But first a short interpolation. I suspect that you feel dissatisfied because the three qualities of the characteristic of consciousness and the three provinces of the mental apparatus do not fall together into three peaceable couples, and you may regard this as in some sense obscuring our findings. I do not think, however, that we should regret it, and we should tell ourselves that we had no right to expect any such smooth arrangement. Let me give you an analogy; analogies, it is true, decide nothing, but they can make one feel more at home. I am imagining a country with a landscape of varying configuration—hill-country, plains, and chains of lakes—, and with a mixed population: it is inhabited by Germans, Magyars and Slovaks, who carry on different activities. Now things might be partitioned in such a way that the Germans, who breed cattle, live in the hill-country, the Magyars, who grow cereals and wine, live in the plains, and the Slovaks, who catch fish and plait reeds, live by the lakes. If the partitioning could be neat and clear-cut like this, a Woodrow Wilson would be delighted by it,[3] it would also be convenient for a lecture in a geography lesson. The probability is, however, that you will find less orderliness and more mixing, if you travel through the region. Germans, Magyars and Slovaks live interspersed all over it; in the hill-country there is agricultural land as well, cattle are bred in the plains too. A few things are naturally as you expected, for fish cannot be caught in the mountains and wine does not grow in the water. Indeed, the picture of the region that you brought with you may on the whole fit the facts; but you will have to put up with deviations in the details.

You will not expect me to have much to tell you that is new about the id apart

[1] [A German physician by whose unconventional ideas Freud was much attracted.]

[2] [In German '*Es*', the ordinary word for 'it.']

[3] [It may be remarked that only a year or so before writing this Freud had finished his collaboration with W. C. Bullitt (then American Ambassador in Berlin) on a study of President Wilson, of whose political judgment he was highly critical.] [*Thomas Woodrow Wilson* was published in 1967 by Houghton Mifflin—*Ed.*]

from its new name. It is the dark, inaccessible part of our personality; what little we know of it we have learnt from our study of the dream-work and of the construction of neurotic symptoms, and most of that is of a negative character and can be described only as a contrast to the ego. We approach the id with analogies: we call it a chaos, a cauldron full of seething excitations. We picture it as being open at its end to somatic influences, and as there taking up into itself instinctual needs which find their psychical expression in it, but we cannot say in what substratum. It is filled with energy reaching it from the instincts, but it has no organization, produces no collective will, but only a striving to bring about the satisfaction of the instinctual needs subject to the observance of the pleasure principle. The logical laws of thought do not apply in the id, and this is true above all of the law of contradiction. Contrary impulses exist side by side, without cancelling each other out or diminishing each other: at the most they may converge to form compromises under the dominating economic pressure towards the discharge of energy. There is nothing in the id that could be compared with negation; and we perceive with surprise an exception to the philosophical theorem that space and time are necessary forms of our mental acts. There is nothing in the id that corresponds to the idea of time; there is no recognition of the passage of time, and—a thing that is most remarkable and awaits consideration in philosophical thought—no alteration in its mental processes is produced by the passage of time. Wishful impulses which have never passed beyond the id, but impressions, too, which have been sunk into the id by repression, are virtually immortal; after the passage of decades they behave as though they had just occurred. They can only be recognized as belonging to the past, can only lose their importance and be reprived of their cathexis of energy, when they have been made conscious by the work of analysis, and it is on this that the therapeutic effect of analytic treatment rests to no small extent.

Again and again I have had the impression that we have made too little theoretical use of this fact, established beyond any doubt, of the unalterability by time of the repressed. This seems to offer an approach to the most profound discoveries. Nor, unfortunately, have I myself made any progress here.

The id of course knows no judgments of value: no good and evil, no morality. The economic or, if you prefer, the quantitative factor, which is intimately linked to the pleasure principle, dominates all its processes. Instinctual cathexes seeking discharge—that, in our view, is all there is in the id. It even seems that the energy of these instinctual impulses is in a state different from that in the other regions of the mind, far more mobile and capable of discharge; otherwise the displacements and condensations would not occur which are characteristic of the id and which so completely disregard the *quality* of what is cathected—what in the ego we should call an idea. We would give much to understand more about these things! You can see, incidentally, that we are in a position to attribute to the id characteristics other than that of its being unconscious, and you can recognize the possibility of portions of the ego and super-ego being unconscious without possessing the same primitive and irrational characteristics.

We can best arrive at the characteristics of the actual ego, in so far as it can be distinguished from the id and from the super-ego, by examining its relation to the outermost superficial portion of the mental apparatus, which we describe as the system *Pcpt.-Cs.* This system is turned towards the external world, it is the medium for the perceptions arising thence, and during its functioning the phenomenon of consciousness arises in it. It is the sense-organ of the entire apparatus; moreover it is receptive not only to excitations from outside but also to those arising from the interior of the mind. We need scarcely look for a justification of the view that the ego is that portion of the id which was modified by the proximity and influence of the external world, which is adapted for the reception of stimuli and as a protective shield against stimuli, comparable to the cortical layer by which a small piece of living substance is surrounded. The relation to the external world has become the decisive factor for the ego; it has taken on the task of representing the external world to the id—fortunately for the id, which could not escape destruction if, in its blind efforts for the satisfaction of its instincts, it disregarded that supreme external power. In accomplishing this function, the ego must observe the external world, must lay down an accurate picture of it in the memory-traces of its perceptions, and by its exercise of the function of 'reality-testing' must put aside whatever in this picture of the external world is an addition derived from internal sources of excitation. The ego controls the approaches to motility under the id's orders; but between a need and an action it has interposed a postponement in the form of the activity of thought, during which it makes use of the mnemic residues of experience. In that way it has dethroned the pleasure principle which dominates the course of events in the id without any restriction and has replaced it by the reality principle, which promises more certainty and greater success.

The relation to time, which is so hard to describe, is also introduced into the ego by the perceptual system; it can scarcely be doubted that the mode of operation of that system is what provides the origin of the idea of time. But what distinguishes the ego from the id quite especially is a tendency to synthesis in its contents, to a combination and unification in its mental processes which are totally lacking in the id. When presently we come to deal with the instincts in mental life we shall, I hope, succeed in tracing this essential characteristic of the ego back to its source. It alone produces the high degree of organization which the ego needs for its best achievements. The ego develops from perceiving the instincts to controlling them; but this last is only achieved by the [psychical] representative of the instinct being allotted its proper place in a considerable assemblage, by its being taken up into a coherent context. To adopt a popular mode of speaking, we might say that the ego stands for reason and good sense while the id stands for the untamed passions.

So far we have allowed ourselves to be impressed by the merits and capabilities of the ego; it is now time to consider the other side as well. The ego is after all only a portion of the id, a portion that has been expediently modified by the proximity of the external world with its threat of danger. From a dynamic point of view it is weak, it has borrowed its energies from the id, and we are not entirely without insight into the methods—we might call them dodges—by which it extracts further amounts of energy from the id. One such method, for instance, is by identifying itself with actual or abandoned objects. The object-cathexes spring from the instinctual demands of the id. The ego has in the first instance to take note of them. But by identifying itself with the object it recommends itself to the id in place of the object and seeks to divert the id's libido on to itself. We have already seen [p. 64] that in the course of its life the ego takes into itself a large number of precipitates like this of former object-cathexes. The ego must on the whole carry out the id's intentions, it fulfils its task by finding out the circumstances in which those intentions can best be achieved. The ego's relation to the id might be compared with that of a rider to his horse. The horse supplies the locomotive energy, while the rider has the privilege of deciding on the goal and of guiding the powerful animal's movement. But only too often there arises between the ego and the id the not precisely ideal situation of the rider being obliged to guide the horse along the path by which it itself wants to go.

There is one portion of the id from which the ego has separated itself by resistances due to repression. But the repression is not carried over into the id: the repressed merges into the remainder of the id.

We are warned by a proverb against serving two masters at the same time. The poor ego has things even worse: it serves three severe masters and does what it can to bring their claims and demands into harmony with one another. These claims are always divergent and often seem incompatible. No wonder that the ego so often fails in its task. Its three tyrannical masters are the external world, the super-ego and the id. When we follow the ego's efforts to satisfy them simultaneously—or rather, to obey them simultaneously—we cannot feel any regret at having personified this ego and having set it up as a separate organism. It feels hemmed in on three sides, threatened by three kinds of danger, to which, if it is hard pressed, it reacts by generating anxiety. Owing to its origin from the experiences of the perceptual system, it is earmarked for representing the demands of the external world, but it strives too to be a loyal servant of the id, to remain on good terms with it, to recommend itself to it as an object and to attract its libido to itself. In its attempts to mediate between the id and reality, it is often obliged to cloak the *Ucs.* commands of the id with its own *Pcs.* rationalizations, to conceal the id's conflicts with reality, to profess, with diplomatic disingenuousness, to be taking notice of reality even when the id has remained rigid and unyielding. On the other hand it is observed at every step it takes by the strict super-ego, which lays down definite standards for its conduct, without taking any account of its difficulties from the direction of the id and the external world, and which, if those standards are not obeyed, punishes it with tense feelings of inferiority and of guilt. Thus the ego, driven by the id, confined by the super-ego, repulsed by reality, struggles to master its economic task of bringing about harmony among the forces and influences working in and upon it; and we can understand how it is that so often we cannot suppress a cry: 'Life is not easy!' If the ego is obliged to admit its weakness, it breaks out in anxiety—realistic anxiety regarding the external world, moral anxiety regarding the super-ego and neurotic anxiety regarding the strength of the passions in the id.

JOHN HOSPERS

What Means This Freedom?

John Hospers, Professor of Philosophy at
the University of Southern California,
has also written *Meaning and Truth in
in the Arts, Human Conduct,* and
Introduction to Philosophical Analysis.

. . . As a preparation for developing my own views on the subject, I want to mention
a factor that I think is of enormous importance and relevance: namely, unconscious
motivation. There are many actions—not those of an insane person (however the
term "insane" be defined), nor of a person ignorant of the effects of his action, nor
ignorant of some relevant fact about the situation, nor in any obvious way mentally
deranged—for which human beings in general and the courts in particular are inclined to hold the doer responsible, and for which, I would say, he should not be
held responsible. The deed may be planned, it may be carried out in cold calculation,
it may spring from the agent's character and be continuous with the rest of his behavior, and it may be perfectly true that he could have done differently *if* he had
wanted to; nonetheless his behavior was brought about by unconscious conflicts
developed in infancy, over which he had no control and of which (without training
in psychiatry) he does not even have knowledge. He may even *think* he knows why
he acted as he did, he may *think* he has conscious control over his actions, he may
even *think* he is fully responsible for them; but he is not. Psychiatric casebooks
provide hundreds of examples. The law and common sense, though puzzled sometimes by such cases, are gradually becoming aware that they exist; but at this early
stage countless tragic blunders still occur because neither the law nor the public in
general is aware of the genesis of criminal actions. The mother blames her daughter
for choosing the wrong men as candidates for husbands; but though the daughter
thinks she is choosing freely and spends a considerable amount of time "deciding"
among them, the identification with her sick father, resulting from Oedipal fantasies
in early childhood, prevents her from caring for any but sick men, twenty or thirty
years older than herself. Blaming her is beside the point; she cannot help it, and she
cannot change it. Countless criminal acts are thought out in great detail; yet the
participants are (without their own knowledge) acting out fantasies, fears, and
defenses from early childhood, over whose coming and going they have no conscious
control.

   Now, I am not saying that none of these persons should be in jails or asylums.
Often society must be protected against them. Nor am I saying that people should

cease the practices of blaming and praising, punishing and rewarding; in general these devices are justified by the results—although very often they have practically no effect; the deeds are done from inner compulsion, which is not lessened when the threat of punishment is great. I am only saying that frequently persons we think responsible are not properly to be called so; we mistakenly think them responsible because we assume they are like those in whom no unconscious drive (toward this type of behavior) is present, and that their behavior can be changed by reasoning, exhorting, or threatening.

I

I have said that these persons are not responsible. But what is the criterion for responsibility? Under precisely what conditions is a person to be held morally responsible for an action? Disregarding here those conditions that have to do with a person's *ignorance* of the situation or the effects of his action, let us concentrate on those having to do with his "inner state." There are several criteria that might be suggested:

1. The first idea that comes to mind is that responsibility is determined by the presence or absence of *premeditation*—the opposite of "premeditated" being, presumably, "unthinking" or "impulsive." But this will not do—both because some acts are not premeditated but responsible, and because some are premeditated and not responsible.

Many acts we call responsible can be as unthinking or impulsive as you please. If you rush across the street to help the victim of an automobile collision, you are (at least so we would ordinarily say) acting responsibly, but you did not do so out of premeditation; you saw the accident, you didn't think, you rushed to the scene without hesitation. It was like a reflex action. But you acted responsibly: unlike the knee jerk, the act was the result of past training and past thought about situations of this kind; that is why you ran to help instead of ignoring the incident or running away. When something done originally from conviction or training becomes habitual, it becomes *like* a reflex action. As Aristotle said, virtue should become second nature through habit: a virtuous act should be performed *as if* by instinct; this, far from detracting from its moral worth, testifies to one's mastery of the desired type of behavior; one does not have to make a moral effort each time it is repeated.

There are also premeditated acts for which, I would say, the person is not responsible. Premeditation, especially when it is so exaggerated as to issue in no action at all, can be the result of neurotic disturbance or what we sometimes call an emotional "block," which the person inherits from long-past situations. In Hamlet's revenge on his uncle (I use this example because it is familiar to all of us), there was no lack, but rather a surfeit, of premeditation; his actions were so exquisitely premeditated as to make Freud and Dr. Ernest Jones look more closely to find out what lay behind them. The very premeditation camouflaged unconscious motives of which Hamlet himself was not aware. I think this is an important point, since it seems that the courts often assume that premeditation is a criterion of responsibility. If failure to kill his uncle had been considered a crime, every court in the land would have convicted Hamlet. Again: a woman's decision to stay with her husband in spite of endless "mental cruelty" is, if she is the victim of an unconscious masochistic "will to punishment," one for which she is not responsible; she is the victim and not the agent, no matter how profound her conviction that she is the agent; she is caught in a masochistic web (of complicated genesis) dating back to babyhood, perhaps a repetition of a comparable situation involving her own parents, a repetition-compulsion that, as Freud said, goes "beyond the pleasure principle." Again: a criminal whose crime was carefully planned step by step is usually considered responsible, but as we shall see in later examples, the overwhelming impulse toward it, stemming from an unusually humiliating ego defeat in early childhood, was as compulsive as any can be.

2. Shall we say, then, that a person is not responsible for his act unless he can *defend it with reasons?* I am afraid that this criterion is no better than the previous one. First, intellectuals are usually better at giving reasons than nonintellectuals, and according to this criterion would be more responsible than persons acting from moral conviction not implemented by reasoning; yet it is very doubtful whether we should want to say that the latter are the more responsible. Second, the giving of reasons itself may be suspect. The reasons may be rationalizations camouflaging unconscious motives of which the agent knows nothing. Hamlet gave many reasons for not doing what he felt it was his duty to do: the time was not right, his uncle's soul might go to heaven, etc. His various "reasons" contradicted one another, and if an overpowering compulsion had not been present, the highly intellectual Hamlet would not have been taken in for a moment by these rationalizations. The real reason, the Oedipal conflict that made his uncle's crime the accomplishment of his own deepest desire, binding their fates into one and paralyzing him into inaction, was unconscious and of course unknown to him. One's intelligence and reasoning power do not enable one to escape from unconsciously motivated behavior; it only gives one greater facility in rationalizing that behavior; one's intelligence is simply used in the interests of the neurosis—it is pressed into service to justify with reasons what one does quite independently of the reasons.

If these two criteria are inadequate, let us seek others.

3. Shall we say that a person is responsible for his action unless it is the *result of unconscious forces* of which he knows nothing? Many psychoanalysts would probably accept this criterion. If it is not largely reflected in the language of responsibility as ordinarily used, this may be due to ignorance of fact: most people do not know that there are such things as unconscious motives and unconscious conflicts causing human beings to act. But it may be that if they did, perhaps they would refrain from holding persons responsible for certain actions.

I do not wish here to quarrel with this criterion of responsibility. I only want to point out the fact that if this criterion is employed a far greater number of actions will be excluded from the domain of responsibility than we might at first suppose. Whether we are neat or untidy, whether we are selfish or unselfish, whether we provoke scenes or avoid them, even whether we can exert our powers of will to change our behavior—all these may, and often do, have their source in our unconscious life.

4. Shall we say that a person is responsible for his act unless it is *compelled?* Here we are reminded of Aristotle's assertion (*Nicomachean Ethics,* Book III) that a person is responsible for his act except for reasons of either ignorance or compulsion.

Ignorance is not part of our problem here (unless it is unconsciously induced ignorance of facts previously remembered and selectively forgotten—in which case the forgetting is again compulsive), but compulsion is. How will compulsion do as a criterion? The difficulty is to state just what it means. When we say an act is compelled in a psychological sense, our language is metaphorical—which is not to say that there is no point in it or that, properly interpreted, it is not true. Our actions are compelled in a literal sense if someone has us in chains or is controlling our bodily movements. When we say that the storm compelled us to jettison the cargo of the ship (Aristotle's example), we have a less literal sense of compulsion, for at least it is open to us to go down with the ship. When psychoanalysts say that a man was compelled by unconscious conflicts to wash his hands constantly, this is also not a literal use of "compel"; for nobody forced his hands under the tap. Still, it is a typical example of what psychologists call *compulsive* behavior: it has unconscious causes inaccessible to introspection, and moreover nothing can change it—it is as inevitable for him to do it as it would be if someone were forcing his hands under the tap. In this it is exactly like the action of a powerful external force; it is just as little within one's conscious control.

In its area of application this interpretation of responsibility comes to much the same as the previous one. And this area is very great indeed. For if we cannot be held responsible for the infantile situations (in which we were after all passive victims), then neither, it would seem, can we be held responsible for compulsive actions occurring in adulthood that are inevitable consequences of those infantile situations. And, psychiatrists and psychoanalysts tell us, actions fulfilling this description are characteristic of all people some of the time and some people most of the time. Their occurrence, once the infantile events have taken place, is inevitable, just as the explosion is inevitable once the fuse has been lighted; there is simply more "delayed action" in the psychological explosions than there is in the physical ones.

(I have not used the word "inevitable" here to mean "causally determined," for according to such a definition every event would be inevitable if one accepted the causal principle in some form or other; and probably nobody except certain philosophers uses "inevitable" in this sense. Rather, I use "inevitable" in its ordinary sense of "cannot be avoided." To the extent, therefore, that adult neurotic manifestations *can* be avoided, once the infantile patterns have become set, the assertion that they are inevitable is not true.)

5. There is still another criterion, which I prefer to the previous ones, by which a man's responsibility for an act can be measured: the degree to which that act can (or could have been) *changed by the use of reasons*. Suppose that the man who washes his hands constantly does so, he says, for hygienic reasons, believing that if he doesn't do so he will be poisoned by germs. We now convince him, on the best medical authority, that his belief is groundless. Now, the test of his responsibility is whether the changed belief will result in changed behavior. If it does not, as with the compulsive hand washer, he is not acting responsibly, but if it does, he is. It is not the *use* of reasons, but their *efficacy in changing behavior,* that is being made the criterion of responsibility. And clearly in neurotic cases no such change occurs; in fact, this is often made the defining characteristic of neurotic behavior: it is unchangeable by any rational considerations.

II

I have suggested these criteria to distinguish actions for which we can call the agent responsible from those for which we cannot. Even persons with extensive knowledge of psychiatry do not, I think, use any one of these criteria to the exclusion of the others; a conjunction of two or more may be used at once. But however they may be combined or selected in actual application, I believe we can make the distinction along some such lines as we have suggested.

But is there not still another possible meaning of "responsibility" that we have not yet mentioned? Even after we have made all the above distinctions, there remains a question in our minds whether we are, in the final analysis, *responsible for any of our actions at all.* The issue may be put this way: How can anyone be responsible for his actions, since they grow out of his character, which is shaped and molded and made what it is by influences—some hereditary, but most of them stemming from early parental environment—that were not of his own making or choosing? This question, I believe, still troubles many people who would agree to all the distinctions we have just made but still have the feeling that "this isn't all." They have the uneasy suspicion that there is a more ultimate sense, a "deeper" sense, in which we are *not* responsible for our actions, since we are not responsible for the character out of which those actions spring. This, of course, is the sense Professor Edwards was describing.

Let us take as an example a criminal who, let us say, strangled several persons and is himself now condemned to die in the electric chair. Jury and public alike hold him fully responsible (at least they utter the words "he is responsible"), for the murders were planned down to the minutest detail, and the defendant tells the jury exactly how he planned them. But now we find out how it all came about; we learn of parents who rejected him from babyhood, of the childhood spent in one foster home after another, where it was always plain to him that he was not wanted; of the constantly frustrated early desire for affection, the hard shell of nonchalance and bitterness that he assumed to cover the painful and humiliating fact of being unwanted, and his subsequent attempts to heal these wounds to his shattered ego through defensive aggression.

> The criminal is the most passive person in this world, helpless as a baby in his motorically inexpressible fury. Not only does he try to wreak revenge on the mother of the earliest period of his babyhood; his criminality is based on the inner feeling of being incapable of making the mother even feel that the child seeks revenge on her. The situation is that of a dwarf trying to annoy a giant who superciliously refuses to see these attempts. . . . Because of his inner feeling of being a dwarf, the criminotic uses, so to speak, dynamite. Of that the giant must take cognizance. True, the "revenge" harms the avenger. He may be legally executed. However, the primary inner aim of forcing the giant to acknowledge the dwarf's fury is fulfilled.[1]

The poor victim is not conscious of the inner forces that exact from him this ghastly toll; he battles, he schemes, he revels in pseudo-aggression, he is miserable, but he does not know what works within him to produce these catastrophic acts of crime. His aggressive actions are the wriggling of a worm on a fisherman's

---

[1] Edmund Bergler, *The Basic Neurosis* (New York: Grune and Stratton, 1949), p. 305.

hook. And if this is so, it seems difficult to say any longer, "He is responsible." Rather, we shall put him behind bars for the protection of society, but we shall no longer flatter our feeling of moral superiority by calling him personally responsible for what he did.

Let us suppose it were established that a man commits murder only if, sometime during the previous week, he has eaten a certain combination of foods—say, tuna fish salad at a meal also including peas, mushroom soup, and blueberry pie. What if we were to track down the factors common to all murders committed in this country during the last twenty years and found this factor present in all of them, and only in them? The example is of course empirically absurd; but may it not be that there is *some* combinations of factors that regularly leads to homicide, factors such as are described in general terms in the above quotation? (Indeed the situation in the quotation is less fortunate than in our hypothetical example, for it is easy to avoid certain foods once we have been warned about them, but the situation of the infant is thrust on him; something has already happened to him once and for all, before he knows it has happened.) When such specific factors are discovered, won't they make it clear that it is foolish and pointless, as well as immoral, to hold human beings responsible for crimes? Or, if one prefers biological to psychological factors, suppose a neurologist is called in to testify at a murder trial and produces X-ray pictures of the brain of the criminal; anyone can see, he argues, that the *cella turcica* was already calcified at the age of nineteen; it should be a flexible bone, growing, enabling the gland to grow.[2] All the defendant's disorders might have resulted from this early calcification. Now, this particular explanation may be empirically false; but who can say that no such factors, far more complex, to be sure, exist?

When we know such things as these, we no longer feel so much tempted to say that the criminal is responsible for his crime; and we tend also (do we not?) to excuse him—not legally (we still confine him to prison) but morally; we no longer call him a monster or hold him personally responsible for what he did. Moreover, we do this in general, not merely in the case of crime: "You must excuse Grandmother for being irritable; she's really quite ill and is suffering some pain all the time." Or: "The dog always bites children after she's had a litter of pups; you can't blame her for it: she's not feeling well, and besides she naturally wants to defend them." Or: "She's nervous and jumpy, but do excuse her: she has a severe glandular disturbance."

Let us note that the more *thoroughly* and *in detail* we know the causal factors leading a person to behave as he does, the more we tend to exempt him from responsibility. When we know nothing of the man except what we see him do, we say he is an ungrateful cad who expects much of other people and does nothing in return, and we are usually indignant. When we learn that his parents were the same way and, having no guilt feelings about this mode of behavior themselves, brought him up to be greedy and avaricious, we see that we could hardly expect him to have developed moral feelings in this direction. When we learn, in addition, that he is not aware of being ungrateful or selfish, but unconsciously represses the memory of events unfavorable to himself, we feel that the situation is unfortunate but "not really his fault." When we know that this behavior of his, which makes

[2] Meyer Levin, *Compulsion* (New York: Simon and Schuster, 1956), p. 403.

others angry, occurs more constantly when he feels tense or insecure, and that he now feels tense and insecure, and that relief from pressure will diminish it, then we tend to "feel sorry for the poor guy" and say he's more to be pitied than censured. We no longer want to say that he is personally responsible; we might rather blame nature or his parents for having given him an unfortunate constitution or temperament.

> In recent years a new form of punishment has been imposed on middle-aged and elderly parents. Their children, now in their twenties, thirties or even forties, present them with a modern grievance: "My analysis proves that *you* are responsible for my neurosis." Overawed by these authoritative statements, the poor tired parents fall easy victims to the newest variations on the scapegoat theory.
>
> In my opinion, his senseless cruelty—which disinters educational sins which had been buried for decades, and uses them as the basis for accusations which the victims cannot answer—is unjustified. Yes "the truth loves to be centrally located" (Melville), and few parents—since they are human—have been perfect. But granting their mistakes, they acted as *their* neurotic difficulties forced them to act. To turn the tables and declare the children not guilty because of the *impersonal* nature of their own neuroses, while at the same time the parents are *personally* blamed, is worse than illogical; it is profoundly unjust.[3]

And so, it would now appear, neither of the parties is responsible: "they acted as their neurotic difficulties forced them to act." The patients are not responsible for their neurotic manifestations, but then neither are the parents responsible for theirs; and so, of course, for their parents in turn, and theirs before them. It is the twentieth-century version of the family curse, the curse on the House of Atreus.

"But," a critic complains, "it's immoral to exonerate people indiscriminately in this way. I might have thought it fit to excuse somebody because he was born on the other side of the tracks, if I didn't know so many bank presidents who were also born on the other side of the tracks." Now, I submit that the most immoral thing in this situation is the critic's caricature of the conditions of the excuse. Nobody is excused merely because he was born on the other side of the tracks. But if he was born on the other side of the tracks *and* was a highly narcissistic infant to begin with *and* was repudiated or neglected by his parents *and* . . . (here we list a finite number of conditions), and if this complex of factors is *regularly* followed by certain behavior traits in adulthood, and moreover *unavoidably* so—that is, they occur no matter what he or anybody else tries to do—then we excuse him morally and say he is not responsible for his deed. If he is not responsible for *A*, a series of events occurring in his babyhood, then neither is he responsible for *B*, a series of things he does in adulthood, provided that *B* inevitably—that is, unavoidably—follows upon the occurrence of *A*. And according to psychiatrists and psychoanalysts, this often happens.

But one may still object that so far we have talked only about neurotic behavior. Isn't nonneurotic or normal or not unconsciously motivated (or whatever you want to call it) behavior still within the area of responsibility? There are reasons for answering "No" even here, for the normal person no more than the neurotic one has caused his own character, which makes him what he is. Granted that neurotics are not responsible for their behavior (that part of it which we call

3 Edmund Bergler, *The Superego* (New York: Grune and Stratton, 1952), p. 320.

neurotic) because it stems from undigested infantile conflicts that they had no part in bringing about, and that are external to them just as surely as if their behavior had been forced on them by a malevolent deity (which is indeed one theory on the subject); but the so-called normal person is equally the product of causes in which his volition took no part. And if, unlike the neurotic's, his behavior is changeable by rational considerations, and if he has the will power to overcome the effects of an unfortunate early environment, this again is no credit to him; he is just lucky. If energy is available to him in a form in which it can be mobilized for constructive purposes, this is no credit to him, for this too is part of his psychic legacy. Those of us who can discipline ourselves and develop habits of concentration of purpose tend to blame those who cannot, and call them lazy and weak-willed; but what we fail to see is that they literally *cannot* do what we expect; if their psyches were structured like ours, they could, but as they are burdened with a tyrannical super-ego (to use psychoanalytic jargon for the moment), and a weak defenseless ego whose energies are constantly consumed in fighting endless charges of the superego, they simply cannot do it, and it is irrational to expect it of them. We cannot with justification blame them for their inability, any more than we can congratulate ourselves for our ability. This lesson is hard to learn, for we constantly and naïvely assume that other people are constructed as we ourselves are.

For example: A child raised under slum conditions, whose parents are socially ambitious and envy families with money, but who nevertheless squander the little they have on drink, may simply be unable in later life to mobilize a drive sufficient to overcome these early conditions. Common sense would expect that he would develop the virtue of thrift; he would make quite sure that he would never again endure the grinding poverty he had experienced as a child. But in fact it is not so: the exact conditions are too complex to be specified in detail here, but when certain conditions are fulfilled (concerning the subject's early life), he will always thereafter be a spendthrift, and no rational considerations will be able to change this. He will listen to the rational considerations and see the force of these, but they will not be able to change him, even if he tries; he cannot change his wasteful habits any more than he can lift the Empire State Building with his bare hands. We moralize and plead with him to be thrifty, but we do not see how strong, how utterly overpowering, and how constantly with him, is the opposite drive, which is so easily manageable with us. But he is possessed by the all-consuming, all-encompassing urge to make the world see that he belongs, that he has arrived, that he is just as well off as anyone else, that the awful humiliations were not real, that they never actually occurred, for isn't he now able to spend and spend? The humiliation must be blotted out; and conspicuous, fleshy, expensive, and wasteful buying will do this; it shows the world what the world must know! True, it is only for the moment; true, it is in the end self-defeating, for wasteful consumption is the best way to bring poverty back again; but the person with an overpowering drive to mend a lesion to his narcissism cannot resist the avalanche of that drive with his puny rational consideration. A man with his back against the wall and a gun at his throat doesn't think of what may happen ten years hence. (Consciously, of course, he knows nothing of this drive; all that appears to consciousness is its shattering effects; he knows only that he must keep on spending—not why—and that he is unable to resist.) He hasn't in him the psychic capacity, the energy to stem the tide of a drive that at the moment is all-powerful. We, seated comfortably away from this flood, sit in judgment on him and blame him and exhort him and criticize him; but he, carried along by the flood, cannot do otherwise than he does. He may fight with all the strength of which he is capable, but it is not enough. And we, who are rational enough at least to exonerate a man in a situation of "overpowering impulse" when we recognize it to be one, do not even recognize this as an example of it; and so, in addition to being swept away in the flood that childhood conditions rendered inevitable, he must also endure our lectures, our criticisms, and our moral excoriation.

But, one will say, he could have overcome his spendthrift tendencies; some people do. Quite true: some people do. They are lucky. They have it in them to overcome early deficiencies by exerting great effort, and they are capable of exerting the effort. Some of us, luckier still, can overcome them with but little effort; and a few, the luckiest, haven't the deficiencies to overcome. It's all a matter of luck. The least lucky are those who can't overcome them, even with great effort, and those who haven't the ability to exert the effort.

But, one persists, it isn't a matter simply of luck; it *is* a matter of effort. Very well then, it's a matter of effort; without exerting the effort you may not overcome the deficiency. But whether or not you are the kind of person who has it in him to exert the effort is a matter of luck.

All this is well known to psychoanalysts. They can predict, from minimal cues that most of us don't notice, whether a person is going to turn out to be lucky or not. "The analyst," they say, "must be able to use the residue of the patient's unconscious guilt so as to remove the symptom or character trait that creates the guilt. The guilt must not only be present, but *available* for use, *mobilizable*. If it is used up (absorbed) in criminal activity, or in an excessive amount of self-damaging tendencies, then it cannot be used for therapeutic purposes, and the prognosis is negative." Not all philosophers will relish the analyst's way of putting the matter, but at least as a physician he can soon detect whether the patient is lucky or unlucky—and he knows that whichever it is, it *isn't the patient's fault*. The patient's conscious volition cannot remedy the deficiency. Even whether he will co-operate with the analyst is really out of the patient's hands: if he continually projects the denying-mother fantasy on the analyst and unconsciously identifies him always with the cruel, harsh forbidder of the nursery, thus frustrating any attempt at impersonal observation, the sessions are useless; yet if it happens that way, he can't help that either. That fatal projection is not under his control; whether it occurs or not depends on how his unconscious identifications have developed since his infancy. He can try, yes—but the ability to try enough for the therapy to have effect is also beyond his control; the capacity to try more than just so much is either there or it isn't—and either way "it's in the lap of the gods."

The position, then, is this: if we *can* overcome the effects of early environment, the ability to do so is itself a product of the early environment. We did not give ourselves this ability; and if we lack it we cannot be blamed for not having it. Sometimes, to be sure, moral exhortation brings out an ability that is there but not being used, and in this lies its *occasional* utility; but very often its use is pointless, because the ability is not there. The only thing that can overcome a desire, as Spinoza said, is a stronger contrary desire; and many times there simply is no wherewithal for producing a stronger contrary desire. Those of us who do have the wherewithal are lucky.

There is one possible practical advantage in remembering this. It may prevent us (unless we are compulsive blamers) from indulging in righteous indignation and committing the sin of spiritual pride, thanking God that we are not as this publican here. And it will protect from our useless moralizings those who are least equipped by nature for enduring them. As with responsibility, so with deserts. Someone commits a crime and is punished by the state; "he deserved it," we say self-righteously—as if we were moral and he immoral, when in fact we are lucky and he is unlucky—forgetting that there, but for the grace of God and a fortunate early environment, go we. Or, as Clarence Darrow said in his speech for the defense in the Loeb-Leopold case:

> I do not believe that people are in jail because they deserve to be. . . . I know what causes the emotional life. . . . I know it is practically left out of some. Without it they cannot act with the rest. They cannot feel the moral shocks which safeguard others. Is [this man] to blame that his machine is imperfect? Who is to blame? I do not know. I have never in my life been interested so much in fixing blame as I have in relieving people from blame. I am not wise enough to fix it.[4]

III

I want to make it quite clear that I have not been arguing for determinism. Though I find it difficult to give any sense to the term "indeterminism," because I do not know what it would be like to come across an uncaused event, let us grant indeterminists everything they want, at least in words—influences that suggest but do not constrain, a measure of acausality in an otherwise rigidly causal order, and so on—whatever these phrases may mean. With all this granted, exactly the same situation faces the indeterminist and the determinist; all we have been saying would still hold true. "Are our powers innate or acquired?"

> Suppose the powers are declared innate; then the villain may sensibly ask whether he is responsible for what he was born with. A negative reply is inevitable. Are they then acquired? Then the ability to acquire them—was *that* innate? or acquired? It is innate? Very well then. . . .[5]

The same fact remains—that we did not cause our characters, that the influences that made us what we are are influences over which we had no control and of whose very existence we had no knowledge at the time. This fact remains for "determinism" and "indeterminism" alike. And it is this fact to which I would appeal, not the specific tenets of traditional forms of "determinism," which seem to me, when analyzed, empirically empty.

"But," it may be asked, "isn't it your view that nothing ultimately *could* be other than it is? And isn't this deterministic? And isn't it deterministic if you say that human beings could never act otherwise than they do, and that their desires and temperaments could not, when you consider their antecedent conditions, be other than they are?"

I reply that all these charges rest on confusions.

1. To say that nothing *could* be other than it is, is, taken literally, nonsense;

---

[4] Levin, *op. cit.*, pp. 439–40, 469.

[5] W. I. Matson, "The Irrelevance of Free-will to Moral Responsibility," *Mind,* LXV (October 1956), p. 495.

and if taken as a way of saying something else, misleading and confusing. If you say, "I can't do it," this invites the question, "No? Not even if you want to?" "Can" and "could" are power words, used in the context of human action; when applied to nature they are merely anthropomorphic. "Could" has no application to nature—unless, of course, it is uttered in a theological context: one might say that God *could* have made things different. But with regard to inanimate nature "could" has no meaning. Or perhaps it is intended to mean that the order of nature is in some sense *necessary*. But in that case the sense of "necessary" must be specified. I know what "necessary" means when we are talking about propositions, but not when we are talking about the sequence of events in nature.

2. What of the charge that we could never have acted otherwise than we did? This, I submit, is simply not true. Here the exponents of Hume-Mill-Schlick-Ayer "soft determinism" are quite right. I could have gone to the opera today instead of coming here; that is, if certain conditions had been different, I should have gone. I could have done many other things instead of what I did, if some condition or other had been different, specifically if my desire had been different. I repeat that "could" is a power word, and "I could have done this" means approximately "I *should* have done this *if* I had wanted to." In this sense, all of us could often have done otherwise than we did. I would not want to say that I should have done differently even if *all* the conditions leading up to my action had been the same (this is generally not what we mean by "could" anyway); but to assert that I could have is empty, for if I *did* act different from the time before, we would automatically say that one or more of the conditions were different, whether we had independent evidence for this or not, thus rendering the assertion imune to empirical refutation. (Once again, the vacuousness of "determinism.")

3. Well, then, could we ever have, not acted, but *desired* otherwise than we did desire? This gets us once again to the heart of the matter we were discussing in the previous section. Russell said, "We can do as we please but we can't please as we please." But I am persuaded that even this statement conceals a fatal mistake. Let us follow the same analysis through. "I could have done *X*" means "I should have done *X* if I had wanted to." "I could have wanted *X*" by the same analysis would mean "I should have wanted *X* if I had wanted to"—which seems to make no sense at all. (What does Russell want? To please as he doesn't please?)

What does this show? It shows, I think, that the only meaningful context of "can" and "could have" is that of *action*. "Could have acted differently" makes sense; "could have desired differently," as we have just seen, does not. Because a word or phrase makes good sense in one context, let us not assume that it does so in another.

I conclude, then, with the following suggestion: that we operate on two levels of moral discourse, which we shouldn't confuse; one (let's call it the upper level) is that of actions; the other (the lower, or deeper, level) is that of the springs of action. Most moral talk occurs on the upper level. It is on this level that the Hume-Mill-Schlick-Ayer analysis of freedom fully applies. As we have just seen, "can" and "could" acquire their meaning on this level; so, I suspect, does "freedom." So does the distinction between compulsive and noncompulsive behavior, and among the senses of "responsibility," discussed in the first section of this paper, according to which we are responsible for some things and not for others. All these distinctions are perfectly valid on this level (or in this dimension) of moral discourse; and it is, after all, the usual one—we are practical beings interested in changing the course of human behavior, so it is natural enough that 99 per cent of our moral talk occurs here.

But when we descend to what I have called the lower level of moral discourse, as we occasionally do in thoughtful moments when there is no immediate need for action, then we must admit that we are ultimately the kind of persons we are because of conditions occurring outside us, over which we had no control. But while this is true, we should beware of extending the moral terminology we used on the other level to this one also. "Could" and "can," as we have seen, no longer have meaning here. "Right" and "wrong," which apply only to actions, have no meaning here either. I suspect that the same is true of "responsibility," for now that we have recalled often forgotten facts about our being the product of outside forces, we must ask in all seriousness what would be added by saying that we are not *responsible* for our own characters and temperaments. What would it mean even? Has it a significant opposite? What would it be like to be responsible for one's own character? What possible situation is describable by this phrase? Instead of saying that it is *false* that we are responsible for our own characters, I should prefer to say that the utterance is meaningless—meaningless in the sense that it describes no possible situation, though it *seems* to because the word "responsible" is the same one we used on the upper level, where it marks a real distinction. If this is so, the result is that *moral* terms—at least the terms "could have" and "responsible"—simply drop out on the lower level. What remains, shorn now of moral terminology, is the point we tried to bring out in Part II: whether or not we have personality disturbances, whether or not we have the ability to overcome deficiences of early environment, is like the answer to the question whether or not we shall be struck down by a dread disease: "it's all a matter of luck." It is important to keep this in mind, for people almost always forget it, with consequences in human intolerance and unnecessary suffering that are incalculable.

JEAN-PAUL SARTRE

Freedom as Choosing Oneself

Jean-Paul Sartre is represented also by the
preceding article "Love and Sexual
Desire."

Common opinion does not hold that to be free means only to choose oneself. A choice is said to be free if it is such that it could have been other than what it is.

From *Being and Nothingness,* by Jean-Paul Sartre, translated by Hazel E. Barnes, Philosophical Library, 1956. Reprinted by permission of the publishers.

I start out on a hike with friends. At the end of several hours of walking my fatigue increases and finally becomes very painful. At first I resist and then suddenly I let myself go, I give up, I throw my knapsack down on the side of the road and let myself fall down beside it. Someone will reproach me for my act and will mean thereby that I was free—that is, not only was my act not determined by any thing or person, but also I could have succeeded in resisting my fatigue longer, I could have done as my companions did and reached the resting place before relaxing. I shall defend myself by saying that I was *too tired*. Who is right? Or rather is the debate not based on incorrect premises? There is no doubt that I could have done otherwise, but that is not the problem. It ought to be formulated rather like this: could I have done otherwise without perceptibly modifying the organic totality of the projects which I am; or is the fact of resisting my fatigue such that instead of remaining a purely local and accidental modification of my behavior, it could be effected only by means of a radical transformation of my being-in-the-world—a transformation, moreover, which is *possible*? In other words: I could have done otherwise. Agreed. But *at what price?*

We are going to reply to this question by first presenting a *theoretical* description which will enable us to grasp the principle of our thesis. We shall see subsequently whether the concrete reality is not shown to be more complex and whether without contradicting the results of our theoretical inquiry, it will not lead us to enrich them and make them more flexible.

Let us note first that the fatigue by itself could not provoke my decision. As we saw with respect to physical pain, fatigue is only the way in which I exist my body. It is not at first the object of a positional consciousness, but it is the very facticity of my consciousness. If then I hike across the country, what is revealed to me is the surrounding world; this is the object of my consciousness, and this is what I transcend toward possibilities which are my own—those, for example, of arriving this evening at the place which I have set for myself in advance. Yet to the extent that I apprehend this countryside with my eyes which unfold distances, my legs which climb the hills and consequently cause new sights and new obstacles to appear and disappear, with my back which carries the knapsack—to this extent I have a non-positional consciousness (of) this body which rules my relations with the world and which signifies my engagement in the world, in the form of fatigue. Objectively and in correlation with this non-thetic consciousness the roads are revealed as interminable, the slopes as *steeper,* the sun as more burning, etc. But I do not yet *think* of my fatigue; I apprehend it as the quasi-object of my reflection. Nevertheless there comes a moment when I do seek to consider my fatigue and to recover it. We really ought to provide an interpretation for this same intention; however, let us take it for what it is. It is not at all a contemplative apprehension of my fatigue; rather, as we saw with respect to pain, I *suffer* my fatigue. That is, a reflective consciousness is directed upon my fatigue in order to live it and to confer on it a value and a practical relation to myself. It is only on this plane that the fatigue will appear to me as bearable or intolerable. It will never be anything in itself, but it is the reflective For-itself which rising up suffers the fatigue as intolerable.

Here is posited the essential question: my companions are in good health—like me; they have had practically the same training as I so that although it is not possible to *compare* psychic events which occur in different subjectivities. I usually conclude—and witnesses after an objective consideration of our bodies-for-others conclude—that they are for all practical purposes "as fatigued as I am." How does it happen therefore that they suffer their fatigue differently? Someone will say that the difference stems from the fact that I am a "sissy" and that the others are not. But although this evaluation undeniably has a practical bearing on the case and although one could take this into account when there arose a question of deciding whether or not it would be a good idea to take me on another expedition, such an evaluation can not satisfy us here. We have seen that to be ambitious is to project conquering a throne or honors; it is not a *given* which would incite one to conquest; it is this conquest itself. Similarly to be a "sissy" can not be a factual given and is only a name given to the way in which I suffer my fatigue. If therefore I wish to understand under what conditions I can suffer a fatigue as unbearable, it will not help to address oneself to so-called factual givens, which are revealed as being only a choice; it is necessary to attempt to examine this choice itself and to see whether it is not explained within the perspective of a larger choice in which it would be integrated as a secondary structure. If I question one of my companions, he will explain to me that he is fatigued, of course, but that he *loves* his fatigue; he gives himself up to it as to a bath; it appears to him in some way as the privileged instrument for discovering the world which surrounds him, for adapting himself to the rocky roughness of the paths, for discovering the "mountainous" quality of the slopes. In the same way it is this light sunburn on the back of his neck and this slight ringing in his ears which will enable him to realize a direct contact with the sun. Finally the feeling of effort is for him that of fatigue overcome. But as his fatigue is nothing but the passion which he endures so that the dust of the highways, the burning of the sun, the roughness of the roads may exist to the fullest, his effort (i.e., this sweet familiarity with a fatigue which he loves, to which he abandons himself and which nevertheless he himself directs) is given as a way of appropriating the mountain, of suffering it to the end and being victor over it. . . .

. . . for Freud the external circumstances and, so to speak, the *history* of the subject will decide whether this or that drive will be fixed on this or that object. It is the child's situation in the family which will determine in him the birth of the Oedipus complex; in other societies composed of families of another type (such as, for example, among primitive peoples on the Coral Islands in the Pacific) this complex could not be formed. Furthermore it is again external circumstances which will decide whether at the age of puberty this complex will be "resolved" or, on the contrary, will remain the pole of the sexual life. Consequently through the intermediacy of history Freud's vertical determinism remains axised on an horizontal determinism. To be sure, a particular symbolic act expresses an underlying, contemporaneous desire just as this desire manifests a more profound complex and all this within the unity of a single psychic process; but the complex nonetheless pre-exists its symbolic manifestation. It is the past which has constituted it such as it is and in accordance with the classic connections, transfer, condensation, etc., which we find mentioned not only in psychoanalysis but in all attempts at a deterministic reconstruction of the psychic life. Consequently the dimension of the future does not exist for psychoanalysis. . . .

. . . Actually we conceive of every act as a *comprehensible* phenomenon, and we do not admit any deterministic "chance" as Freud does. But instead of understanding the considered phenomenon in terms of the past, we conceive of the comprehensive act as a turning back of the future toward the present. The way in which I suffer my fatigue is in no way dependent on the chance difficulty of the slope which I am climbing or on the more or less restless night which I have spent; these factors can contribute to constituting my fatigue itself but not to the way in which I suffer it. . . .

Thus the fundamental act of freedom is discovered; and it is this which gives meaning to the particular action which I can be brought to consider. This constantly renewed act is not distinct from my being; it is a choice of myself in the world and by the same token it is a discovery of the world. This enables us to avoid the perilous reef of the unconscious which psychoanalysis meets at the start. If nothing is in consciousness which is not a consciousness of being, some will say to us by way of objection that then this fundamental choice must of necessity be a conscious choice. They will ask, "Can you maintain that when you yield to fatigue, you are conscious of all the implications which this fact supposes?" We shall reply that we are perfectly conscious of them. Only this consciousness itself must have for its limit the structure of consciousness in general and of the choice which we are making.

So far as the latter is concerned, we must insist on the fact that the question here is not of a deliberate choice. This is not because the choice is *less* conscious or *less* explicit than a deliberation but rather because it is the foundation of all deliberation and because as we have seen, a deliberation requires an interpretation in terms of an original choice. Therefore it is necessary to defend oneself against the illusion which would make of original freedom a *positing* of causes and motives as objects, then a decision from the standpoint of these causes and these motives. Quite the contrary, as soon as there are cause and motive (that is, an appreciation of things and of the structures of the world) there is already a positing of ends and consequently a choice. But this does not mean that the profound choice is thereby unconscious. It is simply one with the consciousness which we have of ourselves. This consciousness, as we know, can be only non-positional; it is we-as-consciousness since it is not distinct from our being. And as our being is precisely our original choice, the consciousness (of) the choice is identical with the self-consciousness which we have. One must be conscious in order to choose, and one must choose in order to be conscious. Choice and consciousness are one and the same thing.

· · ·

The essential consequence of our earlier remarks is that man being condemned to be free carries the weight of the whole world on his shoulders; he is responsible for the world and for himself as a way of being. We are taking the word "responsibility" in its ordinary sense as "consciousness (of) being the incontestable author of an event or of an object." In this sense the responsibility of the for-itself is overwhelming since he[1] is the one by whom it happens that *there is* a world; since he is also the one who makes himself be, then whatever may be the situation in which he finds himself, the for-itself must wholly assume this situation with its peculiar

---

[1] I am shifting to the personal pronoun here since Sartre is describing the for-itself in concrete personal terms rather than as a metaphysical entity. Strictly speaking, of course, this is his position throughout, and the French "il" is indifferently "he" or "it." Tr.

coefficient of adversity, even though it be insupportable. He must assume the situation with the proud consciousness of being the author of it, for the very worst disadvantages or the worst threats which can endanger my person have meaning only in and through my project; and it is on the ground of the engagement which I am that they appear. It is therefore senseless to think of complaining since nothing foreign has decided what we feel, what we live, or what we are.

Furthermore this absolute responsibility is not resignation; it is simply the logical requirement of the consequences of our freedom. What happens to me happens through me, and I can neither affect myself with it nor revolt against it nor resign myself to it. Moreover everything which happens to me is *mine*. By this we must understand first of all that I am always equal to what happens to me *qua* man, for what happens to a man through other men and through himself can be only human. The most terrible situations of war, the worst tortures do not create a non-human state of things; there is no non-human situation. It is only through fear, flight, and recourse to magical types of conduct that I shall decide on the non-human, but this decision is human, and I shall carry the entire responsibility for it. But in addition the situation is *mine* because it is the image of my free choice of myself, and everything which it presents to me is *mine* in that this represents me and symbolizes me. Is it not I who decide the coefficient of adversity in things and even their unpredictability by deciding myself?

Thus there are no *accidents* in a life; a community event which suddenly bursts forth and involves me in it does not come from the outside. If I am mobilized in a war, this war is *my* war; it is in my image and I deserve it. I deserve it first because I could always get out of it by suicide or by desertion; these ultimate possibles are those which must always be present for us when there is a question of envisaging a situation. For lack of getting out of it, I have *chosen* it. This can be due to inertia, to cowardice in the face of public opinion, or because I prefer certain other values to the value of the refusal to join in the war (the good opinion of my relatives, the honor of my family, etc.). Anyway you look at it, it is a matter of a choice. This choice will be repeated later on again and again without a break until the end of the war. Therefore we must agree with the statement by J. Romains, "In war there are no innocent victims."[2] If therefore I have preferred war to death or to dishonor, everything takes place as if I bore the entire responsibility for this war. Of course others have declared it, and one might be tempted perhaps to consider me as a simple accomplice. But this notion of complicity has only a juridical sense, and it does not hold here. For it depended on me that for me and by me this war should not exist, and I have decided that it does exist. There was no compulsion here, for the compulsion could have got no hold on a freedom. I did not have any excuse; for as we have said repeatedly in this book, the peculiar character of human-reality is that it is without excuse. Therefore it remains for me only to lay claim to this war.

But in addition the war is *mine* because by the sole fact that it arises in a situation which I cause to be and that I can discover it there only by engaging myself for or against it, I can no longer distinguish at present the choice which I make of myself from the choice which I make of the war. To live this war is to choose myself through it and to choose it through my choice of myself. There can be no question

---

[2] J. Romains: *Les hommes de bonne volonté;* "Prélude à Verdun."

of considering it as "fours years of vacation" or as a "reprieve," as a "recess," the essential part of my responsibilities being elsewhere in my married, family, or professional life. In this war which I have chosen I choose myself from day to day, and I make it mine by making myself. If it is going to be four empty years, then it is I who bear the responsibility for this.

Finally, as we pointed out earlier, each person is an absolute choice of self from the standpoint of a world of knowledges and of techniques which this choice both assumes and illumines; each person is an absolute upsurge at an absolute date and is perfectly unthinkable at another date. It is therefore a waste of time to ask what I should have been if this war had not broken out, for I have chosen myself as one of the possible meanings of the epoch which imperceptibly led to war. I am not distinct from this same epoch; I could not be transported to another epoch without contradiction. Thus *I am* this war which restricts and limits and makes comprehensible the period which preceded it. In this sense we may define more precisely the responsibility of the for-itself if to the earlier quoted statement, "There are no innocent victims," we add the words, "We have the war we deserve." Thus, totally free, undistinguishable from the period for which I have chosen to be the meaning, as profoundly responsible for the war as if I had myself declared it, unable to live without integrating it in *my* situation, engaging myself in it wholly and stamping it with my seal, I must be without remorse or regrets as I am without excuse; for from the instant of my upsurge into being, I carry the weight of the world by myself alone without anything or any person being able to lighten it.

Yet this responsibility is of a very particular type. Someone will say, "I did not ask to be born." This is a naive way of throwing greater emphasis on our facticity. I am responsible for everything, in fact, except for my very responsibility, for I am not the foundation of my being. Therefore everything takes place as if I were compelled to be responsible. I am *abandoned* in the world, not in the sense that I might remain abandoned and passive in a hostile universe like a board floating on the water, but rather in the sense that I find myself suddenly alone and without help, engaged in a world for which I bear the whole responsibility without being able, whatever I do, to tear myself away from this responsibility for an instant. For I am responsible for my very desire of fleeing responsibilities. To make myself passive in the world, to refuse to act upon things and upon Others is still to choose myself, and suicide is one mode among others of being-in-the-world. Yet I find an absolute responsibility for the fact that my facticity (here the fact of my birth) is directly inapprehensible and even inconceivable, for this fact of my birth never appears as a brute fact but always across a projective reconstruction of my for-itself. I am ashamed of being born or I am astonished at it or I rejoice over it, or in attempting to get rid of my life I affirm that I live and I assume this life as bad. Thus in a certain sense I choose being born. This choice itself is integrally affected with facticity since I am not able not to choose, but this facticity in turn will appear only in so far as I surpass it toward my ends. Thus facticity is everywhere but inapprehensible; I never encounter anything except my responsibility. That is why I can not ask, "*Why* was I born?" or curse the day of my birth or declare that I did not ask to be born, for these various attitudes toward my birth—i.e., toward the *fact* that I realize a presence in the world—are absolutely nothing else but ways of assuming this birth in full responsibility and of making it *mine*. Here again I encounter only myself and my projects so that my abandonment—i.e., my facticity—consists simply in the fact that I am condemned to be wholly responsible for myself. I am the being which *is* in such a way that in its being its being is in question. And this "is" of my being *is* as present and inapprehensible.

Under these conditions since every event in the world can be revealed to me only as an *opportunity* (an opportunity made use of, lacked, neglected, etc.), or better yet since everything which happens to us can be considered as a *chance* (*i.e.,* can appear to us only as a way of realizing this being which is in question in our being) and since others as transcendencies-transcended are themselves only *opportunities* and *chances,* the responsibility of the for-itself extends to the entire world as a peopled-world. It is precisely thus that the for-itself apprehends itself in anguish; that is, as a being which is neither the foundation of its own being nor of the Other's being nor of the in-itselfs which form the world, but a being which is compelled to decide the meaning of being—within it and everywhere outside of it. The one who realizes in anguish his condition as *being* thrown into a responsibility which extends to his very abandonment has no longer either remorse or regret or excuse; he is no longer anything but a freedom which perfectly reveals itself and whose being resides in this very revelation. But as we pointed out at the beginning of this work, most of the time we flee anguish in bad faith.

FURTHER READINGS

ANTHOLOGIES

Jones, W. T., Frederick Sontag, Morton O. Beckner, and Robert Fogelin, Eds., *Approaches to Ethics*, New York, McGraw-Hill, 1962.

Melden, A. I., Ed., *Ethical Theories,* 2nd ed. rev., Englewood Cliffs, N. J., Prentice-Hall, 1967.

Sellers, Wilfrid, and John Hospers Eds., *Readings in Ethical Theory,* 2nd ed., New York, Appleton-Century-Crofts, 1970.

Thomson, Judith Jarvis, and Gerald Dworkin, Eds., *Ethics,* New York, Harper & Row, 1968.

HUMAN DIGNITY

Aristotle, *Nicomachean Ethics,* John Warrington, Ed. and Trans., New York, Dutton, 1963.

Barnes, Hazel, *An Existentialist Ethics,* New York, Knopf, 1967.

Camus, Albert, *The Myth of Sisyphus,* New York, Random House, 1955.

de Beauvoir, Simone, *The Ethics of Ambiguity,* New York, Philosophical Library, 1948; Citadel Books, 1964.

Ewing, A. C., *Ethics,* New York, Collier, 1962.

Frankena, W. D., *Ethics,* Englewood Cliffs, N. J., Prentice-Hall, 1963.

Hospers, John, *Human Conduct,* New York, Harcourt, Brace & World, 1961.

Mill, John Stuart, *Utilitarianism,* Indianapolis, Ind., Liberal Arts, 1957.

Nietzsche, Friedrich, *Beyond Good and Evil,* Helen Zimmern, Trans., London, Allen & Unwin, 1924.

Nowell-Smith, P. H., *Ethics,* Harmondsworth, Eng., Penguin, 1961.

Plato, *Euthyphro* and *The Republic* in *The Collected Dialogues of Plato,* Edith Hamilton and Huntington Cairns, Eds., New York, Bollingen Foundation, 1961.

Ross, W. D., *The Right and the Good,* Oxford, Clarendon, 1961.

Schaff, Adam, *A Philosophy of Man,* New York, Monthly Review Press, 1963.

Singer, Marcus G., *Generalization in Ethics,* New York, Knopf, 1961.

Spinoza, Benedict, *Ethics,* New York, Dutton, 1963.

Warnock, Mary, *Existentialist Ethics,* New York, St. Martin's, 1967.

THE CRISIS IN HUMAN VALUES

Arendt, Hannah, *Eichmann in Jerusalem,* rev. enl. ed., New York, Viking, 1964.

Baie, Kurt, and Nicolas Rescher, Eds., *Values and the Future,* New York, Free Press, 1969.

Bell, Daniel, *Toward the Year 2000,* Boston, Houghton Mifflin, 1968.

Cleaver, Eldridge, *Soul on Ice,* New York, McGraw-Hill, 1968; New York, Delta, 1968.

Crosson, Frederick, and Kenneth M. Sayre, Eds., *The Social Impact of Cybernetics,* Notre Dame, Ind., University Press, 1966; New York, Clarion, 1967.

de Beauvoir, Simone, *The Second Sex,* New York, Knopf, 1953; New York, Bantam, 1961.

DeGeorge, Richard T., Ed., *Ethics and Society,* Garden City, N. Y., Anchor, 1966.

Erikson, Erik, *Identity, Youth, and Crisis,* New York, Norton, 1968.

Fanon, Frantz, *Black Skin, White Masks,* Charles Lam Markmann, Trans., New York, Grove Press, 1967.

Franklin, John Hope, Ed., *The Negro in Twentieth Century America,* New York, Vintage, 1967.

Girvetz, Harry K., Ed., *Contemporary Moral Issues,* 2nd ed., Belmont, Calif., Wadsworth, 1968.

Marcel, Gabriel, *Man Against Mass Society,* G. S. Frazer, Trans., Chicago, Regnery, 1952; Chicago, Gateway, 1962.

Marcuse, Herbert, *One Dimensional Man,* Boston, Beacon, 1964.

Russell, Bertrand, *Authority and the Individual,* London, Allen & Unwin, 1966.

——, *Human Society in Ethics and Politics,* New York, New American Library, 1962.

——, *Marriage and Morals,* New York, Liveright, 1957.

Westin, Alan F., *Privacy and Freedom,* New York, Atheneum, 1968.

Wiener, Norbert, *God and Golem,* Cambridge, Mass., Massachusetts Institute of Technology Press, 1964.

——, *The Human Use of Human Beings,* 2nd ed. rev., Garden City, N. Y., Doubleday, 1954.

FREEDOM

Anthologies

Berofsky, Bernard, Ed., *Free Will and Determinism,* New York, Harper & Row, 1966.

Enteman, Willard, Ed., *The Problem of Free Will,* New York, Scribner, 1967.

Morgenbesser, Sidney, and James J. Walsh, Eds., *Free Will*, Englewood Cliffs, N. J., Prentice-Hall, 1962.

Morris, Herbert, Ed., *Freedom and Responsibility*, Stanford, Calif., Stanford University Press, 1961.

Pears, D. F., Ed., *Freedom and the Will*, New York, St. Martin's, 1963.

Articles and Books

Aristotle, *Nicomachean Ethics*, H. Rackham, Trans., Cambridge, Mass., Harvard, 1926, book III.

Campbell, C. A., "Is Free-Will a Pseudo-Problem?" *Mind*, 60 (1951); also in Berofsky, Morris.

Hampshire, Stuart, *Freedom of the Individual*, New York, Harper & Row, 1965.

James, William, "The Dilemma of Determinism," in *The Will to Believe and Other Essays*, New York, Longmans, Green, 1931.

MacIntyre, Alisdair, *The Unconscious*, London, Routledge & Kegan Paul, 1958.

Melden, A. I., *Free Action*, London, Routledge & Kegan Paul, 1961.

Peters, R. S., *The Concept of Motivation*, London, Routledge & Kegan Paul, 1958.

Schlick, Moritz, *Problems of Ethics*, David Rynin, Trans., Englewood Cliffs, N.J., Prentice-Hall, 1939, chapter 10.

Taylor, Richard, "I Can," *Philosophical Review*, 79 (1960), 78–89; also in Morgenbesser and Walsh.

Section II

POLITICAL

ACTION

Whether man is an inherently vicious creature or whether he possesses a sublime spirit is a question of renewed concern to all who contemplate the world's seemingly endless involvement in local or global wars. Nor does the behavior of man in apparently peaceful societies offer reassurance that he has a spirit in any sense sublime, that he can live peacefully with his fellows. Violence has played a relentless and ever more important role in Western civilization, and particularly in urban civilization.

With the increase in social unrest come increasing demands for the destruction, or at least the "restructuring," of such hallowed institutions as the civil government and the university. Ought such restructuring to occur? If it does occur, should it take the form of revolution? Should institutions be changed by violent means? These are not merely theoretical questions. They are asked and often affirmatively answered, with appeals to violence, by members of racial minorities, by citizens of colonized countries, and by university students.

When these demands are made, some defenders of the institutions under attack rise to argue for the authority of the institution over its members and for its right to impose discipline. More than three hundred years ago Thomas Hobbes defended the authority of a strong and unpermissive government in "Human Aggression and the State." The arguments Hobbes presented are now the subject of intense debate, with positions such as his defended by political conservatives as often as they are attacked by revolutionaries. Thus what Hobbes has to say about the pervasiveness of human aggression and the unjustifiability of revolution remains a timely introduction to the other discussions of revolution and violence in this section.

According to Hobbes, all men are inherently aggressive; and if they were to live ungoverned in a state of nature, they would constantly wage war on one another. To preserve their lives, men banded together to form a social contract in which they relinquished their right to kill one another to a sovereign who, in turn, guaranteed their safety. For this protection, they yielded almost all their individual liberties to the absolute power of the sovereign, but the alternative was to continue living in constant danger of the violence of other men. Hobbes asserts that since the sovereign acquired the power his citizens once used violently against one another, the sovereign's right to rule derives, once again, from his citizen's fear of reprisal against rebellion. And since the sovereign's only obligation to his citizens is to preserve their lives, the only grievance for which he can be justly deposed is his weakness against the aggression of an alien state. Thus, Hobbes asserts, the citizens owe their government absolute loyalty in all matters save their own life and death; for the government alone curbs their destructive impulses and preserves their lives.

Hobbes' assessment of human nature is gloomy indeed, but there is no little evidence to support him. His defenses of governmental authority over the activities of its citizens and governmental force against the aggression of foreign states are strikingly reminiscent of contemporary defenses of strong intelligence and military establishments. Hobbes offers us a shrewd analysis of the inextricable involvement of the right of the government to rule, and the needs and nature of the people that the government undertakes to rule. It is not surprising that the advocates of the kind of drastic political change that Hobbes opposed still have to face squarely the questions of the nature of man and of the authority of the government placed over him.

Nevertheless, citizens still rise up and call for the deposition of civil governments —for revolution. Whether, and how, revolution can be justified, is discussed by the three authors in the subsection that bears that title.

In "Revolution and the General Will" Jean-Jacques Rousseau contends that citizens call for revolution when government has violated the very qualities which make them free men. Human beings are not inherently aggressive, Rousseau contends; they are inherently peaceful and would live most happily could they remain ungoverned. It is only because it becomes inconvenient for a large group of men to make their separate voices heard that they band together and execute a social contract. This contract gives the government they participate in the right to speak for them in matters of common interest. But, Rousseau asserts, should such a government infringe on its own citizens' creative capacities—should it, for example, restrict their right to move peacefully and to organize their lives as they see fit— then such a government has placed its citizens "in chains." Rousseau regards it as a scandal that so many governments, by ignoring the will of their individual citizens, have exceeded what he considers their rightful authority; such governments long ceased to be convenient and should be abolished, he argues.

If governments can overstep their authority, as Rousseau argues, then it becomes necessary to ask how actions against such governments can be justified. Different answers are given by Herbert Marcuse and Albert Camus in their attempts to delineate the relationship between a citizen and his government.

In "Ethics and Revolution" Marcuse argues that violent revolution is justified when a government fails to meet the needs of its people. Individual ethical standards may then be suspended, and even individual suffering may be condoned, if the ultimate end of restructuring the government is at stake.

Camus offers another interpretation of revolution in "The Rebel." Revolution, he argues, is initiated as an individual act. Opposition not only to governmental authority but also to any threat to human solidarity then impels the rebel to assert "I rebel, therefore we exist." Revolutionary change of all kinds, Camus suggests, confirms human existence.

If either the structure of the government or the details of government policy are to be changed, how will the change be brought about? This question is considered in detail in the subsection "Violence."

Marcuse, as we have just seen, advocates the use of violence when no other method would effect changes in an unacceptable government. But this position, which implies approval of violent political action, is not universally held even by other advocates of violence. For example Friedrich Engels, who wrote several works with Karl Marx and who offers an authoritative summary of Marx's position, argues in "Theory of Force" that violence is merely a concomitant to the economic clashes which Marx believed would destroy class distinctions. For Marx and Engels, violence is incidental to the process of political change. It is not condemned, but neither is it glorified—a point on which many contemporary leftists who label themselves "Marxist" evidently disagree.

The question of violent action takes on a spiritual intensity in Frantz Fanon's "Concerning Violence," the first chapter of his widely read *The Wretched of the Earth.* Fanon was a black psychiatrist who bitterly opposed the often brutal French colonial regime in Algeria. Fanon views violent action as a means by which the colonized people might purge themselves of the cowed and degraded role their oppressors had imposed upon them. Thus for Fanon violence is at once a mode of political action and a means by which an oppressed people may recover their self-respect.

Fanon has been read by both student rebels and by black militants, who use his arguments to characterize themselves as "the wretched of the earth." Certainly, students were not oppressed by violence as African natives or American slaves were. But is the only recourse available to people who feel themselves oppressed, whatever they identify as the source of oppression, violent action? Barbara Deming, who herself has served jail sentences for nonviolent civil rights activity, argues in "Revolution and Equilibrium" that this is not the case. She suggests that the phrase "radical and uncompromising action" can be substituted in most of the passages in which Fanon advocates "violent action"; she argues that, in any case, a nonviolent, though radical and uncompromising, action can alter the policies of institutions which abridge human dignity.

It may come as a surprise that something other than violent action may be presented as "radical and uncompromising," but Deming's case can be made even stronger. Much as Fanon argued for a violent answer to the spiritual degradation of oppressed Algerian natives, Mohandas K. Gandhi argues in "Truth-Force (*Satyagraha*)" for a nonviolent answer to the oppression of Indian minorities in South Africa or of the untouchables in India. According to Gandhi, a nonviolent campaign requires a commitment and preparation which is almost religious, as suggested by the very name, *satyagraha* or *truth-force,* coined to distinguish it from other forms of passive resistance. As explained by both Gandhi and by Joan V. Bondurant in "Gandhi's Conquest of Violence," the kind of nonviolent action which Gandhi devoted his life to developing was an attempt to help the oppressed so to purify their own spirits that they might bring their opponents to recognize the moral superiority, or the truth, of their demands. Significantly, as both Gandhi and Bondurant explain, nonviolence is a method chosen by brave men who could have chosen violence, but who adopt nonviolence as a mode of action that brings them closer to the truth.

Finally, in "War and Nonresistance," an article originally written to oppose British involvement in World War I, but which has taken on renewed timeliness in the Vietnam War, Bertrand Russell argues that nations as well as individuals ought to abandon violence as a method of implementing what has been called elsewhere the "territorial imperative." Russell insists that war would cease if nations would cease to regard their boundaries as representative of national pride or patriotism. He adds that no patriotic appeal justifies the sacrifice of individual lives.

The questions considered in this section—the bases of governmental authority, of governmental policy, and of individual opposition to such authority or policy— directly apply to such contemporary events as student revolt, the Black Power movement, and opposition to or support for the Vietnam war. Inevitably, the questions of revolution and violence as modes of political action affect us all.

THOMAS HOBBES

Human Aggression and the State

Thomas Hobbes (1588–1679), English political theorist, made contributions also to philosophical psychology and the philosophy of language. His other major work is *De Cive.*

. . . in the nature of men, we find three principal causes of quarrel. First, competition; second, diffidence; thirdly, glory.

The first, maketh men invade for gain; the second, for safety; and the third,

From *The Leviathan,* by Thomas Hobbes, 1651.

for reputation. The first use violence to make themselves masters of other men's persons, wives, children, and cattle; the second, to defend them; the third, for trifles, as a word, a smile, a different opinion, and any other sign of undervalue, either direct in their persons, or by reflection in their kindred, their friends, their nation, their profession, or their name.

Hereby it is manifest, that during the time men live without a common power to keep them all in awe, they are in that condition which is called war; and such a war, as is of every man, against every man. For WAR, consisteth not in battle only, or the act of fighting; but in a tract of time, wherein the will to contend by battle is sufficiently known; and therefore the notion of *time* is to be considered in the nature of war, as it is in the nature of weather. For as the nature of foul weather lieth not in a shower or two of rain, but in an inclination thereto of many days together; so the nature of war consisteth not in actual fighting, but in the known disposition thereto, during all the time there is no assurance to the contrary. All other time is PEACE.

Whatsoever therefore is consequent to a time of war, where every man is enemy to every man, the same is consequent to the time, wherein men live without other security than what their own strength and their own invention shall furnish them withal. In such condition, there is no place for industry, because the fruit thereof is uncertain: and consequently no culture of the earth; no navigation, nor use of the commodities that may be imported by sea; no commodious building; no instruments of moving, and removing, such things as require much force; no knowledge of the face of the earth; no account of time; no arts; no letters; no society; and which is worst of all, continual fear, and danger of violent death; and the life of man, solitary, poor, nasty, brutish, and short.

It may seem strange to some man that has not well weighed these things, that nature should thus dissociate, and render men apt to invade and destroy one another; and he may, therefore, not trusting to this inference, made from the passions, desire perhaps to have the same confirmed by experience. Let him therefore consider with himself, when taking a journey, he arms himself, and seeks to go well accompanied; when going to sleep, he locks his doors; when even in his house he locks his chests; and this when he knows there be laws, and public officers, armed, to revenge all injuries shall be done him; what opinion he has of his fellow subjects, when he rides armed; of his fellow citizens, when he locks his doors; and of his children, and servants, when he locks his chests. Does he not there as much accuse mankind by his actions, as I do by my words? But neither of us accuse man's nature in it. The desires and other passions of man are in themselves no sin. No more are the actions that proceed from those passions, till they know a law that forbids them: which till laws be made they cannot know: nor can any law be made, till they have agreed upon the person that shall make it.

It may peradventure be thought there was never such a time nor condition of war as this; and I believe it was never generally so, over all the world: but there are many places where they live so now. For the savage people in many places of America, except the government of small families, the concord whereof dependeth on natural lust, have no government at all; and live at this day in that brutish manner as I said before. Howsoever, it may be perceived what manner of life there would be, where there were no common power to fear, by the manner of life, which men that have formerly lived under a peaceful government, use to degenerate into, in a civil war.

But though there had never been any time, wherein particular men were in a condition of war one against another; yet in all times, kings and persons of sovereign authority, because of their independency, are in continual jealousies, and in the state and posture of gladiators; having their weapons pointing, and their eyes fixed on one another; that is, their forts, garrisons, and guns upon the frontiers of their kingdoms; and continual spies upon their neighbors; which is a posture of war. But because they uphold thereby the industry of their subjects, there does not follow from it, that misery, which accompanies the liberty of particular men.

To this war of every man against every man, this also is consequent, that nothing can be unjust. The notions of right and wrong, justice and injustice have there no place. Where there is no common power, there is no law: where no law, no injustice. Force, and fraud, are in war the two cardinal virtues. Justice, and injustice are none of the faculties neither of the body, nor mind. If they were, they might be in a man that were alone in the world, as well as his senses, and passions. They are qualities that relate to men in society, not in solitude. It is consequent also to the same condition, that there be no propriety, no dominion no *mine* and *thine* distinct; but only that to be every man's that he can get, and for so long as he can keep it. And thus much for the ill condition, which man by mere nature is actually placed in; though with a possibility to come out of it, consisting partly in the passions, partly in his reason.

The passions that incline men to peace are fear of death, desire of such things as are necessary to commodious living, and a hope by their industry to obtain them. And reason suggesteth convenient articles of peace, upon which men may be drawn to agreement.

. . .

The final cause, end, or design of men, who naturally love liberty, and dominion over others, in the introduction of that restraint upon themselves, in which we see them live in commonwealths, is the foresight of their own preservation, and of a more contented life thereby; that is to say, of getting themselves out from that miserable condition of war, which is necessarily consequent . . . to the natural passions of men, when there is no visible power to keep them in awe, and tie them by fear of punishment to the performance of their covenants, and observation of those laws of nature set down.

. . .

It is true, that certain living creatures, as bees, and ants, live sociably one with another, which are therefore by Aristotle numbered amongst political creatures; and yet have no other direction, than their particular judgments and appetites; nor speech, whereby one of them can signify to another what he thinks expedient for the common benefit; and, therefore, some man may perhaps desire to know why mankind cannot do the same. To which I answer:

First, that men are continually in competition for honor and dignity, which these creatures are not; and consequently amongst men there ariseth on that ground envy and hatred, and finally war; but amongst these not so.

Secondly, that amongst these creatures, the common good differeth not from the private; and being by nature inclined to their private, they procure thereby the common benefit. But man, whose joy consisteth in comparing himself with other men, can relish nothing but what is eminent.

Thirdly, that these creatures, having not, as man, the use of reason, do not see, nor think they see any fault in the administration of their common business; whereas amongst men, there are very many that think themselves wiser, and able to govern the public better than the rest; and these strive to reform and innovate, one this way, another that way; and thereby bring it into distraction and civil war.

Fourthly, that these creatures, though they have some use of voice in making known to one another their desires, and other affections; yet they want that art of words, by which some men can represent to others that which is good, in the likeness of evil; and evil, in the likeness of good; and augment, or diminish the apparent greatness of good and evil; discontenting men, and troubling their peace at their pleasure.

Fifthly, irrational creatures cannot distinguish between *injury* and *damage;* and, therefore, as long as they be at ease, they are not offended with their fellows, whereas man is then most troublesome, when he is most at ease: for then it is that he loves to show his wisdom, and control the actions of them that govern the commonwealth.

Lastly, the agreement of these creatures is natural; that of men is by covenant only, which is artificial: and, therefore, it is no wonder if there be somewhat else required, besides covenant, to make their agreement constant and lasting; which is a common power, to keep them in awe and to direct their actions to the common benefit.

The only way to erect such a common power, as may be able to defend them from the invasion of foreigners, and the injuries of one another, and thereby to secure them in such sort, as that by their own industry, and by the fruits of the earth, they may nourish themselves and live contentedly is to confer all their power and strength upon one man, or upon one assembly of men, that may reduce all their wills, by plurality of voices, unto one will: which is as much as to say, to appoint one man, or assembly of men, to bear their person; and every one to own, and acknowledge himself to be author of whatsoever he that so beareth their person, shall act, or cause to be acted, in those things which concern the common peace and safety; and therein to submit their wills, every one to his will, and their judgments, to his judgment. This is more than consent, or concord; it is a real unity of them all, in one and the same person, made by covenant of every man with every man, in such manner, as if every man should say to every man, *I authorize and give up my right of governing myself, to this man, or to this assembly of men, on this condition, that thou give up thy right to him, and authorize all his actions in like manner.* This done, the multitude so united in one person, is called a COMMONWEALTH, in Latin CIVITAS. This is the generation of that great LEVIATHAN, or rather, to speak more reverently, of that *mortal god*, to which we owe under the *immortal God*, our peace and defense. For by this authority, given him by every particular man in the commonwealth, he hath the use of so much power and strength conferred on him, that by terror thereof, he is enabled to perform the wills of them all, to peace at home, and mutual aid against their enemies abroad. And in him consisteth the essence of the commonwealth; which, to define it, is *one person, of whose acts as a great multitude, by mutual covenants one with another, have made themselves*

every one the author, to the end he may use the strength and means of them all,
as he shall think expedient, for their peace and common defense.

And he that carrieth this person, is called SOVEREIGN, and said to have *sovereign*
power; and every one besides, his SUBJECT.

The attaining to this sovereign power is by two ways. One, by natural force;
as when a man maketh his children, to submit themselves, and their children, to
his government, as being able to destroy them if they refuse; or by war subdueth
his enemies to his will, giving them their lives on that condition. The other, is when
men agree amongst themselves to submit to some men, or assembly of men, voluntarily, on confidence to be protected by him against all others. This latter may be
called a political commonwealth, or commonwealth by *institution;* and the former,
a commonwealth by *acquisition.*

. . .

But as men, for the attaining of peace, and conservation of themselves thereby,
have made an artificial man, which we call a commonwealth; so also have they
made artificial chains, called *civil laws,* which they themselves, by mutual covenants,
have fastened at one end, to the lips of that man, or assembly, to whom they have
given the sovereign power; and at the other end to their own ears. These bonds in
their own nature but weak, may nevertheless be made to hold, by the danger, though
not by the difficulty of breaking them.

In relation to these bonds only it is, that I am to speak now, of the *liberty* of
subjects. For seeing there is no commonwealth in the *world,* wherein there be rules
enough set down, for the regulating of all the actions and words of men; as being
a thing impossible: it followeth necessarily, that in all kinds of actions by the laws
praetermitted, men have the liberty of doing what their own reasons shall suggest,
for the most profitable to themselves. For if we take liberty in the proper sense, for
corporal liberty; that is to say, freedom from chains and prison, it were very absurd
for men to clamor as they do for the liberty they so manifestly enjoy. Again, if we
take liberty for an exemption from laws, it is no less absurd for men to demand as
they do, that liberty by which all other men may be masters of their lives. And yet,
as absurd as it is, this is it they demand; not knowing that the laws are of no power
to protect them, without a sword in the hands of a man, or men, to cause those laws
to be put in execution. The liberty of a subject lieth therefore only in those things,
which in regulating their actions, the sovereign hath praetermitted: such as is the
liberty to buy, and sell, and otherwise contract with one another; to choose their
own abode, their own diet, their own trade of life, and institute their children as
they themselves think; and the like.

Nevertheless we are not to understand that by such liberty the sovereign power
of life and death is either abolished, or limited. For it has been already shown that
nothing the sovereign representative can do to a subject, on what pretense soever,
can properly be called injustice, or injury; because every subject is author of every
act the sovereign doth; so that he never wanteth right to anything, otherwise, than
as he himself is the subject of God, and bound thereby to observe the laws of nature.
And therefore it may, and doth often happen in commonwealths, that a subject may
be put to death by the command of the sovereign power; and yet neither do the
other wrong; as when Jephtha caused his daughter to be sacrificed: in which, and
the like cases, he that so dieth, had liberty to do the action, for which he is never-

theless, without injury put to death. And the same holdeth also in a sovereign prince, that putteth to death an innocent subject. For though the action be against the law of nature, as being contrary to equity, as was the killing of Uriah, by David; yet it was not an injury to Uriah, but to God. Not to Uriah, because the right to do what he pleased was given him by Uriah himself: and yet to God, because David was God's subject, and prohibited all iniquity by the law of nature: which distinction, David himself, when he repented the fact, evidently confirmed, saying, *To thee only have I sinned*. In the same manner, the people of Athens, when they banished the most potent of their commonwealth for ten years, thought they committed no injustice; and yet they never questioned what crime he had done; but what hurt he would do: nay they commanded the banishment of they knew not whom; and every citizen bringing his oystershell into the market place, written with the name of him he desired should be banished, without actually accusing him, sometimes banished an Aristides, for his reputation of justice; and sometimes a scurrilous jester, as Hyperbolus, to make a jest of it. And yet a man cannot say the sovereign people of Athens wanted right to banish them; or an Athenian the liberty to jest, or to be just.

The liberty, whereof there is so frequent and honorable mention, in the histories, and philosophy of the ancient Greeks, and Romans, and in the writings, and discourse of those that from them have received all their learning in the politics, is not the liberty of particular men; but the liberty of the commonwealth: which is the same with that which every man then should have, if there were no civil laws, nor commonwealth at all. And the effects of it also be the same. For as amongst masterless men, there is perpetual war, of every man against his neighbor; no inheritance, to transmit to the son, nor to expect from the father; no propriety of goods, or lands; no security; but a full and absolute liberty in every particular man; so in states and commonwealths not dependent on one another, every commonwealth, not every man, has an absolute liberty to do what it shall judge, that is to say, what that man, or assembly that representeth it, shall judge most conducing to their benefit. But withal, they live in the condition of a perpetual war, and upon the confines of battle, with their frontiers armed, and cannons planted against their neighbors round about. The Athenians, and Romans were free; that is, free commonwealths: not that any particular men had the liberty to resist their own representative; but that their representative had the liberty to resist or invade other people. There is written on the turrets of the city of Lucca in great characters at this day the word LIBERTAS; yet no man can thence infer that a particular man has more liberty, or immunity from the service of the commonwealth there, than in Constantinople. Whether a commonwealth be monarchical, or popular, the freedom is still the same.

But it is an easy thing for men to be deceived, by the specious name of liberty; and for want of judgment to distinguish, mistake that for their private inheritance, and birthright, which is the right of the public only. And when the same error is confirmed by the authority of men in reputation for their writings on this subject, it is no wonder if it produce sedition, and change of government. In these western parts of the world, we are made to receive our opinions concerning the institution, and rights of commonwealths, from Aristotle, Cicero, and other men, Greeks and Romans, that living under popular states, derived those rights, not from the principles of nature, but transcribed them into their books, out of the practice of their own commonwealths, which were popular; as the grammarians describe the rules of language, out of the practice of the time; or the rules of poetry, out of the poems of Homer and Virgil. And because the Athenians were taught to keep them from desire of changing their government, that they were freemen, and all that lived under monarchy were slaves; therefore Aristotle puts it down in his *Politics*, (*lib. 6 cap. 2.*) *In democracy,* LIBERTY *is to be supposed: for it is commonly held that no man is* FREE *in any other government.* And as Aristotle, so Cicero and other writers have grounded their civil doctrine on the opinions of the Romans, who were taught to hate monarchy, at first, by them that having deposed their sovereign, shared amongst them the sovereignty of Rome; and afterwards by their successors. And by reading of these Greek and Latin authors, men from their childhood have gotten a habit, under a false show of liberty, of favoring tumults, and of licentious controlling the actions of their sovereigns, and again of controlling those controllers; with the effusion of so much blood, as I think I may truly say, there was never anything so dearly bought, as these western parts have bought the learning of the Greek and Latin tongues.

To come now to the particulars of the true liberty of a subject; that is to say, what are the things, which though commanded by the sovereign, he may nevertheless, without injustice, refuse to do; we are to consider, what rights we pass away, when we make a commonwealth; or, which is all one, what liberty we deny ourselves, by owning all the actions, without exception, of the man, or assembly, we make our sovereign. For in the act of our *submission* consisteth both our *obligation* and our *liberty;* which must therefore be inferred by arguments taken from thence; there being no obligation on any man, which ariseth not from some act of his own; for all men equally, are by nature free. And because such arguments, must either be drawn from the express words, *I authorize all his actions,* or from the intention of him that submitteth himself to his power, which intention is to be understood by the end for which he so submitteth; the obligation, and liberty of the subject, is to be derived, either from those words, or others equivalent; or else from the end of the institution of sovereignty, namely, the peace of the subjects within themselves, and their defense against a common enemy.

First, therefore, seeing sovereignty by institution is by covenant of every one to every one; and sovereignty by acquisition, by covenants of the vanquished to the victor, or child to the parent; it is manifest, that every subject has liberty in all those things, the right whereof cannot by covenant be transferred. . . . Covenants, not to defend a man's own body, are void. Therefore:

If the sovereign command a man, though justly condemned, to kill, wound, or maim himself; or not to resist those that assault him; or to abstain from the use of food, air, medicine, or any other thing, without which he cannot live; yet hath that man the liberty to disobey.

If a man be interrogated by the sovereign, or his authority, concerning a crime done by himself, he is not bound, without assurance of pardon, to confess it; because no man . . . can be obliged by covenant to accuse himself.

Again, the consent of a subject to sovereign power is contained in these words, *I authorize, or take upon me, all his actions;* in which there is no restriction at all of his own former natural liberty: for by allowing him to *kill me,* I am not bound to kill myself when he commands me. It is one thing to say, *kill me, or my fellow, if you please;* another thing to say, *I will kill myself, or my fellow.* It followeth therefore, that

No man is bound by the words themselves, either to kill himself, or any other man; and consequently, that the obligation a man may sometimes have, upon the command of the sovereign to execute any dangerous, or dishonorable office, dependeth not on the words of our submission; but on the intention, which is to be understood by the end thereof. When therefore our refusal to obey frustrates the end for which the sovereignty was ordained, then there is no liberty to refuse: otherwise there is.

Upon his ground, a man that is commanded as a soldier to fight against the enemy, though his sovereign have right enough to punish his refusal with death, may nevertheless in many cases refuse, without injustice, as when he substituteth a sufficient soldier in his place: for in this case he deserteth not the service of the commonwealth. And there is allowance to be made for natural timorousness; not only to women, of whom no such dangerous duty is expected, but also to men of feminine courage. When armies fight, there is on one side, or both, a running away; yet when they do it not out of treachery, but fear, they are not esteemed to do it unjustly, but dishonorably. For the same reason, to avoid battle is not injustice, but cowardice. But he that inrolleth himself a soldier, or taketh imprest money, taketh away the excuse of a timorous nature; and is obliged, not only to go to the battle, but also not to run from it, without his captain's leave. And when the defense of the commonwealth requireth at once the help of all that are able to bear arms, everyone is obliged; because otherwise the institution of the commonwealth, which they have not the purpose, or courage to preserve, was in vain.

To resist the sword of the commonwealth, in defense of another man, guilty or innocent, no man hath liberty; because such liberty takes away from the sovereign the means of protecting us and is therefore destructive of the very essence of government. But in case a great many men together have already resisted the sovereign power unjustly, or committed some capital crime, for which every one of them expecteth death, whether have they not the liberty then to join together, and assist, and defend one another? Certainly they have: for they but defend their lives, which the guilty man may as well do as the innocent. There was indeed injustice in the first breach of their duty; their bearing of arms subsequent to it, though it be to maintain what they have done, is no new unjust act. And if it be only to defend their persons, it is not unjust at all. But the offer of pardon taketh from them, to whom it is offered, the plea of self-defense, and maketh their perseverance in assisting, or defending, the rest, unlawful.

As for other liberties, they depend on the silence of the law. In cases where the sovereign has prescribed no rule, there the subject hath the liberty to do, or forbear, according to his own discretion. And therefore such liberty is in some places more, and in some less; and in some times more, in other times less, according as they that have the sovereignty shall think most convenient. As for example, there was a time, when in England a man might enter into his own land, and dispossess such as wrongfully possessed it, by force. But in after times, that liberty of forcible entry was taken away by a statute made, by the king, in parliament. And in some places of the world, men have the liberty of many wives; in other places, such liberty is not allowed.

If a subject have a controversy with his sovereign of debt, or of right of possession of lands or goods, or concerning any service required at his hands, or concerning any penalty, corporal, or pecuniary, grounded on a precedent law; he hath the same liberty to sue for his right, as if it were against a subject; and before such judges, as are appointed by the sovereign. For seeing the sovereign demandeth by force of a former law, and not by virtue of his power, he declareth thereby, that he requireth no more than shall appear to be due by that law. The suit therefore is not contrary to the will of the sovereign, and consequently the subject hath the liberty to demand the hearing of his cause; and sentence, according to that law. But if he demand, or take anything by pretense of his power; there lieth, in that case, no action of law; for all that is done by him in virtue of his power, is done by the authority of every subject, and consequently he that brings an action against the sovereign, brings it against himself.

If a monarch, or sovereign assembly, grant a liberty to all, or any of his subjects, which grant standing, he is disabled to provide for their safety, the grant is void; unless he directly renounce, or transfer the sovereignty to another. For in that he might openly, if it had been his will, and in plain terms, have renounced, or transferred it, and did not; it is to be understood it was not his will, but that the grant proceeded from ignorance of the repugnancy between such a liberty and the sovereign power; and therefore the sovereignty is still retained; and consequently all those powers, which are necessary to the exercising thereof; such as are the power of war and peace, of judicature, of appointing officers and councillors, of levying money, and the rest. . . .

The obligation of subjects to the sovereign is understood to last as long, and no longer, than the power lasteth, by which he is able to protect them. For the right men have by nature to protect themselves, when none else can protect them, can by no covenant be relinquished. The sovereignty is the soul of the commonwealth; which once departed from the body, the members do no more receive their motion from it. The end of obedience is protection; which, wheresoever a man seeth it, either in his own, or in another's sword, nature applieth his obedience to it, and his endeavor to maintain it. And though sovereignty, in the intention of them that make it, be immortal; yet it is in its own nature, not only subject to violent death, by foreign war; but also through the ignorance and passions of men, it hath in it, from the very institution, many seeds of a natural mortality, by intestine discord.

. . .

The law of nature, and the civil law, contain each other, and are of equal extent. For the laws of nature, which consist in equity, justice, gratitude, and other moral virtues on these depending, in the condition of mere nature . . . are not properly laws, but qualities that dispose men to peace, and to obedience. When a commonwealth is once settled, then are they actually laws, and not before; as being then the commands of the commonwealth; and therefore also civil laws: for it is the sovereign power that obliges men to obey them. For in the differences of private men, to declare what is equity, what is justice, and what is moral virtue, and to make them binding, there is need of the ordinances of sovereign power, and punishments to be ordained for such as shall break them; which ordinances are therefore part of the civil law. The law of nature, therefore, is a part of the civil law in all commonwealths of the world. Reciprocally also, the civil law is a part of the dictates of nature. For justice, that is to say, performance of covenant, and giving to every man his own, is a dictate of the law of nature. But every subject in a commonwealth hath covenanted to obey the civil law, (either one with another, as when they assemble to make a common representative, or with the representative itself one by one, when subdued by the sword they promise obedience, that they may receive life). And therefore obedience to the civil law is part also of the law of nature. Civil and natural law are not different kinds, but different parts of law; whereof one part being written, is called civil, the other unwritten, natural. But the right of nature, that is, the natural liberty of man, may by the civil law be abridged, and restrained: nay, the end of making laws, is no other, but such restraint; without the which there cannot possibly be any peace. And law was brought into the world for nothing else, but to limit the natural liberty of particular men, in such manner, as they might not hurt, but assist one another, and join together against a common enemy.

Revolution

JEAN-JACQUES ROUSSEAU

Revolution and the General Will

Jean-Jacques Rousseau (1712–1788) still
influences political and educational theory.
Among his other works is *Émile*.

Man is born free, and yet we see him everywhere in chains. Those who believe themselves the masters of others cease not to be even greater slaves than the people they
govern. How this happens I am ignorant; but, if I am asked what renders it justifiable, I believe it may be in my power to resolve the question.

If I were only to consider force, and the efforts of it, I should say, "When a
people is constrained to obey, and does obey, it does well; but as soon as it can throw
off its yoke, and does throw it off, it does better: for a people may certainly use, for
the recovery of their liberty, the same right that was employed to deprive them of
it: it was either justifiably recovered, or unjustifiably torn from them." But the social
order is a sacred right which serves for the basis of all others. Yet this right comes
not from nature; it is therefore founded on conventions. The question is, what those
conventions are. But, before I come to that point, I must establish the principles which
I have just asserted. . . .

The strongest are still never sufficiently strong to ensure them continual master-
ship, unless they find means of transforming force into right, and obedience into
duty. Hence the right of the strongest—a right which seems ironical in appearance,
but is really established as a principle. But shall we never have an explanation of this
term? Force is a physical power; I do not see what morality can result from its
effects. To yield to force is an act of necessity, not of inclination; or it is at best
only an act of prudence. In what sense then can it be a duty?

Let us suppose for a moment the existence of this pretended right. I see nothing
that can arise from it but inexplicable nonsense. For, if we admit that force constitutes right, the effect changes with the cause: all force which overcomes the first
succeeds to its right. As soon as men can disobey with impunity, they can do so
justifiably; and because the strongest is always in the right, strength is the only thing
men should seek to acquire. But what sort of right is that which perishes with the
force that gave it existence? If it is necessary to obey by force, there can be no occasion
to obey from duty; and when force is no more, all obligation ceases with it. We see,
therefore, that this word "right" adds nothing to force, but is indeed an unmeaning
term.

From *The Social Contract*, by Jean-Jacques Rousseau, edited by Charles Frankel, Hafner, 1951.
Reprinted by permission of the publishers.

If in saying, "Let us obey the powerful," they mean to say, "Let us yield to force," the precept is good, but it is superfluous, for it never is or can be violated. All power, we are told, comes from God. I grant it does; but all diseases likewise come from the same hand, and yet who ever forbade us to call in a physician? If a robber surprises me in a corner of a wood, is it necessary that I should not only give him my purse when forced to do so, but am I in conscience obliged to give it to him, though I should be in a position to escape? For the fact is, the pistol which he holds is also a power.

We must grant, therefore, that force does not constitute right, and that obedience is only due to legitimate powers. Thus everything goes back to my first question.

. . .

I will suppose that men in the state of nature are arrived at that crisis when the strength of each individual is insufficient to overcome the resistance of the obstacles to his preservation. This primitive state can therefore subsist no longer; and the human race would perish unless it changed its manner of life.

As men cannot create for themselves new forces, but merely unite and direct those which already exist, the only means they can employ for their preservation is to form by aggregation an assemblage of forces that may be able to overcome the resistance, to be put in motion as one body, and to act in concert.

This assemblage of forces must be produced by the concurrence of many; but as the force and the liberty of each man are the chief instruments of his preservation, how can he engage them elsewhere without danger to himself, and without neglecting the care which is due himself? This difficulty, which leads directly to my subject, may be expressed in these words:

"Where shall we find a form of association which will defend and protect with the whole common force the person and the property of each associate, and by which every person, while uniting himself with all, shall obey only himself and remain as free as before?" Such is the fundamental problem of which the Social Contract gives the solution.

The articles of this contract are so unalterably fixed by the nature of the act that the least modification renders them vain and of no effect; so that they are the same everywhere, and are everywhere tacitly understood and admitted, even though they may never have been formally announced; until, the social compact being violated, each individual is restored to his original rights, and resumes his native liberty, while losing the conventional liberty for which he renounced it.

The articles of the social contract will, when clearly understood, be found reducible to this single point: the total alienation of each associate, and all his rights, to the whole community; for, in the first place, as every individual gives himself up entirely, the condition of every person is alike; and being so, it would not be to the interest of anyone to render that condition offensive to others.

Nay, more than this, the alienation being made without any reserve, the union is as complete as it can be, and no associate has any further claim to anything: for if any individual retained rights not enjoyed in general by all, as there would be no common superior to decide between him and the public, each person being in some points his own judge, would soon pretend to be so in everything; and thus would the state of nature be continued and the association necessarily become tyrannical or be annihilated.

Finally, each person gives himself to all, and so not to any one individual; and as there is no one associate over whom the same right is not acquired which is ceded to him by others, each gains an equivalent for what he loses, and finds his force increased for preserving that which he possesses.

If, therefore, we exclude from the social compact all that is not essential, we shall find it reduced to the following terms:

> *Each of us places in common his person and all his power under the supreme direction of the general will; and as one body we all receive each member as an indivisible part of the whole.*

From that moment, instead of as many separate persons as there are contracting parties, this act of association produces a moral and collective body, composed of as many members as there are votes in the assembly, which from this act receives its unity, its common self, its life, and its will. This public person, which is thus formed by the union of all other persons, took formerly the name of "city," and now takes that of "republic" or "body politic." It is called by its members "State" when it is passive, "Sovereign" when in activity, and, whenever it is compared with other bodies of a similar kind, it is denominated "power." The associates take collectively the name of "people," and separately, that of "citizens," as participating in the sovereign authority, and of "subjects," because they are subjected to the laws of the State. But these terms are frequently confounded and used one for the other; and it is enough that a man understands how to distinguish them when they are employed in all their precision.

· · ·

The passing from the state of nature to the civil state produces in man a very remarkable change, by substituting justice for instinct in his conduct, and giving to his actions a moral character which they lacked before. It is then only that the voice of duty succeeds to physical impulse, and a sense of what is right, to the incitements of appetite. Man, who had till then regarded none but himself, perceives that he must act on other principles, and learns to consult his reason before he listens to his inclinations. Although he is deprived in this new state of many advantages which he enjoyed from nature, he gains in return others so great, his faculties so unfold themselves by being exercised, his ideas are so extended, his sentiments so exalted, and his whole mind so enlarged and refined, that if, by abusing his new condition, he did not sometimes degrade it even below that from which he emerged, he ought to bless continually the happy moment that snatched him forever from it, and transformed him from a circumscribed and stupid animal to an intelligent being and a man.

In order to draw a balance between the advantages and disadvantages attending his new situation, let us state them in such a manner that they may be easily compared. Man loses by the social contract his *natural* liberty, and an unlimited right to all which tempts him, and which he can obtain; in return he acquires *civil* liberty, and proprietorship of all he possesses. That we may not be deceived in the value of these compensations, we must distinguish natural liberty, which knows no bounds but the power of the individual, from civil liberty, which is limited by the general will; and between possession, which is only the effect of force or of the right of the first occupant, from property, which must be founded on a positive title. In addition we might add to the other acquisitions of the civil state that of moral liberty, which alone renders a man master of himself; for it is *slavery* to be under the impulse of mere appetite, and *freedom* to obey a law which we prescribe for ourselves. But I have already said too much on this head, and the philosophical sense of the word "liberty" is not at present my subject.

. . .

The first and most important consequence of the principles already established is that the general will alone can direct the forces of the State agreeably to the end of its institution, which is the common good; for if the clashing of private interests has rendered the establishing of societies necessary, the agreement of the same interests has made such establishments possible. It is what is common in these different interests that forms the social bond; and if there was not some point in which they all unanimously centered, no society could exist. It is on the basis of this common interest alone that society must be governed.

I say, therefore, that sovereignty, being only the exercise of the general will, can never alienate itself, and that the Sovereign, which is only a collective being, cannot be represented but by itself: the *power* may well be transmitted but not the *will*.

Indeed, if it is not impossible that a private will should accord on some point with the general will, it is at least impossible that such agreement should be regular and lasting; for the private will is inclined by its nature to partiality, and the general will to impartiality. It is even more impossible to guarantee the continuance of this agreement, even if we were to see it always exist; because that existence must be owing not to art but to chance. The Sovereign may indeed say: "My will at present actually agrees with the will of such and such a man, or at least with what he declares to be his will"; but it cannot say, "Our wills shall likewise agree tomorow"; since it would be absurd for the will to bind itself for the future, and since it does not belong to any will to consent to what might be injurious to the being from whom the will proceeds. If, therefore, the people promise unconditionally to obey, the act of making such a promise dissolves their existence, and they lose their quality of a people; for at the moment that there is a master, there is no longer a Sovereign, and from that moment the body politic is destroyed.

I do not say that the commands of chiefs cannot pass for general wills, so long as the Sovereign, being free to oppose them, does not do so. In such cases we must presume from their silence that the people yield their consent. But I shall explain this more at large presently.

. . .

WHETHER THE GENERAL WILL CAN ERR

It follows from what has been said that the general will is always right and tends always to the public advantage; but it does not follow that the deliberations of the people have always the same rectitude. Our will always seeks our own good, but we do not always perceive what it is. The people are never corrupted, but they are often deceived, and only then do they seem to will what is bad.

There is frequently much difference between the *will of all* and the *general will*. The latter regards only the common interest; the former regards private interest, and is indeed but a sum of private will: but remove from these same wills the pluses and minuses that cancel each other, and then the general will remains as the sum of the differences.

If, when the people, sufficiently informed, deliberated, there was to be no communication among them, from the grand total of trifling differences the general will would always result, and their resolutions be always good. But when cabals and partial associations are formed at the expense of the great association, the will of each such association, though *general* with regard to its members, is *private* with regard to the State: it can then be said no longer that there are as many voters as men, but only as many as there are associations. By this means the differences being less numerous, they produce a result less general. Finally, when one of these associations becomes so large that it prevails over all the rest, you have no longer the sum of many opinions dissenting in a small degree from each other, but one great dictating dissentient; from that moment there is no longer a general will, and the predominating opinion is only an individual one.

It is therefore of the utmost importance for obtaining the expression of the general will, that no partial society should be formed in the State, and that every citizen should speak his opinion entirely from himself: such was the unique and sublime system of the great Lycurgus. When there are partial societies, it is politic to multiply their number, that they may be all kept on an equality. This method was pursued by Solon, Numa, and Servius. These are the only precautions that can be taken to make the general will always intelligent, and prevent the people from being deceived.

OF THE LIMITS OF THE SOVEREIGN POWER

If the state or city is only a moral person, the existence of which consists in the union of its members, and if its most important care is that of preserving itself, there is a necessity for its possessing a universally compulsive power, for moving and disposing each part in the manner most convenient to the whole. As nature gives to every man absolute command over all his members, the social compact gives to the body politic absolute command over the members of which it is formed; and it is this power, when directed by the general will, that bears, as I have said before, the name of "sovereignty."

But, besides the public person, we have to consider the private persons who compose it, and whose lives and liberty are naturally independent of it. The point here is to distinguish properly between the respective rights of the citizens and the Sovereign, and between the duties which the former have to fulfil in quality of subjects, and the natural rights which they ought to enjoy in quality of men.

It is granted that all which an individual alienates by the social compact is only that part of his power, his property, and his liberty, the use of which is important to the community; but we must also grant that the Sovereign is the only judge of what is important to the community.

All the services which a citizen can render to the State ought to be rendered as soon as the Sovereign demands them; but the Sovereign cannot, on its side, impose any burden on the subject useless to the community; it cannot even have the inclination to do so; for, under the law of reason, nothing is done without a cause, any more than under the law of nature.

The engagements which bind us to the social body are only obligatory because they are mutual; and their nature is such that in fulfilling them we cannot labour for others without labouring at the same time for ourselves. Wherefore is the general will always right, and wherefore do all the wills invariably seek the happiness of every individual among them, if it is not that there is no person who does not appropriate the word "each" to himself, and who does not think of himself when he is voting for all? This proves that the equality of right, and the idea of justice which it inspires, is derived from the preference which each gives to himself, and consequently from the nature of man; that the general will, to be truly such, ought to be so in its object, as well as its essence: that it ought to come from all, if we are to apply it to all; and that it loses its natural rectitude when it tends towards any one individual and determinate object, because then, judging of what is external to us, we have no true principle of equality to guide us.

In fact, as soon as it is a matter of an individual fact or right, on any point which has not been previously regulated by a general convention, the affair becomes contentious. It is a process wherein the persons interested are one of the parties, and the public the other, but where I do not see any law that must be followed, or any judge who ought to decide. It would be ridiculous in such a case to bring the question to an express decision of the general will, which could only be the conclusion of one party, and consequently, which would be, with respect to the other party, but an external and private will, hurried on that occasion into injustice, and subject to error. Thus, in the same manner as a private will cannot represent the general will, the general will, in its turn, changes its nature if its object is private, and cannot, as the general will, pronounce either on a man or a fact. When the people of Athens, for example, nominated or cashiered their chiefs, decreed honours to one, imposed punishments on another, and, by the multitude of their private decrees, exercised indiscriminately all the acts of government, the people, properly speaking, had then no longer a general will; they acted no longer as Sovereign but as magistrate. This will appear contradictory to common ideas; but I must have time to unfold mine.

We should perceive by this that the generality of the will depends less on the number of voters than on the common interest which unites them; for, in this institution, each necessarily submits to the conditions which he imposes on others—an admirable union of interest and justice, which gives to the common deliberations a character of equity that vanishes in the discussion of all private affairs for want of a common interest to combine and identify the ruling of the judge with that of the party.

By whatever path we return to our principle, we always arrive at the same conclusion—that is, that the social compact establishes among citizens such an equality that they are all engaged under the same conditions, and should all enjoy the same rights. Thus, by the nature of the compact all acts of sovereignty, that is to say, all authentic acts of the general will, oblige or favour all citizens alike in such a manner as evinces that the Sovereign knows no person but the body of the nation, and does not make any distinction among the individuals who compose it. What, therefore, is properly an act of sovereignty? It is not a convention between a superior and an inferior, but a convention of the body with each of its members—a justifiable convention beacuse it has the social contract for its basis; equitable, because it is common to all; beneficial, because it can have no other object but the general good; and solid, because it is guaranteed by the public force and the supreme power. While subjects are under the governance of such conventions only, they obey no one but only their own will: and to enquire how far the respective rights of the Sovereign and citizens extend is to ask how far the citizens can engage with themselves, each towards all, and all towards each.

We see by this that the sovereign power, all absolute, all sacred, all inviolable as it is, neither will, nor can, exceed the bounds of general conventions, and that every man may fully dispose of what is left to him of his property and his liberty by these conventions; so that the Sovereign never has any right to lay a greater charge on one subject than on another, because then the affair would become personal, and in such cases the power of the Sovereign is no longer competent.

These distinctions once admitted, it is evidently false that individuals have made any real renunciation by the social contract. On the contrary, they find their situation, by the effect of that contract, really rendered preferable to what it was before. Instead of making any alienation they have only made an advantageous transition from a mode of living unsettled and precarious to one better and more secure, from a state of natural independence to one of liberty, from possessing the power of injuring others to security for themselves, and from their strength, which others might, by the employment of theirs, overcome, to a right which social union renders invincible. Even their lives, which they have devoted to the State, are continually protected by it; and when they are exposed in its defence, what is it but restoring that which they have received from it? What do they do but what they would do more frequently, and with more danger, in the state of nature, when, living in continual and unavoidable conflicts, they would have to defend at the peril of their lives what was necessary to the preservation of life? All, it is true, must fight for their country when their service is requisite; but then no person has occasion to fight for himself as an individual. And is it not gaining a great advantage to be obliged, for the protection of that to which we owe our security, to incur occasionally only a part of that danger to which we must be again exposed as individuals as soon as we were deprived of it?

HERBERT MARCUSE

Ethics and Revolution

Herbert Marcuse, Professor of
Philosophy at the University
of California at San Diego,
has also written *Reason
and Revolution, Eros and
Civilization,* and *One-
Dimensional Man.*

I propose to discuss the relation between ethics and revolution by taking as guidance the following question: Can a revolution be justified as right, as good, perhaps even as necessary, and justified not merely in political terms (as expedient for certain interests) but in ethical terms, that is to say, justified with respect to the human condition as such, to the potential of man in a given historical situation? This means that ethical terms such as "right" or "good" will be applied to political and social movements, with the hypothesis that the moral evaluation of such movements is (in a sense to be defined) more than subjective, more than a matter of preference. Under this hypothesis, "good" and "right" would mean serving to establish, to promote, or to extend human freedom and happiness in a commonwealth, regardless of the form of government. This preliminary definition combines individual and personal, private and public welfare. It tries to recapture a basic concept of classical political philosophy which has been all too often repressed, namely, that the end of government is not only the greatest possible freedom, but also the greatest possible happiness of man, that is to say, a life without fear and misery, and a life in peace.

Here we encounter the first vexing question, namely, who determines, who can and by what right determine the general interest of a commonwealth, and thereby determine the range and limits of individual freedom and happiness, and the sacrifices imposed upon individual freedom and happiness in the name and on behalf of the commonwealth? For as long as the general and individual welfare do not immediately coincide, the latter will be *made* to conform with the former. And if we ask this question we are at once confronted with an equally serious and embarrassing problem: granted even that freedom is not only an individual and private affair, that it is rather determined by the society, by the state in which we live, what about happiness? Is the happiness of an individual his own private affair, or is it too, in a very definite sense, subject to the limitations and even the definitions imposed upon it by a commonwealth? The extreme position that human happiness is and must remain individual and the individual's own affair cannot be defended if we give it

From *Ethics and Society,* edited by Richard T. DeGeorge. Copyright © 1966 by The Kansas University Endowment Association. Reprinted by permission of Doubleday & Company, Inc.

only a few minutes' thought. There are certainly modes and types of individual happiness which cannot be tolerated by any kind of commonwealth. It is perfectly possible—as a matter of fact we know it to be the fact—that the people who were the master torturers in the Hitler concentration camps were often quite happy doing their job. This is one of the many cases of individual happiness where we do not hesitate to say that it is not merely the individual himself who can be and who can remain the judge of his own happiness. We assume a tribunal which is (actually or morally) entitled to "define" individual happiness.

Now after these preliminary clarifications, let me define what I mean by "revolution." By "revolution" I understand the overthrow of a legally established government and constitution by a social class or movement with the aim of altering the social as well as the political structure. This definition excludes all military coups, palace revolutions, and "preventive" counterrevolutions (such as Fascism and Nazism) because they do not alter the basic social structure. If we define revolution in this way we can move one step forward by saying that such a radical and qualitative change implies violence. Peaceful revolutions, if there are such things, if there can be such things, do not present any problem. We can therefore reformulate the initial question by asking: Is the revolutionary use of violence justifiable as a means for establishing or promoting human freedom and happiness? The question implies a very important assumption, namely, that there are rational criteria for determining the possibilities of human freedom and happiness available to a society in a specific historical situation. If there are no such rational criteria, it would be impossible to evaluate a political movement in terms of its chances to attain a greater extent or a higher degree of freedom and happiness in society.

But postulating the availability of rational standards and criteria for judging the given possibilities of human freedom and happiness means assuming that the ethical, moral standards are *historical* standards. If they are not, they remain meaningless abstractions. Applied to our question, this means that to claim an ethical and moral right, a revolutionary movement must be able to give rational grounds for its chances to grasp real possibilities of human freedom and happiness, and it must be able to demonstrate the adequacy of its means for obtaining this end. Only if the problem is placed in such a historical context, is it susceptible to rational discussion. Otherwise, only two positions remain open, namely, to reject *a priori* or to endorse *a priori* all revolution and revolutionary violence. Both positions, the affirmative as well as the negative one, offend against historical facts. It is, for example, meaningless to say that modern society *could* have come about without the English, American, and French Revolutions. It is also meaningless to say that all revolutionary violence had the same social function and consequences. The violence of the Civil Wars in seventeenth century England, the violence of the first French Revolution certainly had effects and consequences very different from those of the Bolshevik Revolution, and very different from the counterrevolutionary violence perpetrated by the Nazi and Fascist regimes. Moreover, the positions of *a priori* rejecting or *a priori* approving social and political violence would amount to sanctioning any change brought about in history, regardless of whether it would be in a progressive or regressive, liberating or enslaving direction.

A very brief glance at the historical development of our problem may facilitate the discussion. In classical political philosophy, revolutions were not considered as breaks of the historical continuum. Plato as well as Aristotle believed that revolutions were built into the very dynamic of politics, that they belonged to the historical and at the same time natural cycle of birth, growth and decay of political forms. In medieval and early modern philosophy the idea of a natural and divine order either outlawed all resistance to established government, or made resistance against tyranny not only a right but a moral duty and obligation. Then, in the sixteenth and seventeenth centuries, the practically unlimited right to resist a government, even to overthrow a government, was normally claimed by Protestant against Catholic, and by Catholic against Protestant regimes. A most characteristic reaction against these doctrines may be seen in the attitude towards revolution which we find in such different figures as Hobbes and Descartes, namely, that change is always to the worst. Leave the established social and political institutions as they are, for, no matter how bad they may be, the risk of overthrowing them is too great. Descartes, the great revolutionary in thought, was extremely conservative with respect to the "great public bodies." To them, doubt is not supposed to be extended, they are supposed to be left alone. At the same time, philosophers are strongly inclined to endorse a revolution once it has proved to be successful. Representative of this attitude is the case of Kant —certainly not a paragon of opportunism and expediency—who rejected the right of resistance and condemned revolt against established government, but added that, once a revolution has succeeded, a new legal government is established, and man owes obedience to the new revolutionary government just as he owed it to the government which was overthrown by the revolution.

On the other side of the fence, political theory and practice recognize historical situations in which violence becomes the necessary and essential element of progress. This concept is instrumental in the political theory and practice of totalitarian democracy. Robespierre calls for the "despotism of liberty" against the despotism of tyranny: in the fight for freedom, in the interest of the whole against the particular interest of oppression, terror may become a necessity and an obligation. Here, violence, revolutionary violence, appears not only as a political means but as a moral duty. The terror is defined as *counter*violence: it is "legitimate" only in defense against the oppressors and until they are defeated. Similarly, the Marxian concept of proletarian dictatorship is that of a transitional self-cancelling dictatorship: self-cancelling because it is supposed to last only as long as the power of the old ruling classes still combats the construction of the socialist society; after their defeat, the engines of repression were to be stopped. Here too, revolutionary violence is defined as counterviolence. The Marxian concept assumes that the old ruling classes would never voluntarily abdicate their position, that they would be the first to use violence against the revolution, and that revolutionary violence would be the defense against counterrevolutionary violence.

The theory of an educational, transitional dictatorship implies the paradoxical proposition that man must be "forced to be free." Political philosophy has always recognized the moral function of coercion (the coercive power of law, either above the sovereign or identical with the sovereign), but Rousseau provides a radically new justification. Coercion is necessitated by the immoral, repressive conditions under which men live. The basic idea is: how can slaves who do not even know they are slaves free themselves? How can they liberate themselves by their own power, by their own faculties? How can they spontaneously accomplish liberation? They must be taught and must be led to be free, and this the more so the more the society in which they live uses all available means in order to shape and preform their consciousness and to make it immune against possible alternatives. This idea of an educational, preparatory dictatorship has today become an integral element of revolution and of the justification of the revolutionary oppression. The dictatorships which began as revolutionary dictatorships and then perpetuated themselves claim to be in their very essence and structure transitional and preparatory for a stage at which they can be abolished by virtue of their own achievements.

The main argument against the notion of the transitional dictatorship is usually condensed in the question: who educates the educators? By what right do those who actually exercise the dictatorship speak in the name of freedom and happiness as general conditions? This argument by itself is not sufficient, because in a lesser degree it applies even to non-authoritarian societies, where the policy-making top layer is not constantly and effectively controlled from below. However, even if we concede that the majority of men are not yet free today, and that their liberation cannot be spontaneous, the question still remains whether the dictatorial means are adequate to attain the end, namely, liberation. In other words the question of a transitional dictatorship cannot be separated from the general question of whether there can be such a thing as a moral justification of suppression and violence in a revolution. I shall now briefly discuss this question.

The historical revolutions were usually advocated and started in the name of freedom, or rather in the name of greater freedom for more strata of the population. We must first examine this claim strictly on empirical grounds. Human freedom is not and never has been a static condition but an historical condition, a process which involves the radical alteration, and even negation, of established ways of life. The form and content of freedom change with every new stage in the development of civilization, which is man's increasing mastery of man and nature. In both modes, mastery means domination, control; more effective control of nature makes for more effective control of man. Obviously, the possibilities of human freedom and happiness in advanced industrial society today are in no way comparable with those available, even theoretically available, at preceding stages of history. Thus, with respect to the form, extent, degree and content of human freedom, we deal with strictly historical and changing conditions. We can say even more. Measured against the real possibilities of freedom, we always live in a state of relative unfreedom. The wide gap between real possibility and actuality, between the rational and the real has never been closed. Freedom always presupposes liberation, or a step from one state of freedom and unfreedom to a subsequent state. With the advance of technical progress, the later state is *potentially* (but by no means actually!) a *higher* stage, that is, quantitatively and qualitatively. But if this is the case, if freedom always presupposes liberation from unfree and unhappy conditions, it means that this liberation always offends against and ultimately subverts established and sanctioned institutions and interests. In history, they never abdicated voluntarily. Consequently, if and when freedom is a process of liberation, a transition from lower, more restricted forms of freedom to higher forms of freedom, then it always, no matter how, offends against the existing and established state of affairs. And precisely on this ground revolutionary violence has been most effectively justified as counterviolence, that is, as violence necessary in order to secure higher forms of freedom against the resistance of the established forms.

The ethics of revolution thus testifies to the clash and conflict of two historical rights: on the one side, the right of that which *is,* the established commonwealth on which the life and perhaps even the happiness of the individuals depend; and on the other side, the right of that which *can* be and perhaps even *ought* to be because it may reduce toil, misery, and injustice, provided always that this chance can be demonstrated as a real possibility. Such a demonstration must provide rational criteria; we can now add: these must be *historical* criteria. As such, they amount to an "historical calculus," namely, calculation of the chances of a future society as against the chances of the existing society with respect to human progress, that is to say, technical and material progress used in such a way that it increases individual freedom and happiness. Now if such an historical calculus is to have any rational basis, it must, on the one side, take into account the sacrifices exacted from the living generations on behalf of the established society, the established law and order, the number of victims made in defense of this society in war and peace, in the struggle for existence, individual and national. The calculus would further have to take into account the intellectual and material resources available to the society and the manner in which they are actually used with respect to their full capacity of satisfying vital human needs and pacifying the struggle for existence. On the other side, the historical calculus would have to project the chances of the contesting revolutionary movement of improving the prevailing conditions, namely, whether the revolutionary plan or program demonstrates the technical, material, and mental possibility of reducing the sacrifices and the number of victims. Even prior to the question as to the possibility of such a calculus (which, I believe, does exist), its inhuman quantifying character is evident. But its inhumanity is that of history itself, token of its empirical, rational foundation. No hypocrisy should from the beginning distort the examination. Nor is this brutal calculus an empty intellectual abstraction; in fact, at its decisive turns, history became such a calculated experiment.

The ethics of revolution, if there is such a thing, will therefore be in accordance not with absolute, but with historical standards. They do not cancel the validity of those general norms which formulate requirements for the progress of mankind toward humanity. No matter how rationally one may justify revolutionary means in terms of the demonstrable chance of obtaining freedom and happiness for future generations, and thereby justify violating existing rights and liberties and life itself, there are forms of violence and suppression which no revolutionary situation can justify because they negate the very end for which the revolution is a means. Such are arbitrary violence, cruelty, and indiscriminate terror. However, within the historical continuum, revolutions establish a moral and ethical code of their own and in this way become the origin, the fountainhead and source of new general norms and values. In fact some of today's most generally-professed values originated in revolutions, for example, the value of tolerance in the English Civil Wars, the inalienable rights of man in the American and French Revolutions. These ideas become an historical force, first as partial ideas, instruments of a revolutionary movement for specific political ends. Their realization originally involved violence; they then assumed not only partial political but general ethical validity and rejected violence. In this way, revolutions place themselves under ethical standards.

Violence *per se* has never been made a revolutionary value by the leaders of the historical revolutions. His contemporaries rejected Georges Sorel's attempt to cut the link between violence and reason, which was at the same time the attempt to free the class struggle from all ethical considerations. In comparing the violence of the class struggle in its revolutionary phase with the violence of military operations in war, he made the former subject to strategic calculations only: the end was the total defeat of the enemy; violence a means to attain this end—the relation between means and end was a technical one. Sorel's defense of violence this side of good and evil remained isolated from the revolutionary reality of his time; if he had any influence, it was on the side of the counterrevolution. Otherwise, violence was defended, not *per se*, but as part of rational suppression, suppression of counterrevolutionary activity, of established rights and privileges, and, for the society at large, of material and intellectual needs, that is, enforcement of austerity, rationing, censorship.

Now this suppression which includes violence is practiced in the interest of the objectives of the revolution, and these objectives are presented not only as political but also as moral values, ethical imperatives, namely greater freedom for the greater number of people. And in this sense the objectives and the ends of the revolution itself claim general validity and become subject to moral standards and evaluation.

Here we are confronted with the problem of all ethics, namely, the question as to the ultimate sanction of moral values. Or, in plain language, who or what determines the validity of ethical norms? The question becomes acute only with the secularization of the West; it was no problem in the Middle Ages as long as a transcendent sanction of ethics was accepted. The infidels could justly be exterminated, heretics could justly be burned—in spite of all protest. This was justice in terms of the prevailing values, which in turn were those of transcendent ethics. But today, where is the sanction of ethical values—sanction not in terms of the enforcement but in terms of the acceptance of ethical values, the proof of their validity? Sanction today, it seems, rests mainly in a precarious and flexible syndrome of custom, fear, utility, and religion; flexible because, within the syndrome, there is a large range of change. I refer, for example, to the high degree of liberalization in sexual morality which we have witnessed during the last thirty years, or, to the easy suspension of practically all ethical values in so-called emergency situations. The sanction and validity of ethical norms is thus restricted to the normal state of affairs in social and political relations.

Now in terms of the normal established state of affairs, a revolution is by definition immoral; it offends against the right of the existing commonwealth; it permits and even demands deception, cunning, suppression, destruction of life and property, and so on. But a judgment by definition is an inadequate judgment. Ethical standards by virtue of their imperative claim transcend any given state of affairs, and they transcend it, not to any metaphysical entities but to the historical continuum in which every given state of affairs has emerged, by which every given state of affairs is defined, and in which every given state of affairs will be altered and surpassed by other states. And in the historical continuum which defines its place and function, the ethics of revolution appeal to an historical calculus. Can the intended new society, the society intended by the revolution, offer better chances for progress in freedom than the existing society? In the historical continuum, these chances can only be measured by going beyond the given state of affairs, going beyond it not simply into an abstract vacuum of speculation, but going beyond it by calculating the resources, intellectual as well as material, scientific as well as technical, available to a given society, and projecting the most rational ways of utilizing these resources. Now if such projection is possible, then it can yield objective criteria for judging revolutions as to their historical function in terms of progress or regression, in terms of the development of *humanitas.*

A preliminary answer is suggested by a glance at the historical process itself. Historically, the objective tendency of the great revolutions of the modern period was the enlargement of the social range of freedom and the enlargement of the satisfaction of needs. No matter how much the social interpretations of the English and French Revolutions may differ, they seem to agree in that a redistribution of the social wealth took place, so that previously less privileged or underprivileged classes were the beneficiaries of this change, economically and/or politically. In spite of subsequent periods of reaction and restoration, the result and objective function of these revolutions was the establishment of more liberal governments, a gradual democratization of society, and technical progress. I said "objective function" because this evaluation of the revolution is obviously a judgment *ex post facto.* The intention and ideology of the leaders of the revolution, and the drives of the masses may have had quite different aims and motives. By virtue of their objective function, these revolutions attained progress in the sense defined, namely, a demonstrable enlargement of the range of human freedom; they thus established, in spite of the terrible sacrifices exacted by them, an ethical right over and above all political justification.

But if such ethical right and its criteria are always and necessarily after the fact, it serves for nought and leaves us with the irrational choice of either *a priori* accepting or *a priori* rejecting all revolution. Now I submit that, while the historical function of a revolution becomes identifiable only after the fact, its prospective direction, progressive or regressive is, with the certainty of a reasonable *chance,* demonstrable *before* the fact—to the same degree to which the historical conditions of progress are demonstrable. For example, it could be demonstrated—and it was demonstrated before the fact—that the French Revolution of 1789 would give, in terms of the historical calculus, a better chance for the development of human freedom than the Ancien Régime. Contrariwise, it could be demonstrated, and was demonstrated long before the fact, that Fascist and National-Socialist regimes would do the exact opposite, namely, necessarily restrict the range of human freedom. Moreover, and I think this is a very important point, such demonstration of the historical *chances* before the fact becomes increasingly rational with the development of our scientific, technical, and material resources and capabilities, with our progress in the scientific mastery of man and nature. The possibilities and contents of freedom today are coming more and more under the control of man: they are becoming increasingly calculable. And with this advance in effective control and calculability, the inhuman distinction between violence and violence, sacrifice and sacrifice becomes increasingly rational. For throughout history, the happiness and freedom, and even the life of individuals, have been sacrificed. If we consider human life *per se* sacred under all conditions, the distinction is meaningless, and we have to admit that history is *per se* amoral and immoral, because it has never respected the sanctity of human life as such. But in fact we do distinguish between sacrifices which are legitimate and sacrifices which are not legitimate. This distinction is an historical one, and with this qualification, ethical standards are also applicable to violence.

Let me now recapitulate and reformulate. In absolute ethical terms, that is to say, in terms of suprahistorical validity, there is no justification for any suppression and sacrifice for the sake of future freedom and happiness, revolutionary or otherwise. But in historical terms we are confronted with a distinction and a decision. For suppression and sacrifice are daily exacted by all societies, and one cannot start —indeed I would like to say this with all possible emphasis—one cannot start becoming moral and ethical at an arbitrary but expendient point of cut off: the point of revolution. Who can quantify and who can compare the sacrifices exacted by an established society and those exacted by its subversion? Are ten thousand victims more ethical than twenty thousand? Such is in fact the inhuman arithmetic of history, and in this inhuman historical context operates the historical calculus. Calculable are the material and intellectual resources available, calculable are the productive and distributive facilities in a society, and the extent of unsatisfied vital needs and of satisfied nonvital needs. Quantifiable and calculable are the quantity and size of the labor force and of the population as a whole. That is the empirical material at the disposal of the historical calculus. And on the basis of this quantifiable material the question can be asked whether the available resources and capabilities are utilized most rationally, that is to say, with a view to the best possible satisfaction of needs under the priority of vital needs and with a minimum of toil, misery and injustice. If the analysis of a specific historical situation suggests a negative answer, if conditions exist in which technological rationality is impeded or even superseded by repressive political and social interests which define the general welfare, then the reversal of such conditions in favor of a more rational and human use of the available resources would also be a maximalization of the chance of progress in freedom. Consequently, a social and political movement in this direction would, in terms of the calculus, allow the presumption of historical justification. It can be no more than a presumption, subject to correction as the movement actually develops, reveals its potential and establishes new facts, or in other words, as it sustains or as it cuts the links between the means which the revolution employs and the end which it professes to attain.

And this leads to the last question which I want to raise here, namely, can the revolutionary end justify *all* means? Can we distinguish between rational and irrational, necessary and arbitrary, suppression? When can such suppression be called rational in terms of the objective of a respective revolution? I shall briefly illustrate the scope of this question by the Bolshevik Revolution. The professed objective of the Bolshevik Revolution was socialism. It implied the socialization of the means of production, the dictatorship of the proletariat as preparatory to a classless society. In the specific historical situation in which the Bolshevik Revolution occurred, socialism called for industrialization in competition with the advanced capitalist countries of the West, for the building up of the armed forces, and for propaganda on a global scale. Now can we apply a distinction between rational and irrational to these objectives and to the degree of suppression involved in them? In terms of the revolution, rational would be accelerated industrialization, the elimination of non-cooperative layers of management from the economy, the enforcement of work discipline, sacrifices in the satisfaction of needs imposed by the priority of heavy industry in the first stages of industrialization, and suspension of civil liberties if they were used for sabotaging these objectives. And we can reject, without long discussion, as not justifiable, even in terms of the revolution, the Moscow trials, the permanent terror, the concentration camps, and the dictatorship of the Party over the working classes. Further examination would require introducing into the discussion the situation of global coexistence; but time forbids us to do so. We have also made abstractions from the human element in the leadership of the revolution, that is to say, from the so-called historical individuals.

And here I want to add one remark. It seems to me characteristic that, the more calculable and the more controllable the technical apparatus of modern industrial society becomes, the more does the chance of human progress depend on the intellectual and moral qualities of the leaders, and on their willingness and ability to educate the controlled population and to make it recognize the possibility, nay, the necessity of pacification and humanization. For today, the technical apparatus of advanced industrial society is in itself authoritarian, requiring service, submission, subordination to the objective mechanism of the machine system, that is to say, submission to those who control the apparatus. Technology has been made into a powerful instrument of streamlined domination—the more powerful the more it proves its efficiency and delivers the goods. And as such, it serves the politics of domination.

I come to the conclusion. The means-end relation is the ethical problem of revolution. In one sense, the end justifies the means, namely, if they demonstrably serve human progress in freedom. This legitimate end, the only legitimate end, demands the creation of conditions which would facilitate and expedite its realization. And the creation of these conditions may justify sacrifices, as it has justified sacrifices throughout history. But this relation between means and ends is a dialectical one. The end must be operative in the repressive means for attaining the end. But no matter how rational, how necessary, how liberating—revolution involves violence. The nonviolent history is the promise and possibility of a society which is still to be fought for. At present, the triumphant violence seems to be on the other side.

ALBERT CAMUS

The Rebel

Albert Camus (1913–
1960) was a French
novelist and essayist.
He also wrote *The
Myth of Sisyphus,
The Stranger, The
Plague,* and *The Fall.*

What is a rebel? A man who says no, but whose refusal does not imply a renunciation. He is also a man who says yes, from the moment he makes his first gesture of rebellion. A slave who has taken orders all his life suddenly decides that he cannot obey some new command. What does he mean by saying "no"?

He means, for example, that "this has been going on too long," "up to this point yes, beyond it no," "you are going too far," or, again, "there is a limit beyond which you shall not go." In other words, his no affirms the existence of a borderline. The same concept is to be found in the rebel's feeling that the other person "is exaggerating," that he is exerting his authority beyond a limit where he begins to infringe on the rights of others. Thus the movement of rebellion is founded simultaneously on the categorical rejection of an intrusion that is considered intolerable and on the confused conviction of an absolute right which, in the rebel's mind, is more precisely the impression that he "has the right to . . ." Rebellion cannot exist without the feeling that, somewhere and somehow, one is right. It is in this way that the rebel slave says yes and no simultaneously. He affirms that there are limits and also that he suspects—and wishes to preserve—the existence of certain things on this side of the borderline. He demonstrates, with obstinacy, that there is something in him which "is worth while . . ." and which must be taken into consideration. In a certain way, he confronts an order of things which oppresses him with the insistence on a kind of right not to be oppressed beyond the limit that he can tolerate.

In every act of rebellion, the rebel simultaneously experiences a feeling of revulsion at the infringment of his rights and a complete and spontaneous loyalty to certain aspects of himself. Thus he implicitly brings into play a standard of values so far from being gratuitous that he is prepared to support it no matter what the risks. Up to this point he has at least remained silent and has abandoned himself to the form of despair in which a condition is accepted even though it is considered unjust. To remain silent is to give the impression that one has no opinions, that one wants nothing, and in certain cases it really amounts to wanting nothing. Despair, like the absurd, has opinions and desires about everything in general and nothing in particular. Silence expresses this attitude very well. But from the moment that the rebel finds his voice—even though he says nothing but "no"—he begins to desire and to judge. The rebel, in the etymological sense, does a complete turnabout. He acted under the lash of his master's whip. Suddenly he turns and faces him. He opposes what is preferable to what is not. Not every value entails rebellion, but every act of rebellion tacitly invokes a value. Or is it really a question of values?

Awareness, no matter how confused it may be, develops from every act of rebellion: the sudden, dazzling perception that there is something in man with which he can identify himself, even if only for a moment. Up to now this identification was never really experienced. Before he rebelled, the slave accepted all the demands made upon him. Very often he even took orders, without reacting against them, which were far more conducive to insurrection than the one at which he balks. He accepted them patiently, though he may have protested inwardly, but in that he remained silent he was more concerned with his own immediate interests than as yet aware of his own rights. But with loss of patience—with impatience—a reaction begins which can extend to everything that he previously accepted, and which is almost always retroactive. The very moment the slave refuses to obey the humiliating orders of his master, he simultaneously rejects the condition of slavery. The act of rebellion carries him far beyond the point he had reached by simply refusing. He exceeds the bounds that he fixed for his antagonist, and now demands to be treated as an equal. What was at first the man's obstinate resistance now becomes the whole man, who is identified with and summed up in his resistance. The part of himself that he wanted to be respected he proceeds to place above everything else and proclaims it preferable to everything, even to life itself. It becomes for him the supreme good. Having up to now been willing to compromise, the slave suddenly adopts ("because this is how it must be . . .") an attitude of All or Nothing. With rebellion, awareness is born.

But we can see that the knowledge gained is, at the same time, of an "all" that is still rather obscure and of a "nothing" that proclaims the possibility of sacrificing to rebel to this "All." The rebel himself wants to be "all"—to identify himself completely with this good of which he has suddenly become aware and by which he wants to be personally recognized and acknowledged—or "nothing"; in other words, to be completely destroyed by the force that dominates him. As a last resort, he is willing to accept the final defeat, which is death, rather than be deprived of the personal sacrament that he would call, for example, freedom. Better to die on one's feet than to live on one's knees.

Values, according to good authorities, "most often represent a transition from facts to rights, from what is desired to what is desirable (usually through the intermediary of what is generally considered desirable)."[1] The transition from facts to rights is manifest, as we have seen, in rebellion. So is the transition from "this must be" to "this is how I should like things to be," and even more so, perhaps, the idea of the sublimation of the individual in a henceforth universal good. The sudden appearance of the concept of "All or Nothing" demonstrates that rebellion, contrary

[1] Lalande: *Vocabulaire philosophique.*

to current opinion, and though it springs from everything that is most strictly individualistic in man, questions the very idea of the individual. If the individual, in fact, accepts death and happens to die as a consequence of his act of rebellion, he demonstrates by doing so that he is willing to sacrifice himself for the sake of a common good which he considers more important than his own destiny. If he prefers the risk of death to the negation of the rights that he defends, it is because he considers these rights more important than himself. Therefore he is acting in the name of certain values which are still indeterminate but which he feels are common to himself and to all men. We see that the affirmation implicit in every act of rebellion is extended to something that transcends the individual in so far as it withdraws him from his supposed solitude and provides him with a reason to act. But it is already worth nothing that this concept of values as pre-existent to any kind of action contradicts the purely historical philosophies, in which values are acquired (if they are ever acquired) after the action has been completed. Analysis of rebellion leads at least to the suspicion that, contrary to the postulates of contemporary thought, a human nature does exist, as the Greeks believed. Why rebel if there is nothing permanent in oneself worth preserving? It is for the sake of everyone in the world that the slave asserts himself when he comes to the conclusion that a command has infringed on something in him which does not belong to him alone, but which is common ground where all men—even the man who insults and oppresses him—have a natural community.[2]

Two observations will support this argument. First, we can see that an act of rebellion is not, essentially, an egoistic act. Of course, it can have egoistic motives. But one can rebel equally well against lies as against oppression. Moreover, the rebel —once he has accepted the motives and at the moment of his greatest impetus—preserves nothing in that he risks everything, He demands respect for himself, of course, but only in so far as he identifies himself with a natural community.

Then we note that rebellion does not arise only, and necessarily, among the oppressed, but that it can also be caused by the mere spectacle of oppression of which someone else is the victim. In such cases there is a feeling of identification with another individual. And it must be pointed out that this not a question of psychological identification—a mere subterfuge by which the individual imagines that it is he himself who has been offended. On the contrary, it can often happen that we cannot bear to see offenses done to others which we ourselves have accepted without rebelling. The suicides of the Russian terrorists in Siberia as a protest against their comrades' being whipped is a case in point. Nor is it a question of the feeling of a community of interests. Injustices done to men whom we consider enemies can, actually, be profoundly repugnant to us. There is only identification of one's destiny with that of others and a choice of sides. Therefore the individual is not, in himself alone, the embodiment of the values he wishes to defend. It needs all humanity, at least, to comprise them. When he rebels, a man identifies himself with other men and so surpasses himself, and from this point of view human solidarity is metaphysical. But for the moment we are only talking of the kind of solidarity that is born in chains.

---

[2] The community of victims is the same as that which unites victim and executioner. But the executioner does not know this.

It would be possible for us to define the positive aspect of the values implicit in every act of rebellion by comparing them with a completely negative concept like that of resentment as defined by Scheler. Rebellion is, in fact, much more than pursuit of a claim, in the strongest sense of the word. Resentment is very well defined by Scheler as an autointoxication—the evil secretion, in a sealed vessel, of prolonged impotence. Rebellion, on the contrary, breaks the seal and allows the whole being to come into play. It liberates stagnant waters and turns them into a raging torrent. Scheler himself emphasizes the passive aspect of resentment and remarks on the prominent place it occupies in the psychology of women who are dedicated to desire and possession. The fountainhead of rebellion, on the contrary, is the principle of superabundant activity and energy. Scheler is also right in saying that resentment is always highly colored by envy. But one envies what one does not have, while the rebel's aim is to defend what he is. He does not merely claim some good that he does not possess or of which he was deprived. His aim is to claim recognition for something which he has and which has already been recognized by him, in almost every case, as more important than anything of which he could be envious. Rebellion is not realistic. According to Scheler, resentment always turns into either unscrupulous ambition or bitterness, depending on whether it is implanted in a strong person or a weak one. But in both cases it is a question of wanting to be something other than what one is. Resentment is always resentment against oneself. The rebel, on the contrary, from his very step, refuses to allow anyone to touch what he is. He is fighting for the integrity of one part of his being. He does not try, primarily, to conquer, but simply to impose.

Finally, it would seem that resentment takes delight, in advance, in the pain that it would like the object of its envy to feel. Nietzsche and Scheler are right in seeing an excellent example of this in the passage where Tertullian informs his readers that one of the greatest sources of happiness among the blessed will be the spectacle of the Roman emperors consumed in the fires of hell. This kind of happiness is also experienced by the decent people who go to watch executions. The rebel, on the contrary, limits himself, as a matter of principle, to refusing to be humiliated without asking that others should be. He will even accept pain provided his integrity is respected.

It is therefore hard to understand why Scheler completely identifies the spirit of rebellion with resentment. His criticism of the resentment to be found in humanitarianism (which he treats as the non-Christian form of love for mankind) could perhaps be applied to certain indeterminate forms of humanitarian idealism, or to the techniques of terror. But it rings false in relation to man's rebellion against his condition—the movement that enlists the individual in the defense of a dignity common to all men. Scheler wants to demonstrate that humanitarian feelings are always accompanied by a hatred of the world. Humanity is loved in general in order to avoid having to love anybody in particular. This is correct, in some cases, and it is easier to understand Scheler when we realize that for him humanitarianism is represented by Bentham and Rousseau. But man's love for man can be born of other things than a mathematical calculation of the resultant rewards or a theoretical confidence in human nature. In face of the utilitarians, and of Emile's preceptor, there is, for example, the kind of logic, embodied by Dostoievsky in Ivan Karamazov, which progresses from an act of rebellion to metaphysical insurrection. Scheler is aware of this and sums up the concept in the following manner: "There is not enough love in the world to squander it on anything but human beings." Even if this proposition were true, the appalling despair that it implies would merit anything but contempt. In fact, it misunderstands the tortured character of Karamazov's rebellion. Ivan's drama, on the contrary, arises from the fact that there is too much love without an object. This love finding no outlet and God being denied, it is then decided to lavish it on human beings as a generous act of complicity.

Nevertheless, in the act of rebellion as we have envisaged it up to now, an abstract ideal is not chosen through lack of feeling and in pursuit of a sterile demand. We insist that the part of man which cannot be reduced to mere ideas should be taken into consideration—the passionate side of his nature that serves no other purpose than to be part of the act of living. Does this imply that no rebellion is motivated by resentment? No, and we know it only too well in this age of malice. But we must consider the idea of rebellion in its widest sense on pain of betraying it; and in its widest sense rebellion goes far beyond resentment. When Heathcliff, in *Wuthering Heights,* says that he puts his love above God and would willingly go to hell in order to be reunited with the woman he loves, he is prompted not only by youth and humiliation but by the consuming experience of a whole lifetime. The same emotion causes Eckart, in a surprising fit of heresy, to say that he prefers hell with Jesus to heaven without Him. This is the very essence of love. Contrary to Scheler, it would therefore be impossible to overemphasize the passionate affirmation that underlies the act of rebellion and distinguishes it from resentment. Rebellion, though apparently negative, since it creates nothing, is profoundly positive in that it reveals the part of man which must always be defended.

But, to sum up, are not rebellion and the values that it implies relative? Reasons for rebellion do seem to change, in fact, with periods and civilizations. It is obvious that a Hindu pariah, an Inca warrior, a primitive native of central Africa, and a member of one of the first Christian communities had not at all the same ideas about rebellion. We could even assert, with considerable assurance, that the idea of rebellion has no meaning in these particular cases. However, a Greek slave, a serf, a *condottiere* of the Renaissance, a Parisian bourgeois during the Regency, a Russian intellectual at the beginning of the twentieth century, and a contemporary worker would undoubtedly agree that rebellion is legitimate, even if they differed about the reasons for it. In other words, the problem of rebellion seems to assume a precise meaning only within the confines of Western thought. It is possible to be even more explicit by remarking, like Scheler, that the spirit of rebellion finds few means of expression in societies where inequalities are very great (the Hindu caste system) or, again, in those where there is absolute equality (certain primitive societies). The spirit of rebellion can exist only in a society where a theoretical equality conceals great factual inequalities. The problem of rebellion, therefore, has no meaning except within our Western society. One might be tempted to affirm that it is relative to the development of individualism if the preceding remarks had not put us on our guard against this conclusion.

On the basis of the evidence, the only conclusion that can be drawn from Scheler's remark is that, thanks to the theory of political freedom, there is, in the very heart of our society, an increasing awareness in man of the idea of man and, thanks to the application of this theory of freedom, a corresponding dissatisfaction. Actual freedom has not increased in proportion to man's awareness of it. We can only deduce from this observation that rebellion is the act of an educated man who is aware of his own rights. But there is nothing which justifies us in saying that it is only a question of individual rights. Because of the sense of solidarity we have already pointed out, it would rather seem that what is at stake is humanity's gradually increasing self-awareness as it pursues its course. In fact, for the Inca and the pariah the problem never arises, because for them it had been solved by a tradition, even before they had had time to raise it—the answer being that tradition is sacred. If in a world where things are held sacred the problem of rebellion does not arise, it is because no real problems are to be found in such a world, all the answers having been given simultaneously. Metaphysic is replaced by myth. There are no more questions, only eternal answers and commentaries, which may be metaphysical. But before man accepts the sacred world and in order that he should be able to accept it—or before he escapes from it and in order that he should be able to escape from it—there is always a period of soul-searching and rebellion. The rebel is a man who is on the point of accepting or rejecting the sacred and determined on laying claim to a human situation in which all the answers are human—in other words, formulated in reasonable terms. From this moment every question, every word, is an act of rebellion while in the sacred world every word is an act of grace. It would be possible to demonstrate in this manner that only two possible worlds can exist for the human mind: the sacred (or, to speak in Christian terms, the world of grace[3]) and the world of rebellion. The disappearance of one is equivalent to the appearance of the other, despite the fact that this appearance can take place in disconcerting forms. There again we rediscover the *All or Nothing*. The present interest of the problem of rebellion only springs from the fact that nowadays whole societies have wanted to discard the sacred. We live in an unsacrosanct moment in history. Insurrection is certainly not the sum total of human experience. But history today, with all its storm and strife, compels us to say that rebellion is one of the essential dimensions of man. It is our historic reality. Unless we choose to ignore reality, we must find our values in it. Is it possible to find a rule of conduct outside the realm of religion and its absolute values? That is the question raised by rebellion.

We have already noted the confused values that are called into play by incipient rebellion. Now we must inquire if these values are to be found again in contemporary forms of rebellious thought and action, and if they are, we must specify their content. But, before going any farther, let us note that the basis of these values is rebellion itself. Man's solidarity is founded upon rebellion, and rebellion, in its turn, can only find its justification in this solidarity. We have, then, the right to say that any rebellion which claims the right to deny or destroy this solidarity loses simultaneously its right to be called rebellion and becomes in reality an acquiescence in murder. In the same way, this solidarity, except in so far as religion is concerned,

[3] There is of course, an act of metaphysical rebellion at the beginning of Christianity, but the resurrection of Christ and the annunciation of the kingdom of heaven interpreted as a promise of eternal life are the answers that render it futile.

comes to life only on the level of rebellion. And so the real drama of revolutionary thought is announced. In order to exist, man must rebel, but rebellion must respect the limit it discovers in itself—a limit where minds meet and, in meeting, begin to exist. Rebellious thought, therefore, cannot dispense with memory: it is a perpetual state of tension. In studying its actions and its results, we shall have to say, each time, whether it remains faithful to its first noble promise or if, through indolence or folly, it forgets its original purpose and plunges into a mire of tyranny or servitude.

Meanwhile, we can sum up the initial progress that the spirit of rebellion provokes in a mind that is originally imbued with the absurdity and apparent sterility of the world. In absurdist experience, suffering is individual. But from the moment when a movement of rebellion begins, suffering is seen as a collective experience. Therefore the first progressive step for a mind overwhelmed by the strangeness of things is to realize that this feeling of strangeness is shared with all men and that human reality, in its entirety, suffers from the distance which separates it from the rest of the universe. The malady experienced by a single man becomes a mass plague. In our daily trials rebellion plays the same role as does the *"cogito"* in the realm of thought: it is the first piece of evidence. But this evidence lures the individual from his solitude. It founds its first value on the whole human race. I rebel—therefore we exist.

Violence

FRIEDRICH ENGELS

Theory of Force

Friedrich Engels
(1820–1895) wrote
several books in
collaboration with
Karl Marx. This
selection, from an
attack on a then
influential German
socialist, is taken from
a work now consid-
ered an authoritative
exposition of Marx's
thought.

As men first emerged from the animal world—in the narrower sense of the term
—so they made their entry into history; still half animal, brutal, still helpless in
face of the forces of Nature, still ignorant of their own: and consequently as poor
as the animals and hardly more productive than these. There prevailed a certain
equality in the conditions of existence, and for the heads of families also a kind of
equality of social position—at least an absence of social classes—which continued
among the natural agricultural communities of the civilised peoples of a later
period. In each such community there were from the beginning certain common
interests the safeguarding of which had to be handed over to individuals, even
though under the control of the community as a whole: such were the adjudication
of disputes; repression of encroachments by individuals on the rights of others;
control of water supplies, especially in hot countries; and finally, when conditions
were still absolutely primitive, religious functions. Such offices are found in primitive communities of every period—in the oldest German Mark communities and
even today in India. They are naturally endowed with a certain measure of authority and the beginnings of state power. The productive forces gradually increase;
the increasing density of the population creates at one point a community of interests, at another, conflicting interests, between the separate communes, whose group-
ing into larger units brings about in turn a new division of labour, the setting up
of organs to safeguard common interests and to guard against conflicting interests.
These organs which, for the reason that they represent the common interests of the

From *Anti-Dühring: Herr Eugen Dühring's Revolution in Science,* by Friedrich Engels, translated by
Emile Burns, third edition, International Publishers Co., Inc. © 1962. Reprinted by permission of the
publishers.

whole group, have a special position in relation to each individual community—in certain circumstances even one of opposition—soon make themselves even more independent, partly through heredity of functions, which comes about almost as a matter of course in a world where everything happens in a natural way, and partly because they become more and more indispensable owing to the increasing number of conflicts with the other groups. It is not necessary for us to examine here how this independence of social functions in relation to society increased with time until it developed into domination over society; how what was originally the servant developed gradually, where conditions were favourable, into the lord; how this lord, on the basis of different conditions, emerged as an Oriental despot or satrap, the dynast of a Greek tribe, chieftain of a Celtic clan, and so on; and to what extent ultimately used force in this transformation; and how finally the separate individual rulers united into a ruling class. Here we are only concerned with establishing the fact that the exercise of a social function was everywhere the basis of political supremacy; and further that political supremacy has existed for any length of time only when it fulfilled its social functions. However great the number of despotic governments which rose and fell in India and Persia, each was fully aware that its first duty was the general maintenance of irrigation throughout the valleys, without which no agriculture was possible. It was reserved for the enlightened English to lose sight of this in India; they let the irrigation canals and sluices fall into decay, and are now at last discovering, through the regularly recurrent famines, that they have neglected the one activity which might have made their rule in India at least as legitimate as that of their predecessors.

But alongside of this development of classes another was also taking place. The natural division of labour within the family cultivating the soil made possible, at a certain level of well-being, the introduction of one or more strangers as additional labour forces. This was especially the case in countries where the old common ownership of the land had already disappeared or at least the former joint cultivation had given place to the separate cultivation of parcels of land by the respective families. Production had so far developed that the labour power of a man could now produce more than was necessary for its mere maintenance; the means of maintaining additional labour forces existed; likewise the means of employing them; labour power acquired a *value*. But within the community and the association to which it belonged there were no superfluous labour forces available. On the other hand, such forces were provided by war, and war was as old as the simultaneous existence alongside each other of several groups of communities. Up to that time they had not known what to do with prisoners of war, and had therefore simply killed them; at an even earlier period, eaten them. But at the stage of the "economic order" which had now been attained the prisoners acquired a value; their captors therefore let them live and made use of their labour. Thus force, instead of controlling the economic order, was on the contrary pressed into the service of the economic order. *Slavery* was invented. It soon became the predominant form of production among all peoples who were developing beyond the primitive community, but in the end was also one of the chief causes of the decay of that system. It was slavery that first made possible the division of labour between agriculture and industry on a considerable scale, and along with this, the flower of the ancient world, Hellenism. Without slavery, no Greek state, no Greek art, and science; without slavery, no Roman Empire. But without Hellenism and the Roman Empire as a basis, also no modern Europe. We should never forget that our whole economic, political and intellectual development has as its presupposition a state of things in which slavery was as necessary as it was universally recognised. In this sense we are entitled to say: Without the slavery of antiquity, no modern socialism.

It is very easy to inveigh against slavery and similar things in general terms, and to give vent to high moral indignation at such infamies. Unfortunately all that this conveys is only what everyone knows, namely that these institutions of antiquity are no longer in accord with our present-day conditions and our sentiments, which these conditions determine. But it does not tell us one word as to how these institutions arose, why they existed, and what role they have played in history. And when we examine these questions, we are compelled to say—however contradictory and heretical it may sound—that the introduction of slavery under the conditions of that time was a great step forward. For it is a fact that man sprang from the beasts, and had consequently to use barbaric and almost bestial means to extricate himself from barbarism. The ancient communes, where they continued to exist, have for thousands of years formed the basis of the most barbarous form of state, oriental despotism, from India to Russia. It was only where these communities dissolved that the peoples made progress of themselves, and their first economic advance consisted in the increase and development of production by means of slave labour. It is clear that so long as human labour was still so little productive that it provided but a small surplus over and above the necessary means of subsistence, any increase of the productive forces, extension of trade, development of the state and of law, or beginning of art and science, was only possible by means of a greater division of labour. And the necessary basis for this was the great division of labour between the masses discharging simple manual labour and the few privileged persons directing labour, conducting trade and public affairs, and, at a later stage, occupying themselves with art and science. The simplest and most natural form of this division of labour was in fact slavery. In the historical conditions of the ancient world, and particularly of Greece, the advance to a society based on class antagonisms could only be accomplished in the form of slavery. This was an advance even for the slaves; the prisoners of war, from whom the mass of the slaves was recruited, now at least kept their lives, instead of being killed as they had been before, or even roasted, as at a still earlier period.

We may add at this point that all historical antagonisms between exploiting and exploited, ruling and oppressed classes to this very day find their explanation in this same relatively undeveloped productivity of human labour. So long as the really working population was so much occupied in their necessary labour that they had no time left for looking after the common affairs of society—the direction of labour, affairs of the state, legal matters, art, science, etc.—so long was it always necessary that there should exist a special class, freed from actual labour, to manage these affairs; and this special class never failed to impose a greater and greater burden of labour, for its own advantage, on the working masses. Only the immense increase of the productive forces attained through large-scale industry made it possible to distribute labour among all members of society without exception, and thereby to limit the labour time of each individual member to such an extent that all have enough free time left to take part in the general—both theoretical and practical—

affairs of society. It is only now, therefore, that any ruling and exploiting class has become superfluous and indeed a hindrance to social development, and it is only now, too, that it will be inexorably abolished, however much it may be in possession of the "direct force."

When, therefore, Herr Dühring turns up his nose at Hellenism because it was founded on slavery, he might with equal justice reproach the Greeks with having no steam engines and electric telegraphs. And when he asserts that our modern wage-serfdom can only be explained as a somewhat transformed and mitigated heritage of slavery, and not from its own nature (that is, from the economic laws of modern society), either this only means that both wage labour and slavery are forms of subjection and class domination, which every child knows, or it is false. For with equal justice we might say that wage labour is only to be explained as a mitigated form of cannibalism, which is now established as having been the universal primitive form of disposal of vanquished enemies.

The role played in history by force as contrasted with economic development is now clear. In the first place, all political power is originally based on an economic, social function, and increases in proportion as the members of society, through the dissolution of the primitive community, become transformed into private producers, and thus become more and more separated from the administrators of the general functions of society. Secondly, after the political force has made itself independent in relation to society, and has transformed itself from society's servant into its master, it can work in two different directions. Either it works in the sense and in the direction of the regular economic development, in which case no conflict arises between them, the economic development being accelerated. Or, force works against economic development; in this case, as a rule, with but few exceptions, force succumbs to it. These few exceptions are isolated cases of conquest, in which barbarian conquerors have exterminated or driven out the population of a country and have laid waste or allowed to go to ruin productive forces which they did not know how to use. This was what the Christians in Moorish Spain did with the major part of the irrigation works on which the highly-developed agriculture and horticulture of the Moors depended. Every conquest by a more barbarian people naturally disturbs the economic development and destroys numerous productive forces. But in the immense majority of cases where the conquest is permanent, the more barbarian conqueror has to adapt himself to the higher "economic order" as it emerges from the conquest; he is assimilated by the vanquished and in most cases he has even to adopt their language. But where—apart from cases of conquest— the internal public force of a country stands in opposition to its economic development, as at a certain stage has occurred with almost every political power in the past, the contest has always ended with the downfall of the political power. Inexorably and without exception the economic evolution has forced its way through— we have already mentioned the latest and most striking example of this: the Great French Revolution. If, in accordance with Herr Dühring's theory, the economic order and with it the economic constitution of a given country were dependent simply on political force, it is absolutely impossible to understand why after 1848 Friedrich Wilhelm IV could not succeed, in spite of his "magnificent army," in grafting the mediæval guilds and other romantic whims on to the railways, the steam engines and the large-scale industry which was just then developing in his country; or why the tsar of Russia, who is certainly even much more powerful, is not only unable to pay his debts, but cannot even maintain his "force" without continuous loans from the "economic order" of Western Europe.

For Herr Dühring force is the absolute evil; the first act of force is for him the original sin; his whole exposition is a jeremiad on the contamination, which this brought about, of all subsequent history by this original sin; a jeremiad on the shameful perversion of all natural and social laws by this diabolical power, force. That force, however, plays another role in history, a revolutionary role; that, in the words of Marx, it is the midwife of every old society which is pregnant with the new, that it is the instrument by the aid of which social development forces its way through and shatters the dead, fossilised, political forms—of this there is not a word in Herr Dühring. It is only with sighs and groans that he admits the possibility that force will perhaps be necessary for the overthrow of the economic system of exploitation—unfortunately, because all use of force, forsooth, demoralises the person who uses it. And this in spite of the immense moral and spiritual impetus which has resulted from every victorious revolution! And this in Germany, where a violent collision—which indeed may be forced on the people—would at least have the advantage of wiping out the servility which has permeated the national consciousness as a result of the humiliation of the Thirty Years' War. And this parsons' mode of thought—lifeless, insipid and impotent—claims to impose itself on the most revolutionary party that history has known.

FRANTZ FANON

Concerning Violence

Frantz Fanon (1925–1961) was a native African phychiatrist who bitterly opposed French colonial rule in Algeria. He also wrote *Black Skin, White Masks.*

National liberation, national renaissance, the restoration of nationhood to the people, commonwealth: whatever may be the headings used or the new formulas introduced, decolonisation is always a violent phenomenon. At whatever level we study it—relationships between individuals, new names for sports clubs, the human admixture at cocktail parties, in the police, on the directing boards of national or

Reprinted by permission of Grove Press, Inc. Translated from the French by Constance Farrington. Copyright © 1963 by Presence Africaine.

private banks—decolonisation is quite simply the replacing of a certain "species" of men by another "species" of men. Without any period of transition, there is a total, complete and absolute substitution. It is true that we could equally well stress the rise of a new nation, the setting up of a new State, its diplomatic relations, and its economic and political trends. But we have precisely chosen to speak of that kind of *tabula rasa* which characterises at the outset all decolonisation. Its unusual importance is that it constitutes, from the very first day, the minimum demands of the colonised. To tell the truth, the proof of success lies in a whole social structure being changed from the bottom up. The extraordinary importance of this change is that it is willed, called for, demanded. The need for this change exists in its crude state, impetuous and compelling, in the consciousness and in the lives of the men and women who are colonised. But the possibility of this change is equally experienced in the form of a terrifying future in the consciousness of another "species" of men and women: the colonisers.

Decolonisation, which sets out to change the order of the world, is, obviously, a programme of complete disorder. But it cannot come as a result of magical practices, nor of a natural shock, nor of a friendly understanding. Decolonisation, as we know, is a historical process: that is to say that it cannot be understood, it cannot become intelligible nor clear to itself except in the exact measure that we can discern the movements which give it historical form and content. Decolonisation is the meeting of two forces, opposed to each other by their very nature, which in fact owe their originality to that sort of substantification which results from and is nourished by the situation in the colonies. Their first encounter was marked by violence and their existence together—that is to say the exploitation of the native by the settler—was carried on by dint of great array of bayonets and cannon. The settler and the native are old acquaintances. In fact, the settler is right when he speaks of knowing "them" well. For it is the settler who has brought the native into existence and who perpetuates his existence. The settler owes the fact of his very existence, that is to say his property, to the colonial system.

Decolonisation never takes place un-noticed, for it influences individuals and modifies them fundamentally. It transforms spectators crushed with their inessentiality into privileged actors, with the grandoise glare of history's floodlights upon them. It brings a natural rhythm into existence, introduced by new men, and with it a new language and a new humanity. Decolonisation is the veritable creation of new men. But this creation owes nothing of its legitimacy to any supernatural power, the "thing" which has been colonised becomes man during the same process by which it frees itself.

In decolonisation, there is therefore the need of a complete calling in question of the colonial situation. If we wish to describe it precisely, we might find it in the well-known words: "The last shall be first and the first last." Decolonisation is the putting into practice of this sentence. That is why, if we try to describe it, all decolonisation is successful.

The naked truth of decolonisation evokes for us the searing bullets and blood-stained knives which emanate from it. For if the last shall be first, this will only come to pass after a murderous and decisive struggle between the two protagonists. That affirmed intention to place the last at the head of things, and to make them climb at a pace (too quickly, some say) the well-known steps which characterise an organised society, can only triumph if we use all means to turn the scale, including, of course, that of violence.

You do not turn any society, however primitive it may be, upside-down with such a programme if you are not decided from the very beginning, that is to say from the actual formulation of that programme, to overcome all the obstacles that you will come across in so doing. The native who decides to put the programme into practice, and to become its moving force, is ready for violence at all times. From birth it is clear to him that this narrow world, strewn with prohibitions, can only be called in question by absolute violence.

The colonial world is a world divided into compartments. It is probably unnecessary to recall the existence of native quarters and European quarters, of schools for natives and schools for Europeans; in the same way we need not recall Apartheid in South Africa. Yet, if we examine closely this system of compartments, we will at least be able to reveal the lines of force it implies. This approach to the colonial world, its ordering and its geographical lay-out will allow us to mark out the lines on which a decolonised society will be reorganised.

The colonial world is a world cut in two. The dividing line, the frontiers are shown by barracks and police stations. In the colonies it is the policeman and the soldier who are the official, instituted go-betweens, the spokesmen of the settler and his rule of oppression. In capitalist societies the educational system, whether lay or clerical, the structure of moral reflexes handed down from father to son, the exemplary honesty of workers who are given a medal after fifty years of good and loyal service, and the affection which springs from harmonious relations and good behaviour—all these esthetic expressions of respect for the established order serve to create around the exploited person an atmosphere of submission and of inhibition which lightens the task of policing considerably. In the capitalist countries a multitude of moral teachers, counsellors, and "bewilderers" separate the exploited from those in power. In the colonial countries, on the contrary, the policeman and the soldier, by their immediate presence and their frequent and direct action maintain contact with the native and advise him by means of rifle-butts and napalm not to budge. It is obvious here that the agents of government speak the language of pure force. The intermediary does not lighten the oppression, nor seek to hide the domination; he shows them up and puts them into practice with the clear conscience of an upholder of the peace; yet he is the bringer of violence into the home and into the mind of the native.

The zone where the natives live is not complementary to the zone inhabited by the settlers. The two zones are opposed, but not in the service of a higher unity. Obedient to the rules of pure Aristotelian logic, they both follow the principle of reciprocal exclusivity. No conciliation is possible, for of the two terms, one is superfluous. The settlers' town is a strongly-built town, all made of stone and steel. It is a brightly-lit town; the streets are covered with asphalt, and the garbage-cans swallow all the leavings, unseen, unknown and hardly thought about. The settler's feet are never visible, except perhaps in the sea; but there you're never close enough to see them. His feet are protected by strong shoes although the streets of his town are clean and even, with no holes or stones. The settler's town is a well-fed town, an easy-going town; its belly is always full of good things. The settler's town is a town of white people, of foreigners.

The town belonging to the colonised people, or at least the native town, the negro village, the medina, the reservation, is a place of ill fame, peopled by men of evil repute. They are born there, it matters little where or how; they die there, it matters not where, nor how. It is a world without spaciousness; men live there on top of each other, and their huts are built one on top of the other. The native town is a hungry town, starved of bread, of meat, of shoes, of coal, of light. The native town is a crouching village, a town on its knees, a town wallowing in the mire. It is a town of niggers and dirty arabs. The look that the native turns on the settler's town is a look of lust, a look of envy; it expresses his dreams of possession —all manner of possession: to sit at the settler's table, to sleep in the settler's bed, with his wife if possible. The colonised man is an envious man. And this the settler knows very well; when their glances meet he ascertains bitterly, always on the defensive "They want to take our place." It is true, for there is no native who does not dream at least once a day of setting himself up in the settler's place.

This world divided into compartments, this world cut in two is inhabited by two different species. The originality of the colonial context is that economic reality, inequality and the immense difference of ways of life never come to mask the human realities. When you examine at close quarters the colonial context, it is evident that what parcels out the world is to begin with the fact of belonging to or not belonging to a given race, a given species. In the colonies the economic sub-structure is also a superstructure. The cause is the consequence; you are rich because you are white, you are white because you are rich. This is why Marxist analysis should always be slightly stretched every time we have to do with the colonial problem.

Everything up to and including the very nature of precapitalist society, so well explained by Marx, must here be thought out again. The serf is in essence different from the knight, but a reference to divine right is necessary to legitimise this statutory difference. In the colonies, the foreigner coming from another country imposed his rule by means of guns and machines. In defiance of his successful transplantation, in spite of his appropriation, the settler still remains a foreigner. It is neither the act of owning factories, nor estates, nor a bank balance which distinguishes the governing classes. The governing race is first and foremost those who come from elsewhere, those who are unlike the original inhabitants, "the others."

The violence which has ruled over the ordering of the colonial world, which has ceaselessly drummed the rhythm for the destruction of native social forms and broken up without reserve the systems of reference of the economy, the customs of dress and external life, that same violence will be claimed and taken over by the native at the moment when, deciding to embody history in his own person, he surges into the forbidden quarters. To wreck the colonial world is henceforward a mental picture of action which is very clear, very easy to understand and which may be assumed by each one of the individuals which constitute the colonised people. To break up the colonial world does not mean that after the frontiers have been abolished lines of communication will be set up between the two zones. The destruction of the colonial world is no more and no less that the abolition of one zone, its burial in the depths of the earth or its expulsion from the country.

The natives' challenge to the colonial world is not a rational confrontation of points of view. It is not a treatise on the universal, but the untidy affirmation of an original idea propounded as an absolute. The colonial world is a Manichean world. It is not enough for the settler to delimit physically, that is to say with the help of the army and the police force, the place of the native. As if to show the totalitarian character of colonial exploitation the settler paints the native as a sort of quintessence of evil.[1] Native society is not simply described as a society lacking in values. It is not enough for the colonist to affirm that those values have disappeared from, or still better never existed in, the colonial world. The native is declared insensible to ethics; he represents not only the absence of values, but also the negation of values. He is, let us dare to admit, the enemy of values, and in this sense he is the absolute evil. He is the corrosive element, destroying all that comes near him; he is the deforming element, disfiguring all that has to do with beauty or morality; he is the depository of maleficent powers, the unconscious and irretrievable instrument of blind forces. Monsieur Meyer could thus state seriously in the French National Assembly that the Republic must not be prostituted by allowing the Algerian people to become part of it. All values, in fact are irrevocably poisoned and diseased as soon as they are allowed in contact with the colonised race. The customs of the colonised people, their traditions, their myths—above all, their myths—are the very sign of that poverty of spirit and of their constitutional depravity. That is why we must put the DDT which destroys parasites, the bearers of disease, on the same level as the Christian religion which wages war on embryonic heresies and instincts, and on evil as yet unborn. The recession of yellow fever and the advance of evangelisation form part of the same balance-sheet. But the triumphant *communiqués* from the missions are in fact a source of information concerning the implantation of foreign influences in the core of the colonised epople. I speak of the Christian religion, and no one need be astonished. The Church in the colonies is the white people's Church, the foreigner's Church. She does not call the native to God's ways but to the ways of the white man, of the master, of the oppressor. And as we know, in this matter many are called but few chosen.

At times this Manicheism goes to its logical conclusion and dehumanises the native, or to speak plainly it turns him into an animal. In fact, the terms the settler uses when he mentions the native are zoological terms. He speaks of the yellow man's reptilian motions, of the stink of the native quarter, of breeding swarms, of foulness, of spawn, of gesticulations. When the settler seeks to describe the native fully in exact terms he constantly refers to the bestiary. The European rarely hits on a picturesque style; but the native, who knows what is in the mind of the settler, guesses at once what he is thinking of. Those hordes of vital statistics, those hysterical masses, those faces bereft of all humanity, those distended bodies which are like nothing on earth, that mob without beginning or end, those children who seem to belong to nobody, that laziness stretched out in the sun, that vegetative rhythm of life—all this forms part of the colonial vocabulary. General de Gaulle speaks of "the yellow multitudes" and François Mauriac of the black, brown and yellow masses which soon will be unleashed. The native knows all this, and laughs to himself every time he spots an allusion to the animal world in the other's words. For he knows that he is not an animal; and it is precisely at the moment he realises his

[1] We have demonstrated the mechanism of this Manichean world in *Black Skin, White Masks*, New York, Grove Press, 1967.

humanity that he begins to sharpen the weapons with which he will secure its victory.

As soon as the native begins to pull on his moorings, and to cause anxiety to the settler, he is handed over to well-meaning souls who in cultural congresses point out to him the specificity and wealth of Western values. But every time Western values are mentioned they produced in the native a sort of stiffening or muscular lock-jaw. During the period of decolonisation, the native's reason is appealed to. He is offered definite values, he is told frequently that decolonisation need not mean regression, and that he must put his trust in qualities which are well-tried, solid and highly esteemed. But it so happens that when the native hears a speech about Western culture he pulls out his knife—or at least he makes sure it is within reach. The violence with which the supremacy of white values is affirmed and the aggressiveness which has permeated the victory of these values over the ways of life and of thought of the native mean that, in revenge, the native laughs in mockery when Western values are mentioned in front of him. In the colonial context the settler only ends his work of breaking in the native when the latter admits loudly and intelligibly the supremacy of the white man's values. In the period of decolonisation, the colonised masses mock at these very values, insult them and vomit them up.

This phenomenon is ordinarily masked because, during the period of decolonisation, certain colonised intellectuals have begun a dialogue with the bourgeoisie of the colonialist country. During this phase, the indigenous population is discerned only as an indistinct mass. The few native personalities whom the colonialist bourgeois have come to know here and there have not sufficient influence on that immediate discernment to give rise to nuances. On the other hand, during the period of liberation, the colonialist bourgeoisie looks feverishly for contacts with the *élite*, and it is with these *élite* that the familiar dialogue concerning values is carried on. The colonialist bourgeoisie, when it realises that it is impossible for it to maintain its domination over the colonial countries, decides to carry out a rear-guard action with regard to culture, values, techniques and so on. Now what we must never forget is that the immense majority of colonised peoples is oblivious of these problems. For a colonised people the most essential value, because the most concrete, is first and foremost the land: the land which will bring them bread and, above all, dignity. But this dignity has nothing to do with the dignity of the human individual: for that human individual has never heard tell of it. All that the native has seen in his country is that they can freely arrest him, beat him, starve him: and no professor of ethics, no priest has ever come to be beaten in his place, nor to share their bread with him. As far as the native is concerned, morality is very concrete; it is to silence the settler's defiance, to break his flaunting violence—in a word, to put him out of the picture. The well-known principle that all men are equal will be illustrated in the colonies from the moment that the native claims that he is the equal of the settler. One step more, and he is ready to fight to be more than the settler. In fact, he has already decided to eject him and to take his place; as we see it, it is a whole material and moral universe which is breaking up. The intellectual who for his part has followed the colonialist with regard to the universal abstract will fight in order that the settler and the native may live together in peace in a new world. But the thing he does not see, precisely because he is permeated by colonialism and all its ways of thinking is that the settler, from the moment that the colonial context disappears, has no longer any interest in remaining or in co-existing. It is not by chance that, even before any negotiation[2] between the Algerian and French governments has taken place, the European minority which calls itself "liberal" has already made its position clear: it demands nothing more nor less than twofold citizenship. By setting themselves apart in an abstract manner, the liberals try to force the settler into taking a very concrete jump into the unknown. Let us admit it, the settler knows perfectly well that no phraseology can be a substitute for reality.

Thus the native discovers that his life, his breath, his beating heart are the same as those of the settler. He finds out that the settler's skin is not of any more value than a native's skin; and it must be said that this discovery shakes the world in a very necessary manner. All the new, revolutionary assurance of the native stems from it. For if, in fact, my life is worth as much as the settler's, his glance no longer shrivels me up nor freezes me, and his voice no longer turns me into stone. I am no longer on tenterhooks in his presence; in fact, I don't give a damn for him. Not only does his presence no longer trouble me, but I am already preparing such efficient ambushes for him that soon there will be no way out but that of flight.

We have said that the colonial context is characterised by the dichotomy which it imposes upon the whole people. Decolonisation unifies that people by the radical decision to remove from it its heterogenity, and by unifying it on a national, sometimes a racial, basis. We know the fierce words of the Senegalese patriots, referring to the manœuvres of their president, Senghor: "We have demanded that the higher posts should be given to Africans; and now Senghor is Africanising the Europeans." That is to say that the native can see clearly and immediately if decolonisation has come to pass or no, for his minimum demands are simply that the last shall be first.

But the native intellectual brings variants to this petition, and, in fact, he seems to have good reason: higher civil servants, technicians, specialists—all seem to be needed. Now, the ordinary native interprets these unfair promotions as so many acts of sabotage, and he is often heard to declare: "It wasn't worth while, then, our becoming independent. . . ."

In the colonial countries where a real struggle for freedom has taken place, where the blood of the people has flowed and where the length of the period of armed warfare has favoured the backward surge of intellectuals towards bases grounded in the people, we can observe a genuine eradication of the superstructure built by these intellectuals from the bourgeois colonialist environment. The colonialist bourgeoisie, in its narcissistic dialogue, expounded by the members of its universities, had in fact deeply implanted in the minds of the colonised intellectual that the essential qualities remain eternal in spite of all the blunders men may make: the essential qualities of the West, of course. The native intellectual accepted the cogency of these ideas, and deep down in his brain you could always find a vigilant sentinel ready to defend the Greco-Latin pedestal. Now it so happens that during the struggle for liberation, at the moment that the native intellectual comes into touch again with his people, this artificial sentinel is turned into dust. All the Mediterranean values,—the triumph of the human individual, of clarity and of beauty—become lifeless, colourless knick-knacks. All those speeches seem like collections of dead

---

[2] Fanon is writing in 1961. (Transl.)

words; those values which seemed to uplift the soul are revealed as worthless, simply because they have nothing to do with the concrete conflict in which the people is engaged.

Individualism is the first to disappear. The native intellectual had learnt from his masters that the individual ought to express himself fully. The colonialist bourgeoisie had hammered into the native's mind the idea of a society of individuals where each person shuts himself up in his own subjectivity, and whose only wealth is individual thought. Now the native who has the opportunity to return to the people during the struggle for freedom will discover the falseness of this theory. The very forms of organisation of the struggle will suggest to him a different vocabulary. Brother, sister, friend—these are words outlawed by the colonialist bourgeoisie, because for them my brother is my purse, my friend is part of my scheme for getting on. The native intellectual takes part, in a sort of *auto-da-fé,* in the destruction of all his idols: egoism, recrimination that springs from pride, and the childish stupidity of those who always want to have the last word. Such a colonised intellectual, dusted over by colonial culture, will in the same way discover the substance of village assemblies, the cohesion of people's committees, and the extraordinary fruitfulness of local meetings and groupments. Henceforward, the interests of one will be the interests of all, for in concrete fact *everyone* will be discovered by the troops, *everyone* will be massacred—or *everyone* will be saved. The motto "look out for yourself," the atheist's method of salvation, is in this context forbidden.

Self-criticism has been much talked about of late, but few people realise that it is an African institution. Whether in the *djemaas*[3] of Northern Africa or in the meetings of Western Africa, tradition demands that the quarrels which occur in a village should be settled in public. It is communal self-criticism, of course, and with a note of humour, because everybody is relaxed, and because in the last resort we all want the same things. But the more the intellectual imbibes the atmosphere of the people, the more completely he abandons the habits of calculation, of unwonted silence, of mental reservations, and shakes off the spirit of concealment. And it is true that already at that level we can say that the community triumphs, and that it spreads its own light and its own reason.

But it so happens sometimes that decolonisation occurs in areas which have not been sufficiently shaken by the struggle for liberation, and there may be found those same know-all, smart, wily intellectuals. We find intact in them the manners and forms of thought picked up during their association with the colonialist bourgeoisie. Spoilt children of yesterday's colonialism and of today's national governments, they organise the loot of whatever national resources exist. Without pity, they use today's national distress as a means of getting on through scheming and legal robbery, by import-export combines, limited liability companies, gambling on the stock-exchange, or unfair promotion. They are insistent in their demands for the nationalisation of commerce, that is to say the reservation of markets and advantageous bargains for nationals only. As far as doctrine is concerned, they proclaim the pressing necessity of nationalising the robbery of the nation. In this arid phase of national life, the so-called period of austerity, the success of their depredations is swift to call forth the violence and anger of the people. For this same people, poverty-stricken

[3] Village assemblies. (Transl.)

yet independent, comes very quickly to possess a social conscience in the African and international context of today; and this the petty individualists will quickly learn.

In order to assimilate and to experience the oppressor's culture, the native has had to leave certain of his intellectual possessions in pawn. These pledges include his adoption of the forms of thought of the colonialist bourgeoisie. This is very noticeable in the inaptitude of the native intellectual to carry on a two-sided discussion; for he cannot eliminate himself when confronted with an object or an idea. On the other hand, when once he begins to militate among the people he is struck with wonder and amazement; he is literally disarmed by their good faith and honesty. The danger that will haunt him continually is that of becoming the uncritical mouthpiece of the masses; he becomes a kind of yes-man who nods assent at every word coming from the people, which he interprets as considered judgments. Now, the *fellah*, the unemployed man, the starving native do not lay a claim to the truth; they do not *say* that they represent the truth, for they *are* the truth.

Objectively, the intellectual behaves in this phase like a common opportunist. In fact he has not stopped manoeuvring. There is never any question of his being either rejected or welcomed by the people. What they ask is simply that all resources should be pooled. The inclusion of the native intellectual in the upward surge of the masses will in this case be differentiated by a curious cult of detail. That is not to say that the people are hostile to analysis; on the contrary, they like having things explained to them, they are glad to understand a line of argument and they like to see where they are going. But at the beginning of his association with the people the native intellectual over-stresses details and thereby comes to forget that the defeat of colonialism is the real object of the struggle. Carried away by the multitudinous aspects of the fight, he tends to concentrate on local tasks, performed with enthusiasm but most always too solemnly. He fails to see the whole of the movement all the time. He introduces the idea of special disciplines, of specialised functions, of departments within the terrible stone crusher, the fierce mixing machine which a popular revolution is. He is occupied in action on a particular front, and it so happens that he loses sight of the unity of the movement. Thus, if a local defeat is inflicted, he may well be drawn into doubt, and from thence to despair. The people, on the other hand, take their stand from the start on the broad and inclusive positions of *Bread and the land*: how can we obtain the land, and bread to eat? And this obstinate point of view of the masses, which may seem shrunken and limited, is in the end the most worthwhile and the most efficient mode of procedure.

The problem of truth ought also to be considered. In every age, among the people, truth is the property of the national cause. No absolute verity, no discourse on the purity of the soul can shake this position. The native replies to the living lie of the colonial situation by an equal falsehood. His dealings with his fellow-nationals are open; they are strained and incomprehensible with regard to the settlers. Truth is that which hurries on the break-up of the colonialist regime; it is that which promotes the emergence of the nation; it is all that protects the natives, and ruins the foreigners. In this colonialist context there is no truthful behaviour: and the good is quite simply that which is evil for *"them."*

Thus we see that the primary Manicheism which governed colonial society is preserved intact during the period of decolonisation; that is to say that the settler never ceases to be the enemy, the opponent, the foe that must be overthrown. The oppressor, in his own sphere, starts the process, a process of domination, of exploitation and of pillage, and in the other sphere the coiled, plundered creature which is the native provides fodder for the process as best he can, the process which moves uninterruptedly from the banks of the colonial territory to the palaces and the docks of the mother country. In this becalmed zone the sea has a smooth surface, the palmtree stirs gently in the breeze, the waves lap against the pebbles, and raw materials are ceaselessly transported, justifying the presence of the settler: and all the while the native, bent double, more dead than alive, exists interminably in an unchanging dream. The settler makes history; his life is an epoch, an Odyssey. He is the absolute beginning: "This land was created by us"; he is the unceasing cause: "If we leave, all is lost, and the country will go back to the Middle Ages." Over against him torpid creatures, wasted by fevers, obsessed by ancestral customs, form an almost inorganic background for the innovating dynamism of colonial mercantilism.

The settler makes history and is conscious of making it. And because he constantly refers to the history of his mother country, he clearly indicates that he himself is the extension of that mother-country. Thus the history which he writes is not the history of the country which he plunders but the history of his own nation in regard to all that she skims off, all that she violates and starves.

The immobility to which the native is condemned can only be called in question if the native decides to put an end to the history of colonisation—the history of pillage—and to bring into existence the history of the nation—the history of decolonisation.

A world divided into compartments, a motionless, Manicheistic world, a world of statues: the statue of the general who carried out the conquest, the statue of the engineer who built the bridge; a world which is sure of itself, which crushes with its stones the backs flayed by whips: this is the colonial world. The native is a being hemmed in; apartheid is simply one form of the division into compartments of the colonial world. The first thing which the native learns is to stay in his place, and not to go beyond certain limits. This is why the dreams of the native are always of muscular prowess; his dreams are of action and of aggression. I dream I am jumping, swimming, running, climbing; I dream that I burst out laughing, that I span a river in one stride, or that I am followed by a flood of motor-cars which never catch up with me. During the period of colonisation, the native never stops achieving his freedom from nine in the evening until six in the morning.

The colonised man will first manifest this aggressiveness which has been deposited in his bones against his own people. This is the period when the niggers beat each other up, and the police and magistrates do not know which way to turn when faced with the astonishing waves of crime in North Africa. We shall see later how this phenomenon should be judged. When the native is confronted with the colonial order of things, he finds he is in a state of permanent tension. The settler's world is a hostile world, which spurns the native, but at the same time it is a world of which he is envious. We have seen that the native never ceases to dream of putting himself in the place of the settler—not of becoming the settler but of substituting himself for the settler. This hostile world, ponderous and aggressive because it fends off the colonised masses with all the harshness it is capable of, represents not merely a hell from which the swiftest flight possible is desirable, but also a paradise close at hand which is guarded by terrible watchdogs.

The native is always on the alert, for since he can only make out with difficulty the many symbols of the colonial world, he is never sure whether or not he has crossed the frontier. Confronted with a world ruled by the settler, the native is always presumed guilty. But the native's guilt is never a guilt which he accepts; it is rather a kind of curse, a sort of sword of Damocles, for, in his innermost spirit, the native admits no accusation. He is overpowered but not tamed; he is treated as an inferior but he is not convinced of his inferiority. He is patiently waiting until the settler is off his guard to fly at him. The native's muscles are always tensed. You can't say that he is terrorized, or even apprehensive. He is in fact ready at a moment's notice to exchange the rôle of the quarry for that of the hunter. The native is an oppressed person whose permanent dream is to become the persecutor. The symbols of social order—the police, the bugle-calls in the barracks, military parades and the waving flags—are at one and the same time inhibitory and stimulating: for they do not convey the message "Don't dare to budge"; rather, they cry out "Get ready to attack." And, in fact, if the native had any tendency to fall asleep and to forget, the settler's hauteur and the settler's anxiety to test the strength of the colonial system would remind him at every turn that the great show-down cannot be put off indefinitely. That impulse to take the settler's place implies a tonicity of muscles the whole time; and in fact we know that in certain emotional conditions the presence of an obstacle accentuates the tendency towards motion.

The settler-native relationship is a mass relationship. The settler pits brute force against the weight of numbers. He is an exhibitionist. His preoccupation with security makes him remind the native out loud that there he alone is master. The settler keeps alive in the native an anger which he deprives of outlet; the native is trapped in the tight links of the chains of colonialism. But we have seen that inwardly the settler can only achieve a pseudo petrification. The native's muscular tension finds outlet regularly in bloodthirsty explosions—in tribal warfare, in feuds between septs, and in quarrels between individuals.

Where individuals are concerned, a positive negation of common sense is evident. While the settler or the policeman has the right the live-long day to strike the native, to insult him and to make him crawl to them, you will see the native reaching for his knife at the slightest hostile or aggressive glance cast on him by another native; for the last resort of the native is to defend his personality vis-à-vis his brother. Tribal feuds only serve to perpetuate old grudges deep buried in the memory. By throwing himself with all his force into the vendetta, the native tries to persuade himself that colonialism does not exist, that everything is going on as before, that history continues. Here on the level of communal organisations we clearly discern the well-known behaviour patterns of avoidance. It is as if plunging into a fraternal blood-bath allowed them to ignore the obstacle, and to put off till later the choice, nevertheless inevitable, which opens up the question of armed resistance to colonialism. Thus collective autodestruction in a very concrete form is one of the ways in which the native's muscular tension is set free. All these patterns of conduct are those of the death reflex when faced with danger, a suicidal behaviour which proves to the settler (whose existence and domination is by then all the more justified) that these men are not reasonable human beings. In the same way the native manages to by-pass the settler. A belief in fatality removes all blame from the oppressor; the cause of misfortunes and of poverty is attributed to God; He is Fate. In this way the individual accepts the disintegration ordained by God, bows down before the settler and his lot, and by a kind of interior restabilization acquires a stony calm.

Meanwhile, however, life goes on, and the native will strengthen the inhibitions which contain his aggressiveness by drawing on the terrifying myths which are so frequently found in under-developed communities. There are maleficent spirits which intervene every time a step is taken in the wrong direction, leopard-men, serpent-men, six-legged dogs, zombies—a whole series of tiny animals or giants which create around the native a world of prohibitions, of barriers and of inhibitions far more terrifying than the world of the settler. This magical superstructure which permeates native society fulfils certain well-defined functions in the dynamism of the libido. One of the characteristics of under-developed societies is in fact that the libido is first and foremost the concern of a group, or of the family. The feature of communities whereby a man who dreams that he has sexual relations with a woman other than his own must confess it in public and pay a fine in kind or in working days to the injured husband or family is fully described by ethnologists. We may note in passing that this proves that the so-called prehistoric societies attach great importance to the unconscious.

The atmosphere of myth and magic frightens me and so takes on an undoubted reality. By terrifying me, it integrates me in the traditions and the history of my district or of my tribe, and at the same time it reassures me, it give me a status, as it were an identification paper. In underdeveloped countries the occult sphere is a sphere belonging to the community which is entirely under magical jurisdiction. By entangling myself in this inextricable network where actions are repeated with crystalline inevitability, I find the everlasting world which belongs to me, and the perenniality which is thereby affirmed of the world belonging to us. Believe me, the zombies are more terrifying than the settlers; and in consequence the problem is no longer that of keeping oneself right with the colonial world and its barbed-wire entanglements, but of considering three times before urinating, spitting or going out into the night.

The supernatural, magical powers reveal themselves as essentially personal; the settler's powers are infinitely shrunken, stamped with their alien origin. We no longer really need to fight against them since what counts is the frightening enemy created by myths. We perceive that all is settled by a permanent confrontation on the phantasmic plane.

It has always happened in the struggle for freedom that such a people, formerly lost in an imaginary maze, a prey to unspeakable terrors yet happy to lose themselves in a dreamlike torment, such a people becomes unhinged, reorganises itself, and in blood and tears gives birth to very real and immediate action. Feeding the *moud-jahidines*,[4] posting sentinels, coming to the help of families which lack the bare necessities, or taking the place of a husband who has been killed or imprisoned: such are the concrete tasks to which the people is called during the struggle for freedom.

In the colonial world, the emotional sensitivity of the native is kept on the surface of his skin like an open sore which flinches from the caustic agent; and the

---

[4] Highly-trained soldiers who are completely dedicated to the Moslem cause. (Transl.)

psyche shrinks back, obliterates itself and finds outlet in muscular demonstrations which have caused certain very wise men to say that the native is a hysterical type. This sensitive emotionalism, watched by invisible keepers who are however in unbroken contact with the core of the personality, will find its fulfillment through eroticism in the driving forces behind the crisis' dissolution.

On another level we see the native's emotional sensibility exhausting itself in dances which are more or less ecstatic. This is why any study of the colonial world should take into consideration the phenomena of the dance and of possession. The native's relaxation takes precisely the form of a muscular orgy in which the most acute aggressivity and the most impelling violence are canalised, transformed and conjured away. The circle of the dance is a permissive circle: it protects and permits. At certain times on certain days, men and women come together at a given place, and there, under the solemn eye of the tribe, fling themselves into a seemingly unorganised pantomime, which is in reality extremely systematic, in which by various means—shakes of the head, bending of the spinal column, throwing of the whole body backwards—may be deciphered as in an open book the huge effort of a community to exorcise itself, to liberate itself, to explain itself. There are no limits—inside the circle. The hillock up which you have toiled as if to be nearer to the moon; the river bank down which you slip as if to show the connection between the dance and ablutions, cleansing and purification—these are sacred places. There are no limits—for in reality your purpose in coming together is to allow the accumulated libido, the hampered aggressivity to dissolve as in a volcanic eruption. Symbolical killings, fantastic rides, imaginary mass murders—all must be brought out. The evil humours are undamned, and flow away with a din as of molten lava.

One step further and you are completely possessed. In fact, these are actually organised *séances* of possession and exorcism; they include vampirism, possession by djinns, by zombies, and by Legba, the famous god of the Voodoo. This disintegrating of the personality, this splitting and dissolution, all this fulfils a primordial function in the organism of the colonial world. When they set out, the men and women were impatient, stamping their feet in a state of nervous excitement; when they return, peace has been restored to the village; it is once more calm and unmoved.

During the struggle for freedom, a marked alienation from these practices is observed. The native's back is to the wall, the knife is at his throat (or, more precisely, the electrode at his genitals): he will have no more call for his fancies. After centuries of unreality, after having wallowed in the most outlandish phantoms, at long last the native, gun in hand, stands face to face with the only forces which contend for his life—the forces of colonialism. And the youth of a colonised country, growing up in an atmosphere of shot and fire, may well make a mock of, and does not hesitate to pour scorn upon the zombies of his ancestors, the horses with two heads, the dead who rise again, and the djinns who rush into your body while you yawn. The native discovers reality and transforms it into the pattern of his customs, into the practice of violence and into his plan for freedom.

We have seen that this same violence, though kept very much on the surface all through the colonial period, yet turns in the void. We have also seen that it is canalised by the emotional outlets of dance and possession by spirits; we have seen how it is exhausted in fratricidal combats. Now the problem is to lay hold of this violence which is changing direction. When formerly it was appeased by myths and exercised its talents in finding fresh ways of committing mass suicide, now new conditions will make possible a completely new line of action.

Nowadays a theoretical problem of prime importance is being set, on the historical plane as well as on the level of political tactics, by the liberation of the colonies: when can one affirm that the situation is ripe for a movement of national liberation? In what form should it first be manifested? Because the various means whereby decolonisation has been carried out have appeared in many different aspects, reason hesitates and refuses to say which is a true decolonisation, and which a false. We shall see that for a man who is in the thick of the fight it is an urgent matter to decide on the means and the tactics to employ: that is to say, how to conduct and organise the movement. If this coherence is not present there is only a blind will towards freedom, with the terribly reactionary risks which it entails.

What are the forces which in the colonial period open up new outlets and engender new aims for the violence of colonised peoples? In the first place there are the political parties and the intellectual or commercial *élites*. Now, the characteristic feature of certain political structures is that they proclaim abstract principles but refrain from issuing definite commands. The entire action of these nationalist political parties during the colonial period is action of the electoral type: a string of philosophico-political dissertations on the themes of the rights of peoples to self-determination, the rights of man to freedom from hunger and human dignity, and the unceasing affirmation of the principle: "One man, one vote." The national political parties never lay stress upon the necessity of a trial of armed strength, for the good reason that their objective is not the radical overthrowing of the system. Pacifists and legalists, they are in fact partisans of order, the new order—but to the colonialist bourgeoisie they put bluntly enough the demand which to them is the main one: "Give us more power." On the specific question of violence, the *élite* are ambiguous. They are violent in their words and reformist in their attitudes. When the nationalist political leaders *say* something, they make quite clear that they do not really *think* it.

This characteristic on the part of the nationalist political parties should be interpreted in the light both of the make-up of their leaders and the nature of their followings. The rank-and-file of a nationalist party is urban. The workers, primary school-teachers, artisans and small shop-keepers who have begun to profit—at a discount, to be sure—from the colonial set-up, have special interests at heart. What this sort of following demands is the betterment of their particular lot: increased salaries, for example. The dialogue between these political parties and colonialism is never broken off. Improvements are discussed, such as full electoral representation, the liberty of the press, and liberty of association. Reforms are debated. Thus it need not astonish anyone to notice that a large number of natives are militant members of the branches of political parties which stem from the mother country. These natives fight under an abstract watchword: "Government by the workers," and they forget that in their country it should be *nationalist* watchwords which are first in the field. The native intellectual has clothed his aggressiveness in his barely veiled desire to assimilate himself to the colonial world. He has used his aggressiveness to serve his own individual interests.

Thus there is very easily brought into being a kind of class of affranchised slaves, or slaves who are individually free. What the intellectual demands is the right to multiply the emancipated, and the opportunity to organise a genuine class of emancipated citizens. On the other hand, the mass of the people have no intention of standing by and watching individuals increase their chances of success. What they demand is not the settler's position of status, but the settler's place. The immense majority of natives want the settler's farm. For them, there is no question of entering into competition with the settler. They want to take his place.

The peasantry is systematically disregarded for the most part by the propaganda put out by the nationalist parties. And it is clear that in the colonial countries the peasants alone are revolutionary, for they have nothing to lose and everything to gain. The starving peasant, outside the class system, is the first among the exploited to discover that only violence pays. For him there is no compromise, no possible coming to terms; colonisation and decolonisation are simply a question of relative strength. The exploited man sees that his liberation implies the use of all means, and that of force first and foremost.

BARBARA DEMING

Revolution and Equilibrium

Barbara Deming, a civil rights activist, recounts her experiences in a Georgia jail in *Prison Notes*. She has written many other articles on the nonviolent movement in the United States.

> *"What we want to do is to go forward all the time . . . in the company of all men."*
> *"But can we escape becoming dizzy?"*
>
> Frantz Fanon
> in *The Wretched of the Earth*

"Do you want to remain pure? Is that it?" a black man asked me, during an argument about nonviolence. It is not possible to act at all and to remain pure; and that is not what I want, when I commit myself to the nonviolent discipline. There are people who are struggling to change conditions that they find intolerable, trying to find new lives; in the words of Frantz Fanon in *The Wretched of the Earth,* they want "to set afoot a new man." That is what I want too; and I have no wish to be assigned, as it were, separate quarters from those who are struggling in a way different from mine—segregated from my companions rather as, several years ago in Birmingham at the end of a demonstration, I found myself segregated in the very much cleaner and airier white section of the jail. I stand with all who say of present conditions that they do not allow men to be fully human and so they must be changed—all who not only say this but are ready to act.

At a recent conference about the directions the American Left should take, a socialist challenged me: "Can you call degrading the violence used by the oppressed to throw off oppression?" When one is confronted with what Russell Johnson calls accurately "the violence of the status quo"—conditions which are damaging, even murderous, to very many who must live within them—it is degrading for all to allow such conditions to persist. And if the individuals who can find the courage to bring about change see no way in which it can be done without employing violence on their own part—a very much lesser violence, they feel, than the violence to which they will put an end—I do not feel that I can judge them. The judgments I make are not judgments upon men but upon the means open to us—upon the promise these means of action hold or withhold. The living question is: What are the best means for changing our lives—for really changing them?

The very men who speak of the necessity of violence, if change is to be accomplished, are the first, often, to acknowledge the toll it exacts among those who use it—as well as those it is used against. Frantz Fanon has a chapter in *The Wretched of the Earth* entitled "Colonial War and Mental Disorders," and in it he writes, "We are forever pursued by our actions." After describing, among other painful disorders, those suffered by an Algerian terrorist—who made friends among the French after the war and then wondered with anguish whether any of the men he had killed had been men like these—he comments, "It was what might be called an attack of vertigo." Then he asks a poignant question: "But can we escape becoming dizzy? And who can affirm that vertigo does not haunt the whole of existence?"

"Vertigo"—here is a word, I think, much more relevant to the subject of revolutionary action than the word "purity." No, it is not that I want to remain pure; it is that I want to escape becoming dizzy. And here is exactly the argument of my essay: we can escape it. Not absolutely, of course; but we can escape vertigo in the drastic sense. It is my stubborn faith that if, as revolutionaries, we will wage battle without violence, we can remain very much more in control—of our own selves, of the responses to us which our adversaries make, of the battle as it proceeds and of the future we hope will issue from it.

The future—by whom will it be built? By all those whom the struggle has touched and marked. And so the question of how it marks them is not irrelevant. The future will be built even, in part, by those who have fought on the losing side. If it is a colonial struggle, of course, a good many of the adversaries can be expected to leave at the end of a successful revolution; but if it is a civil struggle, those who have been defeated, too, will at least help to make the new society what it is. How will the struggle have touched them? How will it have touched the victors?

Carl Oglesby, in *Containment and Change,* quotes a Brazilian guerrilla: "We are in dead earnest. At stake is the humanity of man." Then he asks, "How can ordinary men be at once warm enough to want what revolutionaries say they want (humanity), cold enough to do without remorse what they are capable of doing (cutting throats), and poised enough in the turbulence of their lives to keep the aspiration and the act both integrated and distinct? How is it that one of these passions does not invade and devour the other?" Yes—the question is one of equilibrium. How does one manage to keep it?

Oglesby would seem to answer that, generally speaking, one cannot expect the rebel to have the poise he describes. "He is an irresponsible man whose irresponsibility has been decreed by others. . . . He has no real views about the future . . . is not by *type* a Lenin, a Mao, a Castro. . . . His motivating vision of change is at root a vision of something absent—not of something that *will* be there . . . a missing landlord, a missing mine owner, a missing sheriff. . . ." Ultimately, says Oglesby, he must *become* responsible. But how? It is in the midst of the struggle that he must at least begin to be, isn't it? And so the very means by which we struggle, and their tendency either to give us poise or to leave us dizzy, is surely, again, relevant.

I think of the words with which Fanon opens the final chapter of *The Wretched of the Earth*: "Come then, comrades; it would be as well to decide at once to change our ways." I quote Fanon often—because he is eloquent, but also because he is quoted repeatedly these days by those who plead the need for violence. It is my conviction that he can be quoted as well to plead for nonviolence. It is true that he declares: "From birth it is clear . . . that this narrow world, strewn with prohibitions, can only be called in question by absolute violence." But I ask all those who are readers of Fanon to make an experiment: Every time you find the word "violence" in his pages, substitute for it the phrase "radical and uncompromising action." I contend that with the exception of a very few passages this substitution can be made, and that the action he calls for could just as well be nonviolent action.

He writes, for example: "Violence alone, violence committed by the people, violence organized and educated by its leaders, makes it possible for the masses to understand social truths and gives the key to them. Without that struggle, without that knowledge of the practice of action, there's nothing but a fancy-dress parade . . . a few reforms at the top . . . and down there at the bottom an undivided mass . . . endlessly marking time." "Knowledge of the practice of action"—*that* is what Fanon sees to be absolutely necessary, to develop in the masses of people an understanding of social truths, accomplish that "work of clarification," "demystification," "enlightening of consciousness" which is the recurring and the deepest theme of his book. This action could be nonviolent action; it could very much better be nonviolent action—if only that action is bold enough.

Here is Fanon as he argues the necessity for "mere rebellion"—which Oglesby has described—to become true revolution: "Racialism and hatred and resentment—'a legitimate desire for revenge'—cannot sustain a war of liberation. Those lightning flashes of consciousness which fling the body into stormy paths or which throw it into an almost pathological trance where the face of the other beckons me on to giddiness, where my blood calls for the blood of the other . . . that intense emotion of the first few hours falls to pieces if it is left to feed on its own substance. . . .

You'll never overthrow the terrible enemy machine, and you won't change human beings if you forgot to raise the standard of consciousness of the rank-and-file."

THE SPIRIT OF INVENTION

The task involves the enlightening of consciousness. But violence "beckons me on to giddiness." I repeat Fanon's words: "It would be as well to decide at once to change our ways." Another man with whom I was arguing the other day declared to me, "You can't turn the clock back now to nonviolence!" Turn the clock back? The clock has been turned to violence all down through history. Resort to violence hardly marks a move forward. It is nonviolence which is in the process of invention, if only people would not stop short in that experiment. Fanon again: "If we want humanity to advance a step further, if we want to bring it up to a different level than that which Europe has shown it, then we must invent and we must make discoveries." It is for that spirit of invention that I plead. And again I would like to ask something of all readers of Fanon. Turn to that last chapter of *The Wretched of the Earth* and read it again. Is he not groping here visibly for a way that departs from violence?

He writes, "We today do everything, so long as we do not imitate Europe." And earlier in the book he has reported, "The argument the native chooses has been furnished by the settler. . . . The native now affirms that the colonialist understands nothing but force." He writes, "We must leave our dreams. . . ." And earlier he has written, "The native is an oppressed person whose permanent dream is to become the persecutor." He writes, "Leave this Europe where they are never done talking of Man, yet murder men everywhere they find them, at the corner of every one of their own streets, in all the corners of the globe. . . . Europe has . . . set her face against all solicitude and all tenderness. . . . So, my brother, how is it that we do not understand that we have better things to do than to follow that same Europe. . . . When I search for Man in the technique and the style of Europe, I see only a succession of negations of man, and an avalanche of murders. . . . Let us combine our muscles and our brains in a new direction. Let us try to create the whole man, whom Europe has been incapable of bringing to triumphant birth. All the elements of a solution . . . have, at different times, existed in European thought. But the action of European men has not carried out the mission which fell to them. We must try to set afoot a new man." And he writes, "It is simply a very concrete question of not dragging men toward mutilation. . . . The pretext of catching up must not be used to push man around, to tear him away from himself or from his privacy, to break and kill him. No, we do not want to catch up with anyone. What we want to do is to go forward all the time, night and day, in the company of Man, in the company of all men."

But how in the company of all men if we are willing to kill? In the passages I have quoted does Fanon not warn us again and again against murder, warn us that murder cannot possibly bring to birth the new man—that it was precisely Europe's propensity for murder that kept her from carrying out the mission we now inherit? What really but radical nonviolence is he here straining to be able to imagine? We must "vomit up" the values of Europe, he has written. Is it not above all the value that Europe and America have put upon violence that we must vomit up? He writes, "It is simply a very concrete question of not dragging men toward mutilation." Yes, very concrete, I urge, because it comes down to the means by which we struggle, comes down to a choice of *which* "practice of action" we are going to study.

At this point suddenly I can hear in my head many voices interrupting me. They all say: "Who among us likes violence? But nonviolence has been tried." It has *not* been tried. We have hardly begun to try it. The people who dismiss it now as irrelevant do not understand what it could be. And, again, they especially do not understand the very much greater control over events that they could find if they would put this "practice of action," rather than violence, to a real test.

What most people are saying just now of course is that nonviolence gives us no control at all over events. "After years of this," says Stokely Carmichael, "we are at almost the same point." Floyd McKissick expresses the same disillusion: all the nonviolent campaigns have accomplished essentially nothing for black people. They have served to integrate a token few into American society. Even those few cannot be said to have been absorbed into the mainstream; they still are not allowed to forget the color of their skins. And the great majority of black people are actually worse off than before. He declares, with reason, "We are concerned about the aspirations of the 90% down there"—those of whom Fanon spoke, the many "endlessly marking time."

PSYCHOLOGICAL FORCES

I won't try to pretend that progress has been made that has not been made. Though I would add to the picture these two men and others paint that there is one sense in which things hardly can be said to be at the same point still. If one speaks of psychological forces that will make a difference—the determination of black people not to accept their situation any longer, the determination of some white people not to accept it either, and a consciousness on the part of other white people that changes are bound to come now, doubts about their ability to prevent them—in these terms all has been in constant motion. And these terms—Fanon for one would stress—are hardly unimportant. Literally, yes, one can speak of gains that seem to mock those who have nearly exhausted themselves in the struggle for them. But I think one has to ask certain questions. Have gains been slight because nonviolent tactics were the wrong tactics to employ—or did many of those leading the battle underestimate the difficulties of the terrain before them? Did they lack at the start a sufficiently radical vision? Can those who have now turned from reliance upon nonviolence say surely that resort to violence over those same years would have brought greater gains?

There are those who are implying this now. One observer who implies it strongly is Andrew Kopkind, writing in *The New York Review of Books* in August [1967] about the uprising in the ghettos. He writes, "Martin Luther King and the 'leaders' who appealed for nonviolence, CORE, the black politicians, the old SNCC *are all* beside the point. Where the point is is in the streets. . . . The insurrections of July have done what everyone in America for thirty years has thought impossible; mass action has convulsed the society and brought smooth government to a halt." He itemizes with awe: they caused tanks to rumble through the heart of the nation's biggest cities, brought out soldiers by the thousands, destroyed billions of dollars worth of property. This violence (or as Dave Dellinger better names it, this counterviolence of the victimized) certainly called out the troops. One thing violence can be counted on to do is bring the antagonist forth in battle dress. The question that hasn't been answered yet is: did this gain the rebels an advantage? It gained them many casualties. The powers-that-be paid their price, too, as Kopkind points out. But it is one thing to be able to state the price the antagonist paid, another to be able to count your own real gains. Kopkind gives us the heady sense of an encounter really joined at last, of battle lines drawn. But in the days of Birmingham, too, people had the excited sense of an engagement entered. Kopkind himself grants, "It is at once obvious that the period of greatest danger is just beginning."

THE GHETTO CHALLENGE

I have slighted, however, one point that he is making, and a very central point: "Poor blacks," he writes, "have stolen the center stage from the liberal elites . . . their actions indict the very legitimacy of [the] government." Yes, this is a fact not to overlook: the people of the ghettos have thrown down a challenge to government that is radical. But Kopkind is writing about two things: the offering of radical challenge and resort to violence. And he writes clearly as though he assumes that such a challenge can only be offered violently. It is with this assumption that I argue.

It is an assumption many share. Carl Oglesby seems to share it. In *Containment and Change* he criticizes "the politics of the appeal to higher power . . . the same thing as prayer . . . a main assumption of which is that [the higher power] is not bad, only misinformed." He appears to see all nonviolent action as covered by this definition. "This way of thinking brought the peasants and priests to their massacre at Kremlin Square in 1905. . . . It rationalized the 1963 March on Washington for jobs and Freedom. The Freedom Rides, the nonviolent sit-ins, and the various Deep South marches were rooted in the same belief: that there was indeed a higher power which was responsive and decent. . . . The Vietnam war demonstrations are no different. . . . The main idea has always been to persuade higher authority . . . to do something. Far from calling higher authority into question, these demonstrations actually dramatize and even exaggerate its power."

He goes on then to describe how the "whimsical" hopes that are entertained about the powerful evaporate: "Sometimes mass-based secular prayer has resulted in change. But more often it has only shown the victim-petitioner that the problem is graver and change harder to get than [he] had imagined. . . . It turns out that the powerful know perfectly well who their victims are . . . and that they have no intention of changing anything. This recognition is momentous, no doubt the spiritual low point of the emergent revolutionary's education. He finds that the enemy is not a few men but a whole system whose agents saturate the society. . . . He is diverted by a most realistic despair. But this despair contains within itself the omen of that final reconstitution of the spirit which will prepare [him] . . . for the shift to insurgency, rebellion, revolution. . . . At the heart of his despair lies the new certainty that there will be no change which he does not produce by himself."

With this description I do not argue at all. It is a very accurate description of the education those protesting in this country have been receiving. May more and more read the lesson. I argue with the contention that nonviolent action can only be prayerful action—must by its nature remain naive. Too often in the past it has confined itself to petition, but there is no need for it to do so—especially now that so many have learned "change [is] harder to get than they had imagined." There have always been those in the nonviolent movement who called for radical moves. As Kopkind writes, "all that has come until now is prologue." But this does not mean that our alternatives have suddenly been reduced. The pressure that nonviolent moves could put upon those who are opposing change, the power that could be exerted this way, has yet to be tested.

POWER AND NONVIOLENCE

I have introduced the word "power" deliberately. When the slogan "Black Power" was first taken up, the statements immediately issued, both for and against it, all seemed to imply that "power" was a word inconsistent with a faith in nonviolence. This was of course the position taken by Stokely Carmichael: "We had to work for power because this country does not function by morality, love and nonviolence, but by power. For too many years, black Americans marched and had their heads broken and got shot. They were saying to the country, 'Look, you guys are supposed to be nice guys and we are only going to do what we are supposed to do. Why . . . don't you give us what we ask?' . . . We demonstrated from a position of weakness. We cannot be expected any longer to march and have our heads broken in order to say to whites: come on, you're nice guys. For you are not nice guys. We have found you out."

Carmichael gives us: the humble appeal to conscience on the one hand, the resort to power on the other. If the choice were really this, anyone who wanted change would certainly have to abandon nonviolent action. For as Bradford Lyttle comments in a paper on Black Power, no, most people are not nice guys. "It isn't necessary to be hit over the head to learn this. . . . Some Christians call the un-niceness of people 'original sin.' It's Freud's 'ego.' Naturalist Konrad Lorenz studies it as aggressiveness and argues convincingly that it's instinctive with men. Whatever the un-niceness may be, it is part of all of us, and our job is to minimize it."

The trouble is that advocates of nonviolence themselves often write in terms that seem to corroborate the picture Carmichael paints. When they actually engage in direct action, they pay great attention to other-than-moral pressures that can be and have to be placed on those with whom they are struggling. But on paper they tend again and again to stress only the appeal that can be made to conscience. Bradford, in his paper on Black Power, notes: "Carmichael's vision isn't limited to Negroes. Machiavelli had it: . . . 'A man who wishes to make a profession of goodness in everything must necessarily come to grief among so many who are not good. Therefore it is necessary . . . to learn how not to be good.'" Then he pleads that to put one's faith in coercive power is tragic, and his argument is: "throughout history, those who have most deeply touched the hearts of hardened men have been the ones who chose not to defend themselves with violence." He, too, seems here to pose a narrow choice: resort to power (learning how not to be good) or appeal to conscience (learning, Carmichael would put it, to do only what we are supposed to do).

THE CHOICE IS WIDER

But the choice is very much wider than this (as Bradford of course knows); and the distinctions that seem to have been set up here are unreal. To resort to power one need not be violent,[1] and to speak to conscience one need not be meek. The most effective action *both* resorts to power *and* engages conscience. Nonviolent action does not have to beg others to "be nice." It can in effect force them to consult their consciences—or to pretend to have them. Nor does it have to petition those in power to do something about a situation. It can face the authorities with a new fact and say: accept this new situation which *we* have created.

If people doubt that there is power in nonviolence, I am afraid that it is due in part to the fact that those of us who believe in it have yet to find for ourselves an adequate vocabulary. The leaflets we pass out tend to speak too easily about love and truth—and suggest that we hope to move men solely by being loving and truthful. The words do describe our method in a kind of shorthand. But who can read the shorthand? It is easy enough to recommend "love." How many, even among those who like to use the word, can literally feel love for a harsh opponent—not merely pretending to while concealing from themselves their own deepest feelings? What *is* possible is to act toward another human being on the assumption that all men's lives are of value, that there is something about any man to be loved, whether one can *feel* love for him or not.[2] It happens that, if one does act on this assumption, it gives one much greater poise in the situation. It is easy enough to speak about truth; but we had better spell out how, in battle, we rely upon the truth. It is not simply that we pay our antagonist the human courtesy of not lying to him. We insist upon telling him truths he doesn't want to hear—telling what seems to us the truth about the injustice he commits. Words are not enough here. Gandhi's term for nonviolent action was "satyagraha"—which can be translated as "clinging to the truth." What is needed is this—to *cling* to the truth as one sees it. And one has to cling with one's entire weigtht. One doesn't simply say, "I have a right to sit here," but acts out that truth—and sits here. One doesn't just say, "If we are customers in this store, it's wrong that we're never hired here," but refuses to be a customer any longer. One doesn't just say, "I don't believe in this war," but refuses to put on a uniform. One doesn't just say, "The use of napalm is atrocious," but refuses to pay for it by

---

[1] Although those in the Movement who issued critical statements against use of the slogan "Black Power" seemed most always to imply that "power" was an improper word, I couldn't help noticing that just that word had a way of slipping into their own publicity releases—an S.C.L.C. release, for example, repudiating the slogan but speaking the next moment of the "political power" they sought through pushing voter registration.

[2] Sometimes, if one disciplines oneself to act upon this assumption, the feeling itself of love for one's enemy enters one, taking one by surprise—a kind of grace. Some readers may ask: why should one want to feel love for one's enemy? But I note that Fanon in *Black Skin, White Masks* writes, "I, the man of color, want only this: . . . That it be possible for me to discover and to love man, wherever he may be."

refusing to pay one's taxes. And so on and so on. One brings what economic weight one has to bear, what political, social, psychological, what physical weight. There is a good deal more involved here than a moral appeal. It should be acknowledged both by those who argue against nonviolence and those who argue for it that we, too, rely upon force.

STOPPING SHORT

If greater gains have not been won by nonviolent action it is because most of those trying it have, quite as Oglesby charges, expected too much from "the powerful"; and so, I would add, they have stopped short of really exercising their peculiar powers—those powers one discovers when one refuses any longer simply to do another's will. They have stopped far too short not only of widespread nonviolent disruption but of that form of noncooperation which is assertive, constructive—that confronts those who are "running everything" with independent activity, particularly independent economic activity. There is leverage for change here that has scarcely begun to be applied.

To refuse one's cooperation is to exert force. One can, in fact, exert so very much force in this way that many people will always be quick to call noncooperators violent. How, then, does one distinguish nonviolent from violent action? It is not that it abstains from force, to rely simply upon moral pressure. It resorts even to what can only be called physical force—when, for example, we sit down and refuse to move, and we force others to cope somehow with all these bodies. The distinction to make is simply that those committed to a nonviolent discipline refuse to injure the antagonist. Of course if nonviolent action is as bold as it must be in any real battle for change, some at least of those resisting the change are bound to *feel* that injury has been done them. For they feel it as injury to be shaken out of the accustomed pattern of their lives. The distinction remains a real one. Perhaps there is another way it could be put. The man who acts violently forces another to do *his* will—in Fanon's words, he tears the other away from himself, pushes him around, often willing to break him, kill him. The man who acts nonviolently insists upon acting out his *own* will, refuses to act out another's—but in this way, only, exerts force upon the other, not tearing him away from himself but tearing from him only that which is not properly his own, the strength which has been loaned to him by all those who have been giving him obedience.

NONVIOLENT OBSTRUCTION

But the distinction I have just made is a little too neat. In almost any serious non-violent struggle, one has to resort to obstructive action. When we block access to buildings, block traffic, block shipments, it can be charged that we go a little further than refusing obedience and impose upon the freedom of action of others. There is some justice to the charge. I nevertheless think it appropriate to speak of non-violent obstruction, but I would revert to my original description as the definitive one: the person committed to nonviolent action refuses to injure the antagonist. It is quite possible to frustrate another's action without doing him injury.[3] And some freedoms are basic freedoms, some are not. To impose upon another man's freedom to kill, or his freedom to help to kill, to recruit to kill, is not to violate his person in a fundamental way.[4]

But I can imagine the impatience of some of my readers with these various scruples. What, they might say, has this to do with fighting battles—battles which are in dead earnest? How can we hope to put any real pressure upon an adversary for whom we show such concern?

A CREATIVE COMBINATION

This is the heart of my argument: We can put *more* pressure on the antagonist for whom we show human concern. It is precisely solicitude for his person *in combination with* a stubborn interference with his actions that can give us a very special degree of control (precisely in our acting both with love, if you will—in the sense that we respect his human rights—and truthfulness, in the sense that we act out fully our objections to his violating *our* rights). We put upon him two pressures— the pressure of our defiance of him and the pressure of our respect for his life— and it happens that in combination these two pressures are uniquely effective.

One effect gained is to "raise the level of consciousness" for those engaged in the struggle—those on both sides. Because the human rights of the adversary are respected, though his actions, his official policies are not, the focus of attention becomes those actions, those policies, and their true nature. The issue cannot be avoided. The antagonist cannot take the interference with his actions personally, because his person is not threatened, and he is forced to begin to acknowledge the reality of the grievance against him. And those in rebellion—committed to the discipline of respect for all men's lives, and enabled by this discipline to avoid that "trance" Fanon describes, "where the face of the other beckons me on to giddiness," is enabled to see more and more clearly that (as Oglesby says) "the enemy is not a few men but a whole system," and to study that system.

THE TWO HANDS

The more the real issues are dramatized, and the struggle raised above the personal, the more control those in nonviolent rebellion begin to gain over their adversary.

---

[3] It is possible, but not always simple. When we stage an act of massive obstruction in a city, for example, there is always the risk that we will prevent some emergency call from being answered—prevent a doctor's car from getting through, perhaps. One has obviously to anticipate such situations and be ready to improvise answers to the human problems raised.

[4] I am uneasy, however, at the way Carl Davidson of S.D.S. words his defense of obstruction. He writes in *New Left Notes* of November 13, 1967: "The institutions our resistance has desanctified and delegitimized, as a result of our action against their oppression of others, have lost all authority and hence all respect. As such, they have only raw coercive power. Since they are without legitimacy in our eyes, they are without rights. Insofar as individuals, such as recruiters, continue to remain in association with those institutions, they run the risk of being given the same treatment. . . . We can assert the Nuremberg decisions and other past criteria of war crimes as the criteria by which we, in conscience, decide whether or not an institution and individuals associated with that institution have lost their

For they are able at one and the same time to disrupt everything for him, making it impossible for him to operate within the system as usual, and to temper his response to this, making it impossible for him simply to strike back without thought and with all his strength. They have as it were two hands upon him—the one calming him, making him ask questions, as the other makes him move.

In any violent struggle one can expect the violence to escalate. It does so automatically, neither side being really able to regulate the process at will. The classic acknowledgement of this fact was made by President Kennedy when he saluted Premier Khrushchev for withdrawing nuclear missiles from Cuba. "I welcome this message," he said, because "developments were approaching a point where events could have become unmanageable." In nonviolent struggle, the violence used against one may mount for a while (indeed, if one is bold in one's rebellion, it is bound to do so), but the escalation is no longer automatic; with the refusal of one side to retaliate, the mainspring of the automaton has been snapped and one can count on reaching a point where de-escalation begins. One can count, that is, in the long run, on receiving far fewer casualties.

THE NUMBER OF CASUALTIES

Nothing is more certain than this and yet, curiously, nothing is less obvious. A very common view is that nonviolent struggle is suicidal. This is, for example, Andrew Kopkind's view: "Turn-the-other-cheek was always a personal standard, not a general rule: people can commit suicide but peoples cannot. Morality, like politics, starts at the barrel of a gun." (A surprising sentence, but by morality he means, no doubt, the assertion of one's rights.) The contention that nonviolent struggle is suicidal hardly stands up under examination. Which rebels suffered more casualties—those who, under Gandhi, managed to throw the British out of India or the so-called Mau Mau who struggled by violence to throw the British out of Kenya? The British were certainly not "nice guys" in their response to the Gandhians. They, and the Indian troops who obeyed their orders, beat thousands of unarmed people, shot and killed hundreds. In the Amritsar Massacre, for example, they fired into an unarmed crowd that was trapped in a spot where no one could escape and killed 379 people, wounding many more. There was a limit, nevertheless, to the violence they could justify to themselves—or felt they could justify to the world. Watching any nonviolent struggle, it is always startling to learn how long it can take the antagonist to set such limits; but he finally does feel constrained to set them—especially if his actions are well publicized. In Kenya, where the British could cite as provocation the violence used against them, they hardly felt constrained to set any limits at all on their actions, and they adopted tactics very similar to those the Americans are using today against the Vietnamese. In that struggle for independence, many thou-

---

legitimacy and their rights." *Can* one give individuals the same treatment that one gives institutions—and deny them *all* respect? If he means that we need not grant individuals the right to oppress others, I am in agreement. But if he means that when we can identify an individual as an oppressor, then we need not treat him as though he had *any* human rights—he alarms me. This formulation would seem to me to lead into grim territory.

sands of Africans fighting in the forest and many thousands of their supporters and sympathizers on the reserves were killed. Many were also tortured.[5]

One can, as I say, be certain if one adopts the discipline of nonviolence that in the long run one will receive fewer casualties. And yet very few people are able to see that this is so. It is worth examining the reasons why the obvious remains unacknowledged. Several things, I think, blind people to the plain truth.

First, something seems wrong to most people engaged in struggle when they see more people hurt on their own side than on the other side. They are used to reading this as an indication of defeat, and a complete mental readjustment is required of them. Within the new terms of struggle, victory has nothing to do with their being able to give more punishment than they take (quite the reverse); victory has nothing to do with their being able to punish the other at all; it has to do simply with being able, finally, to make the other move. Again, the real issue is kept in focus. Vengeance is not the point; change is. But the trouble is that in most men's minds the thought of victory and the thought of punishing the enemy coincide. If they are suffering casualties and the enemy is not, they fail to recognize that they are suffering *fewer* casualties than they would be if they turned to violence.

NONVIOLENT BATTLE

Actually, something seems wrong to many people, I think, when—in nonviolent struggle—they receive any casualties at all. They feel that if they are not hurting anybody, then they shouldn't get hurt themselves. (They shouldn't. But it is not only in nonviolent battle that the innocent suffer.) It is an intriguing psychological fact that when the ghetto uprisings provoked the government into bringing out troops and tanks—and killing many black people, most of them onlookers—observers like Kopkind decided that the action had been remarkably effective, citing as proof precisely the violence of the government's response. But when James Meredith was shot, just for example, any number of observers editorialized: "See, nonviolence doesn't work." Those who have this reaction overlook the fact that nonviolent battle is still battle, and in battle of whatever kind, people do get hurt. If personal safety had been Meredith's main concern, he could, as the saying goes, have stayed at home.

Battle of any kind provokes a violent response—because those who have power are not going to give it up voluntarily. But there is simply no question that—in any long run—violent battle provokes a more violent response and brings greater casualties. Men tend not to think in long-run terms, of course; they tend to think in terms of isolated moments. There will always be such moments that one can cite, in which a particular man might have been safer if he had been armed. If Meredith had been carrying a loaded pistol, he might well have shot his assailant before the man shot him. (He might also well have been ambushed by still more men.) Whatever one can say about overall statistics, some men will always *feel* safer when armed—each able to imagine himself the one among many who would always shoot first.

To recognize that men have greater, not less control in the situation when they have committed themselves to nonviolence requires a drastic readjustment of

[5] See *Mau Mau from Within* by Barrett and Njama.

vision. And this means taking both a long-range view of the field and a very much cooler, more objective one.

Nonviolence can inhibit the ability of the antagonist to hit back. (If the genius of guerrilla warfare is to make it impossible for the other side really to exploit its superior brute force, nonviolence can be said to carry this even further.)

And there is another sense in which it gives one greater leverage—enabling one both to put pressure upon the antagonist and to modulate his response to that pressure. In violent battle the effort is to demoralize the enemy, to so frighten him that he will surrender. The risk is that desperation and resentment will make him go on resisting when it is no longer even in his own interest. He has been driven beyond reason. In nonviolent struggle the effort is of quite a different nature. One doesn't try to frighten the other. One tries to undo him—tries, in the current idiom, to "blow his mind"—only in the sense that one tries to shake him out of former attitudes and force him to appraise the situation now in a way that takes into consideration your needs as well as his. One is able to do this—able in a real sense to change his mind (rather than to drive him out of it)—precisely because one reassures him about his personal safety all the time that one keeps disrupting the order of things that he has known to date. When—under your constant pressure—it becomes to his own interest to adapt himself to change, he is able to do so. Fear for himself does not prevent him. In this sense a liberation movement that is nonviolent sets the oppressor free as well as the oppressed.

THE GENIUS OF NONVIOLENCE

The most common charge leveled against nonviolence is that it counts upon touching the heart of an adversary—who is more than likely to be stony of heart. His heart, his conscience need not be touched. His mind has been. The point is that you prevent him from reacting out of fear—in mindless reflex action. You also prevent him from being able to justify to others certain kinds of actions that he would like to take against you—and may for a while attempt to take. Here one can speak of still another sense in which nonviolence gives one greater control. If the antagonist *is* unjustifiably harsh in his countermeasures, and continues to be, one will slowly win away from him allies and supporters—some of them having consciences more active than his perhaps; or perhaps all of them simply caring about presenting a certain image, caring for one reason or another about public relations. An adversary might seem to be immovable. One could nevertheless move him finally by taking away from him the props of his power—those men upon whose support he depends. The special genius of nonviolence is that it can draw to our side not only natural allies—who are enabled gradually to recognize that they are allies because in confrontation with us their minds are not blurred by fear but challenged (and they begin to refuse orders, as several soldiers did in October at the Pentagon). Even beyond this, it can move to act on our behalf elements in society who have no such natural inclination. When the Quebec to Guantanamo walkers were fasting in jail in Albany, Georgia, the men who finally put most pressure upon the authorities to release them and let them walk through town were clergymen not at all sympathetic either to the walkers as individuals or to the message on their signs and leaflets. Nonviolent tactics can move into action on our behalf men not naturally inclined to act for us; whereas violent tactics draw into actions that do us harm men for whom it is not at all natural to act against us. A painful example of this was Martin Luther King's act of declaring that the authorities were right in calling out troops to deal with the ghetto uprisings. John Gerassi provided another example in a talk I heard him give about revolutionary prospects in Latin America. He told how a plan on the part of a rebel group to gain support among the people by assassinating policemen backfired—because every slain policeman in that society of very large families had so many relatives, all unable to see the death as a political act that might help them, able to see it only as a personal loss. Violence makes men "dizzy"; it disturbs the vision, makes them see only their own immediate losses and fear of losses. Any widespread resort to violence in this country by those seeking change could produce such vertigo among the population at large that the authorities would be sure to be given more and more liberty to take repressive measures—in the name of "Order."

KNOWING THE ENEMY

Some readers might comment that such a development would be educational, for the underlying nature of the society would then stand revealed; and it is necessary to know the enemy. But it is necessary, too, to know that one has a certain power to affect those who stand against us. It would be easy enough to know the worst about them—by acting in a way that allowed them to behave toward us in the worst way that they could. It is more practical, even if it is more difficult, to act in a way that prevents this. If it is important not to be naive about their capacity for doing us harm, it is just as important not to be blind to our own capacity for moderating their action. In histories of the Chinese and Cuban revolutions, there are many accounts of generosity shown by the rebels toward enemy troops—resulting in widespread recruitment from among those troops. It proved very practical to act on the assumption that not all among them need be labeled permanently "enemy." Those engaged in nonviolent battle simply act on this assumption in the boldest degree. They declare, in the words of the Vietnamese Buddhist Thich Nhat Hanh —words that are startling and sound at first naive: "No men are our enemies." By this we do not mean that we think no men will try to destroy us; or that we overlook the fact that men from certain sections of the society are above all likely to try it. We mean, first, of course, that we are committed to try not to destroy them; but we mean furthermore that there is a working chance—if we do refuse to threaten them personally as we struggle with them—that in certain instances at least some of them may be willing to accommodate themselves to the pressure we put on them to change, and so both they and we may be liberated from the state of enmity. We mean that we refuse to cut ourselves off from them in any ultimate human sense— counting it as both decent and practical to do so.

KINDNESS AND REVOLUTION

I have been reading William Hinton's *Fanshen: A Documentary of Revolution in a Chinese Village,* and I have been struck by how many times in the course of his story he reports a decision taken by the revolutionary leaders that greater humanity shown this group or that group will advance the revolution. There is, for example, a decision at one point to be more lenient toward counterrevolutionary suspects among Catholic peasants. "They could never be won if they were isolated and discriminated against. They had to be drawn into full participation." In one dramatic instance it is decided that the attack on middle peasants has been overdone—that the land of many of these families has been wrongly expropriated, and that they must be reclassified as friends rather than enemies of the revolution. "We must make clear to them that they have their . . . rights." Because of this decision, too, things improved, the revolution gained momentum. The decisions which he reports are for the most part taken "to enlarge the united front of the people and to isolate as popular enemies only those diehard elements who could not possibly be mobilized to support a 'land-to-the-tiller' policy." One of the leaders explains, "In proposing any basic social change . . . revolutionaries had to decide who should be brought together and who isolated, who should be called a friend and who an enemy." Experience seemed always to be showing that the more people who were called friends, the better things went. I noted that as time went on leniency began to be advised even toward the gentry and the landlords; it was decided that here, too, the attacks had been at first overdone. "Families cannot be driven from house and home forever." As one leader put it: "We have to show everyone a way out."

This is of course just what nonviolence teaches—not to be naive about the fact that some men more than others will see it as in their interest to try to destroy us, and will often persist and persist in trying to; but to recognize that they never can see it in their interest finally to accommodate themselves to the changes we are forcing unless we give them the liberty to do so. And they will only believe that we offer this liberty, only be able to imagine new lives for themselves, if we have refused to threaten them with any personal injury.[6]

MAN VERSUS FUNCTION

I have had conversations with a Marxist who argues that it is absurd to claim we can avoid personal injury to others in any serious social struggle; for "men are reduced to functional elements": to threaten to deprive a man of his accustomed position in society is to threaten his very person. It will certainly be felt in many instances as just such a threat. But no man is ever reduced quite in his entire being to a functional element in society. And precisely because the rebel who is nonviolent distinguishes, as he struggles with another, between the man himself to whom he offers a certain basic respect (simply *as* another man) and the role that man has been playing, which he refuses to respect, it becomes more possible for the other, too, to begin to make the distinction. It may indeed at first be literally impossible for him to see himself, if he tries to imagine himself functioning in any way but the way that he has been. But the fact that others seem to be able to, makes it easier—especially if so much pressure is put on him that it becomes impossible for him to see himself functioning comfortably any longer in the old way. It is neces-

[6] There is a cliché often applied to the enemy: "All he can understand is force." But men "understand" brute force in the most narrow sense only: They understand that they are being hurt, or may be hurt by it—and so that they had better either surrender or manage to hurt the other side even more. Brute force cannot make the other understand that in a new world he could find a new life for himself.

sary to remember—as Oglesby says—that "the enemy is not a few men but a whole system," to remember that when the men with whom we struggle confront us it is as functional elements in this system that they do so, behaving in a certain sense automatically. It is necessary to know this well. But it is precisely if we refuse to treat them as nothing more than this—if we insist on treating them not as parts of a machine but as men, capable of thought and of change—that we gain a very much greater control in the situation. It is practical, in short, always to be *talking* with the enemy.

Oglesby describes the rebel as one who is quite unwilling to talk. "The rebel is an incorrigible absolutist who has replaced . . . all 'solutions' with the single irreducible demand that . . . those who now have all power shall no longer have any, and that those who now have none—the people, the victimized—shall have all. . . . 'What do you want?' asks the worried, perhaps intimidated master. 'What can I give you?' . . . But the rebel . . . answers, 'I cannot be purchased.' The answer is meant mainly to break off the conference." One reason the rebel wants to break it off, Oglesby explains, is that he has as yet no really clear vision of "the revolutionized, good society," and would be embarrassed to have to confess this. He is not' yet a responsible man. Then Oglesby adds: Ultimately he must become so. I am not quite sure *how*—as Oglesby sees it—he is to become responsible. My own suggestion is, of course, that nonviolent battle in itself teaches one to be.

It is a more difficult way. It does, for example, complicate the process of defining for ourselves and others who can be expected to act as our allies and who can be expected to resist us as harshly as they dare when, of the latter, we have always to be making two points at the same time: (1) here are men toward whom we have to be on our guard and (2) here are men for whom we have to show human concern. It can be done, though, and in very few words. I remember James Bevel addressing a church audience in Birmingham: "We love our white brothers"—pause—"but we don't trust them."

THE FEEL OF AN ACTION

The trouble is that people tend to *feel* that they are taking bolder action when they disdain all conversations with the adversary. We had experience of this often on the Quebec to Guantanamo walk while we were in the South. There were any number of times when, at the edge of a town, we would find ourselves confronted by police who would inform us that we weren't going to be allowed to walk through. We had a constitutional right to walk through, and a few people in the group were always in favor of simply saying, "Try to stop us!" or saying nothing at all—and marching forward. What we actually did, always, was to stop the walk for an hour or two, drive into town and discuss the matter with the chief of police. We would talk very quietly and always show him courtesy, and respect for his *proper* authority (for example, where traffic control was concerned), but in the course of the talk we would let it become clear to him that he would save himself a lot of trouble by letting us walk through; we knew what our rights were and had been to jail before for them and weren't afraid of going again. Time and again, after a certain amount of bluster on the chief's part, we would be allowed to walk. A few people in the group were always dissatisfied with this way. For it *felt like* deferring to the authorities. If we had simply marched forward, of course, feeling very bold, we would not have made our way through the town—we would have made our way right into jail, the authorities doing with us what they liked. The action that felt less bold won us our way.

All this is relevant, I think, to discussions going on now in the Movement about how to pass from protest to resistance, from merely "symbolic" actions to "practical" ones. To define clearly which actions are symbolic—and which more than that— one has often to look twice. A bold foray that is absolutely certain to be stopped is, surely, symbolic action. For example, those who rushed up the steps into the Pentagon on October 21st—to be thrown back at once by the troops, and quite predictably —were surely engaging in symbolic action; whereas those who tried to communicate with the troops confronting them, and were able to cause at least two defections from those troops, were surely engaging in action that was more than symbolic. The whole subject is infinitely complex. I am hardly saying that bold forays are never in order; but I am saying that dialogue with the other side is deeply practical.

HOW MANY WILL ANSWER?

Again I can imagine certain readers interrupting—to remark that I am overlooking, in this essay, one fundamental point. It is all very well to talk of the advantages of nonviolence, they might say, but how many are going to answer the call to such battle? A certain form of struggle can hardly be called practical if one cannot recruit very many men to try it; and to get most men to fight, one has to offer certain things which nonviolent struggle does not offer. I have heard people state, for example, that men from the ghettos would never turn to nonviolence because it does not allow them to speak out the full measure of their hatred for the white man. I have heard others say that few people would turn to it because it does not offer them the chance to feel, for once, like men. How a certain action makes one *feel* is not irrelevant.

But if nonviolent action is boldly taken it does allow men to speak out their deepest feelings; and if it is boldly taken, it does allow them to feel that they are standing up to others like men. It may not permit them to act out their hatred for others by taking revenge; but it allows—it requires—them to act out all the truth they feel about what the other has done, is doing to them, and to act out their determination to change this state of things. In this very process, one's hatred of the other can be forgotten, because it is beside the point; the point is to change one's life. The point is not to give some vent to the emotions that have been destroying one; the point is so to act that one can master them now.

What is it to assert one's manhood—one's human rights? Let me quote Fanon again. He writes in *Black Skin, White Masks*: "I have only one solution: to rise above this absurd drama that others have staged round me," "I have one right alone: that of demanding human behavior from the other." This is, to me, a very accurate description of nonviolent struggle. He writes, "I will impose my whole weight as a man on [the other's] life and show him that I am not that . . . [which] he persists in imagining," "What is needed is to hold oneself, like a sliver, to the heart of the world, to interrupt if necessary the rhythm of the world, to upset, if necessary, the chain of command, but . . . to stand up to the world," "Man is human only to the extent to which he tries to impose his existence on another man in order to be recognized by him." He immediately adds, "If I close the circuit, if I prevent the accomplishment of movement in two directions, I keep the other within himself." He writes, "I do battle for the creation of a human world—that is, a world of reciprocal recognition." The battle for this world, I would plead, is one that *can* only be waged nonviolently.

It is true enough, however, that one of the chief difficulties those who believe in nonviolence must face is how to recruit others to trust themselves to this way. My own conviction is that one can recruit to this form of battle only by setting the very boldest kind of example. Those of us who believe in nonviolent action should listen closely to the words of those who mock it. For if the portrait the latter draw of it is a caricature, and reveals their own ignorance of what such action can be, it reveals, too, a great deal about our own failure to carry experiments with it far enough. We had better look hard at what it is men seek when they turn away from us.

The cry for Black Power, for example, was taken up with swiftness. Why? Because too many—though certainly not all—of the nonviolent actions taken to that date *had* been, as charged, essentially acts of petition; and the necessity of self-assertion was felt very deeply. The gestures of the slave had clearly once and for all to be put from them by black people. And the nonviolent actions in which they had taken part had too often seemed but to repeat those ancient gestures of submission—quite as Carmichael put it: Look, master, we are only going to do what we are supposed to do; we may be on the streets, but see, we're still your good niggers; won't you help us? In this context, the assertion of love for the other seemed too much an echo of the old defensive hypocrisy toward the master: Look, we are your loving servants—who love you, respect you, more than we love, respect our own lives. Only nonviolent actions daring enough to quite shatter that pattern could possibly release either side from the bondage of the old relation.

BOLD ACTION OR NONE

It is not only black people in our society who are suffering now from the sense that their lives are out of their control, and who are going to be satisfied only to take actions that give them some sense of beginning to assert such control. At this point in our history, nonviolent action had better be taken boldly or one need hardly bother to take it at all, for one will be taking it alone.

Those who believe in nonviolence face a sharp challenge. They must decide whether or not we really are engaged in a struggle that is "in dead earnest." If we are, certain consequences follow. One of them is that we must act boldly; another is that we can expect to be hurt. Those who commit themselves to violent struggle take this for granted—which gives them a certain advantage. In the very act of entering battle, they prepare themselves for this—knowing it, very simply, to be the nature of battle. We had better learn, too, to accept that it is. They can claim one other advantage: they are less apt to lose recruits. Fanon writes in *The Wretched of the Earth*, "You could be sure of a new recruit when he could no longer go back into the colonial system—because he had assumed 'the responsibility for violence' and committed some act that made him a hunted man."[7] It is easier to retreat from nonviolent battle. We face the challenge of persisting in spite of this.

THE NEED TO BE AGGRESSIVE

Yes, the challenge to those who believe in nonviolent struggle is to learn to be aggressive enough. Nonviolence has for too long been connected in men's minds with the notion of passivity. "Aggressive" is an ambiguous word, of course, and my statement needs qualifying. In this connection I recommend to all the book *On Aggression* by the Austrian naturalist, Konrad Lorenz. I have quoted Bradford Lyttle's reference to it: "Lorenz studies [the un-niceness of people] as aggressiveness and argues convincingly that it's instinctive with men." Actually, though Lorenz does argue that aggressiveness is instinctive—in men as in animals—he challenges the view that there is anything basically "un-nice" about that instinct. The correct translation of his original title, *Das Sogenannte Böse*, would be *The So-Called Evil Instinct*. He argues that this instinct plays a very positive, life-*promoting* role among animals. Just to give one example: the instinct of each member of a species to fight for its own bit of territory "gives an ideal solution to the problem of the distribution of animals"—so that they don't all crowd into one place and eat up all the food available there and then starve. "The environment is divided between the members of the species in such a way that, within the potentialities offered, everyone can exist." "What a peaceful issue of the evil principle." Aggressiveness may "function in the wrong way" sometimes, by accident, he writes, and cause destruction, but "we have never found that the aim of aggression was the extermination of fellow members of the species." He writes of another, a very special instinct that has been developed in the process of evolution "to oppose aggression . . . and inhibit those of its actions that [*could* be] injurious to the survival of the species." He describes various ritualised "appeasing" gestures that are made by the weaker animal of the species at a certain point in any conflict, and describes how the stronger animal is then automatically restrained from taking advantage of the other and inflicting real injury upon him. He points out the "strangely moving paradox that the most blood-thirsty predators, particularly the Wolf . . . are among the animals with the most reliable killing inhibitions" (toward their own species, that is). For this "built-in safety device" was developed specifically in those creatures who were born heavily armed. And he points out the special dilemma of Man. He is born "harmless," and so "no selection pressure arose in the prehistory of mankind to breed inhibitory mechanisms preventing the killing of his" fellows—and then he invented artificial weapons! Fortunately, Lorenz comments, "inventions and responsibility are both the achievements of the same specifically human faculty of asking questions." Clearly the questions he has asked have, to date, resulted in a more rapid development of invention than of self-discipline, but Lorenz remains optimistic about Man, and sees him as still capable of evolving. "I assert," he writes, "that the long-sought missing link between animals and the really humane being is ourselves"—a hypothesis that I find persuasive.

---

[7] I wrote earlier that one could substitute the phrase "radical uncompromising action" for the word "violence" in Fanon's text with the exception of a very few passages. This is one of those passages.

A BALANCE OF INSTINCTS

What has very clearly worked, in the evolution of animals, to preserve and advance the life of each species, has been a particular *balance* of two instincts. The one, as it were, asserts the individual's right to exist. This is the so-called evil instinct. Lorenz names it "aggression." But just as I would substitute another word for Fanon's "violence," I would substitute another word here—and rename "aggression" "self-assertion." The second instinct restrains the first when it endangers *another's* right to exist. In human terms, the first amounts to respecting one's own person, the second to respecting the person of the other. Lorenz points out, by the way, that the only animals capable of love are those that are "aggressive." One can, it seems, *only* love another "as one loves oneself."

This life-serving balance—this equilibrium between self-assertion and respect for others—has evolved among animals on the physiological plane. In human beings it can be gained only on the plane of consciousness. And the plea this essay makes is precisely that we make the disciplined effort to gain it—all those of us who hope really to change men's lives, who, in Fanon's words, "want humanity to advance a step further," want to "set afoot a new man." My plea is that the key to a revolution that would "go forward all the time . . . in the company of Man, in the company of all men," lies in discovering within ourselves this poise. But it calls equally for the strengthening of *two* impulses—calls both for assertion (for speaking, for acting out "aggressively" the truth, as we see it, of what our rights are) and for restraint toward others (for the acting out of love for them, which is to say of respect for their human rights). May those who say that they believe in nonviolence learn to challenge more boldly those institutions of violence that constrict and cripple our humanity. And may those who have questioned nonviolence come to see that one's rights to life and happiness can only be claimed as inalienable if one grants, in action, that they belong to all men.

MOHANDAS K. GANDHI

Truth-Force (Satyagraha)

Mohandas K. Gandhi (1869–1948) was a lawyer who devoted his life to "experiments with truth" in which he tried to improve the lot of Indians in South Africa, untouchables in India, and Indian subjects of the British colonial regime. His advocacy of nonviolence as an action of the brave won the attention of the late Martin Luther King, Jr. Gandhi wrote an autobiography, but most of his other articles were speeches and newspaper columns, which have been collected in *Non-Violence in Peace and War* and *Satyagraha*. Publication of his complete works is now in progress.

Satyagraha is literally holding on to Truth and it means, therefore, Truth-force. Truth is soul or spirit. It is, therefore, known as soul-force. It excludes the use of violence because man is not capable of knowing the absolute truth and, therefore, not competent to punish. The word was coined in South Africa to distinguish the non-violent resistance of the Indians of South Africa from the contemporary 'passive resistance' of the suffragettes and others. It is not conceived as a weapon of the weak.

Passive resistance is used in the orthodox English sense and covers the suffragette movement as well as the resistance of the Non-conformists. Passive resistance has been conceived and is regarded as a weapon of the weak. Whilst it avoids violence, being not open to the weak, it does not exclude its use if, in the opinion of a passive resister, the occasion demands it. However, it has always been distinguished from armed resistance and its application was at one time confined to Christian martyrs.

Civil Disobedience is civil breach of unmoral statutory enactments. The expression was, so far as I am aware, coined by Thoreau to signify his own resistance to the laws of a slave State. He has left a masterly treatise on the duty of Civil Disobedience. But Thoreau was not perhaps an out and out champion of nonviolence. Probably, also, Thoreau limited his breach of statutory laws to the

From *Satyagraha* and *Non-Violence in Peace and War*, Volume I, by Mohandas K. Gandhi, Navajivan Trust, 1951 and 1942. Reprinted by permission of the publishers.

revenue law, i.e. payment of taxes. Whereas the term Civil Disobedience as practised in 1919 covered a breach of any statutory and unmoral law. It signified the resister's outlawry in a civil, i.e., non-violent manner. He invoked the sanctions of the law and cheerfully suffered imprisonment. It is a branch of Satyagraha.

Non-co-operation predominantly implies withdrawing of co-operation from the State that in the non-co-operator's view has become corrupt and excludes Civil Disobedience of the fierce type described above. By its very nature, non-co-operation is even open to children of understanding and can be safely practised by the masses. Civil Disobedience presupposes the habit of willing obedience to laws without fear of their sanctions. It can, therefore, be practised only as a last resort and by a select few in the first instance at any rate. Non-co-operation, too, like Civil Disobedience is a branch of Satyagraha which includes all non-violent resistance for the vindication of Truth.

. . .

TRUTH

I deal with Truth first of all, as the Satyagraha Ashram owes its very existence to the pursuit and the attempted practice of Truth.

The word *Satya* (Truth) is derived from *Sat*, which means 'being'. Nothing is or exists in reality except Truth. That is why *Sat* or Truth is perhaps the most important name of God. In fact it is more correct to say that Truth is God, than to say that God is Truth. But as we cannot do without a ruler or a general, names of God such as 'King of Kings' or 'the Almighty' are and will remain generally current. On deeper thinking, however, it will be realized, that *Sat* or *Satya* is the only correct and fully significant name for God.

And where there is Truth, there also is knowledge which it true. Where there is no Truth, there can be no true knowledge. That is why the word *Chit* or knowledge is associated with the name of God. And where there is true knowledge, there is always bliss (*Ananda*). Sorrow has no place there. And even as Truth is eternal, so is the bliss derived from it. Hence we know God as *Sat-chit-ananda*, One who combines in Himself Truth, Knowledge and Bliss.

Devotion to this Truth is the sole justification for our existence. All our activities should be centred in Truth. Truth should be the very breath of our life. When once this stage in the pilgrim's progress is reached, all other rules of correct living will come without effort, and obedience to them will be instinctive. But without Truth it would be impossible to observe any principles or rules in life.

Generally speaking, observation of the law of Truth is understood merely to mean that we must speak the truth. But we in the Ashram should understand the word *Satya* or Truth in a much wider sense. There should be Truth in thought, Truth in speech, and Truth in action. To the man who has realized this Truth in its fulness, nothing else remains to be known, because all knowledge is necessarily included in it. What is not included in it is not Truth, and so not true knowledge; and there can be no inward peace without true knowledge. If we once learn how to apply this never-failing test of Truth, we will at once be able to find out what is worth doing, what is worth seeing, what is worth reading.

But how is one to realize this Truth, which may be likened to the philosopher's stone or the cow of plenty? By single-minded devotion (*abhyasa*) and indifference to all other interests in life (*vairugya*)—replies the *Bhagavadgita*. In spite, however, of such devotion, what may appear as truth to one person will often appear as untruth to another person. But that need not worry the seeker. Where there is honest effort, it will be realized that what appear to be different truths are like the countless and apparently different leaves of the same tree. Does not God Himself appear to different individuals in different aspects? Yet we know that He is one. But Truth is the right designation of God. Hence there is nothing wrong in every man following Truth according to his lights. Indeed it is his duty to do so. Then if there is a mistake on the part of any one so following Truth, it will be automatically set right. For the quest of Truth involves *tapas*—self-suffering, sometimes even unto death. There can be no place in it for even a trace of self-interest. In such selfless search for Truth no-body can lose his bearings for long. Directly he takes to the wrong path he stumbles, and is thus redirected to the right path. Therefore the pursuit of Truth is true *bhakti* (devotion). It is the path that leads to God. There is no place in it for cowardice, no place for defeat. It is the talisman by which death itself becomes the portal to life eternal.

In this connection it would be well to ponder over the lives and examples of Harishchandra, Prahlad, Ramachandra, Imam Hasan and Imam Husain, the Christian saints, etc. How beautiful it would be, if all of us, young and old, men and women, devoted ourselves wholly to Truth in all that we might do in our waking hours, whether working, eating, drinking or playing, till dissolution of the body makes us one with Truth? God as Truth has been for me a treasure beyond price; may He be so to every one of us.

AHIMSA OR LOVE

We saw last week how the path of Truth is as narrow as it is straight. Even so is that of *ahimsa*. It is like balancing oneself on the edge of a sword. By concentration an acrobat can walk on a rope. But the concentration required to tread the path of Truth and *ahimsa* is far greater. The slightest inattention brings one tumbling to the ground. One can realize Truth and *ahimsa* only by ceaseless striving.

But it is impossible for us to realize perfect Truth so long as we are imprisoned in this mortal frame. We can only visualize it in our imagination. We cannot, through the instrumentality of this ephemeral body, see face to face Truth which is eternal. That is why in the last resort one must depend on faith.

It appears that the impossibility of full realization of Truth in this mortal body led some ancient seeker after Truth to the appreciation of *ahimsa*. The question which confronted him was: "Shall I bear with those who create difficulties for me, or shall I destroy them?" The seeker realized that he who went on destroying others did not make headway but simply stayed where he was, while the man who suffered those who created difficulties marched ahead, and at times even took the others with him. The first act of destruction taught him that the Truth which was the object of his quest was not outside himself but within. Hence the more he took to violence, the more he receded from Truth. For in fighting the imagined enemy without, he neglected the enemy within.

We punish thieves, because we think they harass us. They may leave us alone;

but they will only transfer their attentions to another victim. This other victim however is also a human being, ourselves in a different form, and so we are caught in a vicious circle. The trouble from thieves continues to increase, as they think it is their business to steal. In the end we see that it is better to endure the thieves than to punish them. The forbearance may even bring them to their senses. By enduring them we realize that thieves are not different from ourselves, they are our brethren, our friends, and may not be punished. But whilst we may bear with the thieves, we may not endure the infliction. That would only induce cowardice. So we realize a further duty. Since we regard the thieves as our kith and kin, they must be made to realize the kinship. And so we must take pains to devise ways and means of winning them over. This is the path of *ahimsa*. It may entail continuous suffering and the cultivating of endless patience. Given these two conditions, the thief is bound in the end to turn away from his evil ways. Thus step by step we learn how to make friends with all the world; we realize the greatness of God—of Truth. Our peace of mind increases in spite of suffering; we become braver and more enterprising; we understand more clearly the difference between what is everlasting and what is not; we learn how to distinguish between what is our duty and what is not. Our pride melts away, and we become humble. Our worldly attachments diminish, and the evil within us diminishes from day to day.

Ahimsa is not the crude thing it has been made to appear. Not to hurt any living thing is no doubt a part of *ahimsa*. But it is its least expression. The principle of *ahimsa* is hurt by every evil thought, by undue haste, by lying, by hatred, by wishing ill to anybody. It is also violated by our holding on to what the world needs. But the world needs even what we eat day by day. In the place where we stand there are millions of microorganisms to whom the place belongs, and who are hurt by our presence there. What should we do then? Should we commit suicide? Even that is no solution, if we believe, as we do, that so long as the spirit is attached to the flesh, on every destruction of the body it weaves for itself another. The body will cease to be only when we give up all attachment to it. This freedom from all attachment is the realization of God as Truth. Such realization cannot be attained in a hurry. The body does not belong to us. While it lasts, we must use it as a trust handed over to our charge. Treating in this way the things of the flesh, we may one day expect to become free from the burden of the body. Realizing the limitations of the flesh, we must strive day by day towards the ideal with what strength we have in us.

It is perhaps clear from the foregoing, that without *ahimsa* it is not possible to seek and find Truth. *Ahimsa* and Truth are so intertwined that it is practically impossible to disentangle and separate them. They are like the two sides of a coin, or rather of a smooth unstamped metallic disc. Who can say, which is the obverse, and which is the reverse? Nevertheless *ahimsa* is the means; Truth is the end. Means to be means must always be within our reach, and so *ahimsa* is our supreme duty. If we take care of the means, we are bound to reach the end sooner or later. When once we have grasped this point, final victory is beyond question. Whatever difficulties we encounter, whatever apparent reverses we sustain, we may not give up the quest for Truth which alone is, being God Himself.

Ahimsa requires certain duties which can be done only by those with a trained physique. It is, therefore, most necessary to consider what kind of physical training a non-violent person should receive.

Very few of the rules applying to a violent army will apply to a non-violent body. A violent army will not have its arms for show but for definitely destructive purposes. A non-violent body will have no use for such weapons and will, therefore, beat its swords into plough-shares and spears into pruning hooks, and will shrink from the thought of using them as lethal weapons. The violent soldier will be trained in the use of violence by being taught to shoot. The non-violent soldier will have no time for this pastime. He will get all his training through nursing the sick, saving those in danger at the risk of his own life, patrolling places which may be in fear of thieves and dacoits, and in laying down his life, if necessary, in dissuading them from their purpose. Even the uniforms of the two will differ. The violent man will wear a coat of mail for his protection, and his uniform will be such as can dazzle people. The uniform of the non-violent man will be simple, in conformity with the dress of the poor, and betokening humility. Its purpose will be just to keep him from heat and cold and rain. A violent soldier's protection will be his arms, no matter how much he takes God's name. He will not shrink from spending millions on armaments. The first and last shield and buckler of the non-violent person will be his unwavering faith in God. And the minds of the two will be as poles asunder. The violent man will always be casting about for plans to work the destruction of his enemy and will pray to God to fulfil his purpose. The national anthem of the British people is worth considering in this connection. It prays to God to save the King, to frustrate the enemy's knavish tricks, and to destroy him. Millions of Englishmen sing this anthem aloud with one voice standing respectfully. If God is the Incarnation of Mercy, He is not likely to listen to such prayer, but it cannot but affect the minds of those who sing it, and in times of war it simply kindles their hatred and anger to white heat. The one condition of winning a violent war is to keep the indignation against the enemy burning fiercely.

In the dictionary of the non-violent there is no such word as an external enemy. But even for the supposed enemy he will have nothing but compassion in his heart. He will believe that no man is intentionally wicked, that there is no man but is gifted with the faculty to discriminate between right and wrong, and that if that faculty were to be fully developed, it would surely mature into non-violence. He will therefore pray to God that He may give the supposed enemy a sense of right and bless him. His prayer for himself will always be that the spring of compassion in him may ever be flowing, and that he may ever grow in moral strength so that he may face death fearlessly.

Thus since the minds of both will differ as the poles, their physical training will also differ in the same degree.

We all know more or less what military training is like. But we have hardly ever thought that non-violent training must be of a different kind. Nor have we ever cared to discover whether in the past such training was given anywhere in the world. I am of opinion that it used to be given in the past and is even now being given in a haphazard way. The various exercises of *Hatha Yoga* are in this direction. The physical training given by means of these imparts among other things physical health, strength, agility, and the capacity to bear heat and cold. Shri Kuvalayanandji is making scientific researches in the technique and, benefits of these exercises. I have no knowledge of the progress he has made, nor do I know whether he is making his experiments with *ahimsa* as his goal. My reference to *Hatha Yoga* is meant only with a view to showing that this ancient type of nonviolent training still exists, though I know that there is room in it for improvement. I do not know either that the author of this science had any idea of mass non-violence. The exercises had at their back the desire for individual salvation. The object of the various exercises was to strengthen and purify the body in order to secure control of the mind. The mass non-violence we are now thinking of applies to people of all religions and therefore the rules that may be framed must be such as can be accepted by all believers in *ahimsa*. And then as we are thinking of a non-violent army, that is to say, of bringing into being a Satyagraha *sangha,* we can but build anew accepting the old as our foundation. Let us then think of the physical training required by a Satyagrahi. If the Satyagrahi is not healthy in mind and body, he may perhaps fail in mustering complete fearlessness. He should have the capacity to stand guard at a single spot day and night; he must not fall ill even if he has to bear cold and heat and rain; he must have the strength to go to places of peril, to rush to scenes of fire, and the courage to wander about alone in desolate jungles and haunts of death; he will bear, without a grumble, severe beatings, starvation and worse, and will keep to his post of duty without flinching; he will have the resourcefulness and capacity to plunge into a seemingly impenetrable scene of rioting; he will have the longing and capacity to run with the name of God on his lips to the rescue of men living on the top storeys of buildings enveloped in flames; he will have the fearlessness to plunge into a flood in order to rescue people being carried off by it or to jump down a well to save a drowning person.

This list can be extended *ad libitum.* The substance of it all is that we should cultivate the capacity to run to the rescue of people in danger and distress and to suffer cheerfully any amount of hardship that may be inflicted upon us. He who accepts this fundamental principle will easily be able to frame rules of physical training for Satyagrahis. I have a firm conviction that the very foundation of this training is faith in God. If that is absent, all the training one may have received is likely to fail at the critical moment.

Let no one poohpooh my statement by saying that the Congress has many people who are ashamed to take the name of God. I am simply trying to state the view in terms of the science of Satyagraha as I have known and developed it. The only weapon of the Satyagrahi is God, by whatsoever name one knows Him. Without Him the Satyagrahi is devoid of strength before an opponent armed with monstrous weapons. Most people lie prostrate before physical might. But he who accepts God as his only Protector will remain unbent before the mightiest earthly power.

As faith in God is essential in a Satyagrahi, even so is *brahmacharya.* Without *brahmacharya* the Satyagrahi will have no lustre, no inner strength to stand unarmed against the whole world. *Brahmacharya* may have here the restricted meaning of conservation of the vital energy brought about by sexual restraint, and not the comprehensive definition I have given of it. He who intends to live on spare diet and without any external remedies, and still wants to have physical strength, has need to conserve his vital energy. It is the richest capital man can ever possess. He who can preserve it ever gains renewed strength out of it. He who uses it up, consciously or unconsciously, will ultimately be impotent. His strength will fail him at the right moment. I have often written about the ways and means of conserving this energy. Let the reader turn to my writings and carry out the instructions. He who lusts with the eye or the touch can never conserve his vital energy, nor the man who lusts after flesh-pots. Those who hope to conserve this energy without strict observance of the rules will no more succeed than those who hope to swim against the current without being exhausted. He who restrains himself physically and sins with his thoughts will fare worse than he who, without professing to observe *brahmacharya*, lives the life of a restrained householder. For he who lusts with the thought will ever remain unsated and will end his life a moral wreck and burden on the earth. Such a one can never be a full Satyagrahi. Nor can one who hankers after wealth and fame.

This is the foundation of the physical training for a Satyagrahi. The detailed structure of the course can easily be built in consonance with this foundation.

It should now be clear that in the physical training of a Satyagrahi there is no room for lethal weapons like the sword or the spear. For far more terrible weapons than we have seen are in existence today, and newer ones are being invented every day. Of what fear will a sword rid him who has to cultivate the capacity to overcome all fear—real or imaginary? I have not yet heard of a man having shed all fear by learning sword-play. Mahavir and others who imbibed *ahimsa* did not do so because they knew the use of weapons, but because, in spite of the knowledge of their use, they shed all fear.

A slight introspection will show that he who has always depended on the sword will find it difficult to throw it away. But having deliberately discarded it he is likely to find his *ahimsa* more lasting than that of him who, not knowing its use, fancies he will not fear it. But that does not mean that in order to be truly non-violent one must beforehand possess and know the use of arms. By parity of reasoning, one might say that only a thief can be honest, only a diseased person can be healthy, and only a dissolute person can be a *brahmachari*. The fact is that we have formed the habit of thinking along traditional grooves and will not get out of them. And as we cannot take a detached view, we cannot draw the right conclusions and get caught in delusive snares.

If I have the time, I hope to present the reader with a model course of training.

. . .

A correspondent writes:

"You say non-violence is for the brave, not for cowards. But, in my opinion, in India the brave are conspicuous by their absence. Even if we claim to be brave, how is the world to believe us when it knows that India has no arms and is therefore incapable of defending herself? What then should we do to cultivate non-violence of the brave?"

The correspondent is wrong in thinking that in India the brave are conspicuous by their absence. It is a matter for shame that because foreigners once labelled us as cowards we should accept the label. Man often becomes what he believes himself to be. If I keep on saying to myself that I *cannot* do a certain thing, it is possible that I may end by really becoming incapable of doing it. On the contrary, if I have the belief that I *can* do it, I shall surely acquire the capacity to do it even if I may not have it at the beginning. Again it is wrong to say that the world today believes us to be cowards. It has ceased to think so since the *satyagraha* campaign. The Congress prestige has risen very high in the West during the past twenty years. The world is watching with astonished interest the fact that, although we have no arms, we are hoping to win Swaraj and have indeed come very near it. Moreover, it sees in our non-violent movement rays of hope for peace in the world and its salvation from the hell of carnage. The bulk of mankind has come to believe that, if ever the spirit of revenge is to vanish and bloody wars are to cease, the happy event can happen only through the policy of non-violence adopted by the Congress. The correspondent's fear and suspicion are, therefore, unfounded.

It will now be seen that the fact that India is unarmed is no obstacle in the path of *ahimsa*. The forcible disarmament of India by the British Government was indeed a grave wrong and a cruel injustice. But we can turn even injustice to our advantage, if God be with us, or if you prefer, we have the skill to do so. And a such thing has happened in India.

Arms are surely unnecessary for a training in *ahimsa*. In fact the arms, if any, have to be thrown away, as the Khansaheb did in the Frontier Province. Those who hold that it is essential to learn violence before we can learn non-violence, would hold that only sinners can be saints.

Just as one must learn the art of killing in the training for violence, so one must learn the art of dying in the training for non-violence. Violence does not mean emancipation from fear, but discovering the means of combating the cause for fear. Non-violence, on the other hand, has no cause for fear. The votary of non-violence has to cultivate the capacity for sacrifice of the highest type in order to be free from fear. He recks not if he should lose his land, his wealth, his life. He who has not overcome all fear cannot practise *ahimsa* to perfection. The votary of *ahimsa* has only one fear, that is of God. He who seeks refuge in God ought to have a glimpse of the *Atman* that transcends the body; and the moment one has a glimpse of the Imperishable *Atman* one sheds the love of the perishable body. Training in non-violence is thus diametrically opposed to training in violence. Violence is needed for the protection of things external, non-violence is needed for the protection of the *Atman,* for the protection of one's honour.

This non-violence cannot be learnt by staying at home. It needs enterprise. In order to test ourselves we should learn to dare danger and death, mortify the flesh, and acquire the capacity to endure all manner of hardships. He who trembles or takes to his heels the moment he sees two people fighting is not non-violent, but a coward. A non-violent person will lay down his life in preventing such quarrels. The bravery of the non-violent is vastly superior to that of the violent. The badge of the violent is his weapon—spear, or sword, or rifle. God is the shield of the non-violent.

This is not a course of training for one intending to learn non-violence. But it is easy to evolve one from the principles I have laid down.

It will be evident from the foregoing that there is no comparison between the two types of bravery. The one is limited, the other is limitless. There is no such thing as out-daring or out-fighting non-violence. Non-violence is invincible. There need be no doubt that this non-violence can be achieved. The history of the past twenty years should be enough to reassure us.

JOAN V. BONDURANT

Gandhi's Conquest of Violence

Joan V. Bondurant, an authority on
Gandhi's thought, has written several other
articles on political theory and Indian
politics.

"I take it, Mr. Gandhi, that you are the author of the satyagraha movement."

"Yes, Sir."

"Will you explain it briefly?"

And so Lord Hunter, as Chairman of the official Committee appointed to inquire into the first nationwide satyagraha movement in India, opened his examination of Mohandas Gandhi.[1] "It is a movement," Gandhi explained, "intended to replace methods of violence and a movement based entirely upon truth. . . ."

It was as a technique of action "intended to replace methods of violence" that satyagraha made its appearance, first in South Africa, and later in India. The philosophy which infused it was not conceived, full-blown, as a logically consistent, systematic statement. But as the technique evolved on the field of social and political action, the philosophical assumptions and the pattern of value fundamental to its operation were laid before those who came to inquire, or to challenge, to adopt or to oppose.

There are a few precepts essential to satyagraha. The degree to which the action technique functions effectively may well be determined by the extent of understanding which the satyagrahi (one engaged in satyagraha) has of these basic elements and the skill with which he applies them in the course of active conflict. The failure to grasp these fundamentals, the failure to discover the manner in which their delicate articulation constitutes the process of satyagraha, may lead to the adoption of outward forms which resemble the Gandhian technique but which are scarcely different from traditional methods of strike, of fasting, or of demonstration. To explore the Gandhian meanings of the concepts *truth, non-violence, self-suffering*, is to approach the fundamentals of Gandhian philosophy. But the further exploration of the relationship of each of these elements to the others and the understanding of such relationships in terms of the role of the individual as satyagraha's ultimate referent, is essential to an understanding of the technique.

"Satyagraha: Its Basic Precepts," from *The Conquest of Violence: The Gandhian Philosophy of Conflict.* Copyright © 1958 by Princeton University Press, pp. 15–35. Reprinted by permission of Princeton University Press.

[1] On 9 January 1920. For the exchange between Lord Hunter and Gandhi, and Sir Chimanlal Setalwad and Gandhi during this examination, see D. G. Tendulkar, *Mahatma Gandhi*, Vol. I (Bombay: Jhaveri and Tendulkar, 1952), pp. 340–343.

TRUTH

"Satyagraha is literally holding on to Truth, and it means therefore Truth-force." What is this "truth" which Gandhi incorporated as an essential element of his premier techniques? How does it become a "force," and how does it relate to man's action on the field of conflict? "It excludes the use of violence," Gandhi asserted, "because man is not capable of knowing the absolute truth and therefore not competent to punish."[2]

The search for truth has long occupied the minds of men. The concept of the infinite, the absolute, has taken many forms, its role in religion and philosophy issuing at times in disquieting dogma. In India, the Hindu tradition holds out to man the possibility of ultimate realization of the absolute: the consummation of man's strivings is his identification with the Godhead, and such is the meaning of man's self-realization. Gandhi, in defining his personal goal, held with other Hindus that his life's endeavor was ultimately to "see God face to face." His acceptance of the absolute followed the Hindu understanding, and his personal view of God was the Hindu view of the all-pervading Brahma. But Gandhi was fully aware that the absolute cannot be known by the yet unfulfilled human mind. Gandhi never claimed to know truth in any absolute sense, and he repeatedly reminded others that man's inability to know the truth required that he maintain an unceasingly open approach to those who would differ with him. He had discovered, early in his application of satyagraha, "that pursuit of truth did not admit of violence being inflicted on one's opponent but that he must be weaned from error by patience and sympathy." For, he added, "what appears to be truth to the one may appear to be error to the other."[3]

To achieve his own self-realization, Gandhi made his life into "numerous experiments with truth." In "holding on to the truth" he did not suggest that such truth need be or could be a universally valid object of acknowledgement. He said, simply,

> . . . I am but a seeker after Truth. I claim to have found the way to it. I claim to be making a ceaseless effort to find it. But I admit that I have not yet found it. To find Truth completely is to realize oneself and one's destiny, that is, to become perfect. I am painfully conscious of my imperfections, and therein lies all the strength I possess, because it is a rare thing for a man to know his own limitations.[4]

And so, Gandhi, in search of an absolute truth, concerned himself more intensively with the means whereby the realization of such truth might be advanced. The "truth" concept which enters into technique of satyagraha is clearly not that of the absolute. As he pursued his experiments with satyagraha the relative character of truth as an operative principle became the stronger. Satyagraha, the technique, developed at once as the tool whereby Gandhi dealt with practical social or political problems and the statement of his philosophical beliefs. Commenting on the derivation of the word satyagraha, Gandhi wrote:

---

[2] M. K. Gandhi, *Speeches and Writings of Mahatma Gandhi* (4th ed.; Madras: Natesan [n.d.]), p. 506.

[3] Jag Parvesh Chander, ed., *Teachings of Mahatma Gandhi* (Lahore: The Indian Printing Works, 1945), p. 494.

[4] Gandhi, *Young India,* November 17, 1921. Also Tendulkar, *op. cit.,* Vol. II, p. 98.

The word 'Satya' (Truth) is derived from 'Sat,' which means being. And nothing is or exists in reality except Truth. That is why 'Sat' or Truth is perhaps the most important name of God. In fact it is more correct to say that Truth is God, than to say that God is Truth. . . . it will be realized that 'Sat' or 'Satya' is the only correct and fully significant name for God.[5]

Early in his public comments on the truth concept, Gandhi had identified God with Truth. In 1925, in a talk with Christian missionaries in Darjeeling, Gandhi had said that for him "God and Truth are convertible terms."[6] The following year in an address at Wardha he had declared: ". . . to me Truth is God and there is no way to find Truth except the way of non-violence."[7] When he was later (in 1931) asked by a group of conscientious objectors in Switzerland why he regarded God as Truth, Gandhi explained how he had come to believe that the phrase "God is Love" was inadequate and how he had further concluded that God is Truth. He then added that he had found it necessary to go a step further and to say that Truth is God.

> You will see the fine distinction between the two statements, 'God is Truth' and 'Truth is God.' I came to that conclusion after a continuous and relentless search after truth which began fifty years ago. I then found that the nearest approach to truth was through love.[8]

This "fine distinction" has been taken by some commentators to be of substantial significance. N. K. Bose interprets the change as relieving a satyagrahi from the necessity of any theological or at least any specific theological belief.

> With his changed creed, he could easily accommodate as fellow-seekers those who looked on Humanity or any other object as their god, and for which they were prepared to sacrifice their all. By enthroning Truth on the highest pedestal, Gandhi thus truly became a catholic, and lost all trace of separateness from every other honest man who worshipped gods other than his own.[9]

It may have been with Gandhi's deliberate change in the structuring of his theological statements that he consciously allowed for the freer construction of satyagraha. Again, this can be but another example of Gandhi's philosophical formulations following upon his practical experiments and his efforts in applied ethics. In the autobiography he wrote:

> There are innumerable definitions of God, because His manifestations are innumerable. They overwhelm me with wonder and awe and for a moment stun me. But I worship God as Truth only. I have not yet found Him, but I am seeking after Him. I am prepared to sacrifice the things dearest to me in pursuit of this quest. . . . But as

[5] *Young India,* July 30, 1931, p. 196. For a note on the distinction between Knowing and Being in the Hindu truth concept, see J. H. Muirhead, "The Hindu Idea of Truth" in S. Radhakrishnan, ed., *Mahatma Gandhi: Essays and Reflections on His Life and Work* (2nd ed.; London: Allen & Unwin [1949]), pp. 197–200.

[6] Tendulkar, *op. cit.,* Vol. II, p. 249.

[7] *Ibid.,* p. 312.

[8] *Ibid.,* Vol. III, p. 176.

[9] N. K. Bose, *Studies in Gandhism* (2nd ed., Calcutta: Indian Associated Publishing Co., 1947), p. 269.

long as I have not realized this Absolute Truth so long must I hold by the relative truth as I have conceived it. That relative truth must meanwhile be my beacon, my shield and buckler.[10]

However inadequate Gandhi's philosophical statements may appear to the philosopher, his efforts to explain his understanding of such concepts as truth have direct bearing upon the development of the technique, satyagraha. He concerned himself with such concepts to the degree that they affected human behavior. In elucidating his view of truth he wrote to a friend:

In "God is Truth," *is* certainly does not mean "equal to" nor does it merely mean, "is truthful." Truth is not a mere attribute of God, but He is That. He is nothing if He is not That. Truth in Sanskrit means *Sat. Sat* means *Is.* Therefore Truth is implied in *Is.* God is, nothing else is. Therefore the more truthful we are, the nearer we are to God. We *are* only to the extent that we are truthful.[11]

Such fragmentary efforts at ontological or epistemological statement were developed in the course of his action in the field of human interrelationships. As Gandhi pursued his experiments with truth, the concept settled solidly into the sphere of ethical consideration. The emphasis became increasingly centered upon the problem of means. The means became more and more specific, while the end—the individual realization of God, which is Truth—increasingly indeterminate. In 1924 Gandhi had written in *Young India*: "I want to see God face to face. God I *know* is Truth. For me the only certain means of knowing God is non-violence—*ahimsa*—love."[12] As Gandhi's experiments proceeded he evolved the concept of non-violence—a concept of means—and as he did so, his concept of God became the freer. But the relative character of Gandhi's concept of God was made explicit as early as 1919 when Gandhi's examination by the Hunter Committee developed the following exchange between the Committee's counsel and Gandhi:

Your satyagraha doctrine, so far as I understand it, involves the pursuit of truth and in that pursuit you invite suffering on yourself and do not cause violence to anybody else.

Yes, Sir.

However honestly a man may strive in his search for truth, his notions of truth may be different from the notions of others. Who then is to determine the truth?

The individual himself would determine that.

Different individuals would have different views as to truth. Would that not lead to confusion?

I do not think so.

Honestly striving after truth differs in every case.

That is why the non-violence part was a necessary corollary. Without that there would be confusion and worse.[13]

[10] M. K. Gandhi, *An Autobiography or The Story of My Experiments with Truth,* translated from the original in Gujarati by Mahadev Desai (Ahmedabad: Navajivan, 1940), p. 4.

[11] From a letter to P. G. Mathew, 9 July 1932, as quoted in *Harijan,* 27 March, 1949, p. 26.

[12] April 3, 1924 as quoted in Chander, *op. cit.,* p. 266.

[13] Tendulkar, *op. cit.,* Vol. I, p. 342. This text also appears in *Young India, 1919–1922* (Madras: S. Ganesan, 1922), pp. 33–36.

The role which non-violence plays as an essential element of satyagraha will be examined below. The Gandhian concept of truth, in its non-absolutistic sense, escapes some of the practical difficulties of ethical relativism through its interrelationship with non-violence as an operative principle in satyagraha.

There is an abundance of evidence that Gandhi adopted a social criterion for judging the truth in a given situation. In his *History of Satyagrahashram,* Gandhi writes with reference to doing penance for a wrong:

> The wrong act must be patent, accepted as such by all and spiritually harmful, and the doer must be aware of it. There should be no penance for inferential guilt. To do so might at times result in dangerous consequences. There should be no room for doubt in regard to the fault. Moreover, one should not do penance for an act, which one regards as wrong as his personal faith or opinion. It is possible that what one holds to be wrong today he might regard as innocent tomorrow. So the wrong must be such as is accepted by society to be so. I might regard the non-wearing of *khadi* to be extremely wrong. But my companion might see nothing wrong in it, or might not magnify it as a virtue, and so might wear it indifferently or not wear it at all. If I regard this as a failure and fast for it, it is not penance but coercion. There can also be no penance where the accused person is not conscious of having committed a wrong.[14]

Here, then, is a suggestion as to how the problem of objectivity is solved in the Gandhian method. While admitting truth to be relative, some objective standard is established. The solution is in terms of "man, the measure." The practical effect of Gandhi's "experiments with truth" is reminiscent of the theoretical solution offered by the German humanistic materialist Feuerbach. The truth which is not absolute—which is not, for Gandhi, God—relates to and partakes of human needs. Individual man searches for truth in terms of the community of which he is a part. "The quest for Truth," said Gandhi, "cannot be prosecuted in a cave."

> When therefore untruth was discovered in the Ashram, I readily pleaded guilty for it myself. That is to say, I have not still attained truth as defined by me. It may be due to ignorance but it is clear that I have not fully understood truth and therefore neither even thought it out nor declared it, still less practised it. But granting all this, was I to leave the Ashram, and resort to some Himalayan cave and impose silence upon myself? That would be sheer cowardice. The quest for truth cannot be prosecuted in a cave. Silence makes no sense where it is necessary to speak. One may live in a cave in certain circumstances, but the common man can be tested only in society.[15]

Gandhi, the social actionist, frequently emphasized those partial manifestations of truth: honesty and integrity.

---

[14] Translated from the Gujarati in *Harijan,* July 4, 1948. The passage occurs in the Hindi translation in Mohandas Karamchand Gandhi, *Satyagraha Ashram ka Itihas,* in Hindi, Ramnarayan Chaudhuri, tr. (Ahmedabad: Navajivan Publishing House [1948]), pp. 17–18.

Gandhi would allow for the employment of certain types of satyagraha directed towards an accused person unaware of his wrong if the matter were felt by the satyagrahi to be of fundamental importance.

[15] Translated from Gujarati in *Harijan,* July 18, 1948. The passage in Hindi occurs in Gandhi, *Satyagraha Ashram ka Itihas,* translated from the original in Gujarati into Hindi by Ramnarayan Chaudhuri (Ahmedabad: Navajivan, 1948), p. 13.

Truthfulness is the master-key. Do not lie under any circumstances whatsoever, keep nothing secret, take your teachers and your elders into your confidence and make a clean breast of everything to them. Bear ill-will to none, do not say an evil thing of anyone behind his back, above all "to thine own-self be true," so that you are false to no one else. Truthful dealings even in the least, little things of life is the only secret of a pure life.[16]

These simpler statements—of honesty and integrity—were derived from an implied social epistemology. Gandhi had identified truth with God. Betokening an uneasiness in the realm of theological dogmatism, he expressed the God of his conception in terms relative to limitless individual interpretations. When conflict resulted, he resorted to the dynamics of human interrelationships for criteria to judge the truth, or its approximation, in a given situation. This led him, necessarily, back to the realm of ethics. To an understanding of the ethical implications of his basic metaphysic, and to action based upon them, Gandhi dedicated his life.

Gandhi's writings and teachings had begun when he sought to describe and then to evolve in a rational, communicable manner the technique of action which he had set in motion on the South African political stage. If truth is God, and God is understood in one way by some, in other ways by others how, then, can one "hold on to truth"? Satyagraha is not a dogma. It is neither static nor substantial. Holding on to truth is a dynamic concept and satyagraha a technique of action. How, then, can one proceed to know and to hold to the truth? How can confusion be avoided if striving after truth differs in every case? The answer Gandhi gave lay in the further precept that truth is inseparable from *ahimsa*.

NON-VIOLENCE

The word *ahimsa* expresses an ancient Hindu, Jain, and Buddhist ethical precept. The negative prefix "a" plus "himsa," loosely meaning "injury," make up the word which is usually translated as non-violence. Yet *ahimsa* is eminently more than a negative notion. As is characteristic of Hindu and Buddhist terminology, the negative wording implies much which remains unexpressed. The full force of *ahimsa*, explicitly stated, means "action based on the refusal to do harm."[17] Albert Schweitzer, in his short study on Indian thought,[18] calls attention to this further meaning of *ahimsa*. Etymologically, *himsa* is the desiderative form of *han* meaning to kill or to damage, so that *himsa* means to wish to kill.[19] *Ahimsa*, then, means renunciation of the will to kill or to damage. Gandhi refined the meaning:

[16] *Young India*, December 25, 1925, as quoted in Chander, *op. cit.*, pp. 559–560.

[17] See Louis Renou, "Gandhi and Indian Civilization" in Kshitis Roy, ed., *Gandhi Memorial Peace Number* (Santiniketan [India]: The Visva-Bharati Quarterly, 1949), pp. 230–238.

[18] *Indian Thought and Its Development*, Mrs. Charles E. B. Russell, tr. (London: Hodder and Stoughton, 1936), p. 79.

[19] *Himsa* is more precisely, derived from the root *hins*, to injure, kill, or destroy, which originally was the desiderative of the root *han*, to slay, kill, or damage. (Monier Monier-Williams, *Sanskrit-English Dictionary, Etymologically and Philologically Arranged*, New ed. enl. and improved [Oxford: Clarendon Press, 1899]).

Cf. Whitney, who notes that the root *hins* is "probably an abbreviated desiderative . . ." of the root *han*. (William Dwight Whitney, *The Roots, Verb-Forms, and Primary Derivatives of the Sanskrit Language* [Leipzig: Breitkopf and Hartel; London: Trübner and Co., 1885]), p. 205.

Ahimsa is not the crude thing it has been made to appear. Not to hurt any living thing is no doubt a part of *ahimsa*. But it is its least expression. The principle of *himsa* is hurt by every evil thought, by undue haste, by lying, by hatred, by wishing ill to anybody.[20]

I accept the interpretation of Ahimsa namely that it is not merely a negative state of harmlessness but it is a positive state of love, of doing good even to the evil-doer. But it does not mean helping the evil-doer to continue the wrong or tolerating it by passive acquiescence. On the contrary, love, the active state of Ahimsa, requires you to resist the wrong-doer by dissociating yourself from him even though it may offend him or injure him physically.[21]

Gandhi here identifies *ahimsa* and love. The proximity of this concept to the Christian charity and to the Greek *agape* is, throughout, apparent. . . . This element in satyagraha has social implications expressed in service and requiring for every satyagraha movement a "constructive program."

The inseparable combination of truth and love in the Gandhian position forms the nucleus of the Gandhian solution to the problem of means.

. . . without *ahimsa* it is not possible to seek and find Truth. *Ahimsa* and Truth are so intertwined that it is practically impossible to disentangle and separate them. They are like the two sides of a coin, or rather of a smooth unstamped metallic disc. Who can say, which is the obverse, and which is the reverse? Nevertheless *ahimsa* is the means; Truth is the end. Means to be means must always be within our reach, and so *ahimsa* is our supreme duty. If we take care of the means, we are bound to reach the end sooner or later. When once we have grasped this point, final victory is beyond question.[22]

Truth is the end, Love a means thereto. We know what is Love or non-violence, although we find it difficult to follow the law of Love. But as for Truth we know only a fraction of it. Perfect knowledge of Truth is difficult of attainment for man even like the perfect practice of nonviolence.[23]

To proceed towards the goal of Truth—truth in the absolute sense—the way must lead through the testing of relative truths as they appear to the individual performer. The testing of truth can be performed only by strict adherence to *ahimsa* —action based upon the refusal to do harm, or, more accurately, upon love. For truth, judged in terms of human needs, would be destroyed, on whichever side it lay, by the use of violence. Non-violence, or *ahimsa,* becomes the supreme value, the one cognizable standard by which true action can be determined.

If there is dogma in the Gandhian philosophy, it centers here: that the only test of truth is action based on the refusal to do harm. Gandhi accepted as his fellow "seekers after truth" persons who espoused various, or no, religions, those who held vastly differing views as to the proper social structuring or constructive programming in a non-violent society. He admitted of error and indecision at many stages of his applied experiment. But the one principle to which he adhered to the end was this

[20] M. K. Gandhi, *From Yeravda Mandir: Ashram Observances,* translated from the original Gujarati by Valji Govindji Desai (3rd ed., Ahmedabad: Navajivan, 1945), p. 7.

[21] *Young India,* January 19, 1921, as quoted in Chander, *op. cit.,* p. 412.

[22] Gandhi, *From Yeravda Mandir: Ashram Observances,* p. 8.

[23] *Ibid.,* p. 19.

theme of *ahimsa*—the supreme and only means to the discovery of social truths. "Those who join the Ashram have to literally accept that meaning," he insisted. And "that meaning" of *ahimsa* took him into a realm much higher than simply non-killing.

> Ahimsa really means that you may not offend anybody, you may not harbor an uncharitable thought even in connection with one who may consider himself to be your enemy. . . . If we resent a friend's action or the so-called enemy's action, we still fall short of this doctrine. . . . If we harbor even this thought, we depart from this doctrine of *ahimsa*. Those who join the Ashram have to literally accept that meaning. That does not mean that we practice that doctrine in its entirety. Far from it. It is an ideal which we have to reach, and it is an ideal to be reached even at this very moment, if we are capable of doing so.[24]

The limitation on human capacity to achieve non-violent action Gandhi recognized. . . . imperfections were expected and, to some extent, tolerated in Gandhian satyagraha movements. When we enquire here into the further meaning of non-violent action, we are brought to the third fundamental element of satyagraha, for

> Non-violence in its dynamic condition means conscious suffering. It does not mean meek submission to the will of the evil-doer, but it means the pitting of one's whole soul against the will of the tyrant. Working under this law of our being, it is possible for a single individual to defy the whole might of an unjust empire. . . .[25]

SELF-SUFFERING

> Love never claims, it ever gives. Love ever suffers, never resents, never revenges itself.[26]

> The test of love is tapasya and tapasya means self-suffering.[27]

The classical Yogic law of self-restraint and self-discipline, and the precept of *tapas* which means penance or austerity are familiar elements in the Indian culture. We shall examine the cultural background in Chapter IV. Here it is enough to understand the meaning of self-suffering or *tapasya*, as a function of satyagraha.

Self-suffering in the Gandhian ethic has several essential characteristics which clearly mark it off from the practice of *tapas* or asceticism undertaken for its own sake. Self-suffering in satyagraha is directed, first of all, towards the moral persuasion of one because of whom it is undertaken. It is not a substitute for inability to use violent means to achieve victory over an opponent; it is not, that is, a "weapon of the weak." Self-suffering is clearly of a different character from cowardice; nor is it to be exercised indiscriminately. Self-suffering differs from violence in that violence consists of doing injury to another.

> Suffering injury in one's own person is . . . of the essence of non-violence and is the chosen substitute for violence to others. It is not because I value life low that I can countenance with joy thousands voluntarily losing their lives for Satyagraha, but because

---

[24] From an address to the YMCA, Madras, February 16, 1916, as quoted in Chander, *op. cit.*, pp. 405–406.

[25] *Young India*, August 11, 1920, as quoted in Chander, *op. cit.*, pp. 409–410.

[26] *Young India*, July 9, 1925, as quoted in Chander, *op. cit.*, p. 352.

[27] *Young India*, June 12, 1922, as quoted in Chander, *op. cit.*, p. 352.

I know that it results in the long run in the least loss of life, and, what is more, it ennobles those who lose their lives and morally enriches the world for their sacrifice.[28]

The insistence upon self-suffering has, then, an element of expediency in it. The resort to self-sacrifice and voluntary submission to injury is a positive policy and is not merely a matter of last resort. Gandhi was careful to distinguish his method from that of passive resistance, which either suggests lack of capacity to employ violence or tends to be a preliminary step to violence. In his exposition of satyagraha in South Africa,[29] Gandhi reports the comments of a well-wisher in introducing him to a public audience. The speaker observed that the Indians had "had recourse to passive resistance which is a weapon of the weak."[30] Gandhi continued to refer to the "non-violence of the weak" throughout his life whenever he wished to criticize his followers, or when he thought—as he tended to in the last months of his life—that he had failed to instill into others the full meaning of satyagraha as the non-violence of the strong. Satyagraha was at its height when those who practiced it were in a position, as they often were, to use violence effectively but refrained from doing so and invited suffering upon themselves.

> Passive resistance may be offered side by side with the use of arms. Satyagraha and brute force, being each a negation of the other, can never go together. In passive resistance there is aways present an idea of harassing the other party and there is a simultaneous readiness to undergo any hardships entailed upon us by such activity; while in Satyagraha there is not the remotest idea of injuring the opponent. Satyagraha postulates the conquest of the adversary by suffering in one's own person.[31]

Gandhi guarded against attracting to his satyagraha movement those who feared to take up arms or felt themselves incapable of resistance. "I do believe," he wrote, "that where there is only a choice between cowardice and violence, I would advise violence."[32] Non-violent conduct, Gandhi insisted, is "never demoralizing," whereas cowardice "always is."[33]

> Non-violence cannot be taught to a person who fears to die and has no power of resistance. A helpless mouse is not non-violent because he is always eaten by pussy. He would gladly eat the murderess if he could, but he ever tries to flee from her. We do not call him a coward because he is made by nature to behave no better than he does. But a man who, when faced by danger, behaves like a mouse, is rightly called a coward. He harbors violence and hatred in his heart and would kill his enemy if he could without being hurt himself. He is a stranger to non-violence.[34]

Just as *ahimsa* carries in the Gandhian ethic the positive meaning of love and goodwill, self-suffering requires the positive attribute of courage. . . . The training of satyagrahis sought to develop courage and to inculcate discipline which could overcome fear. For

---

[28] M. K. Gandhi, *Non-Violence in Peace & War* (2nd ed., Ahmedabad: Navajivan, 1944), p. 49.

[29] M. K. Gandhi, *Satyagraha in South Africa,* translated from the Gujarati by Valji Govindji Desai (Madras: S. Ganesan, 1928), p. 175.

[30] *Loc. cit.*

[31] *Ibid.,* p. 179.

[32] *Young India,* August 11, 1920, as quoted in Chander, *op. cit.,* p. 408.

[33] *Young India,* October 31, 1929.

[34] *Harijan,* July 20, 1935, as quoted in Chander, *op. cit.,* pp. 417–418.

Just as one must learn the art of killing in the training for violence, so one must learn the art of dying in the training for non-violence. . . . The votary of non-violence has to cultivate the capacity for sacrifice of the highest type in order to be free from ear. . . . He who has not overcome all fear cannot practise *ahimsa* to perfection.[35]

Throughout his teachings on self-suffering Gandhi emphasized the need for discrimination in inviting suffering and sacrifice. Submission was never an element of this concept. Submitting to humiliation should be strictly resisted and, where necessary, the greater self-suffering of the body, even unto death, should be invited. In every case a satyagrahi must refuse to do that which his conscience forbids him to do and must preserve the dignity of the individual though it mean loss of property or even life.[36]

The element of self-suffering in satyagraha is, perhaps, of all three fundamentals, the least acceptable to a Western mind. Yet, such sacrifice may well provide the ultimate means of realizing that characteristic so eminent in Western moral philosophy: the dignity of the individual. In proceeding to consider the role of the individual in the Gandhian ethic, one is reminded of the observation of a contemporary Western thinker:

There are two entirely different types of sacrifice. It is one of the tragic facts of life that the demands of our physical self and the aims of our mental self can conflict; that actually we may have to sacrifice our physical self in order to assert the integrity of our spiritual self. This sacrifice will never lose its tragic quality. Death is never sweet, not even if it is suffered for the highest ideal. It remains unspeakably bitter, and still it can be the utmost assertion of our individuality.[37]

THE ROLE OF THE INDIVIDUAL

Gandhi's own life is the best practical example of the role which the individual can play in society. In an age when the place of the individual is being challenged and the specter of total mass-control is raised on every hand, Gandhi has insisted that no power on earth can make a man do a thing against his will. The technique of satyagraha provided the means and suggested the discipline through which resistance could become an active force. The element of self-suffering or sacrifice provided the ultimate alternative. For Gandhi, freedom and preservation of individual integrity were the higher values.

The bond of the slave is snapped the moment he considers himself to be a free being. He will plainly tell the master: "I was your bondslave till this moment, but I am a slave no longer. You may kill me if you like, but if you keep me alive, I wish to tell you that if you release me from the bondage, of your own accord, I will ask for nothing more from you. You used to feed and clothe me, though I could have provided food and clothing for myself by my labour. . . ."[38]

Gandhi's concern for individual freedom does not seek the elevation of the individual ego. His is not the extreme anarchist position of freedom *per se*.

---

[35] *Harijan,* September 1, 1940, as quoted in Chander, *op. cit.,* p. 422.

[36] Gandhi, *Non-Violence in Peace & War,* p. 360.

[37] Eric Fromm, *Escape from Freedom* (New York, Toronto: Rinehart, 1941), p. 268.

[38] From Gandhi's address to the All-India Congress Committee, following the adoption of the famous "Quit India" Resolution, 8 August 1942. Tendulkar, *op. cit.,* Vol. VI, p. 199.

If the individual ceases to count, what is left of society? Individual freedom alone can make a man voluntarily surrender himself completely to the service of society. If it is wrested from him, he becomes an automaton and society is ruined. No society can possibly be built on a denial of individual freedom.[39]

Nor is Gandhi's a strictly voluntaristic ethic. The human will may serve as the ultimate protection against an invaded freedom, but the will is not operating alone. However much voluntarism appears to dominate the Gandhian experiment, there are clear indications that Gandhi understood a certain undeniable influence of social institutions on the individual life. "Goondas [ruffians]," he wrote, "do not drop from the sky, nor do they spring from the earth like evil spirits. They are the product of social disorganization, and society is therefore responsible for their existence. In other words, they should be looked upon as a symptom of corruption in our body politic."[40]

The element which leaves no doubt as to the distance of Gandhi's position from that of the determinist is his insistence upon the power of man's will together with his reason to effect change in his society. We have already hinted that Gandhian satyagraha avoids the practical pitfalls of ethical relativism. It does so by establishing an objective standard of judgment in terms of social criteria. Here I am suggesting that his defense of individual freedom and the power of the individual will, though setting him at unbreachable distance from determinism, does not lead to a strictly voluntaristic ethic. For the Gandhian ethic must not only be decided in terms of socially expressed human needs; it must also be tested by non-violence. A brief examination of the relationship which the various elements in satyagraha bear to one another will indicate the practical procedure.

THE RELATIONSHIP OF THE THREE ELEMENTS IN SATYAGRAHA

The truth concept as it functions in the Gandhian technique of satyagraha has been shown to be that of relative truth. The objective standard by which truth can be judged is a human standard expressed in terms of human needs. The proper means for discovering truth in those terms cannot, then, result in human harm or frustrate rather than fulfill human needs—for in such a procedure truth would become travesty. The discovery of truth, or the resolution of conflict arising out of differences of opinion as to what is truth, must be prosecuted through non-violent action. Action based on the refusal to do harm often requires dealing with violence which may be instigated by the opponent in a conflict. Self-suffering is this further means by which relative truth is tested.

To the three fundamentals of satyagraha may be added certain corollary elements. Truth in satyagraha leads to an ethical humanism. It follows that *ahimsa* (non-violence), which includes the concept of love, leads in turn to social service. Self-suffering—not for its own sake, but for demonstration of sincerity, and flowing from refusal to injure the opponent while at the same time holding to the truth— implies sacrifice and preparation for sacrifice, even to the death.

Such are the principles which infuse the concept "satyagraha." When these

---

[39] *Harijan*, February 1, 1942, as quoted in Chander, *op. cit.*, p. 321.
[40] Gandhi, *Non-Violence in Peace & War*, pp. 390–391.

principles are applied to specific political and social action the tools of civil disobedience—non-cooperation, non-violent strike, constructive program—are devised.

. . .

. . . the element of non-violence in satyagraha is inseparable from a view of
truth which takes as its criterion the needs of man. In the quest for such truth, and
in its propagation, it is therefore not possible, in a proper satyagraha, to inflict harm
on others. In so behaving, truth itself would lose its meaning. He who claims a
different version of truth from the satyagrahi's must be converted by gentleness.
Meanwhile, the satyagrahi must reexamine continuously his own position—for his
opponent may be closer to the truth than he. Self-suffering, the third element of
satyagraha, guarantees the sincerity of the satyagrahi's own opinions, the while it
restrains him from propagating uncertain truths. The objective of satyagraha is to
win the victory over the conflict situation—to discover further truths and to persuade
the opponent, not to triumph over him.

Agreement must, indeed, be achieved. In agreement, the Western relativists
insist, lies certain criterion of truth. Agreement achieved through satyagraha implies
the carrying of full conviction. Holding to the truth means holding to what the
satyagrahi believes to be the truth until he is dissuaded from the position or any
part of it. Meanwhile his effort is steadfastly to persuade his opponent. If he suffers,
if he dies, in this effort, he has applied the principle of self-suffering, and has asserted the truth, as he sees it—for no power on earth can make a man do a thing
against his will.

To avoid possible misinterpretation, it may be well to note here that the effort
of satyagraha to reach agreement, and to hold onto truth until agreement is reached,
does not imply that two or more persons entertaining contradictory beliefs need
become embattled. Gandhi has given much evidence of his willingness to work with
others who disagreed strongly with him. So long as there is no serious conflict emerging from such association or contact, there is no need to resort to satyagraha. The
satyagraha approach is often that of assuming that those who disagree are each simply
holding to a limited view of truth.[41] It is only when beliefs come into serious conflict
—when basic needs or impulses or desires are frustrated—that satyagraha becomes
appropriate.

Gandhi has referred to non-violence as being both the end and the means. In a
prayer speech in New Delhi shortly before his death he commented, once again,
that means and ends are convertible terms.[42] This convertibility in the Gandhian doctrine is based upon non-violence.

A more precise statement of the ends-means relationship operating in satyagraha
is indicated by Shridharani's phrase describing the means as "the end in process and
the ideal in the making."[43] In the operation of satyagraha, where the protagonist
is prepared to revise his opinion and his goal if he is persuaded of their falsity, there
is little room for static ends. Perhaps the most characteristic quality of satyagraha

---

[41] From an address to the YMCA, Madras, February 16, 1916, quoted in Chander, *op. cit.*, pp.
405–406.

[42] M. K. Gandhi, *Delhi Diary: Prayer Speeches from 10-9-'47 to 30-1-'48* (Ahmedabad: Navajivan,
1948), p. 58.

[43] Krishnalal Shridharani, *War Without Violence* (New York: Harcourt, Brace [1939], p. 316. . . .

is the flexibility in ends which an emphasis on means implies. This is not to suggest that a satyagrahi is a weak or easy oppponent. He may persist to the death without relaxing his hold on the original position which he took to be truth. But, significantly, he may easily be won over. His dogma—if such a thing can be alleged of him—lies in adherence to a means, to a technique, which has, as we have seen, specific moral elements at its base. But what action in these terms may mean—what it may lead to as a social, or political, or individual end—is highly unpredictable.

> People say that I have changed my view, that I say today something different from what I said years ago. The fact of the matter is that conditions have changed. I am the same. . . . There has been a gradual evolution in my environment and I react to it as a *Satyagrahi*.[44]

Throughout Gandhi's writings runs the quiet insistence that individual will and reason can effect social and political change. Satyagraha is the technique he developed to point its direction.

BERTRAND RUSSELL

War and Nonresistance

Bertrand Russell (1872–1970) was a world-famous logician, Nobel Prize winner, and social theorist. Known today for his opposition to the testing of the hydrogen bomb, he served a jail sentence for his opposition to British involvement in World War I. This selection was written in 1915 and refers to events which occurred then, but its philosophical position is contemporary.

The principle that it is always wrong to employ force against another human being has been held in its extreme form by Quakers and by Tolstoy, but has always been rejected by the great majority of mankind as inconsistent with the existence of

[44] *Harijan*, January 28, 1939, as quoted in Chander, *op. cit.*, p. 320.

From *Justice in War Time*, by Bertrand Russell, The Open Court Publishing Company, La Salle, Illinois, 1916. Reprinted by permission of the publishers.

civilised society. In this, no doubt, the majority of mankind are in the right. But I think that the occasions where forcible resistance is the best course are much fewer than is generally believed, and that some very great and important advances in civilisation might be made if this were more widely recognised. The so-called "right of self-defence," in particular, seems to have only a very limited sphere of application, and to be often supported by arguments involving both mistakes as to political questions and a wrong conception of the best type of character.

No one who holds that human conduct ought to be such as to promote certain ends—no matter what ends may be selected—will expect any absolute hard-and-fast rules of conduct to which no possible exception can be found. Not to lie, not to steal, not to murder, are very good precepts for ordinary cases: it may be, in view of the likelihood of biassed judgments, that most men will act better if they always follow these precepts unquestioningly than if they consider each case on its merits. Nevertheless, it is obvious that there are cases where lying and stealing are justifiable, and the same must be said of murder by those who hold that some wars are righteous. Tolstoy does not judge conduct by its consequences: he considers actions inherently right or wrong. This makes it possible for him to say that no use of force is ever right. But if we judge conduct, as I think we ought, by its power of promoting what we consider a good life or a good society, we cannot expect such simplicity in our moral precepts, and we must expect all of them to be subject to exceptions. Whatever we may have to say must be regarded as in the nature of practical maxims, to be applied with common sense, not as logically universal rules to be tested by extreme cases.

Broadly speaking, I think the use of force is justifiable when it is ordered in accordance with law by a neutral authority, in the general interest and not primarily in the interest of one of the parties to the quarrel. On this ground, the use of force by the police is justifiable, provided (as is no doubt sometimes the case) the authorities are employing the police in the general interest and not merely in the interest of the holders of power. In international affairs, if there were a Council of the Powers, strong enough to restrain any aggressive nation without great difficulty, any army or navy employed in obedience to its orders might be regarded as a police force, and justified on the same grounds on which the police are justified. I think there is more hope of ultimately achieving universal peace by this method than by the adoption of non-resistance. But this has no bearing upon the question whether non-resistance would be a good policy, if any nation could be induced to adopt it. So long as no Council of the Powers exists, there is no neutral authority to order resistance, and we have to consider the justification of repelling an attack when the nation attacked is the judge in its own cause.

The justification of non-resistance is more easily seen in the case of quarrels between individuals. If I encountered the traditional highwayman, and he demanded my money or my life, I should unhesitatingly give him my money, even if it were in my power to shoot him before he shot me. I should do this, not from cowardice or lack of spirit, but because I would rather part with money than have a man's blood on my conscience. And for the same reason, if I were compelled to engage in a duel, I would rather let my adversary shoot me than shoot him. In this I believe all humane people would agree. At the same time, if he were a worthless fellow, and I had just made an important mathematical discovery which I had not yet had time to record, it might be right to preserve my life at his expense. Arguments of this sort would justify civilised communities in defending themselves against savages. But conflicts between civilised nations are more like conflicts between rival metaphysicians, each of whom considers his own system admirable and the other man's abominable, while to outsiders it is obvious that both are equally fantastic.

In private life, most situations can be met by the double principle of neither employing force nor obeying it. It is a familiar Platonic thesis that the man who inflicts injustice is more to be pitied than the man who suffers it. But such statements are read with a smile, as charming literary paradoxes, and are not taken as a practical wisdom for the guidance of life. Yet the use of force to coerce another man's will, even in those rare cases in which it is justifiable, produces a brutal and tyrannous state of mind, and is more destructive of inward peace than any misfortune that can be inflicted from without. The greatest good that can be achieved in this life is to have will and desire directed to universal ends, purged of the self-assertion which belongs to instinctive will. A man who has once known this good will not consider any private end important enough to be fought for: he may be willing to enter upon a contest of force, but if so, it will be for some end outside his own life, since what is best in his own life cannot be taken from him by another. But although he will not dictate to others for his own ends, he will also not be turned aside from universal ends by others: he will be no more willing to obey than to command. He will preserve his own liberty as scrupulously as he respects the liberty of others.

Exactly similar considerations apply to the conduct of nations, but they are obscured by traditional phrases about "honour," "patriotism," "sacred traditions," or "the protection of women and children." It is assumed that a nation which does not oppose force with force must be actuated by cowardice, and must lose whatever is valuable in its civilisation. Both these are illusions. To oppose force by passive non-obedience would require more courage, and would be far more likely to preserve the best elements of the national life. It would also do far more to discourage the use of force. This would be the way of practical wisdom, if men could be brought to believe it. But I fear men are too much wedded to the belief that patriotism is a virtue, and too fond of proving their superiority to others in a contest of force. People who object to the doctrine that might is right always contend that it will be disproved by showing that might is on their own side. Yet that would only be a disproof if their side were in the wrong, and their argument shows that they really believe the doctrine they are pretending to combat. Those who genuinely disbelieve the doctrine will not attempt to disprove it by getting might on their side.

Let us imagine that England were to disband its army and navy, after a generation of instruction in the principles of passive resistance as a better defence than war. Let us suppose that England at the same time publicly announced that no armed opposition would be offered to an invader, that all might come freely, but that no obedience would be yielded to any commands that a foreign authority might issue. What would happen in this case?

Suppose, to continue the argument, that the German Government wished to take advantage of England's defenceless condition. It would be faced, at the outset, by the opposition of whatever was not utterly brutal in Germany, since no possible cloak could be found to hide the nakedness of aggression. All civilised countries, when they engage in war, find some decent excuse: they fight, almost always, either in self-defence or in defence of the weak. No such excuse could be found in this case. It could no longer be said, as the Germans now say, that England's naval preponderance keeps other nations in bondage, and threatens the very existence of any nation which depends upon imported food. It could no longer be said that we were oppressing India, since India would be able to separate from the British Empire whenever it wished to do so. All the usual pretexts by which aggression is justified would be lacking. When America attacked Spain, it was to liberate the Cubans, against whom Spain was carrying on a war. When England attacked the Transvaal, the Poet Laureate, the *Times,* Messrs. Werner, Beit and Co., and the other imperialist magnates who represented the ancient traditions of the British race, solemnly assured us that our intervention was necessary for the safety of English women in Johannesburg, and for the liberation of the natives from virtual slavery to the Boers. These pleas deceived many people who, though no doubt not unwilling to be deceived, would yet have shrunk from an aggression which could not be in any way disguised. And it was said that the Boers aimed at the conquest of the whole of South Africa: we were told that, if ever England found itself entangled in a European war, Cape Colony would be overrun, and its English colonists would be subjected to a tyranny. In any civilised country, arguments of this kind are always used in justifying even the most aggressive war.

If England had no army and no navy, the Germans would be hard put to it to find a pretext for invasion. All the Liberal elements in Germany would oppose any such enterprise; so would all other nations, unless Germany offered them a share of the plunder. But let us suppose all home opposition overcome, and a force despatched to England to take possession of the country. Such a force, since it would meet with no military opposition, would not need to be large, and would not be in the state of mingled fear and ferocity which characterises an invading army among a hostile population. There would be no difficulty in preserving military discipline, and no opportunity for the rape and rapine which have always been displayed by troops after victory in battle. There would be no glory to be won, not even enough to earn one iron cross. The Germans could not congratulate themselves upon their military prowess, or imagine that they were displaying the stern self-abnegation believed to be shown by willingness to die in the fight. To the soldierly mind, the whole expedition would be ridiculous, causing a feeling of disgust instead of pride. Perhaps a few impudent street-boys might have to have their ears boxed, but otherwise there would be nothing to lend dignity to the expedition.

However, we will suppose the invading army arrived in London, where they would evict the King from Buckingham Palace and the Members from the House of Commons. A few able bureaucrats would be brought over from Berlin to consult with the Civil Servants in Whitehall as to the new laws by which the reign of Kultur was to be inaugurated. No difficulty would be expected in managing so tame a nation, and at first almost all the existing officials would be confirmed in their offices. For the government of a large modern State is a complicated matter, and it would be thought well to facilitate the transition by the help of men familiar with the existing machinery.

But at this point, if the nation showed as much courage as it has always shown in fighting, difficulties would begin. All the existing officials would refuse to cooperate with the Germans. Some of the more prominent would be imprisoned, perhaps even shot, in order to encourage the others. But if the others held firm, if they refused to recognise or transmit any order given by Germans, if they continued to carry out the decrees previously made by the English Parliament and the English Government, the Germans would have to dismiss them all, even to the humblest postman, and call in German talent to fill the breach.

The dismissed officials could not all be imprisoned or shot: since no fighting would have occurred, such wholesale brutality would be out of the question. And it would be very difficult for the Germans suddenly, out of nothing, to create an administrative machine. Whatever edicts they might issue would be quietly ignored by the population. If they ordered that German should be the language taught in schools, the schoolmasters would go on as if no such order had been issued; if the schoolmasters were dismissed, the parents would no longer send the children to school. If they ordered that English young men should undergo military service, the young men would simply refuse; after shooting a few, the Germans would have to give up the attempt in despair. If they tried to raise revenue by customs duties at the ports, they would have to have Germans customs officers; this would lead to a strike of all dock labourers, so that this way of raising revenue would become impossible. If they tried to take over the railways, there would be a strike of the railway servants. Whatever they touched would instantly become paralysed, and it would soon be evident, even to them, that nothing was to be made out of England unless the population could be conciliated.

Such a method of dealing with invasion would, of course, require fortitude and discipline. But fortitude and discipline are required in war. For ages past, education has been largely directed to producing these qualities for the sake of war. They now exist so widely that in every civilised country almost every man is willing to die on the battlefield whenever his Government thinks the moment suitable. The same courage and idealism which are now put into war could quite easily be directed by education into the channel of passive resistance. I do not know what losses England may suffer before the present war is ended, but if they amount to a million no one will be surprised. An immensely smaller number of losses, incurred in passive resitance, would prove to any invading army that the task of subjecting England to alien domination was an impossible one. And this proof would be made once for all, without dependence upon the doubtful accidents of war.

In internal politics, in all democratic countries, the very method we have been considering is constantly practised, with continually increasing success. Even in Russia, it was the general strike which secured the Constitution of 1905. For a generation, terrorists had uselessly copied the methods of militarists by bomb-throwing and assassination; they had achieved nothing except to afford the authorities an excuse for ruthless repression—an excuse not only to the public, but also to their own consciences, since they appeared to themselves, as soldiers do, to be brave men facing death in the public service. After all the years of fruitless violence, it was the method of passive non-obedience which secured the momentary victory, afterwards lost through disunion and a return to violence. And in all the dealings of democratic Governments with labour troubles or with irreconcilable minorities, it is this same power of passive resistance that comes into play. In a civilised, highly organised, highly political State, government is impossible without the consent of the governed. Any object for which a considerable body of men are prepared to starve and die can be achieved by political means, without the need of any resort to force. And if this is true of objects only desired by a minority, it is a thousand times more true of objects desired unanimously by the whole nation.

But it may be said that, even if the Germans could not actually take over the government of England, or rob us of internal self-government, they could do two things which would injure us vitally: they could take away our Empire, and they could levy a tribute by the threat of depriving us of food supplies.

The Germans could not take away the self-governing parts of our Empire, since they would encounter there the same difficulties as would prevent them from governing England. They could take away those parts of our Empire which we hold by force, and this would be a blow to our pride: the oppression of subject races is one of the chief sources of patriotic satisfaction, and one of the chief things for which Germany envies us. But it is not a source of pride to any rational or humane man. European rule over uncivilised races is, in fact, a very sordid affair. The best of the men whom it employs are those engaged in the attempt at government, who live in exile and usually die of fever; the rest grow rich selling rum to natives or making them work in mines. Meanwhile the natives degenerate: some die of drink, some of diseases caught from white men, some of consumption in the mines; those who survive contract the vices of civilisation without losing the vices of barbarism. It can only be a blessing to any nation to be deprived of this source of pride, which is a canker of corruption and immorality in the life of democratic communities.

That the Germans could levy a tribute on England by threatening our food supplies is obviously true. The ethics of such a demand would be exactly the same as that of the highwayman who demands "your money or your life." The same reasons which would lead a reasonable man to give his money rather than shoot or be shot would also lead a reasonable nation to give a tribute rather than resist by force of arms. The greatest sum that foreigners could theoretically exact would be the total economic rent of the land and natural resources of England. In fact, economic rent may be defined as what can be, and historically has been, extorted by such means. The rent now paid to landowners in England is the outcome of the exactions made by William the Conquerer and his barons. The law-courts are the outcome of those set up at that time, and the law which they administer, so far as land is concerned, represents simply the power of the sword. From inertia and lack of imagination, the English at the present day continue to pay to the landowners a vast sum to which they have no right but that of conquest. The working classes, the shopkeepers, manufacturers, and merchants, the literary men, and the men of science—all the people who make England of any account in the world—have at most an infinitesimal and accidental share in the rental of England. The men who have a share use their rents in luxury, political corruption, taking the lives of birds, and depopulating and enslaving the rural districts. This way of life is that which almost all English men and women consider the most admirable: those who are anywhere near achieving it struggle to attain it completely, and those who are more remote read serial stories about it as their ancestors would have read of the joys of Paradise.

It is this life of the idle rich which would be curtailed if the Germans exacted a tribute from England. Everything in England that is not positively harmful would be untouched: wages and other earned incomes could not be diminished without diminishing the productivity of English labour, and so lessening England's capacity for paying tribute. Our snobbish instincts, if the idle rich were abolished, might be driven, by want of other outlet, into the admiration of real merit. And if the Germans could effect this for us, they would well deserve their tribute.

It is very doubtful, indeed, whether the Germans would exact from us a larger tribute than we exact from ourselves in resisting them. There is no knowing what this war will have cost England when it ends, but we shall probably not exaggerate if we place the cost at a thousand million pounds.[1] This represents an annual payment of forty million pounds. All this, together with the annual expenditure on our Army and Navy, we might have paid to the Germans without being any poorer than we shall be when the war ends. This represents an incredibly larger tribute than we derive from India; yet the Germans assure us that we are full of commercial cunning, and that we govern India solely for own profit. If they believe this, it is hardly to be supposed that the receipt of such a tribute would fail to satisfy them. Meanwhile we should have avoided the death of our young men, the moral degradation of almost our whole population, and the lowering of the standard of civilisation slowly achieved through centuries which were peaceful in comparison with our present condition.

But, of course, all that I have been saying is fantastic, degrading, and out of touch with reality. I have been assuming that men are to some extent guided by reason, that their actions are directed to ends such as "life, liberty, and the pursuit of happiness." This is not the case. Death, slavery, and unhappiness (for others) are the chief ends pursued by States in their external relations. It is the preference of such ends to one's own happiness that constitutes patriotism, that shows a man to be free from materialism, and that raises him above the commercial, money-grubbing level of the mere shopkeeper. The Prussian feels himself noble because he is willing to be killed provided men of other nations are killed at the same time. His nobility and his freedom from commercialism consists in the fact that he desires the misery of others more than his own happiness. And there is a Prussian lurking in each of us, ready to make us reject any national advantage which is not purchased by injury to some other nation. It is this lurking Prussian in our instincts who assures us that a policy of non-resistance would be tame and cowardly, unworthy of a great and proud nation, a failure to perform our duty of chastising an exactly similar pride in other nations.

Pride has its place among virtues, in the lives of individuals as well as in the lives of nations. Pride, in so far as it is a virtue, is a determination not to be turned aside from the ends which a man thinks good, no matter what outside pressure may be brought to bear upon him. There is pride in Condorcet, sentenced to the guillotine, spending his last days in writing a book on human progress. There is pride in those who refuse to recant their religious convictions under persecution. Such pride is the noblest form of courage: it shows that self-determination of the will which is the essence of spiritual freedom. But such pride should have as its complement a just conception of what constitutes human welfare, and as its correlative a respect for the freedom of others as absolute as the determination to preserve freedom for ourselves. Exactly the same kind of pride is good in the life of a nation. If we think ill of war, while some other nation thinks well of it, let us show our national pride

---

[1] It is now (September, 1915) evident that this is an underestimate.

by living without war, whatever temptations the other nation may put in our way to live according to their ideals rather than according to our own. The Germans, we are given to understand, hate us with a bitter hatred, and long to believe that we feel towards them as they feel towards us; for unrequited hatred is as bitter as unrequited love. They have made it increasingly difficult not to gratify their desire; but in so far as we can keep our resistance free from bitterness we win a spiritual victory over what deserves to be combated in the enemy, which is far more important than any victory to be won by guns and bayonets.

But this kind of pride is not the kind which patriots exhort us to display. The pride that they admire is the kind which aims at thwarting others; it is the pride of power. Having suspected that the Germans desired Morocco and Mesopotamia, we were proud of the fact that we prevented them from acquiring either. Having found that the Boers desired independence, we were proud of the fact that we made them submit to our rule. This kind of pride consists merely in love of dominion. Dominion and power can only be conclusively shown by compelling others to forego what they desire. By a natural consequence, those in whom the love of power is strong are led to inflict pain and to use force against the perfectly legitimate desires of those whom they wish to subdue. In nations, this nation's history are not those who have benefited mankind, but those who have injured other nations. If we prided ourselves upon the good and not the harm that we have done, we should have put Shakespeare in the Nelson Monument, and given Apsley House to Darwin. But the citizens whom every nation honours most are those who have killed the greatest number of foreigners.

It is this pride of power which makes us unwilling to yield to others in matters of no intrinsic importance. The Germans cherish a desire to own African swamps, of which we have a superfluity. No one in England benefits by the possession of them, except a few financial magnates, mostly of foreign origin. If we were reasonable, we should regard the German desire as a curious whim, which we might gratify without any real national loss. Instead of that, we regard the German desire as a crime, and our resistance to it as a virtue. We teach school children to rejoice because so much of the map is painted red. In order that as much as possible may be painted red, we are willing to sacrifice those ideals of freedom which we have led mankind, and, if necessary, to adopt all the worst features of the Prussian spirit. This is because we fear the external enemy, who kills the body, more than the internal enemy, who kills the soul. The soul of a nation, if it is a free soul, without slavishness and without tyranny, cannot be killed by any outward enemy. And if men would realize this, the panic fear which the nations feel one toward another would be expelled by a better pride than that of diplomatists and warlords.

The armies and navies of the world are kept up by three causes: cowardice, love of dominion, and lust for blood.

It is cowardice that makes it difficult to meet invasion by the method of passive resistance. More courage and discipline is needed for the successful practice of this method than for facing death in the heat of battle. But I am persuaded that there is in England enough courage and enough capacity for discipline to make success in passive resistance possible, if education and moral teaching is directed to that end instead of to warlike prowess. It is cowardice also that makes men prefer the old method of trying to be stronger than your adversary (in which only one party can succeed), rather than a new method requiring imagination and a readjustment of traditional standards. Yet, if men could think outside the well-worn grooves, there are many plain facts which show the folly of conventional statesmanship. Why has Germany invaded France? Because the French have an army. Why has England attacked Germany? Because the Germans have a navy. Yet people persist in thinking that the French army and the German navy contribute to national safety. Nothing could be more obvious than the facts; nothing could be more universal than men's blindness to them.

The second reason for keeping up the armies and navies of the world is love of dominion. The Germans, in the Morocco controversy, announced that nothing of importance was to happen anywhere without their being consulted. We regarded this as monstrous arrogance; but for two centuries we had advanced the same claim as a matter of course. The matters about which diplomatists raise a pother are usually of only microscopic importance to the welfare of ordinary citizens: they are matters involving national "prestige," that is to say, the power of the State to prevent other States from doing as they wish. This power is sometimes partly based on money, but in the main it rests on armies and navies. If our navy had been smaller, we should not have been able to defeat the German desire for an Atlantic port in Morocco. It would have done us no harm if the Germans had acquired Casablanca, but we enjoyed the thought that our fiat kept them out. The procuring of such pleasures is the second purpose served by armies and navies.

The third purpose of armaments—indeed their primary and original purpose, from which all others are derivative—is to satisfy the lust for blood. Fighting is an instinctive activity of males, both animal and human. Human males, being gregarious, naturally fight in packs. It has been found that the pack tends to be more successful against other packs when fighting within the pack is as far as possible prevented. For this purpose, the law and the police have been instituted. But the shedding of human blood is still considered the most glorious thing a man can do, provided he does it in company with the rest of his pack. War, like marriage, is the legally permitted outlet for a certain instinct. But the instinct which leads to war, unlike the instinct which leads to marriage, so far from being necessary to the human race, is wholly harmful among civilized men. It is an instinct which easily becomes atrophied in a settled community: many men have hardly a trace of it. Unfortunately, as men grow older, their affections and their powers of thought decay. For this reason, and also because power stimulates the love of power, the men who have most influence in government are usually men whose passions and impulses are less civilised than those of the average citizen. These men—the great financiers, the Ministers, and some editors of daily papers—use their position, their knowledge, and their power of disseminating misinformation, to arouse and stimulate the latent instinct for bloodshed. When they have succeeded, they say that they are reluctantly forced into war by the pressure of public opinion. Their activities are exactly analogous to those of men who distribute indecent pictures or produce lascivious plays. They ought to be viewed in the same light; but because of the notion that a wish to kill foreigners is patriotic and virtuous, they are honored as men who have deserved well of their country. They provide an outlet for the impulse to homicide. To gratify this impulse is the third and ultimate purpose of armies and navies.

All these three motives for armaments—cowardice, love of dominion, and lust for blood—are no longer ineradicable in civilised human nature. All are diminishing under the influence of modern social organisation. All might be reduced to a degree which could make them almost innocuous, if early education and current moral standards were directed to that end. Passive resistance, if it were adopted deliberately by the will of a whole nation, with the same measure of courage and discipline which is now displayed in war, might achieve a far more perfect protection for what is good in national life than armies and navies can ever achieve, without demanding the courage and waste and welter of brutality involved in modern war.

Nevertheless, it is hardly to be expected that progress will come in this way, because the imaginative effort required is too great. It is much more likely that it will come as the reign of law within the State has come, by the establishment of a central government of the world, able and willing to secure obedience by force, because the great majority of men will recognise that obedience is better than the present international anarchy. A central government of this kind will command assent, not as a partisan but as the representative of the interests of the whole. Very soon, resistance to it would be seen to be hopeless, and wars would cease. Force directed by a neutral authority is not open to the same abuse, or likely to cause the same long-drawn conflicts, as force exercised by quarrelling nations each of which is the judge of its own cause. Although I firmly believe that the adoption of passive instead of active resistance would be good if a nation could be convinced of its goodness, yet it is rather to the ultimate creation of a strong central authority that I should look for the ending of war. But war will only end after a great labour has been performed in altering men's moral ideals, directing them to the good of all mankind, and not only of the separate nations into which men happen to have been born.

FURTHER READINGS

ANTHOLOGIES

Feinberg, Joel, Ed., *Reason and Responsibility,* Belmont, Calif., Dickinson, 1965.

Laslett, Peter, Ed., *Philosophy, Politics, and Society,* 3rd ser., New York, Barnes & Noble, 1967.

Olafson, Frederick A., Ed., *Justice and Social Policy,* Englewood Cliffs, N.J., Prentice-Hall, 1961.

Somerville, John, and Ronald E. Santoni, Eds., *Social and Political Philosophy,* Garden City, N.Y., Anchor, 1963.

Wolff, Robert Paul, Ed., *Political Man and Social Man,* New York, Random House, 1966.

CLASSIC WORKS

Aristotle, *Politics,* Ernest Barker, Trans., Oxford, Clarendon, 1961.

Kant, Immanuel, *The Philosophy of Law,* W. Hastie, Trans., Edinburgh, T. & T. Clark, 1887.

Locke, John, *The Second Treatise on Government* in *Two Treatises on Government,* New York, Hafner, 1956.

Machiavelli, Niccolo, *The Prince and the Discourses,* Luigi Ricci and C. E. Delmond, Trans., New York, Random House, 1940.

Plato, *The Republic, Laws* in *The Collected Dialogues of Plato,* Edith Hamilton and Huntington Cairns, Eds., New York, Bollingen Foundation, 1961.

REVOLUTION AND SOCIAL CHANGE

Arendt, Hannah, *On Revolution,* New York, Viking, 1965.

Bellamy, Edward, *Looking Backward,* Boston, Houghton Mifflin, 1966.

Camus, Albert, *The Rebel,* New York, Knopf, 1956.

———, *Resistance, Rebellion, and Death,* New York, Knopf, 1960.

Huxley, Aldous, *Brave New World and Brave New World Revisited,* New York, Harper Torchbooks, 1965.

Marcuse, Herbert, *An Essay on Liberation,* Boston, Beacon, 1969.

———, *Reason and Revolution,* 2nd ed., New York, Humanities, 1963.

Marx, Karl, *The Communist Manifesto,* Samuel Moore, Trans., Joseph Katz, Ed., New York, Washington Square Press, 1964.

Orwell, George, *Animal Farm,* New York, Harcourt, Brace & World, 1946.

Popper, Karl L., *The Open Society and Its Enemies,* London, Routledge & Kegan Paul, 1949.

Sabine, George H., *A History of Political Theory,* New York, Holt, 1947.

Skinner, B. F., *Walden Two,* New York, Macmillan, 1948.

———, "Utopia and Human Behavior," *The Humanist,* 27 (August, 1967). 120–122, 136–137.

Thoreau, Henry David, *Walden and Civil Disobedience,* New York, Harper & Row, 1965.

Wolff, Robert Paul, *A Critique of Pure Tolerance,* Boston, Beacon, 1963.

VIOLENCE

Arendt, Hannah, "Reflections on Violence," *New York Review of Books,* February 27, 1969, pp. 19–31, and *Journal of International Affairs,* 23 (Winter, 1969), 1–35.

Aron, Raymond, *Peace and War,* Richard Howard and Annette Baker Fox, Trans., Garden City, N.Y., Anchor, 1966.

Carmichael, Stokely, and Charles V. Hamilton, *Black Power,* New York, Random House, 1967.

Deming, Barbara, *Prison Notes,* New York, Grossman, 1966.

Diwakar, R. R., *Satyagraha, Its Technique and History,* Bombay, Hind Kitabs, 1946.

Gandhi, Mohandas K., *Autobiography, or The Story of My Experiments with Truth,* 2nd ed., Ahmedabad, India, Navajivan Trust, 1940.

———, *Non-Violence in Peace and War,* Ahmedabad, India, Navajivan Trust, 1942.

———, *Satyagraha in South Africa,* Ganesan, 1948.

Graham, Hugh Davis, and Ted Robert Carr, Eds., *Violence in America. The Complete Official Report to the National Commission on Causes and Prevention of Violence,* New York, Signet, 1969.

King, Martin Luther, Jr., *Stride Toward Freedom,* New York, Harper & Row, 1958.

Laing, R. D., and D. G. Cooper, *Reason and Violence, A Decade of Sartre's Philosophy 1950–1960,* London, Tavistock, 1964.

Merton, Thomas, "Introduction," in *Gandhi on Non-Violence,* Thomas Merton, Ed., New York, New Directions, 1964.

Payne, Robert, *The Life and Death of Gandhi,* New York, Dutton, 1969.

Russell, Bertrand, *Autobiography,* Vol. 1, Boston, Little, Brown, 1966.

——, *Has Man a Future?,* Harmondsworth, Eng., Penguin, 1962.

——, *War Crimes in Vietnam,* New York, Monthly Review Press, 1967.

Sartre, Jean-Paul, *The Philosophy of Jean-Paul Sartre,* Robert D. Cumming, Ed., New York, Random House, 1965, selections from *The Critique of Dialectical Reason,* pp. 415–483.

Sorel, Georges, *Reflections on Violence,* New York, Collier, 1961.

Tolstoy, Leo, *The Kingdom of God and Peace Essays,* Maude Aylmer, Trans., London, Oxford University Press, 1936.

Section III

MAN AND WORLD

Human beings imagine that nothing else in the universe is like them, yet they imagine themselves enough like other human beings to communicate with one another. People imagine that they dominate this world, in the sense that they can perceive and talk about it; and yet they debate incessantly the basis of their claims to knowledge. Is nothing at all like human beings? Can people, indeed, transcend their lonely isolation from other persons? Do they dare claim to know the inanimate world they survey?

The most audacious attempt to base human domination of the inanimate world on powers possessed only by human beings was offered three centuries ago by René Descartes. So great was the impact of Descartes' definition of the self, "I am a thing that thinks," that it has affected the course of psychology and philosophy ever since. Philosophers of every persuasion still attack or defend Descartes' definition of the human and of human knowledge. Reflective people who may never have heard of Descartes often hold some of the radical views he originated. Thus Descartes' writing help us to formulate the questions discussed at length in this section: What is it to be human? What is our relationship to the world?

For Descartes, even asking these questions requires a total intellectual risk. Asking about our relationship to the world requires us to risk the possibility that there may be no world. Asking about the nature of other people or even oneself requires us to risk the possibility that there may be no one at all, not even the questioner. Yet Descartes tried to show that the methodological doubt he embarked on to try to justify these beliefs would result in a new basis for self-knowledge and knowledge of the world.

According to Descartes, the questioner can hope to surmount the total risk of methodological doubt because of the very kind of risk he takes. I embark on a radical thought-experiment; well, then, if nothing else, I am a thinking being. Through the power of my thought I can construct proofs (not presented here) that there is something outside of me—a god—which guarantees that I am not alone. Because of the guarantee I obtain in this way, I can also be confident that not only my thought but also physical things exist. There are things in the world which I see and hear, there are the faces and bodies of the other people with whom I would communicate, and there is my own body, which my mind inhabits. I am a thing that thinks and I inhabit a material world.

No longer are rational proofs like a proof of the existence of God proposed to justify our knowledge of an inanimate world. Indeed, it now seems odd that anyone should doubt, as Descartes did, that there is an inanimate world. But we do continue to characterize ourselves as things that think, quite unaware of the complications that arise in attempting to refer to our bodies and our minds as if these were completely separate entities. Descartes' separation between body and mind is a key to much current puzzlement about self-identity: Is my mind, for example, *in* my body? Am I my mind or my body? If I am essentially both mind and body, how are they related? This separation is also the key to much of our despair over our alienation from other people, who, like us, are characterized as things that think. These problems are discussed at length in the subsection "Myself and Others."

Who, then, am I? In "Consciousness as Social" Friedrich Nietzsche opens with the suggestion that self-consciousness is awareness of the language and gestures used not only by oneself but by other people as well: it is one's awareness of a social role. On the other hand, in "The Self is a Bundle of Perceptions," David Hume concludes that the self is merely a collection of sense impressions with nothing discernible to hold them together. Neither Nietzsche nor Hume explains what collects or identifies emotional responses, sense impressions, or linguistic expressions as mine alone; but Nietzsche's suggestion leads us to look to a community of persons, rather than to an isolated person, to try to understand self-identity.

If our self-identity depends on our presence in a community of persons, then we assume that other people exist. But do we know anything more about them? Friedrich Waismann poses this question in "Can I Know Another Person's Experiences?" For Waismann, the answer to this question depends on the way we define "person." If a person is a mind in a body, then my experiences are mental and so are the other person's. For example, I perceive the other person's body and he tells me that he is experiencing the color green, but I cannot perceive directly what is in his mind. Thus I cannot know directly his experience of the color green.

Still, as Waismann suggests toward the end of his article, this conception of person does not render all linguistic communication impossible. Even poetry may impart one's experience. Yet if we wish a more satisfactory notion of the knowledge of another person's experience—a solution to what has been called "the problem of other minds"—we shall have to look further.

A notion of dialogue between man and man is carried forward in the next article. In "On Perceiving Persons," Frank A. Tillman argues that there is genuine communication, true interpersonal perception. He begins by criticizing four other attempts to answer these questions and then offers two suggestions of his own. First, our difficulty in showing that communication between persons is possible arises from a conception of persons as minds that just happen to inhabit the bodies that other people perceive. If we give up this dualism, which we have seen developed by both Descartes and Waismann, we will not have to think of another person's experiences as inherently mental and thus inherently inaccessible to everyone else. Second, Tillman shows that there is a great deal of empirical evidence that in different cultures, facial expressions and bodily gestures are used like languages, subject to rules which everyone in his own culture understands. If we interpret bodily gestures as expressive in this way, then it becomes clear that we can know one another's experiences after all.

There remains one question which has recently regained urgency: What, if anything, makes a human being distinct from anything else? It is an affront to our dignity and an insult to our pride to suppose that a computer or robot might do what we do, might express itself as we express ourselves, might *be* indistinguishable from us. Yet Michael Scriven in "Could a Robot Be a Person?" concludes that a robot might be developed to meet all of the critical tests presently met by humans.

In contrast, Noam Chomsky, whose work in linguistics has recently influenced both psychology and philosophy, argues in "Persons, Language, and Automata" that only human beings could meet one test, a test first suggested by Descartes. Only human beings, Chomsky argues, have the capacity to generate and recognize linguistic expression creatively. This "creative aspect of language use" suggests still another departure from Descartes' definition of the person as "a thing that thinks." If Chomsky is right, a person is, instead, a thing that speaks.

Whether or not his use of language uniquely defines the human, an important part of human existence is his use of language and other modes of expression. What can it show us about his place in the world and about his knowledge of it? Classic opposing positions were taken in the eighteenth century by David Hume and Immanuel Kant, and they are still being debated. These, together with several widely varied contemporary responses, are presented in the subsection "Language, Mind, and World."

Hume argues in "The Passive Mind: Custom and Convention" that I inhabit the world as a passive being: my experiences or "ideas" are thrust upon me in a jumble which I cannot control. Then any attempt I offer to interpret the world I experience—to argue that some of my statements about it must be true or to predict that a given configuration of events will always cause some other kind of event to happen—is a vain attempt. The only justification I can offer for such claims is "custom and convention," for there is no order inherent in my statements about the world, or "statements of matters of fact."

In contrast in "The Active Mind: The Judgments of Experience" Kant argues that there is, indeed, an order which I can impose upon my experience of the world.

It stems from the structure of my perceptual experience and is expressed in the form of statements, or propositions, which Kant terms "synthetic *a priori*." Both my knowledge of the world and my expression of this knowledge represent, for Kant, uniquely human contributions.

Since Hume and Kant first questioned the position of men in the world debate has constantly referred to them. Alfred J. Ayer, whose "Language, Meaning, and Reality" shows Hume's influence and presents the recently influential philosophical position called "logical positivism, holds that an examination of language itself offers the key to knowledge. Meaningful propositions (which Ayer called "analytic" and "synthetic") express what is knowable; all other utterances are nonsense and fail to express what is knowable. But John R. Searle, who has taken much inspiration from the work of contemporary English philosopher John L. Austin, argues in "Words, the World, and Human Communication" that it is not the words alone but rather human use of words in context that requires examination. Searle explains that many utterances are "speech acts," subject to conventions as detailed as those that constitute and regulate other kinds of human action. Thus it would appear that not just language but any expressive act would offer the key to human presence in the world.

The emphasis on all modes of expression is carried forward in the concluding article of this section, Maurice Merleau-Ponty's "Expression and Human Existence." There Merleau-Ponty, a philosopher in the existentialist tradition, extends his analysis of the relationship between man and world beyond an analysis of human speech. For Merleau-Ponty, human existence reveals that there is no separation between mind and body, expression and perception, self and world, or self and others. Rather, all exist in a vast community. Human expression, whether through language or through some other form, is the vehicle of human existence in an inhabited world.

Thus renewed hope of resolution is offered for our present loss of self-awareness, our alienation from other people, and our aloofness from the world we inhabit. The authors of the articles in this section suggest new characterizations of the human, of communication, and of the world. Self-knowledge and knowledge of others can be increased as the concepts of self and of knowledge are themselves clarified.

RENÉ DESCARTES

I Am a Thing That Thinks

René Descartes (1596-1650), who
defined man as "a thing that thinks,"
transformed the course of psychology
and philosophy. Among his other works
are the *Discourse on Method* and
Passions of the Soul.

MEDITATION I
OF THE THINGS WHICH MAY BE BROUGHT WITHIN THE SPHERE OF THE DOUBTFUL

It is now some years since I detected how many were the false beliefs that I had
from my earliest youth admitted as true, and how doubtful was everything I had
since constructed on this basis; and from that time I was convinced that I must
once for all seriously undertake to rid myself of all the opinions which I had formerly
accepted, and commence to build anew from the foundation, if I wanted to establish
any firm and permanent structure in the sciences. But as this enterprise appeared
to be a very great one, I waited until I had attained an age so mature that I could
not hope that at any later date I should be better fitted to execute my design. This
reason caused me to delay so long that I should feel that I was doing wrong were
I to occupy in deliberation the time that yet remains to me for action. Today, then,
since very opportunely for the plan I have in view I have delivered my mind from
every care and since I have procured for myself an assured leisure in a peaceable
retirement, I shall at last seriously and freely address myself to the general upheaval of
all my former opinions.

Now for this object it is not necessary that I should show that all of these
are false—I shall perhaps never arrive at this end. But inasmuch as reason already
persuades me that I ought no less carefully to withhold my assent from matters
which are not entirely certain and indubitable than from those which appear to me
manifestly to be false, if I am able to find in each one some reason to doubt, this
will suffice to justify my rejecting the whole. And for that end it will not be requisite
that I should examine each in particular, which would be an endless undertaking;
for owing to the fact that the destruction of the foundations of necessity brings with
it the downfall of the rest of the edifice, I shall only in the first place attack those
principles upon which all my former opinions rested.

Meditations I, II, and VI from *The Philosophical Works of Descartes*, translated by Elizabeth S. Haldane and G. R. T. Ross, Cambridge University Press, 1934. Reprinted by permission of the publishers.

All that up to the present time I have accepted as most true and certain I have learned either from the senses or through the senses; but it is sometimes proved to me that these senses are deceptive, and it is wiser not to trust entirely to any thing by which we have once been deceived.

But it may be that although the senses sometimes deceive us concerning things which are hardly perceptible, or very far away, there are yet many others to be met with as to which we cannot reasonably have any doubt, although we recognise them by their means. For example, there is the fact that I am here, seated by the fire, attired in a dressing gown, having this paper in my hands and other similar matters. And how could I deny that these hands and this body are mine, were it not perhaps that I compare myself to certain persons, devoid of sense, whose cerebella are so troubled and clouded by the violent vapours of black bile, that they constantly assure us that they think they are kings when they are really quite poor, or that they are clothed in purple when they are really without covering, or who imagine that they have an earthenware head or are nothing but pumpkins or are made of glass. But they are mad, and I should not be any the less insane were I to follow examples so extravagant.

At the same time I must remember that I am a man, and that consequently I am in the habit of sleeping, and in my dreams representing to myself the same things or sometimes even less probable things, than do those who are insane in their waking moments. How often has it happened to me that in the night I dreamt that I found myself in this particular place, that I was dressed and seated near the fire, whilst in reality I was lying undressed in bed! At this moment it does indeed seem to me that it is with eyes awake that I am looking at this paper; that this head which I move is not asleep, that it is deliberately and of set purpose that I extend my hand and perceive it; what happens in sleep does not appear so clear nor so distinct as does all this. But in thinking over this I remind myself that on many occasions I have in sleep been deceived by similar illusions, and in dwelling carefully on this reflection I see so manifestly that there are no certain indications by which we may clearly distinguish wakefulness from sleep that I almost in astonishment. And my astonishment is such that it is almost capable of persuading me that I now dream.

Now let us assume that we are asleep and that all these particulars, e.g. that we open our eyes, shake our head, extend our hands, and so on, are but false delusions; and let us reflect that possibly neither our hands nor our whole body are such as they appear to us to be. At the same time we must at least confess that the things which are represented to us in sleep are like painted representations which can only have been formed as the counterparts of something real and true, and that in this way those general things at least, i.e. eyes, a head, hands, and a whole body, are not imaginary things, but things really existent. For, as a matter of fact, painters, even when they study with the greatest skill to represent sirens and satyrs by forms the most strange and extraordinary, cannot give them natures which are entirely new, but merely make a certain medley of the members of different animals; or if their imagination is extravagant enough to invent something so novel that nothing similar has ever before been seen, and that then their work represents a thing purely fictitious and absolutely false, it is certain all the same that the colours of which this is composed are necessarily real. And for the same reason, although these general things, to wit, eyes, a head, hands, and such like, may be imaginary, we are bound at the same time to confess that there are at least some other objects yet more simple and more universal, which are real and true; and of these just in the same way as with certain real colours, all these images of things which dwell in our thoughts, whether true and real or false and fantastic, are formed.

To such a class of things pertains corporeal nature in general, and its extension, the figure of extended things, their quantity or magnitude and number, as also the place in which they are, the time which measures their duration, and so on.

That is possibly why our reasoning is not unjust when we conclude from this that Physics, Astronomy, Medicine, and all other sciences which have as their end the consideration of composite things, are very dubious and uncertain; but that Arithmetic, Geometry and other sciences of that kind which only treat of things that are very simple and very general, without taking great trouble to ascertain whether they are actually existent or not, contain some measure of certainty and an element of the indubitable. For whether I am awake or asleep, two and three together always form five, and the square can never have more than four sides, and it does not seem possible that truths so clear and apparent can be suspected of any falsity.

Nevertheless I have long had fixed in my mind the belief that an all-powerful God existed by whom I have been created such as I am. But how do I know that He has not brought it to pass that there is no earth, no heaven, no extended body, no magnitude, no place, and that nevertheless they seem to me to exist just exactly as I now see them? And, besides, as I sometimes imagine that others deceive themselves in the things which they think they know best, how do I know that I am not deceived every time that I add two and three, or count the sides of a square, or judge of things yet simpler, if anything simpler can be imagined? But possibly God has not desired that I should be thus deceived, for He is said to be supremely good. If, however, it is contrary to His goodness to have made me such that I constantly deceive myself, it would also appear to be contrary to His goodness to permit me to be sometimes deceived, and nevertheless I cannot doubt that He does permit this.

There may indeed be those who would prefer to deny the existence of a God so powerful, rather than believe that all other things are uncertain. But let us not oppose them for the present, and grant that all that is here said of a God is a fable; nevertheless in whatever way they suppose that I have arrived at the state of being that I have reached—whether they attribute it to fate or to accident, or make out that it is by a continual succession of antecedents, or by some other method —since to err and deceive oneself is a defect, it is clear that the greater will be the probability of my being so imperfect as to deceive myself ever, as is the Author to whom they assign my origin the less powerful. To these reasons I have certainly nothing to reply, but at the end I feel constrained to confess that there is nothing in all that I formerly believed to be true, of which I cannot in some measure doubt, and that not merely through want of thought or through levity, but for reasons which are very powerful and maturely considered; so that henceforth I ought not the less carefully to refrain from giving credence to these opinions than to that which is manifestly false, if I desire to arrive at any certainty.

But it is not sufficient to have made these remarks, we must also be careful to keep them in mind. For these ancient and commonly held opinions still revert frequently to my mind, long and familiar custom having given them the right to occupy my mind against my inclination and rendered them almost masters of my belief; nor will I ever lose the habit of deferring to them or of placing my confidence in them, so long as I consider them as they really are, i.e. opinions in some measure doubtful, as I have just shown, and at the same time highly probable, so that there is much more reason to believe in than to deny them. That is why I consider that I shall not be acting amiss, if, taking of set purpose a contrary belief, I allow myself to be deceived, and for a certain time pretend that all these opinions are entirely false and imaginary, until at last, having thus balanced my former prejudices with my latter, my judgment will no longer be dominated by bad usage or turned away from the right knowledge of the truth. For I am assured that there can be neither peril nor error in this course, and that I cannot at present yield too much to distrust, since I am not considering the question of action, but only of knowledge.

I shall then suppose, not that God who is supremely good and the fountain of truth, but some evil genius, not less powerful than deceitful, has employed his whole energies in deceiving me; I shall consider that the heavens, the earth, colours, figures, sound, and all other external things are nought but the illusions and dreams of which this genius has availed himself in order to lay traps for my credulity; I shall consider myself as having no hands, no eyes, no flesh, no blood, nor any senses, yet falsely believing myself to possess all these things; I shall remain obstinately attached to this idea, and if by this means it is not in my power to arrive at the knowledge of any truth, I may at least do what is in my power, and with firm purpose avoid giving credence to any false thing, or being imposed upon by this arch deceiver, however powerful and deceptive he may be. But this task is a laborious one, and insensibly a certain lassitude leads me into the course of my ordinary life. And just as a captive who in sleep enjoys an imaginary liberty, when he begins to suspect that his liberty is but a dream, fears to awaken, and conspires with these agreeable illusions that the deception may be prolonged, so insensibly of my own accord I fall back into my former opinions, and I dread awakening from this slumber, lest the laborious wakefulness which would follow the tranquillity of this repose should have to be spent not in daylight, but in the excessive darkness of the difficulties which have just been discussed.

MEDITATION II
OF THE NATURE OF THE HUMAN MIND; AND
THAT IT IS MORE EASILY KNOWN THAN THE BODY

The Meditation of yesterday filled my mind with so many doubts that it is no longer in my power to forget them. And yet I do not see in what manner I can resolve them; and, just as if I had all of a sudden fallen into very deep water, I am so disconcerted that I can neither make certain of setting my feet on the bottom, nor can I swim and so support myself on the surface. I shall nevertheless make an effort and follow anew the same path as that on which I yesterday entered, i.e. I shall proceed by setting aside all that in which the least doubt could be supposed to exist, just as if I had discovered that it was absolutely false; and I shall ever follow in this road until I have met with something which is certain, or at least, if I can do nothing else, until I have learned for certain that there is nothing in the world that is certain. Archimedes, in order that he might draw the terrestrial globe out of its place, and transport it elsewhere, demanded only that one point should be fixed and immovable; in the same way I shall have the right to conceive high hopes if I am happy enough to discover one thing only which is certain and indubitable.

I suppose, then, that all the things that I see are false; I persuade myself that nothing has ever existed of all that my fallacious memory represents to me. I consider that I possess no senses; I imagine that body, figure, extension, movement and place are but the fictions of my mind. What, then, can be esteemed as true? Perhaps nothing at all, unless that there is nothing in the world that is certain.

But how can I know there is not something different from those things that I have just considered, of which one cannot have the slightest doubt? Is there not some God, or some other being by whatever name we call it, who puts these reflections into my mind? That is not necessary, for is it not possible that I am capable of producing them myself? I myself, am I not at least something? But I have already denied that I had senses and body. Yet I hesitate, for what follows from that? Am I so dependent on body and senses that I cannot exist without these? But I was persuaded that there was nothing in all the world, that there was no heaven, no earth, that there were no minds, nor any bodies: was I not then likewise persuaded that I did not exist? Not at all; of a surety I myself did exist since I persuaded myself of something. But there is some deceiver or other, very powerful and very cunning, who ever employs his ingenuity in deceiving me. Then without doubt I exist also if he deceives me, and let him deceive me as much as he will, he can never cause me to be nothing so long as I think that I am something. So that after having reflected well and carefully examined all things, we must come to the definite conclusion that this proposition: I am, I exist, is necessarily true each time that I pronounce it, or that I mentally conceive it.

But I do not yet know clearly enough what I am, I who am certain that I am; and hence I must be careful to see that I do not imprudently take some other object in place of myself, and thus that I do not go astray in respect of this knowledge that I hold to be the most certain and most evident of all that I have formerly learned. That is why I shall now consider anew what I believed myself to be before I embarked upon these last reflections; and of my former opinions I shall withdraw all that might even in a small degree be invalidated by the reasons which I have just brought forward, in order that there may be nothing at all left beyond what is absolutely certain and indubitable.

What then did I formerly believe myself to be? Undoubtedly I believed myself to be a man. But what is a man? Shall I say a reasonable animal? Certainly not; for then I should have to inquire what an animal is, and what is reasonable; and thus from a single question I should insensibly fall into an infinitude of others more difficult; and I should not wish to waste the little time and leisure remaining to me in trying to unravel subtleties like these. But I shall rather stop here to consider the thoughts which of themselves spring up in my mind, and which were not inspired by anything beyond my own nature alone when I applied myself to the consideration of my being. In the first place, then, I considered myself as having a face, hands, arms, and all that system of members composed of bones and flesh as seen in a corpse which I designated by the name of body. In addition to this I considered that I was nourished, that I walked, that I felt, and that I thought, and I referred all these actions to the soul: but I did not stop to consider what the soul was, or if I did stop, I imagined that it was something extremely rare and subtle like a wind, a flame, or an ether, which was spread throughout my grosser parts. As to body I had no manner of doubt about its nature, but thought I had a very clear knowledge of it; and if I had desired to explain it according to the notions that I had then formed of it, I should have described it thus: By the body I understand all that which can be defined by a certain figure: something which can be confined in a certain place, and which can fill a given space in such a way that every other body will be excluded from it; which can be perceived either by touch, or by sight, or by hearing, or by taste, or by smell: which can be moved in many ways not, in truth, by itself, but by something which is foreign to it, by which it is touched: for to have the power of self-movement, as also of feeling or of thinking, I did not consider to appertain to the nature of body: on the contrary, I was rather astonished to find that faculties similar to them existed in some bodies.

But what am I, now that I suppose that there is a certain genius which is extremely powerful, and, if I may say so, malicious, who employs all his powers in deceiving me? Can I affirm that I possess the least of all those things which I have just said pertain to the nature of body? I pause to consider, I revolve all these things in my mind, and I find none of which I can say that it pertains to me. It would be tedious to stop to enumerate them. Let us pass to the attributes of soul and see if there is any one which is in me. What of nutrition or walking? But if it is so that I have no body it is also true that I can neither walk nor take nourishment. Another attribute is sensation. But one cannot feel without body, and besides I have thought I perceived many things during sleep that I recognised in my waking moments as not having been experienced at all. What of thinking? I find here that thought is an attribute that belongs to me; it alone cannot be separated from me. I am, I exist, that is certain. But how often? Just when I think; for it might possibly be the case if I ceased entirely to think, that I should likewise cease altogether to exist. I do not now admit anything which is not necessarily true: to speak accurately I am not more than a thing which thinks, that is to say a mind or a soul, or an understanding, or a reason, which are terms whose significance was formerly unknown to me. I am, however, a real thing and really exist; but what thing? I have answered: a thing which thinks.

And what more? I shall exercise my imagination. I am not a collection of members which we call the human body: I am not a subtle air distributed through these members, I am not a wind, a fire, a vapour, a breath, nor anything at all which I can imagine or conceive; because I have assumed that all these were nothing. Without changing that supposition I find that I only leave myself certain of the fact that I am somewhat. But perhaps it is true that these same things, which I supposed were nonexistent because they are unknown to me, are really not different from the self which I know. I am not sure about this, I shall not dispute about it now; I can only give judgment on things that are known to me. I know that I exist, and I inquire what I am, I whom I know to exist. But it is very certain that the knowledge of my existence taken in its precise significance does not depend on things whose existence is not yet known to me; consequently it does not depend on those which I can feign in imagination. And indeed the very term *feign* in imagination proves to me my error, for I really do this if I image myself a something, since to imagine is nothing else than to contemplate the figure or image of a corporeal thing. But I already know for certain that I am, and that it may be that all these images, and, speaking generally, all things that relate to the nature of body are nothing but dreams. For this reason I see clearly that I have as little reason to say, "I shall stimulate my imagination in order to know more distinctly what I am," than if I were to say, "I am now awake, and I perceive somewhat that is real and true: but because I do not yet perceive it distinctly enough, I shall go to sleep of express purpose, so that my dreams may represent the perception with greatest truth and evidence." And, thus, I know for certain that nothing of all that I can understand by means of my imagination belongs to this knowledge which I have of myself, and that it is necessary to recall the mind from this mode of thought with the utmost diligence in order that it may be able to know its own nature with perfect distinctness.

But what then am I? A thing which thinks. What is a thing which thinks? It is a thing which doubts, understands, affirms, denies, wills, refuses, which also imagines and feels.

Certainly it is no small matter if all these things pertain to my nature. But why should they not so pertain? Am I not that being who now doubts nearly everything, who nevertheless understands certain things, who affirms that one only is true, who denies all the others, who desires to know more, is averse from being deceived, who imagines many things, sometimes indeed despite his will, and who perceives many likewise, as by the intervention of the bodily organs? Is there nothing in all this which is as true as it is certain that I exist, even though I should always sleep and though He who has given me being employed all His ingenuity in deceiving me? Is there likewise any one of these attributes which can be distinguished from my thought, or which might be said to be separated from myself? For it is so evident of itself that it is I who doubts, who understands, and who desires, that there is no reason here to add anything to explain it. And I have certainly the power of imagining likewise; for although it may happen (as I formerly supposed) that none of the things which I imagine are true, nevertheless this power of imagining does not cease to be really in use, and it forms part of my thought. Finally, I am the same who feels, that is to say, who perceives certain things, as by the organs of sense, since in truth I see light, I hear noise, I feel heat. But it will be said that these phenomena are false and that I am dreaming. Let it be so; still it is at least quite certain that it seems to me that I see light, that I hear noise and that I feel heat. That cannot be false; properly speaking it is what is in me called feeling; and used in this precise sense that is no other thing than thinking.

From this time I begin to know what I am with a little more clearness and distinction than before; but nevertheless it still seems to me, and I cannot prevent myself from thinking, that corporeal things, whose images are framed by thought, which are tested by the senses, are much more distinctly known than that obscure part of me which does not come under the imagination. Although really it is very strange to say that I know and understand more distinctly these things whose existence seems to me dubious, which are unknown to me, and which do not belong to me, than others of the truth of which I am convinced, which are known to me and which pertain to my real nature, in a word, than myself. But I see clearly how the case stands: my mind loves to wander, and cannot yet suffer itself to be retained within the just limits of truth. Very good, let us once more give it the freest rein, so that, when afterwards we seize the proper occasion for pulling up, it may the more easily be regulated and controlled.

Let us begin by considering the commonest matters, those which we believe to be the most distinctly comprehended, to wit, the bodies which we touch and see; not indeed bodies in general, for these general ideas are usually a little more confused, but let us consider one body in particular. Let us take, for example, this piece of wax: it has been taken quite freshly from the hive, and it has not yet lost the sweetness of the honey which it contains; it still retains somewhat of the odour of the flowers from which it has been culled; its colour, its figure, its size are apparent; it is hard, cold, easily handled, and if you strike it with the finger, it will emit a sound. Finally all the things which are requisite to cause us distinctly to recognise a body are met with in it. But notice that while I speak and approach the fire what remained of the taste is exhaled, the smell evaporates, the colour alters, the figure is destroyed, the size increases, it becomes liquid, it heats, scarcely can one handle it, and when one strikes it, no sound is emitted. Does the same wax remain after this change? We must confess that it remains; none would judge otherwise. What then did I know so distinctly in this piece of wax? It could certainly be nothing of all that the senses brought to my notice, since all these things which fall under taste, smell, sight, touch, and hearing, are found to be changed, and yet the same wax remains.

Perhaps it was what I now think, viz. that this wax was not that sweetness of honey, nor that agreeable scent of flowers, nor that particular whiteness, nor that figure, nor that sound, but simply a body which a little while before appeared to me as perceptible under these forms, and which is now perceptible under others. But what, precisely, is it that I imagine when I form such conceptions? Let us attentively consider this, and, abstracting from all that does not belong to the wax, let us see what remains. Certainly nothing remains excepting a certain extended thing which is flexible and movable. But what is the meaning of flexible and movable? Is it not that I imagine that this piece of wax being round is capable of becoming square and of passing from a square to a triangular figure? No, certainly it is not that, since I imagine it admits of an infinitude of similar changes, and I nevertheless do not know how to compass the infinitude by my imagination, and consequently this conception which I have of the wax is not brought about by the faculty of imagination. What now is this extension? Is it not also unknown? For it becomes greater when the wax is melted, greater when it is boiled, and greater still when the heat increases; and I should not conceive according to truth what wax is, if I did not think that even this piece that we are considering is capable of receiving more variations in extension than I have ever imagined. We must then grant that I could not even understand through the imagination what this piece of wax is, and that it is my mind alone which perceives it. I say this piece of wax in particular, for as to wax in general it is yet clearer. But what is this piece of wax which cannot be understood excepting by the mind? It is certainly the same that I see, touch, imagine, and finally it is the same which I have always believed it to be from the beginning. But what must particularly be observed is that its perception is neither an act of vision, nor of touch, nor of imagination, and has never been such although it may have appeared formerly to be so, but only an intuition of the mind, which may be imperfect and confused as it was formerly, or clear and distinct as it is at present, according as my attention is more or less directed to the elements which are found in it, and of which it is composed.

Yet in the meantime I am greatly astonished when I consider [the mind's] proneness to fall into error; for although without giving expression to my thoughts I consider all this in my own mind, words often impede me and I am almost deceived by the terms of ordinary language. For we say that we see the same wax, if it is present, and not that we simply judge that it is the same from its having the same colour and figure. From this I should conclude that I knew the wax by means of vision and not simply by the intuition of the mind; unless by chance I remember that, when looking from a window and saying I see men who pass in the street, I really do not see them, but infer that what I see is men, just as I say that I see wax. And yet what do I see from the window but hats and coats which may cover automatic machines? Yet I judge these to be men. And similarly solely by the faculty of judgment which rests in my mind, I comprehend that which I believed I saw with my eyes.

A man who makes it his aim to raise his knowledge above the common should be ashamed to derive the occasion for doubting from the forms of speech invented by the vulgar; I prefer to pass on and consider whether I had a more evident and perfect conception of what the wax was when I first perceived it, and when I believed I knew it by means of the external senses or at least by the common sense as it is called, that is to say by the imaginative faculty, or whether my present conception is clearer now that I have most carefully examined what it is, and in what way it can be known. It would certainly be absurd to doubt as to this. For what was there in this first perception which was distinct? What was there which might not as well have been perceived by any of the animals? But when I distinguish the wax from its external forms, and when, just as if I had taken from it its vestments, I consider it quite naked, it is certain that although some error may still be found in my judgment, I can nevertheless not perceive it thus without a human mind.

But finally what shall I say of this mind, that is, of myself, for up to this point I do not admit in myself anything but mind? What then, I who seem to perceive this piece of wax so distinctly, do I not know myself, not only with much more truth and certainty, but also with much more distinctness and clearness? For if I judge that the wax is or exists from the fact that I see it, it certainly follows much more clearly that I am or that I exist myself from the fact that I see it. For it may be that what I see is not really wax; it may also be that I do not possess eyes with which to see anything; but it cannot be that when I see, or (for I no longer take account of the distinction) when I think I see, that I myself who think am nought. So if I judge that the wax exists from the fact that I touch it, the same thing will follow, to wit, that I am; and if I judge that my imagination, or some other cause, whatever it is, persuades me that the wax exists, I shall still conclude the same. And what I have here remarked of wax may be applied to all other things which are external to me. And further, if the perception of wax has seemed to me clearer and more distinct, not only after the sight or the touch, but also after many other causes have rendered it quite manifest to me, with how much more distinctness must it be said that I now know myself, since all the reasons which contribute to the knowledge of wax, or any other body whatever, are yet better proofs of the nature of my mind! And there are so many other things in the mind itself which may contribute to the elucidation of its nature, that those which depend on body such as these just mentioned hardly merit being taken into account.

But finally here I am, having insensibly reverted to the point I desired, for, since it is now manifest to me that even bodies are not properly speaking known by the senses or by the faculty of imagination, but by the understanding only, and since they are not known from the fact that they are seen or touched, but only because they are understood, I see clearly that there is nothing which is easier for me to know than my mind. But because it is difficult to rid oneself so promptly of an opinion to which one was accustomed for so long, it will be well that I should halt a little at this point, so that by the length of my meditation I may more deeply imprint on my memory this new knowledge.

MEDITATION VI
OF THE EXISTENCE OF MATERIAL THINGS, AND OF THE REAL DISTINCTION BETWEEN THE SOUL AND BODY OF MAN

Nothing further now remains but to inquire whether material things exist. And certainly I at least know that these may exist in so far as they are considered as the objects of pure mathematics, since in this aspect I perceive them clearly and distinctly. For there is no doubt that God possesses the power to produce everything that I am capable of perceiving with distinctness, and I have never deemed that anything was impossible for Him, unless I found a contradiction in attempting to conceive it clearly. . . .

But I am in the habit of imagining many other things besides this corporeal nature which is the object of pure mathematics, to wit, the colours, sounds, scents, pain, and other such things, although less distinctly. And inasmuch as I perceive these things much better through the senses, by the medium of which, and by the memory, they seem to have reached my imagination, I believe that, in order to examine them more conveniently, it is right that I should at the same time investigate the nature of sense perception, and that I should see if from the ideas which I apprehend by this mode of thought, which I call feeling, I cannot derive some certain proof of the existence of corporeal objects.

And first of all I shall recall to my memory those matters which I hitherto held to be true, as having perceived them through the senses, and the foundations on which my belief has rested; in the next place I shall examine the reasons which have since obliged me to place them in doubt; in the last place I shall consider which of them I must now believe.

First of all, then, I perceived that I had a head, hands, feet, and all other members of which this body—which I considered as a part, or possibly even as the whole, of myself—is composed. Further I was sensible that this body was placed amidst many others, from which it was capable of being affected in many different ways, beneficial and hurtful, and I remarked that a certain feeling of pleasure accompanied those that were beneficial, and pain those which were harmful. And in addition to this pleasure and pain, I also experienced hunger, thirst, and other similar appetites, as also certain corporeal inclinations towards joy, sadness, anger, and other similar passions. And outside myself, in addition to extension, figure, and motions of bodies, I remarked in them hardness, heat, and all other tactile qualities, and, further, light and colour, and scents and sounds, the variety of which gave me the means of distinguishing the sky, the earth, the sea, and generally all the other bodies, one from the other. And certainly, considering the ideas of all these qualities which presented themselves to my mind, and which alone I perceived properly or immediately, it was not without reason that I believed myself to perceive objects quite different from my thought, to wit, bodies from which those ideas proceeded; for I found by experience that these presented themselves to me without my consent being requisite, so that I could not perceive any object, however desirous I might be, unless it were present to the organs of sense; and it was not in my power not to perceive it, when it was present. And because the ideas which I received through the senses were much more lively, more clear, and even, in their own way, more distinct than any of those which I could of myself frame in meditation, or than those I found impressed on my memory, it appeared as though they could not have proceeded from my mind, so that they must necessarily have been produced in me by some other things. And having no knowledge of those objects excepting the knowledge which the ideas themselves gave me, nothing was more likely to occur to my mind than that the objects were similar to the ideas which were caused. And because I likewise remembered that I had formerly made use of my senses rather than my reason, and recognised that the ideas which I formed of myself were not so distinct as those which I perceived through the senses, and that they were most frequently even composed of portions of these last, I persuaded myself easily that I had no idea in my mind which had not formerly come to me through the senses. Nor was it without some reason that I believed that this body (which by a certain special right I call my own) belonged to me more properly and more strictly than any other; for in fact I could never be separated from it as from other bodies; I experienced in it and on account of it all my appetites and affections, and finally I was touched by the feeling of pain and the titillation of pleasure in its parts, and not in the parts of other bodies which were separated from it. But when I inquired, why, from some, I know not what, painful sensation, there follows sadness of mind, and from the pleasurable sensation there arises joy, or why this mysterious pinching of the stomach which I call hunger causes me to desire to eat, and dryness of throat causes a desire to drink, and so on, I could give no reason excepting that nature taught me so; for there is certainly no affinity (that I at least can understand) between the craving of the stomach and the desire to eat, any more than between the perception of whatever causes pain and the thought of sadness which arises from this perception. And in the same way it appeared to me that I had learned from nature all the other judgments which I formed regarding the objects of my senses, since I remarked that these judgments were formed in me before I had the leisure to weigh and consider any reasons which might oblige me to make them.

But afterwards many experiences little by little destroyed all the faith which I had rested in my senses; for I from time to time observed that those towers which from afar appeared to me to be round, more closely observed seemed square, and that colossal statues raised on the summit of these towers appeared as quite tiny statues when viewed from the bottom; and so in an infinitude of other cases I found error in judgments founded on the external senses. And not only in those founded on the external senses, but even in those founded on the internal as well; for is there anything more intimate or more internal than pain? And yet I have learned from some persons whose arms or legs have been cut off, that they sometimes seemed to feel pain in the part which had been amputated, which made me think that I could not be quite certain that it was a certain member which pained me, even although I felt pain in it. And to those grounds of doubt I have lately added two others, which are very general; the first is that I never have believed myself to feel anything in waking moments which I cannot also sometimes believe myself to feel when I sleep, and as I do not think that these things which I seem to feel in sleep proceed from objects outside of me, I do not see any reason why I should have this belief regarding objects which I seem to perceive while awake. The other was that being still ignorant, or rather supposing myself to be ignorant, of the author of my being, I saw nothing to prevent me from having been so constituted by nature that I might be deceived even in matters which seemed to me to be most certain. And as to the grounds on which I was formerly persuaded of the truth of sensible objects, I had not much trouble in replying to them. For since nature seemed to cause me to lean towards many things from which reason repelled me, I did not believe that I should trust much to the teachings of nature. And although the ideas which I receive by the senses do not depend on my will, I did not think that one should for that reason conclude that they proceeded from things different from myself, since possibly some faculty might be discovered in me—though hitherto unknown to me—which produced them.

But now that I begin to know myself better, and to discover more clearly the author of my being, I do not in truth think that I should rashly admit all the matters which the senses seem to teach us, but, on the other hand, I do not think that I should doubt them all universally.

And first of all, because I know that all things which I apprehend clearly and distinctly can be created by God as I apprehend them, it suffices that I am able to apprehend one thing apart from another clearly and distinctly in order to be certain that the one is different from the other, since they may be made to exist in separation at least by the omnipotence of God; and it does not signify by what power this separation is made in order to compel me to judge them to be different: and, therefore, just because I know certainly that I exist, and that meanwhile I do not remark that any other thing necessarily pertains to my nature or essence, excepting that I am a thinking thing, I rightly conclude that my essence consists solely in the fact that I am a thinking thing. And although possibly (or rather certainly, as I shall say in a moment) I possess a body with which I am very intimately conjoined, yet because, on the one side, I have a clear and distinct idea of myself inasmuch as I am only a thinking and unextended thing, and as, on the other, I possess a distinct idea of body, inasmuch as it is only an extended and unthinking thing, it is certain that this I is entirely and absolutely distinct from my body, and can exist without it.

I further find in myself faculties employing modes of thinking peculiar to themselves, to wit, the faculties of imagination and feeling, without which I can easily conceive myself clearly and distinctly as a complete being; while, on the other hand, they cannot be so conceived apart from me, that is without an intelligent substance in which they reside; for in their formal concept, some kind of intellection is comprised, from which I infer that they are distinct from me as its modes are from a thing. I observe also in me some other faculties such as that of change of position, the assumption of different figures and such like, which cannot be conceived, any more than can the preceding, apart from some substance to which they are attached, and consequently cannot exist without it; but it is very clear that these faculties, if it be true that they exist, must be attached to some corporeal or extended substance, and not to an intelligent substance, since in the clear and distinct conception of these there is some sort of extension found to be present, but no intellection at all. There is certainly further in me a certain passive faculty of perception, that is, of receiving and recognising the ideas of sensible things, but this would be useless to me, if there were not either in me or in some other thing another active faculty capable of forming and producing these ideas. But this active faculty cannot exist in me seeing that it does not presuppose thought, and also that those ideas are often produced in me without my contributing in any way to the same, and often even against my will; it is thus necessarily the case that the faculty resides in some substance different from me in which all the reality which is objectively in the ideas that are produced by this faculty is formally or eminently contained, as I remarked before. And this substance is either a body, that is, a corporeal nature in which there is contained formally all that which is objectively in those ideas, or it is God Himself, or some other creature more noble than body in which that same is contained eminently. But, since God is no deceiver, it is very manifest that He does not communicate to me these ideas immediately and by Himself, nor yet by the intervention of some creature in which their reality is not formally, but only eminently, contained. For since He has given me no faculty to recognise that this is the case, but, on the other hand, a very great inclination to believe that they are conveyed to me by corporeal objects, I do not see how He could be defended from the accusation of deceit if these ideas were produced by causes other than corporeal objects. Hence we must allow that corporeal things exist. However, they are perhaps not exactly what we perceive by the senses, since this comprehension by the senses is in many instances very obscure and confused; but we must at least admit that all things which I conceive in them clearly and distinctly, that is to say, all things which, speaking generally, are comprehended in the object of pure mathematics are truly to be recognised as external objects.

As to other things, however, which are either particular only, as, for example, that the sun is of such and such a figure, etc., or which are less clearly and distinctly conceived, such as light, sound, pain and the like, it is certain that although they are very dubious and uncertain, yet on the sole ground that God is not a deceiver, and that consequently He has not permitted any falsity to exist in my opinion which He has not likewise given me the faculty of correcting, I may assuredly hope to conclude that I have within me the means of arriving at the truth even here. And first of all there is no doubt that in all things which nature teaches me there is some truth contained; for by nature, considered in general, I now understand no other thing than either God Himself or else the order and disposition which God has established in created things; and by my nature in particular I understand no other thing than the complexus of all the things which God has given me.

But there is nothing which this nature teaches me more expressly than that I have a body which is adversely affected when I feel pain, which has need of food or drink when I experience the feelings of hunger and thirst, and so on; nor can I doubt there being some truth in all this.

Nature also teaches me by these sensations of pain, hunger, thirst, etc., that I am not only lodged in my body as a pilot in a vessel, but that I am very closely united to it, and so to speak so intermingled with it that I seem to compose with it one whole. For if that were not the case, when my body is hurt, I, who am merely a thinking thing, should not feel pain, for I should perceive this wound by the understanding only, just as the sailor perceives by sight when something is damaged in his vessel; and when my body has need of drink or food, I should clearly understand the fact without being warned of it by confused feelings of hunger and thirst. For all these sensations of hunger, thirst, pain, etc., are in truth none other than certain confused modes of thought which are produced by the union and apparent intermingling of mind and body.

Moreover, nature teaches me that many other bodies exist around mine of which some are to be avoided, and others sought after. And certainly from the fact that I am sensible of different sorts of colours, sounds, scents, tastes, heat, hardness, etc., I very easily conclude that there are in the bodies from which all these diverse sense-perceptions proceed certain variations which answer to them, although possibly these are not really at all similar to them. And also from the fact that amongst these different sense-perceptions some are very agreeable to me and others disagreeable, it is quite certain that my body (or rather myself in my entirety, inasmuch as I am formed of body and soul) may receive different impressions agreeable and disagreeable from the other bodies which surround it. . . .

From this it is quite clear that, notwithstanding the supreme goodness of God, the nature of man, inasmuch as it is composed of mind and body, cannot be otherwise than sometimes a source of deception. For if there is any cause which excites, not in the foot but in some part of the nerves which are extended between the foot and the brain, or even in the brain itself, the same movement which usually is produced when the foot is detrimentally affected, pain will be experienced as though it were in the foot, and the sense will thus naturally be deceived; for since the same movement in the brain is capable of causing but one sensation in the mind, and this sensation is much more frequently excited by a cause which hurts the foot than by another existing in some other quarter, it is reasonable that it should convey to the mind pain in the foot rather than in any other part of the body. And although the parchedness of the throat does not always proceed, as it usually does, from the fact that drinking is necessary for the health of the body, but sometimes comes from quite a different cause, as is the case with dropsical patients, it is yet much better that it should mislead on this occasion than if, on the other hand, it were always to deceive us when the body is in good health; and so on in similar cases.

And certainly this consideration is of great service to me, not only in enabling me to recognise all the errors to which my nature is subject, but also in enabling me to avoid them or to correct them more easily. For knowing that all my senses more frequently indicate to me truth than falsehood respecting the things which concern that which is beneficial to the body, and being able almost always to avail myself of many of them in order to examine one particular thing, and, besides that, being able to make use of my memory in order to connect the present with the past, and of my understanding which already has discovered all the causes of my errors, I ought no longer to fear that falsity may be found in matters every day presented to me by my senses. And I ought to set aside all the doubts of these past days as hyperbolical and ridiculous, particularly that very common uncertainty respecting sleep, which I could not distinguish from the waking state; for at present I find a very notable difference between the two, inasmuch as our memory can never connect our dreams one with the other, or with the whole course of our lives, as it unites events which happen to us while we are awake. And, as a matter of fact, if someone, while I was awake, quite suddenly appeared to me and disappeared as fast as do the images which I see in sleep, so that I could not know from whence the form came nor whither it went, it would not be without reason that I should deem it a spectre or a phantom formed by my brain, rather than a real man. But when I perceive things as to which I know distinctly both the place from which they proceed, and that in which they are, and the time at which they appeared to me, and when, without any interruption, I can connect the perceptions which I have of them with the whole course of my life, I am perfectly assured that these perceptions occur while I am waking and not during sleep. And I ought in no wise to doubt the truth of such matters, if, after having called up all my senses, my memory, and my understanding, to examine them, nothing is brought to evidence by any one of them which is repugnant to what is set forth by the others. For because God is in no wise a deceiver, it follows that I am not deceived in this. But because the exigencies of action often oblige us to make up our minds before having leisure to examine matters carefully, we must confess that the life of man is very frequently subject to error in respect to individual objects, and we must in the end acknowledge the infirmity of our nature.

Myself

and Others

———

FRIEDRICH NIETZSCHE

Consciousness As Social

Friedrich Nietzsche (1844–1900)
wrote literary and philosophical
essays which anticipated the
development of existentialism.
Among these are *The Birth of
Tragedy, Beyond Good and Evil,*
and *Thus Spake Zarathustra.*

The problem of consciousness (or more correctly: of becoming conscious of one-self) meets us only when we begin to perceive in what measure we could dispense with it: and it is at the beginning of this perception that we are now placed by physiology and zoology (which have thus required two centuries to overtake the hint thrown out in advance by Leibnitz). For we could in fact think, feel, will, and recollect, we could likewise "act" in every sense of the term, and nevertheless nothing of it all need necessarily "come into consciousness" (as one says metaphorically). The whole of life would be possible without its seeing itself as it were in a mirror: as in fact even at present the far greater part of our life still goes on without this mirroring,—and even our thinking, feeling, volitional life as well, however painful this statement may sound to an older philosopher. *What* then is *the purpose* of consciousness generally, when it is in the main *superfluous?*—Now it seems to me, if you will hear my answer and its perhaps extravagant supposition, that the subtlety and strength of consciousness are always in proportion to the *capacity for communication* of a man (or an animal), the capacity for communication in its turn being in proportion to the *necessity for communication:* the latter not to be understood as if precisely the individual himself who is master in the art of communicating and making known his necessities would at the same time have to be most dependent upon others for his necessities. It seems to me, however, to be so in relation to whole races and successions of generations: where necessity and need have long compelled men to communicate with their fellows and understand one another rapidly and subtly, a surplus of the power and art of communication is at last acquired, as if it were a fortune which had gradually accumulated, and now waited for an heir to squander it prodigally (the so-called artists are these heirs, in like manner the orators, preachers, and authors: all of them men who come at the end of a long succession, "late-born" always, in the best sense of the word, and as has been said, *squanderers* by their very nature). Granted that this observation is correct, I may proceed further to the conjecture that *consciousness generally has only been developed*

From *The Joyful Wisdom*, by Friedrich Nietzsche, translated by Thomas Common, 1905.

under the pressure of the necessity for communication,—that from the first it has been necessary and useful only between man and man (especially between those commanding and those obeying), and has only developed in proportion to its utility. Consciousness is properly only a connecting network between man and man, —it is only as such that it has had to develop; the recluse and wild-beast species of men would not have needed it. The very fact that our actions, thoughts, feelings and motions come within the range of our consciousness—at least a part of them —is the result of a terrible, prolonged "must" ruling man's destiny: as the most endangered animal he *needed* help and protection; he needed his fellows, he was obliged to express his distress, he had to know how to make himself understood —and for all this he needed "consciousness" first of all: he had to "know" himself what he lacked, to "know" how he felt, and to "know" what he thought. For, to repeat it once more, man, like every living creature, thinks unceasingly, but does not know it; the thinking which is becoming *conscious of itself* is only the smallest part thereof, we may say, the most superficial part, the worst part:—for this conscious thinking alone *is done in words, that is to say, in the symbols for communication,* by means of which the origin of consciousness is revealed. In short, the development of speech and the development of consciousness (not of reason, but of reason becoming self-conscious) go hand in hand. Let it be further accepted that it is not only speech that serves as a bridge between man and man, but also the looks, the pressure and the gestures; our becoming conscious of our sense impressions, our power of being able to fix them, and as it were to locate them outside of ourselves, has increased in proportion as the necessity has increased for communicating them to *others* by means of signs. The sign-inventing man is at the same time the man who is always more acutely self-conscious; it is only as a social animal that man has learned to become conscious of himself,—he is doing so still, and doing so more and more.—As is obvious, my idea is that consciousness does not properly belong to the individual existence of man, but rather to the social and gregarious nature in him; that, as follows therefrom, it is only in relation to communal and gregarious utility that it is finely developed; and that consequently each of us, in spite of the best intention of *understanding* himself as individually as possible, and of "knowing himself," will always just call into consciousness the non-individual in him, namely, his "averageness";—that our thought itself is continuously as it were *outvoted* by the character of consciousness—by the imperious "genius of the species" therein—and is translated back into the perspective of the herd. Fundamentally our actions are in an incomparable manner altogether personal, unique and absolutely individual—there is no doubt about it; but as soon as we translate them into consciousness, they *do not appear so any longer*. . . . This is the proper phenomenalism and perspectivism as I understand it: the nature of *animal consciousness* involves the notion that the world of which we can become conscious is only a superficial and symbolic world, a generalised and vulgarised world;—that everything which becomes conscious *becomes* just thereby shallow, meagre, relatively stupid,—a generalisation, a symbol, a characteristic of the herd; that with the evolving of consciousness there is always combined a great, radical perversion, falsification, superficialisation, and generalisation. Finally, the growing consciousness is a danger, and whoever lives among the most conscious Europeans knows even that it is a disease. As may be conjectured, it is not the antithesis of subject and object with which I am here concerned: I leave that distinction to the epistemologists who have remained entangled in the toils of grammar (popular metaphysics). It is still less the antithesis of "thing in itself" and phenomenon, for we do not "know" enough to be entitled even *to make such a distinction.* Indeed, we have not any organ at all for *knowing,* or for "truth": we "know" (or believe, or fancy) just as much as may be *of use* in the interest of the human herd, the species; and even what is here called "usefulness" is ultimately only a belief, a fancy, and perhaps precisely the most fatal stupidity by which we shall one day be ruined.

DAVID HUME

The Self Is a Bundle of Perceptions

Other selections from David Hume are printed in Section I, "The Primacy of the Person" and in the following subsection, "Language, Mind, and World."

OF PERSONAL IDENTITY

There are some philosophers, who imagine we are every moment intimately conscious of what we call our SELF; that we feel its existence and its continuance in existence; and are certain, beyond the evidence of a demonstration, both of its perfect identity and simplicity. The strongest sensation, the most violent passion, say they, instead of distracting us from this view, only fix it the more intensely, and make us consider their influence on *self* either by their pain or pleasure. To attempt a farther proof of this were to weaken its evidence; since no proof can be deriv'd from any fact, of which we are so intimately conscious; nor is there any thing, of which we can be certain, if we doubt of this.

Unluckily all these positive assertions are contrary to that very experience, which is pleaded for them, nor have we any idea of *self,* after the manner it is here explain'd. For from what impression cou'd this idea be deriv'd? This question 'tis impossible to answer without a manifest contradiction and absurdity; and yet 'tis a question, which must necessarily be answer'd, if we wou'd have the idea of self pass for clear and intelligible. It must be some one impression, that gives rise to every real idea. But self or person is not any one impression, but that to which our several impressions and ideas are suppos'd to have a reference. If any impression gives rise to the idea of self, that impression must continue invariably the same, thro' the

From *A Treatise of Human Nature,* by David Hume, 1739.

whole course of our lives; since self is suppos'd to exist after that manner. But there is no impression constant and invariable. Pain and pleasure, grief and joy, passions and sensations succeed each other, and never all exist at the same time. It cannot, therefore, be from any of these impressions, or from any other, that the idea of self is deriv'd; and consequently there is no such idea.

But farther, what must become of all our particular perceptions upon this hypothesis? All these are different, and distinguishable, and separable from each other, and may be separately consider'd, and may exist separately, and have no need of any thing to support their existence. After what manner, therefore, do they belong to self; and how are they connected with it? For my part, when I enter most intimately into what I call *myself*, I always stumble on some particular perception or other, of heat or cold, light or shade, love or hatred, pain or pleasure. I never can catch *myself* at any time without a perception, and never can observe any thing but the perception. When my perceptions are remov'd for any time, as by sound sleep; so long am I insensible of *myself*, and may truly be said not to exist. And were all my perceptions remov'd by death, and cou'd I neither think, nor feel, nor see, nor love, nor hate after the dissolution of my body, I shou'd be entirely annihilated, nor do I conceive what is farther requisite to make me a perfect non-entity. If any one upon serious and unprejudic'd reflexion, thinks he has a different notion of *himself*, I must confess I can reason no longer with him. All I can allow him is, that he may be in the right as well as I, and that we are essentially different in this particular. He may, perhaps, perceive something simple and continu'd which he calls *himself;* tho' I am certain there is no such principle in me.

But setting aside some metaphysicians of this kind, I may venture to affirm of the rest of mankind, that they are nothing but a bundle or collection of different perceptions, which succeed each other with an inconceivable rapidity, and are in a perpetual flux and movement. Our eyes cannot turn in their sockets without varying our perceptions. Our thought is still more variable than our sight; and all our other senses and faculties contribute to this change; nor is there any single power of the soul, which remains unalterably the same, perhaps for one moment. The mind is a kind of theatre, where several perceptions successively make their appearance; pass, re-pass, glide away, and mingle in an infinite variety of postures and situations. There is properly no *simplicity* in it at one time, nor *identity* in different; whatever natural propension we may have to imagine that simplicity and identity.

FRIEDRICH WAISMANN

Can I Know ᴄAnother Person's Experiences?

Friedrich Waismann (1896-1959), who fled his native Austria
at the beginning of World War II, taught at Cambridge and
Oxford and also wrote *Introduction to Mathematical Thinking.*

. . . Let us turn to a question which is usually cited as an example to show the
existence of insoluble problems. Can the experiences of two persons ever be exactly
compared? Suppose another person and myself are looking at the same green
leaf at the same time. How do I know that we are having the same experience?
that he sees green just as I see it? There seems no possible way of answering the
question; for what I observe in other people are only the signs which they show me,
so how can I be sure that my friend uses words to stand for the same experiences as
those for which I use them? Is it not possible that although we both call the leaf
green, we have different colour experiences on looking at it, that he sees it the
colour which I call 'blue'? Such a difference in our experiences could never be discovered, for we name the colours of objects in the same way, we both agree that
there is rather more yellow in this green than in that, we both find that blue is a
cool colour, red a warm colour—in short, the supposed difference between us would
escape all investigation. Therefore, it is said, we can never know whether two people
are having the same experiences. For me to know this it would be necessary for me
to step outside my own consciousness and to look into the mind of another. This
I can never do, for our minds are absolutely separate, they are monads and have no
windows. Is this not a question which is eternally unanswerable but of which the
meaning is yet perfectly clear and comprehensible? No, it merely appears to be so,
and we shall have gained much if we come to see that it is an illusory question.

Why do we think we understand the sense of the question? Because we think
we know exactly what is meant by every word it contains; that we know,
for example, what an 'experience' is, and what the word 'same' means. But in thinking this we are mistaken. We must, above all, bear in mind that the word 'same' has
not one meaning but many. Even if I know when two intervals in space are the
same, I cannot deduce from this when two intervals of time are the same; I have to
use a new convention in the second case. The word 'same' is used according to
different rules and therefore has a different meaning in each case. If we consider
such examples as 'the same weight', 'the same temperature', and 'the same bright-
ness' we realize that, far from having the same meaning each time, 'same' has in each
of these cases to be explained anew.

From *The Principles of Linguistic Philosophy,* by Friedrich Waismann, ed. by R. Harré, 1965.
Reprinted by permission of St. Martin's Press Inc., The Macmillan Company of Canada Ltd., and Macmillan
& Co., Ltd.

Having realized this, the question at once arises as to what it means to say that two people have the same experiences when they look at a coloured patch. 'This leaf is the same green as that' has a precise sense. The criterion for its truth might, for instance, be that when I look at the two leaves I can see no difference at all between their colours. But what does it mean to say that one man's experience of green is the same as another's experience of it? Does this mean that they describe their experiences in the same words? If so, the question would be in no way perplexing, but would be the easiest thing in the world to answer. But this is certainly not what is meant by the man who thinks the question has a metaphysical sense. He would reply 'Whether or not the two men use the same words is of no interest to me. What I want to know is whether, when they look at a green patch, they have the same *experiences*.' He here takes it for granted that the meaning of the word 'same' is already fixed, and that a particular examination of it in this case in unnecessary. It even seems to him to be absurd pedantry to search for its exact meaning. Yet it is just by refusing this investigation that he fails to find the way to a solution.

The question 'Are the experiences of the two men the same?' has no meaning unless we give it one. There are various ways in which we can do this. What we have said up to now may easily have given the impression that all we have to do is to get rid of the problem by unmasking it as a pseudo-question. This would be a complete misunderstanding. For it is quite as important to examine the problem very carefully to see whether there may not be some sense in the question which the questioner himself is not able to express clearly. We can try to help him by putting forward various suggestions as to what he may in fact mean by his question, in the hope that he will accept one of them.

For instance, we could ask 'Would you agree that two men have the same experiences when they look at a green leaf, if exactly the same processes were taking place in their nervous systems?" If he agrees, he will have given the question a clear meaning, provided we have come to an understanding as to the circumstances in which the processes in nerves shall be called the same. If, however, he rejects this suggestion, we could ask him again what he means by saying 'Do I see green the same as he sees it?' He might reply 'I mean would I see the same as I see now if I felt the sensations my friend feels? I know that it is impossible for me to do this, but nevertheless that is what I mean.' Again we should have to say that he has not made the meaning of the question clear, for the expression 'felt the sensations my friend feels' is as he himself admits, an empty play with words. But he will probably not be satisfied with this; for it will not remove the sting of the question for him. We can try again, as follows, to give his question a meaning in order to express what is in his mind.

The experience of losing all sensation in a part of the body is a familiar one. If, for example, a man's hand is subjected to a local anaesthetic it feels to him dead, like a thing that is not part of his body. Can we not imagine the opposite of this, i.e. that someone should suddenly have sensations in a place where he had never before felt them? Suppose someone assured us with every sign of honesty that every time anyone touched his stick he felt as if it were part of his own body. Should we reply that such a thing is impossible, that he *cannot* have such an experience? If we did, he might ask us 'Have you had every experience there is? How do you know that there cannot be any such sensation?' It is hardly necessary to say that we are not concerned with whether there are in fact any such feelings; we only want to know whether it makes sense to assert that there are; that is to say, whether it is possible to *describe* them. About this there cannot be the slightest doubt, for *we have* described, and could portray to the smallest detail, what it would be like for someone to feel such sensations. One with the imagination of the author of Dr. Jekyll and Mr. Hyde could describe far stranger situations than this, which nevertheless were in the region of the logically possible. Suppose *A* complains of being in pain, and when asked where the pain is, points to *B*'s hand; at the same time, when a certain spot on *B*'s hand is touched *A* cries out in pain. Or *A* wakes up in the morning and finds that his body has altered in an astonishing way: he sees *B*'s face and figure in the mirror. The same morning *B* wakes up and finds he has *A*'s body, though both their memories remain unaltered. Suppose for a moment that *A* and *B* could exchange bodies at will. (Eckermann once told Goethe that he had dreamt of such a thing.) If *A* and *B* wish to know whether they have the same experiences on seeing a green leaf, they have only to change bodies, so that *A* sees out of the eyes of *B* and vice versa. Then (since their memories do not alter) each could tell at once whether he sees the colour the same as before or not.

We now ask the metaphysician whether, supposing such an experiment could be carried out, and *A* and *B* both claimed to have the same experiences as each other on seeing green, he would agree that their experiences were in fact the same. We offer him the possibility of giving a meaning to the phrase 'having another's sensations'. If he says 'Yes, that was what I meant', we know at last what his question is about; and we see at the same time that the giving of meaning consists in showing how the question could in principle be decided. (Not necessarily how it can in fact be decided, because we shall presumably never be in a position to carry out such an experiment as the one we described. Nevertheless, as we have said, the question can in principle be decided; that is to say, we can now give the conditions under which we should answer 'yes', and also those under which we should answer 'no'.) The metaphysician however may still insist that what we have described is irrelevant to his question, because *A* and *B* only compare their *own* experiences in different circumstances, whereas to answer his question, experiences in different consciousnesses must be compared. If so, we can only admit that we have failed so far to find out what he has in mind. We can, however, try to think out other experiences which he would be likely to accept as some sort of 'fusion of the two consciousnesses'.

We might suggest the following for example: It often happens that we suddenly remember a forgotten dream. Let us suppose that I suddenly began to remember all the events that had happened in the previous life of someone else, and that these events came crowding into my mind like submerged memories of my own childhood. That these things I seem to remember really happened to the other person I could find out by asking him. Such an experience might lead us to speak of 'direct contact' or of 'fusion' of two minds.

As soon as we make the sense of the question clear, as soon as we can describe exactly the circumstances in which we should speak of experiences being compared, the perplexing nature of the question disappears. The question may remain *in fact* insoluble, but this merely means that we are not in a position to bring about the circumstances necessary for reaching a solution. This practical insolubility has to be borne. The important point is that the question has lost the aura it had of being in principle insoluble, for perhaps nothing is so intellectually depressing as the knowledge that we have the power to raise questions which we have no power to answer.

Although it is in a sense correct to say 'There are no insoluble questions', it is also misleading, because such a sentence sounds like 'There are no unmeltable metals'. It might lead us to think that we have discovered a property of questions. We shall be less open to misunderstanding if we say that we should use language in such a way that unanswerable questions do not arise.

. . .

. . . the difficulty arises again as soon as we ask ourselves what does it mean to say that two people use the word 'green' in the same way? Are only the *external* circumstances of the use of the word to be counted? Should, then, our criterion for 'using in the same way' consist simply in this: that two people agree in the names they give to the colours of various objects? Or should we say that besides this they must have the same inner experience when they both look at a green surface? The philosophical difficulties connected with the question 'What is communicable?' arise from the second interpretation. We are inclined to say: Even if two persons' use of language coincides as far as the describing of external objects is concerned, this gives no guarantee at all that they attach the same meaning to their words, for in spite of this their experience may be quite different. Only if it were possible to look directly into another man's mind could I find out whether or not he attached the same meaning to his words. And yet this is logically impossible. Each of us is cabined within his own consciousness and cut off from the minds of others by insurmountable barriers. Curious as it is, the term 'communication' is in no wise problematic so long as we use this word practically. The difficulty arises only as soon as we contemplate the use of language from outside. Suddenly, when we talk of communication, a problem seems to loom; and it appears as if before, in practical life, we had ignored a difficulty which we now see. The problem seems, in a sense, to be a scientific one; it concerns, one might say, the *nature* of communication.

The philosopher contemplates the manner in which language works, and there is the problem. It is as if he looked at an object, for instance, a door, through a light-refracting medium so that it appeared to be broken although one could still go in and out through it just the same. In this way the *typical* question arises, 'How is communication possible?' We raise such questions only when the facts *astonish* us, when something about them appears to us paradoxical. There are alternative trains of images which have much the same effect as media with different indices of refraction and make the object appear broken when we look at it partly through one, partly through the other. As long as we think only of the outer conditions of communication, everything seems clear to us; as soon as we contemplate the inner ones, our certainty begins to dwindle. The two images—'outer' and 'inner' circumstances—act like two media of different refractive power through which the object all at once appears broken. We are irritated; we might say 'Certainly, there is communication', only to add after a moment's pause, 'But now, how *can* there be?' We can scarcely avoid having the impression that there is something almost mysterious about the 'I' and the 'you', and about the relation of the consciousness to one another; as if there were something difficult to grasp which resists all attempts of the mind to comprehend it.

'How is communication possible, since it is uncertain whether two people have the same experience on looking at a green leaf?' The confusion is already present in the way the question is put. For what does 'the same experience' mean here? How are we to understand the word 'same' in this context? We shall not say that this question has no meaning, but rather insist that its meaning should be explained to us. This explanation can (as has been shown in Part I) be given in very different ways. Here are some examples:

(i) You say in ordinary life that a colour-blind person 'sees colours in a different way' from the way that normal people do. What urges you to say this sort of thing is the fact that such a person cannot distinguish differences of colour as we do—that if, for example, he is red-green blind, he calls a certain shade of red and a certain shade of green 'the same colour'—in fact, that he uses language differently. This might induce us to suggest the following rule of language: two people looking at the same coloured surface shall be said to have the same or different colour sensations according to whether they follow the same or different rules for their use of colour words. But, if you adopt this criterion, it should be noted that in ascribing to some-one else an *experience* of colour different from your own you *mean* nothing more than that he uses words differently. And now if you say 'He uses words differently *because* he sees the colours differently', it looks as though you have given an explanation of one fact in terms of another. You would only have done this, however, if you had given a meaning to the phrase. 'He sees colour differently' which is *independent* of the way he uses words. This can really be done in many different ways, and in that case the above may be taken as an explanation of why he uses language differently. But if you take the use of language as the criterion for having different experiences, it is then a tautology to say 'He uses words differently *because* he sees colours differently'.

(ii) On the basis of our knowledge of physiology, it is very probable that the physical apparatus connected with seeing differs in some respects in a colour-blind person from the normal, and that processes take place in the light-sensitive parts of the retina which are different in the case of a colour-blind person from those of a normal person. This might suggest the following criterion: two people have the same experience of colour when processes of the same sort take place in their retinas and nervous systems. It would then depend on the result of a scientific test whether or not two people really had the same experience on seeing a green leaf.

If this way of giving a meaning to the phrase 'have the same experience' is not felt to be satisfactory we can refer to other possible explanations. For example:

(iii) 'I have the same experience as Smith has on looking at a leaf' means 'I have the same experience as I have now if I look at the leaf through Smith's eyes while he looks through mine'.

(iv) We have the same experience when I *remember* that Smith's consciousness on seeing the leaf was the same as mine is now (cf. the above remarks).

We are now in a position to deal with the question 'Can I ever be sure that I can make myself understood to other people?' This question is no longer mystifying. The answer to it depends entirely on what you mean by phrases like 'understand', 'make oneself understood', 'communicate'. You have perfect freedom to use such phrases as you please. Supposing you said 'I will say that I understand another person who speaks of colours only if he has the same experience as I have when we both look at the same coloured surface; and the criterion for this sameness of experience shall be that the processes in retina, nerves and brain are the same'. Now, if you say this, you have given an explanation of the word 'understand' in this context, and I learn from it in what circumstances you would say that you understand some-one else and in what circumstances you would not say this. Let us tentatively adopt this use of language. Since such a physiological investigation has not yet been carried out, because of the great difficulties of examining the living organisms, we could not as yet say for certain that we really understood someone else; we could only say that we probably do and leave it to future experiments to decide definitely as to the rightness of this assumption.

Supposing there is a man who declares 'I will say that I understand another person who speaks of colours only if he has the same experiences as I do on looking at a coloured surface, and the criterion for his having the same experience shall be that, if we exchanged bodies so that I looked through his eyes, I should have the same experience as I do now'. This, too, would be a perfectly permissible explana-tion: we should know in what circumstances we were entitled to say that we really understood someone. But in this case there is not the faintest hope of ever carrying out the experiment, and therefore we should never know whether we really under-stood someone or not.

If we had to choose one or other of these different explanations of the word 'understand', which would be the best one to chose? Would it be convenient to make a convention such that we should remain for ever uncertain whether or not we had understood someone else? There can hardly be any doubt as to the answer.

As a matter of fact, we use the words 'understand', 'communicate', 'make our-selves understood,' etc., in such a way that the criterion for understanding is that the other person uses words in the same way that we do. We say, for example, of a colour-blind man that he does not understand colour names as we do, because his use of them differs from ours, and not because different processes may take place in his retina and nervous system. We are not compelled to adopt this convention, but, if we do, the question whether or not we understand other people loses its appearance of mystery. It turns into an empirical question which may be settled in each particular case.

What we object to is the idea of the contents of different people's minds as shut off from each other by insurmountable barriers, so that what is experienced is eternally private and inexpressible—the idea that we are, so to speak, imprisoned behind bars through which only words can escape, as though it were a defect in language that it consists wholly of words.

How misleading is the very form of the question, 'What is communicable?', which makes us expect an answer of the form: this and this is communicable (e.g. the structure of the experience), in contra-distinction to that and that (e.g. its con-tent). It would be better to replace his question by another, namely 'What makes com-munication possible?', i.e. 'What are the determining conditions of communication?' And this leads us to the consideration of a number of fresh points.

REMOVABLE AND IRREMOVABLE BARRIERS TO UNDERSTANDING

What, then, are the conditions under which we can understand each other? Accord-ing to what has been said, the answer seems to be: all that is necessary for mutual understanding is that the two persons should speak the same language. Although this answer is quite correct, it does not remove all our doubts. For we might ask further: *could* two people always use language in the same way? What about the case of a colour-blind man, for example? Can he use our language or we his, or is it possible to translate from one of these two languages into the other? And on what does this depend? To get clear about this, let us examine the way in which the usage of a colour-blind man differs from the normal.

I could show a colour-blind man the various colours, tell him their names, and explain to him how the colour words are to be used in different verbal contexts. Then what would show us that his language differed from ours? He might point to two colours, one a shade of green, the other a shade of red, and say that he saw no difference between them; as in general the relations between his colours would differ from the relations between ours: two shades of yellow that seemed the same to him would look quite different to us, etc. In short, he would be using the words 'same', 'similar', 'dissimilar', 'different' in different circumstances from those in which we used them. Should we conclude from this that he attaches a different meaning to the words 'same', 'different', etc., and means by his colour words the same as we do? Or should we say: the meaning he gives to these words is the same, but the signification of his colour words is different? There is a temptation to choose the former alternative. For, we might say, 'the experience two people have in noticing a similarity need not be the same in quality or in content. The experience he has of noticing the relation between two similar objects (*Beziehungserlebnies*) might well differ from the experience I had of noticing their similarity in the same circumstances'. But this would not be a correct formula. For what is the criterion for the word 'same', having identical meaning? Is it when the word is used in two contexts according to the same rules that the meaning is said to be identical? In that case a colour-blind man means by 'same' what we do. For he learns the use of the word 'same' no differently from anyone else: we show him two things having the same colour in our sense, draw his attention to the two and tell him that such pairs of colours are called 'the same'. We then make him use the expression in different contexts and correct him if necessary, just as we do to anyone else. This is the only way for him to learn the meaning of 'same colour'. But since, in contexts where his use of colour words is normal, he has been taught the rules for the use of 'same' and 'different' exactly as other people have, these words have in his language the same meaning as they have in ours.

But neither alternative would be quite correct. He certainly learns the use of the word 'like' with the same examples as we do, but he goes on to apply it in cases where we should not. To put it differently, the field of the relation 'like' (in his sense) includes the field of the relation 'like' (in our sense) as a proper part of itself; thus in the two cases the word 'like' is used differently.

It would therefore be better to say that, in the language of a colour-blind man, not only do words like 'red', 'green' and 'yellow' have a different use, but also words that are used to express relations between colours, such as 'like', 'unlike', 'similar', etc. As for the colour words, they are used by him in such a way that they are members of a system of less multiplicity. The colour-blind man may distinguish some shades of yellow and call them for example, light yellow, dark yellow, dull yellow, pale yellow, bright yellow, but he will not so distinguish and speak of reddish yellow, or greenish yellow. His colours are, so to speak, embedded in a different background, and therefore the word 'yellow' in his mouth has not exactly the same, but only a similar, meaning to what it has for us.

The relation between these two meanings of the word 'yellow' might perhaps be made clearer by drawing attention to a somewhat analogous relation—although the comparison is, of course, only imperfectly applicable—between two different meanings of the symbol '3'. Compare the meaning of '3' when it is one of the series of natural numbers, with its meaning in a primitive system '1, 2, 3, 4, 5, many'. These two threes are not identical, they only correspond to each other, i.e. they occupy an analogous position in the two systems of numbers. For example, 3 + 2 = 5 in both systems, but 3 + 3 equals 6 in one system and 'many' in the other.

In this connection the following questions suggest themselves: what would it be like for a colour-blind man suddenly to receive normal sight? In what way would his world be changed? Many people would be inclined to say that his colour world had extended. But this would be a misleading way of putting it. For, strictly speaking, it is not a matter of his colour world extending, but rather of his becoming acquainted with a system of greater multiplicity and of his seeing *all* the colours differently. It is not as if his colour world had been incomplete, and as if new colours had been somehow inserted into gaps between the previous ones. We have here two quite different systems between which there are only certain correspondences.

This example shows that there are actually, as it were, barriers to understanding: a colour-blind man and a normal man do live in different worlds and speak different languages that are joined by no bridges of understanding.

Here, however, an objection might be raised. One of the rules of our grammar is that two colour words exclude each other, e.g. 'red' and 'green'. A colour-blind man, on the other hand, since he sees no difference between these colours, would say that the two words were synonymous. But if the difference of experience is to be shown by the different use of language, all we need do is to alter our rules so that 'red' and 'green' become synonyms which lies well in our power, and we should then have to say that we *saw* the colours exactly as he does. This obviously is nonsense; nobody would say that our experience would be altered if we merely altered our rules of grammar. Hence there must be something wrong with the account we have given.

Nietzsche held that the ancient Greeks were colour-blind, since in Homer the word 'kváneos' meant both the colour of the sea and that of the hair of the Achaeans. But such an inference would be rash. To say that the Greeks were colour-blind would have been correct only if they had been unable to *distinguish* between the colour of the sea and that of their hair. In other words, we only call a person colour-blind if, when looking at two different colours, he says 'I can see no difference'. If I call both a light-red patch and a dark-red one 'red', it does not follow that I have the same experience in both cases. This calls attention to the difference between the two sentences:

(i) 'Both colours are called by the same name.'
(ii) 'Both colours are called the same colour.'

The first proposition does not by any means entail the second.

What, then, is the difference between the language of the colour-blind man and the artificial language game in which the words 'red' and 'green' are used synony-mously? The difference is this: if we point to a certain shade of green and a certain shade of red in a colour chart and ask 'Is this colour the same as that?', the colour-blind man would answer 'Yes', whereas a person playing the language game would answer 'No'. The colour-blind person does not see any difference; the person playing the language game is not interested in expressing the difference.

This shows that the two cases are entirely different. Suppose a certain tribe habitually used words according to the rules of our language game, we could yet perfectly well understand them, for we could translate what they said into our own language. They too, if they took the trouble to learn our language, could under-stand us when we talked about colours. But a colour-blind man is in an essentially different position, he is unable to grasp the sense of our colour assertions, because he is unable to learn our language.

From this example we can see that there are barriers to understanding in a different sense: our colour assertions cannot be translated into the primitive language of such a tribe; nevertheless, members of this tribe could attain a full understanding of our remarks by *learning* our language, or else by so *extending* their language that it acquired the same power of expression as ours had. A colour-blind man, on the other hand, could in no way attain the *same* understanding of our assertions as we have. In the first case one might call the barrier 'removable', in the second case 'irremovable'.

To put the point in a more general way, we might say: concerning the relations between two languages there are three distinct possibilities:

(i) Each language can be translated into the other.

(ii) One of the languages (L_1) cannot be translated into the other (L_2), but it can be learned by a speaker of L_2.

(iii) L_1 cannot be learned by a speaker of L_2.

Let us illustrate these differences by a few examples. The text of an ancient Chinese philosopher cannot be translated into any European language; since there are in Chinese words of so comprehensive and various a significance—like the word 'tao'[1]—that they are analogous to none of the words in our language; any attempt at translation would have to use words whose meanings compared with the original would be too narrow, definite and sharply bounded. The thoughts of a Chinese philosopher cannot, therefore, be expressed in any precise sense in a European lan-guage. Here, then, there is something like a barrier to understanding, but one that can be surmounted as soon as we *learn* the uses of such words and, so to speak imitate them in our own language, thus assimilating a new range of ideas. 'Learning the use of a word' will here often mean re-creating the mode of being of an alien people. Or again, the language of mathematics, or of any body of theoretical knowl-edge, cannot be translated into our everyday language. But all these languages could be joined on to or linked up with the basic language, i.e. it is conceivable that the basic language should incorporate new uses of words, so that what was previously inexpressible could now be expressed.

Such 'cohesion' of languages is, however, not always possible. Thus quantum-

1 'tao' means the Way, Principle, Norm, Rule, Order. Cf. I. A. Richards, *Mencius on the Mind*, p. 21 (London, 1932).

mechanics represents a new language which cannot be translated into that of classical mechanics, and cannot be joined on to it. Cohesion of the two languages is impossible, for every attempt to use the concepts of quantum and classical mechanics together in one system necessarily leads to internal contradictions. Classical mechanics is thus in a sense closed and inextensible. By no extension of it is it possible to reach the language of quantum-mechanics. On the other hand, the latter language can, of course, be learned.

The examples of 'tao' and quantum-mechanics illustrate two different ways of reaching a new language: through an extension of the language already in use, and through the acquisition of an entirely new system.

We may call a language unattainable that cannot be learnt in any way. Of course, this 'unattainability' is not due to the language itself, but to us and our experiences. Thus we cannot learn or translate a language which is used by someone to describe experiences from which we are completely cut off, just as a colour-blind man cannot learn our language.

But at this point there arises a doubt which we must consider more carefully. Could we not after all come to a full understanding with a colour-blind man if we both speak the language of physics? By a systematic investigation the colour-blind man could discover in what physical circumstances we used the different colour words and then so use them himself. He could also find out, for example, that this green was rather yellowish and that rather bluish, or that this blue was a bit lighter or more saturated than the other. In a word, he would agree with us in appraisal of the finest shades of colour differences.

Indeed, by examining the microscopic structures of our eyes and nerves and watching our responses he could even give a correct account of the relations between colours. Now, if he uses colour words in exactly the same situations as we do, and arranges colours by their similarities as we do, must we not admit that he speaks our language, and that we understand each other perfectly? There remains, however, *one* difference: that he *verifies* assertions about colours in quite a different way. While we look at something and say 'That is red', he has to conduct a complicated physical investigation at the end of which he, too, says 'That is red'. To the different sorts of verification there here correspond different ways of using words, or, if one pleases, different meanings of the words.

But here we must be especially careful. Our last remark sounds like an assertion, and could easily lead to all sorts of scruples. For someone might object: I see no reason at all why different sorts of verification should correspond to different meanings of words. And now it seems as though we had asserted something and must defend the correctness of our assertion. Let us put the point, therefore, in an undogmatic way and simply draw attention to the following: in the one case a word like 'red' is explained by means of an ostensive definition (by showing a sample, say); in the other case it is explained by stating a definite procedure to be applied to physical measurements. Consequently when we arrive at 'the same proposition', we have *proceeded according to different rules,* and this is all we wished to say. Thus we are no longer speaking of the meaning or of what meaning is, but remain strictly within the confines of grammar. We merely call someone's attention to what he is actually doing, and refrain from making any assertion.

Let us assume that to each colour there corresponds a definite degree of roughness of the surface: to blue, a silky smoothness, to green, the roughness of paper, etc. Then a colour-blind man could learn, by touching, to name correctly the colours of the various objects. He would thus use colour words in the same situations as we did. Should we then say that he understood the meaning of the colour words? Not at all: the difference would be immediately betrayed the moment we asked how he *verified* propositions about colours. This example, I think, throws light on the case of a colour-blind man who used the physical language.

Thus a colour-blind man uses words like 'red' and 'green' according to different rules. Or, more correctly, I too could use these words as he does, and for the simple reason that it may well be the case that my colour perceptions are always correlated with certain of my bodily processes. Always, when I have a sensation of redness, processes of such and such a sort take place in my eyes and nerves, etc. That a parallelism, a correlation between perceptions and bodily processes, exists—this, and this alone, is the experiential basis for the possibility of communicating in this sense with a colour-blind man.

But should I then speak of our 'understanding each other' at all? Normally, in connection with words like 'green' and 'purple', I think of certain qualities that I see, not of waves of such and such frequency. If a colour-blind man 'understands' me, he cannot give to colour words *this* meaning, he must first *reinterpret* my language in order to extract its meaning. To put it more precisely, a normal person understands our words *as we mean them* (he understands the same thing); a colour-blind man understands them by means of a previous *reinterpretation*.

That such a reinterpretation is possible depends, as has been said, on the existence of a 'parallelism'. This alone accounts for the fact that the 'psychological' language which treats of colours as experienced qualities can be co-ordinated to the physical language, so that to every proposition of the former there corresponds one of the latter (though not vice versa)—that the two languages, so to speak, run parallel for part of the way. Let us call such languages 'concordant'.

No one would dispute that there is a difference between the two languages—the psychological and the physical. But it does not always show up so clearly. Suppose there is someone who has an exceptional sense of distance, so that when he looks at any object he can say straight away: the length of that is so-and-so. If we thereupon measure it we find that his assertions are constantly borne out. Or, similarly, suppose that someone has a highly developed sense of number, so that he can give the number of a very large group of objects without counting them. We might then say that he has experiences which we lack; that, for example, he directly perceives the numerical quantity of a group as a sort of quality (a *Gestalt*). Numerals would then play for him a similar rôle to that played by colour words in our language; they would be vocables in a 'psychological' language. We would be unable to learn the way in which he uses numerals; we would have to reinterpret them in order to understand their meaning, and this we could do since, *ex hypothesi,* our two languages are concordant.

But is there really an essential difference here? Am I not able, with practice, to improve my powers of estimating distance and number?[2] Could I not yet say that I am able to learn in a certain sense such a language? What such examples

---

[2] There are here three stages: *measuring* (*counting*), *estimating* and *perceiving exactly,* for both distance and number.

show is that the domain of our experience is not confined within rigid limits—that we can develop new sorts of experience, and in this sense the line drawn between attainable and unattainable languages is a shifting one.

Thus people can 'understand each other' in many different senses:

(i) I understand a sentence in a language familiar to me; I grasp its meaning as soon as I hear it, without any more ado.

(ii) I understand sentences in a foreign language (e.g. Latin) by *translating* them into my own language.

(iii) A translation into my own language is impossible, because my language contains no words equivalent in meaning to those of the original (Chinese); but in this case I can *learn* the foreign language and thus, with a new medium to think in, understand what I have previously been unable to understand.

(iv) There are cases in which I *cannot* learn the language; e.g. I am blind and cannot speak of colours as normal people do. But then I need only to *reinterpret* colour words in terms of wavelengths and frequencies, and I can then use them in exactly the same circumstances as everyone else does. And here again, in a sense, we should understand each other.

(v) Finally, it is conceivable that people should use a language that I *cannot* learn, and which resists all my attempts at reinterpretation. Such a language would to me be quite unattainable—I would be cut off from understanding it as if by an insurmountable barrier. It may well be doubted, however, that there is such a case: for we can use the behaviour of people itself to define the meaning of their words. If those people used a certain word to describe an experience in itself totally foreign to us, we could still recognize when they had it by means of their peculiar behaviour—by their bearing and facial expression, by their tone of voice, their responses, etc. But then I could take the character of this behaviour as an expression of this experience; and if I further discover that the word in question regularly accompanies this behaviour, or if I conclude from the whole context that it refers to it, I can then define the word by means of just this behaviour. Thus it is conceivable that I should manage to extract *some* meaning from their assertions, although in another and more *strict* sense I should not understand. Only if it happened that we could see no connection at all between someone's assertions on the one hand, and all the rest of his behaviour and the situations in the surrounding world on the other—if his use of language followed no apparent rule—only then would the possibility of mutual understanding break down altogether.

Let us assume, for example, that someone has to name the colour of a leaf that he has before him. If he first of all calls it 'green', and a little later 'red', then again 'blue', 'green', 'purple', etc., and all the time in real earnest, with every sign of sincerity, and if we can at no time see any reason for these changes in his assertions, what should we conclude? We could first of all ask him what he means by words like 'red' and 'green.' But if he now explains 'red' by pointing to an object which is and remains red, but in the next minute assures us that the object has changed and is now blue—what then? We should no longer know what to make of his assertions. It may be that we later discover that he is under the influence of certain drugs, or that his eyes are sensitive to certain normally invisible rays, etc. If none of these explanations is forthcoming and he carries on attributing varying colours to things, we could only say: 'he uses words like "red" and "green" quite differently from us, and we do not know what he means by them'. Indeed the situation would be peculiar in so far as the question would arise how he could ever have learned the meaning of colour words. And this leads us to a new series of questions.

HOW CAN WE DESCRIBE OUR SUBJECTIVE EXPERIENCES TO ONE ANOTHER?

The problem of communication is sometimes represented as if each individual first of all spoke a sort of private language which only he could understand, and as if the question then arose as to how all these private languages fitted into the public one. This question springs from a false supposition. It is certainly not the case that each person develops a language which serves him only for describing his own experiences. We already *possess* a common, public language, and it is this that children learn to use.

It will be conducive to clearness if we consider for a moment how we actually come to learn the meaning of words like 'sorrow', 'joy', etc., which stand for subjective personal experiences. Let us examine as simple an example as possible. If I wanted to teach the word 'cold' to someone who has never in his life felt cold—to someone, let us say, who has spent all his life in a uniformly warm climate—I could do it somewhat as follows: I take him into a cold room and say to him 'Now you're feeling cold'. The first question to be asked here is this: in what way does he understand this explanation?, i.e. *what* does he take my words to refer to? To the *feeling* of cold or to the complex of bodily phenomena which are sympathetic of that feeling, such as shivering, paleness, goose-flesh, and so on? A strict behaviourist would probably say 'Both you and he can mean by the word "cold" only that complex of bodily phenomena. For there is nothing to be found over and above these bodily phenomena accompanied by the explanation of the word "cold"; so these alone must determine the meaning of the word.'

To decide this question, let us simply look at the way words are used. Suppose the other person has understood our explanation, i.e. he uses the word 'cold' in the same situations as we do. What then if he says 'I'm cold' when he shows none of the symptoms of being cold? Should we say he has broken the convention and used the word contrary to the rules? Or that he has forgotten the meaning of the word? Or that he is deceiving us? It may be that we doubt whether he is telling the truth. But if we know him to be a trustworthy person and can discover no reason why he should lie to us, we should say: 'he shows no signs of being cold, but he says he is, and he should know best'. In other words, we regard it as perfectly legitimate that someone else should say that he is cold without his showing any bodily symptoms of coldness. And our reason may be that we ourselves remember having felt cold without having shown any perceptible signs of our feeling.

We can now see more clearly how such concepts are acquired. In childhood we learn such words as 'cold', 'warm', 'hungry', 'thirsty', 'toothache', etc., on the occurrence of typical situations. People say to us 'you feel cold', when the bodily symptoms corresponding to this feeling are present, and yet the words stand unequivocally for the experience itself. The possibility of forming such concepts rests entirely on the fact that subjective experience and bodily symptoms nearly always go together; that, for example, a sensation of cold is always, or at least very often, accompanied by shivering and a contraction of blood-vessels. I do not wish to maintain that this connection is of the rigid and unvarying character that is expressed in a law of physics, merely that there is a fairly general correspondence. If there were no such parallelism, if sensations of cold came and went without being associated in any way with bodily phenomena, so that no physical investigations, however careful, could disclose the conditions under which the sensation arose, I could still invent a word to designate this peculiar experience in a 'monologous' language, but I should get into difficulties as soon as I tried to explain its meaning to anyone else. I could only say 'I have just an experience, a feeling or a sensation', without being able to specify *what* experience I had. For if I could so specify it, I would have to refer in some way to the conditions under which the experience could be produced, and this would presuppose a certain degree of correspondence between the experience and some physical phenomena. Without this correspondence a word like 'cold' could be understood only by the person who used it to describe his own experience; it would be a word in a private and not in a common, public language. What makes it possible to communicate our subjective experience is the fact that these experiences generally go together with certain definite bodily phenomena; for on this fact depends the possibility of our learning the words for these experiences.

This correlation is not intrinsically necessary. If there were a kind of experience, inaccessible to all other people, then a person who had it could not communicate it to others; the bridges of understanding would be broken down. The question whether or not there are such experiences may be left undecided. What is important is the fact that we can easily picture to ourselves situations in which there could be no communication. For it is just this which brings home to us that spiritual intercourse depends for its possibility on certain facts of experience.

To sum up: the conditions which make a thing like mutual understanding possible are partly intra-linguistic and partly extra-linguistic. The intra-linguistic condition may be formulated as follows: we must *agree about the rules* according to which we use the words of our language, that is, we must both speak the same language. And to do this is, at least to a certain extent, within our power. The extra-linguistic condition is this: that we should both be so *constituted* that we can speak the same language. And this depends partly on the fact that our bodies are similarly constituted, and have the same sense organs and reactions to stimuli; partly on the fact that our subjective experiences and bodily processes regularly go together; for this is what makes it possible to learn the words which describe experiences. To these must be added a third condition which has not yet been mentioned—the possession of a certain degree of intelligence, or, better, the possession of certain interest, tendencies and dispositions, which are probably biologically useful in the preservation of the species. As Lewis rightly says:[3]

If . . . one examines such a list of basic concepts as the primitive ideas of 'Principia Mathematica', one may see, I think, that the reason I cannot teach my dog the calculus

[3] *Mind and the World Order,* p. 101.

is not because empirical exemplifications of these primitive concepts are not possible, or even familiar, to him, but beacuse he is not capable of making an abstraction which is not dictated directly by instinctive interest, and because a structure of relations must either be very simple or strongly enforced by repetition without exception in order for him to hold it in his mind.

PHYSICAL LANGUAGE

We have seen that the physical language undertakes a reinterpretation of ordinary expressions, and in no way reflects what we mean in ordinary life by such words as 'red' and 'green'. If we compare the physical with ordinary language it is at first not easy to see what advantages it has. On the contrary, it might seem to be much more complicated and to necessitate a laborious reinterpretation of words. But it has *one* feature which gives it a very decided advantage. It is *objective,* i.e. different observers can reach complete unanimity over assertions expressed in this language, whereas this is not the case with the language that treats of colour or tone qualities, feelings, memories and the like. What then is it that gives the physical language its peculiar character?

The physical language uses throughout concepts (like 'wave-length') which are defined by reference to definite procedures of measurement. Each measurement can in principle, however, be reduced to the observation of spatial coincidences, i.e. to observations of the sort 'This pointer now stands opposite this and this graduation mark on the scale'. Now it is a fact that we can all agree about such spatial coincidences, whereas we cannot do so about colours, tones, and memories, etc. It is this fundamental part played by spatial coincidences which invests with objectivity the physical language.

But might it not have been the other way round? Would it be possible for assertions about qualities (colour, tone, etc.) all to agree, and for assertions of spatial coincidence to vary from person to person? Schlick, who raised this question, was of the opinion that it would be possible. 'In our world,' he says,[4] 'the physical language has the property of objectivity and universality which the psychological language seems to lack. We could imagine that it was the other way round, and that psychological concepts . . . were intersubjective, whereas no general agreement could be reached over assertions of spatial coincidence. Such a world would have no resemblance to the real one, but we could nevertheless imagine it.'

Let us give some body to Schlick's suggestion by imagining the following situation: that it is possible to be subject to changes of mood which are in no way connected with, and not to be accounted for, by events in my own personal life. Changes of mood which merely happen to me, a situation in which I am passive, as it were acted upon. In this way I am at one time filled with happiness, at another dejected and yet again suddenly reinvigorated, and so on. And let us further imagine that these periodic changes of mood are felt by all other people at the same times and in exactly the same way as they are by me. Under such conditions a frame of mind would be without private bias, and in speaking of it we would be describing a

[4] *Gesammelte, Aufsätze,* p. 282.

common or perfectly public experience. It seems as if in such a world psychological descriptions would be on the same footing as statements about spatial coincidences—perfectly objective.

So far so good. We have imagined a world in which psychological states are intersubjective, and there has been no difficulty. But how are we to imagine a world in which 'no general agreement could be reached over assertions of spatial coincidence'? What would a world look like in which we could not understand each other's assertions about pointer-readings, or in which our judgements varied systematically as in the case of colour-blindness? Suppose I read a thermometer and see that it stands at 50°. Is it possible for someone else to look at the same thermometer and read it at 60°? i.e. would it be possible for us not to be able to agree about the coincidence of the mercury-column with a mark on the scale? Now this would mean—if we are to describe things in our normal language—that he sees mercury in a place where I see an empty tube, or, in other words, that we cannot agree over the presence, or absence, of a physical object at a certain place. I say 'There is something there'; he says 'There is nothing there'. If I now point with my finger at the place where the mercury-level coincides with a mark on the scale and say 'This is the top of the mercury-column,' he may well see my finger coinciding with some quite different part of the sorroundings. Thus we could not even understand each other in our use of the words 'here' and 'there'! And this, as we see, is a very profound and far-reaching failure of communication; its most elementary device—pointing—now fails us.

This shows us that spatial coincidence plays a very special rôle. We could not even agree on the meaning of names for physical objects, since we learn these names by means of the words 'here' and 'there', used in connection with a pointing gesture. And at this point we begin to wonder whether Schlick was right in thinking that 'psychological concepts . . . were intersubjective, whereas no general agreement could be reached over assertions of spatial coincidence'. But in what would objectivity then consist? Are we to say 'In the fact that all human beings share identical experiences of happiness, and so on'? But how is 'happiness' defined? How do we come to learn the word? Surely only by reference to certain physical happenings which accompany this state of mind, for instance a radiant smile, a jubilant tone of voice, dancing, jumping, etc. But how could we ever learn such things when no agreement can be reached over the most primitive thing—spatial coincidence? Even our pointing would be subjective and at variance with everyone else's. But it goes even farther. For what does it mean to say I *agree* with someone else, or that I *understand* him? And what does it mean to speak at all of *two people*? For notice that the idea of a person and of the delimitation of persons depends ultimately on spatial criteria—and this is true also in the case in which we say that two people inhabit the same body. For what is then meant by 'person' is determined by facial expression, bearing, manner of walking and the like, and how could we distinguish between different persons if we could not even agree about spatial data? It would then lose all meaning to talk of 'agreement between different observers'—unless the notion of a 'person' or an 'observer' were fundamentally altered. Schlick saw this difficulty quite well. He remarks that 'the individuals who speak to each other would not possess spatially extended bodies in the way we are familiar with', but he makes no attempt to show concretely what form the relations would take upon this assumption. Rather he contents himself with the general remark: 'But all this would not be impossible.'

We, on the other hand, must insist that what 'a person' is to mean in this context should be precisely stated, otherwise there is a danger of bandying empty words. Let the reader, for example, try to imagine in detail what it would be like for a person to be a disembodied voice. What, in this case, could be meant by saying that we agree with such a 'person' as to an observation? Suppose we ask the voice, and it answers. But how are we to find out whether or not the voice has really made the observation it reports? In ordinary life it is easy to decide whether or not someone has really observed something. If I say to someone 'The vase on the table has fallen over,' and he asks me 'How can I test this?', I should reply 'Look over there, and then you will see'. But imagine a case in which he looks in a quite different direction and says 'No, the vase has not fallen over,' or says 'I know it has fallen, I don't need to look over there'. In this case I should reply 'You *must* look over there'. Looking in a certain direction is here an essential part of the test. It can be laid down in advance that a person gives a relevant answer only if he looks to see; i.e. it can be laid down—it is a part of grammar—what a person must do in order to test a proposition. But if the observer is nothing but a disembodied voice, none of this applies; we have no longer any method for differentiating between relevant and irrelevant assertions. Is it not already evident here that all similarity with what we normally call 'observing' has vanished?

It is quite possible that we should fail to understand each other's descriptions of *some* experiences, as the example of the colour-blind man shows; but if we fail to communicate the spatial coincidence of objects it is much more serious, since it calls in question the possibility of understanding each other at all. For I would then no longer be sure whether other people understood a pointing gesture accompanied by the word 'here' or 'there' in the same way that I did. In such a language the concept of a physical object as used in everyday life would have to be abandoned; an object would be 'subjective' in the sense that it would exist only for one particular observer and not in general for others. But if we follow up the implications of this thought we shall find it opposed to the very suppositions from which we started, namely that there should be different observers, that there should be more than one person. For, if the concept of a spatial object becomes subjunctive, what can we mean by different people, and what is the criterion for their difference?

What is correct in what Schlick says is that there are *facts of experience* without which it would be impossible to apply the physical language. These are that my perceptions, feelings, etc., regularly coincide with certain processes in my body. On this depends the possibility of translating a proposition which treats of my own subjective experiences into one in an objective language which everyone can understand.

Should we conclude from this that mutual understanding ends exactly at the point where this regular coincidence breaks down? This would be right if the concept of 'regularity' were precise and clearcut. But this concept, too, is by no means sharply bounded. As is well known, our use of this word is partly influenced by practical and aesthetic considerations ('simplicity', 'harmony'). No exact and unambiguous criterion for distinguishing between a 'law-governed' and a 'lawless' world can be discovered, and thus the concept of mutual understanding, too, has no precise boundaries. It would better describe the facts to say that there are *degrees* of understanding, and that the concept defies all attempts to tie it down to a precise definition.

WHAT SORT OF EXPERIENCE IS PRESUPPOSED BY MUTUAL UNDERSTANDING?

In ordinary life we say in general that we can make ourselves understood to one another by means of language. There are, however, cases, especially in dealing with emotions and subjective experiences, where it is doubtful how far language fulfils its purpose, as, for example, in religious and mystical experiences. There is, for example, that sense of horror at one's existence—an anguish roused by the mysterious, irrational, fate-ruled character inherent in the very fact of existence. But to what extent do these words *convey* anything to someone who is unacquainted with such an experience? Is it not also essential to understanding that one should from one's own experience be *acquainted* with the specific colouring of this anguish?

Let us first ask: what would we actually call an 'explanation' in such a case? Would we use the word 'explanation' of a verbal description, such as, to begin with a simple example, 'Sweet is what sugar tastes like', or would an actual introduction to the taste of sugar be what we should call an explanation of sweet? Would it be enough to describe to someone the circumstances in which he can have the experience, or must we actually put him in a position in which he has the experience? In which case would we speak of an 'explanation'? I think in the first case. If, for example, I tell someone 'A "musty" smell is one which you experience in damp and long-shut cupboards', he will understand what the word means even if he has never smelt such a cupboard. What we must apparently distinguish, therefore, is, on the one hand, understanding a word and knowing its meaning; on the other hand, the actual experience which is indicated by the word.

But could I not, then, explain to a blind man that 'white is the colour of snow'? Do I make him understand the word 'white' by this means? Certainly not. To avoid this objection we might propose the following formulation: in order to understand an explanation it is not necessary to have the experience itself, but it is essential that one should be *capable* of having it. Thus the explanation that 'sweet is what sugar tastes like', would also have meaning for a person who happened never to have tasted sugar (but who *could* taste it), while the explanation 'white is the colour of snow' would have no meaning for a blind man. What should we say of this formulation?

I think we may say this: in a certain sense I really do explain to a blind man what 'white' is; in the sense, namely, that he can now use the word as normal people do (e.g. in repeating anecdotes, carrying out certain commissions, making purchases, making up stories, learning the physical properties of white light, and its analysis into the spectrum, etc.). By looking only at this particular part of language nobody would ever notice that a blind man really did not 'know what he was talking about'. What a blind man cannot do is to name the colours of objects shown to him, or pick out a colour, or have the 'correct image' of a colour, etc.

Thus a blind man can in *some* of the cases use colour words as we do, in other cases he cannot. We *have* explained something to him, but we have not explained the *whole* meaning. And is not this also the case with the 'musty' smell, the taste of sugar, and so on? Is it not indeed the case with such expressions as 'sorrow', 'homesickness', 'horror', 'foreboding', and with many feelings and moods that are indefinite and difficult to communicate accurately? We can understand these words to a certain extent, but we cannot appreciate them as fully as one who has himself experienced the feelings. Someone who feels homesick for the first time will probably say 'So this is what people call "homesickness"; now for the first time I am beginning to realize all that that word connotes.' It is as if he previously knew the word only from the outside and now suddenly understands its inner meaning. But what is here called 'understanding' in not only a capacity to react to the word with certain definite feelings, but also the ability to describe imaginatively all the subtle emotional implications of the word. The order of these examples represents merely the experiences of the author. The reader may care to rearrange them more in accordance with his own.

(i) The sensation of the *déjà vu,* i.e. that sudden feeling which sometimes sweeps over us of 'having been here before', as if at some indefinite past time, in just this place, with just these people, we were saying just these things.

(ii) 'When I walk the fields, I am oppressed now and then with an innate feeling that every thing I see has a meaning, if I could but understand it. And this feeling of being surrounded by truths which I cannot grasp amounts to an indescribable awe sometimes'.[5]

(iii) Rimbaud's poem 'Voyelles': 'A noir, E blanc, I rouge, U vert, O Bleu, voyelles...'.

(iv) 'When a person is speaking with someone in complete darkness, the voice of the one who answers sounds distinctly *behind* the darkness, not in the darkness'.[6]

(v) The metaphysical θαῦμα—that sensation of having been flung into this world.

(vi) The description of a conversion crisis: 'I could feel the impression, like a wave of electricity, going through and through me. Indeed it seemed to come in waves and waves of liquid love; for I could not express it in any other way'.[7]

(vii) Gustav Mahler (in a letter to Bruno Walter): 'It's extraordinary! in listening to music—and also in conducting—I hear quite definite answers to all my questions; answers which give me complete quietness and certainty. . . . Or rather I have the distinct feeling that they are not questions at all.'

(viii) The peculiar state of mind which, as described by Dostoevsky, precedes an epileptic fit—a state in which sight seems to be intensified to an abnormal degree, and the whole personality is then pervaded by a surge of indescribable joy—'an inner light' as he calls it.

(ix) The last minutes of a condemned prisoner (again according to Dostoevsky's description): he gazes at the gilded cupolas of a near-by church, at the sunbeams reflected by them, and imagines that they represent the new form of being on which he is about to enter. The thought that in three minutes his being will be fused with theirs moves him to horrified repugnance.

(x) Rilke's poem, 'Ernste Stunde':

> 'Wer jetzt weint irgendwo in der Welt,
> ohne Grund weint in der Welt,
> weint über mich.
>
> . . . . . .

---

[5] Charles Kingsley's *Life,* i. 55, (London, 1877).
[6] W. Metzger, *Psychol. Forsch.* (1929).
[7] Charles G. Finney, *Memoirs* (1876).

> Wer jetzt stirbt irgendwo in der Welt,
> ohne Grund stirbt in der Welt,
> sieht mich an.'

> (Whoever throughout the world, is at this moment weeping,
>   and weeping for no reason, — he is bewailing me . . .
> Whoever throughout the world is at this moment dying, and
>   dying for no reason, — he turns his eyes towards me.)

Still more difficult to communicate are pathological states of mind. Some examples of these are to be found, for example, in William James's *Psychology*:

(i) 'One patient has another self that repeats all his thoughts for him. . . . In another someone "makes" his thoughts for him.'

(ii) 'Another has two bodies lying in different beds.'

(iii) 'Some patients feel as if they had lost parts of their bodies, teeth, brain, stomach, etc. In some the body is made of wood, glass, butter, etc. In some the body does not exist any longer, or is dead, or is a foreign object quite separate from the speaker's self. Occasionally, parts of the body lost their connection with consciousness with the rest, and are treated as belonging to another person and moved by a hostile will. Thus the right hand may fight with the left as with an enemy. Or the cries of the patient himself are assigned to another person with whom the patient expresses sympathy.'

(iv) 'A patient describes his sensations thus: "I was alone, and already a prey to permanent visual trouble, when I was suddenly seized with a visual trouble infinitely more pronounced. Objects grew small and receded to infinite distances—men and things together. I was myself immeasurably far away. I looked about me with terror and astonishment; *the world was escaping from me.*" In addition to being so distant, "objects appeared to me *flat*. When I spoke with anyone, I saw him like an image cut out of paper, with no relief. . . . Constantly it seemed as if my legs did not belong to me . . . I appeared to myself to act automatically by an impulsion foreign to myself. . . . There was inside of me a new being, and another part of myself, the old being, which took no interest in the newcomer. I distinctly remember saying to myself that the sufferings of this new being were to me indifferent. . . . I was another, and I hated, I despised this other; he was perfectly odious to me; it was certainly another who had taken my form and assumed my functions." '

What, then, are we to say in reply to the question how far language serves the purposes of communication—as a bridge built by the mind to lead from consciousness to consciousness? Is it really established that every thought which is expressed in this language is intelligible to everyone else who uses it? In the face of the examples just given, such a view can hardly be advocated. Is everyone, then, in possession of a private language comprehensible to him alone? Not that either. It would be truer to say that our language is suited equally to the purposes of communication. On the whole we manage to make ourselves understood passably. But there are cases, for instance, in conveying certain rare moods and states of minds, where it is doubtful how far language really bridges the chasm between soul and soul.

It is perhaps convenient to think of the vast domain of language as a photograph taken with a long-focus lens. A certain area of such a photograph would be sharp, corresponding to the area of language in which words are adequately fitted for purposes of communication. Such is the language of physics. But beyond this as beyond the sharply focused area of the picture, clearness, definiteness gradually decrease, till the edges of the picture, like the uttermost attainments of language, are blurred into indeterminacy.

FRANK A. TILLMAN

On Perceiving Persons

Frank A. Tillman, Professor of
Philosophy at Vassar College,
is the author of several articles
on analytic philosophy and
existentialism.

Sometimes when I see a facial movement, I see it not as a relic of behavior, a symptom of a mental state, but (depending on context) as anger, jealousy, pain, or depression. A certain configuration of bodily movements seems to *mean* anger or pain, but not the way a low pressure area means bad weather, or spots mean measles. Human behavior we associate with such experiences as anger or pain is not a manifestation or symptom of these states; it is a form of gesture that conforms to the conventions of when, where, and how anger or pain should be expressed by a given culture. These facts suggest that the picture of perceiving other persons should be conceived more on the analogy of reading language than reading a barometer. And the problem of our knowledge of other minds should be viewed as a matter of reducing the ambiguity of a particular structure, a bodily movement, that already has meaning.

This is not the way the problem of our knowledge of other minds is usually conceived. Philosophers and other theorists generally agree that observing behavior is essential to knowing other persons, and some philosophers have even argued that behavior is logically adequate for the job; but behavior itself is conceived as a relatively simple manifestation or symptom of mental states. It is usually assumed that there is a mere *de facto* correlation between behaviour and what it is said to manifest, e.g., anger or pain. According to this picture, behavior, a physical state which constitutes evidence open to all observers, is correlated with experience, a mental state which is open only to one and is hence private. Conceived within this framework, the problem of our knowledge of other minds is the problem of finding a way across or around the gap between behavior and experience. Every philosophical

Reprinted by permission of Quadrangle Books, Inc., from *Phenomenology in America,* edited by James M. Edie, copyright © 1967 by Quadrangle Books, Inc. Revised by the author, 1969.

account of our knowledge of others is a response to this fundamental dualism.

In this essay I want to bring to the center of attention the facts which support another conception of behavior. In doing so I propose to change the framework within which the problem of other minds has been traditionally conceived and to offer solutions to long-standing difficulties associated with it. To this end I shall begin, in Part I, by rehearsing some of the main responses to dualism, and show why these are inadequate. Then I shall offer evidence, in Part II, for the view that the behavior we associate with mental states is conventional. Finally, in Part III, I shall sketch a new picture of perceiving others which is compatible with this evidence and which has philosophical implications for an account of our knowledge of others.

I

There are four responses to the problem of other minds as traditionally conceived. I will deal briefly with a version of behaviourism, intuition, the analogical argument, and the criteriological approach. The first two approaches do real violence to the facts of human experience; the third involves deep conceptual difficulties; and the fourth, though suggestive, leaves the relation between behavior and mental states a mystery.

1. Behaviorism. If we could dispense with the mental component of persons by claiming that propositions about experience are equivalent to propositions about behavior, then there would be no special problem of accounting for our knowledge of others beyond that of knowing behavior. Knowing behavior would simply be a matter of making observations of physical movements or dispositions to move.

It is obvious that this view simplifies the picture of perceiving persons, but it does so at a great price. For this view implies that the basis on which I know my own mental states is the same as the basis on which I know others, namely behavior. But I do not seem to have to observe my own behavior or physical manifestations or to take account of my dispositions in order to recognize that I am in pain or angry. This view also implies that my reports of my own experience of pain or anger are open to the same possibility of error as my reports of another person's mental state. When I am uncertain about another person's pain, I sometimes say, "It seems as if he is in pain," or "I think he is in pain." This is what I should be able to say of myself if my own reports were based on behavior. But it makes no sense to say "I feel as if I am in pain."

The difference between my psychological reports and my reports of the psychological states of others is also evident in the phenomenon of deception, which a behaviorist has trouble explaining. A person may be angry without manifesting anger and he may manifest anger without being angry. As this is the case, it is always reasonable to ask, after observing behavior, whether the person is really in the state in which I perceive him.

So far no one has been able to reconcile these facts with behaviorism. These facts and difficulties suggest that mental states are, after all, quite different from behavior and that psychological concepts cannot be analyzed in terms of the concepts used to characterize behavior.

2. Institution. Is it possible to have as direct an acquaintance with other people's experiences as I have of my own? Behaviorism attempts to reduce this dualism in favor of behavior; the intuitive view attempts to reduce the dualism in favor of experience. According to this view, behavior is never essential to knowing what another person is experiencing; what counts is my direct apprehension of his mental state.

It is obvious that the intuitive approach is no more consistent with the facts than is behaviorism. My report of other people's experiences are not immune to doubt like my own, and I am sometimes fooled by another person's deceitful behavior. Neither of these should be possible if I have the same awareness of another person's experiences as I do of my own. For I should be able to tell if he is fooling and to be sure about his experiences as I am about my own.

No one can explain how one person can experience the contents of another person's mind without making an implicit or explicit reference to behavior or a body. Without some way of identifying a person's experience beyond that of saying that he is a mind that has them, there is no way of making sense of the claim that he knows, in the appropriate sense, what another person experiences. If persons were identified by the experiences they are having, and if two persons are having the same experiences, how could we even say there are two persons without presupposing that there is a way of telling who is one and who is the other, independently of those experiences? But then, contrary to what this view tries to dispense with, behavior is essential to knowing other persons. And no one has yet explained how behavior can be a medium by which one mind somehow apprehends another directly.

3. The Analogical Argument. The facts which cause difficulties for behaviorism and the intuitive approach seem to support a fundamental dualism between experience and behavior. The phenomenon of deception shows that experiences apparently exist independently of behavior. The privileged status of self-observation seems to show that there is a basic asymmetry between my reports of my own experience and my reports of another person's experience. The only relation that could exist between isolated states—behavior on the one hand and experience on the other— is one of simple correlation. It is difficult to see what relation could exist between two different sorts of reports, one in which I am the priveleged knower, the other in which everyone is.

How then is it possible to know the states of others? One classical proposal is the analogical argument which is a form of inductive reasoning. Accordingly, the belief that the body before me is the body of a person or that a particular item of behavior is evidence for saying that a person is angry involves reasoning by analogy with my own case. For example, I notice in my own case that my anger or pain is correlated with certain patterns of behavior in certain circumstances. When I observe these patterns of behavior in others in similar circumstances, I infer that they are having the same experiences.

This model of perceiving persons is attractive because it provides a general account of our understanding of others that seems compatible with the facts. But as an explanation it is inadequate and as a justification of our knowledge of others it is highly unsatisfactory.

The analogical argument does not explain why we generalize so easily on a single case—a single case because there is only one person, namely me, which can be used as a basis—for making inferences to others. It does not explain how the concept of pain or anger has the same meaning when used in such statements as "I am in pain," said by me, and "He is in pain," said by someone about me. Unless they have the same meaning we might as well be talking about two different persons, because my 'I am in pain,' would not contradict 'He is not in pain,' said about me by someone else. Also the analogical argument implies what is not the case, namely, that in order for a child to recognize another person's mental states he must be so enormously precocious that prior to recognizing anger, he has made a point by point comparison between experience and behavior in his own case.

Quite apart from these difficulties, this model of perceiving persons generates deep conceptual troubles that have their origin in the dualism from which the analogical argument takes its start. It forces us to say that a mental state is independent of behavior. It invites the classical skeptical questions, "Are we ever justified in claiming that the body we observe is the body of a person?" and "Is the behavior we observe a sufficient basis for saying that a person is really angry?". It is difficult to see how, using the analogical argument, these questions could be answered. The argument assumes exactly what is necessary to keep doubt going. The user of this version of the argument assumes that there is a correlation between behavior which is public and experience which is private. His argument makes use of public evidence open to all to provide knowledge of that which is open to me. What the skeptic's question comes to is a reminder that no matter how good the analogy is, the evidence is never sufficient, because it is the wrong kind of evidence.

4. The Criteriological Approach. A recent interesting alternative both to behaviorism and the analogical approach attempts to close the gap between behavior and experience. Behavior is said to be a criterion, not a mere symptom of mental states; and the relationship between propositions about behavior and propositions about a person's mental states is held to be stronger than induction. There are at least two ways in which the concept of a criterion is introduced into the discussion of our knowledge of other persons.

First, when behavior is said to be a criterion for ascribing mental states to others what is sometimes meant is that a given configuration of behavior and circumstance is to be accepted as *meaning* that a person is angry or in pain, etc. Thus a proposition specifying certain behavioral conditions is said to provide a criterion for another proposition specifying a mental state. Those who hold this view find that there is a logical relation between these propositions which resides in the element of decision that establishes a convention. This appears to satisfy the need for a relation between propositions about behavior and propositions about mental states that is neither as weak as induction nor as strong as deduction. The problem with this approach, however, is to understand how a relation between propositions can be logical when it is neither inductive nor deductive.

Second, the concept of a criterion is also introduced by saying that behavior is a "logically adequate" criterion for ascribing mental states. In this case, the concept derives its logical force from an argument reminiscent of Kant. For example, it is a fact that we have a concept of pain. But we would not have that concept unless it were possible to teach the use of the concept, to correct someone who has got it wrong, and to translate the concept into another language. But we could do none of these things unless there were an essential connection between behavior and the experience of pain. If this is not clear, try to imagine teaching the use of the word "pain" without making use of external behavior or circumstance. Therefore, it is held, behavior *must* be an adequate criterion for ascribing mental states to others, otherwise we would not possess the concept of pain or of any other mental state.

The concept of a logically adequate criterion at best provides a reason for saying that we are *generally* correct in our ascriptions of pain and such to others. But it does not provide a justification for such an ascription in a particular case. The argument above does not justify my judgment that an item of behavior is adequate for saying that the other person is in pain.

Both of these interpretations of criterion are suggestive. The first suggests that there is a conventional element in ascribing mental states to persons. But in locating the conventional element in the decision of an observer, this view directs attention away from behavior itself. The second suggests that behavior *is* adequate for ascribing mental states, but does so without suggesting how. Neither view provides a justification that behavior is adequate in making judgments about the states of others in particular cases. Neither tells us what behavior must be like in order to be an adequate criterion.

Thus far our knowledge of persons has been conceived within a framework in which behavior is understood as an uncomplicated correlate of mental states. The problem of our knowledge of persons consists in trying to find a way of dealing with the gulf between behavior and mental states—between third-person descriptions of bodily movements and first-person reports of experience. Behaviorism and the intuitive approach attempt to obliterate this gulf; the analogical argument and the criterio-logical approach, each in its way, try to bridge it. All four have tried to provide a justification for our claims to knowledge of others but all four are unsuccessful in various ways.

I think that conceiving the problem within this framework has directed attention away from the actual function of behavior in our experience of persons. In the next section I want to present evidence for the view that behavior is not a mere correlate of experience, but is a meaningful gesture. In a later section I want to show that this is what behavior *must* be like in order to be adequate for our knowledge of persons.

II

The behavior we associate with emotions and sensations is conventional in the sense that it is under our control. It is learned and reinforced by a given culture group. It has a limited range of meaning and its dominant function is communication.

1. The phenomenon of deception proved to be a difficulty for behaviorism, the intuitive approach, and the criteriological view. By contrast, the possibility of deceit provides evidence that behavior is conventional. That I can simulate pain behavior when I am not in pain, and that I can forbear acting in pain when I am, suggests that pain "behavior" is something I accede to and can control and perform. To say that I exhibited pain or anger is not merely to say that my facial muscles moved in fairly well-defined ways. The movement was under my control in the sense

that in most cases I could have inhibited it had I so decided. Of course there are physiological changes which I cannot control or which interfere with my control of postural and facial gestures—increased heartbeat, distribution of blood, suspension of digestion, and simple reflexes. But the fact is that I do manage to inhibit and modify reflexes that involve skeletal muscles. My pain and anger deceptions are very often successful.

This means that there is no simple correlation between my behavior and my mental states. My facial gesture of anger is not a passive indicator, like a swollen jaw or an infected tooth. Human ability and skill intervene and make the movements associated with anger, pain, depression, and so on complex in the way a barometer or other natural sign is not.

But examples of pain and anger deception are the exception. And I should not want to rest my case that our seemingly spontaneous behavior is gestural on such a narrow base. So I shall try to show that we exert more control over ordinary movements associated with mental states than we commonly suppose.

2. Our body is at one and the same time the medium of our emotion and our articulation of it. Even though some of our gestures are causally related to internal and visceral changes and our gestures themselves are partly conditioned by our musculature, our ability and skill intervene. Our gestural movements conform to certain social conventions. We learn very early how deep physiological reflexes must be controlled and what socially acceptable forms they should take. The transformation of the psychological smile of an infant at three weeks into the social smile at two months is a good example.[1] Most of our gestures are based on bodily movements which we have muted or intensified, elaborated and refined, and made to serve specific purposes in conformity with social sanctions and rules: there is a cultural overlay on the whole face of behavior.

It is obvious that a great number of our acts are symbolic or emblematic, e.g., saluting the flag to show allegiance, kneeling to show reverence, thumbing the nose to show contempt. These specific gestures have little or no direct connection with universal biological responses. We are not surprised to find that these gestures have no meaning for people in other cultures; they would be as opaque to some people as the exposure of the tongue in certain pieces of Mayan religious sculpture is to us. Yet it is not at all obvious that the behavior we commonly think of as spontaneous and unmediated is also bound by convention. In fact just the opposite seems to be the case. There would seem to be typical bodily and facial movements that are so prompt and spontaneous that they appear to be simple reflexes. A clear example is anger. The presumed symptoms of anger are reported to be a crouching body, moist forehead, frowning brow, firm lips, clenched fists, grinding teeth. These are thought to be the inborn and constant characteristics of anger which constitute a common basis for understanding between man and man or man and the animals.

There is much evidence for denying that these presumed characteristic manifestations of anger are universal and inborn.

If these were characteristic symptoms of anger, then they would be displayed uniformly by all members of species. (a) But there is no evidence that these presumed

---

[1] R. A. Spitz and K. M. Wolf, "The Smiling Response: A Contribution to the Ontogenesis of Social Relations," *Genetic Psychology*, XXXIV (1957), 57.

characteristics of anger or rage are present in a number of species or even in one species such as man. Very little infra-human behavior corresponds to human gestures; for example, the facial expression of rage in a chimpanzee resembles a smile on a human face. (b) There is also little hope of finding inborn characteristic manifestations of anger in young infants. Studies of infants show that there is little difference between anger and fear responses. If an observer of infant behavior is not able to identify the anger or pain stimulus, he is unable on the basis of observing reactions to tell whether the child is showing pain, anger, or fear.[2] (c) Also, subjects tested in order to determine whether they can identify the emotional behavior of people in other cultures score very low in accuracy, but the same subjects score high in determining the emotional behavior of people in the subjects' own culture. (d) Behavior of psychotics who are angry differs radically from behavior of normals.

If the behavior we associate with anger were universal and inborn, then such cases should not exist. They exist because behavior characteristic of emotion or sensation is learned.

3. The most startling positive evidence that such seeming biological constants as pain, anger, or surprise are conventional is revealed in the radically different ways various groups express themselves. The following examples quicken our sense of strangeness about what we have so long taken for granted as instinctual.

> Shaking the clenched fist is to us a means of showing anger, but to the Bi Bom of Northern Nigeria it is merely a form of greeting.[3]

> The Chinese show anger by opening their eyes widely and staring fixedly at the person who is the object of anger, whereas to us this act would mean surprise or fright, depending on circumstances and other supplementary gestures. It is common for the Chinese to express surprise by sticking out their tongues.[4]

Anthropological literature is rich in alternatives.

> If we saw someone cut his finger, we would not find it strange if we saw him quickly put his finger to his mouth, purse his lips, and grimace. Yet as George Murdoch once reported, an Indian from the Western plains of the United States would find this highly amusing and even silly. It is not his way of showing pain or distress.[5]

Conventional behavior ranges across a very broad spectrum, from behavior which is performed consciously according to rule to behavior which is relatively spontaneous. There are many other sorts of acts which express contempt, embarrassment, surprise, or disappointment which are learned and have significance only to those who are members of the same culture group. For example, the Menomini Indians of Wisconsin express contempt by raising a clenched fist up to the mouth and then suddenly opening the first two fingers of the hand; the Chinese express joy by scratching the ears and cheeks; pulling the ear is a way a Portuguese expresses his admiration of a beautiful girl, but the same action means embarrass-

---

[2] M. Sherman, "The Differentiation of Emotional Responses in Infants," *Journal of Comparative Psychology*, 7 (1927), 265–284.

[3] W. Labarre, "The Cultural Basis of Emotions and Gestures," *Journal of Personality*, XVI (1947), 49–68.

[4] O. Klineberg, "Emotional Expressions in Chinese Literature," *Journal of Abnormal Social Psychology*, XXXIII (1938), 517–520.

[5] From an unpublished lecture at Yale in 1957.

ment for us; Tasmanians stamp the ground with their feet to express surprise; Andaman islanders never smile, but express happiness by weeping. Hissing expresses audience approval in Japan; laughter is not a sign of amusement for the West African, but of embarrassment.

These movements represent a covert culture—codes of the face and body that vary from group to group. Our bodily movements are as colloquial as our language.

4. Expressive conventions are so ubiquitous that we have to be startled into seeing that they are here. I have used observations of anthropologists as a way of showing that a great deal of expressive behavior is as colloquial as our language. I now want to turn to the genesis of expressive behavior in order to show the extent of institutional dependency of certain items of behavior.

From the time a child is born, its undifferentiated needs are directed at an audience, for this behavior contains urgent information that requires communication. And because communication is possible, that is, because there is a responding adult present, a body that is the medium of complex undifferentiated responses is transformed into an articulate system of controlled responses.

When a child is distressed he may make crying noises and thrash about with his arms. He may be in pain, he may be angry, he may be afraid—who knows?— that is to say that no one has placed an interpretation on the situation, and certainly the child has not. When a responding adult picks up the child and comforts it and at the same time interprets the distress (for example, the child is frightened), the child learns how to transform this highly disorganized behavior into an economical device for dealing with his wants. The child soon learns to raise his arms, soon to raise one arm and achieve the same response from the adult. The same kind of development occurs with crying or screaming; the control and foreshortening of these acts become a rudimentary means of communication. Emotional expression and language come into being at the same time.

This process of organizing and articulating disorganized behavior can go on almost indefinitely provided that there is an adult who interprets the child's behavior. The condition for this sort of articulation is the presence of another person. If we were to ask what it is that is being organized, it would be difficult to say. This fact gives little comfort to anyone who is attempting to find mere correlations between behavior and a particular emotion. Even when an item of behavior such as the biological smile (smile reflex) is transformed, at the age of three to six weeks, into the social smile, it is difficult to talk in terms of some "natural" meaning of the biological smile.

The child's ability to control and articulate what was previously merely reflexive occurs at the same time that he begins to recognize the emotional significance of another organism's behavior. There is evidence to show that he probably recognizes his own emotions at the same time he is able to recognize the emotions of others. Long before he is able to discriminate between two simple patterns, such as a cross and a circle, he can perform the much more complex feat of picking out his mother's face from the faces of all other women, and his mother's *smiling* face from her *frowning* face.[6]

---

[6] Joseph L. Stone and Joseph Church, *Childhood and Adolescence*, New York: Random House, 1968, p. 87.

By this complicated process, the adult literally gives meaning to the child's emotions and sensations by helping him to articulate them. Between mother and child there is a kind of "body-English" going on.

Our perception of the expressive states of others depends upon very subtle discriminations of eyebrow and eyelid movements, mouth, head inclinations, hand and finger motion, bodily stances, intonations, non-verbal noises, and context. The process by which these skills are acquired seems to be as complex as the process of language acquisition. There is no science of bodily movement akin to grammar, and yet, as we have shown, the infant is able to make perceptual discriminations of a very refined sort; in this there is an analogy with learning to discriminate complex grammatical distinctions: for example, between "John loves Mary" and "Mary loves John." It is conceivable that a system of perceptual segmentation analogous to grammar could be worked out for bodily movements.

These genetic considerations, and this last point, are intended to forestall any attempt to make *a priori* judgments about what is natural or primitive expressive behavior and to support my conclusion that behavior we associate with emotions is conventional.

5. Feelings, as well as expressions of emotion, are linked to the same social scheme. Experiencing a particular sensation or configuration of them, e.g., pounding heart, visceral disturbances, tremor, flushing, is insufficient for identifying them as a particular emotion, say of anger or elation. It is not just that there is no set of sensations that is uniquely correlated with a particular emotion—that is true—but further, there are no sensations that can be labelled as emotions independently of social context. The context is essential to provide a person with a means of determining what his sensations mean.

An ingenious experiment was devised to demonstrate this.[7] Groups of subjects were given an identical injection of a drug (a substance called "epinephrine," similar to adrenaline) which causes an increase in heart rate and causes tremor and flushing. These reactions perfectly mimic physiological disturbances correlated with a number of emotional states. One group of subjects was informed about the likely effects of the drug; another group was uninformed. Some subjects from both groups were then exposed to different social situations, one designed to induce a sympathetic response to anger, the other designed to induce elation. Afterward the subjects were asked to describe their feelings. Those who had been informed reported experiencing the sensations they were told would follow the injection. Those who were uninformed labeled their sensations "anger" or "elation" in accordance with what was appropriate to the social context. What is significant is that identical bodily disturbances could be interpreted in two widely different ways. The emotion which these subjects identified was given its content by interpreting the significance of the sensation appropriate to a social context.[8]

Although it is difficult to be sure that, as a result of such an injection, each

[7] Stanley Schachter and J. E. Singer, "Cognitive, Social, and Physiological Determinants of Emotional States," *Psychological Review*, 69 (1962), 379–399.

[8] There is also reason to think that cognitive and social factors enter into the identification of pain experiences. See Richard E. Nisbett and Stanley Schachter, "Cognitive Manipulation of Pain," *Journal of Experimental Social Psychology*, 2 (1966), 227–236.

subject had the same bodily sensations, the results are suggestive. They suggest that social and cognitive factors are essential to a person's recognizing his own emotional states.

III

These facts not only add to our understanding of ourselves but also suggest what behavior must be like to be adequate for justifying our knowledge of others. In what follows, I want to work out the implications of these facts, develop a picture of perceiving persons compatible with these implications, and offer some solutions to the long-standing problems we associate with the justification of our knowledge of others.

1. If there is no sharp line between physiology and culture it seems impossibly difficult to find an item of peripheral behavior which we associate with a mental state, but which is not tainted by custom. This is not merely a chronological point; it is also a conceptual point.

Acts which express anger, contempt, joy, or embarrassment are highly institutionalized: they presuppose a whole network of conventions, habits, and rules. How would it be possible to identify an act of surprise independently of these conventions. A particular hand movement or facial feature can be described independently of conventions, but the act constituting surprise cannot. Trying to imagine the act expressing surprise without the framework of rules and conventions is like trying to imagine the act of striking out independently of the game of baseball. And explaining the meaning of expressive movement as if it were a symptom is rather like trying to explain why the American flag is lowered at nightfall on the basis of observed correlations between the flag's going down and the setting of the sun.

An institutional framework of conventions, habits and rules is just as important in considering how a particular sensation counts as a feeling of anger, surprise, elation, pain. As we saw in Part II, section 5 above, an experience of visceral disturbance, or a configuration of other physical states does not constitute anger or any other emotion unless the experience is given a meaning appropriate to a social context. By "meaning appropriate to a social context," I propose that a person must at least (a) believe there is an object (real or imagined) worthy of anger, (b) know the circumstances in which it is appropriate and possible to express anger, and (c) know the appropriate ways of expressing it.

Those who search for a primitive or natural manifestation of emotions in animals or in infants are searching in the wrong place for the wrong thing. Neither the expression nor the feeling of emotion has any meaning apart from the institutional framework.

2. Expressive acts, unlike symptoms or manifestations, have a specific and limited range of meaning; that is, they are conventional. What would it be for an item of behavior to be an expressive act—that is, to be conventional?

An item of behavior P is conventional if it makes sense to say:

(1) What somebody means or meant by using P.

(2) What is meant by P.

These conditions are not equivalent; what P is used to mean depends on, but is not equivalent to, the meaning of P. For example, "The sun is shining" may be used by someone to mean that somebody should draw the blinds, or to explain to someone why the room is warm. In the same way a particular bodily movement such as a frown may be used by someone to mean "I disapprove of your proposal" or in the proper circumstance to mean "Stop your foolish behavior."

The dependency of (1) on (2) can be discerned in the limits of what can be meant by using P. For example, just as it is not possible for anyone to mean by the utterance "The sun in shining," that the angle sum of the triangle is equal to 180° (unless he is using a code), so there are limits to what can be meant by P, when P is a non-linguistic item of behavior. I would not express happiness by frowning (unless it were clear by other means what my intent was); and I would not use a hand salute to mean "My pen is empty." Even if circumstances could be imagined in which I might mean by a hand salute that my pen is empty, this would not show that there were no limits to what a convention means; it would only demonstrate one's ingenuity in getting along with a small repetoire of conventions by reducing the ambiguity of the context by other means.

The limits of conventional expression can also be discerned in the fact that we correct someone who deviates from accepted conventions. If anyone were to express by frowning what we take, on other grounds, to be happiness, we might think that although he is happy, he is also worried. If he assures us that nothing troubles him, then we might say that his facial movement was misleading and correct him. I take it that this kind of coercion is one condition for saying that there are conventions.

That this does not happen very often and that the coercion is not as explicit as this can be explained by the fact that these ways of behaving are learned at a very early age (see Part III, section 3 below).

One would not use a conventional device P for expressing an emotion unless:

(1) One actually has the emotion (But having that emotion involves knowing its meaning appropriate to a social context).

(2) The person using a conventional device P assumes that his audience knows the meaning of P.

(3) The person intends that his real or imagined audience take P as intended; otherwise this person would not use P, but would use some other conventional device.

3. It is a fact that a young child recognizes the meaning of a facial gesture, but he does not learn the meaning of anger, as the analogical approach suggests, on the basis of observed correlations with his own feelings. Nor does he identify his own mental states before he identifies the behavior of another. This view is about as worthless as the genetic hypothesis that in order for there to be a language there must be a first person who learned it. A child cries indiscriminately in pain or anger, but he soon learns the difference (see Part II, section 4).

Being angry involves knowing how to be angry, and the same is true of pain and other states. Knowing how at least involves a knowledge of when and where to be angry or in pain; it involves a knowledge of the customs and sanctions of our group. Even when we are not in pain or angry, we know what we do when we are. This is the basis of our successful deceptions.

If this account is correct, then I am not forced to say what pain is, independently of my bodily behavior. Nor need I maintain that we find out what pain is before we recognize it in another. Since behavior is construed as gesture, it is as important to consider the recipient as the performer. My ability to recognize my pain and your gesture of pain must occur at the same point in the logical order of my understanding. My gestures and my linguistic acts have that much in common.

But conformity to rules is not alone sufficient for a bodily movement to be said to have a meaning analogous to linguistic acts.

There is an obvious gap between the fact that gestures and bodily stances conform to custom and my contention that our bodily movements acquire a socially shared meaning. For example, we learn when and where to expectorate. There are even legal injunctions restricting such activity on public conveyances. But the fact that there are such rules and that people normally conform to them does not turn the act of spitting into a gesture. Yet this act, in suitable circumstances, *can* be a gesture. The act of spitting is a way of showing defiance, denigrating or insulting a person, or desecrating an object.

When an action functions as a gesture, in addition to there being rules in force which both gesturer and recipient acknowledge, there is also an intent—in the case of spitting, the intent to insult or defile. The act succeeds only if the intent is made clear and it is in virtue of the commonly acknowledged rules regulating spitting that this intent is displayed, in this case by breaking them.

I think that the factor of intent is also present in cases of pain, anger, and contempt behavior. When a person is in pain, it is generally his intent to show his pain in socially acceptable ways. The presence of an audience is sometimes essential. A child who has hurt himself cries very little or not at all if no one is present. In adults, involuntary cries of pain in soliloquy occur only in the extreme. When we are in pain we usually use the well-defined acts recognized by our culture for expressing ourselves (see Part II, section 4). An adult male does not cry in pain, but he is likely to grimace. We expect others to respond to our pain or anger, and we sometimes take elaborate steps to control their responses and to prevent, sometimes, their recognizing our obvious intent.

This is the point at which we link our pain and anger behavior with certain moral practices; by acting the way we do we get other people to notice our needs or states of mind, to comfort or console us, or to assuage or relieve our pain and take warning from our anger.

4. If behavior is not merely symptomatic of mental states but is a conventional expression, then we must take a different philosophic attitude toward human bodily behavior. We will also seek a different picture of perceiving persons. (a) To see the human body as a physical object is not at all difficult, but to see it as possessing just physical qualities is a perverse practice in most social circumstances. An exception would be the case in which I become separated from a friend in a large crowd. In trying to find her, I would see people who possess only the attributes—perhaps hair color or height—that she possesses. A physiologist who looks at just the muscle contractions of my face, but not at my anger or my depression, is seeing in an analogous way. This kind of seeing naturally invites the question, "What is the cause?" rather than "What is the facial movement for?" And seeing a facial movement as a symptom of a mental state is just an instance of this sort of selective seeing.

I do not mean to suggest that a philosopher who assumes that behavior is merely symptomatic of mental states is actually seeing this way. But his philosophical account of the perception of others which incorporates that assumption would commit him to holding that this way of viewing behavior is adequate for the perception of persons. I have tried to show why such an attitude toward human behavior is not appropriate to perceiving persons. But if he persists in holding such an attitude, then it is perhaps only because he believes that eventually behavior, as he interprets it, will be the ultimate basis for any satisfactory account of human mental states. I have also tried to show, in Part I, that there is little reason for being satisfied with this way of conceiving behavior.

I believe that the present account of behavior as expressive of mental states will ultimately be more satisfactory. (b) If behavior is not merely symptomatic of a mental state but is gestural in that it conforms to conventions and is used with the intention of conveying something, then we recognize the meaning of a gesture in much the same way as we recognize the meaning of a speech act.

There is a suggestive parallel between the structural ambiguity of a configuration of movements and the ambiguity of a sentence token. For example, if someone uttered the words, "John jumped higher than Mary," then, exclusive of context, those words could mean ambiguously either "John jumped higher than Mary jumped" or "John jumped higher than Mary is tall." The addition of "Then Mary stopped jumping in competition with John," and some extra-linguistic feature of the context, would reduce the ambiguity.

Ambiguity also infects other kinds of structures than sentences. Certain drawings created by psychologists are also ambiguous. Leeper's[9] composite drawing of two women, sometimes called the bride and the mother-in-law, is one example. We perceive alternately the face of two women, the young woman or the older one. The ambiguity of this composite structure can be reduced by placing alongside the drawing a single line, the main curve of which is the outline of one or the other of the two faces. Once the line is perceived, only that face will emerge that the line resembles; and great effort and the use of memory is required to make the other face emerge.[10]

In an analogous way the ambiguity of a gesture can also be reduced. Our attitude toward another is one in which we expect his actions to mean something to us, unless we have reason to think otherwise. By hypothesis, we know the learned conventions we associate with certain mental states. When a particular bodily structure is ambiguous, the problem of the perception of others is the problem of reducing the ambiguity by adding more of the context. It is then sometimes impossible to see another person's gestures as anything but real pain or real anger or some other mental state.

5. In saying that our knowledge of other persons is a matter of reducing the

9 R. W. Leeper, "A Study of a Neglected Portion of the Field of Learning—The Development of Sensory Organization," Journal of Genetic Psychology, 46 (1935), 41–75.

10 The analogy between reducing the ambiguity of a gesture and reducing the ambiguity of a sentence occurred to me while reading J. A. Fodor and R. F. Freed, "Some Types of Ambiguous Tokens," Analysis, XXIV (1963). I owe to them and to N. Chomsky the idea that questions about ambiguity are questions about syntactic and semantic structure. See Noam Chomsky's "Perception and Language," Boston Studies in the Philosophy of Science, Dordrecht, Holland, 1963.

ambiguity of meaningful structures, are we in any better position to show that behavior is adequate to our knowledge of persons?

What chance, for example, does the skeptic have for formulating his question about the existence of other minds? His question is, "Are there entities other than me to which mental states can also be attributed?" To ask this question, the skeptic requires a way of identifying bodily behavior which leaves open the question whether it is the behavior of a person. But since behavior appropriate to mental states is conventional, and since conventions are learned in situations of communication, the concept of expressive behavior already presupposes a plurality of minds.

Doesn't this way of dealing with the skeptic simply beg the question in favor of our picture of perceiving persons? No more, I think, than does the skeptic, who begs a question in favor of his assumptions. For the skeptic has assumed that there is a gap between behavior and experience which leaves open the question whether behavior is the behavior of a person. But the assumption that lies at the root of skepticism is simply that form of dualism which we are trying to displace. The skeptic is simply exploiting that dualistic picture. Recognition of this puts the arguments of the skeptic on another footing. Instead of attempting to answer this form of skepticism, thus assuming that his picture is adequate, we must show that our approach is more adequate than the dualistic picture. I have already indicated some difficulties with one dualistic picture and I am in the process of showing why the picture I advocate is adequate. From the standpoint of my picture of perceiving persons there is no problem of justifying the existence of other persons.

6. Can't we raise reasonable doubts within the framework I am proposing, this time about the contents of another person's experience? It is a fact that a person may perform expressive acts which do not express what he is actually experiencing. Indeed, I have used this fact to support the view that behavior is conventional. A person may express anger or surprise without being angry or surprised; and he may be angry or surprised without expressing it. Doesn't this fact now work against us? For whatever skill I have in reducing the ambiguity of expressive acts, it does not prevent me from being sometimes wrong in ascribing anger or some other state to another person. It appears that we are never sure whether a person *is* angry when he expresses anger or whether he is pretending. A doubt of this sort could throw my whole enterprise into jeopardy, for within my scheme I may have as little success as in any other in justifying our knowledge of other persons.

Contrary to the way it appears, there is a way of dealing with the doubt in question, a way which exploits the fact that behavior we associate with mental states is conventional and learned in contexts of communication.

One answer is helpful but insufficient. The phenomenon of deception itself, that is, the possibility of making a distinction between sham anger and real anger, implies that we do generally recognize real anger or other states. Otherwise the distinction could not exist. In other words, for the distinction to exist it is impossible for all the people to be fooled all of the time. However, all that this guarantees is that we are generally correct in our judgments. It does not establish that what we see in a particular instance is anger and not contempt or something else, or no psychological state at all.

7. The question remains whether we can justifiably ascribe mental states to others in particular cases. Here is where the scheme within which I am working has some distinct advantages.

If behavior were merely correlated with mental states, then the possibilities of falsifying a judgment seem unlimited. When I see a facial movement or a bodily stance, how do I know what the person is feeling? Suppose the behavior I observe is correlated with anger. There is no contradiction involved in saying that a person moves in the way described but he is not angry. What could further justify the judgment that the person is angry? Between behavior and feeling there are no mutual restrictions. There is no way of delimiting what counts as angry behavior and what does not. And there are no limits to what counts as a feeling of anger. Our judgments about what others are feeling, on this view, always go beyond the evidence and there is no further justification for these judgments, beyond that of correlation which itself needs justification.

According to the view I have been developing, behavior is conventional within an institutional framework of customs, habits, and rules. The concept of limit is built into the notion of convention itself. There are limits to what counts as an expression of an emotion; if a person is angry he behaves in certain prescribed ways in the normal case in our culture. There are also limits involved in what counts as a feeling of emotion; if a sensation is recognized by the person whose sensation it is to be a feeling of anger, then that feeling must be appropriate to a prescribed setting. The conditions for the *expression* of emotion in the normal case are the same as those conditions which prescribe what is to count as a *feeling* of emotion in the normal case. These conditions I referred to previously as the institutional framework within which we know when, where, and how emotions are to be expressed.

Now let us return to the question of justification. When I see a particular configuration of behavior which in my culture group expresses anger, there are three possibilities. Either (1) the person is angry, or (2) the person is shamming anger, or (3) his expression is ambiguous. I think the ambiguity can always be reduced; at least there are no logical bars to conceiving it as reducible. That leaves two possibilities. In the case of genuine anger, the context is such that the conditions are fulfilled. In the case of sham anger, there is a temptation to say that it is a bodily expression without the real anger (or successful deceit, the real anger without the expression). Anger, according to this picture, is something that lurks sometimes behind the appearances and sometimes does not. This picture is wrong. For pretended anger is not bodily expression minus a feeling. The whole scheme within which we make and support judgments about a person's emotion has gone awry. Sham anger is a movement which does not count as anger. What counts as anger includes not only the performance of a bit of behavior, but that it should be performed in an appropriate context. The appropriate context includes a pantheon of conditions which are missing in the case of sham anger, the most important of which is the belief that there is an object worthy of anger. In the normal case these are the reasons for saying that a person is shamming.

It is certainly true that there is no contradiction involved in saying that a person expressed anger but was not angry. But there *is* a contradiction in saying that a person expressed anger, and yet gave us no basis for saying he is angry. If there are still doubts, then perhaps the doubter has reverted to another framework which makes states such as anger or pain irretrievably private. If this is so, then consider the following.

8. Reference to an institutional or social scheme makes it easier to explain how the report "I am in pain," said by me, and "He is in pain," said by someone about me, can make the same assertion without destroying the privileged status of first-person reports.

The basis on which I recognize and label my own pain is similar to the basis on which another person recognizes and labels my pain. For there is a common set of conventions and situations appropriate to the expression and recognition of pain. However, my observer and I have access to this single scheme in two different ways. At times sensation is prominent; at other times behavior is. The link between sensation and behavior is the social scheme which we recognize in common and which prescribes the limits of expression and feeling from our two different vantage points. This being so, we must, I think, surrender the view that first-person reports are immune to doubt. For my judgment "I am in pain" or "I am angry" might be revised, not merely because I have mislabeled my sensation, but because I can be wrong in reading the appropriateness of my situation which is the basis for labeling my feeling anger or pain. But from this it does not follow that our privilege is removed, for I can determine what my experience is in a way that no one else can, namely by having the sensations I am currently having in the logical sense in which no one else has my sensations. But this is a privilege without immunity; my judgments of "I am in pain" or "I am angry" are not irretrievably private. For a sensation to mean anything to me I must place an interpretation on it in the same way and in full view of all the factors which an observer of me has.

9. Conclusion. According to my picture of perceiving persons, it is easier to understand why we appear to generalize so freely on a single case—my own—in ascribing mental states to others. I would not generalize on a single case unless I could recognize it as typical. I recognize my case as typical because I identify my own feeling within the same prescribed framework in which I recognize another's. It is because I recognize the common convention of when, where, and how a particular state is to be expressed that I have a basis on which my judgments go beyond the perceptually given.

Our experience of others warrants a better explanation than analogy. It makes unnecessary the radical attempt to simplify our experience of others by reducing their mental states to behavior. There is also less a temptation to think that we need to know another person's states directly in order to really know them. And finally, showing what counts as anger involves more than saying that certain propositions about behavior provide criteria for other propositions ascribing mental states. This is to say that there is a relation between behavior and mental states which shows what behavior must be like if it is to be an adequate basis for justifying our knowledge of others.

MICHAEL SCRIVEN

Could a Robot Be a Person?

Michael Scriven, who teaches at Indiana
University, has written numerous
articles on the philosophy of science.

0. INTRODUCTION

The day was when men sought to discover the secrets of the demigods, the elixirs, spells, and potions of the supernaturally endowed. Perhaps the day will yet come when we, having promoted ourselves to the leading role by discovering there is no one above us, will find ourselves in the role of the magician, the possessor of mysterious powers, and snapping at our heels will be the machines. The question in our mind, and on their tapes, will be: "What is the secret of consciousness?" If they are sufficiently well programmed in the language of mythology, ancient and contemporary, it is perhaps even conceivable that they will refer to their search as the Quest for the Thinking Man's Philtre. In this paper I shall consider what, if any, unique essence characterizes the human brain, what, if any, human property prevents a super-computer from saying 'Anything you can do, I can do better.'

1. THE MEANING OF "MACHINE"

There are many important terms in our language which cannot be explicitly defined, for various reasons, yet can be correctly applied in typical cases. One of these is "machine," another is "science," and there are others such as "truth" and "toothache." We can readily apply such terms in some cases, while in other cases it is hard to decide whether they apply, and there are likely to arise new cases of both sorts. It is possible to introduce some artificial definition—e.g., by requiring that a science be concerned with prediction or experimentation, which will be approximately correct and sometimes convenient. But when dealing with a logical problem, couched in terms which include these words, we can only employ a stipulative definition like this if we can prove in advance that we are not presupposing an answer to the question. For example, if we define "machine" as an inanimate artifactual device, we cannot go on to ask whether machines might one day be conscious. Yet it is not at all obvious that the answer *is* trivially negative in the usual sense of "machine." This definition has other drawbacks: to define a machine in such a way as to require that it be manufactured is both imprecise (why can't a human mother be regarded as manufacturing her offspring?) and too restrictive, since a spontaneously-generated adding machine, complete even to the Marchant label, would present a problem that might leave the physicist and the theologian at a loss for words but not the comptometer operator, who would not hesitate to call it a machine. Similar criticisms apply to requirements about inorganic constituents (which would rule out aeroplanes and cranes with wooden pulley-blocks) and about predictable behavior (which would rule out roulette wheels or radium-driven randomisers).

I shall confine myself to enquiring whether something that *is* manufactured from the usual electronic and mechanical components found in a computer workshop, with possible future refinements and substitutes, must forever lack certain capacities possessed by the brain. I think we can safely say that this would be a machine, without having to commit ourselves to any dubious propositions about what would *not* be a machine. (Whenever possible, I shall try to make the points in terms of an even narrower kind of machine—e.g., contemporary computers.) And in these terms the phrase "thinking machine" is not a trivial contradiction. Incidentally, our answers will leave us uncommitted about the question of whether a biophysicist can produce living creatures from inorganic elements. Although at the moment this appears to be only a technical problem, it is certainly a different problem, since he has a narrower choice of materials and an easier goal than the roboticist in his task of duplicating the brain functions of higher vertebrates. We shall return to the problem of constituents in the next section.

2. & 3. MOVING AND REPRODUCING

A simple question arises immediately. May it not be true that the particular substances of which the brain is composed are enormously more efficient for its tasks than anything we could expect to find in the inventory of a computer workshop? This might be true to a degree that would render machines with powers comparable to men so gigantic that they would be incapable of incorporation in a self-propelling unit comparable to that which the human brain inhabits.

Three comments are in order. First, this is not a very exciting point even if true, since there would be, under this hypothesis, few, if any, human tasks that could not be done by putting mechanical sensors and effectors where the human being would be, and using relays to feed data to and commands from the machine. Even if there are any such tasks, they are not ones that the human can do by virtue of his brain or mind, but by virtue of his body size. Second, there are no very strong reasons for thinking the point valid. Mechanical effectors and sensors can be made both smaller and better than human ones. For instance, they can be ultraviolet sensitive. The use of magnetic imprinting, crystal orientation, subminiaturization, and fail-safe circuitry, has already reduced or will reduce the required volume by several orders of magnitude and there seems no barrier except cost to further progress. Third, if we find that, for example, protein molecules provide the best storage medium, their employment would not necessarily mean we were no longer constructing a machine. Naturally, transplanting a human brain into a robot body is cheating, but the use of some of the same *substances,* either synthesized or extracted from dead tissue, is hardly enough to disqualify the product from being a machine. Our task is to see whether we can make a pseudo-brain—something with performance the same as or better than that of a human brain, but made in a different way, i.e., with largely different components and 'wiring.' There would still be considerable interest in the question of whether we can make a synthetic brain, no holds barred, but there would be less general agreement that it should be called a machine. (Would one call a synthetic flower a machine? A synthetic jellyfish?) I shall restrict our attention to the more difficult task of constructing a mechanical pseudo-brain, which utilizes at most some of the same substances or 'wiring' as the human brain, and thus retains a clearer title to the adjective "mechanical." There is a certain tension between the term "mechanical" and the term "living," so that the more inclined we are to call it alive because of the things it does, the less inclined we shall be to call it a machine. I shall continue to assume that these terms are logically marriageable, although they are uneasy bedfellows, but the substance of my points can be expressed in other ways if this assumption is not granted.

Having thus dealt with very simple behavioral and constitutional considerations, we may proceed to some of the traditionally more favored obstacles to the functional duplication of human mentality by mechanical means.

4. PREDICTING AND CHOOSING

It is a standard sarcasm amongst computer technicians that, contrary to the popular opinion, they are dealing with some of the most unpredictable and unreliable entities known. There are several causes of this. First, there are the errors of inadequate programming, which cannot be dismissed as mere operator errors, since a program often involves tens of thousands of characters in the 'machine language,' not all the consequences of which can be foreseen by the programmer any more than Euclid foresaw all the consequences of his axioms. Secondly, there are mechanical breakdowns within the machine—by no means uncommon, though to some extent their seriousness can be overcome by duplication, fail-safe wiring, and alarm arrangements. Thirdly, there are variations due to uncertainty-principle effects in junctions, relays, thermionic valves, etc. The importance of these variations is commonly slight, but over a long haul they guarantee 'individuality' to a computer. Fourthly, there is the cumulative inaccuracy possible with analogue computers. Fifthly, there is the possibility of deliberately using a randomizer in the circuitry, important in learning circuits. Sixthly, there is the rapidity of operation that makes the fastest computer unpredictable in fact.

It is thus highly unsatisfactory to suggest that computer output behavior is predictable. Even if the addition of "in principle" will get you past some of these objections, it is such a slippery password that its users often find themselves in the wrong camp. Here, I think the only safe conclusion is that computers are "in principle" unpredictable in a way essentially similar to the way human beings are.

The argument that "free-will" is (a) possessed by humans, and (b) implies a unique unpredictability different from that mentioned above, requires both clarification and substantiation, especially its second assertion. I would say it is now readily provable that the kind of free will required to make sense of the idea of responsibility and punishment is perfectly compatible with determinism and third-person predictability, and there is no evidence for any other kind. Hence, even if machines were predictable it would be possible for them to have free will. Since neither they nor human beings are in practice entirely predictable, the argument that only one of the two species has free will needs further grounds, several of which we shall examine under other headings, but none of which appears to provide insuperable differences.

The converse problem to the one just considered is also of relevance to the free-will issue, and serves to clarify the meaning of "predictable in principle." This is the problem of whether a computer can in principle predict everything. If, for the moment, one supposes that a computer can in principle be error-free, the answer is still negative, and thus a further element of similiarity with the human being possessing free will is preserved—the limitation in the power *to* predict. The standard example is the computer with total data and unbounded speed which is connected to a photo-electric cell and phosphor lamp in a certain way and then programmed to predict whether the lamp will be alight five minutes later. The photo-electric cell is focused on the output tape and the lamp so connected that if the output tape reads "yes," the lamp switches off, and if it reads "no," the lamp switches on. The prediction is thus self-invalidating. The other standard case is the prediction of one computer's state by another which is trying to do the same to it; the necessity for a finite time-lag, however brief, between input and output can be shown to produce gross errors under suitable circumstances.

Now these cases have analogues in human experience. The realization that one can do 'just the opposite,' no matter what prediction is announced about one's choice, in trivial matters such as the closing of an eye is a powerful element in the support for free will. (It corresponds, as we shall see, to the first case just described.) One might say that all that is in fact shown by such feelings and freedom is that certain events are not *publicly* predictable. For the prediction can still be made as long as it is not announced to the individual to which it refers. But not only does this remark make less sense in the case of the computer, it also underestimates the importance of the point. For the possibility of falsifying any announced prediction does show that the feeling of free choice is not an "illusion" in any useful sense. "Illusions" can be dispelled, but dispelling a man's "illusion" that his choice is not yet made, that it is still "up to him," is often logically impossible since any announcement about his choice will immediately be falsified. But it is essential to remember that predictability does not eliminate freedom. A virtuous man is no less virtuous because we know he is and hence can guess what he'll do. We are not wrong to praise a man simply because we foresee his actions—we would be wrong only if they were actions over which he had no control (see D. M. MacKay, *On the Logical Indeterminacy of a Free Choice,* Proceedings of the Twelfth International Congress of Philosophy [Venice: 1958]).

The predictability issue, taken either way, is deeply involved in philosophical puzzles of some interest, but it again provides no grounds for supposing the machine to be inferior to the brain, either because its powers of prediction are too great, or because they are too small.

5. CREATING AND DISCOVERING

"Machines only do what we tell them to do. They are incapable of genuinely original thought." As in nearly all these claims, two importantly different points are run together here. These are what I shall call the "performatory" element and the "personality" element. The performatory problem here is whether a computer can produce results which, when translated, provide what would count as an original solution or proof *if it came from a man*. The personality problem is whether we are entitled to call such a result a solution or proof, despite the fact that it did *not* come from a man. The logical trap is this: no *one* performatory achievement will be enough to persuade us to apply the human-achievement vocabulary, but if we refuse to use this vocabulary in each case separately, on this ground, we will, perhaps wrongly, have committed ourselves to avoiding it even when *all* the achievements are simultaneously attained.[1] I shall, for convenience, use the human-achievement vocabulary, but without thereby prejudging the issue. If it transpires that there are *no* essential performatory differences at all, we shall then consider whether we are entitled to apply the terms in their full sense. No single simple property of an object suffices to guarantee that it is an apple, but several *sets* of such properties are sufficient.

The originality point has some sting when we are considering very simple computers, but the moment we have a learning circuit and/or a randomiser for generating trial-and-error runs, the picture is different. We will discuss the learning point in the next section, but I here wish to carry on with the consequences of the randomiser mentioned in the last section, which provides a simple kind of originality. For example, a computer using a randomiser may come up with a solution to a differential equation that no one else has been able to obtain. Is this to count as being original or not (observationally speaking—we ignore for the moment the fact that the result is mechanical in origin)? Certainly we 'built in' the instructions to use the randomiser, but this does not enable us to foretell what results will come out. This is another exercise in the trustworthiness of the "in principle" notion. I shall make only two comments.

First, the randomiser may be of two kinds. If it is a classical randomiser (i.e., of the 'roulette-wheel' type), there is some point to the remark that its outcome is in principle predictable, but none at all to the suggestion that we could ever in practice predict it. Now Euler was an original man, but was he original in any stronger sense than that no one did *in fact* think of his results before him? How could any further claim be supported? Even if it can, there is a stronger source of originality possible for a computer—the use of a quantum randomiser. And to argue that it is in principle possible to predict the outcome of a radium-driven randomiser is even less feasible, because, (a) taken at face value, it is denied by most contemporary physicists, (b) if it means that a deterministic theory might conceivably someday be found, then this is always true, and so the alleged distinction between the man and the machine, in terms of the "in principle" predictability of the latter, becomes vacuous, since one cannot rationally deny the *possibility* of an exact psychological predictive theory.

Of course, more is involved in producing solutions to equations than in producing random numbers, these must have been put through the test of satisfying the equation. But this involves only a routine calculation by the computer. There thus appears to be no reason why a computer cannot produce solutions to problems

---

[1] It is interesting to compare this with the view that none of the arguments for the existence of God are logically sound, but taken all together they are convincing.

that are original in the sense of being (a) historically novel, and (b) in no useful sense predictable. Nevertheless, we feel that originality of this trial-and-error kind is relatively uninteresting. The important kind of originality is that which produces new theories, new conceptual schemes, new works of art. How could a machine possibly do this?

The key notion in the design of a creative machine would be the use of analogy. It has been argued by MacKay that in fact such a machine would have to be of the species referred to as analogue computers (as opposed to digital computers). I shall give some reasons for disagreeing with this in the section on understanding. But whatever type of computer is involved, there is no doubt that it must possess means for the *weighted comparison* of different descriptions. Thus, if it is fed data about the motion of a satellite around a planet, while on a theory-building program, it will register the formal similarity between this kind of motion and the motion of a body attached by a string to a fixed point and given a certain initial tangential velocity. It will, noting no better analogy, examine the consequences of the "theory" that an *invisible* connection exists between the planet and its satellite, the idea of invisibility being well-established in its data banks in connection with magnetic fields, sound waves, etc. Deduction of the consequences of such a hypothesis proves satisfactory for a certain value of the force in the invisible string, a value which depends on its 'length' in a simple way. The analogy with magnetic fields now registers strongly and the computer formulates and successfully tests the law of gravitational attraction.

The crucial difference from the trial-and-error method we first discussed lies not in the absence of trial and error, but in the origin of the candidates for trial; instead of randomly selected elements of a previously obvious class—e.g., the integers—it is necessary to provide a means for electing candidates from the indefinite class of possible hypotheses and then for improving them by adding modifications themselves selected in a similar way. The selection is no longer wholly random, because some candidates have better qualifications than others. What makes them better can be called their antecedent probability, but is perhaps better called the extent of the analogy between their known properties and those required in the situation under study. Any idea of an exact weighting of such analogies, which is perhaps suggested by referring to probabilities, is quite unjustified; the best one can expect is a partial ordering, and since this is all the human brain employs it is clearly adequate.

How would one go about giving the computer data of this kind? A simple beginning would be with curve-fitting problems where loose estimates of the importance of errors of a given magnitude, as against the value of simplicity for computation and theoretical fertility, can be given. The procedure can then be made more complicated in a way involving learning-circuits of the kind to be mentioned in the next section, enabling the computer to adjust the relative weighting of errors and complexity.

The procedure of *trial* is comparatively simple. The definition of the problem (say, the proof of Goldbach's Hypothesis, or the production of an adequate theory for the behavior of liquid helium) itself gives the tests that the successful candidate must pass. The application of these tests is, in the sciences, perfectly routine. There is still the possible difficulty of dealing with cases where several candidates pass the test. Here selection of the best will involve a decision similar to that involved in selecting the best candidates for the tests. This will, for example, occur where ideas such as simplicity are involved, and these make us think of creativity in the arts, where it is clear that we do not have very precise standards for judging the merits of works of art. But the computer's memory banks can with ease be indoctrinated with the canons of free verse, iambic pentameters, or nursery rhymes, and instruction to exploit low-level analogies as if they were high-level ones, and to adjust the result in certain ways by reference to ease of comprehension, richness of associations, and onomatopoeic force, would provide poetry of any acceptable kind. There is no doubt that the subtlety of poetic metaphor and the emotive effect of various rhyme-schemes will not *easily* be compressed into a computer; but they are not easily learned by human beings, and human beings are remarkably disunited about the kind of scaling that would be correct in comparing these virtues (cf. simplicity and fertility of scientific theories). The net effect of these considerations is that there is much less chance that computer verse will be detectable by a literary critic than there was that paintings by chimpanzees would be identifiable by art-critics.

Summing up the discussion of originality, the simplest kind is readily obtainable by a machine and the more complicated kind is obtainable subject to the (feasible but difficult) development of analogy-assessing procedures. Connected with the assessment of analogies is the whole question of mechanical learning, to which we now turn.

6. LEARNING

The usual contemporary computer is essentially a complex instrument, a close relative to the comptometer, and the idea that it does only what we tell it to do is well founded. This idea is more precisely put by saying that it cannot modify its own programming, more loosely by saying it cannot learn by experience. But there are already a few computers, among them modified versions of the IBM 704 and 709, which are more advanced than this. Professor Wiener has referred to them as having "higher-order programming," i.e., as being programmed to modify their basic procedure in certain ways depending on the results obtained from earlier trials. Such machines are already capable of playing a good game of chess, proving theorems in geometry, and so on. The two special features of their design are the provision of assessment rules whereby they can judge the success of various procedures in various situations, and a special kind of instruction. In the chess case, we provide them with the set of possible moves by every chessman, they calculate the results of applying all applicable ones at a particular stage of the game and, using the assessment rules, decide which offers the best option.

A simple assessment rule, used during early stages of a game, would be one which gives greater credit for a position according to the number of pieces deployed, the 'openness' of the position, possibly measured by the number of squares covered. More complex, and more essential, rules will involve assessing a move in terms of its consequences in the light of possible moves by the opponent, the ideal being a move which can be inevitably (i.e., whatever the opponent does) converted into checkmate, less ideal ones resulting in the capture or favorable exchange of pieces.

Thus we instruct the machine to proceed in such a way as to maximize the expectation of checkmate; and we provide certain suggestions as to reliable indicators of a good move, since no computer can actually compute all possible future outcomes of a given move except in some parts of the end game. So far, simple enough; but the special feature of the instructions is that we program the computer to continually reevaluate the suggested *indicators* in the light of its experience in using them to obtain checkmate. It is thus considering hypotheses at two levels. Within a game, it asks: "Is this a good move as far as my current standards of good moves go?"; and after each game, it asks whether a different weighting of the standards would have been more likely to produce success—and if so, it readjusts the weights for future use.

At this stage we have a model of learning by experience. Its application to a chess-playing machine is simpler than to a theory-building machine because the possible moves in chess are a precisely defined family, unlike possible theories. It is true that in computer design it is more difficult to achieve controlled imprecision than precision, whereas the converse might be said to be characteristic of adult humans; and it is the imprecise methods of analogy and suggestion that produce new theories. But the proper analogy to computer design is human education from infancy, not the generation of free associations in adults, and the learner, like the computer, finds it much simpler to follow the exact rules of the syllogism than to evaluate complex analogies. Despite the difficulties, there can be no grounds for radical pessimism about the possibility of combining the devices of originality with those of learning to produce a machine that is cognitively a match for the human being—so far as we have considered the differences between them.

7. UNDERSTANDING AND INTERPRETING

There is a special kind of cognitive barrier that we have not so far considered and which involves a novel difficulty. Naturally, we shall not speak of a machine as 'understanding' a theorem simply because it can type out a proof of it on command. What must it *do* in order to be doing what human beings do who are said to understand a theorem? (Even if it does this, it does not—as we have previously stressed —follow that we should say it understands, for apart from what it *does* there is the question of what it *is;* and it may be argued that such predicates as 'understanding' are inapplicable to machines. But we shall have removed one further *ground* for this argument.) It seems clear to me that the performatory element in the concept of understanding is the capacity to *relate* whatever is said to be understood to a variety of other material in the correct way. Understanding the special theory of relativity involves knowing the relation between its components, the relation of it to other theories, and the relation of it to its applications. Understanding is knowing, but it is knowing certain things. Knowing something is not *ipso facto* understanding something (one knows the date of one's birthday, or the composition of polyurethane, without understanding anything [except a language]). But there is a very large slice of personality in the concept of understanding; we are much more reluctant to apply it to a machine than such a term as "compute." About this slice we cannot dispute; we can only point out that the theory that understanding is a mental sensation, a theory which is heavily ingrained in us, no doubt contributes to our reluctance, but does so illicitly. The point is well, though briefly, discussed in Wittgenstein's *Philosophical Investigations*.

A special difficulty of the concept of understanding arises in connection with the idea of understanding the concept of an irrational number. We here run into the apparent obstacle of the Lowenheim-Skolem Theorem. According to this theorem, it is not possible to give a unique characterization of the reals and hence the irrationals, at least in the following sense: any attempted strict formalization of the real numbers can be shown to be ambiguous in that it can be given at least one interpretation in the rational numbers, i.e., every formalization we produce can be legitimately interpreted in a way contrary to that intended, a way that omits any reference to the irrationals. Now it seems plausible to say that the description of the reals that we give to a computer will be subject to the same irreducible ambiguity, and hence that we shall never be sure that it has actually 'grasped' the *proper* idea of real number, which includes the irrationals, rather than one of the other strictly permissible interpretations. A similar suggestion is made by Nagel and Newman in *Gödel's Proof* when they argue that the Gödel incompleteness theorem presents a serious obstacle to the construction of comprehensive theorem-proving computers; we shall return to this suggestion in a moment. The error in these arguments, as I see it, lies in the idea that the tests of understanding in mathematics are purely syntactical, that the intrasystemic transformations are the only defining properties of the concepts—of number, or proof, or truth. In fact, we can perfectly well regard it as a crucial test of comprehension of the concept of irrational number on the part of man or machine, that he or it immediately identify the square root of two, and π, and the base of natural logarithms as examples of irrational numbers. If this is required, then consideration of the formal properties will guarantee the correct field of entities (other simple requirements on the interpretation of the logical operators would also suffice).

It seems to me that the point is akin to the one arising when we ask whether a blind man can be said fully to understand the meaning of the word "red" when he has mastered (a) the syntactical rules governing color words, and (b) a device which correlates color-differences with musical tones so that he can indirectly differentiate (but not identify) colors reliably. This would *almost* locate the term "red" in the semantic space, but not completely; his interpretation would be invariant under transformations that did not offend current idioms or hue-separation. For example, he could get the color of a particular dahlia wrong although not the natural color of a ripe lemon. (There would be a *series* of tests—linked comparisons —which would uncover the dahlia's color, but he couldn't recognize it immediately.) We are somewhat undecided whether to say that his *comprehension* (of the term "red") is incomplete, or merely his *experience*. Certainly he is not capable of using the term properly in normal circumstances, but neither is a man who has lost his sight—yet the latter understands perfectly well what "red" means. Similarly, the axioms of a formal system provide much but not all of the meaning of "irrational number"; the clincher is the link with examples, the capacity to apply the language correctly in paradigm cases. In certain areas of mathematics, this is guaranteed by the formal rules, but in others the concepts are not merely formal shorthand, but refer to aspects of a complex construction that can readily be *perceived* but not exhaustively eliminated by substituting other, equivalent, concepts. (A related difficulty arises in trying to treat the Peano postulates as defining the integers.) In sum, then, I do not find the existence of a residual ambiguity in an axiomatization of mathematics a good reason for supposing that computers can never understand mathematical concepts.

Similarly, the limitations imposed by the Gödel incompleteness theorem on the formalization of mathematics are, so far as I can see, no more of an obstacle to a mechanical mathematician. As is well known, given any Gödel sentence G which is provably true but undecidable within a system S, it is easy to construct an S^1 within which it is derivable—the uninteresting way being to add G to the system S. Now, Nagel and Newman are struck by the fact that whatever axioms and rules of inference one might give a computer, there would apparently be mathematical truths, such as G, which it could never "reach" from these axioms by the use of these rules. This is true, but their assumption that we could suppose ourselves to have given the machine an adequate idea of mathematical truth when we gave it the axioms and rules of inference is not true. This would be to suppose the formalists were right, and they were shown by Gödel to be wrong. The Gödel theorem is no more an obstacle to a computer than to ourselves. One can only say that mathematics would have been easier if the formalists had been right, and it would in that case be comparatively easy to construct a mechanical mathematician. They weren't and it isn't. But just as we can recognize the truth of the unprovable formula by comparing what it says with what we know to be the case, so can a computer do the same.

It is appropriate here to mention another formal theorem, one which an enthusiastic roboticist might think supports his cause. Craig's theorem has been invoked on occasions to support the view that theories, and hence the necessity for understanding theoretical terms, are dispensable. It does indeed demonstrate the eliminability of certain terms from a given vocabulary under certain conditions. If it is supposed that these conditions correspond to the relationship between theoretical terms and observational terms, the conclusion might follow. But one of the conditions is that there be an absolutely sharp separation between terms of these two kinds. Now, it seems clear that it is part of the nature of theoretical terms that they should sometimes—for example, by progress in techniques of observation—become observable. Another condition requires that the only logically interesting effects of theoretical terms lie in their deduced consequences in the observation vocabulary. Even if deduction were in fact the only vehicle for generating the consequences of theories, this would not be a satisfactory position. The reasons for this require support from a general theory of meaning, but they can be condensed into the comment that part of the meaning of a theory lies in its relation to other theories, and part in its internal logical structure, so that understanding a theory is by no means the same as understanding its empirical consequences. Finally, Craig's theorem has the awkward result that the elimination of theoretical terms is achieved only at the expense of adding an infinite number of axioms in the observation language.

8. ANALYZING

At the practical level, some of the above considerations are already highly relevant. There is a great deal of work now proceeding on the mechanization of translation, abstraction, and indexing. A few words on each topic will perhaps serve to indicate the present situation and its consequences for our inquiry.

8.1 Translation. It is simple enough to build a mechanical *decoder* (or encoder) and they have been in use for many years. If translation were the same as decoding, there would be no special problem. Unfortunately, there are great differences. A code is a way of rendering portions of a single language obscure; decoding consists of applying the key in reverse. But French, except when used by certain people one knows, is not a way of rendering English obscure. It is a way of doing what English also does—describing, explaining, exhorting, ordering, promising, praising, and so on. Since they are both universal languages, and their relation is thus unlike that of mathematics to music, it is reasonable to expect that a *fairly* satisfactory equivalent exists in each for any natural unit in the other. Now, a word or a sentence is not what I have in mind when talking of a natural unit—a word or a sentence is a *phonetically,* or *calligraphically,* or *psychologically* convenient unit. A natural unit is a description, an explanation, an exhortation, etc., produced in a particular context. (Of course, a translation of this depends to some extent on a personal impression of the context, and the linguistic element usually does not fully describe the context.) If we were to suppose that the existence of workable translations of *natural units* implied the existence of workable translations of the *spoken or written* units (i.e., the words and sentences), then a mechanical translator would be a relatively simple problem for the programmer. The discovery that this supposition is unsound is, it seems to me, the chief ground for the present pessimism amongst workers in this area.

But there is no absolute barrier here. In the first place, there are actually many words or groups of words, especially in Western languages, which allow a very general and straightforward translation into corresponding units in other such languages, partly because they are used in only one kind of context. This is especially true in the vital area of technical vocabularies. Secondly, although the language is not always descriptive of a context, it often affords clues to it, so that by taking large enough sections, a translation can be made highly accurate at least for informational purposes. But the translation of poetry is an example of the opposite extreme where a one-many relation holds between a context and associated language complexes. And it is a useful warning, since this is not altogether unlike the situation of theoretical propositions. Finally, provision once being made for the sensory equipment of a robot—a point shortly to be discussed—we would possess a system whose linguists would be of the same kind as our own, and whose translations would therefore be potentially better, their memory being better.

8.2 Abstracting. Mechanical abstractors have already been built in response to the desperate need for systematizing scientific work and publication. They operate on a word (or phrase) frequency count, retaining those words of four letters, or more, that occur most often. This is the most primitive possible device for abstraction and all one can say is that it is surprising how often it nearly does a fair job. (It is not very often.) There are really no short-cuts of this kind that are worth much trouble; we shall not be able to rely—and we need to be able to rely—on abstracting done by someone lacking a first-rate comprehension of the subject being treated. Unfortunately, using such rare individuals for such purposes is intellectually and economically inefficient. The natural solution is mechanization. It is less of a solution than might appear at first sight, since, although the comprehension is feasible as I have argued above, the difficulties are so formidable that the initial cost of such a device will enormously outweigh the cost of discovering and training extra humans for the task. We may indeed find that the super computers of the future will need human servants because they can't afford mechanical aides—a nice twist to the present argument for automation, although perhaps it ranges a little too far into the future to convince the unions today.

8.3 Indexing. Essentially similar problems arise over indexing. Under what headings should an article be referenced or a paragraph be indexed? A simple machine can index an article or passage under all the words in it, or under the most frequent. Both are clearly quite unsatisfactory. The crucial concepts here are those of *relevance* and *importance.* To know which topics an article is relevant to requires more than an understanding of the article—it requires knowledge of all potentially relevant fields. Worse, as our theories change, relevance changes and continual reindexing from scratch is necessary, i.e., all references must be scanned for deletion *and* amplification. It is a tall order to build a machine with the kind of knowledge and speed required for these tasks, but it is increasingly beyond the powers of man to perform such tasks himself, and an increasingly large amount of work is being 'lost' in the technical literature, or expensively duplicated because of the inefficiency of indexing (and cataloguing—a special case). There is really no satisfactory alternative to the machines and we shall have to try them, there being no reason for supposing we cannot succeed but every reason for supposing we shall find it very difficult. It may not be impossible "in principle," but we sometimes abandon our "in principles."

9. DECIDING

In the indexing problem, that matter of relevance is crucial but only half the problem. A particular passage in the *American Journal of Physics* will be relevant to some degree to an uncountable number of topics. If an index is to be useful at all, a subset of these topics must suffice and a decision must be made by the indexer as to the most important of these. If this is to be done sensibly it requires some estimate of importance and some value for a "cutting score," i.e., a level of importance beyond which inclusion in the index is guaranteed and below which it is precluded. As we have suggested earlier, it is a mistake to suppose that a full arithmetization is possible, and partial ordering is all that we need. The issue is really the same as that associated with choosing likely hypotheses and raises no new difficulties for the programmer. The difficulties are bad enough even if not new. The procedure for governing the cutting score by estimates of the maximum permissible size of the index, the seriousness of errors of omission versus excessive bulk, corresponds to the procedure for deciding what hypotheses to consider in a given situation, or, in problem-solving, what maneuvers to try out, if any—e.g., which premises to try out as bases for a mathematical proof.

10. PERCEIVING

The performatory aspect of perception is differentiation of the responses to differentiated stimuli. This is the aim of good scientific instrument design and a computer with its own temperature-recording devices is easily made. The human brain, however, is rather good at detecting similarities and differences of a kind which it would be tremendously difficult to arrange to detect mechanically. For example, the visual recognition of a female acquaintance when she is wearing different clothes, is at varying distances, in varying light and from varying angles, wearing various expressions, hairstyles, and makeup, requires configurational comparisons of great sensitivity and complexity. It is clear enough how one would go about developing a machine with the capacity to perform such tasks, which we do so casually. Here again we would face the "degrees of similarity" problem, and "matching" problems probably best solved by the use of an optical comparator using rapidly varying magnification. A start will have to be made in connection with star-mapping programs using the photomultiplier tubes, and automatic navigation for unmanned interstellar rockets. The recognition of star patterns, regardless of orientation, should not prove too difficult, and the more complex gestalts may be attacked piecemeal.

10.1 Extrasensory Perceiving. Turing apparently thought that telepathy was the one impossibility for the machine. I am not clear whether he thought this because of scepticism about telepathy in humans or because of a 'direct-mental-contact' theory of telepathy, or for some other reason. Neither of the suggested reasons seems altogether satisfactory. The evidence for telepathy in humans is hard to dismiss fairly, but there is no ground for thinking it cannot be regarded as a brain function of a new kind, analogous to the generation of the alpha- and beta-rhythms. We are completely ignorant of the forms of energy or the physical features of the brain that are responsible for telepathy, although intensive work with the electroencephalograph is continuing at Duke and in London. In this respect, ESP represents a more difficult problem for the roboticist than any of the preceding ones, and forms a natural link to the problem of feeling. If it should transpire that no brain elements are responsible for ESP, then it will present a special philosophical problem; but until then, we must assume the contrary and continue the search. We are not at all clear how the memory works, but we do not doubt its existence. It is quite unreasonable to argue as some have done, that because the ESP function has not been localized in the brain, it follows that we should doubt its existence. What I have said about telepathy applies, a fortiori, to the less well-supported phenomena of precognition and psychokinesis.

11. FEELING

The most difficult problem of all those that face the roboticist trying to match human capacity is that of inducing the phenomena of sensation. The difficulty lies not with the outward signs—we have already indicated the way in which these can be achieved. It is the doubt whether there is any actual sensation associated with the wincing, gasping, sighing, and snapping that we succeed in building in for manifestation in 'appropriate' circumstances. A radical behaviorist will not of course be troubled by such doubts, but even the identity theorists would not share his equanimity. We all know what it is to feign feelings and we thus know what it is to behave as if one had a certain feeling although one lacks it—and we wonder if the robot is merely "going through the motions." (It is not, of course, correctly described as "feigning," since this entails an understanding of the nature of not feigning—and we are disputing even this possibility.)

Turing argued ("Computing Machinery and Intelligence," *MIND*, 1950) that if a robot could be so built that remote interrogation could not distinguish it from a human being we would have to agree that it had feelings. This is oversimple, not only because verbal stimuli are too limited for satisfactory proof, but because it seems to make perfectly good sense to say: "It says it is in love because we built it to say so—but is it? It says it is fond of A. E. Housman and thinks Keats is sickly, but does it really *enjoy* Housman?" In making these points in a reply to Turing ("The Mechanical Concept of Mind," *MIND,* 1953), I overlooked two points which now seem to me important and which improve the chances of a decision, although they do not support Turing's view.

In the first place, one must reject the 'argument from design' (androidological version), the argument that because the machine is designed to say it is in love it cannot be supposed that it is *really* in love. For the design may, and perhaps must, have achieved both ends. (To assume the opposite is to adopt a naïve interactionism.) Performatory evidence is not decisive (contra Turing), but neither is it negligible. It fulfills a necessary condition, in a sense which is amplified in my paper in the symposium on "Criteria" in the *Journal of Philosophy,* November 1959. What is a sufficient condition? The answer must be that there is no *logically* sufficient condition statable in terms that can be verified by an external observer. Even a telepath who declares that he directly perceives sensations in the robot exactly as in humans may merely be reacting to brain emanations that are similar. But there are conditions which make doubt profitless although not meaningless—e.g., doubts about the origin of the universe. These conditions are, for the most part, readily imaginable, consisting in the indefinitely sustained and effortless performance and description of emotional conditions, the development of new art forms, the prosecution of novel moral causes (Societies for the Prevention of Cruelty to Robots, etc.), in brief the maintenance and extrapolation of the role of a sensitive man, with dreams and feelings. However, I have thought of a less obvious further test which perhaps merits a separate section.

12. LYING

Remembering that, strictly speaking, to refer to an entity as lying commits one to the personality component as well as the performatory one, I shall use the term to refer to the performatory element for the moment. Now, the substance of my disagreement with Turing was that a machine *might* be made to duplicate sensation-behavior without having the sensation, i.e., the designer could fool the interrogator. But suppose our aim as a designer is not to pass the Turing test, since that is inconclusive, but actually to determine whether robots can be built that have feelings. I suggest that we construct a series of robots called R. George Washington I, II, III, etc. (using Asimov's convention of the R for "Robot" before name), with the following characteristics. They should be taught to use English in the strictest way. They would refer to human beings as being in pain under the usual circumstances, but under what appear to be corresponding circumstances with robots they would use behavorist language, saying that R. Einstein XI had produced the words "I am in pain," etc. And they would use the same care when describing their own states, saying for example: "R. George Washington I has been subjected to overload current" or ". . . has received a potentially damaging stimulus of unknown origin"—it being the named robot speaking. In teaching them to speak in this way, we make it quite clear that other descriptions of themselves may also be appropriate, including those applied to human beings, but we do not assert that they do apply. We also introduce the robot to the concept of truth and falsity and explain that to lie is to utter a falsehood when the truth is known, a practice of value in some circumstances but usually undesirable. We then add a circuit to the robot, at a special ceremony at which we also christen it, which renders lying impossible regardless of conflict with other goals it has been told are important. This makes the robot unsuitable for use as a personal servant, advertising copywriter, or politician, but renders it capable of another service. Having equipped it with all the performatory abilities of humans, fed into its banks the complete works of great poets, novelists, philosophers, and psychologists, we now ask it whether it has feelings. And it tells us the truth since it can do no other. If the answer is "No," we construct further robots on different principles. If the answer is "Yes," we have answered our original question. To the objection that we cannot be sure it understands the question, it seems to me we can reply that we have every good reason for thinking that it does understand, as we have for thinking this of other *people*.

The logical structure of the argument thus consists in standing on a performatory analysis of understanding to reach a conclusion about the nonperformatory issue of sensations. If, with Brentano, one believes there is an irreducible non-behavioral element in such concepts as belief and understanding, and that these, rather than sensations, are the hallmark of mind, my maneuver will not be convincing because it does not refer to that element which his followers translate as intentionality. But one may accept the irreducibility thesis, as I do, and regard the missing element as a compound of the possession of sensations and the possession of personality. This element is not the only one responsible for the irreducibility which also derives from the complexity of the mental-activity concepts in the same way as that which renders theoretical terms not reducible to observational ones. Then we get half of the missing element from the first R. George Washington to say "Yes," and there remains only the question of personality.

13. BEING

What is it to be a person? It can hardly be argued that it is to be human since there can clearly be extraterrestrials of equal or higher culture and intelligence who would qualify as people in much the same way as the peoples of Yucatan and Polynesia. Could an artifact be a person? It seems to me the answer is now clear; and the first R. George Washington to answer "Yes" will qualify. A robot might do many of the things we have discussed in this paper and not qualify. It could not do them all and be denied the accolade. We who must die salute him.

NOAM CHOMSKY

Persons, Language, and Automata

Noam Chomsky, Professor of Linguistics at the Massachusetts Institute of Technology, is the author of Aspects of the Theory of Syntax and Cartesian Linguistics. He also wrote American Power and the New Mandarins.

. . . I would like to focus attention on the question, What contribution can the study of language make to our understanding of human nature? In one or another manifestation, this question threads its way through modern Western thought. In an age that was less self-conscious and less compartmentalized than ours, the nature of language, the respects in which language mirrors human mental processes or shapes the flow and character of thought—these were topics for study and speculation by scholars and gifted amateurs with a wide variety of interests, points of view, and intellectual backgrounds. And in the nineteenth and twentieth centuries, as linguistics, philosophy, and psychology have uneasily tried to go their separate ways, the classical problems of language and mind have inevitably reappeared and have served to link these diverging fields and to give direction and significance to their efforts. There have been signs in the past decade that the rather artificial separation of disciplines may be coming to an end. It is no longer a point of honor for each to demonstrate its absolute independence of the others, and new interests have emerged that permit the classical problems to be formulated in novel and occasionally suggestive ways— for example, in terms of the new perspectives provided by cybernetics and the communication sciences, and against the background of developments in comparative and physiological psychology that challenge long-standing convictions and free the scientific imagination from certain shackles that had become so familiar a part of our intellectual environment as to be almost beyond awareness.

. . .

When we turn to the history of study and speculation concerning the nature of mind and, more specifically, the nature of human language, our attention quite naturally comes to focus on the seventeenth century, "the century of genius," in which the foundations of modern science were firmly established and the problems that still confound us were formulated with remarkable clarity and perspicuity. There are many far from superficial respects in which the intellectual climate of today resembles that of seventeenth-century Western Europe. One, particularly crucial in the present context, is the very great interest in the potentialities and capacities of automata, a problem that intrigued the seventeenth-century mind as fully as it does our own. I mentioned above that there is a slowly dawning realization that a significant gap—more accurately, a yawning chasm—separates the system of concepts of which we have a fairly clear grasp, on the one hand, and the nature of human intelligence, on the other. A similar realization lies at the base of Cartesian philosophy. Descartes also arrived, quite early in his investigations, at the conclusion that the study of mind faces us with a problem of quality of complexity, not merely degree of complexity. He felt that he had demonstrated that understanding and will, the two fundamental properties of the human mind, involved capacities and principles that are not realizable by even the most complex of automata.

It is particularly interesting to trace the development of this argument in the works of the minor and now quite forgotten Cartesian philosophers, like Cordemoy, who wrote a fascinating treatise extending Descartes's few remarks about language, or La Forge, who produced a long and detailed *Traité de l'esprit de l'homme* expressing, so he claimed with some reason, what Descartes would likely have said about this subject had he lived to extend his theory of man beyond physiology. One may question the details of this argument, and one can show how it was impeded and distorted by certain remnants of scholastic doctrine—the framework of substance and mode, for example. But the general structure of the argument is not unreasonable; it is, in fact, rather analogous to the argument against the framework of ideas of the early postwar years, which I mentioned at the outset of this lecture. The Cartesians tried to show that when the theory of corporeal body is sharpened and clarified and extended to its limits, it is still incapable of accounting for facts that are obvious to introspection and that are also confirmed by our observation of the actions of other humans. In particular, it cannot account for the normal use of human language, just as it cannot explain the basic properties of thought. Consequently, it becomes necessary to invoke an entirely new principle—in Cartesian terms, to postulate a second substance whose essence is thought, alongside of body, with its essential properties of extension and motion. This new principle has a "creative aspect," which is evidenced most clearly in what we may refer to as "the creative aspect of language use," the distinctively human ability to express new thoughts and to understand entirely new expressions of thought, within the framework of an "instituted language," a language that is a cultural product subject to laws and principles partially unique to it and partially reflections of general properties of mind. These laws and principles, it is maintained, are not formulable in terms of even the most elaborate extension of the concepts proper to the analysis of behavior and interaction of physical bodies, and they are not realizable by even the most complex automaton. In fact, Descartes argued that the only sure indication that another body possesses a human mind, that it is not a mere automaton, is its ability to use language in the normal way; and he argued that this ability cannot be detected in an animal or an automaton which, in other respects, shows signs of apparent intelligence exceeding those of a human, even though such an organism or machine might be as fully endowed as a human with the physiological organs necessary to produce speech.

I will return to this argument and the ways in which it was developed. But

I think it is important to stress that, with all its gaps and deficiencies, it is an argument that must be taken seriously.

.   .   .

I have tried to call attention to some similarities between the intellectual climate of the seventeenth century and that of today. It is illuminating, I think, to trace in somewhat greater detail the specific course of development of linguistic theory during the modern period, in the context of the study of mind and of behavior in general.

A good place to begin is with the writings of the Spanish physician Juan Huarte, who in the late sixteenth century published a widely translated study on the nature of human intelligence. In the course of his investigations, Huarte came to wonder at the fact that the word for "intelligence," *ingenio*, seems to have the same Latin root as various words meaning "engender" or "generate." This, he argued, gives a clue to the nature of mind. Thus, "One may discern two generative powers in man, one common with the beasts and the plants, and the other participating of spiritual substance. Wit (Ingenio) is a generative power. The understanding is a generative faculty." Huarte's etymology is actually not very good; the insight, however, is quite substantial.

Huarte goes on to distinguish three levels of intelligence. The lowest of these is the "docile wit," which satisfies the maxim that he, along with Leibnitz and many others, wrongly attributes to Aristotle, namely that there is nothing in the mind that is not simply transmitted to it by the senses. The next higher level, normal human intelligence, goes well beyond the empiricist limitation: It is able to "engender within itself, by its own power, the principles on which knowledge rests." Normal human minds are such that "assisted by the subject alone, without the help of any body, they will produce a thousand conceits they never heard spoke of . . . inventing and saying such things as they never heard from their masters, nor any mouth." Thus, normal human intelligence is capable of acquiring knowledge through its own internal resources, perhaps making use of the data of sense but going on to construct a cognitive system in terms of concepts and principles that are developed on independent grounds; and it is capable of generating new thoughts and of finding appropriate and novel ways of expressing them, in ways that entirely transcend any training or experience.

Huarte postulates a third kind of wit, "by means of which some, without art or study, speak such subtle and surprising things, yet true, that were never before seen, heard, or writ, no, nor ever so much as thought of." The reference here is to true creativity, an exercise of the creative imagination in ways that go beyond normal intelligence and may, he felt, involve "a mixture of madness."

Huarte maintains that the distinction between docile wit, which meets the empiricist maxim, and normal intelligence, with its full generative capacities, is the distinction between beast and man. As a physician, Huarte was much interested in pathology. In particular, he notes that the most severe disability of wit that can afflict a human is a restriction to the lowest of the three levels, to the docile wit that conforms to empiricist principles. This disability, says Huarte, "resembles that of Eunuchs, incapable of generation." Under these sad circumstances, in which the intelligence can only receive stimuli transmitted by sense and associate them with one another, true education is of course impossible, since the ideas and principles that permit the growth of knowledge and understanding are lacking. In this case, then, "neither the lash of the rod, nor cries, nor method, nor examples, nor time, nor experience, nor anything in nature can sufficiently excite him to bring forth anything."

Huarte's framework is useful for discussing "psychological theory" in the ensuing period. Typical of later thought is his reference to use of language as an index of human intelligence, of what distinguishes man from animals, and, specifically, his emphasis on the creative capacity of normal intelligence. These concerns dominated rationalist psychology and linguistics. With the rise of romanticism, attention shifted to the third type of wit, to true creativity, although the rationalist assumption that normal human intelligence is uniquely free and creative and beyond the bounds of mechanical explanation was not abandoned and played an important role in the psychology of romanticism, and even in its social philosophy.

As I have already mentioned, the rationalist theory of language, which was to prove extremely rich in insight and achievement, developed in part out of a concern with the problem of other minds. A fair amount of effort was devoted to a consideration of the ability of animals to follow spoken commands, to express their emotional states, to communicate with one another, and even apparently to cooperate for a common goal; all of this, it was argued, could be accounted for on "mechanical grounds," as this notion was then understood—that is, through the functioning of physiological mechanisms in terms of which one could formulate the properties of reflexes, conditioning and reinforcement, association, and so on. Animals do not lack appropriate organs of communication, nor are they simply lower along some scale of "general intelligence."

In fact, as Descartes himself quite correctly observed, language is a species-specific human possession, and even at low levels of intelligence, at pathological levels, we find a command of language that is totally unattainable by an ape that may, in other respects, surpass a human imbecile in problem-solving ability and other adaptive behavior. I will return later to the status of this observation, in the light of what is now known about animal communication. There is a basic element lacking in animals, Descartes argued, as it is lacking in even the most complex automaton that develops its "intellectual structures" completely in terms of conditioning and association—namely Huarte's second type of wit, the generative ability that is revealed in the normal human use of language as a free instrument of thought. If by experiment we convince ourselves that another organism gives evidence of the normal, creative use of language, we must suppose that it, like us, has a mind and that what it does lies beyond the bounds of mechanical explanation, outside the framework of the stimulus-response psychology of the time, which in relevant essentials is not significantly different from that of today, though it falls short in sharpness of technique and scope and reliability of information.

It should not be thought, incidentally, that the only Cartesian arguments for the beast-machine hypothesis were those derived from the apparent inability of animals to manifest the creative aspect of language use. There were also many others—for example, the natural fear of population explosion in the domains of the spirit if every gnat had a soul. Or the argument of Cardinal Melchior de Polignac, who argued that the beast-machine hypothesis followed from the assumption of the goodness of God, since, as he pointed out, one can see "how much more humane is the doctrine that animals suffer no pain." Or there is the argument of Louis Racine, son of the dramatist, who was struck by the following insight: "If beasts had souls and were capable of feelings, would they show themselves insensible to the affront and injustice done them by Descartes? Would they not rather have risen up in wrath against the leader and the sect which so degraded them?" One should add, I suppose, that Louis Racine was regarded by his contemporaries as the living proof that a brilliant father could not have a brilliant son. But the fact is that the discussion of the existence of other minds, and, in contrast, the mechanical nature of animals, continually returned to the creative aspect of language use, to the claim that—as formulated by another minor seventeenth-century figure—"if beasts reasoned, they would be capable of true speech with its infinite variety."

It is important to understand just what properties of language were most striking to Descartes and his followers. The discussion of what I have been calling "the creative aspect of language use" turns on three important observations. The first is that the normal use of language is innovative, in the sense that much of what we say in the course of normal language use is entirely new, not a repetition of anything that we have heard before and not even similar in pattern—in any useful sense of the terms "similar" and "pattern"—to sentences or discourse that we have heard in the past. This is a truism, but an important one, often overlooked and not infrequently denied in the behaviorist period of linguistics to which I referred earlier, when it was almost universally claimed that a person's knowledge of language is representable as a stored set of patterns, overlearned through constant repetition and detailed training, with innovation being at most a matter of "analogy." The fact surely is, however, that the number of sentences in one's native language that one will immediately understand with no feeling of difficulty or strangeness is astronomical; and that the number of patterns underlying our normal use of language and corresponding to meaningful and easily comprehensible sentences in our language is orders of magnitude greater than the number of seconds in a lifetime. It is in this sense that the normal use of language is innovative.

However, in the Cartesian view even animal behavior is potentially infinite in its variety, in the special sense in which the readings of a speedometer can be said, with an obvious idealization, to be potentially infinite in variety. That is, if animal behavior is controlled by external stimuli or internal states (the latter including those established by conditioning), then as the stimuli vary over an indefinite range, so may the behavior of the animal. But the normal use of language is not only innovative and potentially infinite in scope, but also free from the control of detectable stimuli, either external or internal. It is because of this freedom from stimulus control that language can serve as an instrument of thought and self-expression, as it does not only for the exceptionally gifted and talented, but also, in fact, for every normal human.

Still, the properties of being unbounded and free from stimulus control do not, in themselves, exceed the bounds of mechanical explanation. And Cartesian discussion of the limits of mechanical explanation therefore took note of a third property of the normal use of language, namely its coherence and its "appropriateness to the situation"—which of course is an entirely different matter from control by external stimuli. Just what "appropriateness" and "coherence" may consist in we cannot say in any clear or definite way, but there is no doubt that these are meaningful concepts.

We can distinguish normal use of language from the ravings of a maniac or the output of a computer with a random element.

Honesty forces us to admit that we are as far today as Descartes was three centuries ago from understanding just what enables a human to speak in a way that is innovative, free from stimulus control, and also appropriate and coherent. This is a serious problem that the psychologist and biologist must ultimately face and that cannot be talked out of existence by invoking "habit" or "conditioning" or "natural selection."

. . .

It is quite natural to expect that a concern for language will remain central to the study of human nature, as it has been in the past. Anyone concerned with the study of human nature and human capacities must somehow come to grips with the fact that all normal humans acquire language, whereas acquisition of even its barest rudiments is quite beyond the capacities of an otherwise intelligent ape—a fact that was emphasized, quite correctly, in Cartesian philosophy. It is widely thought that the extensive modern studies of animal communication challenge this classical view; and it is almost universally taken for granted that there exists a problem of explaining the "evolution" of human language from systems of animal communication. However, a careful look at recent studies of animal communication seems to me to provide little support for these assumptions. Rather, these studies simply bring out even more clearly the extent to which human language appears to be a unique phenomenon, without significant analogue in the animal world. If this is so, it is quite senseless to raise the problem of explaining the evolution of human language from more primitive systems of communication that appear at lower levels of intellectual capacity. The issue is important, and I would like to dwell on it for a moment.

The assumption that human language evolved from more primitive systems is developed in an interesting way by Karl Popper in his recently published Arthur Compton Lecture, "Clouds and Clocks." He tries to show how problems of freedom of will and Cartesian dualism can be solved by the analysis of this "evolution." I am not concerned now with the philosophical conclusions that he draws from this analysis, but with the basic assumption that there is an evolutionary development of language from simpler systems of the sort that one discovers in other organisms. Popper argues that the evolution of language passed through several stages, in particular a "lower stage" in which vocal gestures are used for expression of emotional state, for example, and a "higher stage" in which articulated sound is used for expression of thought—in Popper's terms, for description and critical argument. His discussion of stages of evolution of language suggests a kind of continuity, but in fact he establishes no relation between the lower and higher stages and does not suggest a mechanism whereby transition can take place from one stage to the next. In short, he gives no argument to show that the stages belong to a single evolutionary process. In fact, it is difficult to see what links these stages at all (except for the metaphorical use of the term "language"). There is no reason to suppose that the "gaps" are bridgeable. There is no more of a basis for assuming an evolutionary development of "higher" from "lower" stages, in this case, than there is for assuming an evolutionary development from breathing to walking; the stages have no significant analogy, it appears, and seem to involve entirely different processes and principles.

A more explicit discussion of the relation between human language and animal communication systems appears in a recent discussion by the comparative ethologist W. H. Thorpe. He points out that mammals other than man appear to lack the human ability to imitate sounds, and that one might therefore have expected birds (many of which have this ability to a remarkable extent) to be "the group which ought to have been able to evolve language in the true sense, and not the mammals." Thorpe does not suggest that human language "evolved" in any strict sense from simpler systems, but he does argue that the characteristic properties of human language can be found in animal communication systems, although "we cannot at the moment say definitely that they are all present in one particular animal." The characteristics shared by human and animal language are the properties of being "purposive," "syntactic," and "propositional." Language is purposive "in that there is nearly always in human speech a definite intention of getting something over to somebody else, altering his behavior, his thoughts, or his general attitude toward a situation." Human language is "syntactic" in that an utterance is a performance with an internal organization, with structure and coherence. It is "propositional" in that it transmits information. In this sense, then, both human language and animal communication are purposive, syntactic, and propositional.

All this may be true, but it establishes very little, since when we move to the level of abstraction at which human language and animal communication fall together, almost all other behavior is included as well. Consider walking: Clearly, walking is purposive behavior, in the most general sense of "purposive." Walking is also "syntactic" in the sense just defined. . . . Furthermore, it can certainly be informative; for example, I can signal my interest in reaching a certain goal by the speed or intensity with which I walk.

It is, incidentally, precisely in this manner that the examples of animal communication that Thorpe presents are "propositional." He cites as an example the song of the European robin, in which the rate of alternation of high and low pitch signals the intention of the bird to defend its territory; the higher the rate of alternation, the greater the intention to defend the territory. The example is interesting, but it seems to me to show very clearly the hopelessness of the attempt to relate human language to animal communication. Every animal communication system that is known (if we disregard some science fiction about dolphins) uses one of two basic principles: Either it consists of a fixed, finite number of signals, each associated with a specific range of behavior or emotional state, as is illustrated in the extensive primate studies that have been carried out by Japanese scientists for the past several years; or it makes use of a fixed, finite number of linguistic dimensions, each of which is associated with a particular nonlinguistic dimension in such a way that selection of a point along the linguistic dimension determines and signals a certain point along the associated nonlinguistic dimension. The latter is the principle realized in Thorpe's bird-song example. Rate of alternation of high and low pitch is a linguistic dimension correlated with the nonlinguistic dimension of intention to defend a territory. The bird signals its intention to defend a territory by selecting a correlated point along the linguistic dimension of pitch alternation—I use the word "select" loosely, of course. The linguistic dimension is abstract, but the principle is clear. A communication system of the second type has an indefinitely large range of potential signals, as does human language. The mechanism and principle, however, are entirely different from those employed by human language to express indefinitely many new thoughts, intentions, feelings, and so on. It is not correct to speak of a "deficiency" of the animal system, in terms of range of potential signals; rather the opposite, since the animal system admits in principle of continuous variation along the linguistic dimension (insofar as it makes sense to speak of "continuity" in such a case), whereas human language is discrete. Hence, the issue is not one of "more" or "less," but rather of an entirely different principle of organization. When I make some arbitrary statement in a human language, say, that "the rise of supranational corporations poses new dangers for human freedom," I am not selecting a point along some linguistic dimension that signals a corresponding point along an associated nonlinguistic dimension, nor am I selecting a signal from a finite behavioral repertoire, innate or learned.

Furthermore, it is wrong to think of human use of language as characteristically informative, in fact or in intention. Human language can be used to inform or mislead, to clarify one's own thoughts or to display one's cleverness, or simply for play. If I speak with no concern for modifying your behavior or thoughts, I am not using language any less than if I say exactly the same things *with* such intention. If we hope to understand human language and the psychological capacities on which it rests, we must first ask what it is, not how or for what purposes it is used. When we ask what human language is, we find no striking similarity to animal communication systems. There is nothing useful to be said about behavior or thought at the level of abstraction at which animal and human communication fall together. The examples of animal communication that have been examined to date do share many of the properties of human gestural systems, and it might be reasonable to explore the possibility of direct connection in this case. But human language, it appears, is based on entirely different principles. This, I think, is an important point, often overlooked by those who approach human language as a natural, biological phenomenon; in particular, it seems rather pointless, for these reasons, to speculate about the evolution of human language from simpler systems—perhaps as absurd as it would be to speculate about the "evolution" of atoms from clouds of elementary particles.

As far as we know, possession of human language is associated with a specific type of mental organization, not simply a higher degree of intelligence. There seems to be no substance to the view that human language is simply a more complex instance of something to be found elsewhere in the animal world. This poses a problem for the biologist, since, if true, it is an example of true "emergence"—the appearance of a qualitatively different phenomenon at a specific stage of complexity of organization. Recognition of this fact, though formulated in entirely different terms, is what motivated much of the classical study of language by those whose primary concern was the nature of mind. And it seems to me that today there is no better or more promising way to explore the essential and distinctive properties of human intelligence than through the detailed investigation of the structure of this unique human possession. A reasonable guess, then, is that if empirically adequate generative grammars can be constructed and the universal principles that govern their structure and organization determined, then this will be an important contribution to human psychology, in ways to which I will turn directly, in detail.

In the course of these lectures I have mentioned some of the classical ideas regarding language structure and contemporary efforts to deepen and extend them. It seems clear that we must regard linguistic competence—knowledge of a language —as an abstract system underlying behavior, a system constituted by rules that interact to determine the form and intrinsic meaning of a potentially infinite number of sentences. Such a system—a generative grammar—provides an explication of the Humboldtian idea of "form of language," which in an obscure but suggestive remark in his great posthumous work, *Über die Verschiedenheit des Menschlichen Sprachbaues,* Humboldt defines as "that constant and unvarying system of processes underlying the mental act of raising articulated structurally organized signals to an expression of thought." Such a grammar defines a language in the Humboldtian sense, namely as "a recursively generated system, where the laws of generation are fixed and invariant, but the scope and the specific manner in which they are applied remain entirely unspecified."

In each such grammar there are particular, idiosyncratic elements, selection of which determines one specific human language; and there are general universal elements, conditions on the form and organization of any human language, that form the subject matter for the study of "universal grammar." Among the principles of universal grammar are those I discussed in the preceding lecture—for example, the principles that distinguish deep and surface structure and that constrain the class of transformational operations that relate them. Notice, incidentally, that the existence of definite principles of universal grammar makes possible the rise of the new field of mathematical linguistics, a field that submits to abstract study the class of generative systems meeting the conditions set forth in universal grammar. This inquiry aims to elaborate the formal properties of any possible human language. The field is in its infancy; it is only in the last decade that the possibility of such an enterprise has been envisioned. It has some promising initial results, and it suggests one possible direction for future research that might prove to be of great importance. Thus, mathematical linguistics seems for the moment to be in a uniquely favorable position, among mathematical approaches in the social and psychological sciences, to develop not simply as a theory of data, but as the study of highly abstract principles and structures that determine the character of human mental processes. In this case, the mental processes in question are those involved in the organization of one specific domain of human knowledge, namely knowledge of language.

· · ·

Are there other areas of human competence where one might hope to develop a fruitful theory, analogous to generative grammar? Although this is a very important question, there is very little that can be said about it today. One might, for example, consider the problem of how a person comes to acquire a certain concept of three-dimensional space, or an implicit "theory of human action," in similar terms. Such a study would begin with the attempt to characterize the implicit theory that underlies actual performance and would then turn to the question of how this theory develops under the given conditions of time and access to data— that is, in what way the resulting system of beliefs is determined by the interplay of available data, "heuristic procedures," and the innate schematism that restricts and conditions the form of the acquired system. At the moment, this is nothing more than a sketch of a program of research.

There have been some attempts to study the structure of other, language-like systems—the study of kinship systems and folk taxonomies comes to mind, for example. But so far, at least, nothing has been discovered that is even roughly comparable to language in these domains.

. . .

Surely the classical questions of language and mind receive no final solution, or even the hint of a final solution, from the work that is being actively pursued today. Nevertheless, these problems can be formulated in new ways and seen in a new light. For the first time in many years, it seems to me, there is some real opportunity for substantial progress in the study of the contribution of the mind to perception and the innate basis for acquisition of knowledge. Still, in many respects, we have not made the first approach to a real answer to the classical problems. For example, the central problems relating to the creative aspect of language use remain as inaccessible as they have always been. And the study of universal semantics, surely crucial to the full investigation of language structure, has barely advanced since the medieval period. Many other critical areas might be mentioned where progress has been slow or nonexistent. Real progress has been made in the study of the mechanisms of language, the formal principles that make possible the creative aspect of language use and that determine the phonetic form and semantic content of utterances. Our understanding of these mechanisms, though only fragmentary, does seem to me to have real implications for the study of human psychology. By pursuing the kinds of research that now seem feasible and by focusing attention on certain problems that are now accessible to study, we may be able to spell out in some detail the elaborate and abstract computations that determine, in part, the nature of percepts and the character of the knowledge that we can acquire —the highly specific ways of interpreting phenomena that are, in large measure, beyond our consciousness and control and that may be unique to man.

Language, Mind,

and World

DAVID HUME

The Passive Mind: Custom and Convention

David Hume also is represented by his preceding articles on
freedom and on personal identity.

Though it be too obvious to escape observation, that different ideas are connected
together; I do not find that any philosopher has attempted to enumerate or class
all the principles of association; a subject, however, that seems worthy of curiosity.
To me, there appear to be only three principles of connexion among ideas, namely,
Resemblance, Contiguity in time or place, and *Cause* or *Effect.*

That these principles serve to connect ideas will not, I believe, be much doubted.
A picture naturally leads our thoughts to the original:[1] the mention of one apart-
ment in a building naturally introduces an enquiry or discourse concerning the
others:[2] and if we think of a wound, we can scarcely forbear reflecting on the pain
which follows it.[3] But that this enumeration is complete, and that there are no
other principles of association except these, may be difficult to prove to the satisfaction of the reader, or even to a man's own satisfaction. All we can do, in such cases,
is to run over several instances, and examine carefully the principle which binds the
different thoughts to each other, never stopping till we render the principle as
general as possible.[4] The more instances we examine, and the more care we employ,
the more assurance shall we acquire, that the enumeration, which we form from the
whole, is complete and entire.

SCEPTICAL DOUBTS CONCERNING THE OPERATIONS
OF THE UNDERSTANDING

All the objects of human reason or enquiry may naturally be divided into two kinds,
to wit, *Relations of Ideas,* and *Matters of Fact.* Of the first kind are the sciences of
Geometry, Algebra, and Arithmetic; and in short, every affirmation which is either
intuitively or demonstratively certain. *That the square of the hypothenuse is equal*

From *Essay Concerning Human Understanding,* by David Hume, 1768.

[1] Resemblance.

[2] Contiguity.

[3] Cause and effect.

[4] For instance, Contrast or Contrariety is also a connexion among Ideas, but it may, perhaps, be
considered as a mixture of *Causation* and *Resemblance.* Where two objects are contrary, the one destroys
the other; that is, the cause of its annihilation, and the idea of the annihilation of an object implies the
idea of its former existence.

to the squares of the two sides, is a proposition which expresses a relation between these figures. *That three times five is equal to the half of thirty,* expresses a relation between these numbers. Propositions of this kind are discoverable by the mere operation of thought, without dependence on what is anywhere existent in the universe. Though there never were a circle or triangle in nature, the truths demonstrated by Euclid would for ever retain their certainty and evidence.

Matters of fact, which are the second objects of human reason, are not ascertained in the same manner; nor is our evidence of their truth, however great, of a like nature with the foregoing. The contrary of every matter of fact is still possible; because it can never imply a contradiction, and is conceived by the mind with the same facility and distinctness, as if ever so conformable to reality. *That the sun will not rise to-morrow* is no less intelligible a proposition, and implies no more contradiction than the affirmation, *that it will rise.* We should in vain, therefore, attempt to demonstrate its falsehood. Were it demonstratively false, it would imply a contradiction, and could never be distinctly conceived by the mind.

It may, therefore, be a subject worthy of curiosity, to enquire what is the nature of that evidence which assures us of any real existence and matter of fact, beyond the present testimony of our senses, or the records of our memory. This part of philosophy, it is observable, has been little cultivated, either by the ancients or moderns; and therefore our doubts and errors, in the prosecution of so important an enquiry, may be the more excusable; while we march through such difficult paths without any guide or direction. They may even prove useful, by exciting curiosity, and destroying that implicit faith and security, which is the bane of all reasoning and free enquiry. The discovery of defects in the common philosophy, if any such there be, will not, I presume, be a discouragement, but rather an incitement, as is usual, to attempt something more full and satisfactory than has yet been proposed to the public.

All reasonings concerning matter of fact seem to be founded on the relation of *Cause and Effect.* By means of that relation alone we can go beyond the evidence of our memory and senses. If you were to ask a man, why he believes any matter of fact, which is absent; for instance, that his friend is in the country, or in France; he would give you a reason; and this reason would be some other fact; as a letter received from him, or the knowledge of his former resolutions and promises. A man finding a watch or any other machine in a desert island, would conclude that there had once been men in that island. All our reasonings concerning fact are of the same nature. And here it is constantly supposed that there is a connexion between the present fact and that which is inferred from it. Were there nothing to bind them together, the inference would be entirely precarious. The hearing of an articulate voice and rational discourse in the dark assures us of the presence of some person: Why? because these are the effects of the human make and fabric, and closely connected with it. If we anatomize all the other reasonings of this nature, we shall find that they are founded on the relation of cause and effect, and that this relation is either near or remote, direct or collateral. Heat and light are collateral effects of fire, and the one effect may justly be inferred from the other.

If we would satisfy ourselves, therefore, concerning the nature of that evidence, which assures us of matters of fact, we must enquire how we arrive at the knowledge of cause and effect.

I shall venture to affirm, as a general proposition, which admits of no exception, that the knowledge of this relation is not, in any instance, attained by reasonings *a priori;* but arises entirely from experience, when we find that any particular objects are constantly conjoined with each other. Let an object be presented to a man of ever so strong natural reason and abilities; if that object be entirely new to him, he will not be able, by the most accurate examination of its sensible qualities, to discover any of its causes or effects. Adam, though his rational faculties be supposed, at the very first, entirely perfect, could not have inferred from the fluidity and transparency of water that it would suffocate him, or from the light and warmth of fire that it would consume him. No object ever discovers, by the qualities which appear to the senses, either the causes which produced it, or the effects which will arise from it; nor can our reason, unassisted by experience, ever draw any inference concerning real existence and matter of fact.

This proposition, that *causes and effects are discoverable, not by reason but by experience,* will readily be admitted with regard to such objects, as we remember to have once been altogether unknown to us; since we must be conscious of the utter inability, which we then lay under, of foretelling what would arise from them. Present two smooth pieces of marble to a man who has no tincture of natural philosophy; he will never discover that they will adhere together in such a manner as to require great force to separate them in a direct line, while they make so small a resistance to a lateral pressure. Such events, as bear little analogy to the common course of nature, are also readily confessed to be known only by experience; nor does any man imagine that the explosion of gunpowder, or the attraction of a loadstone, could ever be discovered by arguments *a priori.* In like manner, when an effect is supposed to depend upon an intricate machinery or secret structure of parts, we make no difficulty in attributing all our knowledge of it to experience. Who will assert that he can give the ultimate reason, why milk or bread is proper nourishment for a man, not for a lion or a tiger?

But the same truth may not appear, at first sight, to have the same evidence with regard to events, which have become familiar to us from our first appearance in the world, which bear a close analogy to the whole course of nature, and which are supposed to depend on the simple qualities of objects, without any secret structure of parts. We are apt to imagine that we could discover these effects by the mere operation of our reason, without experience. We fancy, that were we brought on a sudden into this world, we could at first have inferred that one Billiard-ball would communicate motion to another upon impulse; and that we needed not to have waited for the event, in order to pronounce with certainty concerning it. Such is the influence of custom, that, where it is strongest, it not only covers our natural ignorance, but even conceals itself, and seems not to take place, merely because it is found in the highest degree.

But to convince us that all the laws of nature, and all the operations of bodies without exception, are known only by experience, the following reflections may, perhaps, suffice. Were any object presented to us, and were we required to pronounce concerning the effect, which will result from it, without consulting past observation; after what manner, I beseech you, must the mind proceed in this operation? It must invent or imagine some event, which it ascribes to the object as its effect; and it is plain that this invention must be entirely arbitrary. The mind can never possibly find the effect in the supposed cause, by the most accurate scrutiny and examination. For the effect is totally different from the cause, and consequently can never be discovered in it. Motion in the second Billiard-ball is a quite distinct event from motion in the first: nor is there anything in the one to suggest the smallest hint of the other. A stone or piece of metal raised into the air, and left without any support, immediately falls; but to consider the matter *a priori,* is there anything we discover in this situation which can beget the idea of a downward, rather than an upward, or any other motion, in the stone or metal?

And as the first imagination or invention of a particular effect, in all natural operations, is arbitrary, where we consult not experience; so must we also esteem the supposed tie or connexion between the cause and effect, which binds them together, and renders it impossible that any other effect could result from the operation of that cause. When I see, for instance, a Billiard-ball moving in a straight line towards another; even suppose motion in the second ball should by accident be suggested to me, as the result of their contact or impulse; may I not conceive, that a hundred different events might as well follow from that cause? May not both these balls remain at absolute rest? May not the first ball return in a straight line, or leap off from the second in any line or direction? All these suppositions are consistent and conceivable. Why then should we give the preference to one, which is no more consistent or conceivable than the rest? All our reasonings *a priori* will never be able to show us any foundation for this preference.

In a word, then, every effect is a distinct event from its cause. It could not, therefore, be discovered in the cause, and the first invention or conception of it, *a priori,* must be entirely arbitrary. And even after it is suggested, the conjunction of it with the cause must appear equally arbitrary; since there are always many other effects, which, to reason, must seem fully as consistent and natural. In vain, therefore, should we pretend to determine any single event, or infer any cause or effect, without the assistance of observation and experience.

· · ·

But we have not yet attained any tolerable satisfaction with regard to the question first proposed. Each solution still gives rise to a new question as difficult as the foregoing, and leads us on to farther enquiries. When it is asked, *What is the nature of all our reasonings concerning matter of fact?* the proper answer seems to be, that they are founded on the relation of cause and effect. When again it is asked, *What is the foundation of all our reasonings and conclusions concerning that relation?* it may be replied in one word, Experience. But if we still carry on our sifting humour, and ask, *What is the foundation of all conclusions from experience?* this implies a new question, which may be of more difficult solution and explication.

· · ·

Suppose a person, though endowed with the strongest faculties of reason and reflection, to be brought on a sudden into this world; he would, indeed, immediately observe a continual succession of objects, and one event following another; but he would not be able to discover anything farther. He would not, at first, by any reasoning, be able to reach the idea of cause and effect; since the particular powers, by which all natural operations are performed, never appear to the senses; nor is it reasonable to conclude, merely because one event, in one instance, precedes another, that therefore the one is the cause, the other the effect. Their conjunction may be arbitrary and casual. There may be no reason to infer the existence of one from the appearance of the other. And in a word, such a person, without more experience, could never employ his conjecture or reasoning concerning any matter of fact, or be assured of anything beyond what was immediately present to his memory and senses.

Suppose, again, that he has acquired more experience, and has lived so long in the world as to have observed familiar objects or events to be constantly conjoined together; what is the consequence of this experience? He immediately infers the existence of one object from the appearance of the other. Yet he has not, by all his experience, acquired any idea or knowledge of the secret power by which the one object produces the other; nor is it, by any process of reasoning, he is engaged to draw this inference. But still he finds himself determined to draw it: And though he should be convinced that his understanding has no part in the operation, he would nevertheless continue in the same course of thinking. There is some other principle which determines him to form such a conclusion.

This principle is Custom or Habit. For wherever the repetition of any particular act or operation produces a propensity to renew the same act or operation, without being impelled by any reasoning or process of the understanding, we always say, that this propensity is the effect of *Custom*. By employing that word, we pretend not to have given the ultimate reason of such a propensity. We only point out a principle of human nature, which is universally acknowledged, and which is well known by its effects. Perhaps we can push our enquiries no farther, or pretend to give the cause of this cause; but must rest contented with it as the ultimate principle, which we can assign, of all our conclusions from experience. It is sufficient satisfaction, that we can go so far, without repining at the narrowness of our faculties because they will carry us no farther. And it is certain we here advance a very intelligible proposition at least, if not a true one, when we assert that, after the constant conjunction of two objects—heat and flame, for instance, weight and solidity—we are determined by custom alone to expect the one from the appearance of the other. This hypothesis seems even the only one which explains the difficulty, why we draw, from a thousand instances, an inference which we are not able to draw from one instance, that is, in no respect, different from them. Reason is incapable of any such variation. The conclusions which it draws from considering one circle are the same which it would form upon surveying all the circles in the universe. But no man, having seen only one body move after being impelled by another, could infer that every other body will move after a like impulse. All inferences from experience, therefore, are effects of custom, not of reasoning.

IMMANUEL KANT

The Active Mind: The Judgments of Experience

Another selection from Immanuel Kant appears in Section I, "The Primacy of the Person."

There can be no doubt that all our knowledge begins with experience. For how should our faculty of knowledge be awakened into action did not objects affecting our senses partly of themselves produce representations, partly arouse the activity of our understanding to compare these representations, and, by combining or separating them, work up the raw material of the sensible impressions into that knowledge of objects which is entitled experience? In the order of time, therefore, we have no knowledge antecedent to experience, and with experience all our knowledge begins.

But though all our knowledge begins with experience, it does not follow that it all arises out of experience. For it may well be that even our empirical knowledge is made up of what we receive through impressions and of what our own faculty of knowledge (sensible impressions serving merely as the occasion) supplies from itself. If our faculty of knowledge makes any such addition, it may be that we are not in a position to distinguish it from the raw material, until with long practice of attention we have become skilled in separating it.

This, then, is a question which at least calls for closer examinations, and does not allow of any off-hand answer:—whether there is any knowledge that is thus independent of experience and even of all impressions of the senses. Such knowledge is entitled *a priori,* and distinguished from the *empirical,* which has its sources *a posteriori,* that is, in experience.

The expression '*a priori*' does not, however, indicate with sufficient precision the full meaning of our question. For it has been customary to say, even of much knowledge that is derived from empirical sources, that we have it or are capable of having it *a priori,* meaning thereby that we do not derive it immediately from experience, but from a universal rule—a rule which is itself, however, borrowed by us from experience. Thus we would say of a man who undermined the foundations of his house, that he might have known *a priori* that it would fall, that is, that he need not have waited for the experience of its actual falling. But still he could not know this completely *a priori.* For he had first to learn through experience that bodies are heavy, and therefore fall when their supports are withdrawn.

In what follows, therefore, we shall understand by *a priori* knowledge, not

From *The Critique of Pure Reason,* by Immanuel Kant, translated by Norman Kemp Smith, 1929. Reprinted by permission of St. Martin's Press Inc., The Macmillan Company of Canada Ltd., and Macmillan & Co., Ltd.

knowledge independent of this or that experience, but knowledge absolutely in-dependent of all experience. Opposed to it is empirical knowledge, which is knowl-edge possible only *a posteriori,* that is, through experience. *A priori* modes of knowledge are entitled pure when there is no admixture of anything empirical. Thus, for instance, the proposition, 'every alteration has its cause', while an *a priori* proposition, is not a pure proposition, because alteration is a concept which can be derived only from experience.

WE ARE IN POSSESSION OF CERTAIN MODES OF *A PRIORI* KNOWLEDGE, AND EVEN THE COMMON UNDERSTANDING IS NEVER WITHOUT THEM

What we here require is a criterion by which to distinguish with certainty between pure and empirical knowledge. Experience teaches us that a thing is so and so, but not that it cannot be otherwise. First, then, if we have a proposition which in being thought is thought as *necessary,* it is an *a priori* judgment; and if, besides, it is not derived from any proposition except one which also has the validity of a neces-sary judgment, it is an absolutely *a priori* judgment. Secondly, experience never confers on its judgments true or strict, but only assumed and comparative *univer-sality,* through induction. We can properly only say, therefore, that, so far as we have hitherto observed, there is no exception to this or that rule. If, then, a judgment is thought with strict universality, that is, in such manner that no exception is allowed as possible, it is not derived from experience, but is valid absolutely *a priori.* Empirical universality is only an arbitrary extension of a validity holding in most cases to one which holds in all, for instance, in the proposition, 'all bodies are heavy'. When, on the other hand, strict universality is essential to a judgment, this indicates a special source of knowledge, namely, a faculty of *a priori* knowledge. Necessity and strict universality are thus sure criteria of *a priori* knowledge, and are inseparable from one another. But since in the employment of these criteria the contingency of judgments is sometimes more easily shown than their empirical limitation, or, as sometimes also happens, their unlimited universality can be more convincingly proved than their necessity, it is advisable to use the two criteria separately, each by itself being infallible.

Now it is easy to show that there actually are in human knowledge judgments which are necessary and in the strictest sense universal, and which are therefore pure *a priori* judgments. If an example from the sciences be desired, we have only to look to any of the propositions of mathematics; if we seek an example from the understanding in its quite ordinary employment, the proposition, 'every alteration must have a cause', will serve our purpose. In the latter case, indeed, the very con-cept of a cause so manifestly contains the concept of a necessity of connection with an effect and of the strict universality of the rule, that the concept would be alto-gether lost if we attempted to derive it, as Hume has done, from a repeated associ-ation of that which happens with that which precedes, and from a custom of connecting representations, a custom originating in this repeated association, and constituting therefore a merely subjective necessity. Even without appealing to such examples, it is possible to show that pure *a priori* principles are indispensable for the possibility of experience, and so to prove their existence *a priori.* For whence could experience derive its certainty, if all the rules, according to which it proceeds, were always themselves empirical, and therefore contingent? Such rules could hardly be regarded as first principles. At present, however, we may be content to have established the fact that our faculty of knowledge does have a pure employment, and to have shown what are the criteria of such an employment.

Such *a priori* origin is manifest in certain concepts, no less than in judgments. If we remove from our empirical concept of a body, one by one, every feature in it which is [merely] empirical, the colour, the hardness or softness, the weight, even the impenetrability, there still remains the space which the body (now entirely vanished) occupied, and this cannot be removed. Again, if we remove from our empirical concept of any object, corporeal or incorporeal, all properties which experience has taught us, we yet cannot take away that property through which the object is thought as substance or as inhering in a substance (although this concept of substance is more determinate than that of an object in general). Owing, therefore, to the necessity with which this concept of substance forces itself upon us, we have no option save to admit that it has its seat in our faculty of *a priori* knowledge.

PHILOSOPHY STANDS IN NEED OF A SCIENCE WHICH SHALL DETERMINE THE POSSIBILITY, THE PRINCIPLES, AND THE EXTENT OF ALL *A PRIORI* KNOWLEDGE

But what is still more extraordinary than all the preceding is this, that certain modes of knowledge leave the field of all possible experiences and have the appearance of extending the scope of our judgments beyond all limits of experience, and this by means of concepts to which no corresponding object can ever be given in experience.

It is precisely by means of the latter modes of knowledge, in a realm beyond the world of the senses, where experience can yield neither guidance nor correction, that our reason carries on those enquiries which owing to their importance we consider to be far more excellent, and in their purpose far more lofty, than all that the understanding can learn in the field of appearances. Indeed we prefer to run every risk of error rather than desist from such urgent enquiries, on the ground of their dubious character, or from disdain and indifference. These unavoidable problems set by pure reason itself are *God, freedom,* and *immortality*. The science which, with all its preparations, is in its final intention directed solely to their solution is metaphysics; and its procedure is at first dogmatic, that is, it confidently sets itself to this task without any previous examination of the capacity or incapacity of reason for so great an undertaking.

Now it does indeed seem natural that, as soon as we have left the ground of experience, we should, through careful enquiries, assure ourselves as to the foundations of any building that we propose to erect, not making use of any knowledge that we possess without first determining whence it has come, and not trusting to principles without knowing their origin. It is natural, that is to say, that the question should first be considered, how the understanding can arrive at all this knowledge *a priori*, and what extent, validity, and worth it may have. Nothing, indeed, could be more natural, if by the term 'natural' we signify what fittingly and reasonably ought to happen. But if we mean by 'natural' what ordinarily happens, then on the contrary nothing is more natural and more intelligible than the fact that this enquiry has been so long neglected. For one part of this knowledge, the mathematical, has long been of established reliability, and so gives rise to a favourable presumption as regards the other part, which may yet be of quite different nature. Besides, once we are outside the circle of experience, we can be sure of not being *contradicted* by experience. The charm of extending our knowledge is so great that nothing short of encountering a direct contradiction can suffice to arrest us in our cause; and this can be avoided, if we are careful in our fabrications—which none the less will still remain fabrications. Mathematics gives us a shining example of how far, independently of experience, we can progress in *a priori* knowledge. It does, indeed, occupy itself with objects and with knowledge solely in so far as they allow of being exhibited in intuition. But this circumstance is easily overlooked, since this intuition can itself be given *a priori*, and is therefore hardly to be distinguished from a bare and pure concept. Misled by such a proof of the power of reason, the demand for the extension of knowledge recognises no limits. The light dove, cleaving the air in her free flight, and feeling its resistance, might imagine that its flight would be still easier in empty space. It was thus that Plato left the world of the senses, as setting too narrow limits to the understanding, and ventured out beyond it on the wings of the ideas, in the empty space of the pure understanding. He did not observe that with all his efforts he made no advance—meeting no resistance that might, as it were, serve as a support upon which he could take a stand, to which he could apply his powers, and so set his understanding in motion. It is, indeed, the common fate of human reason to complete its speculative structures as speedily as may be, and only afterwards to enquire whether the foundations are reliable. All sorts of excuses will then be appealed to, in order to reassure us of their solidity, or rather indeed to enable us to dispense altogether with so late and so dangerous an enquiry. But what keeps us, during the actual building, free from all apprehension and suspicion, and flatters us with a seeming thoroughness, is this other circumstance, namely, that a great, perhaps the greatest, part of the business of our reason consists in analysis of the concepts which we already have of objects. This analysis supplies us with a considerable body of knowledge, which, while nothing but explanation or elucidation of what has already been thought in our concepts, though in a confused manner, is yet prized as being, at least as regards its form, new insight. But so far as the matter or content is concerned, there has been no extension of our previously possessed concepts, but only an analysis of them. Since this procedure yields real knowledge *a priori*, which progresses in an assured and useful fashion, reason is so far misled as surreptitiously to introduce, without itself being aware of so doing, assertions of an entirely different order, in which it attaches to given concepts others completely foreign to them, and moreover attaches them *a priori*. And yet it is not known how reason can be in position to do this. Such a question is never so much as thought of. I shall therefore at once proceed to deal with the difference between these two kinds of knowledge.

THE DISTINCTION BETWEEN ANALYTIC AND SYNTHETIC JUDGMENTS

In all judgments in which the relation of a subject to the predicate is thought (I take into consideration affirmative judgments only, the subsequent application to negative judgments being easily made), this relation is possible in two different ways. Either the predicate B belongs to the subject A, as something which is (covertly) contained in this concept A; or B lies outside the concept A, although it does indeed stand in connection with it. In the one case I entitle the judgment analytic, in the other synthetic. Analytic judgments (affirmative) are therefore those in which the connection of the predicate with the subject is thought through identity; those in which this connection is thought without identity should be entitled synthetic. The former, as adding nothing through the predicate to the concept of the subject, but merely breaking it up into those constituent concepts that have all along been thought in it, although confusedly, can also be entitled explicative. The latter, on the other hand, add to the concept of the subject a predicate which has not been in any wise thought in it, and which no analysis could possibly extract from it; and they may therefore be entitled ampliative. If I say, for instance, 'All bodies are extended', this is an analytic judgment. For I do not require to go beyond the concept which I connect with 'body' in order to find extension as bound up with it. To meet with this predicate, I have merely to analyse the concept, that is, to become conscious to myself of the manifold which I always think in that concept. The judgment is therefore analytic. But when I say, 'All bodies are heavy', the predicate is something quite different from anything that I think in the mere concept of body in general; and the addition of such a predicate therefore yields a synthetic judgment.

Judgments of experience, as such, are one and all synthetic. For it would be absurd to found an analytic judgment on experience. Since, in framing the judgment, I must not go outside my concept, there is no need to appeal to the testimony of experience in its support. That a body is extended is a proposition that holds *a priori* and is not empirical. For, before appealing to experience, I have already in the concept of body all the conditions required for my judgment. I have only to extract from it, in accordance with the principle of contradiction, the required predicate, and in so doing can at the same time become conscious of the necessity of the judgment—and that is what experience could never have taught me. On the other hand, though I do not include in the concept of a body in general the predicate 'weight', none the less this concept indicates an object of experience through one of its parts, and I can add to that part other parts of this same experience, as in this way belonging together with the concept. From the start I can apprehend the concept of body analytically through the characters of extension, impenetrability, figure, etc., all of which are thought in the concept. Now, however, looking back on the experience from which I have derived this concept of body, and finding weight to be invariably connected with the above characters, I attach it as a predicate to the concept; and in doing so I attach it synthetically, and am therefore extending my knowledge. The possibility of the synthesis of the predicate 'weight' with the concept of 'body' thus rests upon experience. While the one concept is not contained in the other, they yet belong to one another, though only contingently, as parts of a whole, namely, of an experience which is itself a synthetic combination of intuitions.

But in *a priori* synthetic judgments this help is entirely lacking. [I do not here have the advantage of looking around in the field of experience.] Upon what, then, am I to rely, when I seek to go beyond the concept A, and to know that another concept B is connected with it? Through what is the synthesis made possible? Let us take the proposition, 'Everything which happens has its cause'. In the concept of 'something which happens', I do indeed think an existence which is preceded by a time, etc., and from this concept analytic judgments may be obtained. But the concept of a 'cause' lies entirely outside the other concept, and signifies something different from 'that which happens', and is not therefore in any way contained in this latter representation. How come I then to predicate of that which happens something quite different, and to apprehend that the concepts of cause, though not contained in it, yet belongs, and indeed necessarily belongs, to it? What is here the unknown = X which gives support to the understanding when it believes that it can discover outside the concept A a predicate B foreign to this concept, which it yet at the same time considers to be connected with it? It cannot be experience, because the suggested principle has connected the second representation with the first, not only with greater universality, but also with the character of necessity, and therefore completely *a priori* and on the basis of mere concepts. Upon such synthetic, that is, ampliative principles, all our *a priori* speculative knowledge must ultimately rest; analytic judgments are very important, and indeed necessary, but only for obtaining that clearness in the concepts which is requisite for such a sure and wide synthesis as will lead to a genuinely new addition to all previous knowledge.

IN ALL THEORETICAL SCIENCES OF REASON SYNTHETIC *A PRIORI* JUDGMENTS ARE CONTAINED AS PRINCIPLES

1. *All mathematical judgments, without exception, are synthetic.* This fact, though incontestably certain and in its consequences very important, has hitherto escaped the notice of those who are engaged in the analysis of human reason, and is, indeed, directly opposed to all their conjectures. For as it was found that all mathematical inferences proceed in accordance with the principle of contradiction (which the nature of all apodeictic certainty requires), it was supposed that the fundamental propositions of the science can themselves be known to be true through that principle. This is an erroneous view. For though a synthetic proposition can indeed be discerned in accordance with the principle of contradiction, this can only be if another synthetic proposition is presupposed, and if it can then be apprehended as following from this other proposition; it can never be so discerned in and by itself.

First of all, it has to be noted that mathematical propositions, strictly so called, are always judgments *a priori* not empirical; because they carry with them necessity, which cannot be derived from experience. If this be demurred to, I am willing to limit my statement to *pure* mathematics, the very concept of which implies that it does not contain empirical, but only pure *a priori* knowledge.

We might, indeed, at first suppose that the proposition $7 + 5 = 12$ is a merely analytic proposition, and follows by the principle of contradiction from the concept of a sum of 7 and 5. But if we look more closely we find that the concept of a sum of 7 and 5 contains nothing save the union of the two numbers into one, and in this no thought is being taken as to what that single number may be which combines both. The concept of 12 is by no means already thought in merely thinking this union of 7 and 5; and I may analyse my concept of such a possible sum as long as I please, still I shall never find the 12 in it. We have to go outside these concepts, and call in the aid of the intuition which corresponds to one of them, our five fingers, for instance, or, as Segner does in his *Arithmetic,* five points, adding to the concept of

7, unit by unit, the five given in intuition. For starting with the number 7, and for the concept of 5 calling in the aid of the fingers of my hand as intuition, I now add one by one to the number 7 the units which I previously took together to form the number 5, and with the aid of that figure [the hand] see the number 12 come into being. That 5 should be added to 7, I have indeed already thought in the concept of a sum = 7 + 5, but not that this sum is equivalent to the number 12. Arithmetical propositions are therefore always synthetic. This is still more evident if we take larger numbers. For it is then obvious that, however we might turn and twist our concepts, we could never, by the mere analysis of them, and without the aid of intuition discover what [the number is that] is the sum.

Just as little is any fundamental proposition of pure geometry analytic. That the straight line between two points is the shortest, is a synthetic proposition. For my concept of *straight* contains nothing of quantity, but only of quality. The concept of the shortest is wholly an addition, and cannot be derived, through any process of analysis, from the concept of the straight line. Intuition, therefore, must here be called in; only by its aid is the synthesis possible. What here causes us commonly to believe that the predicate of such apodeictic judgments is already contained in our concept, and that the judgment is therefore analytic, is merely the ambiguous character of the terms used. We are required to join in thought a certain predicate to a given concept, and this necessity is inherent in the concepts themselves. But the question is not what we *ought* to join in thought to the given concept, but what we *actually* think in it, even if only obscurely; and it is then manifest that, while the predicate is indeed attached necessarily to the concept, it is so in virtue of an intuition which must be added to the concept, not as thought in the concept itself.

Some few fundamental propositions, presupposed by the geometrician, are, indeed, really analytic, and rest on the principle of contradiction. But, as identical propositions, they serve only as links in the chain of method and not as principles; for instance, *a* = *a;* the whole is equal to itself; or (*a* + *b*) > *a,* that is, the whole is greater than its part. And even these propositions, though they are valid according to pure concepts, are only admitted in mathematics because they can be exhibited in intuition.

2. *Natural science (physics) contains* a priori *synthetic judgments as principles.* I need cite only two such judgments: that in all changes of the material world the quantity of matter remains unchanged; and that in all communication of motion, action and reaction must always be equal. Both propositions, it is evident, are not only necessary, and therefore in their origin a priori, but also synthetic. For in the concept of matter I do not think its permanence, but only its presence in the space which it occupies. I go outside and beyond the concept of matter, joining to it a priori in thought something which I have not thought *in* it. The proposition is not, therefore, analytic, but synthetic, and yet is thought a priori; and so likewise are the other propositions of the pure part of natural science.

3. *Metaphysics,* even if we look upon it as having hitherto failed in all its endeavours, is yet, owing to the nature of human reason, a quite indispensable science, and *ought to contain* a priori *synthetic knowledge.* For its business is not merely to analyse concepts which we make for ourselves a priori of things, and thereby to clarify them analytically, but to extend our a priori knowledge. And for this purpose we must employ principles which add to the given concept something

that was not contained in it, and through *a priori* synthetic judgments venture out so far that experience is quite unable to follow us, as, for instance, in the proposition, that the world must have a first beginning, and such like. Thus metaphysics consists, at least *in intention,* entirely of *a priori* synthetic propositions.

THE GENERAL PROBLEM OF PURE REASON

Much is already gained if we can bring a number of investigations under the formula of a single problem. For we not only lighten our own task, by defining it accurately, but make it easier for others, who would test our results, to judge whether or not we have succeeded in what we set out to do. Now the proper problem of pure reason is contained in the question: How are *a priori* synthetic judgments possible?

That metaphysics has hitherto remained in so vacillating a state of uncertainty and contradiction, is entirely due to the fact that this problem, and perhaps even the distinction between analytic and synthetic judgments, has never previously been considered. Upon the solution of this problem, or upon a sufficient proof that the possibility which it desires to have explained does in fact not exist at all, depends the succeess or failure of metaphysics. Among philosophers, David Hume came nearest to envisaging this problem but still was very far from conceiving it with sufficient definiteness and universality. He occupied himself exclusively with the synthetic proposition regarding the connection of an effect with its cause (*principium causalitatis*), and he believed himself to have shown that such an *a priori* proposition is entirely impossible. If we accept his conclusions, then all that we call metaphysics is a mere delusion whereby we fancy ourselves to have rational insight into what, in actual fact, is borrowed solely from experience, and under the influence of custom has taken the illusory semblance of necessity. If he had envisaged our problem in all its universality, he would never have been guilty of this statement, so destructive of all pure philosophy. For he would then have recognised that, according to his own argument, pure mathematics, as certainly containing *a priori* synthetic proposition, would also not be possible; and from such an assertion his good sense would have saved him.

In the solution of the above problem, we are at the same time deciding as to the possibility of the employment of pure reason in establishing and developing all those sciences which contain a theoretical *a priori* knowledge of objects, and have therefore to answer the questions:

How is pure mathematics possible?
How is pure science of nature possible?

Since these sciences actually exist, it is quite proper to ask *how* they are possible; for that they must be possible is proved by the fact that they exist.[1] But the poor progress which has hitherto been made in metaphysics, and the fact that no system

---

[1] Many may still have doubts as regards pure natural science. We have only, however, to consider the various propositions that are to be found at the beginning of (empirical) physics, properly so-called, those, for instance, relating to the permanence in the quantity of matter, to inertia, to the equality of action and reaction, etc., in order to be soon convinced that they constitute a *physica pura,* or *rationalis,* which well deserves, as an independent science, to be separately dealt with in its whole extent, be that narrow or wide.

yet propounded can, in view of the essential purpose of metaphysics, be said really to exist, leaves everyone sufficient ground for doubting as to its possibility.

Yet, in a certain sense, this *kind of knowledge* is to be looked upon as given; that is to say, metaphysics actually exists, if not as a science, yet still as natural disposition (*metaphysica naturalis*). For human reason, without being moved merely by the idle desire for extent and variety of knowledge, proceeds impetuously, driven on by an inward need, to question such as cannot be answered by any empirical employment of reason, or by principles thence derived. Thus in all men, as soon as their reason has become ripe for speculation, there has always existed and will always continue to exist some kind of metaphysics. And so we have the question:

How is metaphysics, as natural disposition, possible?

that is, how from the nature of universal human reason do those questions arise which pure reason propounds to itself, and which it is impelled by its own need to answer as best it can?

But since all attempts which have hitherto been made to answer these natural questions—for instance, whether the world has a beginning or is from eternity— have always met with unavoidable contradictions, we cannot rest satisfied with the mere natural disposition to metaphysics, that is, with the pure faculty of reason itself, from which, indeed, some sort of metaphysics (be it what it may) always arises. It must be possible for reason to attain to certainty whether we know or do not know the objects of metaphysics, that is, to come to a decision either in regard to the objects of its enquiries or in regard to the capacity or incapacity of reason to pass any judgment upon them, so that we may either with confidence extend our pure reason or set to it sure and determinate limits. This last question, which arises out of the previous general problem, may, rightly stated, take the form:

How is metaphysics, as science, possible?

Thus the critique of reason, in the end, necessarily leads to scientific knowledge; while its dogmatic employment, on the other hand, lands us in dogmatic assertions to which other assertions, equally specious, can always be opposed—that is, in *scepticism.*

This science cannot be of any very formidable prolixity, since it has to deal not with the objects of reason, the variety of which is inexhaustable, but only with itself and the problems which arise entirely from within itself, and which are imposed upon it by its own nature, not by the nature of things which are distinct from it. When once reason has learnt completely to understand its own power in respect of objects which can be presented to it in experience, it should easily be able to determine, with completeness and certainty, the extent and the limits of its attempted employment beyond the bounds of all experience.

We may, then, and indeed we must, regard as abortive all attempts, hitherto made, to establish a metaphysic *dogmatically.* For the analytic part in any such attempted system, namely, the mere analysis of the concepts that inhere in our reason *a priori,* is by no means the aim of, but only a preparation for, metaphysics proper, that is, the extension of its *a priori* synthetic knowledge. For such a purpose, the analysis of concepts is useless, since it merely shows what is contained in these concepts, not how we arrive at them *a priori*. A solution of this latter problem is required, that we may be able to determine the valid employment of such concepts in regard to the objects of all knowledge in general. Nor is much self-denial needed to give up these claims, seeing that the undeniable, and in the dogmatic procedure of reason also unavoidable, contradictions of reason with itself have long since undermined the authority of every metaphysical system yet propounded. Greater firmness will be required if we are not to be deterred by inward difficulties and outward opposition from endeavouring, through application of a method entirely different from any hitherto employed, at last to bring to a prosperous and fruitful growth a science indispensable to human reason—a science whose every branch may be cut away but whose root cannot be destroyed. . . .

ALFRED J. AYER

Language, Meaning, and Reality

Sir Alfred J. Ayer is a Fellow of New College and Wykeham Professor of Logic at the University of Oxford. He has also written *Foundations of Empirical Knowledge, The Problem of Knowledge,* and *The Concept of a Person.*

The traditional disputes of philosophers are, for the most part, as unwarranted as they are unfruitful. The surest way to end them is to establish beyond question what should be the purpose and method of a philosophical enquiry. And this is by no means so difficult a task as the history of philosophy would lead one to suppose. For if there are any questions which science leaves it to philosophy to answer, a straightforward process of elimination must lead to their discovery.

We may begin by criticising the metaphysical thesis that philosophy affords us knowledge of a reality transcending the world of science and common sense. Later on, when we come to define metaphysics and account for its existence, we shall find that it is possible to be a metaphysician without believing in a transcendent reality; for we shall see that many metaphysical utterances are due to the commission of logical errors, rather than to a conscious desire on the part of their authors to go beyond the limits of experience. But it is convenient for us to take the case of those who believe that it is possible to have knowledge of a transcendent reality as a start-

From *Language, Truth, and Logic,* by Alfred Jules Ayer, Dover Publications, Inc., New York, 1951, and Victor Gollancz, Ltd., London, 1936. Reprinted by permission of the publishers.

ing-point for our discussion. The arguments which we use to refute them will subsequently be found to apply to the whole of metaphysics.

One way of attacking a metaphysician who claimed to have knowledge of a reality which transcended the phenomenal world would be to enquire from what premises his propositions were deduced. Must he not begin, as other men do, with the evidence of his senses? And if so, what valid process of reasoning can possibly lead him to the conception of a transcendent reality? Surely from empirical premises nothing whatsoever concerning the properties, or even the existence, of anything super-empirical can legitimately be inferred. But this objection would be met by a denial on the part of the metaphysician that his assertions were ultimately based on the evidence of his senses. He would say that he was endowed with a faculty of intellectual intuition which enabled him to know facts that could not be known through sense-experience. And even if it could be shown that he was relying on empirical premises, and that his venture into a nonempirical world was therefore logically unjustified, it would not follow that the assertions which he made concerning this nonempirical world could not be true. For the fact that a conclusion does not follow from its putative premise is not sufficient to show that it is false. Consequently one cannot overthrow a system of transcendent metaphysics merely by criticising the way in which it comes into being. What is required is rather a criticism of the nature of the actual statements which comprise it. And this is the line of argument which we shall, in fact, pursue. For we shall maintain that no statement which refers to a "reality" transcending the limits of all possible sense-experience can possibly have any literal significance; from which it must follow that the labours of those who have striven to describe such a reality have all been devoted to the production of nonsense.

It may be suggested that this is a proposition which has already been proved by Kant. But although Kant also condemned transcendent metaphysics, he did so on different grounds. For he said that the human understanding was so constituted that it lost itself in contradictions when it ventured out beyond the limits of possible experience and attempted to deal with things in themselves. And thus he made the impossibility of a transcendent metaphysic not, as we do, a matter of logic, but a matter of fact. He asserted, not that our minds could not conceivably have had the power of penetrating beyond the phenomenal world, but merely that they were in fact devoid of it. And this leads the critic to ask how, if it is possible to know only what lies within the bounds of sense-experience, the author can be justified in asserting that real things do exist beyond, and how he can tell what are the boundaries beyond which the human understanding may not venture, unless he succeeds in passing them himself. As Wittgenstein says, "in order to draw a limit to thinking, we should have to think both sides of this limit,"[1] a truth to which Bradley gives a special twist in maintaining that the man who is ready to prove that metaphysics is impossible is a brother metaphysician with a rival theory of his own.[2]

Whatever force these objections may have against the Kantian doctrine, they have none whatsoever against the thesis that I am about to set forth. It cannot here be said that the author is himself overstepping the barrier he maintains to be im-

[1] *Tractatus Logico-Philosophicus*, Preface.
[2] Bradley, *Appearance and Reality*, 2nd ed., p. 1.

passable. For the fruitlessness of attempting to transcend the limits of possible sense-experience will be deduced, not from a psychological hypothesis concerning the actual constitution of the human mind, but from the rule which determines the literal significance of language. Our charge against the metaphysician is not that he attempts to employ the understanding in a field where it cannot profitably venture, but that he produces sentences which fail to conform to the conditions under which alone a sentence can be literally significant. Nor are we ourselves obliged to talk nonsense in order to show that all sentences of a certain type are necessarily devoid of literal significance. We need only formulate the criterion which enables us to test whether a sentence expresses a genuine proposition about a matter of fact, and then point out that the sentences under consideration fail to satisfy it. And this we shall now proceed to do. We shall first of all formulate the criterion in somewhat vague terms, and then give the explanations which are necessary to render it precise.

The criterion which we use to test the genuineness of apparent statements of fact is the criterion of verifiability. We say that a sentence is factually significant to any given person, if, and only if, he knows how to verify the proposition which it purports to express—that is, if he knows what observations would lead him, under certain conditions, to accept the proposition as being true, or reject it as being false. If, on the other hand, the putative proposition is of such a character that the assumption of its truth, or falsehood, is consistent with any assumption whatsoever concerning the nature of his future experience, then, as far as he is concerned, it is, if not a tautology, a mere pseudo-proposition. The sentence expressing it may be emotionally significant to him; but it is not literally significant. And with regard to questions the procedure is the same. We enquire in every case what observations would lead us to answer the question, one way or the other; and, if none can be discovered, we must conclude that the sentence under consideration does not, as far as we are concerned, express a genuine question, however strongly its grammatical appearance may suggest that it does.

As the adoption of this procedure is an essential factor in the argument of this book, it needs to be examined in detail.

In the first place, it is necessary to draw a distinction between practical verifiability, and verifiability in principle. Plainly we all understand, in many cases believe, propositions which we have not in fact taken steps to verify. Many of these are propositions which we could verify if we took enough trouble. But there remain a number of significant propositions, concerning matters of fact, which we could not verify even if we chose; simply because we lack the practical means of placing ourselves in the situation where the relevant observations could be made. A simple and familiar example of such a proposition is the proposition that there are mountains on the farther side of the moon.[3] No rocket has yet been invented which would enable me to go and look at the farther side of the moon, so that I am unable to decide the matter by actual observation. But I do know what observations would decide it for me, if, as is theoretically conceivable, I were once in a position to make them. And therefore I say that the proposition is verifiable in principle, if not in practice, and is accordingly significant. On the other hand, such a metaphysical pseudo-proposition as "the Absolute enters into, but is itself incapable of, evolution

[3] This example has been used by Professor Schlick to illustrate the same point.

and progress,"[4] is not even in principle verifiable. For one cannot conceive of an observation which would enable one to determine whether the Absolute did, or did not, enter into evolution and progress. Of course it is possible that the author of such a remark is using English words in a way in which they are not commonly used by English-speaking people, and that he does, in fact, intend to assert something which could be empirically verified. But until he makes us understand how the proposition that he wishes to express would be verified, he fails to communicate anything to us. And if he admits, as I think the author of the remark in question would have admitted, that his words were not intended to express either a tautology or a proposition which was capable, at least in principle, of being verified, then it follows that he has made an utterance which has no literal significance even for himself.

A further distinction which we must make is the distinction between the "strong" and the "weak" sense of the term "verifiable." A proposition is said to be verifiable, in the strong sense of the term, if, and only if, its truth could be conclusively established in experience. But it is verifiable, in the weak sense, if it is possible for experience to render it probable. In which sense are we using the term when we say that a putative proposition is genuine only if it is verifiable?

It seems to me that if we adopt conclusive verifiability as our criterion of significance, as some positivists have proposed,[5] our argument will prove too much. Consider, for example, the case of general propositions of law—such propositions, namely, as "arsenic is poisonous"; "all men are mortal"; "a body tends to expand when it is heated." It is of the very nature of these propositions that their truth cannot be established with certainty by any finite series of observations. But if it is recognised that such general propositions of law are designed to cover an infinite number of cases, then it must be admitted that they cannot, even in principle, be verified conclusively. And then, if we adopt conclusive verifiability as our criterion of significance, we are logically obliged to treat these general propositions of law in the same fashion as we treat the statements of the metaphysician.

In face of this difficulty, some positivists[6] have adopted the heroic course of saying that these general propositions are indeed pieces of nonsense, albeit an essentially important type of nonsense. But here the introduction of the term "important" is simply an attempt to hedge. It serves only to mark the authors' recognition that their view is somewhat too paradoxical, without in any way removing the paradox. Besides, the difficulty is not confined to the case of general propositions of law, though it is there revealed most plainly. It is hardly less obvious in the case of propositions about the remote past. For it must surely be admitted that, however strong the evidence in favour of historical statements may be, their truth can never become more than highly probable. And to maintain that they also constituted an important, or unimportant, type of nonsense would be unplausible, to say the very least. Indeed, it will be our contention that no proposition, other than a tautology, can possibly be anything more than a probable hypothesis. And if this is correct, the

---

[4] A remark taken at random from *Appearance and Reality*, by F. H. Bradley.

[5] e.g. M. Schlick, "Positivismus und Realismus," *Erkenntnis*, Vol. I, 1930. F. Waismann, "Logische Analyse des Warscheinlichkeitsbegriffs," *Erkenntnis*, Vol. I, 1930.

[6] e.g. M. Schlick, "Die Kausalität in der gegenwärtigen Physik," *Naturwissenschaft*, Vol. 19, 1931.

principle that a sentence can be factually significant only if it expresses what is conclusively verifiable is self-stultifying as a criterion of significance. For it leads to the conclusion that it is impossible to make a significant statement of fact at all.

Nor can we accept the suggestion that a sentence should be allowed to be factually significant if, and only if, it expresses something which is definitely confutable by experience.[7] Those who adopt this course assume that, although no finite series of observations is ever sufficient to establish the truth of a hypothesis beyond all possibility of doubt, there are crucial cases in which a single observation, or series of observations, can definitely confute it. But, as we shall show later on, this assumption is false. A hypothesis cannot be conclusively confuted any more than it can be conclusively verified. For when we take the occurrence of certain observations as proof that a given hypothesis is false, we presuppose the existence of certain conditions. And though, in any given case, it may be extremely improbable that this assumption is false, it is not logically impossible. We shall see that there need be no self-contradiction in holding that some of the relevant circumstances are other than we have taken them to be, and consequently that the hypothesis has not really broken down. And if it is not the case that any hypothesis can be definitely confuted, we cannot hold that the genuineness of a proposition depends on the possibility of its definite confutation.

Accordingly, we fall back on the weaker sense of verification. We say that the question that must be asked about any putative statement of fact is not, Would any observations make its truth or falsehood logically certain? but simply, Would any observations be relevant to the determination of its truth or falsehood? And it is only if a negative answer is given to this second question that we conclude that the statement under consideration is nonsensical.

To make our position clearer, we may formulate it in another way. Let us call a proposition which records an actual or possible observation an experiential proposition. Then we may say that it is the mark of a genuine factual proposition, not that it should be equivalent to an experiential proposition, or any finite number of experiential propositions, but simply that some experiential propositions can be deduced from it in conjunction with certain other premises without being deducible from those other premises alone.[8]

This criterion seems liberal enough. In contrast to the principle of conclusive verifiability, it clearly does not deny significance to general propositions or to propositions about the past. Let us see what kinds of assertion it rules out.

A good example of the kind of utterance that is condemned by our criterion as being not even false but nonsensical would be the assertion that the world of sense-experience was altogether unreal. It must, of course, be admitted that our senses do sometimes deceive us. We may, as the result of having certain sensations, expect certain other sensations to be obtainable which are, in fact, not obtainable. But, in all such cases, it is further sense-experience that informs us of the mistakes that arise out of sense-experience. We say that the senses sometimes deceive us, just because the expectations to which our sense-experiences give rise do not always accord with what we subsequently experience. That is, we rely on our senses to

---

[7] This has been proposed by Karl Popper in his *Logik der Forschung*.

[8] This is an over-simplified statement, which is not literally correct. . . .

substantiate or confute the judgements which are based on our sensations. And therefore the fact that our perceptual judgements are sometimes found to be erroneous has not the slightest tendency to show that the world of sense-experience is unreal. And, indeed, it is plain that no conceivable observation, or series of observations, could have any tendency to show that the world revealed to us by sense-experience was unreal. Consequently, anyone who condemns the sensible world as a world of mere appearance, as opposed to reality, is saying something which, according to our criterion of significance, is literally nonsensical.

An example of a controversy which the application of our criterion obliges us to condemn as fictitious is provided by those who dispute concerning the number of substances that there are in the world. For it is admitted both by monists, who maintain that reality is one substance, and by pluralists, who maintain that reality is many, that it is impossible to imagine any empirical situation which would be relevant to the solution of their dispute. But if we are told that no possible observation could give any probability either to the assertion that reality was one substance or to the assertion that it was many, then we must conclude that neither assertion is significant. We shall see later on that there are genuine logical and empirical questions involved in the dispute between monists and pluralists. But the metaphysical question concerning "substance" is ruled out by our criterion as spurious.

A similar treatment must be accorded to the controversy between realists and idealists, in its metaphysical aspect. A simple illustration, which I have made use of in a similar argument elsewhere,[9] will help to demonstrate this. Let us suppose that a picture is discovered and the suggestion made that it was painted by Goya. There is a definite procedure for dealing with such a question. The experts examine the picture to see in what way it resembles the accredited works of Goya, and to see if it bears any marks which are characteristic of a forgery; they look up contemporary records for evidence of the existence of such a picture, and so on. In the end, they may still disagree, but each one knows what empirical evidence would go to confirm or discredit his opinion. Suppose, now, that these men have studied philosophy, and some of them proceed to maintain that this picture is a set of ideas in the perceiver's mind, or in God's mind, others that it is objectively real. What possible experience could any of them have which would be relevant to the solution of this dispute one way or the other? In the ordinary sense of the term "real," in which it is opposed to "illusory," that reality of the picture is not in doubt. The disputants have satisfied themselves that the picture is real, in this sense, by obtaining a correlated series of sensations of sight and sensations of touch. Is there any similar process by which they could discover whether the picture was real, in the sense in which the term "real" is opposed to "ideal"? Clearly there is none. But, if that is so, the problem is fictitious according to our criterion. This does not mean that the realist-idealist controversy may be dismissed without further ado. For it can legitimately be regarded as a dispute concerning the analysis of existential propositions, and so as involving a logical problem which, as we shall see, can be definitively solved. What we have just shown is that the question at issue between idealists and realists becomes fictious when, as is often the case, it is given a metaphysical interpretation.

[9] Vide "Demonstration of the Impossibility of Metaphysics," *Mind,* 1934, p. 339.

There is no need for us to give further examples of the operation of our criterion of significance. For our object is merely to show that philosophy, as a genuine branch of knowledge, must be distinguished from metaphysics. We are not now concerned with the historical question how much of what has traditionally passed for philosophy is actually metaphysical. We shall, however, point out later on that the majority of the "great philosophers" of the past were not essentially metaphysicians, and thus reassure those who would otherwise be prevented from adopting our criterion by considerations of piety.

As to the validity of the verification principle, in the form in which we have stated it, a demonstration will be given in the course of this book. For it will be shown that all propositions which have factual content are empirical hypotheses; and that the function of an empirical hypothesis is to provide a rule for the anticipation of experience. And this means that every empirical hypothesis must be relevant to some actual, or possible, experience, so that a statement which is not relevant to any experience is not an empirical hypothesis, and accordingly has no factual content. But this is precisely what the principle of verifiability asserts.

It should be mentioned here that the fact that the utterances of the metaphysician are nonsensical does not follow simply from the fact that they are devoid of factual content. It follows from that fact, together with the fact that they are not *a priori* propositions. And in assuming that they are not *a priori* propositions, we are once again anticipating the conclusions of a later chapter in this book. For it will be shown there that *a priori* propositions, which have always been attractive to philosophers on account of their certainty, owe this certainty to the fact that they are tautologies. We may accordingly define a metaphysical sentence as a sentence which purports to express a genuine proposition, but does, in fact, express neither a tautology nor an empirical hypothesis. And as tautologies and empirical hypotheses form the entire class of significant propositions, we are justified in concluding that all metaphysical assertions are nonsensical. Our next task is to show how they come to be made.

The use of the term "substance," to which we have already referred, provides us with a good example of the way in which metaphysics mostly comes to be written. It happens to be the case that we cannot, in our language, refer to the sensible properties of a thing without introducing a word or phrase which appears to stand for the thing itself as opposed to anything which may be said about it. And, as a result of this, those who are infected by the primitive superstition that to every name a single real entity must correspond assume that it is necessary to distinguish logically between the thing itself and any, or all, of its sensible properties. And so they employ the term "substance" to refer to the thing itself. But from the fact that we happen to employ a single word to refer to a thing, and make that word the grammatical subject of the sentences in which we refer to the sensible appearances of the thing, it does not by any means follow that the thing itself is a "simple entity," or that it cannot be defined in terms of the totality of its appearances. It is true that in talking of "its" appearances we appear to distinguish the thing from the appearances, but that is simply an accident of linguistic usage. Logical analysis shows that what makes these "appearances" the "appearances of" the same thing is not their relationship to an entity other than themselves, but their relationship to one another. The metaphysician fails to see this because he is misled by a superficial grammatical feature of his language.

A simpler and clearer instance of the way in which a consideration of grammar leads to metaphysics is the case of the metaphysical concept of Being. The origin of our temptation to raise questions about Being, which no conceivable experience would enable us to answer, lies in the fact that, in our language, sentences which express existential propositions and sentences which express attributive propositions may be of the same grammatical form. For instance, the sentences "Martyrs exist" and "Martyrs suffer" both consist of a noun followed by an intransitive verb, and the fact that they have grammatically the same appearance leads one to assume that they are of the same logical type. It is seen that in the proposition "Martyrs suffer," the members of a certain species are credited with a certain attribute, and it is sometimes assumed that the same thing is true of such a proposition as "Martyrs exist." If this were actually the case, it would, indeed, be as legitimate to speculate about the Being of martyrs as it is to speculate about their suffering. But, as Kant pointed out,[10] existence is not an attribute. For, when we ascribe an attribute to a thing, we covertly assert that it exists: so that if existence were itself an attribute, it would follow that all positive existential propositions were tautologies, and all negative existential propositions self-contradictory; and this is not the case.[11] So that those who raise questions about Being which are based on the assumption that existence is an attribute are guilty of following grammar beyond the boundaries of sense.

A similar mistake has been made in connection with such propositions as "Unicorns are fictitious." Here again the fact that there is a superficial grammatical resemblance between the English sentences "Dogs are faithful" and "Unicorns are fictitious," and between the corresponding sentences in other languages, creates the assumption that they are of the same logical type. Dogs must exist in order to have the property of being faithful, and so it is held that unless unicorns in some way existed they could not have the property of being fictitious. But, as it is plainly self-contradictory to say that fictitious objects exist, the device is adopted of saying that they are real in some non-empirical sense—that they have a mode of real being which is different from the mode of being of existent things. But since there is no way of testing whether an object is real in this sense, as there is for testing whether it is real in the ordinary sense, the assertion that fictitious objects have a special non-empirical mode of real being is devoid of all literal significance. It comes to be made as a result of the assumption that being fictitious is an attribute. And this is a fallacy of the same order as the fallacy of supposing that existence is an attribute, and it can be exposed in the same way.

In general, the postulation of real non-existent entities results from the superstition, just now referred to, that, to every word or phrase that can be the grammatical subject of a sentence, there must somewhere be a real entity corresponding. For as there is no place in the empirical world for many of these "entities," a special non-empirical world is invoked to house them. To this error must be attributed, not only the utterances of a Heidegger, who bases his metaphysics on the assumption that "Nothing" is a name which is used to denote something peculiarly

[10] Vide *The Critique of Pure Reason,* "Transcendental Dialectic," Book II, Chapter iii, section 4.
[11] This argument is well stated by John Wisdom, *Interpretation and Analysis,* pp. 62, 63.

mysterious,[12] but also the prevalence of such problems as those concerning the reality of propositions and universals whose senselessness, though less obvious, is no less complete.

These few examples afford a sufficient indication of the way in which most metaphysical assertions come to be formulated. They show how easy it is to write sentences which are literally nonsensical without seeing that they are nonsensical. As thus we see that the view that a number of the traditional "problems of philosophy" are metaphysical, and consequently fictitious, does not involve any incredible assumptions about the psychology of philosophers.

Among those who recognise that if philosophy is to be accounted a genuine branch of knowledge it must be defined in such a way as to distinguish it from metaphysics, it is fashionable to speak of the metaphysician as a kind of misplaced poet. As his statements have no literal meaning, they are not subject to any criteria of truth or falsehood: but they may still serve to express, or arouse, emotion, and thus be subject to ethical or aesthetic standards. And it is suggested that they may have considerable value, as means of moral inspiration, or even as works of art. In this way, an attempt is made to compensate the metaphysician for his extrusion from philosophy.[13]

I am afraid that this compensation is hardly in accordance with his deserts. The view that the metaphysician is to be reckoned among the poets appears to rest on the assumption that both talk nonsense. But this assumption is false. In the vast majority of cases the sentences which are produced by poets do have literal meaning. The difference between the man who uses language scientifically and the man who uses it emotively is not that the one produces sentences which are incapable of arousing emotion, and the other sentences which have no sense, but that the one is primarily concerned with the expression of true propositions, the other with the creation of a work of art. Thus, if a work of science contains true and important propositions, its value as a work of science will hardly be diminished by the fact that they are inelegantly expressed. And similarly, a work of art is not necessarily the worse for the fact that all the propositions comprising it are literally false. But to say that many literary works are largely composed of falsehoods, is not to say that they are composed of pseudo-propositions. It is, in fact, very rare for a literary artist to produce sentences which have no literal meaning. And where this does occur, the sentences are carefully chosen for their rhythm and balance. If the author writes nonsense, it is because he considers it most suitable for bringing about the effects for which his writing is designed.

The metaphysician, on the other hand, does not intend to write nonsense. He lapses into it through being deceived by grammar, or through commiting errors of reasoning, such as that which leads to the view that the sensible world is unreal. But it is not the mark of a poet simply to make mistakes of this sort. There are some, indeed, who would see in the fact that the metaphysician's utterances are

---

[12] Vide *Was ist Metaphysik*, by Heidegger: criticised by Rudolf Carnap in his "Überwindung der Metaphysik durch logische Analyse der Sprache," *Erkenntnis*, Vol. II, 1932.

[13] For a discussion of this point, see also C. A. Mace, "Representation and Expression," *Analysis*, Vol. I, No. 3; and "Metaphysics and Emotive Language," *Analysis*, Vol. II, Nos. 1 and 2.

senseless a reason against the view that they have aesthetic value. And, without going so far as this, we may safely say that it does not constitute a reason for it.

It is true, however, that although the greater part of metaphysics is merely the embodiment of humdrum errors, there remain a number of metaphysical passages which are the work of geniune mystical feeling; and they may more plausibly be held to have moral or aesthetic value. But, as far as we are concerned, the distinction between the kind of metaphysics that is produced by a philosopher who has been duped by grammer, and the kind that is produced by a mystic who is trying to express the inexpressible, is of no great importance: what is important to us is to realise that even the utterances of the metaphysician who is attempting to expound a vision are literally senseless; so that henceforth we may pursue our philosophical researches with as little regard for them as for the more inglorious kind of metaphysics which comes from a failure to understand the workings of our language.

JOHN R. SEARLE

Words, the World, and Human Communication

John R. Searle is Professor of Philosophy at the University of California at Berkeley. He is the author of *Speech Acts.*

How do words relate to the world? How is it that when one man emits a noise he can be said to mean something by that noise and another man can be said to understand what he means? How can we distinguish a meaningful string of sounds or marks from a meaningless one? And what exactly is involved in a string's being meaningful? And what is involved in its meaning just what it does and not something else? How is it possible, for example, that when I say "Smith went to the party" I mean Smith went to the party and not Brown stayed home or Jones got sick? What is the difference between saying something and meaning it and saying it without meaning it?

Such questions are as old as philosophy. We must not assume that in the forms I have stated them they even make sense. Still, in some form or other some such questions must make sense; for we do know that people communicate, that they do say things and sometimes mean what they say, that they are on occasion at least understood, that people's utterances do relate to the world in ways we can describe

From "Human Communication Theory and the Philosophy of Language: Some Remarks" by John R. Searle in *Human Communication Theory* edited by Frank E. X. Dance. Copyright © 1967 by Holt, Rinehart and Winston, Inc. Reprinted by permission of the publishers.

by characterizing the utterances as being true, false, exaggerated, stupid, or meaningless, or whatnot. And if these things do happen, it follows that it is possible for them to happen, and if it is possible for them to happen, it ought to be possible to pose and answer the questions that examine that possibility.

One of the oldest and most appealing approaches is this: words get their meaning by standing for things. What the word stands for is what it means. If the word or longer expression is a proper name like Charles de Gaulle or Mount Everest, the meaning of the word or expression is simply the particular object for which it stands. If the word is a general term like "red" or "triangle," it stands for some abstract entity such as redness or triangularity.

Some words, called syncategorematic, such words as "if," "but," "however," "not," "and," etc., may not stand for anything but have meaning only as connecting other expressions that really do stand for things. But most words have meaning only by standing for things, be they concrete or abstract things. This approach to meaning goes back as far as Plato's *Dialogues,* and its most sophisticated and rigorous variation is in Wittgenstein's *Tractatus Logico-philosophicus.*[1]

It is really quite unsatisfactory. Frege[2] pointed out that meaning could not in general be equated with standing for (or designating, naming, denoting, referring to), because, for example, both the expressions "the morning star" and "the evening star" stand for the same planet but the two expressions have different meanings. They have one reference but two different senses. And Wittgenstein[3] himself later pointed out that even for proper names when the bearer of the name dies or is destroyed or otherwise ceases to exist, we do not say the meaning of the name is destroyed. If Mr. N. N. dies, the meaning of "Mr. N. N." does not die. If it did, it would be meaningless to say "Mr. N. N. died." So even in the case of proper names the meaning of the expression is not the same as the object for which it stands.

A second approach is to suppose that meanings are introspectible entities of some sort. Locke,[4] for example, argues that words get their meanings by standing for ideas in the mind. In the case of singular terms these ideas are mental pictures or images of the objects designated by the term, in the case of general terms like "red" or "triangle" the ideas are abstract or general ideas. Abstract ideas, according to Locke,[5] contain what is common to all of the particular instances of a thing, without containing what is peculiar to each. Subsequent theorists such as Berkeley[6] and Hume[7] argued that abstract or general ideas were impossible to form, that one could not have a mental picture of triangles in general but only a mental picture

---

[1] Ludwig Wittgenstein, *Tractatus Logico-philosophicus,* London: K. Paul, Trench, Trubner & Co., Ltd., 1922.

[2] Gottlob Frege, "On Sense and Reference," *Translations from the Philosophical Writings of Gottlob Frege,* P. Geach and M. Black, Oxford: Blackwell & Mott, Ltd., 1952, pp. 52–78.

[3] Ludwig Wittgenstein, *Philosophical Investigations,* tr. G. E. M. Anscombe, New York: Crowell Collier and Macmillan, 1953, § 39, 40, pp. 19, 20.

[4] John Locke, *An Essay Concerning Human Understanding,* Oxford: Clarendon Press, 1894, Vol. II, Book III, Chapter 2.

[5] John Locke, *An Essay Concerning Human Understanding.*

[6] George Berkeley, *The Principles of Human Knowledge,* London: A. Brown & Sons, Ltd., 1937, Introduction, § 6–25.

[7] David Hume, *A Treatise on Human Nature,* Oxford: Clarendon Press, 1965, Book I, Part I, § viii.

of a triangle with determinate character. This particular idea could then be made "general in its representation," but it could not itself be a general idea.

Such imagist theories as those of Locke, Berkeley, and Hume conceive of the relation between words and the world on the following model. The word stands for the mental picture and the mental picture resembles objects in the world, whether actual or possible objects. But the essential connection between words and the world is made via the mental picture. It is arbitrary what sounds we use to stand for the pictures, but the mental pictures themselves are related to the world via a natural nonarbitrary relation of resemblance.

Such imagist theories of meaning have been subjected to devastating criticism, and are no longer widely held. It seems to be simply false that people's speaking is accompanied by such images, and if true, it appears to be irrelevant to the meaning and meaningfulness of what they say. If it should happen, for example, that my utterance of the word "horse" is always accompanied in my mind by an image of an airplane, that is quite irrelevant to whether or not I know the meaning of the word "horse" and use it correctly. If I can use the word correctly I know its meaning, and what images accompany my use of it, or whether any images accompany its use, are logically speaking quite irrelevant to its meaning and to whether I know its meaning. Furthermore, the existence of a mental image, even if it were invariably correlated with a particular word, does not determine the use to which that image is put, so that the same mental image could have any number of different uses, and thus would not uniquely determine the meaning of a word. In sum, it is psychologically false that there are invariably mental images accompanying the use of words, it is logically neither necessary not sufficient to determine the meaning of a word that there should be such images, and finally, even if there were such images, they would not be enough to determine the use of words. These and other considerations might incline one to say that the meaning of a word is really its use in the language, a view that many philosophers now accept and that we shall shortly consider.

Yet another objection to the imagist theory is its total lack of explanatory power. If we are concerned with the question "How do words stand for things?" it is no answer at all to be told "First they stand for images that resemble the things the words stand for" for that only raises the original question in a new form: "How do words stand for images?"

The most widely held contemporary philosophical theory of meaning is that the meaning of a word is either identical with or at any rate closely associated with its use. Wittgenstein, the father of this theory, writes:

> For a large class of cases—though not for all—in which we employ the word "meaning" it can be defined thus: the meaning of a word is its use in the language.[8]

The difficulty with this view is that the notion of use is so vague as to be almost worthless as an analytical tool for discussing meaning. The same sentence, and hence the same words with the same literal meaning, may on one occasion be used to compliment one person and on another occasion be used to insult another person. They may be used to annoy, convince, amuse, bore, and so on. So if it is use we are talking about we will first have to distinguish the different kinds of uses

---

[8] Ludwig Wittgenstein, *Philosophical Investigations,* § 43, p. 20.

which expressions or strings of expressions may have and sort out which are relevant to meaning and which are not.

I find the notion of "use" useful only as an antidote against referential or imagist theories of meaning, but as a positive "theory" in its own right it is too crude for our purposes. However, it does suggest an approach to problems in communication, which many philosophers, notably J. L. Austin,[9] have begun to explore in recent years. This approach can be characterized by saying that it conceives of the speaking of a language as a human activity. Rather than concentrating on the linguistic forms, one concentrates on the speech acts that are performed in the utterance of those linguistic forms. In what follows I want to state, justify, and explain some of the general principles that seem to me form a part (only a part) of the answers to the cluster of questions with which I began this paper, and that may justifiably be regarded as deriving from the tradition that associates meaning and use. Instead of the notion of "use," however, it distinguishes the different kinds of "speech acts" one can be said to perform in the utterance of expressions and thus, hopefully, avoids the obscurity of the notion of "use."

I shall simply state these principles categorically and then try to explain what they mean and why I think they are true.

1. *Speaking a language is engaging in a rule-governed form of behavior.*

Obviously speaking a language is engaging in a form of behavior: talking is a human activity. But it is not so obvious that that form of activity is governed by rules. Ultimately the proof that that is the case will have to come from showing that the hypothesis that human linguistic behavior is rule governed explains the data of speech behavior better than any alternative hypothesis. In certain areas, particularly syntax, we are well on the way to having explained a great deal of data on this hypothesis. That speakers are able to produce an unlimited number of new sentences, sentences they have never heard or seen before, and that they are able to recognize what is a sentence and what is not a sentence, is explicable by the fact that they have internalized a system of rules. This hypothesis is supported by our ability to actually formulate rules that account for these abilities,[10] and by the failure of alternative hypotheses to account for such data.[11]

The hypothesis that speaking is a form of behavior, though obvious, is crucially important for our investigations. For it implies that our account is incomplete as long as it deals only with language as a formal system. Our study is insufficient as long as it deals only with the formal structure purely as a formal system, for the formal structure exists for the purpose of and is manifested in the linguistic behavior of the speaking subjects. Of course the *actual* behavior of the speaker may only be an imperfect manifestation of the underlying structure since speakers' performances

---

9 See especially: J. L. Austin, *How to Do Things with Words,* Cambridge, Mass.: Harvard University Press, 1962.

10 Noam Chomsky, "A Transformational Approach to Syntax," *Proceedings of the Third Texas Conference on Problems of Linguistic Analysis in English, 1958,* ed. A. A. Hill, Austin, Texas: The University of Texas, 1962, pp. 124–158. Reprinted in *The Structure of Language,* eds. Jerry A. Fodor and Jerrold J. Katz, Englewood Cliffs, N.J.: Prentice Hall, Inc., 1964.

11 Noam Chomsky, "A Review of B. F. Skinner's 'Verbal Behavior'," New York: Appleton-Century-Crofts, 1957, in *Language,* 35, No. 1, 1959, pp. 26–58. Reprinted in *The Structure of Language,* eds. Jerry A. Fodor and Jerrold J. Katz, Englewood Cliffs, N.J.: Prentice Hall, Inc., 1964.

are frequently marred by memory lapses, sloppy pronunciation, half-finished sentences, false starts, and a variety of other speech ills. To eliminate these irrelevant aspects from our study, we need to concentrate on *idealized* forms of speech behavior.[12]

The speakers of a language may be "unconscious" of the rules in the sense that they could not formulate them, but they are nonetheless acting in accordance with the rules. The behavior is intentional rule-governed behavior, although the agent may be unable to state what the rules are. If I teach a child to play simple games, he will learn to act in accordance with the rules of those games, although he may not, in general, be able to formulate those rules. Similarly a child may learn to speak in accordance with the rule: the wh-inversion transformation only applies once to a given phrase marker, without ever learning to formulate that rule. So it is no objection to this approach to say that the speakers of a language can't be acting in accordance with rules because they cannot state the rules: much rule-governed behavior is performed without any explicit awareness of what the rules are. We have to *discover* the rules we have been following, but that is no objection to the view that we have been following them.

2. *The minimal unit of communication is the illocutionary act.*

It is tempting and indeed common to think of that which communicates as essentially signs, marks, symbols, words, sentences, or some other such thing. What one forgets when one so thinks is that in order to take such a thing as a message, as a unit of human linguistic communication, one must regard its production as the performance of a speech act. If I hear a sound, and I take that sound to be a part of linguistic communication, say as a greeting, a warning, or a command, then necessarily my so regarding that sound presupposes that I regard the sound as having been produced by beings more or less similar to myself and produced with certain kinds of intentions.

To regard the sound as a natural phenomenon, like the wind in the trees, precludes me from regarding it as an instance of linguistic communication, even though a particular sound made by the wind in the trees may be audibly indistinguishable from a whispered sentence. Similarly in order for me to regard the marks I see on a piece of paper as an instance of linguistic communication, I have to regard those marks as the product of a certain kind of act, as having been produced with certain intentions and for certain purposes. If I am convinced that the marks are the result of a mold on the paper, I cannot regard them as a linguistic message, as an instance of linguistic communication. It is not the sign or symbol or word that communicates but it is the production of instances of these in speech acts.[13] This adds further depth to point 1. If the fundamental unit of communication is a speech act, then regarding language within the general range of human acts, actions, and activities is not merely an idiosyncratic methodological device but is essential for understanding communication.

Now if speaking a language is a form of behavior and if it is necessary to so

---

[12] For a discussion of this distinction between actual performance and idealized competence see: Noam Chomsky, "Aspects of the Theory of Syntax," *Massachusetts Institute of Technology, Research Laboratory of Electronics. Special Technical Report. No. 11,* Cambridge, Mass.: M.I.T. Press, 1965.

[13] Cf. J. R. Searle, "What is a Speech Act?," *Philosophy in America,* ed. Max Black, Ithaca, N.Y.: Cornell University Press, 1965.

regard it in order to understand communication, certain questions naturally arise; first, which of these behavioral units are the minimal complete units capable of standing on their own; and secondly, into what sorts of units does this behavior naturally segment? The obvious answer to the first question is: statements, commands, questions, promises, remarks, explanations, orders, comments, requests, and things like them. Austin[14] baptized these with the name "illocutionary acts."

They need to be distinguished from acts like referring, as, for example, when I refer to John in saying "John came yesterday." Here the reference to John is not by itself a complete speech act capable of standing on its own but is only part of the larger complete illocutionary act of making the statement that John came yesterday.

The syntactical correlate of this point is that sentences and not words are the units of the complete speech act. Words occur intelligibly only in sentences. (They may be one word sentences such as "Look!," but even here we need to distinguish the word from the imperative intonation contour of its utterance, the morpheme of stress, and the sentence boundary that surrounds the word. All of these are parts of the sentence, and the word without them is not the sentence.)

Furthermore, it is necessary to distinguish both of these kinds of acts from acts that involve the consequence or effects of illocutionary acts. Acts such as persuading, convincing, annoying, amusing, or boring our audience may indeed be things we can do with words, but they are acts that go beyond uttering, meaning, and getting the hearer to understand what is meant, which are the essential elements involved in performing illocutionary acts. Austin[15] called these acts involving further effects on the hearer *perlocutionary acts*. The failure to distinguish the perlocutionary from the illocutionary is one of the chief weaknesses of the meaning-is-use theory of meaning.

3. *Saying something and meaning it involves saying it plus:*

(a) *intending to produce certain illocutionary effects in a hearer (which effects are a function of the rules governing the sentence uttered);*

(b) *intending to produce these effects by getting the hearer to recognize intention a, and*

(c) *intending to get him to recognize intention a by means of his knowledge of the rules governing the sentence uttered.*[16]

Everybody is aware that there is a difference between just saying something and saying something and meaning it. But how exactly can we characterize that difference? Well, one might say, saying something and meaning it is a matter characteristically of intending to produce certain effects in a hearer, which effects we could describe as his *understanding*. But that gets us nowhere in an effort to explicate the concept of *meaning*, since the understanding we are trying to produce is an understanding of what the speaker means. So we must try to unpack this notion of understanding.

Understanding the speaker's utterance will involve recognizing certain of the

---

[14] J. L. Austin, *How to Do Things with Words.* Lecture VIII.

[15] *Ibid.*

[16] This analysis of meaning is inspired by (but not identical with) that given by H. P. Grice in his article "Meaning," *Philosophical Review*, Ithaca, New York: Cornell University, Vol. LXVI, No. 3 (July, 1957) pp. 377–388.

speaker's intentions. For example, if I say, "It's hot in here" and mean it, then if my hearer understands me, he will recognize that it is my intention to get him to know that I am telling him, in the utterance of that sentence, that it is hot in here. And it is a peculiar and important feature of illocutionary acts that recognizing the intention with which the utterance is made is a crucial part of the achievement of that intention, since it is by means of the recognition of that intention that one achieves the intention. If you recognize my intention in uttering, "It's hot in here" as getting you to know that you are being told that it is hot in here, then as soon as you recognize that intention you do know that you are being so told, for it is by means of that recognition that you acquire that knowledge. And how do you recognize the speaker's intention? If he utters a sentence, which is part of a language you understand, you recognize his intention by means of your knowledge of the meaning (i.e., rules governing the utterance of) the sentence uttered. So there are really three parts to meaning *It's hot in here* when I say, "It's hot in here," and mean it:

(a) intending to get the hearer to know that I am telling him that it's hot in here;

(b) intending to get him to know that by means of his recognition of intention *a*;

(c) intending to get him to recognize intention *a* by means of his knowledge of the rules governing the elements of the sentence uttered.

And this is just a special case of the general conditions set by the definition above.

Two further points: First, it is important to emphasize that the intended effects of meaning are illocutionary not perlocutionary effects. When I tell you that it's hot in here, I may tell you that with the intention of getting you to turn on the air-conditioner. But your turning on the air-conditioner is a perlocutionary effect of the utterance, and the intention to produce that effect is not part of meaning, "It's hot in here" when I say, "It's hot in here" and mean it.

The same holds true incidentally of saying and meaning, "Turn on the air-conditioner." The illocutionary effect of that utterance is that the hearer should know he is being told (ordered, requested, and so on) to turn on the air-conditioner. Characteristically the intended perlocutionary effect of these illocutionary acts is to get the hearer to turn on the air-conditioner, but saying and meaning "Turn on the air-conditioner" do not necessarily involve intending to produce that effect, since, in odd cases, I may say, "Turn on the air-conditioner" and not intend that the speaker should actually do it (if I know for example that it is broken, and I wish to deceive him). So the necessarily intended effects of "meaning" are illocutionary and not perlocutionary.

Secondly, we have so far only dealt with literal meaning. Figurative speech may be characterized as speech where the intended illocutionary effects differ from those specified by the rules for the use of the sentence uttered. In an important sense figurative speech is parasitic on literal speech since one could not utter a sentence meaning it figuratively if it did not have a literal meaning as a basis for the figurative use.

4. *Whatever can be meant can be said.*

Philosophers and poets sometimes lament the inadequacy of language to express the precise meaning they wish to convey. And certainly there is some point to this, since any natural language provides us with a finite set of words and syntactical forms for saying what we mean. But where there is in a given language an upper bound on the expressible, where there are thoughts that simply cannot be expressed in a given language, or in any language, it is a contingent fact and not a necessary truth. It is always in principle, if not in fact, possible to add new words or other elements to the language for saying what was previously inexpressible. There is no theoretical upper boundary on the number of lexical elements or complexity of syntactical structures that languages can bear. When a speaker means X, he can in principle, if not always in fact, come to be able to say literally X. If he does not know enough of the language he is speaking to be able to say X in that language, he can learn enough, and if, more radically, the language lacks the resources for saying X, those resources can be added to it.

This is an important principle, for it has the consequence that the study of the meaning of sentences and the study of speech acts are not two different studies but one and the same study from two points of view. For every possible speech act a speaker may wish to perform, there is a possible sentence (or set of sentences) the literal utterance of which would, under appropriate conditions, be a performance of that speech act.

There are not two distinct semantic studies, one a study of the meaning of sentences and another a study of the performances of speech acts; for just as it is part of our notion of the meaning of a sentence that a literal utterance of that sentence with that meaning in a certain content would be the performance of a particular illocutionary act, so it is part of our notion of an illocutionary act that there is a possible sentence, the utterance of which in a certain context would in virtue of its meaning constitute a performance of that illocutionary act. A great deal of useless dispute has been spent between those who concentrate on linguistic forms and those who concentrate on speech acts as the object of semantic study. The real insight of the tradition of Wittgenstein and Austin is not that we can neglect the formal elements in the study of semantics but that in studying them we should remember that their meaning is tied to their role in linguistic behavior. As Wittgenstein[17] said, "Language is an instrument."

This principle does not imply that whatever can be said can be understood by others, for that would exclude the possibility of a private language, a language that it was logically impossible for anyone but the speaker to understand. Such language may indeed be logically impossible, but I do not wish to argue the point here.

5. *Systems of semantic rules are constitutive and not regulative.* When we first think about rules and rule-governed behavior, we are inclined to fasten on to examples such as the traffic rules that regulate driver and pedestrian behavior. Such rules exist to regulate an independently existing form of behavior. Some rules and systems of rules exist not just to regulate an existing form of behavior, but their existence creates the very possibility of the behavior they regulate. For example, the rules of games such as baseball or football make possible the playing of the games. Without the rules of football there would be no such thing as the playing of

---

[17] Ludwig Wittgenstein, *Philosophical Investigations*, § 569, p. 151.

football, and similarly, within the game the rules concerning scoring do not just regulate how a team scores, but rather they define such notions as "'touchdown" or "field goal," and create the possibility of there being such things by determining that such and such forms of behavior count as a touchdown or a field goal.

Rules that in this sense create the possibility of new forms of behavior are called "constitutive rules" to distinguish them from regulative rules, which regulate independently existing behavior. The constitutive rules of an activity are such that engaging in the activity is constituted by acting in accordance with the rules, or at any rate with a sufficiently large subset of the rules. The connection between the rules and the activity is thus an analytic one: e.g., football is defined as a game played according to such and such rules, and within the game words such as "touchdown" and "offside" are defined by the rules concerning scoring and penalties. Constitutive rules normally come in systems, and although individual rules within the system may be regulative, the system as a whole is constitutive. For example, the infield-fly rule in baseball is a regulative rule within the system of rules of baseball, but the system of rules of which it is a part is constitutive of baseball.

The semantical and syntactical rules of a language are similarly constitutive. The rules of English syntax define such notions as "sentence in English," for they provide us with a system such that acting in accordance with that system constitutes uttering English sentences. The rules of semantics are similarly constitutive, for acting in accordance with them constitutes performing such illocutionary acts as promising, making statements, giving orders, and so on. The form of constitutive rules is not always the same as that of regulative rules. Regulative rules generally have an imperative character: "Do such and such," or "under conditions C, do such and such." The form of constitutive rules is often: "Under certain conditions C, doing such and such counts as X." Thus, under certain conditions the utterance of a certain string of words counts as the making of a promise. It is the joint mastery of rules of this form that enable the hearer to recognize in the utterance of the string the speaker's intention to produce certain effects in him, and thus to produce those effects. And, as we have seen, the production of such effects in such a fashion is an essential feature of linguistic communication.

It is important to emphasize the constitutive character of linguistic rules, for no set of purely regulative rules could account for linguistic behavior since there is no antecedently existing activity of speaking a language to be regulated by the rules. The possibility of speaking the language only exists within a system of constitutive rules.

CONCLUSION

I have stated five principles concerning the philosophy of language. Taken together these principles provide us with a model for speech behavior, a model that if fully worked out would explicate the relationships between meaning, saying, sentences, illocutionary acts, constitutive linguistic rules, and understanding utterances. In outline the model shapes up like this. Speaking is rule-governed intentional behavior. The behavior consists in performing illocutionary acts in accordance with constitutive rules by uttering sentences. In its internal structure the successfully performed illocutionary act involves the speaker's uttering a sentence and meaning something in that utterance and the hearer's understanding the utterance. On the speaker's side, meaning something is a matter of intending to produce certain illocutionary effects in the hearer, and on the hearer's side understanding the utterance consists in recognizing these intentions and thereby achieving the intended effect. The bridge between the speaker and the hearer is provided by their common language of which the uttered sentence is a part. Here is how that bridge works: understanding the sentence is knowing its meaning. Its meaning is determined entirely by semantical rules, rules that concern both its syntactical structure and its lexical elements. These rules specify both the conditions of the correct utterance of the sentence and what the utterance counts as. If the utterance is meant literally, the speaker's intended illocutionary effect will be determined by the rules, for in a literal utterance the illocutionary effect is simply the knowledge that the states of affairs specified by the rules obtain. For example, if the utterance is of the form, "I hereby promise such and such," then the intended illocutionary effect of a literal utterance of that sentence is among other things that the bearer should know that a promise is being made to him, which effect is determined by the rules for the form, "I hereby promise." Thus, if the utterance is meant literally, the sentence meaning, determined by the rules, will produce the illocutionary effect of the speaker's meaning. And the achievement of those effects is simply the hearer's understanding the utterance.

If this model is at all adequate its further refinement should enable us to explain a good deal of linguistic data. To develop the model we need to actually try to state the rules for performing various kinds of speech acts. To do so would be to explain a great deal of data concerning the various kinds of illocutionary acts, but furthermore we should then be able to extend the account to explain how nonliteral speech works. Successful figurative speech is not a random departure from literal speech but is related to it in certain systematic ways, or at any rate that it is so related is a hypothesis that could be worked out by attempting to show how the rules for literal speech provide a basis for conveying different illocutionary effects by departing from the rules in certain ways. So the research projects immediately implicit in the model involve both a development of the rules for performing illocutionary acts and the further application of the theory to the study of nonliteral speech.

MAURICE MERLEAU-PONTY

Expression and Human Existence

Maurice Merleau-Ponty (1908–1961) was
Professor of Philosophy at the Collège de
France and the author of several influential
works in the tradition of existentialism and
phenomenology. Among them are *The
Structure of Behavior, The Primacy of
Perception,* and *The Phenomenology of
Perception,* from which this selection is taken.

. . . That which is called an idea is necessarily linked to an act of expression, and
owes to it its appearance of autonomy. It is a cultural object, like the church, the
street, the pencil or the Ninth Symphony. It may be said in reply that the church
can be burnt down, the street and pencil destroyed, and that, if all the scores of the
Ninth Symphony and all musical instruments were reduced to ashes, it would
survive only for a few brief years in the memory of those who have heard it,
whereas on the other hand the idea of the triangle and its properties are imperishable. In fact, the idea of the triangle with its properties, and of the quadratic
equation, have their historical and geographical area, and, if the tradition in which
they have been handed down to us, and the cultural instruments which bear them
on, were to be destroyed, fresh acts of creative expression would be needed to
revive them in the world. What is true, however, is that, once they have made
their first appearance, subsequent 'appearances', if successful, add nothing and if
unsuccessful, subtract nothing, from the quadratic equation, which remains an
inexhaustible possession among us. But the same may be said of the Ninth Symphony, which lives on in its intelligible abode, as Proust has said, whether it is
played well or badly; or rather which continues its existence in a more occult time
than natural time. The time of ideas is not to be confused with that in which books
appear and disappear, and musical works are printed or lost: a book which has
always been reprinted one day ceases to be read, a musical work of which there
were only a few copies extant is suddenly much sought after. The existence of
the idea must not be confused with the empirical existence of the means of expression, for ideas endure or fall into oblivion, and the intelligible sky subtly changes
colour. We have already drawn a distinction between empirical speech—the word
as a phenomenon of sound, the fact that a certain word is uttered at a certain

From *The Phenomenology of Perception,* by Maurice Merleau-Ponty, translated by Colin Smith,
1962. New York: Humanities Press Inc., London: Routledge & Kegan Paul Ltd. Reprinted by permission
of the publishers.

moment by a certain person, which may happen independently of thought—and transcendental or authentic speech, that by which an idea begins to exist. But if there had been no mankind with phonatory or articulatory organs, and a respiratory apparatus—or at least with a body and the ability to move himself, there would have been no speech and no ideas. What remains true is that in speech, to a greater extent than in music or painting, thought seems able to detach itself from its material instruments and acquire an eternal value. There is a sense in which all triangles which will ever exist through the workings of physical causality will always have angles the sum of which equals two right angles, even if a time comes when men have forgotten their geometry, and there is not a single person left who knows any. But in this case it is because speech is applied to nature, whereas music, and painting, like poetry, create their own object, and as soon as they become sufficiently aware of themselves, deliberately confine themselves within the cultural world. Prosaic, and particularly scientific, utterance is a cultural entity which at the same time lays claim to translate a truth relating to nature in itself. Now we know that this is not the case, for modern criticism of the sciences has clearly shown the constructive element in them. 'Real', i.e. perceived, triangles, do not necessarily have, for all eternity, angles the sum of which equals two right angles, if it is true that the space in which we live is no less amenable to non-Euclidean than to Euclidean geometry. Thus there is no fundamental difference between the various modes of expression, and no privileged position can be accorded to any of them on the alleged ground that it expresses a truth in itself. Speech is as dumb as music, music as eloquent as speech. Expression is everywhere creative, and what is expressed is always inseparable from it. There is no analysis capable of making language crystal clear and arraying it before us as if it were an object. The act of speech is clear only for the person who is actually speaking or listening; it becomes obscure as soon as we try to bring explicitly to light those reasons which have led us to understand thus and not otherwise. We can say of it what we have said of perception, and what Pascal says about opinions: in all three cases we have the same miracle of an immediately apprehended clarity, which vanishes as soon as we try to break it down to what we believe to be its component elements. I speak, and I understand myself and am understood quite unambiguously; I take a new grip on my life, and others take a new grip on it too. I may say that 'I have been waiting for a long time', or that someone 'is dead', and I think I know what I am saying. Yet if I question myself on time or the experience of death, which were implied in my words, there is nothing clear in my mind. This is because I have tried to speak about speech, to re-enact the act of expression which gave significance to the words 'dead' and 'time', to extend the brief hold on my experience which they ensure for me. These second or third order acts of expression, like the rest, have indeed in each case their convincing clarity, without, however, ever enabling me to dispel the fundamental obscurity of what is expressed, or to eliminate the distance separating my thought from itself. Must we conclude from this that, born and developed in obscurity, yet capable of clarity, language is nothing but the obverse of an infinite Thought, and the message of that Thought as communicated to us? This would mean losing contact with the analysis which we have just carried out, and reaching a conclusion in conflict with what has been established as we have gone along. Language transcends us and yet we speak. If we are led to conclude from this that there exists a transcendent thought spelt out by our words, we are supposing that an attempt at expression is brought to completion, after saying that it can never be so, and invoking an absolute thought, when we have just shown that any such thought is beyond our conception. It is the principle of Pascal's apologetics, but the more it is shown that man is without absolute power, the more any assertion of an absolute is made, not probable, but on the contrary suspect. In fact analysis demonstrates, not that there is behind language a transcendent thought, but that language transcends itself in speech, that speech itself *brings about* that concordance between me and myself, and between myself and others, on which an attempt is being made to base that thought.

. . .

. . . The laws of our thought and our self-evident truths are certainly facts, but they are not detachable from us, they are implied in any conception that we may form of being and the possible. It is not a question of confining ourselves to phenomena, of imprisoning consciousness in its own states, while retaining the possibility of another being beyond apparent being, nor of treating our thought as one fact among many, but of defining being as that which appears, and consciousness as a universal fact. I think, and this or that thought appears to me as true; I am well aware that it is not unconditionally true, and that the process of making it totally explicit would be an endless task; but the fact remains that at the moment I think, I think something, and that any other truth, in the name of which I might wish to discount this one, must, if it is to be called a truth for me, square with the 'true' thought of which I have experience. If I try to imagine Martians, or angels, or some divine thought outside the realm of my logic, this Martian, angelic or divine thought must figure in my universe without completely disrupting it. My thought, my self-evident truth is not one fact among others, but a value-fact which envelops and conditions every other possible one.

. . .

. . . Our situation, then, is as follows: in order to know that we think, it is necessary in the first place that we actually should think. Yet this commitment does not dispel all doubts, for my thoughts do not deprive me of my power to question; a word or an idea, considered as events in my history, have meaning for me only if I take up this meaning from within. I know that I think through such and such particular thoughts that I have, and I know that I have these thoughts because I carry them forward, that is, because I know that I think in general. The aim at a transcendent objective and the view of myself aiming at it, the awareness of the connected and of connecting are in a circular relationship. The problem is how I can be the constituting agent of my thought in general, failing which it would not be thought by anybody, would pass unnoticed and would therefore not be thought at all—without ever being that agent of my particular thoughts, since I never see them come into being in the full light of day, but merely know myself through them. The question is how subjectivity can be both dependent yet irremovable.

Let us tackle this by taking language as our example. There is a consciousness of myself which makes use of language and is humming with words. I read, let us say, the *Second Meditation*. It concerns the self, but rather the idea of the self which is, strictly speaking, neither mine nor, for that matter, Descartes', but that of any reflecting man. By following the meaning of the words and the argument, I reach the conclusion that indeed because I think, I am; but this is merely a verbal *cogito*, for I have grasped my thought and my existence only through the medium of language, and the true formula of this *cogito* should be: 'One thinks, therefore one is.' The wonderful thing about language is that it promotes its own oblivion: my eyes follow the lines on the paper, and from the moment I am caught up in their meaning, I lose sight of them. The paper, the letters on it, my eyes and body are there only as the minimum setting of some invisible operation. Expression fades out before what is expressed, and this is why its mediating rôle may pass unnoticed, and why Descartes nowhere mentions it. Descartes, and *a fortiori* his reader, begin their meditation in what is already a universe of discourse. This certainty which we enjoy of reaching, beyond expression, a truth separable from it and of which expression is merely the garment and contingent manifestation, has been implanted in us precisely by language. It appears as a mere sign only once it has provided itself with a meaning, and the coming to awareness, if it is to be complete, must rediscover the expressive unity in which both signs and meaning appear in the first place. When a child cannot speak, or cannot yet speak the adult's language, the linguistic ritual which unfolds around him has no hold on him, he is near us in the same way as is a spectator with a poor seat at the theatre; he sees clearly enough that we are laughing and gesticulating, he hears the nasal tune being played, but there is nothing at the end of those gestures or behind those words, nothing *happens* for him. Language takes on a meaning for the child when it *establishes a situation* for him. A story is told in a children's book of the disappointment of a small boy who put on his grandmother's spectacles and took up her book in the expectation of being able himself to find in it the stories which she used to tell him. The tale ends with these words: 'Well, what a fraud! Where's the story? I can see nothing but black and white.' For the child the 'story' and the thing expressed are not 'ideas' or 'meanings', nor are speaking or reading 'intellectual operations'. The story is a world which there must be some way of magically calling up by putting on spectacles and leaning over a book. The power possessed by language of bringing the thing expressed into existence, of opening up to thought new ways, new dimensions and new landscapes, is, in the last analysis, as obscure for the adult as for the child. In every successful work, the significance carried into the reader's mind exceeds language and thought as already constituted and is magically thrown into relief during the linguistic incantation, just as the story used to emerge from grandmother's book. In so far as we believe that, through thought, we are in direct communication with a universe of truth in which we are at one with others, in so far as Descartes' text seems merely to arouse in us thoughts already formed, and that we never learn anything from outside, and finally in so far as a philosopher, in a meditation purporting to be thoroughgoing, never even mentions language as the condition of the *reading* of the *cogito*, and does not invite us more unmistakably to pass from the idea to the practice of the *cogito*, it is because we take the process of expression for granted, and count it among our acquisitions. The *cogito* at which we arrive by reading Descartes (and even the one which Descartes effects in relation to expression and when, looking back on his past life, he fastens it down, objectifies it and 'characterizes' it as indubitable) is, then, a spoken *cogito,* put into words and understood in words, and for this very reason not attaining its objective, since that part of our existence which is engaged in fixing our life in conceptual forms, and thinking of it as indubitable, is escaping focus and thought. Shall we therefore conclude that language envelops us, and that we are led by it, much as the realist believes he is subject to the determinism of the external world, or as the theologian believes he is led on by Providence? This would be to forget half the truth. For after all, words, 'cogito' and 'sum' for example, may well have an empirical and statistical meaning, for it is the case that they are not directed specifically to my own experience, but form the basis of a general and anonymous thought. Nevertheless, I should find them not so much derivative and inauthentic as meaningless, and I should be unable even to read Descartes' book, were I not, before any speech can begin, in contact with my own life and thought, and if the spoken *cogito* did not encounter within me a tacit *cogito.* This silent *cogito* was the one Descartes sought when writing his *Meditations.* He gave life and direction to all those expressive operations which, by definition, always miss their target since, between Descartes' existence and the knowledge of it which he acquires, they interpose the full thickness of cultural acquisitions. And yet Descartes would not even have tried to put these expressive operations into operation had he not in the first place caught a glimpse of his existence. The whole question amounts to gaining a clear understanding of the unspoken *cogito,* to putting into it only what is really there, and not making language into a product of consciousness on the excuse that consciousness is not a product of language.

Neither the word nor the meaning of the word is, in fact *constituted* by consciousness. Let us make this clear. The word is certainly never reducible to one of its embodiments. The word 'sleet', for example, is not the set of characters which I have just written on the paper, nor that other set of signs that I once read in a book for the first time, nor again the sound that runs through the air when I pronounce it. Those are merely reproductions of the word, in which I recognize it but which do not exhaust it. Am I then to say that the word 'sleet' is the unified idea of these manifestations, and that it exists only for my consciousness and through a synthesis of identification? To do so would be to forget what psychology has taught us about language. To speak, as we have seen, is not to call up verbal images and articulate words in accordance with the imagined model. By undertaking a critical examination of the verbal image, and showing that the speaking subject plunges into speech without imagining the words he is about to utter, modern psychology eliminates the word as a representation, or as an object for consciousness, and reveals a motor presence of the word which is not the knowledge of the word. The word 'sleet', when it is known to me, is not an object which I recognize through any identificatory synthesis, but a certain use made of my phonatory equipment, a certain modulation of my body as a being in the world. Its generality is not that of the idea, but that of a behavioural style 'understood' by my body in so far as the latter is a behaviour-producing power, in this case a phoneme-producing one. One day I 'caught on' to the word 'sleet', much as one imitates a gesture, not, that is, by analysing it and performing an articulatory or phonetic action corresponding to each part of the word as heard, but by hearing it as a single modulation of the world of sound, and because this acoustic entity presents itself as 'something to pronounce' in virtue of the all-embracing correspondence existing between my perceptual potentialities and my motor ones, which are elements of my indivisible and open existence. The word has never been inspected, analysed, known and constituted, but caught and taken up by a power of speech and, in the last analysis, by a motor power given to me along with the first experience I have of my body and its perceptual and practical fields. As for the meaning of the word, I learn it as I learn to use a tool, by seeing it used in the context of a certain situation. The word's meaning is not compounded of a certain number of physical characteristics belonging to the object; it is first and foremost the aspect taken on by the object in human experience, for example my wonder in the face of these hard, then friable, then melting pellets falling ready-made from the sky. Here we have a meeting of the human and the non-human and, as it were, a piece of the world's behaviour, a certain version of its style, and the generality of its meaning as well as that of the vocable is not the generality of the concept, but of the world as typical. Thus language presupposes nothing less than a consciousness of language, a silence of consciousness embracing the world of speech in which words first receive a form and meaning. This is why consciousness is never subordinated to any empirical language, why languages can be translated and learned, and finally, why language is not an attribute of external origin, in the sociologist's sense. Behind the spoken *cogito,* the one which is converted into discourse and into essential truth, there lies a tacit *cogito,* myself experienced by myself. But this subjectivity, albeit imperious, has upon itself and upon the world only a precarious hold. It does not constitute the world, it divines the world's presence round about it as a field not provided by itself; nor does it constitute the word, but speaks as we sing when we are happy; nor again the meaning of the word, which instantaneously emerges for it in its dealing with the world and other men living in it, being at the intersection of many lines of behaviour, and being, even once 'acquired', as precise and yet as indefinable as the significance of a gesture. The tacit *cogito,* the presence of oneself to oneself, being no less than existence, is anterior to any philosophy, and knows itself only in those extreme situations in which it is under threat: for example, in the dread of death or of another's gaze upon me. What is believed to be thought about thought, as pure feeling of the self, cannot yet be thought and needs to be revealed. The consciousness which conditions language is merely a comprehensive and inarticulate grasp upon the world, like that of the infant at its first breath, or of the man about to drown and who is impelled towards life, and though it is true that all particular knowledge is founded on this primary view, it is true also that the latter waits to be won back, fixed and made explicit by perceptual exploration and by speech. Silent consciousness grasps itself only as a generalized 'I think' in face of a confused world 'to be thought about'. Any particular seizure, even the recovery of this generalized project by philosophy, demands that the subject bring into action powers which are a closed book to him and, in particular, that he should become a speaking subject. The tacit *cogito* is a *cogito* only when it has found expression for itself.

Such formulations may appear puzzling: if ultimate subjectivity cannot think of itself the moment it exists, how can it ever do so? How can that which does not think take to doing so? And is not subjectivity made to amount to a thing or a force which produces its effects without being capable of knowing it? We do not mean that the primordial *I* completely overlooks itself. If it did, it would indeed be a thing, and nothing could cause it subsequently to become consciousness. We have merely withheld from it objective thought, positing consciousness of the world and of itself. What do we mean by this? Either these words mean nothing at all, or else they mean that we refrain from assuming an explicit consciousness which duplicates and sustains the confused grasp of primary subjectivity upon itself and upon its world. My vision, for example, is certainly 'thinking that I see', if we mean thereby that it is not simply a bodily function like digestion or respiration, a collection of processes so grouped as to have a significance in a larger system, but that it is itself that system and that significance, that anteriority of the future to the present, of the whole to its parts. There is vision only through anticipation and intention, and since no intention could be a true intention if the object towards which it tends were given to it ready made and with no motivation, it is true that all vision assumes in the last resort, at the core of subjectivity, a total project or a logic of the world which empirical perceptions endow with specific form, but to which they cannot give rise. But vision is not thinking that one sees, if we understand thereby that it itself links up with its object, and that it becomes aware of itself as absolutely transparent, and as the originator of its own presence in the visible world. The essential point is clearly to grasp the project towards the world that we are. What we have said above about the world's being inseparable from our views of the world should here help us to understand subjectivity conceived as inherence in the world. There is no *hylé,* no sensation which is not in communication with other sensations or the sensations of other people, and *for this very reason* there is no *morphe,* no apprehension or apperception, the office of which is to give significance to a matter that has none, and to ensure the *a priori* unity of my experience, and experience shared with others. Suppose that my friend Paul and I are looking at a landscape. What precisely happens? Must it be said that we have both private sensations, that we know things but cannot communicate them to each other—that, as far as pure, lived-through experience goes, we are each incarcerated in our separate perspectives—that the landscape is not numerically the same for both of us and that it is a question only of a specific identity? When I consider my perception itself, before any objectifying reflection, at no moment am I aware of being shut up within my own sensations. My friend Paul and I point out to each other certain details of the landscape; and Paul's finger, which is pointing out the church tower, is not a finger-for-me that I *think of* as oriented towards a church-tower-for-me, it is Paul's finger which itself shows me the tower that Paul sees, just as, conversely, when I make a movement towards some point in the landscape that I can see, I do not imagine that I am producing in Paul, in virtue of some pre-established harmony, inner visions merely analogous to mine: I believe, on the contrary, that my gestures invade Paul's world and guide his gaze. When I think of Paul, I do not think of a flow of private sensations indirectly related to mine through the medium of interposed signs, but of someone who has a living experience of the same world as mine, as well as the same history, and with whom I am in communication through that world and that history. Are we to say, then, that what we are concerned with is an ideal unity, that my world is the same as Paul's, just as the quadratic equation spoken of in Tokyo is the same as the one spoken of in Paris, and that in short the ideal nature of the world guarantees its intersubjective value? But ideal unity is not satisfactory either, for it exists no less between Mount Hymettus seen by the ancient Greeks and the same mountain seen by me. Now it is no use my telling myself, as I contemplate those russet mountain sides, that the Greeks saw them too, for I cannot convince myself that they are the same ones. On the other hand, Paul and I 'together' see this landscape, we are jointly present in it, it is the same for both of us, not only as an intelligible significance, but as a certain accent of the world's style, down to its very thisness. The unity of the world crumbles and falls asunder under the influence of that temporal and spatial distance which the ideal unity can cover while remaining (in theory) unimpaired. It is precisely because the landscape makes its impact upon me and produces feelings in me, because it reaches me in my uniquely individual being, because it is my own view of the landscape, that I enjoy possession of the landscape itself, and the landscape for Paul as well as for me. Both universality and the world lie at the core of individuality and the subject, and this will never be understood as long as the world is made into an ob-ject. It is understood immediately if the world is the *field* of our experience, and if we are nothing but a view of the world, for in that case it is seen that the most intimate vibration of our psycho-physical being already announces the world, the quality being the outline of a thing, and the thing the outline of the world. A world which, as Malebranche puts it, never gets beyond being an 'unfinished work', or which, as Husserl says of the body, is 'never completely constituted', does not require, and even rules out, a constituting subject. There must be, corresponding to this adumbration of being which appears through the concordant aspects of my own experience, or of the experience I share with others—experience which I presume capable of being consummated through indefinite horizons, from the sole fact that my phenomena congeal into a thing, and display, as they occur, a certain consistency of style—there must be, then, corresponding to this open unity of the world, an open and indefinite unity of subjectivity. Like the world's unity, that of the *I* is invoked rather than experienced each time I perform an act of perception, each time I reach a self-evident truth, and the universal *I* is the background against which these effulgent forms stand out: it is through one present thought that I achieve the unity of all my thoughts. What remains, on the hither side of my particular thoughts, to constitute the tacit *cogito* and the original project towards the world, and what, ultimately, am I in so far as I can catch a glimpse of myself independently of any particular act? I am a field, an experience. One day, once and for all, something was set in motion which, even during sleep, can no longer cease to see or not to see, to feel or not to feel, to suffer or be happy, to think or rest from thinking, in a word to 'have it out' with the world. There then arose, not a new set of sensations or states of consciousness, not even a new monad or a new perspective, since I am not tied to any one perspective but can change my point of view, being under compulsion only in that I must always have one, and can have only one at once—let us say, therefore, that there arose a fresh *possibility of situations*. The event of my birth has not passed completely away, it has not fallen into nothingness in the way that an event of the objective world does, for it committed a whole future, not as a cause determines its effect, but as a situation, once created, inevitably leads on to some outcome. There was henceforth a new 'setting', the world received a fresh layer of meaning. In the home into which a child is born, all objects change their significance; they begin to await some as yet indeterminate treatment at his hands; another and different person is there, a new personal history, short or long, has just been initiated, another account has been opened. My first perception, along with the horizons which surrounded it, is an ever-present event, an unforgettable tradition; even as a thinking subject, I still am that first perception, the continuation of that same life inaugurated by it. In one sense, there are no more acts of consciousness or distinct *Erlebnisse* in a life than there are separate things in the world. Just as, as we have seen, when I walk round an object, I am not presented with a succession of perspective views which I subsequently co-ordinate thanks to the idea of one single flat projection, there being merely a certain amount of 'shift' in the thing which, in itself, is journeying through time, so I am not myself a succession of 'psychic' acts, not for that matter a nuclear *I* who bring them together into a synthetic unity, but one single experience inseparable from itself, one single 'living cohesion',[1] one single temporality which is engaged, from birth, in making itself progressively explicit, and in confirming that cohesion in each successive present. It is this advent or again this event of transcendental kind that the *cogito* reveals. The primary truth is indeed 'I think', but only provided that we understand thereby 'I belong to myself'[2] while belonging to the world. When we try to go deeper into subjectivity, calling all things into question and suspending all our beliefs, the only form in which a glimpse is vouchsafed to us of that non-human ground through which, in the words of Rimbaud, 'we are not of the world', is as the horizon of our particular commitments, and as the potentiality of something in the most general sense, which is the world's phantom. Inside and outside are inseparable. The world is wholly inside and I am wholly outside myself. When I perceive this table, the perception of the top must not overlook that of the legs, otherwise the object would be thrown out of joint. When I hear a melody, each of its moments must be related to its successor, otherwise there would be no melody. Yet the table is there with its external parts, and succession is of the essence of melody. The act which draws together at the same time takes away and holds at a distance, so that I touch myself only by escaping from myself. In a thought of his which is famous, Pascal shows that in one way I understand the world, and in another it understands me. We must add that it is in the *same* way: I understand the world because there are for me things near and far, foregrounds and horizons, and because in this way it forms a picture and acquires significance before me, and this finally is because I am situated in it and it understands me. We do not say that the *notion* of the world is inseparable from that of the subject, or that the subject *thinks himself* inseparable from the idea of his body and the idea of the world; for, if it were a matter of no more than a conceived relationship, it would *ipso facto* leave the absolute independence of the subject as thinker intact, and the subject would not be in a situation. If the subject *is* in a situation, even if he is no more than a possibility of situations, this is because he forces his ipseity into reality only by actually being a body, and entering the world through that body. In so far as, when I reflect on the essence of subjectivity, I find it bound up with that of the body and that of the world, this is because my existence as subjectivity is merely one with my existence as a body and with the existence of the world, and because the subject that I am, when taken

---

[1] 'Zusammenhang des Lebens,' Heidegger, *Sein und Zeit,* p. 388.
[2] Heidegger, *Sein und Zeit,* pp. 124–5.

concretely, is inseparable from this body and this world. The ontological world and body which we find at the core of the subject are not the world or body as idea, but on the one hand the world itself contracted into a comprehensive grasp, and on the other the body itself as a knowing-body.

But, it will be asked, if the unity of the world is not based on that of consciousness, and if the world is not the outcome of a constituting effort, how does it come about that appearances accord with each other and group themselves together into things, ideas and truths? And why do our random thoughts, the events of our life and those of collective history, at least at certain times assume common significance and direction, and allow themselves to be subsumed under one idea? Why does my life succeed in drawing itself together in order to project itself in words, intentions and acts? This is the problem of rationality. The reader is aware that, on the whole, classical thought tries to explain the concordances in question in terms of a world in itself, or in terms of an absolute mind. Such explanations borrow all the forces of conviction which they can carry from the phenomenon of rationality, and therefore fail to explain that phenomenon, or ever to achieve greater clarity than it possesses. Absolute Thought is no clearer to me than my own finite mind, since it is through the latter that I conceive the former. We are in the world, which means that things take shape, an immense individual asserts itself, each existence is self-comprehensive and comprehensive of the rest. All that has to be done is to recognize these phenomena which are the ground of all our certainties. The belief in an absolute mind, or in a world in itself detached from us is no more than a rationalization of this primordial faith.

FURTHER READINGS

ANTHOLOGIES IN THE THEORY OF KNOWLEDGE

Canfield, John V., and Franklin H. Donnell, Eds., *Readings in the Theory of Knowledge,* New York, Appleton-Century-Crofts, 1964.

Nagel, Ernest, and Richard Brandt, Eds., *Meaning and Knowledge,* New York, Harcourt, Brace & World, 1965.

Stroll, Avrum, Ed., *Epistemology,* New York, Harper & Row, 1967.

MYSELF AND OTHERS

Anthologies in the Philosophy of Mind

Anderson, Alan Ross, Ed., *Minds and Machines,* Englewood Cliffs, N.J., Prentice-Hall, 1964.

Crosson, Frederick J., and Kenneth M. Sayre, Eds., *Philosophy and Cybernetics,* Notre Dame, Ind., University Press, 1967.

Flew, Antony, Ed., *Body, Mind, and Death,* New York, Collier, 1964.

Hampshire, Stuart, Ed., *Philosophy of Mind,* New York, Harper & Row, 1966.

Hook, Sidney, Ed., *Dimensions of Mind,* New York, Collier, 1961.
Morick, Harold, Ed., *Other Minds,* Glenview, Ill., Scott, Foresman, 1970.
Tillman, Frank A., Ed., *Philosophy of Mind,* New York, Harper & Row, 1970.

Articles and Books

Aristotle, *De Anima,* in *The Basic Works of Aristotle,* Richard McKeon, Ed., New York, Random House, 1966.
Ayer, A. J., *The Concept of a Person and Other Essays,* New York, St. Martin's, 1964.
Campell, A. Co., *Selfhood and Godhood,* New York, Macmillan, 1957.
Danto, Arthur C., *Nietzsche as Philosopher,* New York, Macmillan, 1965, chapter 4.
Dreyfus, Hubert, "Phenomenology and Artificial Intelligence," in *Phenomenology in America,* James Edie, Ed., Chicago, Quadrangle Books, 1967.
Fingarette, Herbert, *The Self in Transformation,* New York, Basic Books, 1963.
MacMurray, John, *The Self as Agent,* New York, Harper & Row, 1957.
Malcolm, Norman, "Knowledge of Other Minds," in *Journal of Philosophy, 55* (1958), and in Norman Malcolm, *Knowledge and Certainty,* Englewood Cliffs, N.J., Prentice-Hall, 1963.
Reeves, J. W., *Body and Mind in Western Thought,* Harmondsworth, Eng., Penguin, 1958.
Ryle, Gilbert, *The Concept of Mind,* New York, Barnes & Noble, 1949.
Sartre, Jean-Paul, *The Transcendence of the Ego,* New York, Noonday, 1957.
Turing, A. M., "Computing Machinery and Intelligence," *Mind, 59* (1950), 433–460, and in Anderson.
White, Alan R., *The Philosophy of Mind,* New York, Random House, 1967.
Wittgenstein, Ludwig, *The Blue and Brown Books,* Oxford, Blackwell, 1953, pp. 46–74.
———, *Philosophical Investigations,* Oxford, Blackwell, 1953, pp. 833–1043.

LANGUAGE, MIND, AND WORLD

Alston, William, *Philosophy of Language,* Englewood Cliffs, N.J., Prentice-Hall, 1964.
Austin, John L., *How to do Things with Words,* Cambridge, Mass., Harvard University Press, 1962.
———, "Other Minds," in *Philosophical Papers,* Oxford, Clarendon, 1961.
———, *Sense and Sensibilia,* Oxford, Clarendon, 1961.
Ayer, A. J., *Foundations of Empirical Knowledge,* London, Macmillan, 1940.
———, *The Problem of Knowledge,* Harmondsworth, Eng., Penguin, 1956.
Berkeley, George, *Principles of Human Knowledge,* Indianapolis, Ind., Liberal Arts, 1957.
———, *Three Dialogues between Hylas and Philonious,* Indianapolis, Ind., Liberal Arts, 1954.
Cornforth, Maurice, *Marxism and Linguistic Philosophy,* New York, International Publishers, 1965.
Danto, A. C., *What Philosophy Is,* New York, Harper & Row, 1968.
Ewing, A. C., *The Fundamental Questions of Philosophy,* New York, Collier, 1962.
Henle, Paul, Ed., *Language, Thought, and Culture,* Ann Arbor, Mich., University of Michigan Press, 1959.
Hirst, R. J., *The Problems of Perception,* New York, Macmillan, 1959.

————, Ed., *Perception and the External World*, New York, Macmillan, 1965.

Husserl, Edmund, *The Paris Lectures*, Peter Koestenbaum, Trans., The Hague, Martinus Nijhoff, 1964.

Kaplan, Abraham, *The New World of Philosophy*, New York, Random House, 1961.

Lauer, Quentin, *Phenomenology, Its Genesis and Prospect*, New York, Harper Torchbooks, 1965. Originally published under the title *The Triumph of Subjectivity*.

Lee, Dorothy, "Lineal and Nonlineal Codifications of Reality," in Edward Carpenter and Marshall McLuhan, Eds., *Explorations in Communication*, Boston, Beacon, 1960; Beacon Paperbacks, 1966.

McLuhan, Marshall, *Understanding Media*, New York, McGraw-Hill, 1964.

Manser, Anthony, *Sartre: A Philosophic Study*, London, Athlone Press, 1966.

Nakhnikian, George, Introduction to Edmund Husserl's *The Idea of Phenomenology*, in William Alston and George Nakhnikian, Eds., *Readings in Twentieth Century Philosophy*, New York, Free Press, 1963.

Russell, Bertrand, *The Problems of Philosophy*, New York, Holt, 1912.

Sartre, Jean-Paul, *Imagination*, Forrest Williams, Trans., Ann Arbor, Mich., University of Michigan Press, 1962.

————, *The Psychology of Imagination*, Bernard Frechtman, Trans., New York, Philosophical Library, 1948.

Somerville, John, *The Philosophy of Marxism*, New York, Random House, 1967.

Taylor, Richard, *Metaphysics*, Englewood Cliffs, N.J., Prentice-Hall, 1963.

Whiteley, C. H., *An Introduction to Metaphysics*, New York, Barnes & Noble, 1950.

Wilson, John, *Language and the Pursuit of Truth*, London, Cambridge, 1956.

Wood, Ledger, *The Analysis of Knowledge*, Princeton, N.J., Princeton University Press, 1941.

Woozley, A. D., *Theory of Knowledge*, London, Hutchinson, 1962.

Section IV

RELIGIOUS

COMMITMENT

Human dignity and human identity are not self-sustaining concepts. Human actions are often hopelessly inept and futile; and all human life is perishable. Thus we come to look for something beyond our humanity to give it worth and hope. This search leads many to a religious commitment.

Religious commitment is increasingly complicated and imperiled in this age. For one thing, religious beliefs taught to children are questioned when the children grow up and critically compare their own experiences with the tenets of their earlier faith. For another, many are no longer taught an institutional religion. Finally, anyone who sustains a religious commitment discovers that it will fly in the face of common sense, accepted standards of meaningful discourse, logical proof, and scientific evidence.

This last challenge to religious commitment is the most troublesome. In his "Lectures on Religious Belief" Ludwig Wittgenstein—a philosopher whose logical and conceptual analyses have had unequaled influence on the discipline for the last several decades—turns the full power of his intelligence to considering just what constitutes religious commitment. He finds that the usual standards of meaningful discourse—standards he himself did much to develop—do not apply to religious discourse. For example, although it would ordinarily be thought nonsensical for one to assert he has seen a man known to have died, it is not nonsensical in the same way for a Christian to claim as a central tenet of his faith that the dead shall be raised. Indeed, the defining characteristic of religious discourse is its utter disregard for the usual criteria of meaning and proof. For this reason a person's utterance of religious statements surely expresses a commitment that transcends the human: It does not adhere to criteria imposed by our limited intelligence, but relies on a faith which goes beyond it.

Not unexpectedly, it is a fascination with the very irrationality of such commitment, as well as a search for a more profound justification of human dignity, that impels many toward religion. The very experience of suspending one's criteria for proof must be exhilarating; and if it accompanies an enlightenment not accessible merely to our intelligence, it is greatly to be valued. The experience of believing becomes as important as the belief itself. These possibilities are discussed in the subsection "Religious Experience."

A search for the profound experience has recently led to claims that hallucinogenic drugs can induce it. In "Psychedelic Drugs and Religious Experience" two psychologists, R. E. L. Masters and Jean Houston, discuss the results of their controlled experiments with mescaline, LSD, and peyote, on more than two hundred subjects who reported drug-induced religious experiences. Masters and Houston discovered that both mystical and religious experience under the influence of drugs are possible, but rare; they occur only after long spiritual preparation. They conclude that drugs alone cannot produce the depth of insight or wisdom many seek in religious experience; drugs offer no shortcut to enlightenment.

Of course, the search for religious experience did not begin with the recent widespread use of LSD. There have been reports of such experience, and particularly of mystical experiences, throughout the ages. In "The Reality of the Unseen" William James, a physician who became a psychologist and philosopher, devotes particular attention to the mystic's experience of self-annihilation. To this he contrasts the testimony of those who found their own religious experiences rational. James draws on many examples of both kinds of religious experience to identify the elements common to both.

In some religious experience there is an element of awe which is subjective, rather than rational. Yet it is not mystical, for there is no annihilation of consciousness. Søren Kierkegaard dramatically describes such an experience in "The Concept of Dread." It is a vertigo like that felt by the person who stands on the edge of the abyss and feels impelled to leap into it. An act of religious belief is itself a kind of leap into the abyss, for only faith assures the believer that he will not perish.

Finally, a religious experience expressed rationally can still involve a symbolic redescription of all experience. This is illustrated in Albert Einstein's "A Scientist's Cosmology." Einstein, of course, formulated a radically revised physical description of the universe in his general theory of relativity; here he offers a description of another sort that ascribes to the universe an order or design greater than what a scientist could hope to observe.

An essential element in religious experience is its attempt to remove the doubts which arise from events in our lives. Such doubts pose a particular problem for Christians and Jews, for both religions affirm the existence of a personal God who is both ultimately good and ultimately powerful. Yet all of us suffer the cruelties of natural disaster or of evil men. Why does not a good God use his omnipotence to prevent them? The fact that He does not (for we do suffer) generates a crisis of faith.

The nature and extent of this crisis is described dramatically in a chapter from Fyodor Dostoyevsky's *The Brothers Karamazov*. In the famous "The Grand Inquisitor" an anonymous Christ is depicted as being interrogated by officials of the Spanish Inquisition. Christ himself, it is charged, would now be branded as a heretic. How could God allow this?

In "Evil and the God of Love" John Hick presents an answer for the Christian: Evil does exist, and we cannot explain it away as illusion, as was sometimes traditionally done. On the other hand, God is the God of love. Our religious faith in Him despite the presence of evil requires an expansion and an evolution of our own belief.

In "Jewish Faith and the Holocaust" Emil L. Fackenheim faces the challenge that the Nazi imprisonment and murder of six million Jews in concentration camps presents to Jewish faith. Jews dare not abandon their faith on account of this atrocity, Fackenheim argues, for such an abandonment of faith would constitute the unimaginable—a victory, after all, for the Nazis who were trying to remove Judaism from the face of the earth.

Finally, in a metaphor that captures the spirit of doubt in the present age and that has recently captured the imagination of theologians, Friedrich Nietzsche contends that massive moral failure, such as that which we are presently experiencing, signifies that "God is dead."

Can any unshakable proof for the existence of God be offered to demolish doubt? This question is considered in the subsection "The Existence of God." In the Middle Ages, in attempts that still fascinate committed believers, two theologians tried to apply logic to this problem. The existence of God is self-evident, argues Saint Anselm in his famous ontological proof, for the very nature of the idea that I have of Him requires me to acknowledge that He exists beyond my thought. On the other hand, Saint Thomas Aquinas offers no less than five proofs, all from evidence to be found in the world, that God is the author of such indisputably present phenomena as motion and cause, and that God indisputably exists.

Saint Thomas' fifth proof is the argument from design, the argument that there is an order in nature from which we may infer the existence of a Supreme Being who created it. This argument, as John Stuart Mill points out at the beginning of "The Argument from Design," evokes respect because of its scientific character. But Mill also points out that no scientific demonstration—in this case an inductive analogy—can establish an unshakable and indisputably certain conclusion. Thus the argument from design, too, must fail to establish that God necessarily exists.

Can any proof for the existence of God succeed? Not if the only God whose existence such a proof could establish is a rational God far removed from the religious experience believers seek. In the final article, "The Irrelevance to Religion of Philosophic Proofs for the Existence of God," Steven M. Cahn contends that the proofs can neither convince the unbeliever nor, in their lapses in logic, sustain the doubter. Cahn argues that neither religious men nor skeptics are swayed by logic; religious belief rests on other than rational grounds.

The fabric of religious experience is not captured by rational proof or by descriptive discourse. Religous commitment transcends the control of our intelligence and yet remains intensely personal.

LUDWIG WITTGENSTEIN

Lectures on Religious Belief

Ludwig Wittgenstein (1889–1951), an Austrian-born former engineering student, became a philosopher after studying with Bertrand Russell. He wrote the *Tractatus Logico-Philosophicus* to investigate the possibility of using formal logic to solve philosophical problems. In a later work, *Philosophical Investigations,* he repudiated that approach and applied an analysis of "ordinary," or spoken, language to problems in the philosophy of mind. This selection is a set of lecture notes in which his students recorded his application of ordinary-language analysis to problems in theology.

I

An Austrian general said to someone: "I shall think of you after my death, if that should be possible." We can imagine one group who would find this ludicrous, another who wouldn't.

(During the war, Wittgenstein saw consecrated bread being carried in chromium steel. This struck him as ludicrous.)

Suppose that someone believed in the Last Judgment, and I don't, does this

From *Lectures and Conversations on Aesthetics, Psychology and Religious Belief*, by Ludwig Wittgenstein, edited by Cyril Barrett from notes taken by Yorick Smythies, Ruch Rhees, and James Taylor, University of California Press and Basil Blackwell, 1967. Reprinted by permission of Basil Blackwell, Publisher.

mean that I believe the opposite to him, just that there won't be such a thing? I would say: "not at all, or not always."

Suppose I say that the body will rot, and another says "No. Particles will rejoin in a thousand years, and there will be a Resurrection of you."

If some said: "Wittgenstein, do you believe in this?" I'd say: "No." "Do you contradict the man?" I'd say: No."

If you say this, the contradiction already lies in this.

Would you say: "I believe the opposite", or "There is no reason to suppose such a thing"? I'd say neither.

Suppose someone were a believer and said: "I believe in a Last Judgment," and I said: "Well, I'm not so sure. Possibly." You would say that there is an enormous gulf between us. If he said "There is a German aeroplane overhead," and I said "Possibly I'm not so sure," you'd say we were fairly near.

It isn't a question of my being anywhere near him, but on an entirely different plane, which you could express by saying: "You mean something altogether different, Wittgenstein."

The difference might not show up at all in any explanation of the meaning.

Why is it that in this case I seem to be missing the entire point?

Suppose somebody made this guidance for this life: believing in the Last Judgment. Whenever he does anything, this is before his mind. In a way, how are we to know whether to say he believes this will happen or not?

Asking him is not enough. He will probably say he has proof. But he has what you might call an unshakeable belief. It will show, not by reasoning or by appeal to ordinary grounds for belief, but rather by regulating for in all his life.

This is a very much stronger fact—foregoing pleasures, always appealing to this picture. This in one sense must be called the firmest of all beliefs, because the man risks things on account of it which he would not do on things which are by far better established for him. Although he distinguishes between things well-established and not well-established.

Lewy: Surely, he would say it is extremely well-established.

First, he may use "well-established" or not use it at all. He will treat this belief as extremely well-established, and in another way as not well-established at all.

If we have a belief, in certain cases we appeal again and again to certain grounds, and at the same time we risk pretty little—if it came to risking our lives on the ground of this belief.

There are instances where you have a faith—where you say "I believe"—and on the other hand this belief does not rest on the fact on which our ordinary every-day beliefs normally do rest.

How should we compare beliefs with each other? What would it mean to compare them?

You might say: "We compare the states of mind."

How do we compare states of mind? This obviously won't do for all occasions. First, what you say won't be taken as the measure for the firmness of a belief? But, for instance, what risks you would take?

The strength of a belief is not comparable with the intensity of a pain.

An entirely different way of comparing beliefs is seeing what sorts of grounds he will give.

A belief isn't like a momentary state of mind. "At 5 o'clock he had very bad toothache."

Suppose you had two people, and one of them, when he had to decide which course to take, thought of retribution, and the other did not. One person might, for instance, be inclined to take everything that happened to him as a reward or punishment, and another person doesn't think of this at all.

If he is ill, he may think: "What have I done to deserve this?" This is one way of thinking of retribution. Another way is, he thinks in a general way whenever he is ashamed of himself: "This will be punished."

Take two people, one of whom talks of his behaviour and of what happens to him in terms of retribution, the other one does not. These people think entirely differently. Yet, so far, you can't say they believe different things.

Suppose someone is ill and he says: "This is a punishment," and I say: "If I'm ill, I don't think of punishment at all." If you say: "Do you believe the opposite?"—you can call it believing the opposite, but it is entirely different from what we would normally call believing the opposite.

I think differently, in a different way. I say different things to myself. I have different pictures.

It is this way: if someone said: "Wittgenstein, you don't take illness as punishment, so what do you believe?"—I'd say: "I don't have any thoughts of punishment."

There are, for instance, these entirely different ways of thinking first of all—which needn't be expressed by one person saying one thing, another person another thing.

What we call believing in a Judgment Day or not believing in a Judgment Day—The expression of belief may play an absolutely minor role.

If you ask me whether or not I believe in a Judgment Day, in the sense in which religious people have belief in it, I wouldn't say: "No. I don't believe there will be such a thing." It would seem to me utterly crazy to say this.

And then I give an explanation: "I don't believe in . . .", but then the religious person never believes what I describe.

I can't say. I can't contradict that person.

In one sense, I understand all he says—the English words "Good", "separate", etc. I understand. I could say: "I don't believe in this," and this would be true, meaning I haven't got these thoughts or anything that hangs together with them. But not that I could contradict the thing.

You might say: "Well, if you can't contradict him, that means you don't understand him. If you did understand him, then you might." That again is Greek to me. My normal technique of language leaves me. I don't know whether to say they understand one another or not.

These controversies look quite different from any normal controversies. Reasons look entirely different from normal reasons.

They are, in a way, quite inconclusive.

The point is that if there were evidence, this would in fact destroy the whole business.

Anything that I normally call evidence wouldn't in the slightest influence me.

Suppose, for instance, we knew people who foresaw the future; made forecasts for years and years ahead; and they described some sort of a Judgment Day.

Queerly enough, even if there were such a thing, and even if it were more convincing than I have described but, belief in this happening wouldn't be at all a religious belief.

Suppose that I would have to forego all pleasures because of such a forecast. If I do so and so, someone will put me in fires in a thousand years, etc. I wouldn't budge. The best scientific evidence is just nothing.

A religious belief might in fact fly in the face of such a forecast, and say "No. There it will break down."

As it were, the belief as formulated on the evidence can only be the last result—in which a number of ways of thinking and acting crystallize and come together.

A man would fight for his life not to be dragged into the fire. No induction. Terror. That is, as it were, part of the substance of the belief.

That is partly why you don't get in religious controversies, the form of controversy where one person is *sure* of the thing, and the other says: "Well, possibly."

You might be surprised that there hasn't been opposed to those who believe in Resurrection those who say "Well, possibly."

Here believing obviously plays much more this role: suppose we said that a certain picture might play the role of constantly admonishing me, or I always think of it. Here, an enormous difference would be between those people for whom the picture is constantly in the foreground, and the others who just didn't use it at all.

Those who said: "Well, possibly it may happen and possibly not" would be on an entirely different plane.

This is partly why one would be reluctant to say: "These people rigorously hold the opinion (or view) that there is a Last Judgment". "Opinion" sounds queer.

It is for this reason that different words are used: 'dogma', 'faith'.

We don't talk about hypothesis, or about high probability. Nor about knowing.

In a religious discourse we use such expressions as: "I believe that so and so will happen," and use them differently to the way in which we use them in science.

Although, there is a great temptation to think we do. Because we do talk of evidence, and do talk of evidence by experience.

We could even talk of historic events.

It has been said that Christianity rests on an historic basis.

It has been said a thousand times by intelligent people that indubitability is not enough in this case. Even if there is as much evidence as for Napoleon. Because the indubitability wouldn't be enough to make me change my whole life.

It doesn't rest on an historic basis in the sense that the ordinary belief in historic facts could serve as a foundation.

Here we have a belief in historic facts different from a belief in ordinary historic facts. Even, they are not treated as historical, empirical, propositions.

Those people who had faith didn't apply the doubt which would ordinarily apply to *any* historical propositions. Especially propositions of a time long past, etc.

What is the criterion of reliability, dependability? Suppose you give a general description as to when you say a proposition has a reasonable weight of probability. When you call it reasonable, is this *only* to say that for it you have such and such evidence, and for others you haven't?

For instance, we don't trust the account given of an event by a drunk man.

Father O'Hara[1] is one of those people who make it a question of science.

Here we have people who treat this evidence in a different way. They base things on evidence which taken in one way would seem exceedingly flimsy. They base enormous things on this evidence. Am I to say they are unreasonable? I wouldn't call them unreasonable.

I would say, they are certainly not *reasonable,* that's obvious.

'Unreasonable' implies, with everyone, rebuke.

I want to say: they don't treat this as a matter of reasonability.

Anyone who reads the Epistles will find it said: not only that it is not reasonable, but that it is folly.

Not only is it not reasonable, but it doesn't pretend to be.

What seems to me ludicrous about O'Hara is his making it appear to be *reasonable.*

Why shouldn't one form of life culminate in an utterance of belief in a Last Judgment? But I couldn't either say "Yes" or "No" to the statement that there will be such a thing. Nor "Perhaps," nor "I'm not sure."

It is a statement which may not allow of any such answer.

If Mr. Lewy is religious and says he believes in a Judgment Day, I won't even know whether to say I understand him or not. I've read the same things as he's read. In a most important sense, I know what he means.

If an atheist says: "There won't be a Judgment Day, and another person says there will," do they mean the same?—Not clear what criterion of meaning the same is. They might describe the same things. You might say, this already shows that they mean the same.

We come to an island and we find beliefs there, and certain beliefs we are inclined to call religious. What I'm driving at is, that religious beliefs will not. . . . They have sentences, and there are also religious statements.

These statements would not just differ in respect to what they are about. Entirely different connections would make them into religious beliefs, and there can easily be imagined transitions where we wouldn't know for our life whether to call them religious beliefs or scientific beliefs.

You may say they reason wrongly.

In certain cases you would say they reason wrongly, meaning they contradict us. In other cases you would say they don't reason at all, or "It is an entirely different kind of reasoning." The first, you would say in the case in which they reason in a similar way to us, and make something corresponding to our blunders.

Whether a thing is a blunder or not—it is a blunder in a particular system. Just as something is a blunder in a particular game and not in another.

You could also say that where we are reasonable, they are not reasonable—meaning they don't use *reason* here.

If they do something very like one of our blunders, I would say, I don't know. It depends on further surroundings of it.

It is difficult to see, in cases in which it has all the appearances of trying to be reasonable.

---

[1] Contribution to a Symposium on *Science and Religion* (London: Gerald Howe, 1931, pp. 107–116).

I would definitely call O'Hara unreasonable. I would say, if this is religious belief, then it's all superstition.

But I would ridicule it, not by saying it is based on insufficient evidence. I would say: here is a man who is cheating himself. You can say: this man is ridiculous because he believes, and bases it on weak reasons.

II

The word 'God' is amongst the earliest learnt—pictures and catechisms, etc. But not the same consequences as with pictures of aunts. I wasn't shown [that which the picture pictured].

The word is used like a word representing a person. God sees, rewards, etc.

"Being shown all these things, did you understand what this word meant?" I'd say: "Yes and no. I did learn what it didn't mean. I made myself understand. I could answer questions, understand questions when they were put in different ways—and in that sense could be said to understand."

If the question arises as to the existence of a god or God, it plays an entirely different role to that of the existence of any person or object I ever heard of. One said, had to say, that one *believed* in the existence, and if one did not believe, this was regarded as something bad. Normally if I did not believe in the existence of something no one would think there was anything wrong in this.

Also, there is this extraordinary use of the word 'believe'. One talks of believing and at the same time one dosen't use 'believe' as one does ordinarily. You might say (in the normal use): "You only believe—oh well. . . ." Here it is used entirely differently; on the other hand it is not used as we generally use the word 'know'.

If I even vaguely remember what I was taught about God, I might say: "Whatever believing in God may be, it can't be believing in something we can test, or find means of testing." You might say: "This is nonsense, because people say they believe on *evidence* or say they believe on religious experiences." I would say: "The mere fact that someone says they believe on evidence doesn't tell me enough for me to be able to say now whether I can say of a sentence 'God exists' that your evidence is unsatisfactory or insufficient."

Suppose I know someone, Smith. I've heard that he has been killed in a battle in this war. One day you come to me and say: "Smith is in Cambridge." I inquire, and find you stood at Guildhall and saw at the other end a man and said: "That was Smith." I'd say: "Listen. This isn't sufficient evidence." If we had a fair amount of evidence he was killed I would try to make you say that you're being credulous. Suppose he was never heard of again. Needless to say, it is quite impossible to make inquiries: "Who at 12.05 passed Market Place into Rose Crescent?" Suppose you say: "He was there". I would be extremely puzzled.

Suppose there is a feast on Mid-Summer Common. A lot of people stand in a ring. Suppose this is done every year and then everyone says he has seen one of his dead relatives on the other side of the ring. In this case, we could ask everyone in the ring. "Who did you hold by the hand?" Nevertheless, we'd all say that on that day we see our dead relatives. You could in this case say: "I had an extraordinary experience. I had the experience I can express by saying: 'I saw my dead cousin'." Would we say you are saying this on insufficient evidence? Under certain circumstances I would say this, under other circumstances I wouldn't. Where what is said sounds a bit absurd I would say: "Yes, in this case insufficient evidence." If altogether absurd, then I wouldn't.

Suppose I went to somewhere like Lourdes in France. Suppose I went with a very credulous person. There we see blood coming out of something. He says: "There you are, Wittgenstein, how can you doubt?" I'd say: "Can it only be explained one way? Can't it be this or that?" I'd try to convince him that he'd seen nothing of any consequence. I wonder whether I would do that under all circumstances. I certainly know that I would under normal circumstances.

"Oughtn't one after all to consider this?" I'd say: "Come on. Come on." I would treat the phenomenon in this case just as I would treat an experiment in a laboratory which I thought badly executed.

"The balance moves when I will it to move." I point out it is not covered up, a draught can move it, etc.

I could imagine that someone showed an extremely passionate belief in such a phenomenon, and I couldn't approach his belief at all by saying: "This could just as well have been brought about by so and so" because he could think this blasphemy on my side. Or he might say: "It is possible that these priests cheat, but nevertheless in a different sense a miraculous phenomenon takes place there."

I have a statue which bleeds on such and such a day in the year. I have red ink, etc. "You are a cheat, but nevertheless the Deity uses you. Red ink in a sense, but not red ink in a sense."

Cf. Flowers at seance with label. People said: "Yes, flowers are materialized with label." What kind of circumstances must there be to make this kind of story not ridiculous?

I have a moderate education, as all of you have, and therefore know what is meant by insufficient evidence for a forecast. Suppose someone dreamt of the Last Judgment, and said he now knew what it would be like. Suppose someone said: "This is poor evidence." I would say: "If you want to compare it with the evidence for it's raining to-morrow it is no evidence at all." He may make it sound as if by stretching the point you may call it evidence. But it may be more than ridiculous as evidence. But now, would I be prepared to say: "You are basing your belief on extremely slender evidence, to put it mildly." Why should I regard this dream as evidence—measuring its validity as though I were measuring the validity of the evidence for meteorological events?

If you compare it with anything in Science which we call evidence, you can't credit that anyone could soberly argue: "Well, I had this dream . . . therefore . . . Last Judgment." You might say: "For a blunder, that's too big." If you suddenly wrote numbers down on the blackboard, and then said: "Now, I'm going to add," and then said: "2 and 21 is 13," etc. I'd say: "This is no blunder."

There are cases where I'd say he's mad, or he's making fun. Then there might be cases where I look for an entirely different interpretation altogether. In order to see what the explanation is I should have to see the sum, to see in what way it is done, what he makes follow from it, what are the different circumstances under which he does it, etc.

I mean, if a man said to me after a dream that he believed in the Last Judgment, I'd try to find what sort of impression it gave him. One attitude: "It will be in about 2,000 years. It will be bad for so and so and so, etc." Or it may be one of terror. In the case where there is hope, terror, etc., would I say there is insufficient evidence if he says: "I believe . . ."? I can't treat these words as I normally treat 'I believe so and so'. It would be entirely beside the point, and also if he said his friend so and so and his grandfather had had the dream and believed, it would be entirely beside the point.

I would not say: "If a man said he dreamt it would happen to-morrow," would he take his coat?, etc.

Case where Lewy has visions of his dead friend. Cases where you don't try to locate him. And case where you try to locate him in a business-like way. Another case where I'd say: "We can pre-suppose we have a broad basis on which we agree."

In general, if you say: "He is dead" and I say: "He is not dead" no-one would say: "Do they mean the same thing by 'dead'?" In the case where a man has visions I wouldn't offhand say: "He means something different."

Cf. A person having persecution mania.

What is the criterion for meaning something different? Not only what he takes as evidence for it, but also how he reacts, that he is in terror, etc.

How am I to find out whether this proposition is to be regarded as an empirical proposition—'You'll see your dead friend again?' Would I say: "He is a bit superstitious?" Not a bit.

He might have been apologetic. (The man who stated it categorically was more intelligent that the man who was apologetic about it).

'Seeing a dead friend,' again means nothing much to me at all. I don't think in these terms. I don't say to myself: "I shall see so and so again" ever.

He always says it, but he doesn't make any search. He puts on a queer smile. "His story had that dreamlike quality." My answer would be in this case "Yes," and a particular explanation.

Take "God created man." Pictures of Michelangelo showing the creation of the world. In general, there is nothing which explains the meanings of words as well as a picture, and I take it that Michelangelo was a good as anyone can be and did his best, and here is the picture of the Deity creating Adam.

If we ever saw this, we certainly wouldn't think this the Deity. The picture has to be used in an entirely different way if we are to call the man in that queer blanket 'God', and so on. You could imagine that religion was taught by means of these pictures. "Of course, we can only express ourselves by means of pictures." This is rather queer . . . I could show Moore the pictures of a tropical plant. There is a technique of comparison between picture and plant. If I showed him the picture of Michelangelo and said: "Of course, I can't show you the real thing, only the picture." . . . The absurdity is, I've never taught him the technique of using this picture.

It is quite clear that the rôle of pictures of Biblical subjects and rôle of the picture of God creating Adam are totally different ones. You might ask this question: "Did Michelangelo think that Noah in the ark looked like this, and that God creating Adam looked like this?" He wouldn't have said that God or Adam looked as they looked in this picture.

It might seem as though, if we asked such a question as: "Does Lewy *really* mean what so and so means when he says so and so is alive?"—it might seem as though there were two sharply divided cases, one in which he would say he didn't mean it literally. I want to say this is not so. There will be cases where we will differ, and where it won't be a question at all of more or less knowledge, so that we can come together. Sometimes it will be a question of experience, so you can say: "Wait another 10 years." And I would say: "I would disencourage this kind of reasoning" and Moore would say: "I wouldn't disencourage it." That is, one would *do* something. We would take sides, and that goes so far that there would really be great differences between us, which might come out in Mr. Lewy saying: "Wittgenstein is trying to undermine reason," and this wouldn't be false. This is actually where such questions rise.

III

Today I saw a poster saying: " 'Dead' Undergraduate speaks."

The inverted commas mean: "He isn't really dead." "He isn't what people call dead. They call it 'dead' not quite correctly."

We don't speak of "door" in quotes.

It suddenly struck me: "If someone said 'He isn't really dead, although by the ordinary criteria he is dead'—couldn't I say "He is not only dead by the ordinary criteria; he is what we all call 'dead'."

If you now call him 'alive', you're using language in a queer way, because you're almost deliberately preparing misunderstandings. Why don't you use some other word, and let "dead" have the meaning it already has?

Suppose someone said: "It didn't always have this meaning. He's not dead according to the old meaning" or "He's not dead according to the old idea".

What is it, to have different ideas of death? Suppose you say: "I have the idea of myself being a chair after death" or "I have the idea of myself being a chair in half-an-hour"—you all know under what circumstances we say of something that it has become a chair.

Cf. (1) "This shadow will cease to exist."

(2) "This chair will cease to exist." You say that you know what this chair ceasing to exist is like. But you have to think. You may find that there isn't a use for this sentence. You think of the use.

I imagine myself on the death-bed. I imagine you all looking at the air above me. You say "You have an idea".

Are you clear when you'd say you had ceased to exist?

You have six different ideas [of 'ceasing to exist'] at different times.

If you say: "I can imagine myself being a disembodied spirit. Wittgenstein, can you imagine yourself as a disembodied spirit?"—I'd say: "I'm sorry. I [so far] connect nothing with these words."

I connect all sorts of complicated things with these words. I think of what people have said of sufferings after death, etc.

"I have two different ideas, one of ceasing to exist after death, the other of being a disembodied spirit."

What's it like to have two different ideas? What is the criterion for one man having one idea, another man having another idea?

You gave me two phrases, "ceasing to exist", "being a disembodied spirit". "When I say this, I think of myself having a certain set of experiences." What is it like to think of this?

If you think of your brother in America, how do you know that what you think is, that the thought inside you is, of your brother being in America? Is this an experiential business?

Cf. How do you know that what you want is an apple? [Russell].

How do you know that you believe that your brother is in America?

A pear might be what satisfied you. But you wouldn't say: "What I wanted was an apple."

Suppose we say that the thought is some sort of process in his mind, or his saying something, etc.—then I could say: "All right, you call this a thought of your brother in America, well, what is the connection between this and your brother in America?"

Lewy: You might say that this is a question of convention.

Why is it that you don't doubt that it is a thought of your brother in America?

One process [the thought] seems to be a shadow or a picture of something else.

How do I know that a picture is a picture of Lewy?—Normally by its likeness to Lewy, or; under certain circumstances, a picture of Levy may not be like him, but like Smith. If I give up the business of being like [as a criterion], I get into an awful mess, because anything may be his portrait, given a certain method of projection.

If you said that the thought was in some way a picture of his brother in America—Yes, but by what method of projection is it a picture of this? How queer it is that there should be no doubt what it's a picture of.

If you're asked: "How do you know it is a thought of such and such?" the thought that immediately comes to your mind is one of a shadow, a picture. You don't think of a causal relation. The kind of relation you think of is best expressed by "picture", "shadow", etc.

The word "picture" is even quite all right—in many cases it is even in the most ordinary sense, a picture. You might translate my very words into a picture.

But the point is this, suppose you drew this, how do I know it is my brother in America? Who says it is him—unless it is here ordinary similarity?

What is the connection between these words, or any thing substitutable for them, with my brother in America?

The first idea [you have] is that you are looking at your own thought, and are absolutely sure that it is a thought that so and so. You are looking at some mental phenomenon, and you say to yourself "obviously this is a thought of my brother being in America". It seems to be a super-picture. It seems, with thought, that there is no doubt whatever. With a picture, it still depends on the method of projection, whereas here it seems that you get rid of the projecting relation, and are absolutely certain that this is thought of that.

Smythies's muddle is based on the idea of a super—picture.

We once talked about how the idea of certain superlatives came about in Logic. The idea of a super-necessity, etc.

"How do I know that this is the thought of my brother in America?"—that *what* is the thought?

Suppose my thought consists of my *saying* "My brother is in America"—how do I know that I *say* my brother is in America?

How is the connection made?—We imagine at first a connection like strings.

Lewy: The connection is a convention. The word designates.

You must explain "designates" by examples. We have learnt a rule, a practice, etc.

Is thinking of something like painting or shooting at something?

It seems like a projection connection, which seems to make it indubitable, although there is not a projection relation at all.

If I said "My brother is in America"—I could imagine there being rays projecting from my words to my brother in America. But what if my brother isn't in America?—then the rays don't hit anything.

[If you say that the words refer to my brother by expressing the proposition that my brother is in America—the proposition being a middle link between the words and what they refer to]—What has the proposition, the mediate link, got to do with America?

The most important point is this—if you talk of painting, etc. your idea is that the connection exists *now*, so that it seem as though as long as I do this thinking, this connection exists.

Whereas, if we said it is a connection of convention, there would be no point in saying it exists while we think. There is a connection by convention—What do we mean?—This connection refers to events happening at various times. Most of all, it refers to a technique.

["Is thinking something going on at a particular time, or is it spread over the words?" "It comes in a flash." "Always?—it sometimes does come in a flash, although this may be all sorts of different things".]

If it does refer to a technique, then it can't be enough, in certain cases, to explain what you mean in a few words; because there is something which might be thought to be in conflict with the idea going on from 7 to 7.5, namely the practice of using it [the phrase.]

When we talked of: "So and so is an automaton", the strong hold of that view was [due to the idea] that you could say: "Well, I know what I mean" . . . , as though you were looking at something happening while you said the thing, entirely independent of what came before and after, the application [of the phrase]. It looked as though you could talk of understanding a word, without any reference to the technique of its usage. It looked as though Smythies said he could understand the sentence, and that we then had nothing to say.

What was it like to have different ideas of death?—What I meant was—Is having an idea of death something like having a certain picture, so that you can say "I have an dea of death from 5 to 5.1 etc."? "In whatever way anyone will use this word, I have now a certain idea"—if you call this "having an idea", then it is not what is commonly called "having an idea", because what is commonly called "having an idea", has a reference to the technique of the word, etc.

We are all here using the word "death", which is a public instrument, which has a whole technique [of usage]. Then someone says he has an idea of death. Something queer; because you might say "You are using the word 'death', which is an instrument functioning in a certain way."

If you treat this [your idea] as something private, with what right are you calling it an idea of death?—I say this, because we, also, have a rght to say what is an idea of death.

He might say "I have my own private idea of death"—why call this an 'idea of death' unless it is something you connect with death. Although this [your 'idea'] might not interest us at all. [In this case,] it does not belong on the game played with 'death', which we all know and understand.

If what he calls his "idea of death" is to become relevant, it must become part of our game.

'My idea of death is the separation of the soul from the body'—if we know what to do with these words. He can also say: "I connect with the word 'death' a certain picture—a woman lying in her bed"—that may not be of some interest.

If he connects

with death, and this was his idea, this might be interesting psychologically.

"The separation of soul from body" [only had a public interest.] This may act like black curtains or it may not act like black curtains. I'd have to find out what the consequences [of your saying it] are. I am not, at least, at present at all clear. [You say this]—"So what?"—I know these words, I have certain pictures. All sorts of things go along with these words.

If he says this, I won't know yet what consequences he will draw. I don't know what he opposes this to.

Lewy: "You oppose it to being extinguished."

If you say to me—"Do you cease to exist?"—I should be bewildered, and would not know what exactly this is to mean. "If you don't cease to exist, you will suffer after death", there I begin to attach ideas, perhaps ethical ideas of responsibility. The point is, that although these are well-known words, and although I can go from one sentence to another sentence, or to pictures [I don't know what consequences you draw from this statement].

Suppose someone said: "What do you believe, Wittgenstein? Are you a sceptic? Do you know whether you will survive death?" I would really, this is a fact, say "I can't say. I don't know", because I haven't any clear idea what I'm saying when I'm saying "I don't cease to exist," etc.

Spiritualists make one kind of connection.

A Spiritualist says "Apparition" etc. Although he gives me a picture I don't like, I do get a clear idea. I know that much, that some people connect this phrase with a particular kind of verification. I know that some people don't—religious people e.g.—they don't refer to a verification, but have entirely different ideas.

A great writer said that, when he was a boy, his father set him a task, and he suddenly felt that nothing, not even death, could take away the responsibility [in doing this task]; this was his duty to do, and that even death couldn't stop it being his duty. He said that this was, in a way, a proof of the immortality of the soul—because if this lives on [the responsibility won't die.] The idea is given by what we call the proof. Well, if this is the idea, [all right].

If a Spiritualist wishes to give *me* an idea of what he means or doesn't mean by 'survival', he can say all sorts of things—

[If I ask what idea he has, I may be given what the Spiritualists say or I may be given what the man I quoted said, etc., etc.]

I would at least [in the case of the Spiritualist] have an idea of what this sentence is connected up with, and get more and more of an idea as I see what he does with it.

As it is, I hardly connect anything with it at all.

Suppose someone, before going to China, when he might never see me again, said to me: "We might see one another after death"—would I necessarily say that I don't understand him? I might say [want to say] simply, "Yes. I *understand* him entirely."

Lewy: "In this case, you might only mean that he expressed a certain attitude."

I would say "No, it isn't the same as saying 'I'm very fond of you' "—and it may not be the same as saying anything else. It says what it says. Why should you be able to substitute anything else?

Suppose I say: "The man used a picture."

"Perhaps now he sees he was wrong." What sort of remark is this?

"God's eye sees everything"—I want to say of this that it uses a picture.

I don't want to belittle him [the person who says it.]

Suppose I said to him "You've been using a picture", and he said "No, this is not all"—mightn't he have misunderstood me? What do I want to do [by saying this]? What would be the real sign of disagreement? What might be the real criterion of his disagreeing with me?

Lewy: "If he said: 'I've been making preparations [for death].' "

Yes, this might be a disagreement—if he himself were to use the world in a way in which I did not expect, or were to draw conclusions I did not expect him to draw. I wanted only to draw attention to a particular technique of usage. We should disagree, if he was using a technique I didn't expect.

We associate a particular use with a picture.

Smythies: 'This isn't all he does—associate a use with a picture.'

Wittgenstein: Rubbish. I meant: what conclusions are you going to draw? etc. Are eyebrows going to be talked of, in connection with the Eye of God?

He could just as well have said so and so"—this [remark] is foreshadowed by the word "attitude". He couldn't just as well have said something else.

If I say he used a picture, I don't want to say anything he himself wouldn't say. I want to say that he draws these conclusions.

Isn't it as important as anything else, what picture he does use?

Of certain pictures we say that they might just as well be replaced by another —e.g. we could, under certain circumstances, have one projection of an ellipse drawn instead of another.

[He *may* say]: "I would have been prepared to use another picture, it would have had the same effect. . . ."

The whole *weight* may be in the picture.

We can say in chess that the exact shape of the chess-men plays no rôle. Suppose that the main pleasure was, to see people ride; then, playing it in writing wouldn't be playing the same game. Someone might say: "All he's done is change the shape of the head"—what more could he do?

When I say he's using a picture I'm merely making a *grammatical* remark: [What I say] can only be verified by the consequences he does or does not draw.

If Smythies disagrees, I don't take notice of this disagreement.

All I wished to characterize was the conventions he wished to draw. If I wished to say anything more I was merely being philosophically arrogant.

Normally, if you say "He is an automaton" you draw consequences, if you stab him, [he'll feel pain]. On the other hand, you may not wish to draw any such consequences, and this is all there is to it—except further muddles.

Religious

Experience

_____

R. E. L. MASTERS AND JEAN HOUSTON

Psychedelic Drugs and Religious Experience

R. E. L. Masters and Jean Houston are psychologists who have
conducted detailed controlled investigations of drug-induced
hallucination. Masters has also written *Eros and Evil* and
Forbidden Sexual Behavior and Morality. Dr. Houston has
written several other articles on the drug experience.

One of the most important questions raised by the psychedelic drugs is whether
authentic religious and mystical experiences occur among the drug subjects. To
this question the answer must be *Yes*—but we feel an extended discussion is warranted and that many qualifications are in order.

In our experience, the most profound and transforming psychedelic experiences have been those regarded by the subjects as religious. And in depth of feeling,
sense of revelation, semantically, and in terms of reorientation of the person the
psychedelic religious and religious-type experiences certainly seem to show significant
parallels with the more orthodox religious experiences. These parallels alone would
be sufficient to demand extensive and careful study.

Undoubtedly it would be the supreme irony of the history of religion should it
be proved that the ordinary person could by the swallowing of a pill attain to those
states of exhalted consciousness a lifetime of spiritual exercises rarely brings to the
most ardent and adept seeker of mystical enlightenment. Considering the present
rapid assimilation on a mass cultural level of new discoveries, therapies, and ideologies, it then might not be long before the vested religious interests would finally
have to close up shop. And no less renowned a prophet than the late Aldous Huxley
has suggested that humanity at large may in fact come to avail itself of psychedelic
drugs as a surrogate for religion.

Since his statement appeared in 1954, the controversy has raged between those
like Huxley, Gerald Heard, and Alan Watts who believe that in these chemicals
the evolutionary acceleration of man's spiritual nature is now at hand, and other
writers such as R. C. Zaehner who contend that these drugs at the most produce a
very minor sort of nature mysticism and moreover tend to vitiate higher forms of
religious and mystic expectations.[1]

[1] See, for example, Huxley, Aldous, *The Doors of Perception* and *Heaven and Hell*. Harper & Row,
New York, 1963; Heard, Gerald, *The Five Ages of Man*. Julian Press, New York, 1964; Watts, Alan,
The Joyous Cosmology. Pantheon Books, New York, 1962; and Zaehner, R., *Mysticism, Sacred and
Profane*, Oxford University Press, New York, 1961.

Before considering this debate in the light of our own findings, it should be of value to examine briefly something of the history of artificially induced states of mystical and religious consciousness. We do this in order to demonstrate to the reader the unbroken line of continuity in the history of "provoked mysticism."

Since the time when man first discovered that he was a thinking organism in a manifold world, he has sought to marshal his analytic capacity to control the manifold and discover its natural laws. As a parallel movement to this analytic process there developed as an undercurrent another way of knowing—one that sought to discover man's essential nature and his true relationship to the creative forces behind the universe, and to discern where his fulfillment lay. For the sake of achieving this integral knowledge men have willingly submitted themselves to elaborate ascetic procedures and have trained for years to laboriously master Yoga and meditation techniques. They have practiced fasting, flagellation, and sensory deprivation, and, in so doing, may have attained to states of heightened mystical consciousness, but also have succeeded in altering their body chemistry. Recent physiological investigations of these practices in a laboratory setting tend to confirm the notion that provoked alterations in body chemistry and body rhythm are in no small way responsible for the dramatic changes in consciousness attendant upon these practices. The askesis or ascetic discipline of fasting,[2] for example, makes for vitamin and sugar deficiencies which acts to lower the efficiency of what Huxley calls the cerebral reducing valve.

Similarly, the practice of flagellation will tend to release quantities of histamine, adrenalin, and the toxic decomposition products of protein—all of which work to induce shock and hallucination. With regard to sensory deprivation, the work of D. O. Hebb at McGill University in Canada and that of John Lilly at the National Institutes of Health in Washington demonstrates on the laboratory level how the elimination of external sensory stimuli can result in the subjective production of fantastic visionary experiences similar to those reported by St. Anthony during his vigil in the desert or the cave-dwelling Tibetan and Indian hermits who live out great segments of their lives in complete isolation. Other techniques of "provoked mysticism" include breathing exercises rhythmically performed to alter the composition of the blood and provide a point of concentration, extended chanting (which increases the carbon dioxide content of the blood), hypnosis, prayer dancing (employing body oscillations which induce trance and presumed physical changes), the spinning frenzy of the whirling dervishes, and so on.

The most comprehensive and consciously controlled system of disciplines is, of course, the Hatha Yoga which incorporates the practices of posture regulation, breathing exercises, and meditation. Its immediate aim is to bring under conscious control all physiological processes, so that the body can function with maximum efficiency. Its ultimate aim is to arouse what is called *Kundalini,* a universal vital energy which is supposed to gain its access to the body at the base of the spine. When aroused and controlled, it is said to activate the psychic centers and thus make available to the yogi unusual powers. It is claimed that if this energy can be directed to the head center (the thousand-petalled lotus), a mystical state is attained and the

---

[2] For a discussion of the physiology of fasting and the psychological changes it produces, see Keys, Ansel, *The Biology of Human Starvation.* University of Minnesota Press, 1950.

yogi becomes aware of a mystical unitive consciousness. To this end the early Sanskrit psychophysical researchers developed a remarkable knowledge of physiological processes and their relation to body control.

Thirty years ago, in a volume entitled *Poisons Sacrés, Ivresses Divines,* Philippe de Felice provided considerable documentation to support the ages-old connection between the occurrence of religious-type experiences and the eating of certain vegetable substances. He wrote that the employment of these substances for religious purposes is so extraordinarily widespread as to be "observed in every region of the earth among primitives no less than among those who have reached a high pitch of civilization. We are therefore dealing not with exceptional facts, which might justifiably be overlooked, but with a general and, in the widest sense of the word, a human phenomenon, the kind of phenomenon which cannot be disregarded by anyone who is trying to discover what religion is and what are the deep needs which it must satisfy."[3]

De Felice advanced the thesis that one of the earliest known of the substances, the *soma* of the Vedic hymns, may have been indirectly responsible for the development of Hatha Yoga. The *soma* appears to have been some kind of creeping plant which the Aryan invaders brought down with them from Central Asia about 1500 B.C. The plant occupied an integral position in the myth and ritual structure of Vedic religion, was regarded as divinity, and was itself ritually consumed to bring the worshiper to a state of divine exhilaration and incarnation. "We have drunk soma and become immortal," hymns the early Vedic author. "We have attained the light, the gods discovered." According to de Felice, as the Aryans moved deeper into India the gods proved more difficult to find as the *soma* plant, like fine wine, would not travel. The exercises of the Hatha Yoga school, he suggests, may have been created as an attempt to fill the "somatic" gap and achieve that physiological state of being conducive to religious states of consciousness similar to those brought on by the ingestion of the sacred food. The larger implication of this thesis is that vegetable-provoked mysticism exists as a state prior to askesis-provoked mysticism —that early man may have come upon his first instances of consciousness change through his random eating of herbs and vegetables. Certainly this thesis can never move beyond the realm of conjecture, although the fact remains that naturally occurring mind-changing substances are found the world over and are much more likely to have been experimented with before the creation of any system of mind-changing exercises.

For millennia man has been involved in the ritual ingestion of substances reputed to produce an awareness of a sacramental reality and has come to incorporate these substances into the myth and ritual pattern of the culture in which they occur. The words *haoma, soma, peyote,* and *teonanacatl,* all of which refer to God's flesh, are significant semantic referrents to the religious experiences believed to be inherent in the sacred foods.

One of the major archaeological discoveries of recent years has been the digging up on the Guatemalan highlands of a great many stone figures representing mushrooms out of whose stem emerges the head of a god. Thus the mushroom appears to have been hypostatized as deity as early as 1500 B.C. These figures occur

[3] De Felice, Philippe, *Poisons Sacrés, Ivresses Divines.* Editions Albin, Paris, 1936, p. 363.

as Aztec artifacts as late as the ninth century A.D. However, the earlier figures are technically and stylistically of finer craftsmanship, indicating a flourishing cult in the early pre-classical period. By the sixteenth and seventeenth centuries of our era reports of such a mushroom cult occur in the writings of Spanish explorers and priests. They naturally regarded these rites as demonically derived celebrations and soon made certain that they were driven underground. The rites, as noted, continue to survive today among the Mazatec Indians of southern Mexico where the ancient liturgy and ritual ingestion is still performed in remote huts before tiny congregations.

In recent years the cult has been subject to a great deal of publicity owing chiefly to the efforts of that well-known mycophile R. Gordon Wasson. In thirty years of search for the secret of the mushroom throughout the world, he and his wife believed that they uncovered the mystery among the Mazatec communicants. They persuaded a *curandera* or cult shaman to allow them to participate in the ceremony and swallow the sacred food. Recalling his experience, Wasson wrote that "as your body lies in the darkness, heavy as lead, your spirit seems to soar and leave the hut, and with the speed of thought to travel where it listeth, in time and space, accompanied by the shaman's singing and by the ejaculations of her percussive chant. What you are seeing and what you are hearing takes on the modalities of music, the music of the sphere . . . as your body lies there . . . your soul is free, loses all sense of time, alert as it never was before, living eternity in a night, seeing infinity in a grain of sand. What you have seen and heard is cut as with a burin in your memory, never to be effaced. At last you know what the ineffable is, and what ecstacy means."[4]

In a monumental study of the mushroom, *Mushrooms, Russia, and History,* the Wassons claimed to discover its sacramental usages in cultures widely distributed from the Levant to China; and they state that it even was known to the Norsemen of the Icelandic culture.[5] In addition to the Mexican cult, the rite continues today among certain shamanistic tribes in Siberia, the ritual object of the cult being the hallucinogenic mushroom *Amanita muscaria*. Because this variety of mushroom occurs widely throughout Europe, Wasson has advanced the hypothesis that it might provide an answer to the secret of the Elusinian mysteries. From certain Greek writings and from a Pompeian fresco there are indications that the initiate drank a potion and then, in the depths of the night, beheld a great vision. Aristides, in the second century A.D., speaks of the ineffable visions and the awesome and luminous experience of the initiates. Wasson finds significance in the fact that the Greeks frequently referred to mushrooms as the "food of the gods," *broma theon,* and that Porphyrius is quoted as having called them "nurslings of the gods," *theotrophos.*

However interesting is the notion of a mushroom-inspired Hellenic mystery, we suspect that Wasson's mycophiliac zeal exceeds his academic rigor when he suggests that Plato came upon his theory of an ideal world of archetypes after having

[4] Wasson, R.G., "The Hallucinogenic Fungi of Mexico: An Inquiry into the Origins of the Religious Idea among Primitive Peoples," *Botanical Museum leaflets Harvard University,* 19, No. 7, Cambridge, Mass., Feb. 17, 1961, pp. 156–157.

[5] Wasson, R.G., and Wasson, V., *Mushrooms, Russia and History,* Pantheon Books, New York, 1957.

spent a night at the temple of Eleusis drinking a mushroom potion.

The history of transcendental experience bears testimony to the thin line that often separates the sublime from the demonic, and to the frequency with which the one may cross over into the other. In demonic terms the visionary foods were extensively used, for example, by witches, especially during the period 1450 to 1750. As remarked, the witches drank and rubbed on their bodies concoctions the principal ingredients of which were the *Solanaceae* drugs contained in such plants as the thorn apple, mandragora, deadly nightshade, the henbanes, and others. The drug concoctions were employed at the Sabbats to produce hallucinations and disorientation, and also were taken at home for the purpose of inducing dreams and imagery of flying, orgiastic revels, and intercourse with incubi. So vivid were the nightmares and hallucinations produced by these drugs that witches frequently confessed to crimes they had only dreamed about but thought they had committed in the flesh.

The peyote ceremonies of the Native American Church have received sufficient treatment elsewhere in this book.

The historic sacrality of the visionary vegetables has since given way to the modern notoriety of the synthetic derivatives—especially, LSD, psilocybin, and mescaline. With regard to religious experiences as otherwise, one confronts these contemporary compounds with a host of puzzling questions. How, for example, may one reconcile the extremes of enthusiasm on the part of those who claim to find in these drugs a near-panacea for all ills and the key to mystical illumination with the vehement antagonism of those who are convinced that at best the drug-state mimics schizophrenia while at worst the drugs may wreak irreparable havoc with the psyche and possibly also irreparably damage the brain? Again the whole question arises as to whether these substances are consciousness-expanders or merely mind-distorters? In Savage's well-known phrase, do they provide "Instant Grace, Instant Insanity, or Instant Analysis?"[6] Finally, there is the tragic-comic denouement that these altercations have won for the drugs a pariah mystique. The problem with such a mystique is, of course, that it dictates that the pariah must go underground and there fester in cultic movements.

The contemporary quest for the artificial induction of religious experiences through the use of psycho-chemicals became a controversial issue with the publication of Huxley's *Doors of Perception* in 1954. In that book Huxley with his usual genius for the quixotic offered the suggestion that visionary vegetables in their modern synthetic forms could provide a new spiritual stimulation for the masses: one that was surer than church-going and safer than alcohol. The actual experimental testing of the claims for the psycho-chemical-as-religious-surrogate occurred in 1962 on an occasion now known as "The Miracle of Marsh Chapel." As a part of his work on a Harvard University doctoral dissertation in the Philosophy of Religion, Dr. Walter Pahnke, an M.D., set out to test a typology of mysticism based on the categories of mystical experience summarized by W. T. Stace in his classic study of the subject.[7] Pahnke designed his experiment to test this typology on subjects who

---

[6] Quoted in Harman, W.W., "The Issue of the Consciousness-Expanding Drugs," *Main Currents in Modern Thought*, 20, No. 1, Sept.-Oct., 1963, p. 6.

[7] Stace, W.T., *Mysticism and Philosophy*, J.P. Lippincott Company, Philadelphia and New York, 1940.

were given psilocybin in a religious setting. The subjects in question were twenty theology students who had never had the drug before and ten guides with considerable psychedelic experience. The theology students were divided into five groups of four persons, with two guides assigned to each group. After a preparatory gathering the groups moved upstairs to the chapel and the three-hour Good Friday service that awaited them. It was on this occasion that two of the subjects in each group and one of the guides were given 30 micrograms of psilocybin, a fairly strong dose of that drug. The effects of psilocybin are very similar to those of LSD. The second guide and the two remaining subjects received a placebo containing nicotinic ingredients which provided the subject with a tingling sensation but produced no psychedelic effects. The drug was given in a triple-blind framework, meaning that neither subjects, guides, nor the experimenter knew which ten were getting the psilocybin and which ten were members of the control group and received placebos. The Good Friday sermon was preached and the subjects were left in the chapel to listen to organ music and to await whatever experiences they were to have.

What subsequently occurred has been described as "bizarre," "outrageous," and "deeply inspiring." As Pahnke's dissertation has not yet been published, we will not to be able to describe at this time the events that transpired in the chapel. However, it is permissible to say that nine subjects from the psilocybin group reported having religious experiences which they considered to be genuine while one of the subjects who had been given a placebo also claimed to have experienced phenomena of a religious nature. Typical of the responses was this excerpt from a report written shortly after the experiment by one of the subjects: "I felt a deep union with God. . . . I carried my Bible to the altar and tried to preach. The only words I mumbled were peace, peace, peace. I felt I was communicating beyond words."

In order to provide some material for a meaningful critique of this experiment the subjects' reports were read by three college-graduate housewives who were not informed as to the nature and background of the reports, but were asked to assign to each a rating of *strong, moderate, slight,* or *none,* according to which of these terms best applied to a subject's statement in the light of each of the nine elements of mystical experience listed in the mystical typology provided by Pahnke. According to Pahnke, the statistical results of these ratings indicated that "those subjects who received psilocybin experienced phenomena which were indistinguishable from if not identical with . . . the categories defined by our typology of mysticism.[8]

Various other studies would seem to attest to the mystico-religious efficacy of the psychedelic drugs. For example, in an attempt to explore the "revelatory potentialities of the human nervous system," Dr. Timothy Leary and his associates arranged for 69 full-time religious professionals to take psilocybin in a supportive setting. Leary has subsequently reported that over seventy-five percent of these sub-

---

[8] Pahnke, Walter N., *Drugs and Mysticism: An Analysis of the Relationship between Psychedelic Drugs and the Mystical Consciousness.* A thesis presented to the Committee on Higher Degrees in History and Philosophy of Religion, Harvard University, June, 1963. This thesis is available at the Harvard University Library, Cambridge, Massachusetts, although restricted for five years. Before this time persons may write the author at 277 West 14 Place, Chicago Heights, Illinois, for permission to obtain a microfilm of the thesis.

jects stated after their sessions that they had experienced "intense mystico-religious reactions, and considerably more than half claim that they have had the deepest spiritual experience of their life."[9]

In another study by two Californians, a psychiatrist and a psychologist respectively, Oscar Janiger and William McGlothlin reported on a study involving 194 LSD subjects (121 volunteers and 73 as part of a program in psychotherapy). The drug was given in a nonreligious setting so that presumably religious expectations did not influence the subjects as was the case with the Leary experiment. Below is a statistical abstract of their findings, based on a questionnaire answered by the subjects ten months after their sessions:

	JANIGER-MC GLOTHLIN (NONRELIGIOUS SETTING) N=194 Percent
Increased interest in morals, ethics . . . :	35
Increased interest in other universal concepts (meaning of life):	48
Change in sense of values:	48
LSD should be used for	
becoming aware of oneself:	75
gaining new meaning to life:	58
getting people to understand each other:	42
An experience of lasting benefit:	58

It also should be added that ten months after having taken the drug twenty-four percent of the 194 subjects still spoke of their experiences as having been "religious."[10]

Two other similar studies should be mentioned because of the remarkable percentages reported with regard to the subjects' feeling that they had had a religious-type experience. Both experiments were conducted by psychiatrists but whereas one provided a supportive environment for the session, the other not only was supportive but also was structured in part to provide the subject with religious stimuli. This second procedure resulted in significantly higher percentages of subjects reporting religious experiences.[11]

Taken altogether these findings must be regarded as remarkable. In the five studies just cited between thirty-two and seventy-five percent of psychedelic subjects will report religious-type experiences if the setting is supportive; and in a

[9] Leary, T., "The Religious Experience: Its Production and Interpretation," *Psychedelic Review,* Vol. I, No. 3 (1964), p. 325.

[10] McGlothlin, W.H., *Long-Lasting Effects of LSD on Certain Attitudes in Normals.* Printed for private distribution by the RAND Corporation.

[11] Ditman, K.S., Hayman, M., and Whittlesay, J.R.B., "Nature and Frequency of Claims Following LSD," *Journal of Nervous and Mental Disease,* Vol. 134 (1962), pp. 336–352. And: Savage, C., Harman, W. W., Fadiman, J., and Savage, E., "A Follow-up Note on the Psychedelic Experience." Paper delivered at a meeting of the American Psychiatric Association, St. Louis, Missouri, May, 1963.

	DITMAN AND HAYMAN (SUPPORTIVE ENVIRONMENT)	SAVAGE (SUPPORTIVE ENVIRONMENT AND SOME RELIGIOUS STIMULI)
	N=74 *Percent*	N=96 *Percent*
Feel it (LSD) was the greatest thing that ever happened to me:	49	85
A religious experience:	32	83
A greater awareness of God or a Higher Power, or an Ultimate Reality:	40	90

setting providing religious stimuli, from seventy-five to ninety percent report experiences of a religious or even mystical nature.

The reader is surely by this time wondering what to make of the claims of these researchers. Are they psychedelic Svengalis employing suggestion to play upon the sensitized psyches of their hypersuggestible subjects, imposing whatever delusions they might need or wish to impose? Or may it be that they themselves are deluded and fail to understand that in present-day America a man or woman will put a check next to "had a religious experience" if a drug has helped him or her to feel in some impressive way "different" than usual? There can be no doubt that the psychedelic drugs give the subject experiences very "different" from any the average person is likely to have had. For the most part the drug-state resembles neither the effects to be gotten from alcohol nor those resulting from amphetamines and tranquilizers. Does the present-day subject, then, having little or no familiarity with what is meant by the terms "religious" and "mystical" (other than something undefinedly exciting), adopt these words by default to describe the novel phenomena he has encountered during his session (and finds conveniently present on the questionnaire)? The Eastern scholar R. C. Zaehner offers a sophisticated version of this argument in his book attacking Huxley's position, *Mysticism, Sacred and Profane.* In this work Zaehner presents a closely reasoned and scholarly look at the classical records of religious and mystical experience and concludes that drug-induced mysticism falls so far short of the experiences of saints and holy men that a subject is badly misleading himself if he feels that he has undergone an authentic religious experience. "Preternatural" experience, the experience of transcendence and union with that which is apprehended as lying beyond the multiplicity of the world, is very common experience indeed, Zaehner argues. Not only is it common to nature mystics, but it recurs regularly with poets, monists, manic-depressives, and schizophrenics. Whether one is dealing with the "cosmic emotion" of the nature mystic, the "almost hysterical expression of superhuman ecstasy" found in a poet like Rimbaud, the bliss of subject-object dissolution, or the rapture of psychologically dissociated states, one is dealing exclusively with "preternatural" phenomena and not with authentic religious or mystical experience. Zaehner deems all psychedelic drug experience, be it madness, monism, or nature mysticism, to lie entirely within the province of such preternatural experience.

The further implication of Zaehner's thesis is that these drugs can never induce theistic states of religious and mystical experience which he regards as the supreme and authentic religious experience. The other two forms of mystical experience which Zaehner recognizes, nature mysticism in which the soul is united with the natural world and monistic mysticism in which the soul dissolves into an impersonal Absolute, are infinitely inferior states of religious awareness as compared to theistic mysticism in which the soul confronts the living, personal God.

Here Zaehner's position is clearly open to criticism. Apart from questioning the value hierarchy which Zaehner ascribes to the three kinds of mysticism, one might take him to task for suppressing the evidence for drug-induced theistic mysticism. As is well known, the peyote rituals of the Native American Church are frequently productive of theistic religious experiences. James Slotkin, an anthropologist, has noted that the Indians during these ceremonials "see visions, which may be of Christ Himself. Sometimes they hear the voice of the Great Spirit. Sometimes they become aware of the presence of God and of those personal shortcomings which must be corrected if they are to do His will."[12] (Slotkin, it should be added, had observed the Indians' rites and been a participant in them.) And, in any case, the phenomenon of specifically theistic versions of psychedelic mysticism is an ancient and widespread tradition.

Needless to say, Zaehner's arguments have provided ammunition for many theologians and churchmen who refer to religious experiences induced with the help of psychedelic drugs as "chemical religion," "cheap and lazy religion," "instant mysticism," etc., and who charge that the use of the drugs for such a purpose amounts to "irreverently storming the gates of heaven." However, there is no avoiding the fact that Zaehner's critique has the ring of an eleventh hour *tour de force*. One philosopher sympathetic to the use of the drugs for religious purposes says that "Zaehner's refusal to admit that drugs can induce experiences descriptively indististinguishable from those which are spontaneously religious is the current counterpart of the seventeenth-century theologians' refusal to look through Galileo's telescope or, when they did, their persistence in dismissing what they saw as machinations of the devil. . . . When the fact that drugs can trigger religious experiences becomes incontrovertible, discussion will move to the more difficult question of how this new fact is to be interpreted."[13]

In our own experience, the evidence would seem to support the contentions of those who assert that an authentic religious experience may occur within the context of the psychedelic drug-state. However, we are certainly less exuberant than some other researchers when it comes to the question of the frequency of such experiences. It is not here a question of our having had fewer subjects who claim to have had a religious experience—over forty-five percent have made this claim;

[12] Slotkin, J., *The Peyote Religion*. Free Press, Glencoe, Illinois, 1956.

[13] Smith, Huston, "Do Drugs Have Religious Import?" *The Journal of Philosophy,* Vol. LXI, No. 18, Sept. 17, 1964. This article has been reprinted in Solomon, D. (Ed.), *LSD: The Consciousness-Expanding Drug,* G.P. Putnam's Sons, New York, 1964, and the above quotation may be found on p. 159 of that volume.

rather, because of the criteria employed, a large number of these claims have been rejected by us. The difference therefore is one of criteria rather than of testimonial opulence.

In our attempt to develop unbiased criteria for the authentic religious experience we have employed the usual measuring devices; however, we have also found it important to place some emphasis on what we have termed the "depth level" of the experience. The literature of nondrug religious and mystical experience appears to lend considerable support to this criterion. It is significant to note, for example, that in this traditional literature the writers repeatedly deal with and emphasize the stages on the way to mystical enlightenment and describe these with metaphors suggesting striking analogies to the psychodynamic levels hypothesized in our psychedelic research. Again and again, the literature reveals comparable gradations or levels of experience as the mystic moves from acute bodily sensations and sensory enhancement to a heightened understanding of his own psychodynamic processes, through a stage inhabited by visionary and symbolic structures, until at last he achieves the very depths of his being and the luminous vision of the One. This level is described as the source and the ground of the self's unfolding and represents the level of confrontation with Ultimate Reality. The most important of the experiences reported by William James in *The Varieties of Religious Experience* are of this type in which the person seems to be encountered on the most profound level of his being by the Ground of Being. Religious experience can be defined, then, as that experience which occurs when the "depths of one's being" are touched or confronted by the "Depth of Being." Mystical experience differs from this in degree, not in kind. This latter occurs when one's personal depths dissolve into the "transpersonal" depths—when one is unified at one's deepest level with the source level of reality.

Mystics and religious personalities have repeatedly warned against accepting states of sensory and psychological alteration or visionary phenomena as identical with the depths of the spiritual consciousness. These warnings go unheeded today by many investigators of the psychedelic experience who seem to accept the subject's experiences of heightened empathy and increased sensory awareness as proofs of religious enlightenment. Doubtless some of these experiences are analogous in some way to religious and mystical experiences. But religious analogues are still not religious experiences. At best they are but stages on the way to religious experiences. And a major problem in this research to date is that it has been conducted by persons unfamiliar with the nature and content of the religious experience. Thus claims are made that can be misleading.

For example, a subject may have a euphoria-inducing experience of empathy with a chair, a painting, a person, or a shoe. This may result in protestations of transcendental delight as chair, painting, person, and shoe are raised to platonic forms and the subject assumes himself to be mystically enlightened. Too often in these and similar situations the guide will offer reassurance to the subject and so reinforce his belief that he is having a religious experience. But by doing this, the guide may prevent the subject from descending to a deeper level of his being where a genuinely religious and transformative experience then might be had.

Given this type of misunderstanding, it is no wonder that the psychedelic drugs have resulted in a proliferation of "fun" mystics and armchair pilgrims who loudly claim mystical mandates for experiences that are basically nothing more than routine instances of consciousness alteration. The mandate being falsely and shallowly derived, the subsequent spiritual hubris can be horrendous, the subject announcing to whoever will listen that all mystic themes, all religious concepts, all meanings, and all mysteries now are accessible and explainable by virtue of his "cosmic revelation." It is frequent and funny, if also unfortunate, to encounter young members of the Drug Movement who claim to have achieved a personal apotheosis when, in fact, their experience appears to have consisted mainly of depersonalization, dissociation, and similar phenomena. Such individuals seek their beatitude in regular drug-taking, continuing to avoid the fact that their psychedelic "illumination" is not the sign of divine or cosmic approval they suppose it to be, but rather a flight from reality. Euphoria then may ensue as a result of the loss of all sense of responsibility; and this can and often does lead to orgies of spiritual pride and self-indulgence by those who now see themselves as the inheritors of *It!* In fact, they come to spend several days a week with *It!* And all mundane concerns, all earthly "games" seem superflous and are abandoned insofar as circumstances will allow.

The situation is complicated by the fact that many such persons are caught up in a quasi-Eastern mystique through which they express their disenchantment with the declining Western values and with the proliferating technology, the fear of becoming a machine-man, and the yearning for some vision of wholeness to turn the tide of rampant fragmentation. This vision they pursue by means of a wholesale leap to the East without, however, having gained the stability, maturity, and elasticity needed to assimilate the Eastern values. Few have the spiritual sophistication of a Huxley or have spent as many years of study and training in quest of methods of achieving the spontaneity and integration elaborated in the teachings of some schools of Vedanta and Mahayana Buddhism. Thus the leap out of the "games" and everyday "roles" of Western reality is usually into a nebulous chaos seen as Eastern "truth." It is an added misfortune that the psychedelic drugs may genuinely give some inkling of the complexity of Eastern consciousness, although the vista usually uncovered is no revelation but merely a glimpse—one that would require years of dedicated study before it could be implemented and made effective in day-to-day existence.

To at least some extent the responsibility for this seduction of the innocent must lie with such authors as Huxley, Alan Watts, and others who in their various writings imposed upon the psychedelic experience essentially Eastern ideas and terminology which a great many persons then assumed to be the sole and accurate way of approaching and interpreting such experience. Armed with such terminology and ideation, depersonalization is mistranslated into the Body of Bliss, empathy or pseudo-empathy becomes a Mystic Union, and spectacular visual effects are hailed as the Clear Light of the Void.

It should by now be evident why the authors discount as belonging to the class of authentic religious and mystical experience a good many cases in which the data of altered sensory perception and other ordinary drug-state phenomena are hypostatised by the subject as having sacramental or religious significance. Among our own cases, that of the young woman in the opening chapter who perceived the objects around her in terms of "holy pots" and a "numinous peach" is clearly not an example of religious experience as the rest of her account goes on to make clear. This subject is indulging in a commonplace practice of psychedelic subjects—the describing of various uncommon experiences in terms of sacramental metaphors.

This is not to suggest that religious insight and religious-type experience never occur in combination with an experience of sensory enhancement. The interpretation accompanying the perception may result in revelatory insights. A famous case in point is the divinity school professor contemplating a rose: "As I looked at the rose it began to glow," he said, "and suddenly I felt I understood the rose. A few days later when I read the Biblical account of Moses and the burning bush it suddenly made sense to me." Thus within the framework of the psychedelic experience one man's glowing rose can be another man's epiphany.

. . .

PSYCHEDELIC DRUGS AND MYSTICAL EXPERIENCE

Of mysticism it often has been said that it begins in mist and ends in schism; and to this statement, the psychedelic variety is no exception. A part of the blame for the historical abundance of misty schisms may lie with the ambiguities inherent in the mystical experience itself. As writers and mystics alike have noted, there are two distinct and differing types of mystical experience available—the inward and the outward way. Variously termed introvertive and extrovertive, introspective and extrospective, both involve the apprehension of an Ultimate Unity with which the seeker unites or identifies. The outward way differs from the inward in that whereas the one attempts to discover the Ultimate Unity in the external world, the other introspects into the depths of the self therein to meet and yield to the Ground of Being. Mystics and writers are unanimous in declaring the inward way the superior mysticism. The outward variety is considered at most a preparation for the true mystic pilgrimage inward.

In his classic study of mysticism, the noted philosopher W. T. Stace distinguishes between the two types of mysticism and terms them extrovertive and introvertive. He suggests seven common characteristics of introvertive mystical states of mind as evidenced from a wide sampling of the literature of mystical experience. According to Stace, these seven characteristics are:

1. The Unitary Consciousness, from which all the multiplicity of sensuous or conceptual or other empirical content has been excluded, so that there remains only a void and empty unity. This is the one basic, essential, nuclear characteristic, from which most of the others inevitably follow.
2. Being nonspatial and nontemporal. This of course follows from the nuclear characteristic listed above.
3. Sense of objectivity or reality.
4. Feelings of blessedness, joy, peace, happiness, etc.
5. Feeling that what is apprehended is holy, sacred, or divine.
6. Paradoxicality.
7. Alleged by mystics to be ineffable.[14]

14 Stace, W.T., *Mysticism and Philosophy*, pp. 110–111.

Extrovertive mysticism differs from the introvertive variety in only the first two characteristics. In extrovertive mysticism, according to Stace's typology, there is no Unitary Consciousness but only a unifying vision "expressed abstractly by the formula 'All is One.' The One is, in extrovertive mysticism, perceived through the physical senses, in or through the multiplicity of objects." The nonspatial and nontemporal character of introvertive mysticism has no place in the extrovertive variety in which there is a "concrete apprehension of the One as being an inner subjectivity in all things, described variously as life, or consciousness, or a living Presence. The discovery that nothing is really dead,"[15] is also a crucial revelation for the extrovertive mystic.

In the psychedelic drug-state there also may occur major and minor forms of mysticism, these being roughly equivalent to Stace's descriptions of the extrovertive and introvertive varieties. The drug subject is also prone, however, to another experiential possibility of mystical awareness, one which is nothing more than an analogue of mystical experience differing from the religious analogues already described mainly in the degree of identification and the intensity with which the subject responds to persons, objects, and various drug-state phenomena. These mystical analogues we do not regard as authentic mystical or religious experiences. At best they are experiences of intense empathic communion often rendered more impressive still by such accompanying drug-state phenomena as ego loss and body dissolution. That these are profoundly moving and impressive experiences explains in part why it is that they are so often confused with authentic states of mystical awareness.

In our investigations we have discovered that religious professionals are especially given to this kind of confusion, perhaps because of their strong desire to have first-hand experience of a phenomenon with which they may have had only theoretical familiarity. As often has been true in the past, at the opportunity of moving from theory into practice the scholar and theologian will all too often mistake the sow's ear for the silk purse.

In discussing the extrovertive mystical experience as it occurs in the psychedelic state, we will limit ourselves to an examination of one of its most frequently recurring types—a type experienced by almost one half of all our LSD subjects and which we will term *cosmological* mysticism. Cosmological mysticism is essentially an ecstatic experience of Nature and Process which leaves the subject with a sense of having acquired important insight into, as well as identity with, the fundamental nature and structure of the universe. Rarely transformative of the person as integral level experience may be transformative, it is not a religious experience either, since it rarely involves an individual encounter with That which is perceived as God or Being. Pantheistic terms are frequently employed, but what the subject expresses is likely to be the pervasiveness of energy states rather the plentitude of deity.

COSMOLOGICAL MYSTICISM

In its best sense cosmological mysticism is an experience of Reality illumined from within, an experience in which, to quote Blake's words, "the doors of perception

---

[15] Stace, *ibid.,* p. 79.

are cleansed" so that "everything appears to man as it is, infinite."[16] It is an experience that has inspired poets and nature mystics to revel in the Immanence in things and to speak of:

> . . . a sense sublime
> of something far more deeply interfused,
> Whose swelling is the light of setting suns,
> And the round ocean and the living air,
> And the blue sky, and in the mind of man:
> A motion and a spirit, that impels
> All thinking things, all objects of all thought,
> And rolls through all things.[17]

With the great mystics of the past this is familiar terrain and is regarded as a way station along the Mystic Path. The Protestant mystic, Jacob Boehme, was especially prone to the raptures of cosmological mysticism, for as Evelyn Underhill remarks:

"In Boehme's life . . . there were three distinct onsets of illumination; all of the pantheistic and external type. . . . About the year 1600 occurred the second illumination, initiated by a trancelike state of consciousness, the result of gazing at a polished disk. . . . This experience brought with it that particular and lucid vision of the inner reality of the phenomenal world in which, as he says, he looked into the deepest foundations of things. . . . He believed that it was only a fancy, and in order to banish it from his mind he went out upon the green. But here he remarked that he gazed into the very heart of things . . . viewing the herbs and grass of the field in his inward light, he saw into their essences, use, and properties, which were discovered to him by their lineaments, figures, and signatures. . . ."[18]

It is not uncommon for the psychedelic subject to feel that he, too, gazes into the very heart of things to discover therein the "essences, use, and properties," the "lineaments, figures, and signatures." He, too, may be certain that he perceives the "hidden unity in the Eternal Being" and knows directly the mysterious workings of Nature which science is only beginning to guess at. This sense of acquiring real knowledge of the processes of life while in the drug-state, is at first glance one of the more baffling phenomena of the state we have termed cosmological mysticism.

In a curious article entitled "The Religious Experience: Its Production and Interpretation," Timothy Leary asserts that "those aspects of the psychedelic experience which subjects report to be ineffable and ecstatically religious involve a direct awareness of the processes which physicists and biochemists and neurologists measure." Leary believes[19] that the data of the drug session provide psychedelic correlates remark-

---

[16] William Blake, "The Marriage of Heaven and Hell," xxii.

[17] William Wordsworth, "Tintern Abbey."

Compare with this the similar sentiments in Robert Browning when he has the young David sing:

> "I but open my eyes,—and perfection, no more and no less,
> In the kind I imagined full-fronts me, and God is seen God
> In the star, in the stone, in the flesh, in the soul and the clod."
> ("Saul," xvii.)

[18] Underhill, E., *Mysticism*, Meridian Books, New York, 1955, pp. 255–256.

[19] Leary, T., "The Religious Experience: Its Production and Interpretation," *Psychedelic Review*, 1, No. 3, 1964, pp. 324–346.

ably similar to the most advanced scientific thinking with regard to 1) the ultimate power question, 2) the life question, 3) the human-destiny question, and 4) the ego question. Leary had defined religious experience as the "ecstatic, incontrovertibly certain, subjective discovery of answers to these four basic questions." He argues that since psychedelic correlates correspond so favorably to current scientific findings, the subject who achieves such information in the course of his session is undoubtedly undergoing an authentic religious or mystical experience according to the Leary definition.

Our own position is that while we have witnessed the same kind of phenomena Leary describes, we would be very hesitant to suggest as he does that in the ecstatic-psychedelic state genetic codes are unlocked, nuclear enigmas revealed, and the virtual infinity of intracellular communication lines perceived and in some sense understood. Further, we must argue that his criteria for what constitutes religious and mystical experience are not adequate as criteria for the authentic experience. As mystics through the ages have known and shown, much that is accepted as evidence by Leary is but a part of the exotica accompanying certain minor forms of mysticism.

To take a brief look at some of this exotica, we find drug subjects with little or no scientific training describing evolutionary processes in some detail, spelling out the scenery of microcosm and macrocosm in terms roughly equivalent to those used by the modern physicist, empathizing with primal states of matter and energy and then recounting this experience in terms more reminiscent of Heisenberg than of an hallucinatory state. Since this book already is replete with subjects' descriptions of just such experiences, there is no need to burden the reader with further "documentation" of this kind.

Still the question remains: Where is this information coming from? Is it a gift of God? of Grace? of hyper-neuronal ecstasy? Is it a result of our twelve billion brain cells astronomically interconnecting at the speed of light and now galvanized by a psychedelic drug to ever more prodigious computations—to tune in finally on the Process Itself? Or perhaps may it be, as some theorists propose, that the cell has its knowledge that Knowledge does not know? In regard to this last suggested explanation, it might be argued that it is a well-known fact of biophysics that there is a kind of purposiveness to all bodily processes, be they ever so microscopic. It might be, then, that in the sensitized psychedelic state the subject picks up some sense of this purposiveness from his physical processes which he then dramatizes in terms of the drama of birth, growth, decay, and death. Or could it even be that the subject becomes aware of the purposiveness and then transforms this insight into a scientific spectacular from information dimly remembered or subliminally recorded?

Whatever the explanation may be, we believe that it is fair to say that we are here facing the same problem that was met with in the preceding chapter. There, it will be recalled, we described several instances of remarkably accurate and sometimes esoteric historical descriptions provided by persons who seemed largely ignorant of that kind of information. Just as one might have recourse to a "collective unconscious" in explaining the historical evocations, so with regard to the present phenomena one can easily fall into a kind of Jungian physicalism, proposing *a priori* knowledge of energy and nuclear and cellular processes. Claiming unconscious *a priori* knowledge is a very seductive stance, but it does not exhaust the possibilities. A more probable speculation would propose the drug-induced activation of memory patterns dealing with scientific data. As we observed in the previous chapter, the average American is exposed through his reading of newspapers, magazines, TV-watching, to enormous amounts of exoteric and esoteric information concerning a vast range of subject matter. This information is haphazardly absorbed, consciously forgotten, but cumulatively stored in regions of the mind accessible under certain conditions. As the surprising emergence of historical data into a subject's consciousness may constitute subliminal triumphs of *Time, Life, Newsweek,* so the scientific arcana of cosmological mysticism may be similarly attributed.

Having offered some suggestions as to the "where" of this material, it still remains to inquire after the "why." Why should a religious or mystic-type experience have as an important part of its content the metaphors and meanings of science? The reason, we will speculate, is this: Since man has been man he has limned his understanding of life through mythological motifs, finding in the myth both dimensional perspective and the emotional force necessary to interpret his world. As the mythopoeics of one age become inadequate for a succeeding age, the myth assumes a broader and sometimes more factual base from which it either develops or decays. Today the mythic mantle has passed in many cases from gods and heroes and has fallen upon the extraordinary hypotheses of inner and outer space. The new scientific knowledge concerning molecule and galaxy, DNA and RNA, force field and wave length, creation and evolution, provides the *stuff* of myth-making and constitutes part of the present domain of "sacred knowledge." It is for this reason then that we believe that after the psychedelic subject has paid eidetic and ideational lip service to traditional (but demythologized) myths and deities, he often will center his emotion and conviction upon the mythologized vistas of sacramentalized science. As we have shown throughout this book, it is a commonplace for the subject to apprehend the world both mythically and empathically. Cosmological mysticism would appear to be the mythic and empathic apprehension of the world, often scientifically conceptualized by virtue of the subject's normal or subliminal familiarity with the terms and "sacred" hypotheses of the new science. Cosmological mysticism is also the mythopoeic eye ecstatically encountering these hypotheses (the dogmatics of the myth) in the data of the world and so experiencing these data as revelatory though coherent, mystical though precise.

Introvertive Mystical Experience. Among our psychedelic drug subjects the authentic and introvertive mystical state as described by Stace has appeared to occur at the deepest phenomenological stratum of the subject's experience. This deep stratum, of the integral level, may be reached rather quickly when the movement is towards introvertive mystical experience. Sensory level phenomena are especially rich and typically include some variety of cosmological mysticism which may be an important first step towards the more profound mystical state yet to come. After that, the subject moves quickly through comparatively unimporant recollective-analytic materials to the symbolic experiences carrying him to the threshold of what for want of a better term we will call the *Mysterium* of the integral level. This Mysterium almost always is experienced as the source level of reality. Here, the semantics of theological discourse become the visceral realities of the subject; and such well-known concepts as the "primordial essence" and the "ultimate Ground of Being" take on an immediacy and clarity hitherto unknown.

Out of our total of 206 subjects we believe that six have had this (introvertive mystical) experience. It is of interest to observe that those few subjects who attain to this level of mystical apprehension have in the course of their lives either actively sought the mystical experience in meditation and other spiritual disciplines or have for many years demonstrated a considerable interest in integral levels of consciousness. It also should be noted that all of these subjects were over forty years of age, were of superior intelligence, and were well-adjusted and creative personalities. It would appear, therefore, that where there is an intellectual and other predisposition, a belief in the validity of religious and mystical experience, and the necessary maturity and capacity to undergo such experience, then we have the conditions favorable to the psychedelic-mystical state.

Reports from the subjects concerning the structure and development of their mystical experience show a remarkable similarity. Along with generally confirming the characteristics of the introvertive mystical experience as Stace describes it, they also agree as to many particulars met with, too, in the classical literature of mysticism. In almost every case the experience is initiated with a sense of the ego dissolving into boundless being. This process is almost always attended by an experience of the subject being caught up in a torrent of preternatural light. S-4, a forty-nine-year-old woman (LSD), gives a typical description of this light:

"My body became the body of bliss, diaphanous to the rhythms of the universe. All around and passing through me was the Light, a trillion atomized crystals shimmering in blinding incandescence. I was carried by this Light to an Ecstasy beyond and suddenly I was no longer I but a part of the Divine Workings. There was no time, no space, no 'I,' no 'You,' only—the Becoming of Being."

Another common aspect of the experience is the subject's becoming aware of himself as continuous with the energy of the universe. This is frequently described with words to the effect that the person was part of a dynamic continuum. It is also experienced as a state in which the subject feels himself to be filled by divinity. We find this illustrated in the experience of another LSD subject, S-5, a fifty-two-year-old engineer, who writes:

"Although consciousness of self seemed extinguished, I knew that the boundaries of my being now had been dissolved and that all other boundaries also were dissolved. All, including what had been myself, was an ever more rapid molecular whirling that then became something else, a pure and seething energy that was the whole of Being. This energy, neither hot nor cold, was experienced as a white and radiant fire. There seemed no direction to this whirling, only an acceleration of speed, yet one knew that along this dynamic continuum the flux of Being streamed inexorably, unswervingly toward the One.

"At what I can only call the 'core' of this flux was God, and I cannot explain how it was that I, who seemed to have no identity at all, yet experienced myself as *filled with God,* and then as (whatever this may mean) *passing through God* and into a Oneness wherein it seemed God, Being, and a mysterious unnameable One constituted together what I can only designate the ALL. What 'I' experienced in this ALL so far transcends my powers of description that to speak, as I must, of an ineffably rapturous Sweetness is an approximation not less feeble than if I were to describe a candle and so hope to capture with my words all of the blazing glory of the sun."

It is characteristic of the subject during the mystical state to feel that the categories of time are strained by the tensions of eternity. "Everything was touched with eternity," said one subject. "Time was no longer. Eternity had burst in," said another. "Eternity had flooded the gates of time," said still another.

The subject experiences the world as transfigured and unified. He describes himself as having been caught up in an undifferentiated unity wherein the knower, the knowledge, and the known are experienced as a single reality. In the following case we have an account by a subject whose whole experience largely typifies the range of phenomena encountered in the psychedelic experience. The subject, S-6, is a highly sensitive and intelligent woman in her late fifties. She wrote the following "Subjective Report" about twenty-nine hours after taking 75 micrograms of LSD:

"For those interested in the type of experience that was mine I should like to record, in the interest of 'preparation,' 'motivation,' that I have, for over twenty-five years, been drawn to the philosophy and literature of ancient China, India, and Tibet, and have practiced the science of meditation. After reading the published account of Aldous Huxley's experience under mescaline, I hoped some day to have a similar opportunity to know the true meaning of an expanded consciousness. After waiting some years, this was given. Under guidance and in the company of beloved friends, I was given 75 gamma of LSD.

"Lying on a comfortable couch, in a room of great serenity, filled with roses, pansies, and hydrangea, I felt almost immediately a sense of profound relaxation and a great inner peace. I watched the sunlight on the ceiling as it played through the shadow of the windowpanes reflected there.

"Soon a shell-pink rose was given to me to observe. I sat up to do this and though quite prepared for the phenomenon given to most everyone under this influence, I was overwhelmed by the life that pulsated through this fragile, delicate flower. Its petals rhythmically expanding and contracting and hues of pink rushing into its heart and out again. It was spellbinding, and as I re-emerged into a three-dimensional world I looked with awe upon what I considered a live, fresh flower and realized that it was only a 'still life' in comparison to that which had been given. I asked whether my hand was trembling, so alive was this quivering rose. Later, I observed the rich, deep velvet tones of a large-faced pansy with the same 'inner seeing' only its heart became a fathomless tunnel of light.

"Now I no longer wanted the abstractions of this kind of glory, for deep within was the thirst for a greater knowing into the ancient Wisdom teaching I had long wrestled with. Closing my eyes, my position was suddenly shifted to some Oriental posture—legs folded across—palms facing up—wrists meeting under chin—it was pleasant—as if it were a prankish, almost impish moment into some former incarnation. Then followed this verbatim description (from notes made at the time) of what came out as 'The First Absorption'—The longing of my soul to experience the Reality of Oneness with the Absolute was my paramount hope and motivation in taking LSD—that some breakthrough might be given. Also, long had I contemplated whether Identity is sustained in the final Absorption. With these thoughts, I became a diffused light that broke into a brilliant glittering, quivering thing—then it burst— bringing a shower of dazzling rays—each ray filled with a myriad of colors—gold, purple, emerald, ruby—and each ray charged with a current—throwing off sparkling lights—there was the Ecstasy—all identification with self dissolved. There was no sense of time-space. Only an awareness of Being. At last I cried: 'I cannot endure this any longer. It is enough.' Someone whispered: 'You are given that which you can endure.' Then I wept. I recall there were 'instances' of a returning awareness. At no time was there a sense of the individualized self. I never knew when 'I' entered the stream. Only the emergence out of it.

"I joined the group who were having a late (?) lunch (there *is* no time) on the terrace. A friend asked whether I would like to have something and I said no and made a remark about those 'historic figures' reputed to have lived a life without partaking of food and wondered how this could be. Instantly, I became a vessel—a mighty force of energy, sparkling, crystal-like, and pure, came pouring into me. I remember thinking or saying—'This is the pure source of energy—right from the very mouth of Godhead. The current entered into me—through the fingers first, then coursed through my entire body and all of me seemed electrified. I felt energized, knew to an overwhelming degree the meaning of regeneration and thought 'this is how it's done.' Why should this have to go into the earth, to be converted into food—to be digested and again converted into energy, when one may have it pure and glorified. I saw it dissipate itself into the earth and rise with incredible speed into a spiral going up, up, up, and then I spoke of the Whirling Dervishes and understood the Cosmic meaning of all nature dances and how man and nature merge into one.

"I was reminded that I had not yet known the joy of being outdoors, in the grass and under the trees. We went out beyond the house where I lay in the grass, felt its wondrous texture with my fingers and toes, then rose to stand under a cedar tree. Embracing its branches and burying my head, I was overcome by the crisp, pungent fragrance of the cedar. At that moment an icy wind began to blow over and through me and I was shifted to some solitary height, measureless, boundless, and indescribable. There I shivered and in that instant there came a repeat of the former, shatteringly ecstatic experience of an exploding shower of sparkling light, pouring into me illuminating rays of glittering jeweled tones—emeralds, amethyst, ruby, and gold.

"We returned indoors. I again stretched out on the couch, exhausted, spent. In conversation I mentioned everything that I had ever sought to experience in the realm of 'other world' had been given—although the 'between worlds' had not. Instantly I became aware of a formless mass hovering above the gross body. At first it appeared with a cloud-like dimness—the texture gradually became more and more delicate and finally translucent. There was a sense of buoyancy—an inexpressible joy. I thought 'this may be suspended animation.' Unlike the two earlier experiences, this awareness had form. It was lovely and one knew why meditation at this level could be indefinitely sustained. I do not recall that 'it' had identity. I believe not.

"After the guides felt the peak had been reached, it was explained that I would descend quietly and cold cloths were applied to my head which now was throbbing. The ache became concentrated at the center of my forehead—between the eyes. This became so penetrating that I placed the third finger of my left hand on the spot and pressed down with all my strength. In so doing the finger became an iron shaft that kept pushing down, down, down. It was excruciatingly painful and remained so. All the while I felt something was 'being done.' The sense of several faceless, formless, and nameless presences were around the area making a concerted effort to keep the shaft going deeper and deeper. The pain increased and I cried out: 'No more today, please. Don't give it all in one day.' And suddenly the pain reached such intensity that it was no longer a pain. Questions were asked by voices in the room and someone mentioned the third eye episode and asked was it similar and what did it mean to me. I felt the shaft and said simply, 'an initiation.' It diffused itself by streaming to the base of the skull and dividing. The ache back of each ear was awful until it flowed into many little veins and entered some subterranean passage. The area between the eyes felt as if some surgery had been performed, the wound stitched and with the anesthetic waning, was left tender and sore."

Although the experience of introvertive drug-state mysticism are integral level experiences, they rarely yield any such radical transformation of the subject's inner and outer life as ordinarily results from the integral level religious experiences. The reason for this may be that those few subjects who are sufficiently prepared for and able to attain to introvertive mystical states are already persons of exceptional mental and emotional maturity and stability. The present potential of the person already has been in large measure realized. It is also possible, however, that the aforementioned tendency of these subjects to avoid or minimize work with psychodynamic materials may preclude the possibility of a transforming experience.

Apparently, introvertive mystical experience, at least in the case of the psychedelic subject, does not occur except in those instances where preparation has been considerable and a state of readiness for the mystical experience has been established. It may be significant that in each of our six cases of introvertive mysticism, the subject probably was, at the time of the session, near the peak of his or her preparation and readiness to undergo a profound mystical experience. Thus the function of the drug-state seems to have been that of giving the subject the final push off the mystical brink on which he or she already was standing.

We have said that the psychedelic mystical experience closely resembled the seven-point typology of mystical experience set forth by Stace. In fact, when Stace recently was asked if he thought the psychedelic mystical experience to be similar to traditional mystical experience, he responded that "It's not a matter of it being *similar* to mystical experience; it *is* mystical experience."[20] To this judgment we would like to introduce a qualification we feel to be significant to the future development and understanding of states of religious and mystical consciousness.

Our qualification has to do with the *culmination* of the mystical experience—since we feel that the psychedelic and traditional varieties afford a virtually identical experience of non-sensuous, atemporal Unitary Consciousness—but with the developmental process of the experience, since here we have observed the psychedelic type to differ diametrically from the traditional. These differences of process are evidenced in the following important manner:

In nondrug introvertive mysticism, whether of the Eastern or Western variety, the seeker attempts a long, arduous process of gradually emptying his mind of all its empirical content; that is, of all events, associations, sensations, images, symbols—until the mind becomes a virtual vacuum which then can be "filled" with the Mystic Void. By thus systematically ridding the mind of its multiplicity the traditional adept attains to the pure essence of the Undifferentiated Unity, the One without a second. But in the psychedelic experience, it would appear that just the opposite

[20] Quoted by Houston Smith, *op. cit.,* p. 159.

happens. Consciousness expands and reaches outward to encompass a wealth of phenomena unprecedented in the subject's experience. The empirical content of the subject's mind is vitalized, the multiplicity compounded, and the fullness of awareness increases to an intensity that may seem almost too great to be borne. Then, with the crossing-over into the integral, consciousness abruptly and spontaneously contracts, narrowing to a focal point of awareness, which being so compacted then explodes into the mystic state of One Single Reality. The process is such that the phenomena condense into the Noumenon, the many into the One, the particulars into Essence.

While it is impossible at this time to make comparative qualitative judgments concerning psychedelic and traditional mysticism, it appears to us evident that the process leading toward Mystical Culmination is far richer in the case of the psychedelic subject than is the *via negativa* or path of obliteration of the traditional mystic. This is an area in which our conclusions have not yet crystallized and to the consideration of which we plan to give much further attention. However, we do feel it possible to suggest that the disparate processes involved in these two mysticisms may do much to explain the withdrawal from life of many of the traditional mystics as compared to the psychedelic mystic's oft observed tendency to move towards a fullness of experience.

In the case of our six subjects who experienced the introvertive mystical state, the only significant change in post-session behavior observed by either us or the subject was a change toward increasing concern with and appreciation of the particulars of existence. For if one were to note any single deficiency characteristic of all of these subjects, it would be the somewhat abstracted attitude they had acquired as a result of their years of preparational devotions. The beneficial effect of the psychedelic mystical experience, then, was to take the subject through a process of experiencing Essence in such a way that it illuminated all of existence, making him more interested in and responsive to the phenomena of existence than he had been before. Thus, instead of retreating from the phenomenal world, as often occurs with the traditional mystic, the psychedelic subject was inspired by the process of his experience to a flight *towards* reality.

WILLIAM JAMES

The Reality of the Unseen

William James (1842–1910), a
physician turned philosopher and
psychologist, wrote *The Will to
Believe* and other works which
greatly influenced the American
pragmatic tradition.

Were one asked to characterize the life of religion in the broadest and most general terms possible, one might say that it consists of the belief that there is an unseen order, and that our supreme good lies in harmoniously adjusting ourselves thereto. This belief and this adjustment are the religious attitude in the soul. I wish during this hour to call your attention to some of the psychological peculiarities of such an attitude as this, of belief in an object which we cannot see. All our attitudes, moral, practical, or emotional, as well as religious, are due to the 'objects' of our consciousness, the thing which we believe to exist, whether really or ideally, along with ourselves. Such objects may be present to our senses, or they may be present only to our thought. In either case they elicit from us a *reaction;* and the reaction due to things of thought is notoriously in many cases as strong as that due to sensible presences. It may be even stronger.

* * *

... It is as if there were in the human consciousness a *sense of reality, a feeling of objective presence, a perception* of what we may call *'something there,'* more deep and more general than any of the special and particular 'senses' by which the current psychology supposes existent realities to be originally revealed. If this were so, we might suppose the senses to waken our attitudes and conduct as they so habitually do, by first exciting this sense of reality; but anything else, any idea, for example, that might similarly excite it, would have that same prerogative of appearing real which objects of sense normally possess. So far as religious conceptions were able to touch this reality-feeling, they would be believed in in spite of criticism, even though they might be so vague and remote as to be almost unimaginable, even though they might be such non-entities in point of *whatness,* as Kant makes the objects of his moral theology to be.

The most curious proofs of the existence of such an undifferentiated sense of reality as this are found in experiences of hallucination. It often happens that an hallucination is imperfectly developed: the person affected will feel a 'presence' in the room, definitely localized, facing in one particular way, real in the most emphatic

From *The Varieties of Religious Experience,* by William James, 1902.

sense of the word, often coming suddenly, and as suddenly gone; and yet neither seen, heard, touched, nor cognized in any of the usual 'sensible' ways. Let me give you an example of this, before I pass to the objects with whose presence religion is more peculiarly concerned.

An intimate friend of mine, one of the keenest intellects I know, has had several experiences of this sort. He writes as follows in response to my inquiries:—

"I have several times within the past few years felt the so-called 'consciousness of a presence.' The experiences which I have in mind are clearly distinguishable from another kind of experience which I have had very frequently, and which I fancy many persons would also call the 'consciousness of a presence.' But the difference for me between the two sets of experience is as great as the difference between feeling a slight warmth originating I know not where, and standing in the midst of a conflagration with all the ordinary senses alert.

"It was about September, 1884, when I had the first experience. On the previous night I had had, after getting into bed at my rooms in College, a vivid tactile hallucination of being grasped by the arm, which made me get up and search the room for an intruder; but the sense of presence properly so called came on the next night. After I had got into bed and blown out the candle, I lay awake awhile thinking on the previous night's experience, when suddenly I *felt* something come into the room and stay close to my bed. It remained only a minute or two. I did not recognize it by any ordinary sense, and yet there was a horribly unpleasant 'sensation' connected with it. It stirred something more at the roots of my being than any ordinary perception. The feeling had something of the quality of a very large tearing vital pain spreading chiefly over the chest, but within the organism—and yet the feeling was not *pain* so much as *abhorrence*. At all events, something was present with me, and I knew its presence far more surely than I have ever known the presence of any fleshly living creature. I was conscious of its departure as of its coming: an almost instantaneously swift going through the door, and the 'horrible sensation' disappeared.

"On the third night when I retired my mind was absorbed in some lectures which I was preparing, and I was still absorbed in these when I became aware of the actual presence (though not of the *coming*) of the thing that was there the night before, and of the 'horrible sensation.' I then mentally concentrated all my effort to charge this 'thing,' if it was evil, to depart, if it was *not* evil, to tell me who or what it was, and if it could not explain itself, to go, and that I would compel it to go. It went as on the previous night, and my body quickly recovered its normal state.

"On two other occasions in my life I have had precisely the same 'horrible sensation.' Once it lasted a full quarter of an hour. In all three instances the certainty that there in outward space there stood *something* was indescribably *stronger* than the ordinary certainty of companionship when we are in the close presence of ordinary living people. The something seemed close to me, and intensely more real than any ordinary perception. Although I felt it to be like unto myself, so to speak, or finite, small, and distressful, as it were, I didn't recognize it as any individual being or person."

Of course such an experience as this does not connect itself with the religious sphere. Yet it may upon occasion do so; and the same correspondent informs me that at more than one other conjuncture he had the sense of presence developed with equal intensity and abruptness, only then it was filled with a quality of joy.

"There was not a mere consciousness of something there, but fused in the central happiness of it, a startling awareness of some ineffable good. Not vague either, not like the emotional effect of some poem, or scene, or blossom, or music, but the sure knowledge of the close presence of a sort of mighty person, and after it went, the memory persisted as the one perception of reality. Everything else might be a dream, but not that."

. . .

Of the more habitual and so to speak chronic sense of God's presence the following sample from Professor Starbuck's manuscript collection may serve to give an idea. It is from a man aged forty-nine,—probably thousands of unpretending Christians would write an almost identical account.

"God is more real to me than any thought or thing or person. I feel his presence positively, and the more as I live in closer harmony with his laws as written in my body and mind. I feel him in the sunshine or rain; and awe mingled with a delicious restfulness most nearly describes my feelings. I talk to him as to a companion in prayer and praise, and our communion is delightful. He answers me again and again, often in words so clearly spoken that it seems my outer ear must have carried the tone, but generally in strong mental impressions. Usually a text of Scripture, unfolding some new view of him and his love for me, and care for my safety. I could give hundreds of instances, in school matters, social problems, financial difficulties, etc. That he is mine and I am his never leaves me, it is an abiding joy. Without it life would be a blank, a desert, a shoreless, trackless waste."

I subjoin some more examples from writers of different ages and sexes. They are also from Professor Starbuck's collection, and their number might be greatly multiplied. The first is from a man twenty-seven years old:—

"God is quite real to me. I talk to him and often get answers. Thoughts sudden and distinct from any I have been entertaining come to my mind after asking God for his direction. Something over a year ago I was for some weeks in the direst perplexity. When the trouble first appeared before me I was dazed, but before long (two or three hours) I could hear distinctly a passage of Scripture: 'My grace is sufficient for thee.' Every time my thoughts turned to the trouble I could hear this quotation. I don't think I ever doubted the existence of God, or had him drop out of my consciousness. God has frequently stepped into my affairs very perceptibly, and I feel that he directs many little details all the time. But on two or three occasions he has ordered ways for me very contrary to my ambitions and plans."

Another statement (none the less valuable psychologically for being so decidedly childish) is that of a boy of seventeen:—

"Sometimes as I go to church, I sit down, join in the service, and before I go out I feel as if God was with me, right side of me, singing and reading the Psalms with me. . . . And then again I feel as if I could sit beside him, and put my arms around him, kiss him, etc. When I am taking Holy Communion at the altar, I try to get with him and generally feel his presence."

I let a few other cases follow at random:—

"God surrounds me like the physical atmosphere. He is closer to me than my my own breath. In him literally I live and move and have my being."—

"There are times when I seem to stand in his very presence, to talk with him. Answers to prayer have come, sometimes direct and overwhelming in their revelation of his presence and powers. There are times when God seems far off, but this is always my own fault."—

"I have the sense of a presence, strong, and at the same time soothing, which hovers over me. Sometimes it seems to enwrap me with sustaining arms."

Such is the human ontological imagination, and such is the convincingness of what it brings to birth. Unpicturable beings are realized, and realized with an intensity almost like that of an hallucination. They determine our vital attitude as decisively as the vital attitude of lovers is determined by the habitual sense, by which each is haunted, of the other being in the world. A lover has notoriously this sense of the continuous being of his idol, even when his attention is addressed to other matters and he no longer represents her features. He cannot forget her; she uninterruptedly affects him through and through.

I spoke of the convincingness of these feelings of reality, and I must dwell a moment longer on that point. They are as convincing to those who have them as any direct sensible experiences can be, and they are, as a rule, much more convincing than results established by mere logic ever are. One may indeed be entirely without them; probably more than one of you here present is without them in any marked degree; but if you do have them, and have them at all strongly, the probability is that you cannot help regarding them as genuine perceptions of truth, as revelations of a kind of reality which no adverse argument, however unanswerable by you in words, can expel from your belief. The opinion opposed to mysticism in philosophy is sometimes spoken of as *rationalism*. Rationalism insists that all our beliefs ought ultimately to find for themselves articulate grounds. Such grounds, for rationalism, must consist of four things: (1) definitely stable abstract principles; (2) definite facts of sensation; (3) definite hypotheses based on such facts; and (4) definite inferences logically drawn. Vague impressions of something indefinable have no place in the rationalistic system, which on its positive side is surely a splendid intellectual tendency, for not only are all our philosophies fruits of it, but physical science (amongst other good things) is its result.

Nevertheless, if we look on man's whole mental life as it exists, on the life of men that lies in them apart from their learning and science, and that they inwardly and privately follow, we have to confess that the part of it of which rationalism can give an account is relatively superficial. It is the part that has the *prestige* undoubtedly, for it has the loquacity, it can challenge you for proofs, and chop logic, and put you down with words. But it will fail to convince or convert you all the same, if your dumb intuitions are opposed to its conclusions. If you have intuitions at all, they come from a deeper level of your nature than the loquacious level which rationalism inhibits. Your whole subconscious life, your impulses, your faiths, your needs, your divinations, have prepared the premises, of which your consciousness now feels the weight of the result; and something in you absolutely *knows* that that result must be truer than any logic-chopping rationalistic talk, however clever, that may contradict it. This inferiority of the rationalistic level in founding belief is just as manifest when rationalism argues for religion as when it argues against it. That vast literature of proofs of God's existence drawn from the order of nature, which a century ago seemed so overwhelmingly convincing, to-day does little more than gather dust in libraries, for the simple reason that our generation has ceased to believe in the kind of God it argued for. Whatever sort of a being God may be, we *know* to-day that he is nevermore that mere external inventor of 'contrivances' intended to make manifest his 'glory' in which our great-grandfathers took such satisfaction, though just how we know this we cannot possibly make clear by words either to others or to ourselves. I defy any of you here fully to account for your persuasion if a God exist he must be a more cosmic and tragic personage than that Being.

The truth is that in the metaphysical and religious sphere, articulate reasons are cogent for us only when our inarticulate feelings of reality have already been impressed in favor of the same conclusion. Then, indeed, our intuitions and our reason work together, and great world-ruling systems, like that of the Buddhist or of the Catholic philosophy, may grow up. Our impulsive belief is here always what sets up the original body of truth, and our articulately verbalized philosophy is but its showy translation into formulas. The unreasoned and immediate assurance is the deep thing in us, the reasoned argument is but a surface exhibition. Instinct leads, intelligence does but follow. If a person feels the presence of a living God after the fashion shown by my quotations, your critical arguments, be they never so superior, will vainly set themselves to change his faith.

Please observe, however, that I do not yet say that it is *better* that the subconscious and non-rational should thus hold primacy in the religious realm. I confine myself to simply pointing out that they do so hold it as a matter of fact.

SØREN KIERKEGAARD

The Concept of Dread

Søren Kierkegaard (1813–1855) was a Danish existentialist theologian. Among his many works, some pseudonymous, are *Either/Or, Fear and Trembling,* and *Concluding Unscientific Postscript.*

One may liken dread to dizziness. He whose eyes chances to look down into the yawning abyss becomes dizzy. But the reason for it is just as much his eye as it is the precipice. For suppose he had not looked down.

Thus dread is the dizziness of freedom which occurs when the spirit would posit the synthesis, and freedom then gazes down into its own possibility, grasping at finiteness to sustain itself. In this dizziness freedom succumbs. Further than this psychology cannot go and will not. That very instant everything is changed, and when freedom rises again it sees that it is guilty. Between these two instants lies the leap, which no science has explained or can explain. He who becomes guilty in dread becomes as ambiguously guilty as it is possible to be.

.   .   .

In one of Grimm's Fairy Tales there is the story of a youth who went out in search of adventures for the sake of learning what it is to fear or be in dread. We will let that adventurer go his way without troubling ourselves to learn whether in the course of it he encountered the dreadful. On the other hand I would say that learning to know dread is an adventure which every man has to affront if he would not go to perdition either by not having known dread or by sinking under it. He therefore who has learned rightly to be in dread has learned the most important thing.

If a man were a beast or an angel, he would not be able to be in dread. Since he is a synthesis he can be in dread, and the greater the dread, the greater the man. This, however, is not affirmed in the sense in which men commonly understand dread, as related to something outside a man, but in the sense that man himself produces dread. Only in this sense can we interpret the passage where it is said of Christ that he was in dread [ængstes] even unto death, and the place also where he says to Judas, "What thou doest, do quickly." Not even the terrible word upon which even Luther dreaded to preach, "My God, my God, why hast thou forsaken me?"—not even this expresses suffering so strongly. For this word indicates a situation in which Christ actually is; the former sayings indicate a relation to a situation which is not yet actual.

Dread is the possibility of freedom. Only this dread is by the aid of faith absolutely educative, laying bare as it does all finite aims and discovering all their deceptions. And no Grand Inquisitor has in readiness such terrible tortures as has dread, and no spy knows how to attack more artfully the man he suspects, choosing the instant when he is weakest, nor knows how to lay traps where he will be caught and ensnared, as dread knows how, and no sharp-witted judge knows how to interrogate, to examine the accused, as dread does, which never lets him escape, neither by diversion nor by noise, neither at work nor at play, neither by day nor by night.

He who is educated by dread is educated by possibility, and only the man who is educated by possibility is educated in accordance with his infinity. Possibility is therefore the heaviest of all categories. One often hears, it is true, the opposite affirmed, that possibility is so light but reality is heavy. But from whom does one hear such talk? From a lot of miserable men who never have known what possibility is, and who, since reality showed them that they were not fit for anything and never would be, mendaciously bedizened a possibility which was so beautiful, so enchanting; and the only foundation of this possibility was a little youthful tomfoolery of which they might rather have been ashamed. Therefore by this possibility which is said to be light one commonly understands the possibility of luck, good fortune, etc. But this is not possibility, it is a mendacious invention which human depravity falsely embellishes in order to have reason to complain of life, of providence, and as a pretext for being self-important. No, in possibility everything is possible, and he who truly was brought up by possibility has comprehended the dreadful as well as the smiling. When such a person, therefore, goes out from the school of possibility, and knows more thoroughly than a child knows the alphabet that he can demand of life absolutely nothing, and that terror, perdition, annihilation, dwell next door to every man, and has learned the profitable lesson that every dread which alarms [ængste] may the next instant become a fact, he will then interpret reality differently, he will extol reality, and even when it rests upon him heavily he will remember that after all it is far, far lighter than the possibility was. Only thus can possibility educate; for finiteness and the finite relationships in which the individual is assigned a place, whether it be small and commonplace or world-historical, educate only finitely, and one can always talk them around, always get a little more out of them, always chaffer, always escape a little way from them, always keep a little apart, always prevent oneself from learning absolutely from them; and if one is to learn absolutely, the individual must in turn have the possibility in himself and himself fashion that from which he is to learn, even though the next instant it does not recognize that it was fashioned by him, but absolutely takes the power from him.

But in order that the individual may thus absolutely and infinitely be educated by possibility, he must be honest towards possibility and must have faith. By faith I mean what Hegel in his fashion calls very rightly "the inward certainty which anticipates infinity." When the discoveries of possibility are honestly administered, possibility will then disclose finitudes and idealize them in the form of infinity in the individual who is overwhelmed by dread, until in turn he is victorious by the anticipation of faith.

What I say here appears perhaps to many an obscure and foolish saying, since they even boast of never having been in dread. To this I would reply that doubtless one should not be in dread of men, of finite things, but that only the man who has gone through the dread of possibility is educated to have no dread—not because he avoids the dreadful things of life, but because they always are weak in comparison with those of possibility. If on the other hand the speaker means that the great thing about him is that he has never been in dread, then I shall gladly initate him into my explanation, that this comes from the fact that he is spirit-less.

If the individual cheats the possibility by which he is to be educated, he never reaches faith; his faith remains the shrewdness of finitude, as his school was that of finitude. But men cheat possibility in every way—if they did not, one has only to stick one's head out of the window, and one would see enough for possibility to begin its exercises forthwith. There is an engraving by Chodowiecki which represents the surrender of Calais as viewed by the four temperaments, and the theme of the artist was to let the various impressions appear mirrored in the faces which express the various temperaments. The most commonplace life has events enough, no doubt, but the question is whether the possibility in the individuality is honest towards itself. It is recounted of an Indian hermit who for two years had lived upon dew, that he came once to the city, tasted wine, and then became addicted to drink. This story, like every other of the sort, can be understood in many ways, one can make it comic, one can make it tragic; but the man who is educated by possibility has more than enough to occupy him in such a story. Instantly he is absolutely identified with that unfortunate man, he knows no finite evasion by which he might escape. Now the dread of possibility holds him as its prey, until it can deliver him saved into the hands of faith. In no other place does he find repose, for every other point of rest is mere nonsense, even though in men's eyes it is shrewdness. This is the reason why possibility is so absolutely educative. No man has ever become so unfortunate in reality that there was not some little residue left to him, and, as common sense observes quite truly, if a man is canny, he will find a way. But he who went through the curriculum of misfortune offered by possibility lost everything, absolutely everything, in a way that no one has lost it in reality. If in this situation he did not behave falsely towards possibility, if he did not attempt to talk around the dread which would save him, then he received everything back again, as in reality no one ever did even if he received everything double, for the pupil of possibility received infinity, whereas the soul of the other expired in the finite. No one ever sank so deep in reality that he could not sink deeper, or that there might not be one or another sunk deeper than he. But he who sank in the possibility has an eye too dizzy to see the measuring rod which Tom, Dick, and Harry hold out as a straw to the drowning man; his ear is closed so that he cannot hear what the market price for men is in his day, cannot hear that he is just as good as most of them. He sank absolutely, but then in turn he floated up from the depth of the abyss, lighter now than all that is oppressive and dreadful in life. Only I do not deny that he who is educated by possibility is exposed—not to the danger of bad company and dissoluteness of various sorts, as are those who are educated by the finite, but—to one danger of downfall, and that is self-slaughter. If at the beginning of his education he misunderstands the anguish of dread, so that it does not lead him to faith but away from faith, then he is lost. On the other hand, he who is educated by possibility remains with dread, does not allow himself to be deceived by its countless counterfeits, he recalls the past precisely; then at last the attacks of dread, though they are fearful, are not such that he flees from them. For him dread becomes a serviceable spirit which against its will leads him whither he would go. Then when it announces itself, when it craftily insinuates that it has invented a new instrument of torture far more terrible than anything employed before, he does not recoil, still less does he attempt to hold it off with clamor and noise, but he bids it welcome, he hails it solemnly, as Socrates solemnly flourished the poisoned goblet, he shuts himself up with it, he says, as a patient says to the surgeon when a painful operation is about to begin, "Now I am ready." Then dread enters into his soul and searches it thoroughly, constraining out of him all the finite and the petty, and leading him hence whither he would go.

When one or another extraordinary event occurs in life, when a world-historical hero gathers heroes about him and accomplishes heroic feats, when a crisis occurs and everything becomes significant, then men wish to be in it, for these are things which educate. Quite possibly. But there is a much simpler way of being educated much more fundamentally. Take the pupil of possibility, set him in the midst of the Jutland heath where nothing happens, where the greatest event is that a partridge flies up noisily, and he experiences everything more perfectly, more precisely, more profoundly, than the man who was applauded upon the stage of universal history, in case he was not educated by possibility.

Then when the individual is by possibility educated up to faith, dread will eradicate what it has itself produced. Dread discovers fate, but when the individual would put his confidence in fate, dread turns about and takes fate away; for fate is like dread, and dread is like possibility . . . a witch's letter. If the individuality is not by itself transformed with relation to fate, it will always retain a dialectical remnant, which no finitude can eradicate, any more than a man will lose faith in the lottery who does not lose it by his own act but is supposed to lose it for the fact that he constantly loses what he gambles. Even in relation to the most trifling things dread is promptly at hand so soon as the individual would sneak away from something, would except something by chance. In itself it is a trifle and external, the individuality can learn nothing about it from the finite, but to cut the process short dread instantly plays the trump of infinity, that of the category, and the individuality cannot take the trick. Such an individual cannot possibly fear fate in an outward sense, its changeableness and its rebuffs, for in him dread has already fashioned fate and taken away from him everything that any fate could take away. Socrates says in the dialogue of *Cratylus* that it is dreadful to be deceived by oneself, because one always has the deceiver with one. So one can say that it is good fortune to have with one such a deceiver as dread, which deceives piously and weans the child before finiteness begins to bungle it. Even if in our time an individuality is not thus educated by possibility, our age has after all a characteristic which is notably helpful to one who has a deeper nature and desires to learn the good. The more peaceful and quiet an age is, the more precisely everythings follows its regular course, so that the good has its reward, all the more easily can an individual be deceived with regard to the question whether the goal of its striving, though it be a beautiful one, may not be a finite goal. In these times, on the contrary, one need not be more than sixteen years of age to perceive that he who now has to tread the stage of life is pretty much in the same fix as the man who went down to Jericho and fell among thieves. He then who does not wish to sink in the wretchedness of the finite is constrained, in the deepest sense, to assault the infinite. Such a preliminary orientation is analogous to education in possibility, and such an orientation cannot possibly come about except by the help of possibility. So when shrewdness has brought to a close its innumerable calculations, upon the assumption of winning the game—then comes dread, even before the game was in reality lost or won, and against the devil dread makes the sign of the cross, then there is nothing shrewdness can do, and all its most sagacious combinations vanish like a ghost before that figure which dread fashions by the omnipotence of possibility. Even in relation to the most trifling matters, so soon as the individuality would make an artful turn which is only artful, would steal away from something, and there is every probability that it will succeed, for reality is not so sharp an examiner as dread—then dread is at hand. If it is sent away on the plea that this is a trifle, then dread makes this trifle as notable as the village of Marengo became in the history of Europe, because there the great Battle of Marengo was fought. In case an individuality is not thus weaned away from shrewdness by its own act, then this is never thoroughly accomplished, for finitude explains only piecemeal, never totally, and the man whose shrewdness was always at fault (and even this is impossible in reality) may seek the reason for his failure in a lack of shrewdness and strive to become all the shrewder. So also it is with regard to guilt, which is the second thing dread discovers. The man who merely by finiteness learns to recognize his guilt is lost in finiteness, and in the end the question whether one is guilty or not cannot be decided except in an external, juridical, exceedingly imperfect way. He therefore who only learns to recognize his guilt by analogy with the decisions of the police justice or the supreme court never really comprehends that he is guilty; for if a man is guilty, he is infinitely guilty. Therefore if such an individual who is educated only by finiteness does not get a verdict from the police and a verdict of public opinion that he is guilty, he becomes about the most ludicrous and pitiable of all men, a paragon of virtue who is a little better than people generally are, but not nearly so good as the parson. What help does such a man need in life? Why, even before he is dead he can almost take his place in a gallery of wax figures. From finiteness one can learn much, but one cannot learn dread, except in a very mediocre and depraved sense. On the other hand, he who truly has learned to be in dread will tread as in a dance when the dreads of finiteness strike up their tune, and the disciples of finiteness lose their wits and their courage. Thus it is life often deceives. . . .

ALBERT EINSTEIN

A Scientist's Cosmology

Albert Einstein (1879–1955),
world-famous physicist, formulated
the general theory of relativity.

Everything that the human race has done and thought is concerned with the satisfaction of deeply felt needs and the assuagement of pain. One has to keep this constantly in mind if one wishes to understand spiritual movements and their development. Feeling and longing are the motive force behind all human endeavor and human creation, in however exalted a guise the latter may present themselves to us. Now what are the feelings and needs that have led men to religious thought and belief in the widest sense of the words? A little consideration will suffice to show us that the most varying emotions preside over the birth of religious thought and experience. With primitive man it is above all fear that evokes religious notions —fear of hunger, wild beasts, sickness, death. Since at this stage of existence under-

From "Religion and Science," in *Ideas and Opinions*, by Albert Einstein, tr. by Sonja Bargmann, Crown, 1954. © 1955 by the Estate of Albert Einstein. Reprinted by permission of the Estate. This selection appeared in a slightly different form in *The New York Times Magazine*, November 9, 1930

standing of causal connections is usually poorly developed, the human mind creates illusory beings more or less analogous to itself on whose wills and actions these fearful happenings depend. Thus one tries to secure the favor of these beings by carrying out actions and offering sacrifices which, according to the tradition handed down from generation to generation, propitiate them or make them well disposed toward a mortal. In this sense I am speaking of a religion of fear. This, though not created, is an important degree stabilized by the formation of a special priestly caste which sets itself up as a mediator between the people and the beings they fear, and erects a hegemony on this basis. In many cases a leader or ruler or a privileged class whose position rests on other factors combines priestly functions with its secular authority in order to make the latter more secure; or the political rulers and the priestly caste make common cause in their own interests.

The social impulses are another source of the crystallization of religion. Fathers and mothers and the leaders of larger human communities are mortal and fallible. The desire for guidance, love, and support prompts men to form the social or moral conception of God. This is the God of Providence, who protects, disposes, rewards, and punishes; the God who, according to the limits of the believer's outlook, loves and cherishes the life of the tribe or of the human race, or even life itself; the comforter in sorrow and unsatisfied longing; he who preserves the souls of the dead. This is the social or moral conception of God.

The Jewish scriptures admirably illustrate the development from the religion of fear to moral religion, a development continued in the New Testament. The religions of all civilized peoples, especially the peoples of the Orient, are primarily moral religions. The development from a religion of fear to moral religion is a great step in people's lives. And yet, that primitive religions are based entirely on fear and the religions of civilized peoples purely on morality is a prejudice against which we must be on our guard. The truth is that all religions are a varying blend of both types, with this differentiation: that on the higher levels of social life the religion of morality predominates.

Common to all these types is the anthropomorphic character of their conception of God. In general, only individuals of exceptional endowments, and exceptionally high-minded communities, rise to any considerable extent above this level. But there is a third stage of religious experience which belongs to all of them, even though it is rarely found in a pure form: I shall call it cosmic religious feeling. It is very difficult to elucidate this feeling to anyone who is entirely without it, especially as there is no anthropomorphic conception of God corresponding to it.

The individual feels the futility of human desires and aims and the sublimity and marvelous order which reveal themselves both in nature and in the world of thought. Individual existence impresses him as a sort of prison and he wants to experience the universe as a single significant whole. The beginnings of cosmic religious feeling already appear at an early stage of development, e.g., in many of the Psalms of David and in some of the Prophets. Buddhism, as we have learned especially from the wonderful writings of Schopenhauer, contains a much stronger element of this.

The religious geniuses of all ages have been distinguished by this kind of religious feeling, which knows no dogma and no God conceived in man's image; so that there can be no church whose central teachings are based on it. Hence it is precisely among the heretics of every age that we find men who were filled with this highest kind of religious feeling and were in many cases regarded by their contemporaries as atheists, sometimes also as saints. Looked at in this light, men like Democritus, Francis of Assisi, and Spinoza are closely akin to one another.

How can cosmic religious feeling be communicated from one person to another, if it can give rise to no definite notion of a God and no theology? In my view, it is the most important function of art and science to awaken this feeling and keep it alive in those who are receptive to it.

We thus arrive at a conception of the relation of science to religion very different from the usual one. When one views the matter historically, one is inclined to look upon science and religion as irreconcilable antagonists, and for a very obvious reason. The man who is thoroughly convinced of the universal operation of the law of causation cannot for a moment entertain the idea of a being who interferes in the course of events—provided, of course, that he takes the hypothesis of causality really seriously. He has no use for the religion of fear and equally little for social or moral religion. A God who rewards and punishes is inconceivable to him for the simple reason that a man's actions are determined by necessity, external and internal, so that in God's eyes he cannot be responsible, any more than an inanimate object is responsible for the motions it undergoes. Science has therefore been charged with undermining morality, but the charge is unjust. A man's ethical behavior should be based effectually on sympathy, education, and social ties and needs; no religious basis is necessary. Man would indeed be in a poor way if he had to be restrained by fear of punishment and hope of reward after death.

It is therefore easy to see why the churches have always fought science and persecuted its devotees. On the other hand, I maintain that the cosmic religious feeling is the strongest and noblest motive for scientific research. Only those who realize the immense efforts and, above all, the devotion without which pioneer work in theoretical science cannot be achieved are able to grasp the strength of the emotion out of which alone such work, remote as it is from the immediate realities of life, can issue. What a deep conviction of the rationality of the universe and what a yearning to understand, were it but a feeble reflection of the mind revealed in this world, Kepler and Newton must have had to enable them to spend years of solitary labor in disentangling the principles of celestial mechanics! Those whose acquaintance with scientific research is derived chiefly from its practical results easily develop a completely false notion of the mentality of the men who, surrounded by a skeptical world, have shown the way to kindred spirits scattered wide through the world and the centuries. Only one who has devoted his life to similar ends can have a vivid realization of what has inspired these men and given them the strength to remain true to their purpose in spite of countless failures. It is cosmic religious feeling that gives a man such strength. A contemporary has said, not unjustly, that in this materialistic age of ours the serious scientific workers are the only profoundly religious people.

Doubt

FYODOR DOSTOYEVSKY

The Grand Inquisitor

Fyodor Dostoyevsky (1821–
1881) was a Russian novelist
whose other major works
include *The Idiot, The
Possessed,* and *Crime and
Punishment.*

"Even this must have a preface—that is, a literary preface," laughed Ivan, "and I
am a poor hand at making one. You see, my action takes place in the sixteenth
century, and at that time, as you probably learnt at school, it was customary in poetry
to bring down heavenly powers on earth. Not to speak of Dante, in France, clerks,
as well as the monks in the monasteries, used to give regular performances in which
the Madonna, the saints, the angels, Christ, and God Himself were brought on
the stage. In those days it was done in all simplicity. In Victor Hugo's 'Notre Dame
de Paris' an edifying and gratuitous spectacle was provided for the people in the
Hotel de Ville of Paris in the reign of Louis XI in honour of the birth of the
dauphin. It was called *Le bon jugement de la très sainte et gracieuse Vierge Marie,*
and she appears herself on the stage and pronounces her *bon jugement.* Similar
plays, chiefly from the Old Testament, were occasionally performed in Moscow too,
up to the times of Peter the Great. But besides plays there were all sorts of legends
and ballads scattered about the world, in which the saints and angels and all the
powers of Heaven took part when required. In our monasteries the monks busied
themselves in translating, copying, and even composing such poems—and even under
the Tatars. There is, for instance, one such poem (of course, from the Greek),
'The Wanderings of Our Lady through Hell,' with descriptions as bold as Dante's.
Our Lady visits Hell, and the Archangel Michael leads her through the torments.
She sees the sinners and their punishment. There she sees among others one noteworthy set of sinners in a burning lake; some of them sink to the bottom of the
lake so that they can't swim out, and 'these God forgets'—an expression of extraordinary depth and force. And so Our Lady, shocked and weeping, falls before
the throne of God and begs for mercy for all in Hell—for all she has seen there,
indiscriminately. Her conversation with God is immensely interesting. She be-
seeches Him, she will not desist, and when God points to the hands and feet of
her Son, nailed to the Cross, and asks, 'How can I forgive His tormentors?' she
bids all the saints, all the martyrs, all the angels and archangels to fall down with

From *The Brothers Karamazov,* by Fyodor Dostoyevsky, translated by Constance Garnett, Random
House, Inc., 1950. British edition published by William Heinemann, Ltd., and reprinted by permission.

her and pray for mercy on all without distinction. It ends by her winning from God a respite of suffering every year from Good Friday till Trinity day, and the sinners at once raise a cry of thankfulness from Hell, chanting, 'Thou art just, O Lord, in this judgment.' Well, my poem would have been of that kind if it appeared at that time. He comes on the scene in my poem, but He says nothing, only appears and passes on. Fifteen centuries have passed since He promised to come in His glory, fifteen centuries since His prophet wrote, 'Behold, I come quickly'; 'Of that day and that hour knoweth no man, neither the Son, but the Father,' as He Himself predicted on earth. But humanity awaits him with the same faith and with the same love. Oh, with greater faith, for it is fifteen centuries since man has ceased to see signs from Heaven.

> No signs from Heaven come to-day
> To add to what the heart doth say.

There was nothing left but faith in what the heart doth say. It is true there were many miracles in those days. There were saints who performed miraculous cures; some holy people, according to their biographies, were visited by the Queen of Heaven herself. But the devil did not slumber, and doubts were already arising among men of the truth of these miracles. And just then there appeared in the north of Germany a terrible new heresy. 'A huge star like to a torch' (that is, to a church) 'fell on the sources of the waters and they became bitter.' These heretics began blasphemously denying miracles. But those who remained faithful were all the more ardent in their faith. The tears of humanity rose up to Him as before, awaited His coming, loved Him, hoped for Him, yearned to suffer and die for Him as before. And so many ages mankind had prayed with faith and fervour, 'O Lord our God, hasten Thy coming,' so many ages called upon Him, that in His infinite mercy He deigned to come down to His servants. Before that day He had come down, He had visited some holy men, martyrs and hermits, as is written in their 'Lives.' Among us, Tyutchev, with absolute faith in the truth of his words, bore witness that

> Bearing the Cross, in slavish dress,
> Weary and worn, the Heavenly King
> Our mother, Russia, came to bless,
> And through our land went wandering.

And that certainly was so, I assure you.

"And behold, He deigned to appear for a moment to the people, to the tortured, suffering people, sunk in iniquity, but loving Him like children. My story is laid in Spain, in Seville, to the most terrible time of the Inquisition, when fires were lighted every day to the glory of God, and 'in the splendid auto da fé the wicked heretics were burnt.' Oh, of course, this was not the coming in which He will appear according to His promise at the end of time in all His heavenly glory, and which will be sudden 'as lightning flashing from east to west.' No, He visited His children only for a moment, and there where the flames were crackling round the heretics. In His infinite mercy He came once more among men in that human shape in which He walked among men for three years fifteen centuries ago. He came down to the 'hot pavement' of the southern town in which on the day before almost a hundred heretics had, *ad majorem gloriam Dei*, been burnt by the cardinal, the Grand Inquisitor, in a magnificent *auto da fé*, in the presence of the king, the court, the knights, the cardinals, the most charming ladies of the court, and the whole population of Seville.

"He came softly, unobserved, and yet, strange to say, every one recognised Him. That might be one of the best passages in the poem. I mean, why they recognised Him. The people are irresistibly drawn to Him, they surround Him, they flock about Him, follow Him. He moves silently in their midst with a gentle smile of infinite compassion. The sun of love burns in His heart, light and power shine from His eyes, and their radiance, shed on the people, stirs their hearts with responsive love. He holds out His hands to them, blesses them, and a healing virtue comes from contact with Him, even with His garments. An old man in the crowd, blind from childhood, cries out, 'O Lord, heal me and I shall see Thee!' and, as it were, scales fall from his eyes and the blind man sees Him. The crowd weeps and kisses the earth under His feet. Children throw flowers before Him, sing, and cry hosannah. 'It is He—it is He!' all repeat. 'It must be He, it can be no one but Him!' He stops at the steps of the Seville cathedral at the moment when the weeping mourners are bringing in a little open white coffin. In it lies a child of seven, the only daughter of a prominent citizen. The dead child lies hidden in flowers. 'He will raise your child,' the crowd shouts to the weeping mother. The priest, coming to meet the coffin, looks perplexed, and frowns but the mother of the dead child throws herself at His feet with a wail. 'If it is Thou, raise my child!' she cries, holding out her hands to Him. The procession halts, the coffin is laid on the steps at His feet. He looks with compassion, and His lips once more softly pronounce, 'Maiden, arise!' and the maiden arises. The little girl sits up in the coffin and looks round, smiling with wide-open wondering eyes, holding a bunch of white roses they had put in her hand.

"There are cries, sobs, confusion among the people, and at that moment the cardinal himself, the Grand Inquisitor, passes by the cathedral. He is an old man, almost ninety, tall and erect, with a withered face and sunken eyes, in which there is still a gleam of light. He is not dressed in his gorgeous cardinal's robes, as he was the day before, when he was burning the enemies of the Roman Church—at that moment he was wearing his coarse, old, monk's cassock. At a distance behind him come his gloomy assistants and slaves and the 'holy guard.' He stops at the sight of the crowd and watches it from a distance. He sees everything; he sees them set the coffin down at His feet, sees the child rise up, and his face darkens. He knits his thick grey brows and his eyes gleam with a sinister fire. He holds out his finger and bids the guards take Him. And such is his power, so completely are the people cowed into submission and trembling obedience to him, that the crowd immediately make way for the guards, and in the midst of deathlike silence they lay hands on Him and lead Him away. The crowd instantly bows down to the earth, like one man, before the old inquisitor. He blesses the people in silence and passes on. The guards lead their prisoner to the close, gloomy vaulted prison in the ancient palace of the Holy Inquisition and shut Him in it. The day passes and is followed by the dark, burning 'breathless' night of Seville. The air is 'fragrant with laurel and lemon.' In the pitch darkness the iron door of the prison is suddenly opened and the Grand Inquisitor himself comes in with a light in his hand.

He is alone; the door is closed at once behind him. He stands in the doorway and for a minute or two gazes into His face. At last he goes up slowly, sets the light on the table and speaks.

" 'Is it Thou? Thou?' but receiving no answer, he adds at once, 'Don't answer, be silent. What canst Thou say, indeed? I know too well what Thou wouldst say. And Thou hast no right to add anything to what Thou hadst said of old. Why, then, art Thou come to hinder us? For Thou hast come to hinder us, and Thou knowest that. But dost Thou know what will be to-morrow? I know not who Thou art and care not to know whether it is Thou or only a semblance of Him, but to-morrow I shall condemn Thee and burn Thee at the stake as the worst of heretics. And the very people who have to-day kissed Thy feet, to-morrow at the faintest sign from me will rush to heap up the embers of Thy fire. Knowest Thou that? Yes, maybe Thou knowest it,' he added with thoughtful penetration, never for a moment taking his eyes off the Prisoner."

"I don't quite understand, Ivan. What does it mean?" Alyosha, who had been listening in silence, said with a smile. "Is it simply a wild fantasy, or a mistake on the part of the old man—some impossible *quiproquo?*"

"Take it as the last," said Ivan, laughing, "if you are so corrupted by modern realism and can't stand anything fantastic. If you like it to be a case of mistaken identity, let it be so. It is true," he went on, laughing, "the old man was ninety, and he might well be crazy over his set idea. He might have been struck by the appearance of the Prisoner. It might, in fact, be simply his ravings, the delusion of an old man of ninety, over-excited by the *auto da fé* of a hundred heretics the day before. But does it matter to us after all whether it was a mistake of identity or a wild fantasy? All that matters is that the old man should speak out, should speak openly of what he has thought in silence for ninety years."

"And the Prisoner too is silent? Does He look at him and not say a word?"

"That's inevitable in any case," Ivan laughed again. "The old man has told Him He hasn't the right to add anything to what He has said of old. One may say it is the most fundamental feature of Roman Catholicism, in my opinion at least. 'All has been given by Thee to the Pope,' they say, 'and all, therefore, is still in the Pope's hands, and there is no need for Thee to come now at all. Thou must not meddle for the time, at least.' That's how they speak and write too—the Jesuits, at any rate. I have read it myself in the works of their theologians. 'Hast Thou the right to reveal to us one of the mysteries of that world from which Thou hast come?' my old man asks Him, and answers the question for Him. 'No, Thou hast not; that Thou mayest not add to what has been said of old and mayest not take from men the freedom which Thou didst exalt when Thou wast on earth. Whatsoever Thou revealest anew will encroach on men's freedom of faith; for it will be manifest as a miracle, and the freedom of their faith was dearer to Thee than anything in those days fifteen hundred years ago. Didst Thou not often say then, "I will make you free"? But now Thou hast seen these "free" men,' the old man adds suddenly, with a pensive smile. 'Yes, we've paid dearly for it,' he goes on, looking sternly at Him, 'but at last we have completed that work in Thy name. For fifteen centuries we have been wrestling with Thy freedom, but now it is ended and over for good. Dost Thou not believe that it's over for good? Thou lookest meekly at me and deignest not even to be wroth with me. But let me tell Thee that now, to-day, people are more persuaded than ever that they have perfect freedom, yet they have brought their freedom to us and laid it humbly at our feet. But that has been our doing. Was this what Thou didst? Was this Thy freedom?'"

"I don't understand again," Alyosha broke in. "Is he ironical, is he jesting?"

"Not a bit of it! He claims it as a merit for himself and his Church that at last they have vanquished freedom and have done so to make men happy. 'For now' (he is speaking of the Inquisition, of course) 'for the first time it has become possible to think of the happiness of men. Man was created a rebel; and how can rebels be happy? Thou wast warned,' he says to Him. 'Thou hast had no lack of admonitions and warnings, but Thou didst not listen to those warnings; Thou didst reject the only way by which men might be made happy. But, fortunately, departing Thou didst hand on the work to us. Thou hast promised, Thou hast established by Thy word, Thou hast given to us the right to bind and to unbind, and now, of course, Thou canst not think of taking it away. Why, then, hast Thou come to hinder us?'"

"And what's the meaning of 'no lack of admonitions and warnings'?" asked Alyosha.

"Why, that's the chief part of what the old man must say."

"'The wise and dread spirit, the spirit of self-destruction and non-existence,' the old man goes on, 'the great spirit talked with Thee in the wilderness, and we are told in the books that he "tempted" Thee. Is that so? And could anything truer be said than what he revealed to Thee in three questions and what Thou didst reject, and what in the books is called "the temptation"? And yet if there has ever been on earth a real stupendous miracle, it took place on that day, on the day of the three temptations. The statement of those three questions was itself the miracle. If it were possible to imagine simply for the sake of argument that those three questions of the dread spirit had perished utterly from the books, and that we had to restore them and to invent them anew, and to do so had gathered together all the wise men of the earth—rulers, chief priests, learned men, philosophers, poets—and had set them the task to invent three questions, such as would not only fit the occasion, but express in three words, three human phrases, the whole future history of the world and of humanity—dost Thou believe that all the wisdom of the earth united could have invented anything in depth and force equal to the three questions which were actually put to Thee then by the wise and mighty spirit in the wilderness? From those questions alone, from the miracle of their statement, we can see that we have here to do not with the fleeting human intelligence, but with the absolute and eternal. For in those three questions the whole subsequent history of mankind is, as it were, brought together into one whole, and foretold, and in them are united all the unsolved historical contradictions of human nature. At the time it could not be so clear, since the future was unknown; but now that fifteen hundred years have passed, we see that everything in those three questions was so justly divined and foretold, and has been so truly fulfilled, that nothing can be added to them or taken from them.

"'Judge Thyself who was right—Thou or he who questioned Thee then? Remember the first question; its meaning, in other words, was this: "Thou wouldst go into the world, and art going with empty hands, with some promise of freedom which men in their simplicity and their natural unruliness cannot even understand, which they fear and dread—for nothing has ever been more insupportable for a man and a human society than freedom. But seest Thou these stones in this parched and barren wilderness? Turn them into bread and mankind will run after Thee like a flock of sheep, grateful and obedient, though for ever trembling, lest Thou withdraw Thy hand and deny them Thy bread." But Thou wouldst not deprive man of freedom and didst reject the offer, thinking, what is that freedom worth, if obedience is bought with bread? Thou didst reply that man lives not by bread alone. But dost Thou know that for the sake of that earthly bread the spirit of the earth will rise up against Thee and will strive with Thee and overcome Thee, and all will follow him, crying, "Who can compare with this beast? He has given us fire from heaven!" Dost Thou know that the ages will pass, and humanity will proclaim by the lips of their sages that there is no crime, and therefore no sin; there is only hunger? "Feed men, and then ask of them virtue!" that's what they'll write on the banner, which they will raise against Thee, and with which they will destroy Thy temple. Where Thy temple stood will rise a new building; the terrible tower of Babel will be built again, and though, like the one of old, it will not be finished, yet Thou mightest have prevented that new tower and have cut short the sufferings of men for a thousand years; for they will come back to us after a thousand years of agony with their tower. They will seek us again, hidden underground in the catacombs, for we shall be again persecuted and tortured. They will find us and cry to us, "Feed us, for those who have promised us fire from heaven haven't given it!" And then we shall finish building their tower, for he finishes the building who feeds them. And we alone shall feed them in Thy name, declaring falsely that it is in Thy name. Oh, never, never can they feed themselves without us! No science will give them bread so long as they remain free. In the end they will lay their freedom at our feet, and say to us, "Make us your slaves, but feed us." They will understand themselves, at last, that freedom and bread enough for all are inconceivable together, for never, never will they be able to share between them! They will be convinced, too, that they can never be free, for they are weak, vicious, worthless and rebellious. Thou didst promise them the bread of Heaven, but, I repeat again, can it compare with earthly bread in the eyes of the weak, ever sinful and ignoble race of man? And if for the sake of the bread of Heaven thousands and tens of thousands shall follow Thee, what is to become of the millions and tens of thousands of millions of creatures who will not have the strength to forego the earthly bread for the sake of the heavenly? Or dost Thou care only for the tens of thousands of the great and strong, while the millions, numerous as the sands of the sea, who are weak but love Thee, must exist only for the sake of the great and strong? No, we care for the weak too. They are sinful and rebellious, but in the end they too will become obedient. They will marvel at us and look on us as gods, because we are ready to endure the freedom which they have found so dreadful and to rule over them—so awful it will seem to them to be free. But we shall tell them that we are Thy servants and rule in Thy name. We shall deceive them again, for we will not let Thee come to us again. That deception will be our suffering, for we shall be forced to lie.

"'This is the significance of the first question in the wilderness, and this is what Thou hast rejected for the sake of that freedom which Thou has exalted above everything. Yet in this question lies hid the great secret of this world.

Choosing "bread," Thou wouldst have satisfied the universal and everlasting craving of humanity—to find some one to worship. So long as man remains free he strives for nothing so incessantly and so painfully as to find some one to worship. But man seeks to worship what is established beyond dispute, so that all men would agree at once to worship it. For these pitiful creatures are concerned not only to find what one or the other can worship, but to find something that all would believe in and worship; what is essential is that all may be *together* in it. This craving for *community* of worship is the chief misery of every man individually and of all humanity from the beginning of time. For the sake of common worship they've slain each other with the sword. They have set up gods and challenged one another, "Put away your gods and come and worship ours, or we will kill you and your gods!" And so it will be to the end of the world, even when gods disappear from the earth; they will fall down before idols just the same. Thou didst know, Thou couldst not but have known, this fundamental secret of human nature, but Thou didst reject the one infallible banner which was offered Thee to make all men bow down to Thee alone—the banner of earthly bread: and Thou hast rejected it for the sake of freedom and the bread of Heaven. Behold what Thou didst further. And all again in the name of freedom! I tell Thee that man is tormented by no greater anxiety than to find some one quickly to whom he can hand over that gift of freedom with which the ill-fated creature is born. But only one who can appease their conscience can take over their freedom. In bread there was offered Thee an invincible banner; give bread, and man will worship Thee, for nothing is more certain than bread. But if some one else gains possession of his conscience—oh! then he will cast away Thy bread and follow after him who has ensnared his conscience. In that Thou wast right. For the secret of man's being is not only to live but to have something to live for. Without a stable conception of the object of life, man would not consent to go on living, and would rather destroy himself than remain on earth, though he had bread in abundance. That is true. But what happened? Instead of taking men's freedom from them, Thou didst make it greater than ever! Didst Thou forget that man prefers peace, and even death, to freedom of choice in the knowledge of good and evil? Nothing is more seductive for man than his freedom of conscience, but nothing is a greater cause of suffering. And behold, instead of giving a firm foundation for setting the conscience of man at rest for ever, Thou didst choose all that is exceptional, vague and enigmatic; Thou didst choose what was utterly beyond the strength of men, acting as though Thou didst not love them at all—Thou who didst come to give Thy life for them! Instead of taking possession of men's freedom, Thou didst increase it, and burdened the spiritual kingdom of mankind with its sufferings for ever. Thou didst desire man's free love, that he should follow Thee freely, enticed and taken captive by Thee. In place of the rigid ancient law, man must hereafter with free heart decide for himself what is good and what is evil, having only Thy image before him as his guide. But didst Thou not know he would at last reject even Thy image and Thy truth, if he is weighed down with the fearful burden of free choice? They will cry aloud at last that the truth is not in Thee, for they could not have been left in greater confusion and suffering than Thou hast caused, lying upon them so many cares and unanswerable problems.

"'So that, in truth, Thou didst Thyself lay the foundation for the destruction of Thy kingdom, and no one is more to blame for it. Yet what was offered Thee? There are three powers, three powers alone, able to conquer and to hold captive for ever the conscience of these impotent rebels for their happiness—those forces are miracle, mystery and authority. Thou hast rejected all three and hast set the example for doing so. When the wise and dread spirit set Thee on the pinnacle of the temple and said to Thee, "If Thou wouldst know whether Thou art the Son of God then cast Thyself down, for it is written: the angels shall hold him up lest he fall and bruise himself, and Thou shalt know then whether Thou art the Son of God and shalt prove then how great is Thy faith in Thy Father." But Thou didst refuse and wouldst not cast Thyself down. Oh! of course, Thou didst proudly and well, like God; but the weak, unruly race of men, are they gods? Oh, Thou didst know then that in taking one step, in making one movement to cast Thyself down, Thou wouldst be tempting God and have lost all Thy faith in Him, and wouldst have been dashed to pieces against that earth which Thou didst come to save. And the wise spirit that tempted Thee would have rejoiced. But I ask again, are there many like Thee? And couldst Thou believe for one moment that men, too, could face such a temptation? Is the nature of men such, that they can reject miracle, and at the great moments of their life, the moments of their deepest, most agonising spiritual difficulties, cling only to the free verdict of the heart? Oh, Thou didst know that Thy deed would be recorded in books, would be handed down to remote times and the utmost ends of the earth, and Thou didst hope that man, following Thee, would cling to God and not ask for a miracle. But Thou didst not know that when man rejects miracle he rejects God too; for man seeks not so much God as the miraculous. And as man cannot bear to be without the miraculous, he will create new miracles of his own for himself, and will worship deeds of sorcery and witchcraft, though he might be a hundred times over a rebel, heretic and infidel. Thou didst not come down from the Cross when they shouted to Thee, mocking and reviling Thee, "Come down from the cross and we will believe that Thou art He." Thou didst not come down, for again Thou wouldst not enslave man by a miracle, and didst crave faith given freely, not based on miracle. Thou didst crave for free love and not the base raptures of the slave before the might that has overawed him for ever. But Thou didst think too highly of men therein, for they are slaves, of course, though rebellious by nature. Look round and judge; fifteen centuries have passed, look upon them. Whom hast Thou raised up to Thyself? I swear, man is weaker and baser by nature than Thou hast believed him! Can he, can he do what Thou didst? By showing him so much respect, Thou didst, as it were, cease to feel for him, for Thou didst ask far too much from him —Thou who hast loved him more than Thyself! Respecting him less, Thou wouldst have asked less of him. That would have been more like love, for his burden would have been lighter. He is weak and vile. What though he is everywhere now rebelling against our power, and proud of his rebellion? It is the pride of a child and a schoolboy. They are little children rioting and barring out the teacher at school. But their childish delight will end; it will cost them dear. They will cast down temples and drench the earth with blood. But they will see at last, the foolish children, that, though they are rebels, they are impotent rebels, unable to keep up their own rebellion. Bathed in their foolish tears, they will recognise at last that He who created them rebels must have meant to mock at them. They will say this in despair, and their utterance will be a blasphemy which will make them more unhappy still, for man's nature cannot bear blasphemy, and in the end always avenges it on itself. And so unrest, confusion and unhappiness—that is the present lot of man after Thou didst bear so much for their freedom! Thy great prophet tells in vision and in image, that he saw all those who took part in the first resurrection and that there were of each tribe twelve thousand. But if there were so many of them, they must have been not men but gods. They had borne Thy cross, they had endured scores of years in the barren, hungry wilderness, living upon locusts and roots—and Thou mayest indeed point with pride at those children of freedom, of free love, of free and splendid sacrifice for Thy name. But remember that they were only some thousands; and what of the rest? And how are the other weak ones to blame, because they could not endure what the strong have endured? How is the weak soul to blame that it is unable to receive such terrible gifts? Canst Thou have simply come to the elect and for the elect? But if so, it is a mystery and we cannot understand it. And if it is a mystery, we too have a right to preach a mystery, and to teach them that it's not the free judgment of their hearts, not love that matters, but a mystery which they must follow blindly even against their conscience. So we have done. We have corrected Thy work and have founded it upon *miracle, mystery* and *authority*. And men rejoiced that they were again led like sheep, and that the terrible gift that had brought them such suffering, was, at last, lifted from their hearts. Were we right teaching them this? Speak! Did we not love mankind, so meekly acknowledging their feebleness, lovingly lightening their burden, and permitting their weak nature even sin with our sanction? Why hast Thou come now to hinder us? And why dost Thou look silently and searchingly at me with Thy mild eyes? Be angry. I don't want Thy love, for I love Thee not. And what use is it for me to hide anything from Thee? Don't I know to Whom I am speaking? All that I can say is known to Thee already. And is it for me to conceal from Thee our mystery? Perhaps it is Thy will to hear it from my lips. Listen, then. We are not working with Thee, but with *him*—that is our mystery. It's long—eight centuries—since we have been on *his* side and not on Thine. Just eight centuries ago, we took from him what Thou didst reject with scorn, that last gift he offered Thee, showing Thee all the kingdoms of the earth. We took from him Rome and the sword of Cæsar, and proclaimed ourselves sole rulers of the earth, though hitherto we have not been able to complete our work. But whose fault is that? "Oh, the work is only beginning, but it has begun. It has long to await completion and the earth has yet much to suffer, but we shall triumph and shall be Cæsars, and then we shall plan the universal happiness of man. But Thou mightest have taken even then the sword of Cæsar. Why didst Thou reject that last gift? Hadst Thou accepted that last counsel of the mighty spirit, Thou wouldst have accomplished all that man seeks on earth—that is, some one to worship, some one to keep his conscience, and some means of uniting all in one unanimous and harmonious ant-heap, for the craving for universal unity is the third and last anguish of men. Mankind as a whole has always striven to organise a universal state. There have been many great nations with great histories, but the more highly they were developed the more unhappy they were, for they felt more acutely than other people the craving for worldwide union. The great conquerors, Timours and

Ghenghis-Khans, whirled like hurricanes over the face of the earth striving to subdue its people, and they too were but the unconscious expression of the same craving for universal unity. Hadst Thou taken the world and Cæsar's purple, Thou wouldst have founded the universal state and have given universal peace. For who can rule men if not he who holds their conscience and their bread in his hands? We have taken the sword of Cæsar, and in taking it, of course, have rejected Thee and followed *him*. Oh, ages are yet to come of the confusion of free thought, of their science and cannibalism. For having begun to build their tower of Babel without us, they will end, of course, with cannibalism. But then the beast will crawl to us and lick our feet and spatter them with tears of blood. And we shall sit upon the beast and raise the cup, and on it will be written, "Mystery." But then, and only then, the reign of peace and happiness will come for men. Thou art proud of Thine elect, but Thou hast only the elect, while we give rest to all. And besides, how many of those elect, those mighty ones who could become elect, have grown weary waiting for Thee, and have transferred and will transfer the powers of their spirit and the warmth of their heart to the other camp, and end by raising their *free* banner against Thee, Thou didst Thyself lift up that banner. But with us all will be happy and will no more rebel nor destroy one another as under Thy freedom. Oh, we shall persuade them that they will only become free when they renounce their freedom to us and submit to us. And shall we be right or shall we be lying? They will be convinced that we are right, for they will remember the horrors of slavery and confusion to which Thy freedom brought them. Freedom, free thought and science, will lead them into such straits and will bring them face to face with such marvels and insoluble mysteries, that some of them, the fierce and rebellious, will destroy themselves, others, rebellious but weak, will destroy one another, while the rest, weak and unhappy, will crawl fawning to our feet and whine to us: "Yes, you were right, you alone possess His mystery, and we come back to you, save us from ourselves!"

" 'Receiving bread from us, they will see clearly that we take the bread made by their hands from them, to give it to them, without any miracle. They will see that we do not change the stones to bread, but in truth they will be more thankful for taking it from our hands than for the bread itself! For they will remember only too well that in old days, without our help, even the bread they made turned to stones in their hands, while since they have come back to us, the very stones have turned to bread in their hands. Too, too well they know the value of complete submission! And until men know that, they will be unhappy. Who is most to blame for their not knowing it, speak? Who scattered the flock and sent it astray on unknown paths? But the flock will come together again and will submit once more, and then it will be once for all. Then we shall give them the quiet humble happiness of weak creatures such as they are by nature. Oh, we shall persuade them at last not to be proud, for Thou didst lift them up and thereby taught them to be proud. We shall show them that they are weak, that they are only pitiful children, but that childlike happiness is the sweetest of all. They will become timid and will look to us and huddle close to us in fear, as chicks to the hen. They will marvel at us and will be awestricken before us, and will be proud at our being so powerful and clever, that we have been able to subdue such a turbulent flock of thousands of millions. They will tremble impotently before our wrath, their minds will grow fearful, they will be quick to shed tears like women and children, but they will be just as ready at a sign from us to pass to laughter and rejoicing, to happy mirth and childish song. Yes, we shall set them to work, but in their leisure hours we shall make their life like a child's game, with children's songs and innocent dance. Oh, we shall allow them even sin, they are weak and helpless, and they will love us like children because we allow them to sin. We shall tell them that every sin will be expiated, if it is done with our permission, that we allow them to sin because we love them, and the punishment for these sins we take upon ourselves. And we shall take it upon ourselves, and they will adore us as their saviours who have taken on themselves their sins before God. And they will have no secrets from us. We shall allow or forbid them to live with their wives and mistresses, to have or not to have children—according to whether they have been obedient or disobedient —and they will submit to us gladly and cheerfully. The most painful secrets of their conscience, all, all they will bring to us, and we shall have an answer for all. And they will be glad to believe our answer, for it will save them from the great anxiety and terrible agony they endure at present in making a free decision for themselves. And all will be happy, all the millions of creatures except the hundred thousand who rule over them. For only we, we who guard the mystery, shall be unhappy. There will be thousands of millions of happy babes, and a hundred thousand sufferers who have taken upon themselves the curse of the knowledge of good and evil. Peacefully they will die, peacefully they will expire in Thy name, and beyond the grave they will find nothing but death. But we shall keep the secret, and for their happiness we shall allure them with the reward of heaven and eternity. Though if there were anything in the other world, it certainly would not be for such as they. It is prophesied that Thou wilt come again in victory. Thou wilt come with Thy chosen, the proud and strong, but we will say that they have only saved themselves, but we have saved all. We are told that the harlot who sits upon the beast, and holds in her hands the *mystery,* shall be put to shame, that the weak will rise up again, and will rend her royal purple and will strip naked her loathsome body. But then I will stand up and point out to Thee the thousand millions of happy children who have known no sin. And we who have taken their sins upon us for their happiness will stand up before Thee and say: "Judge us if Thou canst and darest." Know that I fear Thee not. Know that I too have been in the wilderness, I too have lived on roots and locusts, I too prized the freedom with which Thou hast blessed men, and I too was striving to stand among Thy elect, among the strong and powerful, thirsting "to make up the number." But I awakened and would not serve madness. I turned back and joined the ranks of those *who have corrected Thy work.* I left the proud and went back to the humble, for the happiness of the humble. What I say to Thee will come to pass, and our dominion will be built up. I repeat, to-morrow Thou shalt see that obedient flock who at a sign from me will hasten to heap up the hot cinders about the pile on which I shall burn Thee for coming to hinder us. For if any one has ever deserved our fires, it is Thou. To-morrow I shall burn Thee. Dixi.'"

Ivan stopped. He was carried away as he talked and spoke with excitement; when he had finished, he suddenly smiled.

Alyosha had listened in silence; towards the end he was greatly moved and seemed several times on the point of interrupting, but restrained himself. Now his words came with a rush.

"But . . . that's absurd!" he cried, flushing. "Your poem is in praise of Jesus, not in blame of Him—as you meant it to be. And who will believe you about freedom? Is that the way to understand it? That's not the idea of it in the Orthodox Church. . . . That's Rome, and not even the whole of Rome, it's false— those are the worst of the Catholics, the Inquisitors, the Jesuits! . . . And there could not be such a fantastic creature as your Inquisitor. What are these sins of mankind they take on themselves? Who are these keepers of the mystery who have taken some curse upon themselves for the happiness of mankind? When have they been seen? We know the Jesuits, they are spoken ill of, but surely they are not what you describe? They are not that at all, not at all. . . . They are simply the Romish army for the earthly sovereignty of the world in the future, with the Pontiff of Rome for Emperor . . . that's their ideal, but there's no sort of mystery or lofty melancholy about it. . . . It's simple lust of power, of filthy earthly gain, of domination—something like a universal serfdom with them as masters—that's all they stand for. They don't even believe in God perhaps. Your suffering in- quisitor is a mere fantasy."

"Stay, stay," laughed Ivan, "how hot you are! A fantasy you say, let it be so! Of course it's a fantasy. But allow me to say: do you really think that the Roman Catholic movement of the last centuries is actually nothing but the lust of power, of filthy earthly gain? Is that Father Païssy's teaching?"

"No, no, on the contrary, Father Païssy did once say some thing rather the same as you . . . but of course it's not the same, not a bit the same," Alyosha hastily corrected himself.

"A precious admission, in spite of your 'not a bit the same.' I ask you why your Jesuits and Inquisitors have united simply for vile material gain? Why can there not be among them one martyr oppressed by great sorrow and loving humanity? You see, only suppose that there was one such man among all those who desire nothing but filthy material gain—if there's only one like my old inquisitor, who had himself eaten roots in the desert and made frenzied efforts to subdue his flesh to make himself free and perfect. But yet all his life he loved humanity, and suddenly his eyes were opened, and he saw that it is no great moral blessedness to attain perfection and freedom, if at the same time one gains the conviction that millions of God's creatures have been created as a mockery, that they will never be capable of using their freedom, that these poor rebels can never turn into giants to complete the tower, that it was not for such geese that the great idealist dreamt his dream of harmony. Seeing all that he turned back and joined—the clever people. Surely that could have happened?"

"Joined whom, what clever people?" cried Alyosha, completely carried away. "They have no such great cleverness and no mysteries and secrets. . . . Perhaps noth- ing but Atheism, that's all their secret. Your inquisitor does not believe in God, that's his secret!"

"What if it is so! At last you have guessed it. It's perfectly true that that's the whole secret, but isn't that suffering, at least for a man like that, who has wasted his whole life in the desert and yet could not shake off his incurable love of humanity? In his old age he reached the clear conviction that nothing but the advice of the great dread spirit could build up any tolerable sort of life for feeble, unruly, incomplete, empirical creatures created in jest.' And so, convinced of this, he sees that he must follow the counsel of the wise spirit, the dread spirit of death and destruction, and therefore accept lying and deception, and lead men consciously to death and destruction, and yet deceive them all the way so that they may not notice where they are being led, that the poor blind creatures may at least on the way think themselves happy. And note, the deception is in the name of Him in Whose ideal the old man had so fervently believed all his life long. Is not that tragic? And if only one such stood at the head of the whole army 'filled with the lust of power only for the sake of filthy gain'—would not one such be enough to make a tragedy? More than that, one such standing at the head is enough to create the actual leading idea of the Roman Church with all its armies and Jesuits, its highest idea. I tell you frankly that I firmly believe that there has always been such a man among those who stood at the head of the movement. Who knows, there may have been some such even among the Roman Popes. Who knows, perhaps the spirit of that accursed old man who loves mankind so obstinately in his own way, is to be found even now in a whole multitude of such old men, existing not by chance but by agreement, as a secret league formed long ago for the guarding of the mystery, to guard it from the weak and the unhappy, so as to make them happy. No doubt it is so, and so it must be indeed. I fancy that even among the Masons there's something of the same mystery at the bottom, and that that's why the Catholics so detest the Masons as their rivals breaking up the unity of the idea, while it is so essential that there should be one flock and one shepherd. . . . But from the way I defend my idea I might be an author impatient of your criticism. Enough of it."

"You are perhaps a Mason yourself!" broke suddenly from Alyosha. "You don't believe in God," he added, speaking this time very sorrowfully. He fancied besides that his brother was looking at him ironically. "How does your poem end?" he asked, suddenly looking down. "Or was it the end?"

"I meant to end it like this. When the Inquisitor ceased speaking he waited some time for his Prisoner to answer him. His silence weighed down upon him. His silence weighed down upon him. He saw that the Prisoner had listened intently all the time, looking gently in his face and evidently not wishing to reply. The old man longed for Him to say something, however bitter and terrible. But He suddenly approached the old man in silence and softly kissed him on his bloodless aged lips. That was all his answer. The old man shuddered. His lips moved. He went to the door, opened it, and said to Him: 'Go, and come no more. . . . come not at all, never, never!' And he let Him out into the dark alleys of the town. The Prisoner went away."

JOHN HICK

Evil and the God of Love

John Hick, who teaches at
Princeton Theological Seminary, is
the author and editor of several
books and articles on the
philosophy of religion.

THE NEGATIVE TASK OF THEODICY

At the outset of an attempt to present a Christian theodicy—a defence of the goodness of God in face of the evil in His world—we should recognize that, whether
or not we can succeed in formulating its basis, an implicit theodicy is at work
in the Bible, at least in the sense of an effective reconciliation of profound faith in
God with a deep involvement in the realities of sin and suffering. The Scriptures
reflect the characteristic mixture of good and evil in human experience. They record
every kind of sorrow and suffering from the terrors of childhood to the 'stony griefs
of age: cruelty, torture, violence, and agony; poverty, hunger, calamitous accident;
disease, insanity, folly; every mode of man's inhumanity to man and of his painfully
insecure existence in the world. In these writings there is no attempt to evade
the clear verdict of human experience that evil is dark, meanacingly ugly, heart-
rending, crushing. And the climax of this biblical history of evil was the execution
of Jesus of Nazareth. Here were pain and violent destruction, gross injustice, the
apparent defeat of the righteous, and the premature death of a still-young man.
But further, for Christian faith, this death was the slaying of God's Messiah, the one
in whom mankind was to see the mind and heart of God made flesh. Here, then, the
problem of evil rises to its ultimate maximum; for in its quality this was an evil than
which no greater can be conceived. And yet throughout the biblical history of evil,
including even this darkest point, God's purpose of good was moving visibly or
invisibly towards its far-distant fulfilment. In this faith the prophets saw both
personal and national tragedy as God's austere but gracious disciplining of His
people. And even the greatest evil of all, the murder of the son of God, has been
found by subsequent Christian faith to be also, in an astounding paradox, the
greatest good of all, so that through the centuries the Church could dare to sing

From *Evil and the God of Love,* by John Hick, Harper & Row, The Macmillan Co. of Canada Ltd.,
and Macmillan & Co., Ltd., 1966. Copyright 1966 by John Hick. Reprinted by permission of the publishers.
    [1] 'O certe necessarium Adae peccatum, quod Christi morte deletum est! O felix culpa, quae talem
ac tantum meruit habere redemptorem!' (O truly necessary sin of Adam, which is cancelled by Christ's
death! O fortunate crime (*or,* O happy fault), which merited [to have] such and so great a redeemer!)

on the eve of its triumphant Easter celebrations, 'O felix culpa, quae talem ac tantum meruit habere redemptorem'.[1] For this reason there is no room within the Christian thought-world for the idea of tragedy in any sense that includes the idea of finally *wasted* suffering and goodness.[2]

In all this a Christian theodicy is latent; and our aim must be to try to draw it out explicitly. The task, like that of theology in general, is one of 'faith seeking understanding', seeking in this case an understanding of the grounds of its own practical victory in the face of the harsh facts of evil. Accordingly, from the point of view of apologetics, theodicy has a negative rather than a positive function. It cannot profess to create faith, but only to preserve an already existing faith from being overcome by this dark mystery. For we cannot share the hope of the older schools of natural theology of inferring the existence of God from the evidences of nature; the one main reason for this, as David Hume made clear in his *Dialogues*, is precisely the fact of evil in its many forms. For us today the live question is whether this renders impossible a rational belief in God: meaning by this, not a belief in God that has been arrived at by rational argument (for it is doubtful whether a religious faith is ever attained in this way), but one that has arisen in a rational individual in response to some compelling element in his experience, and decisively illuminates and is illuminated by his experience as a whole. The aim of a Christian theodicy must thus be the relatively modest and defensive one of showing that the mystery of evil, largely incomprehensible though it remains, does not render irrational a faith that has arisen, not from the inferences of natural theology, but from participation in a stream of religious experience which is continuous with that recorded in the Bible.

THE TRADITIONAL THEODICY BASED UPON CHRISTIAN MYTH

We can distinguish, though we cannot always separate, three relevant facets of the Christian religion: Christian experience, Christian mythology, and Christian theology.

Religious experience is 'the whole experience of religious persons',[3] constituting an awareness of God acting towards them in and through the events of their lives and of world history, the interpretative element within which awareness is the cognitive aspect of faith. And distinctively *Christian experience,* as a form of this, is the Christian's seeing of Christ as his 'Lord and Savior', together with the pervasive recreative effects of this throughout his life, transforming the quality of his experience and determining his responses to other people. Christian faith is thus a distinctive consciousness of the world and of one's existence with it, radiating from and

---

These famous phrases occur in the Roman Missal in the *Exultet* for the evening before Easter Day. The date and authorship of this *Exultet* are uncertain. It has been attributed, but without adequate evidence, to St. Augustine, to St. Ambrose, and to Gregory the Great. As part of the Easter liturgy it goes back at least to the seventh century and possibly to the beginnings of the fifth century. On its history see Arthur O. Lovejoy, *Essays in the History of Ideas,* 1948 (New York: Capricorn Books, 1960), pp. 286–7.

[2] Cf. D. D. Raphael, *The Paradox of Tragedy* (London: George Allen & Unwin Ltd., 1960), pp. 43 f.

[3] William Temple, *Nature, Man and God* (London: Macmillan & Co. Ltd., 1934), p. 334.

illuminated by a consciousness of God in Christ. It is because there are often a successful facing and overcoming of the challenge of evil at this level that there can, in principle at least, be an honest and serious—even though tentative and incomplete—Christian theodicy.

By *Christian mythology* I mean the great persisting imaginative pictures by means of which the corporate mind of the Church has expressed to itself the significance of the historical events upon which its faith is based, above all the life, death, and resurrection of Jesus who was the Christ. The function of these myths is to convey in universally understandable ways the special importance and meaning of certain items of mundane experience.

By *Christian theology* I mean the attempts by Christian thinkers to speak systematically about God on the basis of the data provided by Christian experience. Thus it is a fact of the Christian faith-experience that 'God was in Christ';[4] and the various Christological theories are attempts to understand this by seeing it in the context of other facts both of faith and of nature. Again, it is another facet of this basic fact of faith that in Christ God was 'reconciling the world unto Himself';[5] and the various atonement theories are accordingly attempts to understand this further aspect of the experience. The other departments of Christian doctrine stand in a similar relationship to the primary data of Christian experience.

In the past, theology and myth have been closely twined together. For the less men knew about the character of the physical universe the harder it was for them to identify myth as myth, as distinct from history or science. This fact has profoundly affected the development of the dominant tradition of Christian theodicy. Until comparatively recent times the ancient myth of the origin of evil in the fall of man was quite reasonably assumed to be history. The theologian accordingly accepted it as providing 'hard' data, and proceeded to build his theodicy upon it. This mythological theodicy was first comprehensively developed by Augustine, and has continued substantially unchanged within the Roman Catholic Church to the present day. It was likewise adopted by the Reformers of the sixteenth century and has been virtually unquestioned as Protestant doctrine until within approximately the last hundred years. Only during this latest period has it been possible to identify as such its mythological basis, to apply a theological criticism to it, and then to go back to the data of Christian experience and build afresh, seeking a theodicy that can hope to make sense to Christians in our own and succeeding centuries.

But first, in order to see how the hitherto dominant theodicy has arisen, and why it is now utterly unacceptable, we must trace the outline of the mythology that underlies it. The story of the fall of man is part of a more comprehensive cosmic story. In this great amalgam of Jewish and Christian themes, God created spiritual beings, the angels and archangels, to be His subjects and to love and serve Him in the heavenly spheres. But a minority of them revolted against God in envy of His supremacy, and were defeated and cast into an abode suited to their now irreconcilably evil natures. Either to replenish the citizenry of heaven thus depleted by the expulsion of Satan and his followers, or as an independent venture of creation, God

---

[4] II Corinthians v. 19.
[5] Ibid.

made our world, and mankind within it consisting initially of a single human pair. This first man and woman, living in the direct knowledge of God, were good, happy, and immortal, and would in due course have populated the earth with descendants like themselves. But Satan, in wicked spite, successfully tempted them to disobey their Creator, who then expelled them from this paradisal existence into a new situation of hardship, danger, disease, and inevitable death. This was the fall of man, and as a result of it the succeeding members of the human race have been born as fallen creatures in a fallen world, participating in the effects of their first parents' rebellion against their Maker. But God in Christ has made the atonement for man's sin that His own eternal justice required and has offered free forgiveness to as many as will commit themselves to Christ as their Savior. At the last judgement, when faith and life alike will be tested, many will enter into eternal life whilst others, preferring their own darkness to God's light, will linger in a perpetual living death.

This great cosmic drama is the official Christian myth. With only minor variations it has constituted the accepted framework of thought of the great majority of Christians in the past, and still fulfills this role for the great majority today. By means of it Christian faith, which began as a crucial response of trust towards one in whom the disciples had experienced God directly at work on earth, broadened out into a comprehensive vision of the universe. The great creation-fall-redemption myth has thus brought within the scope of the simplest human soul a pictorial grasp of the universal significance of the life and death of Jesus. Jesus himself was not a mythological figure; he lived in Palestine and his life and death and resurrection made their impact upon living people, and through them upon others in a long succession of faith down to ourselves today. But the cosmic picture, sketched by St. Paul and completed by St. Augustine, of the beginning of our present human situation in the fall of humanity from a condition of paradisal perfection into one of sin and pain and death, and of its end in the separation of mankind into those destined for the eternal bliss or torment of heaven or hell, is a product of the religious imagination. It expresses the significance of the present reality of sin and sorrow by seeing them as flowing from a first dramatic act of rebellion; and the significance of the experience of reconciliation with God by means of the picture of a juridical arrangement taking place within the councils of the Trinity and being transacted in time on the cross of Christ; and the significance of man's inalienable personal responsibility by the picture of a divine administration directing souls to their appropriate final destinations.

This great cosmic drama in three acts has constituted a valid myth in the sense that it has successfully fulfilled the conserving and communicating function of a myth in the minds of countless people. By means of natural images it has vividly brought home to the simplest understandings the claim that Christ stands at the centre of the universe and is of crucial importance for all men. And when religious myths thus work effectively it is as absurd to criticize them for being myths rather than science or history as it would be for us today to insist that they *are* science or history and to proceed to draw scientific or historical conclusions from them.

Because we can no longer share the assumption, upon which traditional Christian theodicy has been built, that the creation–fall myth is basically authentic history,[6] we inevitably look at that theodicy critically and see in it inadequacies to which in the past piety has tended to blind the eyes of faith.

For, in general, religious myths are not adapted to the solving of problems. Their function is to illumine by means of unforgettable imagery the religious significance of some present or remembered fact of experience. But the experience which myth thus emphasizes and illumines is itself the locus of mystery. Hence it is not surprising that Christian mythology mirrors Christian experience in presenting but not resolving the profound mystery of evil. Nor is it surprising that when this pictorial presentation of the problem has mistakenly been treated as a solution to it, the 'solution' has suffered from profound incoherences and contradictions.

This traditional solution (representing the theological, in distinction from the philosophical, side of Augustine's thought on the theodicy problem) finds the origin of evil, as we have seen, in the fall, which was the beginning both of sin and, as its punishment, of man's sorrows and sufferings. But this theory, so simple and mythologically satisfying, is open to insuperable scientific, moral, and logical objections. To begin with less fundamental aspects of the traditional solution, we know today that the conditions that were to cause human disease and mortality and the necessity for man to undertake the perils of hunting and the labours of agriculture and building, were already part of the natural order prior to the emergence of man and prior therefore to any first human sin, as were also the conditions causing such further 'evils' as earthquake, storm, flood, drought, and pest. And, second, the policy of punishing the whole succeeding human race for the sin of the first pair is, by the best human moral standards, unjust and does not provide anything that can be recognized by these standards as a theodicy. Third, there is a basic and fatal incoherence at the heart of the mythically based 'solution'. The Creator is preserved from any responsibility for the existence of evil by the claim that He made men (or angels) as free and finitely perfect creatures, happy in the knowledge of Himself, and subject to no strains or temptations, but that they themselves inexplicably and inexcusably rebelled against Him. But this suggestion amounts to a sheer self-contradiction. It is impossible to conceive of wholly good beings in a wholly good world becoming sinful. To say that they do is to postulate the self-creation of evil *ex nihilo*! There must have been some moral flaw in the creature or in his situation to set up the tension of temptation; for creaturely freedom in itself and in the absence of any temptation cannot lead to sin. Thus the very fact that the creature sins refutes the suggestion that until that moment he was a finitely perfect being living in an ideal creaturely relationship to God. And indeed (as we have already seen) the two greatest upholders of this solution implicitly admit the contradiction. Augustine, who treats of evil at its first occurrence in the fall of Satan and his followers, has to explain the eruption of sin in supposedly perfect angels by holding that God had in effect predestined their revolt by withholding from them the assurance of eternal bliss with which, in contrast, He had furnished the angels who remained steadfast.[7] And Calvin, who treats the subject primarily at the point of the fall of man, holds that 'all are not created in equal condition; rather, eternal

---

[6] One of the most eloquent recent presentations of the traditional conception of a temporal fall of man is that of C. S. Lewis in *The Problem of Pain* (London: The Centenary Press, 1940), pp. 65 f.

[7] *C.G.*, bk. xi, chaps. 11 and 13; bk. xii, chap. 9. . . .

life is foreordained for some, eternal damnation for others'.[8] Thus the myth, when mistakenly pressed to serve as a theodicy, can be saved only by adding to it the new and questionable doctrine of an absolute divine predestination. And this in turn only leads the theodicy to contradict itself. For its original intention was to blame evil upon the misuse of creaturely free will. But now this misuse is itself said to fall under the divine predestinating decrees. Thus the theodicy collapses into radical incoherence, and its more persistent defenders have become involved in ever more desperate and implausible epicycles of theory to save it. For example, to salvage the view of the fall of man as a temporal event that took place on this earth some definite (if unknown) number of years ago, it has been suggested that after emerging from his subhuman precursors man lived in the paradisal state for only a very brief period, lasting perhaps no more than a matter of hours. Again, attempts have been made to protect the fall doctrine from the encroachments of scientific research by locating the primal calamity in a pre-mundane sphere. In the third century Origen had taught that some of the spirits whom God created rebelled against the divine majesty and were cast down into the material world to constitute our human race;[9] and in the nineteenth century the German Protestant theologian Julius Müller, impressed by the overwhelming difficulties of affirming an historical fall, in effect revived Origen's theory as an explanation of the apparently universal evil propensities of man. All men are sinful, he suggested, because in another existence prior to the present life they have individually turned away from God.[10]

The difficulties and disadvantages of such a view are, I think, not far to seek. The theory is without grounds in Scripture or in science, and it would have claim to consideration only if it could provide a solution, even if a speculative one, to the question of the origin of moral evil. But in fact it is not able to do this. It merely pushes back into an unknown and unknowable realm the wanton paradox of finitely perfect creatures, dwelling happily and untempted in the presence of God, turning to sin. Whether on earth or in heaven, this still amounts to the impossible self-creation of evil *ex nihilo*. If evil could thus create itself out of nothing in the midst of a wholly good universe, it could do so in a mundane Garden of Eden as easily as, or perhaps more easily than, in the highest heaven. Nothing, then, is gained for theodicy by postulating a pre-mundane fall of human souls.

As a variation which he regarded as superior to the notion of a pre-mundane fall of individuals, N. P. Williams proposed the idea of 'a collective fall of the race-soul of humanity at an indefinitely remote past.'[11] This collective fall occurred, according to Williams, during the long period between the first emergence of man as a biological species and his subsequent development to the point at which there were primitive societies, and therefore moral laws which could be transgressed. 'We must', he says, 'postulate some unknown factor or agency which interfered to arrest the development of corporate feeling, just when man was becoming man, some mysterious and maleficent influence which cut into the stream of the genetic evolution of our race at some point during the twilit age which separates pre-

---

8 *Inst.*, bk. III, chap. xxi, para. 5. . . .

9 *De Principiis*, bk. II, chap. i, para. I. Cf. ibid., chap. ix, para. 6.

10 *The Christian Doctrine of Sin*, bk. IV, chap. 4. Cf. bk. III, pt. i, chap. 3, sect. I, and chap. 4, sect. 3

11 N. P. Williams, *The Ideas of the Fall and of Original Sin*, p. 513.

human from human history.'[12] This evil influence which attacked and corrupted mankind is also 'the mysterious power which vitiates the whole of sub-human life with cruelty and selfishness',[13] and thus accounts not only for moral evil but also for the disorder, waste, and pain in nature.[14] Accordingly the original calamity was not merely a fall of man but of the Life-Force itself, which we must conceive 'as having been at the beginning, when it first sprang forth from the creative fecundity of the Divine Being, free, personal, and selfconscious'.[15] This World-Soul was created good, but 'at the beginning of Time, and in some transcendental and incomprehensible manner, it turned away from God and in the direction of Self, thus shattering its own interior being, which depended upon God for its stability and coherence, and thereby forfeiting its unitary self-consciousness, which it has only regained, after aeons of myopic striving, in sporadic fragments which are the separate minds of men and perhaps of superhuman spirits.'[16]

Williams is, I think, justified in claiming that such a speculation cannot be excluded *ab initio* as impermissible to a responsible Christian theologian. As he points out,

> Such a substitution of the idea of a corruption of the whole cosmic energy at at some enormously remote date for the idea of a voluntary moral suicide of Man in comparatively recent times would be no greater a revolution than that which was effected by St. Anselm, when he substituted a satisfactional theory of the Atonement for the view which regarded the death of Christ as a ransom paid to the Devil—a view which had behind it the venerable authority of a thousand years of Christian history.[17]

Williams' suggestion preserves the central thought of the Augustinian fall doctrine that the ultimate source of evil lies in an original conscious turning away from God on the part of created personal life. But precisely because of its faithfulness to that tradition his theory fails to throw any new light upon the problem of evil. Whether the self-creation of evil *ex nihilo* be located in an historical Adam and Eve, or in a multitude of souls in a pre-mundane realm, or in a single world-soul at the beginning of time, it is equally valueless from the point of view of theodicy. In order for a soul or souls to fall there must be, either in them or in their environment, some flaw which produces temptation and leads to sin; and this flaw in the creation cannot be traced back to any other ultimate source than the Creator of all that is. Thus Williams' theory is open to the same objection as Müller's: namely, that it is a speculation whose only point would be to solve or lighten the problem of evil, but that it fails to do this.[18]

[12] N. P. Williams, *The Ideas of the Fall and of Original Sin,* pp. 518–19.

[13] Ibid., p. 520.

[14] The application of the notion of a pre-mundane fall to evil in nature will be discussed below, pp. 367 f.

[15] Williams, op. cit., p. 525.

[16] Ibid., p. 526.

[17] Ibid., p. 524.

[18] A pre-mundane fall has been propounded by Canon Peter Green in *The Problem of Evil* (London: Longmans, Green & Co., 1920), chap. 7, and in *The Pre-Mundane Fall* (London: A. R. Mowbray & Co., 1944); and by C. W. Formby in *The Unveiling of the Fall* (London: Williams & Norgate, 1923).

THE 'VALE OF SOUL-MAKING' THEODICY

Fortunately there is another and better way. As well as the 'majority report' of the Augustinian tradition, which has dominated Western Christendom, both Catholic and Protestant, since the time of Augustine himself, there is the 'minority report' of the Irenaean tradition. This latter is both older and newer than the other, for it goes back to St. Irenaeus and others of the early Hellenistic Fathers of the Church in the two centuries prior to St. Augustine, and it has flourished again in more developed forms during the last hundred years.

Instead of regarding man as having been created by God in a finished state, as a finitely perfect being fulfilling the divine intention for our human level of existence, and then falling disastrously away from this, the minority report sees man as still in process of creation. Irenaeus himself expressed the point in terms of the (exegetically dubious) distinction between the 'image' and the 'likeness' of God referred to in Genesis i. 26: 'Then God said, Let us make man in our image, after our likeness.'[19] His view was that man as a personal and moral being already exists in the image, but has not yet been formed into the finite likeness of God. By this 'likeness' Irenaeus means something more than personal existence as such; he means a certain valuable quality of personal life which reflects finitely the divine life. This represents the perfecting of man, the fulfilment of God's purpose for humanity, the 'bringing of many sons to glory',[20] the creating of 'children of God' who are 'fellow heirs with Christ' of his glory.[21]

And so man, created as a personal being in the image of God, is only the raw material for a further and more difficult stage of God's creative work. This is the leading of men as relatively free and autonomous persons, through their own dealings with life in the world in which He has placed them, towards that quality of personal existence that is the finite likeness of God. The features of this likeness are revealed in the person of Christ, and the process of man's creation into it is the work of the Holy Spirit. In St. Paul's words, 'And we all, with unveiled faces, beholding the glory of the Lord, are being changed into his likeness (εἰκών) from one degree of glory to another; for this comes from the Lord who is the Spirit';[22] or again, 'For God knew his own before ever they were, and also ordained that they should be shaped to the likeness (εἰκών) of his Son.'[23] In Johannine terms, the movement from the image to the likeness is a transition from one level of existence, that of animal life (*Bios*), to another and higher level, that of eternal life (*Zoe*), which includes but transcends the first. And the fall of man was seen by Irenaeus as a failure within the second phase of this creative process, a failure that has multiplied the perils and complicated the route of the journey in which God is seeking to lead mankind.

In the light of modern anthropological knowledge some form of two-stage con-

---

[19] *A.H.* v. vi. 1. Cf. pp. 217 f. above.
[20] Hebrews ii. 10
[21] Romans viii. 17.
[22] II Corinthians iii. 18.
[23] Romans viii. 29. Other New Testament passages expressing a view of man as undergoing a process of spiritual growth within God's purpose, are: Ephesians ii. 21; iii. 16; Colossians ii. 19; I John iii. 2; II Corinthians iv. 16.

ception of the creation of man has become an almost unavoidable Christian tenet. At the very least we must acknowledge as two distinguishable stages the fashioning of *homo sapiens* as a product of the long evolutionary process, and his sudden or gradual spiritualization as a child of God. But we may well extend the first stage to include the development of man as a rational and responsible person capable of personal relationship with the personal Infinite who has created him. This first stage of the creative process was, to our anthropomorphic imaginations, easy for divine omnipotence. By an exercise of creative power God caused the physical universe to exist, and in the course of countless ages to bring forth within it organic life, and finally to produce out of organic life personal life; and when man had thus emerged out of the evolution of the forms of organic life, a creature had been made who has the possibility of existing in conscious fellowship with God. But the second stage of the creative process is of a different kind altogether. It cannot be performed by omnipotent power as such. For personal life is essentially free and self-directing. It cannot be perfected by divine fiat, but only through the uncompelled responses and willing co-operation of human individuals in their actions and reactions in the world in which God has placed them. Men may eventually become the perfected persons whom the New Testament calls 'children of God', but they cannot be created ready-made as this.

The value-judgment that is implicitly being invoked here is that one who has attained to goodness by meeting and eventually mastering temptations, and thus by rightly making responsible choices in concrete situations, is good in a richer and more valuable sense than would be one created *ab initio* in a state either of innocence or of virtue. In the former case, which is that of the actual moral achievements of mankind, the individual's goodness has within it the strength of temptations overcome, a stability based upon an accumulation of right choices, and a positive and responsible character that comes from the investment of costly personal effort. I suggest, then, that it is an ethically reasonable judgment, even though in the nature of the case not one that is capable of demonstrative proof, that human goodness slowly built up through personal histories of moral effort has a value in the eyes of the Creator which justifies even the long travail of the soul-making process.

The picture with which we are working is thus developmental and teleological. Man is in process of becoming the perfected being whom God is seeking to create. However, this is not taking place—it is important to add—by a natural and inevitable evolution, but through a hazardous adventure in individual freedom. Because this is a pilgrimage within the life of each individual, rather than a racial evolution, the progressive fulfilment of God's purpose does not entail any corresponding progressive improvement in the moral state of the world. There is no doubt a development in man's ethical situation from generation to generation through the building of individual choices into public institutions, but this involves an accumulation of evil as well as of good.[24] It is thus probable that human life was lived on much the same moral plane two thousand years ago or four thousand

---

[24] This fact is symbolized in early Christian literature both by the figure of the Antichrist, who continually opposes God's purposes in history, and by the expectation of cataclysmic calamity and strife in the last days before the end of the present world order.

years ago as it is today. But nevertheless during this period uncounted millions of souls have been through the experience of earthly life, and God's purpose has gradually moved towards its fulfilment within each one of them, rather than within a human aggregate composed of different units in different generations.

If, then, God's aim in making the world is 'the bringing of many sons to glory',[25] that aim will naturally determine the kind of world that He has created. Antitheistic writers almost invariably assume a conception of the divine purpose which is contrary to the Christian conception. They assume that the purpose of a loving God must be to create a hedonistic paradise; and therefore to the extent that the world is other than this, it proves to them that God is either not loving enough or not powerful enough to create such a world. They think of God's relation to the earth on the model of a human being building a cage for a pet animal to dwell in. If he is humane he will naturally make his pet's quarters as pleasant and healthful as he can. Any respect in which the cage falls short of the veterinarian's ideal, and contains possibilities of accident or disease, is evidence of either limited benevolence or limited means, or both. Those who use the problem of evil as an argument against belief in God almost invariably think of the world in this kind of way. David Hume, for example, speaks of an architect who is trying to plan a house that is to be as comfortable and convenient as possible. If we find that 'the windows, doors, fires, passages, stairs, and the whole economy of the building were the source of noise, confusion, fatigue, darkness, and the extremes of heat and cold' we should have no hesitation in blaming the architect. It would be in vain for him to prove that if this or that defect were corrected greater ills would result: 'still you would assert in general, that, if the architect had had skill and good intentions, he might have formed such a plan of the whole, and might have adjusted the parts in such a manner, as would have remedied all or most of these inconveniences'.[26]

But if we are right in supposing that God's purpose for man is to lead him from human *Bios*, or the biological life of man, to that quality of *Zoe*, or the personal life of eternal worth, which we see in Christ, then the question that we have to ask is not, Is this the kind of world that an all-powerful and infinitely loving being would create as an environment for his human pets? or, Is the architecture of the world the most pleasant and convenient possible? The question that we have to ask is rather, Is this the kind of world that God might make as an environment in which moral beings may be fashioned, through their own free insights and responses, into 'children of God'?

Such critics as Hume are confusing what heaven ought to be, as an environment for perfected finite beings, with what this world ought to be, as an environment for beings who are in process of becoming perfected. For if our general conception of God's purpose is correct the world is not intended to be a paradise, but rather the scene of a history in which human personality may be formed towards the pattern of Christ. Men are not to be thought of on the analogy of animal pets, whose life is to be made as agreeable as possible, but rather on the analogy of human children, who are to grow to adulthood in an environment whose primary and overriding purpose

25 Hebrews ii. 10.
26 *Dialogues Concerning Natural Religion*, pt. xi. Kemp-Smith's ed. (Oxford: Clarendon Press, 1935), p. 251.

is not immediate pleasure but the realizing of the most valuable potentialities of human personality.

Needless to say, this characterization of God as the heavenly Father is not a merely random illustration but an analogy that lies at the heart of the Christian faith. Jesus treated the likeness between the attitude of God to man, and the attitude of human parents at their best towards their children, as providing the most adequate way for us to think about God. And so it is altogether relevant to a Christian understanding of this world to ask, How does the best parental love express itself in its influence upon the environment in which children are to grow up? I think it is clear that a parent who loves his children, and wants them to become the best human beings that they are capable of becoming, does not treat pleasure as the sole and supreme value. Certainly we seek pleasure for our children, and take great delight in obtaining it for them; but we do not desire for them unalloyed pleasure at the expense of their growth in such even greater values as moral integrity, unselfishness, compassion, courage, humour, reverence for the truth, and perhaps above all the capacity for love. We do not act on the premise that pleasure is the supreme end of life; and if the development of these other values sometimes clashes with the provision of pleasure, then we are willing to have our children miss a certain amount of this, rather than fail to come to possess and to be possessed by the finer and more precious qualities that are possible to the human personality. A child brought up on the principle that the only or the supreme value is pleasure would not be likely to become an ethically mature adult or an attractive or happy personality. And to most parents it seems more important to try to foster quality and strength of character in their children than to fill their lives at all times with the utmost possible degree of pleasure. If, then, there is any true analogy between God's purpose for his human creatures, and the purpose of loving and wise parents for their children, we have to recognize that the presence of pleasure and the absence of pain cannot be the supreme and overriding end for which the world exists. Rather, this world must be a place of soul-making. And its value is to be judged, not primarily by the quantity of pleasure and pain occurring in it at any particular moment, but by its fitness for its primary purpose, the purpose of soul-making.[28]

In all this we have been speaking about the nature of the world considered simply as the God-given environment of man's life. For it is mainly in this connection that the world has been regarded in Irenaean and in Protestant thought.[29] But such a way of thinking involves a danger of anthropocentrism from which the

[28] The phrase 'the vale of Soul-making' was coined by the poet John Keats in a letter written to his brother and sister in April 1819. He says, 'The common cognomen of this world among the misguided and superstitious is "a vale of tears" from which we are to be redeemed by a certain arbitrary interposition of God and taken to Heaven—What a little circumscribed straightened notion! Call the world if you Please "The vale of Soul-making".' In this letter he sketches a teleological theodicy. 'Do you not see', he asks, 'how necessary a World of Pains and troubles is to school an Intelligence and make it a Soul?' (*The Letters of John Keats,* ed. by M. B. Forman. London: Oxford University Press, 4th ed., 1952, pp. 334–5.)

[29] Thus Irenaeus said that 'the creation is suited to [the wants of] man; for man was not made for its sake, but creation for the sake of man' (*A.H.* v. xxix, 1), and Calvin said that 'because we know that the universe was established especially for the sake of mankind, we ought to look for this purpose in his governance also'. (*Inst.* i. xvi. 6.)

Augustinian and Catholic tradition has generally been protected by its sense of the relative insignificance of man within the totality of the created universe. Man was dwarfed within the medieval world-view by the innumerable hosts of angels and archangels above him—unfallen rational natures which rejoice in the immediate presence of God, reflecting His glory in the untarnished mirror of their worship. However, this higher creation has in our modern world lost its hold upon the imagination. Its place has been taken, as the minimizer of men, by the immensities of outer space and by the material universe's unlimited complexity transcending our present knowledge. As the spiritual environment envisaged by Western man has shrunk, his physical horizons have correspondingly expanded. Where the human creature was formerly seen as an insignificant appendage to the angelic world, he is now seen as an equally insignificant organic excrescence, enjoying a fleeting moment of consciousness on the surface of one of the planets of a minor star. Thus the truth that was symbolized for former ages by the existence of the angelic hosts is today impressed upon us by the vastness of the physical universe, countering the egoism of our species by making us feel that this immense prodigality of existence can hardly all exist for the sake of man—though, on the other hand, the very realization that it is not all for the sake of man may itself be salutary and beneficial to man!

However, instead of opposing man and nature as rival objects of God's interest, we should perhaps rather stress man's solidarity as an embodied being with the whole natural order in which he is embedded. For man is organic to the world; all his acts and thoughts and imaginations are conditioned by space and time; and in abstraction from nature he would cease to be human. We may, then, say that the beauties and sublimities and powers, the microscopic intricacies and macroscopic vastnesses, the wonders and the terrors of the natural world and of the life that pulses through it, are willed and valued by their Maker in a creative act that embraces man together with nature. By means of matter and living flesh God both builds a path and weaves a veil between Himself and the creature made in His image. Nature thus has permanent significance; for God has set man in a creaturely environment, and the final fulfilment of our nature in relation to God will accordingly take the form of an embodied life within 'a new heaven and a new earth'.[30] And as in the present age man moves slowly towards that fulfilment through the pilgrimage of his earthly life, so also 'the whole creation' is 'groaning in travail', waiting for the time when it will be 'set free from its bondage to decay'.[31]

And yet however fully we thus acknowledge the permanent significance and value of the natural order, we must still insist upon man's special character as a personal creature made in the image of God; and our theodicy must still centre upon the soul-making process that we believe to be taking place within human life.

This, then, is the starting-point from which we propose to try to relate the realities of sin and suffering to the perfect love of an omnipotent Creator. And as will become increasingly apparent, a theodicy that starts in this way must be eschatological in its ultimate bearings. That is to say, instead of looking to the past for its clue to the mystery of evil, it looks to the future, and indeed to that ultimate

30 Revelation xxi. 1.
31 Romans viii. 21–22.

future to which only faith can look. Given the conception of a divine intention working in and through human time towards a fulfilment that lies in its completeness beyond human time, our theodicy must find the meaning of evil in the part that it is made to play in the eventual outworking of that purpose; and must find the justification of the whole process in the magnitude of the good to which it leads. The good that outshines all ill is not a paradise long since lost but a kingdom which is yet to come in its full glory and permanence.

From this point of view we must speak about moral evil; about pain, including that of the lower animals; about the higher and more distinctively human forms of suffering; and about the relation between all this and the will of God as it has been revealed in Jesus Christ.

EMIL L. FACKENHEIM

Jewish Faith and the Holocaust

Emil L. Fackenheim, Professor of Philosophy at the University of Toronto, has also written *The Religious Dimension in Hegel's Thought* and *Quest for Past and Future*.

I

Within the past two centuries, three events have shaken and are still shaking Jewish religious existence—the Emancipation and its after-effects, the Nazi Holocaust, and the rise of the first Jewish state in two thousand years—and of these, two have occurred in our own generation. From the point of view of Jewish religious existence, as from so many other points of view, the Holocaust is the most shattering. Doubtless the Emancipation and all its works have posed and continue to pose powerful challenges, with which Jewish thought has been wrestling all along—scientific agnosticism, secularism, assimilation, and the like. The Emancipation represents, however, a challenge *ab extra*, from without, and for all its well-demonstrated power to weaken and undermine Jewish religious existence I have long been convinced that the challenge can be met, religiously and intellectually. The state of Israel, by contrast, is a challenge *ab intra*, from within—at least to much that Jewish existence has been throughout two millennia. But this challenge is positive—the

From *Commentary*, vol. 46, no. 2, later incorporated in chapter "These Twenty Years: A Reappraisal," in *Quest for Past and Future*, Indiana University Press, 1968. Copyright © 1968 by Emil L. Fackenheim. Reprinted by permission of the publishers and the author.

fact that in one sense (if not in many others) a long exile has ended. That it represents a positive challenge was revealed during and immediately after the Six-Day War, when biblical (i.e., pre-exilic) language suddenly came to life.

The Holocaust, too, challenges Jewish faith from within, but the negativism of its challenge is total, without light or relief. After the events associated with the name of Auschwitz, everything is shaken, nothing is safe.

To avoid Auschwitz, or to act as though it had never occurred, would be blasphemous. Yet how face it and be faithful to its victims? No precedent exists either within Jewish history or outside it. Even when a Jewish religious thinker barely begins to face Auschwitz, he perceives the possibility of a desperate choice between the faith of a millennial Jewish past, which has so far persisted through every trial, and faithfulness to the victims of the present. But at the edge of this abyss there must be a great pause, a lengthy silence, and an endurance.

II

Men shun the scandal of the particularity of Auschwitz. Germans link it with Dresden; American liberals, with Hiroshima, Christians deplore anti-Semitism-in-general, while Communists erect monuments of victims-of-Fascism-in-general, depriving the dead of Auschwitz of their Jewish identity even in death. Rather than face Auschwitz, men everywhere seek refuge in generalities, comfortable precisely because they are generalities. And such is the extent to which reality is shunned that no cries of protest are heard even when in the world community's own forum obscene comparisons are made between Israeli soldiers and Nazi murderers.

The Gentile world shuns Auschwitz because of the terror of Auschwitz—and because of real or imagined implication in the guilt for Auschwitz. But Jews shun Auschwitz as well. Only after many years did significant Jewish responses begin to appear. Little of real significance is being or can be said even now. Perhaps there should still be silence. It is certain, however, that the voices, now beginning to be heard, will grow ever louder and more numerous. For Jews now know that they must ever after remember Auschwitz, and be its witnesses to the world. Not to be a witness would be a betrayal. In the murder camps the victims often rebelled with no other hope than that one of them might escape to tell the tale. For Jews now to refrain from telling the tale would be unthinkable. Jewish faith still recalls the Exodus, Sinai, the two destructions of the Temple. A Judaism which survived at the price of ignoring Auschwitz would not deserve to survive.

It is because the world shrinks so fully from the truth that once a Jew begins to speak at all he must say the most obvious. Must he say that the death of a Jewish child at Auschwitz is no more lamentable than the death of a German child at Dresden? He must say it. And in saying it, he must also refuse to dissolve Auschwitz into suffering-in-general, even though he is almost sure to be considered a Jewish particularist who cares about Jews but not about mankind. Must he distinguish between the mass-killing at Hiroshima and that at Auschwitz? At the risk of being thought a sacrilegious quibbler, he must, with endless patience, forever repeat that Eichmann was moved by no such "rational" objective as victory when he diverted trains needed for military purposes in order to dispatch Jews to their death. He must add that there was no "irrational" objective either. Torquemada burned bodies in order to save souls. Eichmann sought to destroy both bodies and souls. Where else and at what other time have executioners ever separated those to be murdered now from those to be murdered later to the strain of Viennese waltzes? Where else has human skin ever been made into lampshades, and human body-fat into soap—not by isolated perverts but under the direction of ordinary bureaucrats? Auschwitz is a unique descent into hell. It is an unprecedented celebration of evil. It is evil for evil's sake.

A Jew must bear witness to this truth. Nor may he conceal the fact that Jews in their particularity were the singled-out victims. Of course, they were by no means the sole victims. And a Jew would infinitely prefer to think that to the Nazis, Jews were merely a species of the genus "inferior race." This indeed was the theme of Allied wartime propaganda, and it is still perpetuated by liberals, Communists, and guilt-ridden Christian theologians. Indeed, "liberal"-minded Jews themselves perpetuate it. The superficial reason is that this view of Auschwitz unites victims of all races and creeds: it is "brotherly" propaganda. Under the surface, however, there broods at least in Jewish if not in some Gentile minds an idea horrible beyond all description. Would even Nazis have singled out Jews for such a terrible fate unless Jews had done *something* to bring it upon themselves? Most of the blame attaches to the murderers: must not at least some measure of blame attach to the victims as well? Such are the wounds which Nazism has inflicted on some Jewish minds. And such is the extent to which Nazism has defiled the world that, while it should have destroyed every vestige of anti-Semitism in every Gentile mind on earth, Auschwitz has, in some Gentile minds, actually increased it.

These wounds and this defilement can be confronted only with the truth. And the ineluctable truth is that Jews at Auschwitz were not a species of the genus "inferior race," but rather the prototype by which "inferior race" was defined. Not until the Nazi revolution had become an anti-Jewish revolution did it begin to succeed as a movement; and when all its other works came crashing down only one of its goals remained: the murder of Jews. This is the scandal which requires, of Germans, a ruthless examination of their whole history; of Christians, a pitiless reckoning with the history of Christian anti-Semitism; of the whole world, an inquiry into the grounds of its indifference for twelve long years. Resort to theories of suffering-in-general or persecution-in-general permits such investigations to be evaded.

Yet even where the quest for explanations is genuine there is not, and never will be, an adequate explanation. Auschwitz is the scandal of evil for evil's sake, an eruption of demonism without analogy; and the singling-out of Jews, ultimately, is an unparalleled expression of what the rabbis call groundless hate. This is the rock on which throughout eternity all rational explanations will crash and break apart.

How can a Jew respond to thus having been singled out, and to being singled out even now whenever he tries to bear witness? Resisting rational explanations, Auschwitz will forever resist religious explanations as well. Attempts to find rational causes succeed at least up to a point, and the search for the religious, ideological, social, and economic factors leading to Auschwitz must be relentlessly pressed. In contrast, the search for a purpose in Auschwitz is foredoomed to total failure. Not that good men in their despair have not made the attempt. Good Orthodox Jews have resorted to the ancient "for our sins are we punished," but

this recourse, unacceptable already to Job, is in this case all the more impossible. A good Christian theologian sees the purpose of Auschwitz in a divine reminder of the sufferings of Christ, but this testifies to a moving sense of desperation—and to an incredible lapse of theological judgment. A good Jewish secularist will connect the Holocaust with the rise of the state of Israel, but while to see a causal connection here is possible and necessary, to see a purpose is intolerable. A total and uncompromising sweep must be made of these and other explanations, all designed to give purpose to Auschwitz. No purpose, religious or non-religious, will ever be found in Auschwitz. The very attempt to find one is blasphemous.

Yet it is of the utmost importance to recognize that seeking a purpose is one thing, but seeking a response quite another. The first is wholly out of the question. The second is inescapable. Even after two decades any sort of adequate response may as yet transcend the power of any Jew. But his faith, his destiny, his very survival will depend on whether, in the end, he will be able to respond.

How can a Jew begin to seek a response? Looking for precedents, he finds none either in Jewish or in non-Jewish history. Jewish (like Christian) martyrs have died for their faith, certain that God needs martyrs. Job suffered despite his faith, able to protest within the sphere of faith. Negro Christians have died for their race, unshaken in a faith which was not at issue. The one million Jewish children murdered in the Nazi Holocaust died neither because of their faith, nor in spite of their faith, nor for reasons unrelated to faith. They were murdered because of the faith of their great-grandparents. Had these great-grandparents abandoned their Jewish faith, and failed to bring up Jewish children, then their fourth-generation descendants might have been among the Nazi executioners, but not among their Jewish victims. Like Abraham of old, European Jews some time in the mid-19th century offered a human sacrifice, by the mere minimal commitment to the Jewish faith of bringing up Jewish children. But unlike Abraham they did not know what they were doing, and there was no reprieve. This is the brute fact which makes all comparisons odious or irrelevant. This is what makes Jewish religious existence today unique, without support from analogies anywhere in the past. This is the scandal of the particularity of Auschwitz which, once confronted by Jewish faith, threatens total despair.

I confess that it took me twenty years until I was able to look at this scandal, but when at length I did, I made what to me was, and still is, a momentous discovery: that while religious thinkers were vainly struggling for a response to Auschwitz, Jews throughout the world—rich and poor, learned and ignorant, religious and non-religious—had to some degree been responding all along. For twelve long years Jews had been exposed to a murderous hate which was as groundless as it was implacable. For twelve long years the world had been lukewarm or indifferent, unconcerned over the prospect of a world without Jews. For twelve long years the whole world had conspired to make Jews wish to cease to be Jews wherever, whenever, and in whatever way they could. Yet to this unprecedented invitation to group-suicide Jews responded with an unexpected will-to-live—with, under the circumstances, an incredible commitment to Jewish group survival.

In ordinary times, a commitment of this kind may be a mere mixture of nostalgia and vague loyalties not far removed from tribalism; and, unable to face

Auschwitz, I had myself long viewed it as such, placing little value on a Jewish survival which was, or seemed to be, only survival for survival's sake. I was wrong, and even the shallowest Jewish survivalist philosophy of the postwar period was right by comparison. For in the age of Auschwitz a Jewish commitment to Jewish survival is in itself a monumental act of faithfulness, as well as a monumental, albeit as yet fragmentary, act of faith. Even to do no more than remain a Jew after Auschwitz is to confront the demons of Auschwitz in all their guises, and to bear witness against them. It is to believe that these demons cannot, will not, and must not prevail, and to stake on that belief one's own life and the lives of one's children, and of one's children's children. To be a Jew after Auschwitz is to have wrested hope—for the Jew and for the world—from the abyss of total despair. In the words of a speaker at a recent gathering of Bergen-Belsen survivors, the Jew after Auschwitz has a second *Shema Yisrael*: no second Auschwitz, no second Bergen-Belsen, no second Buchenwald—anywhere in the world, for anyone in the world!

What accounts for this commitment to Jewish existence when there might have been, and by every rule of human logic should have been, a terrified and demoralized flight from Jewish existence? Why, since Auschwitz, have all previous distinctions among Jews—between religious and secularist, Orthodox and liberal—diminished in importance, to be replaced by a new major distinction between Jews committed to Jewish survival, willing to be singled out and counted, and Jews in flight, who rationalize this flight as a rise to humanity-in-general? In my view, nothing less will do than to say that a commanding Voice speaks from Auschwitz, and that there are Jews who hear it and Jews who stop their ears.

The ultimate question is: where was God at Auschwitz? For years I sought refuge in Buber's image of an eclipse of God. This image, still meaningful in other respects, no longer seems to me applicable to Auschwitz. Most assuredly no *redeeming* Voice is heard from Auschwitz, or ever will be heard. However, a *commanding* Voice is being heard, and has, however faintly, been heard from the start. Religious Jews hear it, and they identify its source. Secularist Jews also hear it, even though perforce they leave it unidentified. At Auschwitz, Jews came face to face with absolute evil. They were and still are singled out by it, but in the midst of it they hear an absolute commandment: *Jews are forbidden to grant posthumous victories to Hitler*. They are commanded to survive as Jews, lest the Jewish people perish. They are commanded to remember the victims of Auschwitz, lest their memory perish. They are forbidden to despair of man and his world, and to escape into either cynicism or otherworldliness, lest they cooperate in delivering the world over to the forces of Auschwitz. Finally, they are forbidden to despair of the God of Israel, lest Judaism perish. A secularist Jew cannot make himself believe by a mere act of will, nor can he be commanded to do so; yet he can perform the commandment of Auschwitz. And a religious Jew who has stayed with his God may be forced into new, possibly revolutionary, relationships with Him. One possibility, however, is wholly unthinkable. A Jew may not respond to Hitler's attempt to destroy Judaism by himself cooperating in its destruction. In ancient times, the unthinkable Jewish sin was idolatry. Today, it is to respond to Hitler by doing his work.

In the Midrash, God is, even in time of unrelieved tragedy, only "seemingly" powerless, for the Messiah is still expected. In Elie Wiesel's *Night,* God hangs on the gallows, and for the hero of Wiesel's *The Gates of the Forest,* A Messiah who is able to come, and yet at Auschwitz failed to come, is not to be conceived. Yet this same hero asserts that precisely because it is too late we are commanded to hope. He also says the Kaddish, "that solemn affirmation, filled with grandeur and serenity, by which man returns to God His crown and His scepter." But how a Jew after Auschwitz can return these to God is not yet known. Nor is it yet known how God can receive them.

III

The Nazi Holocaust has brought Jews and Christians closer together—and set them further apart. The first truth is comforting and obvious. The second is painful, complex, and obscure, but perhaps in the end more necessary to confront. The gulf between Jews and Christians which Hitler succeeded in creating can be bridged only if it is recognized. But to bridge it is of incalculable importance for the future of both Judaism and Christianity.

Since an objective grasp of this issue is almost impossible, I had better state my views in terms of my own subjective development. Twenty years ago I believed that what once separated Jew and Christian was now dwarfed by what united them—namely their opposition to Nazism. I was of course not unaware of phenomena like the Nazi "German-Christian" church, or of the fact that respectable and indeed outstanding theologians were part of it. But so far as my native Germany was concerned, it was not the Christian Nazis who mattered to me; it was rather the Christian anti-Nazis, however small their number—not the "German-Christian" but rather the German confessional church. And what mattered theologically was thinkers like Barth and Tillich, able to recognize Nazi idolatry and to fight it courageously and unequivocally. To this day I still revere Kierkegaard, the first Christian thinker to perceive the nature and extent of modern idolatry, who would surely have been put into a concentration camp had he lived and written in Nazi Germany. To this day I am supported in my Judaism by the faithfulness of Christians to their Christianity. And when a new generation of Christian theologians arises to proclaim the death of God I feel, as a Jew, abandoned and betrayed.

The ancient rabbis recognized "righteous Gentiles" as being equal to the high priest in the sight of God; but they had no real acquaintance with Christianity and, of course, none with Islam. Medieval Jewish thinkers recognized Christianity and Mohammedanism as valid monotheistic religions, and considering the state of medieval Jewish-Christian and Jewish-Moslem relations, it is surprising that they did. But since the experience of Nazism and of Christian opposition to Nazism (which goes back to my adolescence), I have been convinced that there is now a need for Jewish recognition that the Christian (and the Mohammedan) not only affirms the One God but also stands in a living relation to Him. Where to go from here I cannot say. I never could accept Rosenzweig's famous "double covenant" doctrine, according to which all except Jews (who are already "with the Father") need the Son in order to find Him. How can a modern Jew pray for the conversion of the whole non-Jewish world to Christianity when even pre-modern

Jews could pay homage to Moslem monotheism? Rosenzweig's doctrine seems altogether outmoded at a time when Christians themselves are beginning to replace missionary efforts with inter-religious dialogue, and I wonder whether even for Rosenzweig this doctrine was more than a stage in his self-emancipation from modern paganism.

Thus, though I very much feel the need for a Jewish doctrine of Christianity, I am left without one and must for the time being rest content only with openness to Jewish-Christian dialogue. As regards the prospect of such dialogue, I confess that I have over the years become less optimistic in the hope that the long age of Christian triumphalism over Judaism is truly being superseded by an age of Jewish-Christian dialogue. In view of recent Christian developments, such as ecclesiastical declarations deploring anti-Semitism and absolving Jews of the charge of deicide, this may seem a strange, and even perverse, personal opinion. Yet I think that recent events have shown it to be realistic.

To most impartial observers it has always been a plain fact that, ever since the Age of Enlightenment, it was secularists who spearheaded the struggle for Jewish emancipation; organized Christian forces sometimes accepted emancipation, often opposed it, but rarely if ever led the fight. This fact, plain to so many, I myself failed to see (or refused to accept) until quite recently. I saw the distinction between the new Nazi and the old Christian anti-Semitism, but could not bear to admit a relation between them. In the grim years of Nazism and immediately thereafter, I found it humanly impossible to see enemies on every side. Twenty-five years later, however, it is necessary to confront yet another painful truth.

I will confine myself to two examples, both concerning German Christians opposed to Nazism. In 1933, many Jews then in Germany, myself included, made a veritable saint of Cardinal Faulhaber, crediting him with opposing both Nazism and Nazi anti-Semitism. This image remained with me for many years. I had read the Cardinal's relevant sermons, but had somehow not noticed what they said. Not until about three years ago, when I came upon Guenter Lewy's masterful *The Catholic Church and Nazi Germany,* did I realize that Faulhaber had confined his defense to the Jews of the Old Testament, and had gone out of his way to make clear that he was not defending his Jewish contemporaries. To quote Lewy:

> We must distinguish, he told the faithful, between the people of Israel before the death of Christ, who were vehicles of divine revelation, and the Jews after the death of Christ, who have become restless wanderers over the earth. But even the Jewish people of ancient times could not justly claim credit for the wisdom of the Old Testament. So unique were these laws that one was bound to say: "People of Israel, this did not grow in your own garden of your own planting. This condemnation of usurious land-grabbing, this war against the oppression of the farmer by debt, this prohibition of usury, is not the product of your spirit."

Rarely has the Christian belief in the revealed character of the Hebrew Bible been put to so perverse a use.

My second example is even more painful, for it involves none other than the universally beloved Dietrich Bonhoeffer, brave anti-Nazi Christian witness and martyr to his cause. Even now I find it hard to believe that he should have confined his attack on Nazi Aryan legislation to its application to converted Jews; and I find it even harder to believe that these words were written by Bonhoeffer in Nazi Germany in response to Nazi anti-Semitism:

> Now the measures of the state toward Judaism in addition stand in quite special context for the church. The church of Christ has never lost sight of the thought that the "chosen people," who nailed the redeemer of the world to the cross, must bear the curse for its action through a long history of suffering. . . .

Rather than comment myself, I prefer to cite the comment of the American Christian theologian, J. Coert Rylaarsdam:

> We all think of Dietrich Bonhoeffer as a good Christian, even a martyr, perhaps. With great courage he insisted on "the crown rights of the Redeemer" within his own church. Moreover, he insisted that Jews who had converted to Christianity were entitled to the same rights in the church as other Christians, a position by no means unanimously held in the church of Hitler's Germany. Nevertheless, standing in the Christian tradition of the curse, Bonhoeffer did not hesitate to appeal to it to rationalize Hitler's program for Jews faithful to their own faith.

To keep the record straight, one must add that the passages in question were written in 1933 (when, according to his friend Eberhard Bethge, Bonhoeffer still suffered from "lack of reality-relatedness"), that his opposition to Nazism became more complete as it came to assume secular-political expression, and, indeed, that he took personal risks to save Jewish lives. Even so, I know of no evidence yet (though I would dearly love to hear of any) to the effect that Bonhoeffer ever totally repudiated the Christian "tradition of the curse." From the very beginning he opposed the encroachment of racism upon the church and spoke up for Jews converted to Christianity. By 1940 he charged that the church "was silent when she should have cried out because the blood of the innocent was crying aloud to heaven . . . she is guilty of the deaths of the weakest and most defenseless brothers of Jesus Christ." But during the most grievous Jewish martyrdom in all of history, did he ever repudiate a millennial Christian tradition, and seek a bond (even if only in his own mind) with "Jews faithful to their own faith," because, and not in spite of, their faithfulness? How different would Bonhoeffer's struggle have been if he had repudiated the "Christian tradition of the curse" from the start! How different would Jewish fate have been in our time had his whole church repudiated it!

In America, to be sure, it has always been different, and the churches of the 1960's differ everywhere from those of the 1940's, there being historic changes in the making in Christian attitudes toward Jews. The question is, however, whether American differences are not mainly due to the effect of secular democracy, and also whether the changes in Christian attitudes toward Jews possess the radicalism which, after Auschwitz, is a categorical imperative. Here again, only ruthless truthfulness can save the future of Jewish-Christian dialogue. And the truth, as I am now forced to see it, is that the organized Christian forces will find it easiest to drop the ancient charge of deicide, harder to recognize roots of anti-Semitism in the New Testament, and hardest of all to face up to the fact that Jews and Judaism are both still alive. Confronted with the awkward fact of Jewish survival after the advent of Christianity, theologians have looked upon Judaism as a fossil, an anachronism, a shadow. It is not easy to reverse a doctrine which has persisted for two millennia (assuming not only religious, but also, as in Toynbee, secular, and, as in Marx, anti-religious forms), and to recognize that both Jews and Judaism have maintained an unbroken existence throughout the entire Christian era. But how can a Jew, however he may strain his ears, hear God speak to the Christian church, if even after Auschwitz this ancient calumny is not at length totally and categorically rejected? And how, he wonders, can a Christian enter into dialogue with a Jew unless he recognizes that the person across the table is no shadow but alive?

These questions became traumatically vivid for any Jew committed to Jewish-Christian dialogue during the momentous events of May and June 1967, when the state of Israel, the most incontestable proof that the Jewish people still lives, was threatened with destruction. The secular Western press understood well enough that Israel was fighting for her life. Yet only a handful of Christian spokesmen showed the same understanding. Why should Christian spokesmen have remained neutral as between Israel's claim to the right to live and Arab claims to the right to destroy her—if not because of old, unconscious, theologically-inspired doubts as to whether the "fossil" Israel did indeed have the right to live? Why has there always been much Christian concern for Arab refugees from Israel, but none whatever for Jewish refugees from Arab countries—if not because of old, no longer consciously remembered ecclesiastical doctrines to the effect that Jews (unlike Arabs) must be kept landless, and therefore rightless? Why were ecclesiastical authorities untroubled by two decades of Moslem control of the Christian holy places (and of Arab desecration of Jewish holy places), and yet now so deeply distressed by Jewish control?

But a still more ultimate question is raised by the events of 1967. For two long weeks in May the worldwide Jewish community perceived the specter of a second Jewish Holocaust in a single generation. For two weeks it listened to the same words emanating from Cairo and Damascus which had once emanated from Berlin, largely composed, one may be sure, by pupils of Joseph Goebbels. For two weeks it longed for Christian words of apprehension and concern. But whereas some such words came from secular sources, from the churches there was little but silence. Once again, Jews were alone. This fact, transcending as it does all politics, is a trauma for Jews regardless of political persuasion—non-Zionists and even anti-Zionists as well as Zionists. Moreover, it stands between Jews and Christians even now, for when Jews ask why there was no moral Christian outcry against a second Auschwitz they are still widely misunderstood, as demanding of Christians that they side politically with Israel against the Arab states.

Any Jew pondering this ultimate question must surely reject the idea that the Christian churches abandoned Jews knowingly to a second Holocaust. What, then, was revealed by the Christian silence in the spring of 1967? Not, I believe, an old Christian anti-Semitism, but rather a new Jewish-Christian problem—the fearful truth that Hitler, against his will bringing Jews and Christians closer, also had his will in setting them further apart.

A Jew at Auschwitz was murdered because he was a Jew; a Christian was murdered only if he was a saint: but there are few saints among either Jews or Christians. Hitler gave a new and perverse reality to the ancient Jewish doctrine that anyone born a Jew is a Jew. He also gave a new and perverse reality to the ancient Christian doctrine that one becomes a Christian only through an act of voluntary commitment—and, with diabolical cunning as well as terror, he led Christians into temptation. Hitler tried to create an abyss between Jews and Christians; he succeeded; and—this is the horror—he continues to enjoy posthumous successes. The Jew after Auschwitz exists with the knowledge of abandonment; the Christian cannot bear to face his responsibility for this abandonment. He knows that, as a Christian, he should voluntarily have gone to Auschwitz, where his own Master would have been dragged, voluntarily or involuntarily, and he is wracked by a sense of guilt the deeper the less he has cause to feel it. Hence the Christian failure to face Auschwitz. Hence Christian recourse to innocuous generalities. Hence, too, Christian silence in May 1967. If in May 1967 the Christian community did not cry out against a second Auschwitz, it was not because of its indifference to the words emanating from Cairo and Damascus, but rather because it did not hear them. It failed to recognize the danger of a second Holocaust because it has yet to recognize the fact of the first.

To bridge the Jewish-Christian gulf which Hitler has succeeded in creating is a task of incalculable importance, and at a Jewish-Christian colloquium prior to the events of May 1967 I attempted a hesitant step in that direction. I said there that if every Christian in Hitler's Europe had followed the example of the King of Denmark and decided to put on the yellow star, there would today be neither confusion nor despair in the church, nor talk of the death of God. I said with every emphasis at my command that, as a Jew after Auschwitz, I did not and could not speak as a judge, but only as a witness. To remove every trace of ambiguity or doubt I stated not politely, but quite truthfully, that I had been sixteen years of age when Hitler came to power, and had not known then, any more than I knew now, whether I would have become a Nazi had I been born a Gentile. Yet a leading Christian thinker, himself a lifelong anti-Nazi, mistook my statement for a case of Jewish triumphalism. So wide still is the gulf between Jews and Christians which Hitler opened decades ago. So close are we to handing him further, posthumous victories.

IV

On another public occasion, in March 1967, I asked the following question:

> Would we [like Job] be able to say that the question of Auschwitz will be answered in any sense whatever in case the eclipse of God were ended and He appeared to us? An impossible and intolerable question.

Less than three months later this purely hypotheical question had become actual, when at Jerusalem the threat of total annihilation gave way to sudden salvation, atheists spoke of miracles, and hardboiled Western reporters resorted to biblical images.

The question *is* impossible and intolerable. Even Job's question is not answered by God's presence, and to him children are restored. The children of Auschwitz will not be restored, and the question of Auschwitz will not be answered by a saving divine presence.

And yet, is a Jew after Auschwitz permitted to despair of salvation because of Auschwitz? Is it permitted him to cast out all hope and all joy? But on the other side, can there be any hope and any joy, purchased at the price of forgetting? Any one of these responses would be further victories handed to Hitler, and are thus impossible.

It was into precisely this impossible and intolerable contradiction that believing Jews were placed by the events at Jerusalem in May and June 1967. Those events cast into clear relief the whole as yet unassimilated fact of an embattled, endangered, but nevertheless free Jewish state, emerging from ashes and catastrophe. Solely because of the connection of the events of May and June with Auschwitz did a military victory (rarely applauded in Judaism, and never for its own sake) acquire an inescapable religious dimension.

In this context, let me quote from a letter I recently received from Professor Harold Fisch of Bar-Ilan University in Israel:

> May I report to you a conversation I had last summer with a colleague, a psychologist, who had served during the war as an artillery officer in Sinai. I asked him how he accounted for the remarkable heroism of the quite ordinary soldier of the line, for, as you may know, exemplary heroism was the normal thing at that time; mere carrying out of duty was the exception. Where, I asked him, was the psychological spring? To my surprise, he answered that what deeply motivated each and every soldier was the memory of the Holocaust, and the feeling that *above all this must never happen again.* There had been an ominous similarity between the statements of Arab leaders, their radio, and newspapers, and the remembered threats of the Nazis: we had entered into a *Shoah* (holocaust) psychosis, all around us enemies threatening us with extermination and having both the means and the will to carry out their threat. As the ring closed in and help seemed far, one noticed one's neighbors who had been in Auschwitz and Bergen-Belsen going about white-faced. It was all too obvious what was the source of their dread. The years in between had momentarily fallen away, and they were back in that veritable nightmare world. The dark night of the soul was upon us. *And it was the commandment which the Lord of history had, so to speak, pronounced at Auschwitz which saved us.* [Italics added.] I told my friend that I could not entirely accept his explanation because I knew that a majority of the soldiers had no personal or family recollections of the European Holocaust: they had come from North Africa or Yeman, or even the neighboring Arab countries where at that time such horrors were unknown. How could they feel the force of the analogy as could the survivors of Buchenwald? He told me that the intervening twenty years had brought it about that the Holocaust had become a collective experience pressing consciously and unconsciously on the minds of all, even the young, for whom Jewish history in the Diaspora had come to an end with the beginnings of Israeli independence.

It is solely because of this connection of the events of May and June with Auschwitz that a Jew must both tremble and rejoice. He must tremble lest he permit any light after Auschwitz to relieve the darkness of Auschwitz. He must rejoice, lest he add to the darkness of Auschwitz. Rejoicing after Auschwitz and because of Auschwitz, the Jew must be a Jew, *am Yisrael chai* ("the people Israel, alive"), a witness to the world, preparing a way for God.

FRIEDRICH NIETZSCHE

God Is Dead

Another selection
from Friedrich
Nietzsche appears
in the previous
sub-section, "Man
and World."

WHAT OUR CHEERFULNESS SIGNIFIES

The most important of more recent events—that "God is dead," that the belief
in the Christian God has become unworthy of belief—already begins to cast its
first shadows over Europe. To the few at least whose eye, whose *suspecting*
glance, is strong enough and subtle enough for this drama, some sun seems to
have set, some old, profound confidence seems to have changed into doubt: our
old world must seem to them daily more darksome, distrustful, strange and
"old." In the main, however, one may say that the event itself is far too great,
too remote, too much beyond most people's power of apprehension, for one to
suppose that so much as the report of it could have *reached* them; not to speak
of many who already knew *what* had taken place, and what must all collapse
now that this belief had been undermined,—because so much was built upon it,
so much rested on it, and had become one with it: for example, our entire
European morality. This lengthy, vast and uninterrupted process of crumbling,
destruction, ruin and overthrow which is now imminent: who has realised it
sufficiently to-day to have to stand up as the teacher and herald of such a
tremendous logic of terror, as the prophet of a period of gloom and eclipse, the
like of which has probably never taken place on earth before? . . . Even we, the
born riddle-readers, who wait as it were on the mountains posted 'twixt to-day
and to-morrow, and engirt by their contradiction, we, the firstlings and premature
children of the coming century, into whose sight especially the shadows which
must forthwith envelop Europe *should* already have come—how is it that even
we, without genuine sympathy for this period of gloom, contemplate its advent
without any *personal solicitude or fear*? Are we still, perhaps, too much under
the *immediate effects* of the event—and are these effects, especially as regards
ourselves, perhaps the reverse of what was to be expected—not at all sad and
depressing, but rather like a new and indescribable variety of light, happiness,
relief, enlivenment, encouragement, and dawning day? . . . In fact, we philos-

From *The Joyful Wisdom*, by Friedrich Nietzsche, translated by Thomas Common, 1905.

ophers and "free spirits" feel ourselves irradiated as by a new dawn by the report that the "old God is dead"; our hearts overflow with gratitude, astonishment, presentiment and expectation. At last the horizon seems open once more, granting even that it is not bright; our ships can at last put out to sea in face of every danger; every hazard is again permitted to the discerner; the sea, *our* sea, again lies open before us; perhaps never before did such an "open sea" exist.—

TO WHAT EXTENT EVEN WE ARE STILL PIOUS

It is said with good reason that convictions have no civic rights in the domain of science: it is only when a conviction voluntarily condescends to the modesty of an hypothesis, a preliminary standpoint for experiment, or a regulative fiction, that its access to the realm of knowledge, and a certain value therein, can be conceded,—always, however, with the restriction that it must remain under police supervision, under the police of our distrust.—Regarded more accurately, however, does not this imply that only when a conviction *ceases* to be a conviction can it obtain admission into science? Does not the discipline of the scientific spirit just commence when one no longer harbours any conviction? . . . It is probably so: only, it remains to be asked whether, *in order that this discipline may commence,* it is not necessary that there should already be a conviction, and in fact one so imperative and absolute, that it makes a sacrifice of all other convictions. One sees that science also rests on a belief: there is no science at all "without premises." The question whether *truth* is necessary, must not merely be affirmed beforehand, but must be affirmed to such an extent that the principle, belief, or conviction finds expression, that "there is *nothing more necessary* than truth, and in comparison with it everything else has only secondary value."—This absolute will to truth: what is it? Is it the will *not to allow ourselves to be deceived*? Is it the will *not to deceive*? For the will to truth could also be interpreted in this fashion, provided one included under the generalisation, "I will not deceive," the special case, "I will not deceive myself." But why not deceive? Why not allow oneself to be deceived?—Let it be noted that the reasons for the former eventuality belong to a category quite different from those for the latter: one does not want to be deceived oneself, under the supposition that it is injurious, dangerous, or fatal to be deceived,—in this sense science would be a prolonged process of caution, foresight and utility; against which, however, one might reasonably make objections. What? is not-wishing-to-be-deceived really less injurious, less dangerous, less fatal? What do you know of the character of existence in all its phases to be able to decide whether the greater advantage is on the side of absolute distrust, or of absolute trustfulness? In case, however, of both being necessary, much trusting *and* much distrusting, whence then should science derive the absolute belief, the conviction on which it rests, that truth is more important than anything else, even than every other conviction? This conviction could not have arisen if truth *and* untruth had both continually proved themselves to be useful: as is the case. Thus—the belief in science, which now undeniably exists, cannot have had its origin in such a utilitarian calculation, but rather *in spite of* the fact of the inutility and dangerousness of the "Will to truth," of "truth at all costs," being continually demonstrated. "At all costs": alas, we understand that sufficiently well, after having sacrificed and slaughtered one belief after another at this altar!—Consequently, "Will to truth" does *not* imply, "I will not allow myself to be deceived," but—there is no other alternative—"I will not deceive, not even myself": *and thus we have reached the realm of morality.* For, let one just ask oneself fairly: "Why wilt thou not deceive?" especially if it should seem—and it does seem—as if life were laid out with a view to appearance, I mean, with a view to error, deceit, dissimulation, delusion, self-delusion; and when on the other hand it is a matter of fact that the great type of life has always manifested itself on the side of the most unscrupulous πολύτροποι. Such an intention might perhaps, to express it mildly, be a piece of Quixotism, a little enthusiastic craziness; it might also, however, be something worse, namely, a destructive principle, hostile to life. . . . "Will to Truth,"—that might be a concealed Will to Death.—Thus the question, Why is there science? leads back to the moral problem: *What in general is the purpose of morality*, if life, nature, and history are "non-moral"? There is no doubt that the conscientious man in the daring and extreme sense in which he is presupposed by the belief in science, *affirms thereby a world other than* that of life, nature, and history; and in so far as he affirms this "other world," what? must he not just thereby—deny its counterpart, this world, *our* world? . . . But what I have in view will now be understood, namely, that it is always a *metaphysical belief* on which our belief in science rests,—and that even we knowing ones of to-day, the godless and anti-metaphysical, still take *our* fire from the conflagration kindled by a belief a millennium old, the Christian belief, which was also the belief of Plato, that God is truth, that the truth is divine. . . . But what if this itself always becomes more untrustworthy, what if nothing any longer proves itself divine, except it be error, blindness, and falsehood;—what if God himself turns out to be our most persistent lie?—

The Existence

of God

_____

SAINT ANSELM

God's Existence Is Logically Necessary

Saint Anselm (1033–1109) was Archbishop of
Canterbury.

Some time ago, at the urgent request of some of my brethren, I published a brief
work,[1] as an example of meditation on the grounds of faith. I wrote it in the role
of one who seeks, by silent reasoning with himself, to learn what he does not know.
But when I reflected on this little book, and saw that it was put together as a long
chain of arguments, I began to ask myself whether *one* argument might possibly
be found, resting on no other argument for its proof, but sufficient in itself to prove
that God truly exists, and that he is the supreme good, needing nothing outside
himself, but needful for the being and well-being of all things. I often turned my
earnest attention to this problem, and at times I believed that I could put my finger
on what I was looking for, but at other times it completely escaped my mind's eye,
until finally, in despair, I decided to give up searching for something that seemed
impossible to find. But when I tried to put the whole question out of my mind, so
as to avoid crowding out other matters, with which I might make some progress,
by this useless preoccupation, then, despite my unwillingness and resistance, it began
to force itself on me more persistently than ever. Then, one day, when I was worn
out by my vigorous resistance to the obsession, the solution I had ceased to hope for
presented itself to me, in the very turmoil of my thoughts, so that I enthusiastically
embraced the idea which in my disquiet, I had spurned.

I thought that the proof I was so glad to find would please some readers if it
were written down. Consequently, I have written the little work that follows, dealing with this and one or two other matters, in the role of one who strives to raise
his mind to the contemplation of God and seeks to understand what he believes.
Neither this essay nor the other one I have already mentioned really seemed to me to
deserve to be called a book or to bear an author's name; at the same time, I felt
that they could not be published without some title that might encourage anyone
into whose hands they fell to read them, and so I gave each of them a title. The
first I called *An Example of Meditation on the Grounds of Faith*, and the second
Faith Seeking Understanding.

From *A Scholastic Miscellany*, edited and translated by Eugene R. Fairweather, Vol. X, Library
of Christian Classics. Published simultaneously in Great Britain and the United States of America by
S.C.M. Press, Ltd., London, and The Westminster Press, Philadelphia. First published in 1956. Used by
permission.
1 The *Monologion*, probably Anselm's first work, was written at Bec in the second half of 1076.
(Translator's note.)

But when both of them had been copied under these titles by a number of people, I was urged by many people—and especially by Hugh, the reverend archbishop of Lyons, apostolic legate in Gaul, who ordered this with apostolic authority —to attach my name to them. In order to do this more fittingly, I have named the first *Monologion* (or *Soliloquy*), and the second *Proslogion* (or *Address*).

GOD TRULY IS

And so, O Lord, since thou givest understanding to faith, give me to understand— as far as thou knowest it to be good for me—that thou dost exist, as we believe, and that thou art what we believe thee to be. Now we believe that thou art a being than which none greater can be thought. Or can it be that there is no such being, since "the fool hath said in his heart, 'There is no God' "? But when this same fool hears what I am saying—"A being than which none greater can be thought"—he understands what he hears, and what he understands is in his understanding, even if he does not understand that it exists. For it is one thing for an object to be in the understanding, and another thing to understand that it exists. When a painter considers beforehand what he is going to paint, he has it in his understanding, but he does not suppose that what he has not yet painted already exists. But when he has painted it, he both has it in his understanding and understands that what he has now produced exists. Even the fool, then, must be convinced that a being than which none greater can be thought exists at least in his understanding, since when he hears this he understands it, and whatever is understood is in the understanding. But clearly that than which a greater cannot be thought cannot exist in the understanding alone. For if it is actually in the understanding alone, it can be thought of as existing also in reality, and this is greater. Therefore, if that than which a greater cannot be thought is in the understanding alone, this same thing than which a greater cannot be thought is that than which a greater can be thought. But obviously this is impossible. Without doubt, therefore, there exists, both in the understanding and in reality, something than which a greater cannot be thought.

GOD CANNOT BE THOUGHT OF AS NONEXISTENT

And certainly it exists so truly that it cannot be thought of as nonexistent. For something can be thought of as existing, which cannot be thought of as not existing, and this is greater than that which *can* be thought of as not existing. Thus, if that than which a greater cannot be thought can be thought of as not existing, this very thing than which a greater cannot be thought is *not* that than which a greater cannot be thought. But this is contradictory. So, then, there truly is a being than which a greater cannot be thought—so truly that it cannot even be thought of as not existing.

And *thou* art this being, O Lord our God. Thou so truly are, then, O Lord my God, that thou canst not even be thought of as not existing. And this is right. For if some mind could think of something better than thou, the creature would rise above the Creator and judge its Creator; but this is altogether absurd. And indeed, whatever is, except thyself alone, can be thought of as not existing. Thou alone, therefore, of all beings, has being in the truest and highest sense, since no other being so truly exists, and thus every other being has less being. Why, then, has "the fool said in his heart, 'There is no God,'" when it is so obvious to the rational mind that, of all beings, thou dost exist supremely? Why indeed, unless it is that he is a stupid fool?

HOW THE FOOL HAS SAID IN HIS HEART
WHAT CANNOT BE THOUGHT

But how did he manage to say in his heart what he could not think? Or how is it that he was unable to think what he said in his heart? After all, to say in one's heart and to think are the same thing. Now if it is true—or, rather, since it is true—that he thought it, because he said it in his heart, but did not say it in his heart, since he could not think it, it is clear that something can be said in one's heart or thought in more than one way. For we think of a thing, in one sense, when we think of the word that signifies it, and in another sense, when we understand the very thing itself. Thus, in the first sense God can be thought of as nonexistent, but in the second sense this is quite impossible. For no one who understands what God is can think that God does not exist, even though he says these words in his heart—perhaps without any meaning, perhaps with some quite extraneous meaning. For God is that than which a greater cannot be thought, and whoever understands this rightly must understand that he exists in such a way that he cannot be nonexistent even in thought. He, therefore, who understands that God thus exists cannot think of him as nonexistent.

Thanks be to thee, good Lord, thanks be to thee, because I now understand by thy light what I formerly believed by thy gift, so that even if I were to refuse to believe in thy existence, I could not fail to understand its truth.

REPLY TO THE CRITICISMS OF GAUNILO

. . . But, you say, suppose that someone imagined an island in the ocean, surpassing all lands in its fertility. Because of the difficulty, or rather the impossibility, of finding something that does not exist, it might well be called "Lost Island." By reasoning like yours, he might then say that we cannot doubt that it truly exists in reality, because anyone can easily conceive it from a verbal description.[2] I state confidently that if anyone discovers something for me, other than that "than which a greater cannot be thought," existing either in reality or in thought alone, to which the logic of my argument can be applied, I shall find his lost island and give it to him, never to be lost again. But it now seems obvious that this being than which a greater cannot be thought cannot be thought of as nonexistent, because it exists by such a sure reason of truth. For otherwise it would not exist at all. In short, if anyone says that he thinks it does not exist, I say that when he thinks this, he either thinks of something than which a greater cannot be thought or he does not think. If he does not think, he does not think of what he is not thinking of as nonexistent. But if he does think, then he thinks of something which cannot be thought of as nonexistent. For if it could be thought of as nonexistent, it could be thought of as having a beginning and an end. But this is impossible. Therefore, if

[2] Cf. Gaunilo, *Pro insipiente,* 6.

anyone thinks of it, he thinks of something that cannot even be thought of as nonexistent. But he who thinks of this does not think that it does not exist; if he did, he would think what cannot be thought. Therefore, that than which a greater cannot be thought cannot be thought of as nonexistent.

You say, moreover, that when it is said that the highest reality cannot be *thought of* as nonexistent, it would perhaps be better to say that it cannot be *understood* as nonexistent, or even as possibly nonexistent. But it is more correct to say, as I said, that it cannot be thought. For if I had said that the reality itself cannot be understood not to exist, perhaps you yourself, who say that according to the very definition of the term what is false cannot be understood, would object that nothing that is can be understood as nonexistent. For it is false to say that what exists does not exist. Therefore it would not be peculiar to God to be unable to be understood as nonexistent. But if some one of the things that most certainly are can be understood as nonexistent, other certain things can similarly be understood as nonexistent. But this objection cannot be applied to "thinking," if it is rightly considered. For although none of the things that exist can be understood not to exist, still they can all be thought of as nonexistent, except that which most fully is. For all those things—and only those—which have a beginning or end or are composed of parts can be thought of as nonexistent, along with anything that does not exist as a whole anywhere or at any time (as I have already said). But the only being that cannot be thought of as nonexistent is that in which no thought finds beginning or end or composition of parts, but which any thought finds as a whole, always and everywhere.

You must realize, then, that you can think of yourself as nonexistent, even while you know most certainly that you exist. I am surprised that you said you did not know this. For we think of many things as nonexistent when we know that they exist, and of many things as existent when we know that they do not exist—all this not by a real judgment, but by imagining that what we think is so. And indeed, we can think of something as nonexistent, even while we know that it exists, because we are able at the same time to think the one and know the other. And yet we cannot think of it as nonexistent, while we know that it exists, because we cannot think of something as at once existent and nonexistent. Therefore, if anyone distinguishes these two senses of the statement in this way, he will understand that nothing, as long as it is known to exist, can be thought of as nonexistent, and that whatever exists, except that than which a greater cannot be thought, can be thought of as nonexistent, even when it is known to exist. So, then it is peculiar to God to be unable to be thought of as nonexistent, and nevertheless many things, as long as they exist, cannot be thought of as nonexistent. . . .

SAINT THOMAS AQUINAS

Five Proofs for the Existence of God

Saint Thomas Aquinas (c. 1225–1274) wrote
Summa Theologica, Summa Contra Gentiles, and
other works to try to reconcile Aristotelian
philosophy with Roman Catholic theology.

. . . I answer that, The existence of God can be proved in five ways.

The first and more manifest way is the argument from motion. It is certain, and evident to our senses, that in the world some things are in motion. Now whatever is moved is moved by another, for nothing can be moved except it is in potentiality to that towards which it is moved whereas a thing moves inasmuch as it is in act. For motion is nothing else than the reduction of something from potentiality to actuality. But nothing can be reduced from potentiality to actuality, except by something in a state of actuality. Thus that which is actually hot, as fire, makes wood, which is potentially hot, to be actually hot, and thereby moves and changes it. Now it is not possible that the same thing should be at once in actuality and potentiality in the same respect, but only in different respects. For what is actually hot cannot simultaneously be potentially hot; but it is simultaneously potentially cold. It is therefore impossible that in the same respect and in the same way a thing should be both mover and moved, i.e., that it should move itself. Therefore, whatever is moved must be moved by another. If that by which it is moved be itself moved, then this also must needs be moved by another, and that by another again. But this cannot go on to infinity, because then there would be no first mover, and consequently, no other mover, seeing that subsequent movers move only inasmuch as they are moved by the first mover, as the staff moves only because it is moved by the hand. Therefore, it is necessary to arrive at a first mover, moved by no other; and this everyone understands to be God.

The second way is from the nature of efficient cause. In the world of sensible things we find there is an order of efficient causes. There is no case known (neither is it, indeed, possible) in which a thing is found to be the efficient cause of itself; for so it would be prior to itself, which is impossible. Now in efficient causes it is not possible to go on to infinity, because in all efficient causes following in order, the first is the cause of the intermediate cause, and the intermediate is the cause of the ultimate cause, whether the intermediate cause be several, or one only. Now to take away the cause is to take away the effect. Therefore, if there be no first cause

From the *Summa Theologica,* by St. Thomas Aquinas, translated by the Fathers of the English Dominican Province, Benziger Brothers, New York, publishers and copyright owners, 1936. Reprinted by permission of the publishers.

among efficient causes, there will be no ultimate, nor any intermediate, cause. But if in efficient causes it is possible to go on to infinity, there will be no first efficient cause, neither will there be an ultimate effect, nor any intermediate efficient causes; all of which is plainly false. Therefore it is necessary to admit a first efficient cause, to which everyone gives the name of God.

The third way is taken from possibility and necessity, and runs thus. We find in nature things that are possible to be and not to be, since they are found to be generated, and to be corrupted, and consequently, it is possible for them to be and not to be. But it is impossible for these always to exist, for that which can not-be at some time is not. Therefore, if everything can not-be, then at one time there was nothing in existence. Now if this were true, even now there would be nothing in existence, because that which does not exist begins to exist only through something already existing. Therefore, if at one time nothing was in existence, it would have been impossible for anything to have begun to exist; and thus even now nothing would be in existence—which is absurd. Therefore, not all beings are merely possible, but there must exist something the existence of which is necessary. But every necessary thing either has its necessity caused by another, or not. Now it is impossible to go on to infinity in necessary things which have their necessity caused by another, as has been already proved in regard to efficient causes. Therefore we cannot but admit the existence of some being having of itself its own necessity, and not receiving it from another, but rather causing in others their necessity. This all men speak of as God.

The fourth way is taken from the gradation to be found in things. Among beings there are some more and some less good, true, noble, and the like. But *more* and *less* are predicated of different things according as they resemble in their different ways something which is the maximum, as a thing is said to be hotter according as it more nearly resembles that which is hottest; so that there is something which is truest, something best, something noblest, and, consequently, something which is most being, for those things that are greatest in truth are greatest in being, as it is written in *Metaph.* II (*Metaph.* Ia, 1 993b30). Now the maximum in any genus is the cause of all in that genus, as fire, which is the maximum of heat, is the cause of all hot things, as is said in the same book (993b25). Therefore there must also be something which is to all beings the cause of their being, goodness, and every other perfection; and this we call God.

The fifth way is taken from the governance of the world. We see that things which lack knowledge, such as natural bodies, act for an end, and this is evident from their acting always, or nearly always in the same way, so as to obtain the best result. Hence it is plain that they achieve their end, not fortuitously, but designedly. Now whatever lacks knowledge cannot move towards an end, unless it be directed by some being endowed with knowledge and intelligence; as the arrow is directed by the archer. Therefore some intelligent being exists by whom all natural things are directed to their end; and this being we call God.

JOHN STUART MILL

The Argument From Design

Another selection by John Stuart Mill
appears in Section I, "The Primacy of
the Person."

... We now at last reach an argument of a really scientific character, which does not shrink from scientific tests, but claims to be judged by the established canons of Induction. The Design argument is wholly grounded on experience. Certain qualities, it is alleged, are found to be characteristic of such things as are made by an intelligent mind for a purpose. The order of Nature, or some considerable parts of it, exhibit these qualities in a remarkable degree. We are entitled, from this great similarity in the effects, to infer similarity in the cause, and to believe that things which it is beyond the power of man to make, but which resemble the works of man in all but power, must also have been made by Intelligence, armed with a power greater than human.

I have stated this argument in its fullest strength, as it is stated by its most thoroughgoing assertors. A very little consideration, however, suffices to show that though it has some force, its force is very generally overrated. Paley's illustration of a watch puts the case much too strongly. If I found a watch on an apparently desolate island, I should indeed infer that it had been left there by a human being; but the inference would not be from marks of design, but because I already knew by direct experience that watches are made by men. I should draw the inference no less confidently from a foot print, or from any relic however insignificant which experience has taught me to attribute to man: as geologists infer the past existence of animals from coprolites, though no one sees marks of design in a coprolite. The evidence of design in creation can never reach the height of direct induction; it amounts only to the inferior kind of inductive evidence called analogy. Analogy agrees with induction in this, that they both argue that a thing known to resemble another in certain circumstances (call those circumstances A and B) will resemble it in another circumstance (call it C). But the difference is that in induction, A and B are known, by a previous comparison of many instances, to be the very circumstances on which C depends, or with which it is in some way connected. When this has not been ascertained, the argument amounts only to this, that since it is not known with which of the circumstances existing in the known case C is connected, they may as well be A and B as any others; and therefore there is a greater probability of C in cases where we know that A and B exist, than in cases of which we

From *Three Essays on Religion*, by John Stuart Mill, 1874.

know nothing at all. This argument is of a weight very difficult to estimate at all, and impossible to estimate precisely. It may be very strong, when the known points of agreement, A and B &c. are numerous and the known points of difference few; or very weak, when the reverse is the case: but it can never be equal in validity to a real induction. The resemblances between some of the arrangements in nature and some of those made by man are considerable, and even as mere resemblances afford a certain presumption of similarity of cause: but how great that presumption is, it is hard to say. All that can be said with certainty is that these likenesses make creation by intelligence considerably more probable than if the likenesses had been less, or than if there had been no likenesses at all.

This mode, however, of stating the case does not do full justice to the evidence of Theism. The Design argument is not drawn from mere resemblances in Nature to the works of human intelligence, but from the special character of those resemblances. The circumstances in which it is alleged that the world resembles the works of man are not circumstances taken at random, but are particular instances of a circumstance which experience shows to have a real connection with an intelligent origin, the fact of conspiring to an end. The argument therefore is not one of mere analogy. As mere analogy it has its weight, but it is more than analogy. It surpasses analogy exactly as induction surpasses it. It is an inductive argument.

This, I think, is undeniable, and it remains to test the argument by the logical principles applicable to Induction. For this purpose it will be convenient to handle, not the argument as a whole, but some one of the most impressive cases of it, such as the structure of the eye, or of the ear. It is maintained that the structure of the eye proves a designing mind. To what class of inductive arguments does this belong? and what is its degree of force?

The species of inductive arguments are four in number, corresponding to the four Inductive Methods; the Methods of Agreement, of Difference, of Residues, and of Concomitant Variations. The argument under consideration falls within the first of these divisions, the Method of Agreement. This is, for reasons known to inductive logicians, the weakest of the four, but the particular argument is a strong one of the kind. It may be logically analysed as follows:

The parts of which the eye is composed, and the collocations which constitute the arrangement of those parts, resemble one another in this very remarkable property, that they all conduce to enabling the animal to see. These things being as they are, the animal sees: if any one of them were different from what it is, the animal, for the most part, would either not see, or would not see equally well. And this is the only marked resemblance that we can trace among the different parts of this structure, beyond the general likeness of composition and organization which exists among all other parts of the animal. Now the particular combination of organic elements called an eye had, in every instance, a beginning in time and must therefore have been brought together by a cause or causes. The number of instances is immeasurably greater than is, by the principles of inductive logic, required for the exclusion of a random concurrence of independent causes, or speaking technically, for the elimination of chance. We are therefore warranted by the canons of induction in concluding that what brought all these elements together was some cause common to them all; and inasmuch as the elements agree in the single circumstance of conspiring to produce sight, there must be some connection by way of causation between the cause which brought those elements together, and the fact of sight.

This I conceive to be a legitimate inductive inference, and the sum and substance of what Induction can do for Theism. The natural sequel of the argument would be this. Sight, being a fact not precedent but subsequent to the putting together of the organic structure of the eye, can only be connected with the production of that structure in the character of a final, not an efficient cause; that is, it is not Sight itself but an antecedent Idea of it, that must be the efficient cause. But this at once marks the origin as proceeding from an intelligent will.

I regret to say, however, that this latter half of the argument is not so inexpugnable as the former half. Creative forethought is not absolutely the only link by which the origin of the wonderful mechanism of the eye may be connected with the fact of sight. There is another connecting link on which attention has been greatly fixed by recent speculations, and the reality of which cannot be called in question, though its adequacy to account for such truly admirable combinations as some of those in Nature, is still and will probably long remain problematical. This is the principle of "the survival of the fittest."

This principle does not pretend to account for the commencement of sensation or of animal or vegetable life. But assuming the existence of some one or more very low forms of organic life, in which there are no complex adaptations nor any marked appearances of contrivance, and supposing, as experience warrants us in doing, that many small variations from those simple types would be thrown out in all directions, which would be transmissible by inheritance, and of which some would be advantageous to the creature in its struggle for existence and others disadvantageous, the forms which are advantageous would always tend to survive and those which are disadvantageous to perish. And thus there would be a constant though slow general improvement of the type as it branched out into many different varieties, adapting it to different media and modes of existence, until it might possibly, in countless ages, attain to the most advanced examples which now exist.

It must be acknowledged that there is something very startling, and *prima facie* improbable in this hypothetical history of Nature. It would require us, for example, to suppose that the primæval animal of whatever nature it may have been, could not see, and had at most such slight preparation for seeing as might be constituted by some chemical action of light upon its cellular structure. One of the accidental variations which are liable to take place in all organic beings would at some time or other produce a variety that could see, in some imperfect manner, and this peculiarity being transmitted by inheritance, while other variations continued to take place in other directions, a number of races would be produced who, by the power of even imperfect sight, would have a great advantage over all other creatures which could not see and would in time extirpate them from all places, except, perhaps, a few very peculiar situations underground. Fresh variations supervening would give rise to races with better and better seeing powers until we might at last reach as extraordinary a combination of structures and functions as are seen in the eye of man and of the more important animals. Of this theory when pushed to this extreme point, all that can now be said is that it is not so absurd as it looks, and that the analogies which have been discovered in experience, favourable to its possibility, far exceed what any one could have supposed beforehand. Whether it will ever be possible to say more than this, is at present uncertain. The theory if admitted would be in no way whatever inconsistent with Creation. But it must be acknowledged that it would greatly attenuate the evidence for it.

Leaving this remarkable speculation to whatever fate the progress of discovery may have in store for it, I think it must be allowed that, in the present state of our knowledge, the adaptations in Nature afford a large balance of probability in favour of creation by intelligence. It is equally certain that this is no more than a probability; and that the various other arguments of Natural Theology which we have considered, add nothing to its force. Whatever ground there is, revelation apart, to believe in an Author of Nature, is derived from the appearances in the universe. Their mere resemblance to the works of man, or to what man could do if he had the same power over the materials of organized bodies which he has over the materials of a watch, is of some value as an argument of analogy: but the argument is greatly strengthened by the properly inductive considerations which establish that there is some connection through causation between the origin of the arrangements of nature and the ends they fulfil; an argument which is in many cases slight, but in others, and chiefly in the nice and intricate combinations of vegetable and animal life, is of considerable strength.

STEVEN M. CAHN

The Irrelevance to Religion of Philosophic Proofs for the Existence of God

Steven M. Cahn, who teaches philosophy at New York University, is the author of *Fate, Logic, and Time* and the editor of a book in the philosophy of religion.

Philosophic proofs for the existence of God have a long and distinguished history. Almost every major Western philosopher has been seriously concerned with defending or refuting such proofs. Furthermore, many contemporary philosophers have exhibited keen interest in such proofs. A survey of the philosophical literature of the past decade reveals quite a concentration of work in this area.[1]

One might expect that religious believers would be vitally interested in dis-

From "The Irrelevance to Religion of Philosophic Proofs for the Existence of God," by Steven M. Cahn, from *American Philosophical Quarterly*, Vol. 6, No. 2, April, 1969. Reprinted by permission of the publisher and the author.

[1] For a partial bibliography, see Robert C. Coburn's "Recent Work in Metaphysics," *American Philosophical Quarterly*, vol. 1 (1964), pp. 218–220. Two comprehensive treatments of the subject are Wallace I. Matson's *The Existence of God* (Ithaca, Cornell University Press, 1966) and Antony Flew's *God and Philosophy* (London, Hutchinson & Co., 1966).

cussions of this subject. One might suppose that when a proof of God's existence is presented and eloquently defended, believers would be most enthusiastic, and that when a proof is attacked and persuasively refuted, believers would be seriously disappointed. But this is not at all the case. Religious believers seem remarkably uninterested in philosophic proofs for the existence of God. They seem to consider discussion of such proofs as a sort of intellectual game which has no relevance to religious belief or activity. And this view is shared by proponents of both super- naturalist and naturalist varieties of religion. For example, Søren Kierkegaard, a foremost proponent of supernaturalist religion, remarked: "Whoever therefore attempts to demonstrate the existence of God . . . [is] an excellent subject for a comedy of the higher lunacy!"[2] The same essential point is made in a somewhat less flamboyant manner by Mordecai M. Kaplan, a foremost proponent of natu- ralist religion, who remarks that the "immense amount of mental effort to prove the existence of God . . . was in vain, since unbelievers seldom become believers as a result of logical arguments."[3]

In what follows, I wish to explain just why religious believers have so little interest in philosophic proofs for the existence of God. I wish to show that their lack of interest is entirely reasonable, and that whatever the philosophic relevance of such proofs, they have little or no relevance to religion.

The three classic proofs for the existence of God are the ontological, the cosmological, and the teleological. Each of these proofs is intended to prove some- thing different. The ontological argument is intended to prove the existence (or necessary existence) of the most perfect conceivable Being. The cosmological argument is intended to prove the existence of a necessary Being who is the Prime Mover or First Cause of the Universe. The teleological argument is intended to prove the existence of an all-good designer and creator of the universe.

Suppose we assume, contrary to what most philosophers, I among them, be- lieve, that all of these proofs are valid. Let us grant the necessary existence (what- ever that might mean) of the most perfect conceivable Being, a Being who is all-good and is the designer and creator of the universe. What implications can be drawn from this fact which would be of relevance to human life? In other words, what difference would it make in men's lives if God existed?[4]

Perhaps some men would feel more secure in the knowledge that the uni- verse had been planned by an all-good Being. Others, perhaps, would feel insecure, realizing the extent to which their very existence depended upon the will of this Being. In any case, most men, either out of fear or respect, would wish to act in accordance with the moral code advocated by this Being.

Note, however, that the proofs for the existence of God provide us with no hint whatever as to which actions God wishes us to perform, or what we ought to do so as to please or obey Him. We may affirm that God is all-good and yet have no way of knowing what the highest moral standards are. All we may be

2 *Philosophical Fragments,* tr. by David F. Swenson (Princeton, Princeton University Press, 1936), ch. III, p. 34.

3 *The Future of the American Jew* (New York, The Macmillan Company, 1948), p. 171.

4 I am not concerned here with the implications of God's omniscience and omnipotence for man's free will. It is possible to interpret these divine attributes in such a way as not to entail the loss of man's free will, and for the purposes of this essay, I shall assume such an interpretation.

sure of is that whatever these standards may be, God always acts in accordance with them. One might assume that God would have implanted the correct moral standards in men's minds, but this seems doubtful in view of the wide variance in men's moral standards. Which of these numerous standards, if any, is the correct one is not known, and no appeal to a proof for the existence of God will cast the least light upon the matter.

For example, assuming that it can be proven that God exists, is murder immoral? One might argue that since God created man, it is immoral to murder, since it is immoral to destroy what God in His infinite wisdom and goodness has created. This argument, however, fails on several grounds. First, if God created man, He also created germs, viruses, disease-carrying rats, and man-eating sharks. Does it follow from the fact that God created these things that they ought not to be eliminated? Secondly, if God arranged for men to live, He also arranged for men to die. Does it follow from this that by committing murder we are assisting the work of God? Thirdly, if God created man, He provided him with the mental and physical capacity to commit murder. Does it follow from this that God wishes men to commit murder? Clearly, the attempt to deduce moral precepts from the fact of God's existence is but another case of trying to do what Hume long ago pointed out to be logically impossible, viz., the deduction of normative judgments from factual premisses. No such deduction is valid, and, thus, any moral principle is consistent with the existence of God.

The fact that the proofs of God's existence afford no means of distinguishing good from evil has the consequence that no man can be sure of how to obey God and do what is best in His eyes. One may hope that his actions are in accord with God's standards, but no test is available to check on this. Some seemingly good men suffer great ills, and some seemingly evil men achieve great happiness. Perhaps in a future life these things are rectified, but we have no way of ascertaining which men are ultimately rewarded and which are ultimately punished.

One can imagine that if a group of men believed in God's existence, they would be most anxious to learn His will, and consequently, they would tend to rely upon those individuals who claimed to know the will of God. Diviners, seers, and priests would be in a position of great influence. No doubt competition between them would be severe, for no man could be sure which of these oracles to believe. Assuming that God made no effort to reveal His will by granting one of these oracles truly superhuman powers (though, naturally, each oracle would claim that he possessed such powers), no man could distinguish the genuine prophet from the fraud.

It is clear that the situation I have described is paralleled by a stage in the actual development of religion. What men wanted at this stage was some way to find out the will of God. Individual prophets might gain a substantial following, but prophets died and their vital powers died with them. What was needed on practical grounds was a permanent record of God's will as revealed to His special prophet. And this need was eventually met by the writing of holy books, books in which God's will was revealed in a permanent fashion.

But there was more than one such book. Indeed, there were many such books. Which was to be believed? Which moral code was to be followed? Which prayers were to be recited? Which rituals were to be performed? Proofs for the existence of God are silent upon these crucial matters.

There is only one possible avenue to God's will. One must undergo a personal experience in which one senses the presence of God and apprehends which of the putative holy books is the genuine one. But it is most important not to be deceived in this experience. One must be absolutely certain that it is God whose presence one is experiencing and whose will one is apprehending. In other words, one must undergo a self-validating experience, one which carries its own guarantee of infallibility.

If one undergoes what he believes to be such an experience, he then is certain which holy book is the genuine one, and consequently he knows which actions, prayers, and rituals God wishes him to engage in. But notice that if he knows this, he has necessarily validated the existence of God, for unless he is absolutely certain that he has experienced God's presence, he cannot be sure that the message he has received is true. Thus, he has no further need for a proof of God's existence.

For one who does not undergo what he believes to be such a self-validating experience, several possibilities remain open. He may accept the validity of another person's self-validating experience. He thereby accepts the holy book which has been revealed as genuine, and he thereby also accepts the existence of God, since unless he believed that this other person had experienced the presence of God, he would not accept this person's opinion as to which is the genuine book.

It is possible, however, that one does not accept the validity of another person's supposedly self-validating experience. This may be due either to philosophical doubts concerning the logical possibility of such an experience[5] or simply to practical doubts that anyone has, in fact, ever undergone such an experience. In either case, adherence to a particular supernatural religion is unreasonable.

But having no adherence to a supernatural religion does not imply that one does not still face the serious moral dilemmas which are inherent in life. How are these dilemmas to be solved? To believe that God exists is of no avail, for one cannot learn His will. Therefore, one must use one's own judgment. But this need not be solely an individual effort. One may join others in a communal effort to propound and promulgate a moral code. Such a group may have its own distinctive prayers and rituals which emphasize various aspects of the group's beliefs. Such a naturalistic religious organization does not depend upon its members' belief in the existence of God, for such a belief is irrelevant to the religious aims and activities of the group.

Is it surprising then that proponents of both supernaturalist and naturalist religion are uninterested in philosophic proofs for the existence of God? Not at all. A supernaturalist believes in God because of a personal self-validating experience which has shown him (or someone he trusts) not only that God exists, but also what His will is. A philosophic proof of the existence of God is thus of no use to the supernaturalist. If the proof is shown to be valid, it merely confirms what he already knows on the much stronger evidence of personal experience. If the proof is shown to be invalid, it casts no doubt on a self-validating experience.

---

[5] Such doubts are forcefully expressed in C. B. Martin's *Religious Belief* (Ithaca, Cornell University Press, 1959), ch. V.

On the other hand, a naturalist believes either that no one has learned or that no one can learn the will of God. If, therefore, a proof for the existence of God is shown to be valid, this has no implications for the naturalist, for such a proof does not provide him with any information which he can utilize in his religious practice. If, on the contrary, a proof for the existence of God is shown to be invalid, this casts no doubt on the naturalist's religious views, since these views have been formulated independently of a belief in the existence of God.

Who, then, is concerned with philosophic proofs for the existence of God? First, there are those who believe that if such proofs are invalid, religion is thereby undermined. This is, as I have shown, a wholly erroneous view. Neither supernaturalist nor naturalist religion depends at all upon philosophic proofs for the existence of God. To attack religion on the grounds that it cannot provide a philosophic proof for the existence of God is an instance of *ignoratio elenchi*.

Secondly, there are those who believe that if the philosophic proofs for the existence of God are invalid, our moral commitments are necessarily undermined. This is also, as I have shown, a wholly erroneous view. It is, however, a common view, and one which underlies the so-called moral argument for the existence of God. According to this argument, it is only if one believes in the existence of God that one can reasonably commit oneself to respect the importance of moral values. This argument is invalid, however, for, as I have shown, belief in the existence of God is compatible with any and all positions on moral issues. It is only if one can learn the will of God that one can derive any moral implications from His existence.

Thirdly, there are philosophers who discuss proofs for the existence of God because of the important philosophical issues which are brought to light and clarified in such discussions. So long as philosophers are aware of the purpose which their discussions serve, all is well and good. It is when philosophers and others use discussions of this sort as arguments for and against religion that they overstep their bounds. Religion may be rationally attacked or defended, but to refute philosophic proofs for the existence of God is not to attack religion, and to support philosophic proofs for the existence of God is not to defend religion.

FURTHER READINGS

ANTHOLOGIES

Alston, William P., Ed., *Religious Belief and Philosophical Thought,* New York, Harcourt, Brace & World, 1963.

Cahn, Steven M., Ed., *Philosophy of Religion,* New York, Harper & Row, 1970.

Flew, Antony, and Alisdair MacIntyre, Eds., *New Essays in Philosophical Theology,* New York, Macmillan, 1955.

Hick, John, Ed., *Classical and Contemporary Readings in the Philosophy of Religion,* 2nd ed., Englewood Cliffs, N.J., Prentice-Hall, 1970.

Smart, Ninian, Ed., *Historical Selections in the Philosophy of Religion,* New York, Harper & Row, 1962.

RELIGIOUS EXPERIENCE

Baillie, John, *Our Knowledge of God,* New York, Scribner, 1962.

Buber, Martin, *I and Thou,* 2nd edition, Ronald Gregor Smith, Trans., New York, Scribner, 1956.

Dewey, John, *A Common Faith,* New Haven, Conn., Yale University Press, 1934.

Fackenheim, Emil L., *Quest for Past and Future,* Bloomington, Ind., Indiana University Press, 1968.

Freud, Sigmund, *Totem and Taboo,* New York, Vintage, 1946.

Heschel, Abraham, *God in Search of Man,* New York, Harper Torchbooks, 1966.

Hick, John, *Philosophy of Religion,* Englewood Cliffs, N.J., Prentice-Hall, 1963.

Huxley, Julian, *The Doors of Perception and Heaven and Hell,* New York, Harper & Row, 1956.

Kierkegaard, Søren, *Fear and Trembling and Sickness unto Death,* Garden City, N.Y., Anchor, 1954.

Leary, Timothy, Ralph Metzner, and Richard Alpert, *The Psychedelic Experience,* New Hyde Park, N.Y., University Books, 1964.

Levi-Strauss, Claude, *Totemism,* Rodney Needham, Trans., Boston, Beacon, 1963.

Santayana, George, *Sceptism and Animal Faith,* New York, Dover, 1955.

Stace, W. T., *Mysticism and Philosophy,* Philadelphia, Lippincott, 1960.

Teilhard de Chardin, Pierre, *The Phenomenon of Man,* New York, Harper & Row, 1959.

Tillich, Paul, *The Courage to Be,* New Haven, Conn., Yale University Press, 1952.

Underhill, Evelyn, *Mysticism,* New York, Dutton, 1911.

Weil, Simone, *Gravity and Grace,* New York, Putnam, 1952.

Zaehner, Arthur, *Mysticism, Sacred and Profane,* Oxford, Oxford University Press, 1961.

DOUBT

Altizer, Thomas J., Ed., *Toward a New Christianity: Readings in the Death of God Theology,* New York, Harcourt, Brace & World, 1967.

Freud, Sigmund, *The Future of an Illusion,* Garden City, N.Y., Doubleday, 1961.

Hume, David, *Dialogues Concerning Natural Religion,* New York, Hafner, 1948.

Leibniz, Gottfied Wilhelm, *Theodicy,* E. M. Huggard, Trans., London, Routledge & Kegan Paul, 1951.

Lewis, C. S., *The Problem of Pain,* New York, Macmillan, 1950.

Pike, Nelson, Ed., *God and Evil,* Englewood Cliffs, N.J., Prentice-Hall, 1964.

Robinson, John T., *Honest to God,* London, SCM Press, 1963.

Russell, Bertrand, *Why I Am Not a Christian,* New York, Simon and Schuster, 1966.

Schonfeld, Hugh J., *The Passover Plot,* New York, Bernard Geis, 1966.

THE EXISTENCE OF GOD

Anthologies

Burrill, Donald, Ed., *The Cosmological Argument,* Garden City, N.Y., Anchor, 1967.

Hick, John, Ed., *The Existence of God,* New York, Collier, 1964.

Hick, John, and Arthur C. McGill, *The Many-Faced Argument: Recent Studies on the Ontological Argument for the Existence of God,* New York, Macmillan, 1967.

Plantingea, Alvin, Ed., *The Ontological Argument,* Garden City, N.Y., Anchor, 1965.

Proofs and Criticisms

Aristotle, *Metaphysics,* Richard Hope, Trans., Ann Arbor, Mich., University of Michigan Press, 1960, book lambda.

Aquinas, St. Thomas, *On the Truth of the Catholic Faith, Book One, God*, Anton C. Pegis, Trans., Garden City, N.Y., Doubleday, 1955, *Summa Contra Gentiles,* book 1, chapters 10 and 11.

Descartes, René, Meditations, III and V, in *The Philosophical Works of Descartes,* New York, Cambridge, 1934.

Hume, David, *Dialogues Concerning Natural Religion,* New York, Hafner, 1948.

Kant, Immanuel, *Critique of Pure Reason,* Norman Kemp Smith, Trans., New York, St. Martin's, 1965, "Transcendental Dialectic," Book 2, Chapter 3.

Kierkegaard, Søren, *Philosophical Fragments,* David Swenson, Trans., Princeton, N.J., Princeton University Press, 1936, pp. 31–36.

Russell, Bertrand, and F. C. Copleston, "The Existence of God—a Debate," in Paul Edwards and Arthur Pap, Eds., *A Modern Introduction to Philosophy,* New York, Free Press, 1965.

Wisdom, John, "Gods," in Antony Flew, Ed., *Logic and Language,* Garden City, N.Y., Anchor, 1965; also in Hick.

Alternative Topics

The Contemporary Crisis

Major Fields of Philosophy

Philosophic Problems